A History of
the Supreme Court

A History of
the Supreme Court

BERNARD SCHWARTZ

OXFORD UNIVERSITY PRESS
New York   Oxford

Oxford University Press

Oxford   New York
Athens   Auckland   Bangkok   Bombay
Calcutta   Cape Town   Dar es Salaam   Delhi
Florence   Hong Kong   Istanbul   Karachi
Kuala Lumpur   Madras   Madrid   Melbourne
Mexico City   Nairobi   Paris   Singapore
Taipei   Tokyo   Toronto

and associated companies in
Berlin   Ibadan

Library of Congress Cataloging-in-Publication Data
Schwartz, Bernard, 1923–
A history of the Supreme Court / Bernard Schwartz.
p.   cm.   Includes bibliographical references and index.
ISBN 0-19-508099-8
ISBN 0-19-509387-9 (pbk.)
1. United States.   Supreme Court—History.   I. Title.
KF8742.S39   1993   347.73'26'09—dc20   [347.3073509]   92-44097

5 7 9 10 8 6

Printed in the United States of America
on acid-free paper

Semper uxori suae

Preface

There is no good one-volume history of the United States Supreme Court. The Holmes Devise history is too massive to be usable except for scholars engaged in research, and other histories, such as that by Robert Mc-Closkey, are too short and hence largely superficial. I hope that this book will correct the situation. It tells the story of the Court over the years since its first session in 1790. The emphasis is on the history of the Court in relation to the development of the nation. The theme is that of the Court as both a mirror and a motor—reflecting the development of the society which it serves and helping to move that society in the direction of the dominant jurisprudence of the day.

The organization of the book is chronological. In addition to the chapters on the Court under the different Chief Justices, there are chapters on four watershed cases—landmark cases that bring into sharp focus both how the Court operates and the impact of major decisions upon the nation and on the Court itself. My hope is that the audience for this book will not be limited to specialists in the subject. I have tried to write in a nontechnical manner to make the work less forbidding to the general reader who is normally "turned off" by a book written by a law professor. War, according to the famous aphorism, is too important a matter to be left to the generals. The work of the Supreme Court is similarly too significant in a country such as ours to be left only to the lawyers and law professors. This is particularly true of the historical functioning of the highest tribunal. It is scarcely possible to understand American history fully without an understanding of the part played in that history by the Supreme Court. In so

many cases, the decisions of the Court have become a vital part of the story
of the nation's development.

I will be more than rewarded for my efforts if this survey of the
Supreme Court's history proves useful to the growing number of those
who desire to learn more about the institution that plays such a vital part in
the polity.

Tulsa, Okla.   B. S.
1993

Contents

A History of
the Supreme Court

Introduction:
"The Very Essence of
Judicial Duty"

"Human history," says H. G. Wells, "is in essence a history of ideas."[1] To an American interested in constitutional history, the great theme in the country's development is the idea of law as a check upon governmental power. The institution that best embodies this idea is the United States Supreme Court. But the Court itself is the beneficiary of a constitutional heritage that starts centuries earlier in England.

Seedtime of Judicial Review

Chief Justice John Marshall tells us that the power to determine constitutionality "is of the very essence of judicial duty."[2] To an American interested in the development of the Marshall concept, as good a starting point as any is the dramatic assertion of the supremacy of law by Sir Edward Coke on November 13, 1608.[3] For it was on that day that James I confronted "all the Judges of England and Barons of the Exchequer" with the claim that, since the judges were but his delegates, he could take any case he chose, remove it from the jurisdiction of the courts, and decide it in his royal person. The judges, as James saw it, were "his shadows and ministers . . . and the King may, if he please, sit and judge in Westminster Hall in any Court there and call their Judgments in question."[4]

"To which it was answered by me," states Chief Justice Coke, "in the presence, and with the clear consent of all the Judges . . . that the King in his own person cannot adjudge any case . . . but that this ought to be determined and adjudged in some Court of Justice, according to the law and custom of England." To this James made the shrewd reply "that he thought the law was founded upon reason, and that he and others had reason as well as the Judges."

Coke then delivered his justly celebrated answer, "that true it was, that God had endowed His Majesty with excellent science, and great endowments of nature; but His Majesty was not learned in the laws of his realm of England, and causes which concern the life, or inheritance, or goods, or fortunes of his subjects, are not to be decided by natural reason but by the artificial reason and judgment of law, which law is an act which requires long study and experience, before that a man can attain to the cognisance of it: that the law was the golden met-wand and measure to try the causes of the subjects."[5]

It is hardly surprising that the King was, in Coke's description "greatly offended." "This means," said James, "that I shall be under the law, which it is treason to affirm." "To which," replied Coke, "I said, that Bracton saith, *quod Rex non debet esse sub homine, sed sub Deo et lege* [that the King should not be under man but under God and law]."

Needless to say, the King's anger only increased. According to one onlooker, in fact, "[H]is Majestie fell into that high indignation as the like was never knowne in him, looking and speaking fiercely with bended fist, offering to strike him, etc."[6]

James's indignation was well justified. Coke's articulation of the supremacy of law was utterly inconsistent with royal pretensions to absolute authority. In the altercation between Coke and the King, indeed, there is personified the basic conflict between power and law which underlies all political history. Nor does it affect the importance of Coke's rejection of James's claim that, with the King's fist raised against him, Coke was led personally to humble himself. That he "fell flatt on all fower"[7] to avoid being sent to the Tower does not alter the basic boldness of his clear assertion that the law was supreme even over the Crown.

Nor did Coke stop with affirming that even the King was not above the law. In *Dr. Bonham's Case*[8]—perhaps the most famous case decided by him—Coke seized the occasion to declare that the law was above the Parliament as well as above the King. Dr. Bonham had practiced physic without a certificate from the Royal College of Physicians. The College Censors committed him to prison, and he sued for false imprisonment. The college set forth in defense its statute of incorporation, which authorized it to regulate all physicians and punish with fine and imprisonment practitioners not admitted by it. The statute in question, however, gave the college one-half of all the fines imposed. This, said Coke, made the college not only judges, but also parties, in cases coming before them, and it is an established maxim of the common law that no man may be judge in his own cause.

But what of the statute, which appeared to give the college the power to judge Dr. Bonham? Coke's answer was that even the Parliament could not confer a power so contrary to common right and reason. In his words, "[I]t appears in our books, that in many cases, the common law will controul Acts of Parliament, and sometimes adjudge them to be utterly void: for when an Act of Parliament is against common right and reason, or repugnant, or impossible to be performed, the common law will controul it, and adjudge such Act to be void."[9]

Modern scholars have debated the exact meaning of these words. To the men of the formative era of American constitutional history, on the other hand, the meaning was clear. Chief Justice Coke was stating as a rule of positive law that there was a fundamental law which limited Crown and Parliament indifferently. Had not my Lord Coke concluded that when an Act of Parliament is contrary to that fundamental law, it must be adjudged void? Did not this mean that when the British government acted toward the Colonies in a manner contrary to common right and reason, its decrees were of no legal force?

The men of the American Revolution were nurtured upon Coke's writings. *"Coke's Institutes,"* wrote John Rutledge of South Carolina, "seem to be almost the foundation of our law."[10] Modern writers may characterize Coke as an obsolete writer whom the British Constitution has outgrown. Americans of the eighteenth century did not have the benefit of such ex post facto criticism. To them, Coke was the contemporary colossus of the law—"our juvenile oracle," John Adams termed him in an 1816 letter[11]—who combined in his own person the positions of highest judge, commentator on the law, and leader of the Parliamentary opposition to royal tyranny. Coke's famous *Commentary upon Littleton,* said Jefferson, "was the universal elementary book of law students and a sounder Whig never wrote nor of profounder learning in the orthodox doctrines of . . . British liberties."[12] When Coke, after affirming the supremacy of the law to royal prerogative, announced, "It is not I, Edward Coke, that speaks it but the records that speak it,"[13] men on the western side of the Atlantic took as the literal truth his assertion that he was only declaring, not making law.

Coke's contribution to constitutionalism was thus a fundamental one. He stated the supremacy of law in terms of positive law. And it was in such terms that the doctrine was of such import to the Founders of the American Republic. When they spoke of a government of laws and not of men, they were not indulging in mere rhetorical flourish.

Otis and Unconstitutionality

The influence of Coke may be seen at all of the key stages in the development of the conflict between the Colonies and the mother country. From Whitehall Palace, to which King James had summoned the judges in 1608, to the Council Chamber of the Boston Town House a century and a half later was not really so far as it seemed. "That council chamber," wrote John

Adams over half a century after the event, "was as respectable an apartment as the House of Commons or the House of Lords in Great Britain. . . . In this chamber, round a great fire, were seated five Judges, with Lieutenant Governor Hutchinson at their head, as Chief Justice, all arrayed in their new, fresh, rich robes of scarlet English broadcloth; in their large cambric bands, and immense judicial wigs."[14] For it was in this chamber that, in 1761, James Otis delivered his landmark attack in *Lechmere's Case*[15] against general writs of assistance.

The Otis argument in *Lechmere's Case* has been characterized as the opening gun of the American Revolution. In it, Otis with "a torrent of impetuous eloquence . . . hurried away everything before him." He argued the cause, Otis declared, "with the greater pleasure . . . as it is in opposition to a kind of power, the exercise of which, in former periods of English history, cost one King of England his head, and another his throne."[16] If Patrick Henry came close to treason in his famous 1765 speech attacking the Stamp Act, he at least had an excellent model in this Otis speech.

To demonstrate the illegality of the writs of assistance, Otis went straight back to Coke. As Horace Gray (later a Justice of the Supreme Court) put it in an 1865 comment, "His main reliance was the well-known statement of Lord Coke in *Dr. Bonham's Case*."[17] This may be seen clearly from John Adams's summary of the Otis argument: "As to acts of Parliament. An act against the Constitution is void: an Act against natural Equity is void; and if an Act of Parliament should be made in the very words of the petition, it would be void. The . . . Courts must pass such Acts into disuse."[18]

The Otis oration, exclaimed Adams, "breathed into this nation the breath of life," and "[t]hen and there the child Independence was born."[19] To which we may add that then and there American constitutional law was born. For Otis, in Justice Gray's words, "denied that [Parliament] was the final arbiter of the justice and constitutionality of its own acts; and . . . contended that the validity of statutes must be judged by the courts of justice; and thus foreshadowed the principle of American constitutional law, that it is the duty of the judiciary to declare unconstitutional statutes void."[20]

Coke's biographer tells us that he would have been astonished at the uses to which *Dr. Bonham's Case* was put.[21] Certain it is that Otis and those who followed in his steps went far beyond anything the great English jurist had expressly intended. Yet had not Coke's own attitude been stated in his picturesque phrase: "Let us now peruse our ancient authors, for out of the old fields must come the new corne."?[22] That is precisely what Americans have done in using Coke as the foundation for the constitutional edifice which, starting with Otis's argument, they have erected. Coke himself would not have been disturbed by the fact that, though the fields were old, the corn was new.

State Precursors

Throughout the Revolutionary period, Americans relied upon their possession of the rights of Englishmen and the claim that infringement upon those rights was unconstitutional and void. That claim could not, however, rest upon a secure legal foundation until the rights of Americans were protected in written organic instruments. Such protection came with the adoption of written constitutions and bills of rights in the states, as soon as independence had severed their ties with the mother country.

How were the rights guaranteed by these new constitutions to be enforced? The American answer to this question was, of course, ultimately, judicial review. That answer was first given during the period between the Revolution and the ratification of the Federal Constitution. By the end of the period, an increasing number of Americans accepted the view that laws might "be so unconstitutional as to justify the Judges in refusing to give them effect."[23] Oliver Ellsworth, later the third Chief Justice of the United States, was stating far from radical doctrine when he asserted in the 1788 Connecticut ratifying convention, "If the United States go beyond their powers, if they make a law which the Constitution does not authorize, it is void and the judicial power . . . will declare it to be void."[24]

Between 1780 and 1787 cases in a number of states saw direct assertions of judicial power to rule on constitutionality. There has been some dispute about whether these cases really involved judicial review. Much of the difficulty in assessing their significance arises from the fact that no meaningful reporting of cases in the modern sense existed at the time these cases were heard and decided. Reported opinions were mainly skimpy or nonexistent. For most of these early cases, recourse has to be had to other materials (such as newspapers and pamphlets) rather than to law reports of the modern type.

The first of the pre-Constitution review cases was the 1780 New Jersey case of *Holmes v. Walton.*[25] A 1778 statute, aimed at traffic with the enemy, permitted trial by a six-man jury and provided for punishment by property seizures. The statute was attacked on the ground that it was "contrary to the constitution of New Jersey." The claim was upheld by the court, though the actual decision has been lost. From other materials, it appears that the decision was based on the unconstitutionality of the six-man jury.[26] Some recent commentators have attacked the conclusion that *Holmes v. Walton* set a precedent for judicial review. It was, however, widely thought of as such at the time the Federal Constitution and Bill of Rights were adopted. Soon after the case was decided "a petition from sixty inhabitants of the county of Monmouth" was presented to the New Jersey Assembly. It complained that "the justices of the Supreme Court have set aside some of the laws as unconstitutional." In 1785, Gouverneur Morris sent a message to the Pennsylvania legislature that mentioned "a law as once passed in New Jersey, which the judges pronounced unconstitutional, and therefore void."[27] In addition, there is an 1802 case that states that in *Holmes v. Walton,* an "act upon solemn argument was adjudged to be unconstitutional and in that case inoperative."[28] At the least, these indicate that comtemporaries did regard *Holmes v. Walton* as a precedent for judicial review.

The second case involving judicial review was *Commonwealth v. Caton,*[29] decided in 1782 by the Virginia Court of Appeals. It has been widely assumed, relying on the report of the case in Call's Virginia Reports, that *Caton* was the strongest early precedent for judicial review. The language in Call is, indeed, unequivocal. "[T]he judges, were of opinion, that the court had power to declare any resolution or act of the legislature, or of either branch of it to be unconstitutional and void; and, that the resolution of the house of delegates, in this case, was inoperative, as the senate had not concurred in it."[30]

Call's report on *Caton* was not published until 1827; it was based upon the reporter's reconstruction of the case from surviving records, notes, and memoranda. There are significant differences between the Call report and the contemporary notes of Edmund Pendleton, who presided over the *Caton* court. According to Pendleton's account, only one of the eight judges ruled that the statute at issue was unconstitutional, though two others did assert judicial power to declare a law void for repugnancy to the Constitution. The two judges in question were Chancellor George Wythe and Pendleton himself. Wythe, perhaps the leading jurist of the day, delivered a ringing affirmation of review authority, declaring that if a statute conflicted with the Constitution, "I shall not hesitate, sitting in this place, to say, to the general court, Fiat justitia, ruat coelum; and, to the usurping branch of the legislature, you attempt worse than a vain thing."[31] Pendleton also stated that the "awful question" of voiding a statute was one from which "I will not shrink, if ever it shall become my duty to decide it."[32]

The *Caton* Court did not exercise the power to hold a law unconstitutional; the majority held "that the Treason Act was not at Variance with the Constitution but a proper exercise of the Power reserved to the Legislature by the latter."[33] Yet three judges did assert power in the courts to void statutes on constitutional grounds, including the two most prestigious members of the court. And it was Wythe's words, in particular, Pendleton's biographer tells us, that were "preserved in the court reports, and they were never forgotten by lawyers and students of government, by whom they were repeated again and again to men who would arrogate to themselves unconstitutional powers or seek to circumvent constitutional limitations."[34]

The most noted of the pre-Constitution review cases[35] was the 1784 New York case of *Rutgers v. Waddington.*[36] It was noted in its day because of Alexander Hamilton's argument for the defendant and because the court's opinion, published at the time, made a considerable stir. It is the best documented of these early cases. Strictly speaking, *Rutgers v. Waddington* did not involve a review of constitutionality but only of judicial power to annul a state statute contrary to a treaty and the law of nations. The statute in question provided for a trespass action against those who had occupied property during the British occupation of New York and barred defendants from any defense based on the following of military orders. Waddington was a British merchant who had occupied Mrs. Rutgers's abandoned property under license of the Commander-in-Chief of the British army of occupation. Hamilton argued that the statutory bar was in conflict both with the law of nations (since defendant had occupied the premises under British authority and thus derived the right of the military occupier over abandoned property sanctioned by the law of war) and the peace treaty with Britain. As stated by the editor of Hamilton's legal papers, he urged that "a court must apply the law that related to a higher authority in derogation of that which related to a lesser when the two came in conflict."[37]

The court agreed that the statute could not override a treaty or international law and refused to apply it to the extent that there was any conflict. Whether or not *Rutgers v. Waddington* may be regarded as a precedent for judicial review, its lesson was not lost on the Framers' Convention; by the Supremacy Clause state judges were directed to set aside state laws that conflicted with treaties. Certainly, Hamilton's assertion of review power in the courts made *Rutgers v. Waddington* "a marker on the long road that led to judicial review."[38]

The next case involving judicial review was the 1786 Rhode Island case of *Trevett v. Weeden*. That case, too, was unreported, but it was widely known through a 1787 pamphlet published by James M. Varnum (better known as one of Washington's generals), who argued the case against the statute.[39] Varnum's argument received wide dissemination and demonstrated the unconstitutionality of a legislative attempt to deprive Weeden of his right to trial by jury. Weeden, a butcher, was prosecuted under a statute making it an offense to refuse to accept paper money of the state in payment for articles offered for sale—in this case, meats. Appearing for the defense Varnum resorted to the modern distinction between the constitution and ordinary statute law,[40] arguing that the principles of the constitution were superior because they "were ordained by the people anterior to and created the powers of the General Assembly." It was the duty of the courts to measure laws of the legislature against the constitution. The judiciary's task was to "reject all acts of the Legislature that are contrary to the trust reposed in them by the people."[41] That the Rhode Island judges agreed with Varnum is shown by the following brief newspaper account:

> The court adjourned to next morning, upon opening of which, Judge Howell, in a firm, sensible, and judicious speech, assigned the reasons which induced him to be of the opinion that the information was not cognizable by the court, declared himself independent as a judge, the penal law to be repugnant and unconstitutional, and therefore gave it as his opinion that the court could not take cognizance of the information! Judge Devoe was of the same opinion. Judge

Tillinghast took notice of the striking repugnancy of the expressions of the act . . . and on that ground gave his judgment the same way. Judge Hazard voted against taking cognizance. The Chief Justice declared the judgment of the court without giving his own opinion.[42]

The clearest pre-Constitution case involving review power was the North Carolina case of *Bayard v. Singleton*,[43] decided in May 1787, just before the Philadelphia Convention. The contemporary account in the North Carolina Reports shows that the judges there realized the implications of what they were doing when they held that a statute contrary to the guaranty of trial by jury in cases involving property in the North Carolina Declaration of Rights "must of course . . . stand as abrogated and without any effect." No "act they could pass, could by any means repeal or alter the constitution" so long as the constitution remains "standing in full force as the fundamental law of the land."[44]

James Iredell, later a Justice of the Supreme Court, had been attorney for the plaintiff in *Bayard v. Singleton*. While attending the Framers' Convention, Richard Dobbs Spaight wrote to Iredell condemning the *Bayard* decision as a "usurpation," which "operated as an absolute negative on the proceedings of the Legislature, which no judiciary ought ever to possess." Iredell replied that "it has ever been my opinion, that an act inconsistent with the Constitution was void; and that the judges, consistently with their duties could not carry it into effect." Far from a "usurpation," the power to declare unconstitutional laws void flowed directly from the judicial duty of applying the law: "[E]ither . . . the *fundamental unrepealable* law must be obeyed, by the rejection of an act unwarranted by and inconsistent with it, or you must obey an act founded on authority not given by the people." The exercise of review power, said Iredell, was unavoidable. "It is not that the judges are appointed arbiters . . . but when an act is necessarily brought in judgment before them, they must, unavoidably, determine one way or another. . . . Must not they say whether they will obey the Constitution or an act inconsistent with it?"[45]

To be sure, these pre-Constitution assertions of review power did not go unchallenged. After *Rutgers v. Waddington,* the New York Assembly passed a resolution attacking the asserted power of the courts.[46] An open letter in a newspaper went even further, asserting, "That there should be a power vested in courts of judicature whereby they might controul the supreme Legislative power we think is absurd in itself. Such power in courts would be destructive of liberty, and remove all security of property."[47]

The reaction to *Trevett v. Weeden* was even stronger. The Rhode Island Legislature ordered the judges to appear before it "to render their reasons for adjudging an act of the General Assembly unconstitutional, and so void."[48] Then, as Madison was to explain it to the Framers' Convention, "In Rhode Island the judges who refused to execute an unconstitutional law were displaced, and others substituted, by the Legislature who would be willing instruments of the wicked and arbitrary plans of their masters."[49]

The important thing, however, is that despite such opposition, the judges did exercise the review power during the pre-Constitution period. The judicial groundwork was thus laid for the assertion of the power that has made the U.S. Supreme Court the fulcrum of our constitutional system.

Constitution and Ratification

The men who came to Philadelphia in the sultry summer of 1787 had the overriding aim of making such alterations in the constitutional structure as would, in the words of the Confederation Congress calling the convention, "render the Federal Constitution adequate to the exigencies of Government."[50] To accomplish that goal, they drafted a new charter providing for a Federal Government endowed with the authority needed to enable it to operate effectively.

The Articles of Confederation had concentrated all the governmental authority provided for under it in a unicameral legislative body. Before the Constitution, "Congress was the general, supreme, and controlling council of the nation, the centre of union, the centre of force, and the sun of the political system."[51] In the Confederation, there was no separate Executive and the only federal courts were those Congress might set up for piracy and felony on the high seas and for appeals in prize cases.

From the beginning of their deliberations, the Framers agreed that the new government they were creating should be based upon the separation of powers. It was, Madison told the Convention, "essential . . . that the Legislative: Executive: and Judicial powers be separate . . . [and] independent of each other."[52] Accordingly, the Virginia Plan drafted by him, which served as the basis for the new Constitution, provided expressly: "That a national government ought to be established consisting of a supreme legislative, judiciary and executive."[53]

In basing their deliberations upon Madison's plan, the Framers decided, at almost the outset of their deliberations, that there should be a federal judiciary and that it should be "supreme." The resolutions introduced to give effect to the plan provided that "a National Judiciary be established," to consist of both a supreme tribunal and inferior tribunals.[54] The federal courts were thus to be modeled upon the colonial and state court systems—consisting, as they did, of both inferior courts and a central high court.

Although attention was paid to the judiciary during the Convention debates, "[t]o one who is especially interested in the judiciary, there is surprisingly little on the subject to be found in the records of the convention."[55] The only serious objection was that to inferior federal courts, which some saw as an encroachment upon the states. The difficulty was resolved by a compromise: inferior courts were not required, but Congress was permitted to create them.[56]

The Framers were, of course, familiar with the preindependence judicial system, under which appeals could be taken to a central appellate tribunal. The proposal for a Federal Supreme Court was adopted with practically no discussion. The Convention considered and rejected a number of motions that would have been inconsistent with the judicial function and might have impaired the independence of the new supreme tribunal— notably one to set up a Council of Revision composed of the Executive and "a convenient number of the National Judiciary" to veto acts passed by Congress, as well as one "that all acts before they become laws should be submitted both to the Executive and Supreme Judiciary Departments."[57] There was debate about who should appoint the federal judges as well as their jurisdiction. In the end, however, the Judiciary Article was adopted essentially as it had been drafted by those who sought a strong national government—especially by its principal draftsman, Oliver Ellsworth.

The Constitution does not, to be sure, specifically empower the federal courts to review the constitutionality of laws. But it does contain provisions upon which judicial review authority can be based. The jurisdiction vested in the new judiciary extends to all "Cases . . . arising under this Constitution, the Laws of the United States, and Treaties." Even more important was the Supremacy Clause of article VI, added on motion of John Rutledge, who was appointed to the first Supreme Court and also served briefly as the second Chief Justice. The supremacy of the Constitution was expressly proclaimed as the foundation of the constitutional structure. And since only "Laws . . . made in pursuance" of the Constitution were given the status of "supreme law," laws repugnant to the Constitution were excluded from the imperative of obedience.

At various times during their debates, the Framers asserted that, in Elbridge Gerry's words, "the Judiciary . . . by their exposition of the laws" would have "a power of deciding on their Constitutionality."[58] Those who did so included Gerry himself, James Wilson,[59] and James Madison,[60] as well as opponents of the Constitution such as Luther Martin[61] and George Mason.[62] Even those who were troubled by such a power in the courts conceded that they saw no workable alternative. As John Dickinson put it, "He thought no such power ought to exist. He was at the same time at a loss what expedient to substitute."[63]

Madison, too, saw dangers in judicial review, which, he said in 1788, "makes the Judiciary Department paramount in fact to the Legislature, which was never intended and can never be proper."[64] Yet Madison also concluded his discussion of the matter by stating, "A law violating a constitution established by the people themselves, would be considered by the Judges as null and void."[65]

During the ratification debates of 1787–1788, both supporters and opponents of the Constitution assumed that judicial review would be an essential feature of the new organic order. "If they were to make a law not warranted by any of the powers enumerated," declared John Marshall in the Virginia ratifying convention, "it would be considered by the judges as an infringement of the Constitution which they are to guard. . . . They would declare it void."[66]

The Anti-Federalist *Brutus* letters, which Hamilton sought to answer in *The Federalist,* agreed with Marshall. If Congress, Brutus wrote, should "pass laws, which, in the judgment of the court, they are not authorized to do by the constitution, the court will not take notice of them . . . they cannot therefore execute a law, which, in their judgment, opposes the constitution."[67]

To opponents of the Constitution, judicial review was one of the new instrument's great defects. Because of it, Brutus wrote, "I question whether the world ever saw . . . a court of justice invested with such immense powers" as the Supreme Court.[68] There would be no power to control their decisions. In such a situation and vested with full judicial independence, the new Justices would "feel themselves independent of Heaven itself."[69]

The most effective defense of the federal judiciary and its review power was, of course, that by Hamilton in *The Federalist*—itself called forth by the challenge presented by the *Brutus* argument. Most important for our purposes was the defense of judicial review in No. 78 of *The Federalist*. Hamilton's essay there stands as the classic pre-Marshall statement on the subject. American constitutional law has never been the same since it was published.

Hamilton's *Federalist* reasoning on review is based upon the very nature of the Constitution as a limitation upon the powers of government. "Limitations of this kind can be preserved in practice in no other way than through the medium of the courts of justice; whose duty it must be to declare all acts contrary to the manifest tenor of the constitution void. Without this, all the reservations of particular rights or privileges would amount to nothing."[70]

The courts, Hamilton urged, were designed to keep the legislature within constitutional limits. "The interpretation of the laws is the proper and peculiar province of the courts. A constitution is, in fact, and must be regarded by the judges as a fundamental law. It must therefore belong to them to ascertain its meaning, as well as the meaning of any particular act proceeding from the legislative body. If there should happen to be an irreconcilable variance between the two, that which has the superior obligation and validity ought, of course, to be preferred: in other words, the constitution ought to be preferred to the statute; the intention of the people to the intention of their agents."[71]

Hamilton's reasoning here, and even his very language, formed the foundation for the *Marbury v. Madison*[72] confirmation of judicial review as the core principle of the constitutional system. The *Marbury* opinion can, indeed, be read as more or less a gloss upon *The Federalist,* No. 78.

Judiciary Act

The Constitution's Judiciary Article was, of course, not self-executing. Before the federal courts, including the Supreme Court, could come into existence, they had to be provided for by statute. The first Congress passed the necessary law when it enacted the Judiciary Act of 1789—the law that both created the Supreme Court and set forth its jurisdiction. The key members of the Senate committee that drafted the statute were Oliver Ellsworth, later the third Chief Justice, and William Paterson, who was to become a Supreme Court Justice. The principal draftsman was Ellsworth; according to a senatorial opponent, "this Vile Bill is a child of his."[73]

The 1789 statute resolved the issue of whether there should be inferior federal courts in favor of their creation. It established the federal judiciary with a Supreme Court, consisting of six Justices, at its apex, and a two-tiered system of inferior courts, with district courts in each state at the base, and three circuit courts grouped into three circuits—the eastern, the middle, and the southern, each composed of two Supreme Court Justices and one district judge. The federal courts were given only limited jurisdiction; as it was put by a member of the Senate drafting committee, "it will not extend to a tenth part of the causes which *might* by the constitution come into the Federal Court."[74]

There was again little discussion on the establishment of the Supreme Court, though some opponents sought to reduce the number of Justices and even to dispense with a Chief Justice. The jurisdiction of the Court was provided for in the form it has retained throughout its history. Crucial was the fact that the Court was given appellate jurisdiction not only over the lower federal courts, but also, under section 25 of the Judiciary Act, over the state courts in cases involving federal questions. "A vital chapter of American history," Justice Frankfurter tells us, "derives from the famous twenty-fifth section of the Judiciary Act."[75] From 1789 to our own day, the Supreme Court's power to review state court decisions has been what the Court historian characterized as "the keystone of the whole arch of federal judicial power."[76] Because of section 25, indeed, William Paterson could state, in his notes on the Judiciary Bill debate, "The powers of the Supreme Court are great—they are to check the excess of Legislation."[77]

With the passage of the first Judiciary Act, the stage was set for the Supreme Court to play its part in the unfolding drama of the new nation's development. The actual scenario would, however, depend upon the personnel of the new tribunal and the manner in which they performed their awesome constitutional role.

1

The First Court, 1790–1801

Chief Justice Warren E. Burger once said "that he himself should be in a wig and gown, and had been cheated out of it by Thomas Jefferson."[1] The question of the Justices' attire was a controversial issue when the United States Supreme Court first met. As was to be expected, Hamilton was for the English wig and gown. Jefferson was against both, but he said that if the gown was to be worn, "For Heaven's sake, discard the monstrous wig which makes the English judges look like rats peeping through benches of oakum!"[2]

Jefferson's opposition (as well as that by other public figures, including Aaron Burr) carried the day. One of the first Justices, William Cushing, came to New York for the first Court session wearing his old-fashioned judicial wig. His appearance with it caused a commotion: "The boys followed him in the street, but he was not conscious of the cause until a sailor, who came suddenly upon him, exclaimed, 'My eye! What a wig!'" Then, we are told, Cushing, "returning to his lodgings, . . . obtained a more fashionable covering for his head. He never again wore the professional wig."[3] Nor did any of the other Supreme Court Justices.

When, on February 2, 1790, the Supreme Court met in its first public session in the Royal Exchange, at the foot of Broad Street in New York City, the Justices did not wear wigs. But they were elegantly attired in black and red robes, "the elegance, gravity and neatness of which were the subject of remark and approbation with every spectator."[4] The elegance of the Justices' attire could, however, scarcely serve to conceal the relative ineffectiveness of the first Supreme Court, at least by comparison with what that tribunal was later to become. To understand the Court's position, it is necessary to look at the new judicial department not through twentieth-century spectacles but through the eyes of men living a decade after the Constitution went into effect. "The judiciary," wrote Hamilton in *The Federalist,* "is beyond comparison the weakest of the three departments of power."[5] This remark was amply justified by the situation of the fledgling Supreme Court.

It is hard for us today to realize that, at the beginning at least, a seat on the supreme bench was anything but the culmination of a legal career that it has since become. John Jay, the first Chief Justice, resigned to become Governor of New York, and Alexander Hamilton declined Jay's post, being "anxious to renew his law practice and political activities in New York." John Rutledge resigned his seat on the first Supreme Court to become Chief Justice of the South Carolina Court of Common Pleas. "[S]ince Marshall's time," as Justice Felix Frankfurter tells us, "only a madman would resign the chief justiceship to become governor"—much less a state judge.[6]

The weakness of the early Supreme Court is forcefully demonstrated by the fact that, in the building of the new capital, that tribunal was completely overlooked and no chamber provided for it. When the seat of government was moved to Washington, the high bench crept into an undignified committee room in the Capitol beneath the House Chamber.

Getting Under Way

With the opening of the Supreme Court, the tripartite governmental structure provided by the Framers was at last fully operative. Two days after the first session, a New York merchant wrote to a British friend, "Our Supreme Court was Opened the 2 Instant . . . we [are] now in Every Respect a Nation."[7]

The Supreme Court itself is established directly by the Constitution, which provides expressly for the existence of "one supreme Court." The Court could not, however, come into operation until the details of its organization and operation were provided by Congress. The Judiciary Act of 1789 set up a Supreme Court consisting of a Chief Justice and five Associate Justices and set forth the jurisdiction vested in it. But the President still had to appoint its members before the Court could come into existence.

President Washington took his responsibility in nominating Supreme Court Justices most seriously. In a famous letter to Edmund Randolph, the first Attorney General, Washington declared, "Impressed with a conviction, that the due administration of justice is the firmest pillar of good government, I have considered the first arrangement of the judicial department as essential to the happiness of our country, and to the stability of its political system." Because of this, the President wrote in his letters to his Supreme Court appointees, "I have thought it my duty to nominate for the high offices in that department, such men as I conceived would give dignity and lustre to our national character."[8] Despite Washington's clear comprehension of the responsibility of making suitable appointments to the first Court, he found it most difficult to get men of stature to accept. The low prestige of the Court led a number of his first choices to prefer other positions.

John Jay was apparently the President's first choice as Chief Justice. A few months before the appointment, Vice President Adams had written, "I am fully convinced that Services, Hazard, Abilities and Popularity, all properly weighed, the Balance, is in favour of Mr. Jay."[9] Jay accepted the position, though he was concerned about the salary. While the appointment was pending, the Secretary of the Senate wrote to a Senator, "The Keeper of the Tower [i.e., Jay] is waiting to see which Salary is best, that of Lord Chief Justice or Secretary of State."[10]

In choosing the five Associate Justices, Washington followed the practice, since followed by many Presidents, of geographic representation. A letter he sent to Hamilton the day after his nominations emphasized the geographic dispersion of Court seats.[11] His choice for Chief Justice was from New York. The other appointees were from South Carolina (John Rutledge, Chief Justice of the state's Chancery Court), Pennsylvania (James Wilson, one of the first American law professors, who had played a leading part in the Constitutional Convention), Massachusetts (William Cushing, Chief Justice of the state's highest court), Maryland (Robert H. Harrison, Chief Judge of the Maryland General Court), and Virginia (John Blair, a judge on the Virginia Supreme Court of Appeals).

Though all the nominees were speedily confirmed by the Senate, Harrison declined the appointment because of poor health. He died two months later. "Poor Col. Harrison," wrote Washington to Lafayette, "who was appointed one of the Judges of the Supreme Court, and declined, is lately dead."[12] In Harrison's place, Washington chose James Iredell of North Carolina, who had served as a state judge and attorney general and had been a leader in the struggle for ratification of the Constitution in his state.

In a letter soon after his appointment, the new Justice described the functioning of the fledgling Court:

> There are to be 2 Sessions of the Supreme Court held at the seat of Gov. in each year & a Circuit Court twice a year in each State. The United States are divided into three Circuits—one, called the [Middle], consisting of New Jersey, Pennsylvania, Delaware, Maryland & Virginia; and the Southern, consisting at present of South Carolina & Georgia, to which I imagine North Carolina will be added. [There was also an Eastern Circuit, consisting of New York and the New England states.] The Circuit Courts are to consist of two Judges of the Supreme Court, and a Judge in each State appointed by the President who has in other respects a separate jurisdiction of a limited kind—Any two of these may constitute a Quorum.[13]

As already seen, the Supreme Court began its first sittings on February 2, 1790. During that session and the next two terms, there were no cases docketed for argument and the Justices had little to do. "There is little business but to organise themselves," wrote Congressman Abraham Baldwin, "and let folks look on and see they are ready to work at them."[14] De Witt Clinton confirmed this assessment. In a letter to his brother, he stated, "The Supreme Court of the U. States is now in session and ha[ve] done no other business than admitting a few Counsellors and making a few rules."[15]

One of the new Court's rules irked the young Clinton:

> One of their orders "that all process shall run in the name of the President" tho' apparently unimportant smells strongly of monarchy—You know that in G. Britain some writs are prefaced with "George the 3d by the Grace of God & c." A federal process beginning with "George Washington by the grace of God & c." will make the American President as important in Law forms as the British King.[16]

Despite the early Court's lack of business, Justice Iredell could still say when he was appointed, "The duty will be severe."[17] That was true because of the arduous duty of serving in the circuit courts. The 1789 Judiciary Act placed on the members of the highest Court the obligation of personally sitting on the circuit courts that had been set up on a territorial basis throughout the country. At a time when travel was so difficult, the imposition upon the Supreme Court Justices of this circuit duty was most burdensome. In February 1792, Justice Cushing complained in a letter to Washington about the hardships involved in his judicial travels: "The travelling is difficult this Season:—I left Boston, the 13th of Jan in a Phaeton, in which I made out to reach Middleton as the Snow of the 18th began, which fell so deep there as to oblige me to take a Slay, & now again wheels seem necessary."[18]

The situation with regard to one Justice was graphically described in a 1798 letter by Samuel Chase, who had been appointed to the Court two years earlier. He would, Chase wrote,

> shew the very great burthen imposed on one of the Judges Mr. Iredell lives at Edenton, in North Carolina. When he is appointed to attend the Middle Circuit, he holds the Circuit Court for New Jersey at Trenton, on 1st of April; and, at Philadelphia, on the 11th of the same month; he then passes through the State of Delaware (by Annapolis) to hold the Court, on 22nd of May, at Richmond, in Virginia (267 miles.); from thence he must return, the same distance to hold Circuit Court on 27th June, at New Castle in Delaware. . . . A permanent system should not impose such hardship on any officer of Government.[19]

"I will venture to say," Iredell himself wrote in 1791, "no Judge can conscientiously undertake to ride the Southern Circuit constantly, and perform the other parts of his duty. . . . I rode upon the last Circuit 1900 miles: the distance from here and back again is 1800."[20]

When Jay resigned as Chief Justice, one of the reasons, according to a letter from a Congressman, was "the system of making the Judges of the Supreme Court ride the Circuits throughout the Union; this has induced Mr. Jay to quit the Bench; he was Seven months in the Year from his family travelling about the Country."[21] In a letter the previous year, Jay had expressed resentment at being "placed in an office . . . which takes me from my Family half the Year, and obliges me to pass too considerable a part of my Time on the Road, in Lodging Houses, & Inns."[22]

Thomas Johnson of Maryland, who had been appointed to Justice Rutledge's seat in 1791, actually resigned a year later because of the burden of circuit duty. "I cannot resolve," Johnson wrote in his resignation letter, "to spend six Months in the Year of the few I may have left from my Family on Roads at Taverns chiefly and often in Situations where the most moderate Desires are disappointed: My Time of Life Temper and other Circumstances forbid it."[23]

Finally, the Justices themselves publicly complained about what they termed, in a 1792 letter to Washington, "the burdens laid upon us so excessive that we cannot forbear representing them in strong and explicit terms."[24] At the same time, they wrote a remonstrance to Congress which declared, "That the task of holding twenty seven circuit Courts a year, in the different States, from New Hampshire to Georgia, besides two Sessions of the Supreme Court at Philadelphia, in the two most severe seasons of the year, is a task which considering the extent of the United States, and the small number of judges, is too burthensome."[25]

In addition, the remonstrance urged the unfairness of a system in which the Justices sat on appeals from decisions which they had made on circuit: "That the distinction made between the Supreme Court and its Judges, and appointing the same men finally to correct in one capacity, the errors which they themselves may have committed in another, is a distinction unfriendly to impartial justice, and to that confidence in the supreme Court, which it is so essential to the public Interest should be reposed in it."[26]

Though the Justices asked "that the system may be so modified as that they may be relieved from their present painful and improper situation."[27] Congress gave them only what has been called "but a half loaf and a meagre one at that."[28] A 1793 statute dispensed with the attendance of more than one Supreme Court Justice at each Circuit Court. This, wrote Justice Cushing, "eases off near half the difficulty. . . . The Justices are now impowered, at each Session of the Supreme Court, to assign a Circuit to a Single Judge, so that a Judge need go but one Circuit in a Year." But that was all Congress was prepared to do. It did not make what Cushing called the "radical alteration of the present Itinerant System for the better," for which the Justices had hoped. In fact, a law which, in Cushing's phrase, "may take off the fatigues of travelling & the inconvenience of so much absence from home"[29] would not take effect for another century.

Early Decisions

One of the reasons why Congress was unwilling, despite the Justices' remonstrance, to relieve them of circuit duties, was the fact that the Supreme Court itself had little work to do. As her son Thomas wrote in a 1799 letter to Abigail Adams, "The Supreme Court of the United States adjourned this day—Little business was done, because there was little to do."[30] During its first decade, the Supreme Court decided relatively few cases. In the first three years of its existence, in fact, the Court had practically no business to transact; it was not until February 1793 that the Justices decided their first case.

A half year earlier, on August 11, 1792, the Justices had delivered their first opinions in *Georgia v. Brailsford*.[31] The Justices adopted the English practice of delivering their opinions seriatim—a practice which they followed until John Marshall's day. Interestingly, in this first case in which opinions were delivered, the first opinion was a dissent by Justice Johnson, thus establishing at the outset the right of Justices to express publicly their disagreement with the result reached by the Court.

Brailsford granted Georgia a temporary injunction. The decision was described by Edmund Randolph in a letter to Madison which contained an unflattering picture of the first Court:

> The State of Georgia applied for an injunction to stop in the Marshal's hands a sum of money which had been recovered in the last circuit court by a British subject, whose estate had been confiscated. It was granted with a demonstration to me of these facts; that the premier [Jay] aimed at the cultivation of Southern popularity; that the professor [Wilson] knows not an iota of equity; that the North Carolinian [Iredell] repented of the first ebullitions of a warm temper; and that it will take a score of years to settle, with such a mixture of judges, a regular course of chancery.[32]

The first important decision of the Supreme Court was that rendered in February 1793 in *Chisholm v. Georgia*.[33] Chisholm was a citizen of South Carolina and his suit was based upon a claim for the delivery of goods to the state for which no payment had been received. Counsel for Georgia appeared and presented a written remonstrance denying the Court's jurisdiction, "but, in consequence of positive instructions, they declined taking any part in arguing the question." The case was then argued by Randolph, who represented Chisholm. (It was common at the time for the Attorney General to represent private clients; indeed, Randolph's official salary was so small that he depended for his livelihood upon such private clients.)

"This great cause,"[34] as the first *Chisholm* opinion (that by Justice Iredell) characterized it, presented the crucial issue of whether a state could be sued in a federal court by citizens of another state. The Court's answer was given unequivocally in favor of its jurisdiction in such a case in opinions by Justices Blair, Wilson, and Cushing and Chief Justice Jay (Justice Iredell alone dissenting). The most important opinion was delivered by

Justice Wilson. Unfortunately, it suffers from the pedantry and exaggerated rhetoric present in all of Wilson's writing—these defects, as much as his delivery of law lectures at the College of Philadelphia, led to his sobriquet of "the professor," as seen in the quoted Randolph letter. With all its faults, however, the Wilson *Chisholm* opinion remains a powerful justification both of the Court's decision and of the United States as a nation, not merely a league of sovereign states.

Wilson's opinion resoundingly rejected the state assertion of immunity from suit. After going into his conception of a state as a "body of free persons united together for their common benefit," Wilson asked, "Is there any part of this description, which intimates in the remotest manner, that a state, any more than the men who compose it, ought not to do justice and fulfil engagements?" Wilson declared that if a free individual is amenable to the courts, the same should be true of the state. "If the dignity of each singly, is undiminished, the dignity of all jointly must be unimpaired." States are subject to the same rules of morality as individuals. If a dishonest state willfully refuses to perform a contract, should it be permitted "to insult . . . justice" by being permitted to declare, "I am a sovereign state"?[35]

In *Chisholm,* Wilson recognized that though the immediate issue of state subjection to suit was important, it was outweighed by one "more important still; and . . . no less radical than this—'do the people of the United States form a nation?'" Wilson's opinion answered this question with a categorical affirmative. In *Chisholm,* he repudiated the concept of state sovereignty in language as strong as that later delivered by Chief Justice Marshall himself. Sovereignty, he asserted, is not to be found in the states, but in the people. The Constitution was made by the "People of the United States," who did not surrender any sovereign power to the states. "As to the purposes of the union, therefore, Georgia is not a sovereign state."[36]

The people, Wilson concluded, intended to set up a nation for national purposes. They never intended to exempt the states from national jurisdiction. Instead, they provided expressly, "The judicial power of the United States shall extend to controversies, between a state and citizens of another state." Wilson asked, "[C]ould this strict and appropriated language, describe, with more precise accuracy, the cause now depending before the tribunal?"[37]

The *Chisholm* decision, we are told, "fell upon the country with a profound shock."[38] Indeed, it led to such a furor in the states that the Eleventh Amendment (prohibiting suits by individuals against states) was at once proposed and adopted. Though the immediate holding in *Chisholm v. Georgia* was thus overruled, the Court's reasoning there remains of basic importance for what it tells us about the nature of the Union. To decide the case, the Court really had to determine the crucial issue of state sovereignty. If Georgia was intended to be a sovereign state under the Constitution, it could not be sued. In deciding that Georgia was subject to suit, the Court was rejecting the claim that the state was vested with the traits of sovereignty. "As to the purposes of the Union," to repeat the declaration of Justice Wilson, "Georgia is not a sovereign state."

Judicial Review

It is, of course, known to even the beginner in constitutional history that the power of the Supreme Court to review the constitutionality of acts of Congress was established by Chief Justice Marshall's landmark opinion in *Marbury v. Madison.*[39] Yet even Marshall—legal colossus though he was— did not write on a blank slate. On the contrary, the law laid down by Marshall in *Marbury v. Madison* was inextricably woven with that expounded by his contemporaries and predecessors. Judicial review, as an essential element of the law, was part of the legal tradition of the time, derived from both the colonial and revolutionary experience. With the appearance during the Revolution of written constitutions, the review power began to be stated in modern terms. Between the Revolution and *Marbury v. Madison,* state courts asserted or exercised the power in at least twenty cases.[40] Soon after the Constitution went into effect, assertions of review authority were made by a number of federal judges.[41]

Even more important, the Supreme Court began to lay the foundation for judicial review soon after it went into operation. Of particular significance in this respect were three cases decided during the 1790s. The first was *Ware v. Hylton.*[42] A 1777 Virginia law decreed the confiscation of all debts owed to British subjects. Despite it, an action was brought on a debt due before the Revolution from an American to a British subject. Plaintiff relied upon the Treaty of Peace with Britain under which "creditors, on either side, shall meet with no lawful impediment to the recovery of the full value of all *bona fide* debts, heretofore contracted."

A letter from Justice Iredell to his wife called the case "the great Virginia cause."[43] John Marshall argued in favor of the Virginia law and maintained that "the judicial authority can have no right to question the validity of a law; unless such a jurisdiction is expressly given by the constitution."[44] As Marshall's biographer notes, "It is an example of the 'irony of fate' that in this historic legal contest Marshall supported the theory which he had opposed throughout his public career thus far, and to demolish which his entire after life was given."[45] Had Marshall's *Ware v. Hylton* assertion prevailed, the American system of constitutional law would have developed along lines altogether different from the course taken.

The Court, however, rejected Marshall's argument and ruled that the Treaty of Peace with Britain overrode conflicting provisions of state law on the debts owed by Americans to British subjects. "A treaty cannot be the supreme law of the land," declared Justice Chase, "if any act of a state Legislature can stand in its way. . . . It is the declared will of the people of the United States that every treaty made, by the authority of the United States, shall be superior to the constitution and laws of any individual state; and their will alone is to decide."[46]

Ware v. Hylton asserted review power over a state law. A similar power was exercised in *Calder v. Bull,*[47] where a Connecticut law that set aside a probate decree disapproving a will and granting a new trial was attacked as a violation of the Ex Post Facto Clause. The Court held that the law was not an ex post facto law, since the Ex Post Facto Clause reaches only laws that are criminal in nature; the constitutional prohibition, in Justice Iredell's words, "extends to criminal, not to civil cases."[48]

The opinions delivered, nevertheless, left no doubt of the Court's power to strike down the state law, if it had been found to violate the Constitution. "I cannot," declared Justice Chase, "subscribe to the omnipotence of a state Legislature or that it is absolute and without control. . . . An act of the Legislature (for I cannot call it a law) contrary to the great first principles of the social compact, cannot be considered a rightful exercise of legislative authority."[49]

In his opinion, Justice Chase stated that he was not "giving an opinion, at this time, whether this court has jurisdiction to decide that any law made by Congress, contrary to the Constitution of the United States, is void."[50] It was not, to be sure, until *Marbury v. Madison* that the Court came down categorically in favor of such a review power. It was, however, in *Hylton v. United States,*[51] almost a decade before Marshall's classic *Marbury* opinion, that the Court first ruled on the constitutionality of a federal law.

Hylton arose under article I, section 9: "No Capitation, or other direct, Tax shall be laid, unless in Proportion to the Census or Enumeration herein before directed to be taken." This means that direct taxes must be apportioned among the states on the basis of their respective populations. Yet this does not tell us what is a "direct tax" within the constitutional provision. During the Framers' Convention, "Mr. King asked what was the precise meaning of *direct* taxation? No one answered."[52]

In *Hylton v. United States,* it was argued that a fixed federal tax on all carriages used for the conveyance of persons was a direct tax and hence invalid, because it was not apportioned among the states according to population. The Court unanimously held that the tax at issue was not a direct tax within the meaning of article I, section 9. According to the opinions rendered, since the Direct-Tax Clause constitutes an exception to the general taxing power of Congress, it should be strictly construed. No tax should be considered "direct" unless it could be conveniently apportioned. "As all direct taxes must be apportioned," said Justice Iredell, "it is evident, that the constitution contemplated none as direct, but such as could be apportioned. If this cannot be apportioned, it is, therefore, not a direct tax in the sense of the constitution. That this tax cannot be apportioned is evident."[53]

Justice Paterson, himself one of the Framers, who had been appointed to the Court after Justice Johnson resigned, stated that the constitutional provision on direct taxes had been intended to allay the fears of the southern states lest their slaves and lands be subjected to special taxes not equally apportioned among the northern states.[54] From this, it was a natural step to the view, expressed by all the Justices, that the "direct taxes contemplated by the constitution, are only two, to wit, a capitation, or poll tax, simply, without regard to property, profession or any other circumstance; and a tax on land."[55]

More important than the *Hylton* holding is the fact that the case was the first in which an act of Congress was reviewed by the Supreme Court. It is true that Justice Chase stated that "it is unnecessary, at this time, for me to determine, whether this court constitutionally possesses the power to declare an act of Congress void, on the ground of its being made contrary to, and in violation of, the constitution."[56] But the mere fact that the Justices considered the claim that the federal statute was "unconstitutional and void"[57] indicates that they believed that the Court did possess the review power. As such, *Hylton* was an important step on the road to *Marbury v. Madison.*

What the Court Does Not Do

Justice Louis D. Brandeis used to say that what the Supreme Court did not do was often more important than what it did do.[58] The fact that the highest tribunal acts as a law court has been more important than any other factor in determining the things that it does not do in our constitutional system. The Framers deliberately withheld from the Supreme Court power that was purely political in form, such as a forthright power to veto or revise legislation. Instead, they delegated to the Court "The judicial Power" alone—a power which, by the express language of article III, extends only to the resolution of "Cases" and "Controversies." This, Justice Robert H. Jackson once noted,[59] is the most significant and the least comprehended limitation upon the way in which the Court can act. Judicial power, the Court pointed out in 1911, "is the right to determine actual controversies arising between adverse litigants, duly instituted in the courts of proper jurisdiction."[60] The result of the constitutional restriction is that the Court's only power is to decide lawsuits between opposing litigants with real interests at stake, and its only method of proceeding is by the conventional judicial process. "The Court from the outset," says Chief Justice Charles Evans Hughes, "has confined itself to its judicial duty of deciding actual cases."[61]

Of course, in a system such as ours, where the highest Court plays so prominent a political role, there might be great advantages in knowing at once the legal powers of the Government. It would certainly be convenient for the parties and the public to know promptly whether a particular statute is valid. The desire to secure these advantages led to strong efforts at the Constitutional Convention to associate the Supreme Court as a Council of Revision in the legislative process; but these attempts failed and, ever since, it has been deemed, both by the Court itself and by most students of its work, that the disadvantages of such a political role by the judiciary were far greater than its advantages.

Similarly, from the beginning, the Court has rejected the notion that it could avoid the difficulties inherent in long-delayed judicial invalidation of legislation by an advisory opinion procedure. The very first Court felt constrained to withhold even from the "Father of his Country" an advisory opinion on questions regarding which Washington was most anxious to have illumination from the highest tribunal.[62] In 1793 President Washington, through a letter sent to the Justices by Secretary of State Jefferson, sought the advice of the Supreme Court on a series of troublesome "abstract questions" in the realm of international law "which have already occurred, or may soon occur." Chief Justice Jay and his associates first postponed their answer until the sitting of the Court and then, three weeks later, replied politely but firmly, declining to give the requested answers.

According to the Justices' letter to Washington, both "the lines of separation drawn by the Constitution between the three departments of the government . . . and our being judges of a court in the last resort, are considerations which afford strong arguments against the propriety of our extra-judicially deciding the questions alluded to."[63] This, says Chief Justice Hughes, was a statement that the Court "considered it improper to declare opinions on questions not growing out of a case before it."[64]

The Justices' refusal has served as a precedent against the giving of advisory opinions by the Court. Ever since that time, it has, in Chief Justice Harlan F. Stone's phrase, been the Court's "considered practice not to decide abstract, hypothetical or contingent questions."[65] A party cannot, in other words, bring an action for what Justice Oliver Wendell Holmes once called a "mere declaration in the air";[66] on the contrary, "A case or controversy in the sense of a litigation ripe and right for constitutional adjudication by this Court implies a real contest—an active clash of views, based upon an adequate formulation of issues, so as to bring a challenge to that which Congress has enacted inescapably before the Court."[67]

A few years earlier, in *Hayburn's Case*,[68] the Justices had decided that they might not, as judges, render decisions that were subject to revision by some other body or officer. They gave effect to this view even though it meant the effective nullification of a federal statute providing for veterans' pensions.

The statute, passed by Congress in 1792, authorized the federal circuit courts to determine the pension claims of invalid veterans of the Revolution and certify their opinions to the Secretary of War, who might then grant or deny the pensions as he saw fit. *Hayburn's Case* was argued in the Supreme Court, but that tribunal never rendered decision, for Congress intervened by providing another procedure for the relief of the pensioners.[69] But the statute at issue was considered in the different circuit courts and their opinions are given in a note to *Hayburn's Case* by the reporter.

All of the circuit courts (with five of the six Justices sitting) concurred in the holding that they could not validly execute the statute as courts set up under article III. The strongest position was taken by Justices Wilson and Blair sitting in the Pennsylvania Circuit Court. In Chief Justice Taney's words, they "refused to execute [the statute] altogether."[70] They entered an order in a case involving Hayburn as the invalid claimant: "[I]t is considered by the Court that the same be not proceeded upon."[71] Then they sent a letter to the President, undoubtedly drafted by Justice Wilson, which gave the reasons for their action. It asserted that "the business directed by this act is not of a judicial nature." For the court to act under the law would mean that it "proceeded *without* constitutional authority."[72]

That was true, "Because, if, upon the business, the court had proceeded, its *judgments* . . . might, under the same act, have been revised and controuled . . . by an officer in the executive department. Such revision and controul we deemed radically inconsistent with the independence of that judicial power which is vested in the courts; and, consequently, with that important principle which is so strictly observed by the Constitution of the United States."[73]

After Hayburn presented a memorial petitioning Congress for relief, Congressman Elias Boudinot explained the action to the House of Representatives:

It appeared that the Court . . . looked on the law . . . as an unconstitutional one; inasmuch as it directs the Secretary of War to state the mistakes of the Judge to Congress for their revision; they could not, therefore, accede to a regulation tending to render the Judiciary subject to the Legislative and Executive powers, which, from a regard for liberty and the Constitution, ought to be kept carefully distinct, it being a primary principle of the utmost importance that no decision of the Judiciary Department should under any pretext be brought in revision before either the Legislative or Executive Departments of the government, neither of which have, in any instance, a revisionary authority over the judicial proceedings of the Courts of Justice.[74]

According to Chief Justice Taney, *Hayburn's Case* established that the power conferred upon the federal courts by the 1792 statute "was no judicial power within the meaning of the Constitution, and was, therefore, unconstitutional and could not lawfully be exercised by the courts."[75] Since *Hayburn's Case,* it has been settled that the federal judges may not act in cases where their judgments are subject to revision by the executive or legislative department. The alternative is what District Judge Peters, who sat with Justices Wilson and Blair in the circuit court, termed "the danger of Executive control over the judgments of Courts"[76]—something avoided by the judges' strong stand in *Hayburn's Case.*

The judges' action in *Hayburn's Case* was also an important step on the road to *Marbury v. Madison.* This, said Boudinot in his statement to the House, was "the first instance in which a Court of Justice had declared a law of Congress to be unconstitutional."[77] It was widely recognized that the action of the judges was one, in the phrase of a newspaper, "declaring an act of the present session of Congress, unconstitutional."[78] Writing to Henry Lee, Madison referred to the review power and said that the judges' "pronouncing a law providing for Invalid Pensioners unconstitutional and void" was "an evidence of its existence."[79] At any rate, cases such as *Hayburn's Case* as well as those discussed in the last section were early recognitions of the judicial possession of the review power.

Chief Justices Rutledge and Ellsworth

The first national capital was New York and, as seen, the Supreme Court first met in that city early in 1790. A year later, in February 1791, after the seat of government had moved to Philadelphia, the Court held its sessions there, first in the State House and then in the new City Hall just east of Independence Hall, where both the Supreme Court and the state and city courts sat.

There were significant personnel changes while the Court sat in Philadelphia. As already seen, Thomas Johnson of Maryland was appointed in place of John Rutledge, who had resigned in 1791 to become Chief Justice of the South Carolina Court of Common Pleas. Johnson, however, resigned a year later because he found the circuit duties too strenuous, and his seat was filled by William Paterson, one of the Framers, who was then Governor of New Jersey. Samuel Chase of Maryland was elevated to the Court in 1796 in place of Justice Blair, who had resigned because of ill health. Then, when James Wilson died in 1798, President Adams selected Bushrod Washington, the first President's nephew, who had become a leader of the Virginia Bar. Justice Washington was to serve for thirty-two years as one of the pillars of the Marshall Court. Mention should also be made of the appointment in 1799 of Alfred Moore, a North Carolina judge, to fill the vacancy caused by the death of Justice Iredell.

Even more important were the personnel changes that occurred in the Chief Justiceship. John Jay is, of course, one of the leading names in early American history. He was not, however, a success as the head of the Supreme Court. In part this was due to the lack of business in the early Court, as well as the burden of circuit duty. One must conclude, as Edmund Randolph did in a 1792 letter to Madison, that Jay may have been "clear . . . in the expression of his ideas, but . . . they do not abound in legal subjects."[80]

Jay also set a bad example in the early Court by indicating that he did not consider his judicial position all that important. In 1794, Jay accepted an appointment as Special Ambassador to England, where he negotiated the treaty that bears his name. Though his appointment was denounced as a violation of the separation of powers, Jay did not resign as Chief Justice while carrying out his diplomatic assignment. Jay's successor, Oliver Ellsworth, also served as Minister to France without resigning as Chief Justice. These extrajudicial appointments had an inevitable negative effect upon the prestige of the fledgling Court. "That the *Chief Justiceship* is a sinecure," wrote the *Philadelphia Aurora,* "needs no other evidence, than that in one case the duties were *discharged* by one person who resided at the same time in England; and by another during a year's residence in France."[81]

While he was absent in England, Jay was nominated for Governor of New York and elected to that office soon after his return in 1795. He resigned as Chief Justice to accept the Governorship. A striking indication of the relative importance of the two positions at the time is given in the characterization by a New York newspaper of Jay's new office as a "promotion."[82]

President Washington had difficulty in filling the Chief Justiceship. John Rutledge, who had resigned from the Court to become Chief Justice of the South Carolina Court of Common Pleas, wrote to Washington that he was now willing to be Jay's successor. The President gave him a recess appointment, and Rutledge sat as Chief Justice during the August 1795 Term. However, the Senate voted against his confirmation, both because of his vitriolic attack upon the Jay Treaty in a Charleston speech and rumors of what John Adams called his "accellerated and increased . . . Disorder of the Mind."[83]

Washington next nominated Justice Cushing, the Senate confirmed the nomination, and Cushing actually received his commission. But then, as summarized by Adams in a letter to his wife, "Judge Cushing declines the Place of Chief-Justice on Account of his Age and declining Health."[84] Another indication of the contemporary reputation of the highest judicial position is seen in the comment of a Rhode Island official, "It is generally thought that Neighbor Cushing gave a Clear proof of his Understanding when he refused the Chief Justiceship."[85]

The President then chose Oliver Ellsworth of Connecticut, who had been a member of the Continental Congress, a state judge, and a Senator. He had been an important participant in the Framers' Convention, as well as a leader in the ratification struggle. As Senator he had been the principal author of the Judiciary Act of 1789.

The Ellsworth appointment met with general approval. "The appointment of the C.J.," Adams wrote to his wife, "was a wise Measure," even though, by it, "we loose the clearest head and most diligent hand we had [in the Senate]."[86] Senator Jonathan Trumbull agreed in a letter to his brother John, a famous painter, that Ellsworth's appointment was "a great Loss this to the Senate!" At the same time, he wrote, it was "a valuable acquisition to the Court—an acquisition which has been much needed."[87]

The leading history of the early Court states that Ellsworth was the first to make the position of Chief Justice a place of leadership.[88] His tenure was, however, too short for him to establish a true leadership role. About the only sign of the Justices' following Ellsworth's lead was the indication in the reported cases that his predilection for brief opinions was not without effect.[89]

Chief Justice Ellsworth's most important opinion (about the only significant one he delivered on the Supreme Court) laid down a basic rule on the Court's own jurisdiction. The case was *Wiscart v. D'Auchy*,[90] decided in 1796. The question at issue was whether an equity decree was reviewable in the Supreme Court by a writ of error or an appeal. In the course of the case, the Court considered the nature of its appellate jurisdiction. Chief Justice Ellsworth, in an oft-cited passage, declared that the Court's appellate jurisdiction depended entirely upon statute: "If Congress has provided no rule to regulate our proceedings, we cannot exercise an appellate jurisdiction; and if the rule is provided, we cannot depart from it."[91] Therefore, said Ellsworth, the only question in determining whether the Supreme Court has appellate jurisdiction in a given case is whether Congress has established a rule regulating its exercise in such a case.

The Ellsworth view on the matter was rejected by Justice Wilson, who urged, in a dissenting opinion, that the Supreme Court's appellate jurisdiction was derived from the Constitution: "The appellate jurisdiction, therefore, flowed, as a consequence, from this source; nor had the legislature any occasion to do, what the constitution had already done."[92] Even in the absence of congressional provision, therefore, according to Wilson, the appellate jurisdiction of the Supreme Court may be exercised, resting as it does upon the strong ground of the Constitution itself.

Interestingly enough, both Ellsworth and Wilson had been prominent members of the Framers' Convention. Yet less than a decade after the basic document was drafted, they disagreed sharply on the organic nature of the appellate jurisdiction of the nation's highest tribunal. Subsequent cases confirm the correctness of Chief Justice Ellsworth's view. "By the constitution of the United States," declared the Court in 1847, "the Supreme Court possesses no appellate power in any case, unless conferred upon it by act of Congress."[93] Two decades later, the Court was, if anything, even more blunt, asserting, "In order to create such appellate jurisdiction in any case, two things must concur: the Constitution must give the capacity to take it and an act of Congress must supply the requisite authority." The Supreme Court's appellate jurisdiction is thus "wholly the creature of legislation."[94]

His *Wiscart v. D'Auchy* opinion shows both Chief Justice Ellsworth's legal ability and his potential for molding our public law. But he was able to sit in the court's center chair for less than four years, and during much of that time he was absent because of illness. As a 1798 letter from his brother to Oliver Wolcott, Jr., characterized it, "Mr. Ellsworth . . . is considerably unwell, and I understand quite hypocondriac."[95]

During Ellsworth's last year as Chief Justice, he served as special envoy in France. The Court could barely function during that period. At its August 1800 Term, the last in Philadelphia, not only was Ellsworth absent, but also absent were Justice Cushing, who was ill, and Justice Chase, who was in Maryland working for President Adams's reelection. This led to bitter anti-Federalist attacks, such as that in the *Aurora* which condemned "[t]he suspension of the highest court of judicature in the United States, to allow a *Chief Justice* to add NINE THOUSAND DOLLARS a year to his salary, and to permit Chase to make electioneering harangues in favor of Mr. *Adams.*"[96] Even Adams's son wrote to his cousin that Chase was "too much engaged in Electioneering."[97]

Not in the best of condition when appointed, Ellsworth's health completely broke down on his journey to France. The Chief Justice described his condition in a letter sent from Le Havre to Wolcott: "Sufferings at sea, and by a winter's journey thro' Spain, gave me an obstinate gravel, which by wounding the kidneys, has drawn & fixed my wandering gout to those parts. My pains are constant, and at times excruciating."[98] On the same day, October 16, 1800, Ellsworth sent to President Adams a letter resigning the office of Chief Justice.

Judiciary Act of 1801

Circuit duty, we have seen, was the great albatross of the early Supreme Court. It is true that the problem of the Supreme Court Justices sitting on circuit was resolved by the Judiciary Act of 1801. That law provided for the creation of six new Circuit Courts to be staffed entirely by newly appointed judges. Unfortunately, however, the new statute was an integral part of the controversy between the Federalists and the Jeffersonians that dominated the political scene at the turn of the century. The desirable reform of relieving Supreme Court members of their circuit duties was less important than the creation by the lame-duck Federalist Congress of a whole new court system, with vacancies in the new tribunals to be filled by deserving members of the defeated party. The bill was enacted into law on February 13, 1801; within two weeks President Adams had filled the new positions with Federalists; and by March 2 (two days before Jefferson took office) the Senate had confirmed the appointments. The new judges, many of whose commissions were actually filled out on the last day of Adams's term of office, were derisively known as the "midnight judges."

The newly elected Jeffersonians greeted the 1801 statute with indignation. They could scarcely concur in the Federalist attempt to entrench themselves in the life-tenure judiciary by the Midnight Judges Bill. Instead, the Jeffersonian Congress did away with what they called the "army of judges" by abolishing the new courts soon after Jefferson took office, without making any provision for the displaced judges. They did so by a simple Act of March 8, 1802, repealing the 1801 Judiciary Act and providing for the revival of the former circuit court system.

Lost in the partisan controversy was the desirable reform effected by the 1801 act in relieving Supreme Court Justices of circuit court duty. Instead, the obligation of sitting on the circuits continued as a burden upon the members of the highest bench. It was only after that burden was finally removed in 1891 that the Supreme Court was able fully to assert its role as guardian of the constitutional system. Though judicial review was established in 1803, it did not really become an important practical factor in the polity until the 1890s.

The Federalists themselves bitterly attacked the 1802 repealing statute as one which, in Gouverneur Morris's characterization, "renders the judicial system manifestly defective and hazards the existence of the Constitution."[99] The Federalist argument was, however, rejected by the Supreme Court in *Stuart v. Laird*,[100] in a laconic opinion which stated only that Congress had constitutional authority to establish, as the members chose, such inferior tribunals as they deemed proper, and to transfer a cause from one such tribunal to another. "In this last particular," said the Court, "there are no words in the constitution to prohibit or restrain the exercise of legislative power."[101]

2

Marshall Court, 1801–1836

On the north and south walls of the Supreme Court Chamber in Washington are carved two marble panels depicting processions of historical lawgivers. Of the eighteen figures on the panels only one is there because of his work as a judge, and he is the one American represented: John Marshall. This is more than mere coincidence, for it sharply illustrates a basic difference between the making of law in the United States and in other countries. The great lawgivers in other systems have been mighty monarchs of the type of Hammurabi and Justinian, divinely inspired prophets like Moses, philosophers such as Confucius, or scholars like Hugo Grotius and Sir William Blackstone. We in the United States have certainly had our share of the last two types of lawgiver—particularly among the men who drew up the organic documents upon which our polity is based. Significantly enough, however, it is not a Jefferson or a Madison who is depicted as *the* American lawgiver, but the great Chief Justice who, more than any one person, has left his imprint upon the development of our constitutional law.

Marshall's Appointment

In the autumn of 1800, not long before Marshall's appointment as Chief Justice, the United States Government moved to Washington, D.C. The new capital was still in the early stages of construction and except for the north wing of the Capitol and the still unfinished White House, there was, as a Congressman wrote, "nothing to admire but the beauties of nature."[1]

At least buildings had been erected for the Legislature and Executive. The same was not true of the Judiciary. When the Federal City was planned, the Supreme Court was completely overlooked and no chamber provided for it: "When the seat of government was transferred to Washington, the court crept into an humble apartment"[2] in what had been designed as a House Committee room.

The failure to provide adequate housing for the Supreme Court "provides further evidence that the Court was not regarded as an institution of great importance in the federal system."[3] Indeed, the outstanding aspect of the Court's work during its first decade was its relative unimportance. When Marshall came to the central judicial chair in 1801, the Court was but a shadow of what it has since become. When he died in 1836, it had been transformed into the head of a fully coordinate department, endowed with the ultimate authority of safeguarding the ark of the Constitution.

Marshall it was who gave to the Constitution the impress of his own mind, and the form of our constitutional law is still what it is because he shaped it.[4] "Marshall," declared John Quincy Adams at news of his death, "by the ascendancy of his genius, by the amenity of his deportment, and by the imperturbable command of his temper, has given permanent and systematic character to the decisions of the Court, and settled many great constitutional questions favorably to the continuance of the Union." It was under Marshall's leadership that the Supreme Court transmuted the federal structure created by the Founders into a nation strong enough to withstand even the shock of civil war. To quote Adams's not unbiased view again, "Marshall has cemented the Union which the crafty and quixotic democracy of Jefferson had a perpetual tendency to dissolve."[5]

Marshall's appointment as Chief Justice was one of the happy accidents that change the course of history. In the first place, had Justice Cushing not declined the appointment or had Chief Justice Ellsworth not made the arduous journey to France, there would have been no vacancy in the Chief Justiceship until well after President Adams's term had expired. After Chief Justice Ellsworth's resignation, the President offered his place to John Jay. The Senate confirmed the appointment and, had Jay accepted, there would, of course, still have been no place for Marshall on the Court. Jay, however, also refused the position both because he wanted to retire to his farm in Bedford, New York, and because his acceptance in "a System so defective would give some Countenance to the neglect and Indifference with which the opinions and Remonstrances of the Judges on this important Subject have been treated."[6]

After Jay declined the Chief Justiceship, it was widely expected that the President would nominate Justice Paterson. Marshall later wrote, "On the resignation of Chief Justice Ellsworth I recommended Judge Patteson [*sic*] as his successor."[7] Adams, however, refused to select him. According to Marshall, "The President objected to him, and assigned as his ground of objection that the feelings of Judge Cushing would be wounded by passing him and selecting a junior member of the bench."[8] The real reason for

Adams's refusal, however, was that, as a letter to Hamilton stated, "Either Judge Paterson or General Pinckney ought to have been appointed, but both those worthies are your friends."9 Adams was unwilling to consider any person in the Hamiltonian faction of his party.

Marshall himself tells us what happened next: "When I waited on the President with Mr. Jays letter declining the appointment he said thoughtfully 'Who shall I nominate now'? I replied that I could not tell, as I supposed that his objection to Judge Paterson remained. He said in a decided tone 'I shall not nominate him.' After a moments hesitation he said, 'I believe I must nominate you'. . . . Next day I was nominated."10

The Marshall appointment was both completely unexpected and resented by Adams's own party, which believed that Judge Paterson should have been given the position. "With grief, astonishment & almost indignation," Jonathan Dayton, a Federalist Senator, wrote to Judge Paterson, "I hasten to inform you, that, contrary to the hopes and expectations of us all, the President has this morning nominated Gen. Marshall. . . . The eyes of all parties had been turned upon you, whose pretensions he knew were, in every respect the best, & who, he could not be ignorant, would have been the most acceptable to our country."11

The feeling in the Senate against the nomination was so strong, Dayton went on, that "I am convinced . . . that they would do it [i.e., reject the nomination] if they could be assured that thereby *you* would be called to fill it." The Senate suspended the nomination for a week, but finding the President inflexibly opposed to Paterson and fearing, in Dayton's words, "that the rejection of this might induce the nomination of some other character more improper, and more disgusting,"12 the Senate yielded and unanimously confirmed Marshall's appointment.

Judge Paterson had not wanted to be Chief Justice and went out of his way to praise the Marshall appointment. "Mr. Marshall," Paterson replied to Dayton, "is a man of genius, of strong reasoning powers, and a sound, correct lawyer. His talents have at once the lustre and solidity of gold."13 Paterson wrote to Marshall to the same effect in congratulating him on his appointment,14 and, Marshall writes, "I felt truly grateful for the real cordiality towards me"15 displayed by his new colleague.

Some time before Marshall's appointment, James Kent heard some friends of Hamilton say that Hamilton was in "every way, suited" to be Chief Justice. Kent, writing to Hamilton's wife about the incident, affirmed, "Of all this there could be no doubt." But, Kent concluded, Hamilton's "versatile talents, adapted equally for the bench & the bar, the field, the Senate house & the Executive cabinet, were fortunately called to act in a more complicated, busy & responsible Station."16

This estimate by the man who, next to Marshall, was then the nation's preeminent jurist, is still another indication of the low state of the early Supreme Court. All this, however, was to change after Marshall became Chief Justice. It was Marshall who established the role of the Supreme Court as the authoritative expounder of the Constitution, and it was he who exercised this role to lay the legal foundations of a strong nation, endowed with all the authority needed to enable it to govern effectively.

Marshall's Background

On the morning of Jefferson's first inauguration, Marshall wrote to Charles C. Pinckney, "Of the importance of the judiciary at all times but more especially the present I am very fully impressed & I shall endeavor in the new office to which I am called not to disappoint my friends."[17] Certainly, Marshall as Chief Justice was anything but a disappointment to his "friends." Years after John Adams had nominated Marshall to be Chief Justice, he said, "My gift of John Marshall to the people of the United States was the proudest act of my life. . . . I have given to my country . . . a Hale, a Holt, or a Mansfield."[18]

Almost two centuries later, no one doubts Marshall's preeminence in our law. "If American law," says Justice Oliver Wendell Holmes, "were to be represented by a single figure, skeptic and worshipper alike would agree without dispute that the figure could be one alone, and that one, John Marshall."[19] Marshall's was the task of translating the constitutional framework into the reality of decided cases. He was not merely the expounder of our constitutional law; he was its author, its creator. "Marshall found the Constitution paper and he made it power," said James A. Garfield. "He found a skeleton, and he clothed it with flesh and blood."[20] What Justice Story termed "the extraordinary judgments of Mr. Chief Justice Marshall upon constitutional law"[21] laid the foundation of our constitutional edifice. Ever since, that structure has been associated with the Marshall name and has remained the base upon which the American polity functions.

If we look to the background of the man himself, however, he certainly seemed ill equipped for the task to which he was ultimately called. One who reads the modest account of his early life in his famous autobiographical letter to Joseph Story is bound to be amazed at the meagerness of his education and training, both generally and in the law itself. His only formal schooling consisted of a year under the tuition of a clergyman, as well as another under a tutor who resided with his family. For the rest, his learning was under the superintendence of his father, who, Marshall concedes, "had received a very limited education."[22]

His study for the Bar was equally rudimentary. During the winter of 1779–1780, while on leave from the Army, "I availed myself of this inactive interval for attending a course of law lectures given by Mr. Wythe, and of lectures of Natural philosophy given by Mr. Madison then President of William and Mary College."[23] He attended law lectures for less than three months[24]—a time so short, according to his leading biographer, that, in the opinion of the students, "those who finish this study [of law] in a few months, either have strong natural parts or else they know little about it."[25] We may doubt, indeed, whether Marshall was prepared even to take full advantage of so short a law course. He had just fallen in love with his wife-to-be, and his notebook (which is preserved) indicates that his thoughts were at least as much upon his sweetheart as upon the lecturer's wisdom.[26]

Shakespeare, according to Alfred North Whitehead, wrote better poetry for not knowing too much. It may appear paradoxical to make the same assertion with regard to the greatest of American judges, for judicial ability normally depends, in large measure, upon the depth of legal learning. It must, however, be emphasized that Marshall's was not the ordinary judicial role. Great judges are typically not radical innovators. "I venture to suggest," states Justice Felix Frankfurter, "that had they the mind of such originators, the bench is not the place for its employment. Transforming thought implies too great a break with the past, implies too much discontinuity, to be imposed upon society by one who is entrusted with enforcing its law."[27]

Marshall's role, on the other hand, was as much that of legislator as judge. His was the task of translating the constitutional framework into the reality of decided cases. As one commentator puts it, "[H]e hit the Constitution much as the Lord hit the chaos, at a time when everything needed creating."[28] The need was for formative genius—for the transfiguring thought that the judge normally is not called upon to impose on society. Had he been more the trained lawyer, thoroughly steeped in technical learning and entangled in the intricacies of the law, he might not have been so great a judge; for his role called for the talent and the insight of a statesman capable of looking beyond the confines of strict law to the needs of a vigorous nation entered upon the task of occupying a continent.

One aspect of Marshall's education should not be overlooked, though it was far removed from the traditional type of schooling. This was his service as a soldier of the Revolution. It was, his biographer informs us, his military experience—on the march, in camp, and on the battlefield—that taught Marshall the primary lesson of the necessity of strong, efficient government: "Valley Forge was a better training for Marshall's peculiar abilities than Oxford or Cambridge could have been."[29] Above all, his service with Washington confirmed in him the overriding loyalty to an effective Union. Love of the Union and the maxim "United we stand, divided we fall," he once wrote, were "imbibed . . . so thoroughly that they constituted a part of my being. I carried them with me into the army . . . in a common cause believed by all to be most precious, and where I was confirmed in the habit of considering America as my country and Congress as my government."[30] In his most powerful opinions, it has been well said, Marshall appears to us to be talking, not in terms of technical law, but as one of Washington's soldiers who had suffered that the nation might live.

When all is said and done, nevertheless, an element of wonder remains as we contemplate Marshall's work. The magisterial character of his opinions marching with measured cadence to their inevitable logical conclusion has never been equaled, much less surpassed, in judicial history. Clarity, conciseness, eloquence—these are the Marshall hallmarks, which made his opinions irresistible, combined as they were with what Edward S. Corwin termed his "tiger instinct for the jugular vein,"[31] his rigorous pursuit of logical consequences, his power of stating a case, his scorn of qualifying language, the pith and balance of his phrasing, and the developing momentum of his argument. His is the rare legal document whose words can be read and meaning understood by the layman as well as the learned practitioner. And all this from a man almost without formal schooling, either in literature or the law. Were we not historically certain of the fact, we might have as much doubt that such an individual, possessed as he was only of raw genius and the courage to use it, really wrote the masterful opinions that served as the doctrinal foundation of a great nation as some have expressed with regard to the authorship by an unschooled Elizabethan actor of the supreme literary products of the English language.

The Chief Justice

The Supreme Court met for the first time in Washington on Februrary 2, 1801. Since only Justice Cushing was present, the Court *Minutes* state, "A sufficient number of Justices [was] not . . . convened to constitute a quorum"[32] and the Court was adjourned. A quorum was present on the rainy winter morning of February 4 and the Court proceeded to the business of the day: the swearing in of the new Chief Justice, who then took his seat upon the bench.

Aside from Marshall's induction, the February 1801 Term saw little done by the Court. Nor did the press take much notice either of the new Chief Justice's appointment or of the sessions at which he first presided. The February 5, 1801, issue of the *National Intelligencer,* then the leading Washington newspaper, noted only "The Justices of the Supreme Court have made a court, Marshall, Cushing, Chase, and Washington."[33] The lack of press interest illustrates both the Court's low prestige at the time and the fact that it had not yet begun to play its important role in the constitutional structure.

The Court's lack of prestige was strikingly shown by the fact that, as seen, no chamber was provided for it when the new capital was being built. Instead, soon after it convened, the House resolved "[t]hat leave be given to the Commissioners of the City of Washington to use one of the rooms on the first floor of the Capitol for holding the present session of the Supreme Court of the United States."[34] A similar resolution was passed by the Senate.

The room assigned to the Court pursuant to these resolutions was one of the first-floor committee rooms, under the south end of the hall assigned to the House of Representatives. The room measured thirty to thirty-five feet; it had two windows. The chamber was heated by a fireplace set in the wall. Where the bench was located has not been ascertained.[35] We do know, however, that the bench was not raised—a feature present in most courtrooms. The room itself, Benjamin Latrobe, the architect of the Capitol, wrote to Madison, was only half finished and "meanly furnished, very inconvenient."[36]

Here, in the bare quarters of Committee Room 2, the Court sat when Marshall took his seat. The new Chief Justice was a commanding figure in the courtroom—tall, erect, though slightly ungainly if not awkward. His black hair was tied in a queue, after the fashion of the day, but his clothes were frequently disheveled, his appearance anything but that of a man impressed with his high station. William Wirt tells us that, "in his whole appearance, and demeanor; dress, attitudes, gesture; sitting, standing or walking; he is as far removed from the idolized graces of lord Chesterfield, as any other gentleman on earth."[37]

In the courtroom, according to Joseph Story, Marshall's outstanding characteristic was the "quiet, easy dignity" with which he presided. "You heard him," Story wrote, "pronounce the opinion of the Court in a low, but modulated voice, unfolding in luminous order every topic of argument, trying its strength, and measuring its value, until you felt yourself in the presence of the very oracle of the law."[38]

Marshall's accomplishments as Chief Justice were directly related to his overriding conception of law. To Marshall, the law was essentially a social instrument—with the Constitution itself to be shaped to special and particular ends. The Constitution was not to be applied formalistically; it must be applied in light of what it is for. Marshall never doubted that the overriding purpose behind the organic instrument was to establish a nation that was endowed with all the necessary governmental powers. Marshall, wrote John Quincy Adams in his diary at the Chief Justice's death, "settled many great constitutional questions favorably to the continuance of the Union. Marshall has cemented the Union."[39]

The key to the Marshall conception is his seminal dictum: "[W]e must never forget that it is a *constitution* that we are expounding."[40] Justice Frankfurter once termed this the "most important, single sentence in American Constitutional Law." It set the theme for constitutional construction—that the Constitution is not to be read as "an insurance clause in small type, but a scheme of government . . . intended for the undefined and unlimited future."[41]

Just after Marshall assumed his Court seat, Charles Cotesworth Pinckney complained in a letter that "attempts are making to construe away the Energy of our Constitution, to unnerve our Government, & to overthrow that system by which we have risen to our present prosperity."[42] Marshall's Court tenure was devoted to defeating these attempts. It is customary to designate a particular Supreme Court by the name of its Chief Justice. Such designation was more than formalism when Marshall presided over the Court. From the time when he first took his judicial place to his death thirty-four years later, it was emphatically *the Marshall Court* that stood at the head of the judiciary. Throughout his judicial career, Marshall's consistent aim was to use the Supreme Court to lay the constitutional foundation of an effective nation. Before this aim could be realized, the prestige and power of the Court itself had to be increased, for the bench to which Marshall was first appointed could hardly hope to play the positive role in welding the new nation that the great Chief Justice conceived.

As soon as Marshall began to discharge his duties as head of the highest Court, Beveridge's classic biography informs us, "he quietly began to strengthen the Supreme Court."[43] Before Marshall, the Court followed the English practice of having opinions pronounced by each of the Justices. "For the first time," says Beveridge, "the Chief Justice disregarded the custom of the delivery of opinions by the Justices seriatim, and, instead, calmly assumed the function of announcing, himself, the views of that tribunal."[44] Marshall did so in the very first case decided by his Court. "Opinions of the Court" were made the primary vehicle for announcing decisions, with the opinion in virtually all important cases delivered by the Chief Justice himself.[45]

The change from a number of individual opinions to the Court opinion was admirably suited to strengthen the prestige of the fledgling Court. Marshall saw that the needed authority and dignity of the Court could be attained only if the principles it proclaimed were pronounced by a united tribunal. To win conclusiveness and fixity for its decisions, he strove for a Court with a single voice. How well he succeeded is shown by the reception accorded Justice William Johnson, who sought to express his own views in dissent. "During the rest of the Session," he plaintively affirmed in a letter to Jefferson, "I heard nothing but lectures on the indecency of judges cutting at each other, and the loss of reputation which the Virginia appellate court had sustained by pursuing such a course."[46]

Yet, though American constitutional decisions have thus, since Marshall's innovation, been the offspring of the Supreme Court as a whole, it is important to bear in mind that their expression is individual. As Justice Frankfurter said, "The voice of the Court cannot avoid imparting to its opinions the distinction of its own accent. Marshall spoke for the Court. But *he* spoke."[47] And this enabled him to formulate in his own way the landmarks of American constitutional law.

Judicial Review

The first such landmark was, of course, *Marbury v. Madison* (1803),[48] where Marshall asserted for the judicial department the power needed to enable it to forge the constitutional bonds of a strong nation. In 1974, Chief Justice Burger circulated a draft opinion in which he referred to "the power of judicial review first announced by this Court under the authority of Article III in *Marbury*."[49] In a July 18, 1974, letter to the Chief Justice, Justice Byron R. White objected to the draft's implication that *Marbury v. Madison* had created judicial review. "Because I am one of those who thinks that the Constitution on its face provides for judicial review, especially if construed in the light of what those who drafted it said at the time or later, I always wince when it is inferred that the Court created the power or even when it is said that the 'power of judicial review [was] first announced in *Marbury v. Madison.*' . . . But perhaps this is only personal idiosyncrasy."[50]

Despite the White disclaimer, there is no doubt that it was *Marbury v. Madison* that made judicial review positive constitutional doctrine. It was the decision in that case that established the power of the Supreme Court to rule on the constitutionality of a congressional act. *Marbury v. Madison* arose out of the passage of the Judiciary Act of 1801 during the last days of John Adams's Federalist Administration. As seen in the last chapter, that law provided for the appointment of a large number of new federal circuit judges. A second law, passed a few days later, established courts in the District of Columbia, with the judges there also to be appointed by the outgoing President. The bills angered the Jeffersonians, who were about to assume office. In the words of the pro-Jefferson *Philadelphia Aurora,* they would allow Adams, in his last days in the Presidency, to provide "sinecure places and pensions for thorough going Federal partisans." That, of course, was the intention of Adams, who wished to fill the judiciary with men who would carry on Federalist principles. As Henry Adams put it, "the Federalists felt bound to exclude Republicans from the bench, to prevent the overthrow of those legal principles in which, as they believed, national safety dwelt."[51]

Acting under the new laws, President Adams appointed over fifty men—all right-thinking Federalists. Among them, selected as a justice of the peace for the District of Columbia was a member of a prominent Maryland family, a banker and large landowner named William Marbury.

The Senate confirmed the appointees, and the outgoing President signed their commissions of office. It was now the job of the Secretary of State, John Marshall—who had just been appointed and sworn in as Chief Justice—to place the Great Seal of the United States on the commissions and deliver them. Because of the pressure of last-minute duties, Marshall overlooked delivering the commissions of the justices of the peace and the new President, Thomas Jefferson, ordered his Secretary of State, James Madison, not to deliver them.

Marbury then brought an action for mandamus against Madison, asking the court to order Madison to deliver his commission. Marbury brought the action directly in the Supreme Court under section 13 of the Judiciary Act of 1789, which gave the Court original jurisdiction in mandamus cases against federal officials.

The case appeared only to raise the question of whether the Court could issue a mandamus against the Secretary of State. Seemingly, the Court could either disavow having such power over the Executive branch and dismiss Marbury's application, or it could order Madison to deliver the commission to him. The first course would have meant abdicating the essentials of "The judicial Power" conferred on the Court by the Constitution. But the second course would have been no better. While it would have declared the Court's authority to hold the Executive to the law, it would have remained only a "paper declaration," for the Court would have no power to enforce its mandate.

That Marshall was able to choose neither course was a tribute to his judicial statesmanship. He escaped from the dilemma by ruling that section 13 of the Judiciary Act was unconstitutional on the ground that, since the original jurisdiction conferred upon the Supreme Court by the Constitution was exclusive, it could not be enlarged by congressional law. Thus the Court could deny Marbury's application, not because the Executive branch was above the law (Marshall's opinion, on the contrary, contained a strong repudiation of that claim), but because the Court itself did not possess the original jurisdiction to issue the writ that Marbury requested.

To reach that decision and rule that the congressional law was invalid, the Court was asserting that it had power to review the constitutionality of acts of Congress. From a strategic point of view, the Court could not have chosen a better case through which to declare that power. Since its decision did not rule in favor of Marbury, there was nothing that would bring on a direct conflict with the Jefferson Administration.

More than that, the assertion of the greatest of all judicial powers—review of laws—was made in a case that ruled against authority that had been granted to the Court. The Jeffersonians found it hard to attack the decision in which the Court declined—even from Congress—a jurisdiction to which it was not entitled by the Constitution. "To the public of 1803," Charles Warren tells us, "the case represented the determination of Marshall and his Associates to interfere with the authority of the Executive, and it derived its chief importance then from that aspect." On the other hand, "To the lawyers of today, the significance of Marshall's opinion lies in its establishment of the power of the Court to adjudicate the validity of an Act of Congress—the fundamental decision in the American system of constitutional law."[52]

Marbury v. Madison is *the* great case in American constitutional law because it was the first case to establish the Supreme Court's power to review constitutionality. Indeed, had Marshall not confirmed review power at the outset in his magisterial manner, it is entirely possible it would never have been insisted upon, for it was not until 1857 that the authority to invalidate a federal statute was next exercised by the Court.[53] Had the Marshall Court not taken its stand, more than sixty years would have passed without any question arising as to the omnipotence of Congress. After so long a period of judicial acquiescence in congressional supremacy, it is probable that the opposition then would have been futile.

To be sure, Marshall in *Marbury* merely confirmed a doctrine that was part of the American legal tradition of the time, derived from both the colonial and Revolutionary experience. One may go further. Judicial review was the inarticulate major premise upon which the movement to draft constitutions and bills of rights was ultimately based. The doctrine of unconstitutionality had been asserted by Americans even before the first written constitutions, notably by James Otis in his 1761 attack on general writs of assistance[54] and by Patrick Henry in 1763 when he challenged the right of the Privy Council to disallow the Virginia Two-penny Act.[55] The Otis-Henry doctrine was a necessary foundation, both for the legal theory underlying the American Revolution and the constitutions and bills of rights that it produced.

The doctrine could, however, become a principle of positive law only after independence, when written constitutions were adopted that contained binding limitations, beyond the reach of governmental power. Judicial review started to become a part of the living law during the decade before the adoption of the Federal Constitution. Cases in at least five states between 1780 and 1787 involved direct assertions of the power of judicial review.[56] Marshall himself could affirm, in his *Marbury* opinion, not that the Constitution establishes judicial review, but only that it "confirms and strengthens the principle."[57] Soon after the Constitution went into effect, further assertions of review authority were made by a number of federal judges, including members of the Supreme Court sitting on circuit. In addition, the first Supreme Court itself, as we saw in the last chapter, decided cases such as *Hylton v. United States,*[58] which were based upon its possession of review power. Hence, when Madison introduced the proposed amendments that became the Federal Bill of Rights, he could recognize expressly that the new guaranties would be enforced by the courts. For Madison, as for his compatriots generally, judicial review was an implicit aspect of the constitutional structure.

That Marshall's opinion in *Marbury v. Madison* was not radical innovation does not at all detract from its importance. The great Chief Justice, like Jefferson in writing the Declaration of Independence, may have merely set down in clear form what had already been previously declared. Yet, as Marshall's biographer observes, Thomas Jefferson and John Marshall as private citizens in Charlottesville and Richmond might have written declarations and opinions all their lives, and today none but the curious student would know that such men had ever lived.[59] It is the authoritative positions which those two Americans happened to occupy that have given immortality to their enunciations. If Marshall's achievement in *Marbury v. Madison* was not transformation but only articulation, what has made it momentous is the fact that it was magisterial articulation as positive law by the highest judicial officer of the land.

Marshall's *Marbury* reasoning is a more elaborate version of that used by Hamilton in *The Federalist,* No. 78. But it was Marshall, not Hamilton, who elevated that reasoning to the constitutional plane, and he did so in terms so firm and clear that the review power has never since been legally doubted. As the encomium of a leading constitutional scholar puts it, "There is not a false step in Marshall's argument." Instead, his "presentation of the case . . . marches to its conclusion with all the precision of a demonstration from Euclid."[60]

In Marshall's *Marbury* opinion, the authority to declare constitutionality flows inexorably from the judicial duty to determine the law: "It is emphatically the province and duty of the judicial department to say what the law is. . . . If two laws conflict with each other, the courts must decide that case comformably to the law, disregarding the constitution; or conformably to the constitution, disregarding the law; the court must determine which of these conflicting rules governs the case. This is of the very essence of the judicial duty."[61] One may go further and say that judicial review, as declared in *Marbury v. Madison,* has become the sine qua non of the American constitutional machinery: draw out this particular bolt, and the machinery falls to pieces.

Addressing the court in the 1627 *Five Knights' Case,* the Attorney General, arguing for the Crown, asked, "Shall any say, The King cannot do this? No, we may only say, He will not do this."[62] It was precisely to ensure that in the American system one would be able to say "The State *cannot* do this" that the people enacted a written Constitution containing basic limitations upon the powers of government. Of what avail would such limitations be, however, if there were no legal machinery to enforce them? Even a Constitution is naught but empty words if it cannot be enforced by the courts. It is judicial review that makes constitutional provisions more than mere maxims of political morality.

Review Power over States

To hold as Marshall did in *Marbury v. Madison* that the Supreme Court can review the constitutionality of acts of Congress is, however, to lay down only half of the doctrine of judicial review. According to a noted statement by Justice Holmes, indeed, it is the less important half. "I do not think," he asserted, "the United States would come to an end if we lost our power to declare an Act of Congress void. I do think the Union would be imperilled if we could not make that declaration as to the laws of the several states."[63] The power to pass on the validity of state legislation is a necessary part of the review power if the Constitution is truly to be maintained as supreme law throughout the country.

In was in the 1810 case of *Fletcher v. Peck*[64] that the Supreme Court first exercised the power to hold a state law unconstitutional. In ruling that a Georgia statute violated the Contract Clause of the Constitution, Marshall, who delivered the opinion, declared categorically that the state could not be viewed as a single, unconnected sovereign power, on whom no other restrictions are imposed than those found in its own constitution. On the contrary, it is a member of the Union, "and that Union has a constitution the supremacy of which all acknowledge, and which imposes limits to the legislatures of the several states, which none claim a right to pass."[65]

In *Fletcher v. Peck,* Marshall, in Beveridge's description, laid the second stone in the structure of American constitutional law. Yet even this was still not enough to enable the Supreme Court to maintain the Constitution as the supreme law of the land. In addition to the power to review the validity of legislative acts of both the nation and the states, review power over the judgments of the state courts is also necessary. In a system in which state judicatures coexist with those of the nation, vested with equal competence to pronounce judgment on constitutional issues, it is essential that their judgments be subjected to the overriding control of the highest tribunal. The review power over state courts is necessary if the Supreme Court is to uphold national supremacy when it conflicts with state law or is challenged by state authority.

The appellate power of the Supreme Court over state court decisions, in order to harmonize them with the Constitution, laws, and treaties of the United States, was established in two memorable decisions by the Marshall Court. The first was rendered in 1816 in *Martin v. Hunter's Lessee*.[66] That case arose out of the refusal of the highest court of Virginia to obey the mandate issued by the Supreme Court in an earlier case in which the Virginia court's decision had been reversed on the ground that it was contrary to a treaty of the United States. The Virginia judges had asserted that they were not subject to the highest bench's appellate power "under a sound construction of the constitution of the United States" and ruled that the provision of the first Judiciary Act which "extends the appellate jurisdiction of the Supreme Court to this court, is not in pursuance of the constitution of the United States."

The Supreme Court, in an opinion by Justice Story, categorically rejected the holding that it could not be vested with appellate jurisdiction over state court decisions. Marshall did not deliver the opinion because a personal interest in the case led him to decline to participate. There is no doubt, however, that Story's opinion was strongly influenced by the Marshall view on judicial power. Beveridge tells us, indeed, that it was commonly supposed that Marshall "practically dictated" Story's opinion.[67] Be that as it may, the opinion was certainly one that, save for some turgidity of language, the great Chief Justice could have written.

Five years later, in the case of *Cohens v. Virginia*,[68] Marshall was given the opportunity to demonstrate that such was the case. Defendants there had been convicted in a Virginia court of violating that state's law prohibiting the sale of lottery tickets. They sought a writ of error from the Supreme Court on the ground that, since the lottery in question had been authorized by an act of Congress, the state prohibitory law was invalid since it conflicted with federal law. Again it was claimed that the highest Court had no appellate power over the state courts. With typical force, Marshall declared that such an argument was contrary to the Constitution. The states, he affirmed, are not independent sovereignties; they are members of one great nation—a nation endowed by the basic document with a government competent to attain all national objects. "The exercise of the appellate power over those judgments of the state tribunals which may contravene the constitution or laws of the United States, is, we believe, essential to the attainment of those objects."[69] Let the nature and objects of the Union be considered, let the great principles on which the constitutional framework rests be examined, and the result must be that the Court of the nation must be given the power of revising the decisions of local tribunals on questions which affect the nation.

According to Marshall's biographer, the opinion in *Cohens v. Virginia* is "one of the strongest and most enduring strands of that mighty cable woven by him to hold the American people together as a united and imperishable nation."[70] Certain it is that Marshall's masterful opinion conclusively settled the competence of the high bench to review the decisions of state courts. Since *Cohens v. Virginia,* state attempts to make themselves the final arbiters in cases involving the Constitution, laws, and treaties of the United States have been foredoomed to defeat before the bar of the highest Court.

With the decision in *Cohens v. Virginia,* the structure of judicial power erected by the Marshall Court was completed. The authority of the judicial department to enforce the Constitution against both the national and state governments became an accepted part of American constitutional law. All governmental acts, whether of the nation or the states, now had to run the gantlet of review by the Supreme Court to determine whether they were constitutional. And that Court itself was now the veritable supreme tribunal of the land, for it was vested with the last word over the state, as well as the federal, judiciaries.

National Power

For Marshall, judicial review, like law itself, was a means not an end. The end was the attainment of the goal intended by "the framers of the Constitution, who were his compatriots"[71]—an effective national government endowed with vital substantive powers, the lack of which had rendered the Articles of Confederation sterile. Judicial review was the tool that enabled Marshall to translate this goal into legal reality.

To Marshall, the overriding end to be served by our public law was nationalism in the broad sense of that term. The law was to be employed to lay down the doctrinal foundations of an effective nation. That end was attained through a series of now-classic decisions that had two principal aims: to ensure that the nation possessed the powers needed to enable it to govern effectively; and to ensure federal supremacy vis-à-vis state powers.

The key case in this respect was *McCulloch v. Maryland,*[72] decided in 1819. It established the doctrine of implied powers in our constitutional law, resolving in the process the controversy between those who favored a strict and those who favored a broad construction of the Necessary-and-Proper Clause of the Constitution. That clause, after enumerating the specific powers conferred on Congress, authorizes it "to make all laws which shall be necessary and proper for carrying into execution the foregoing powers, and all other powers vested by this Constitution in the government of the United States." Conflicting approaches had been taken to the clause by Jefferson and Hamilton. Jefferson had adopted a strict view, emphasizing the word *necessary* in the clause: it endowed the Federal Government only with those powers indispensable for the exercise of its enumerated powers. The broader Hamilton view maintained that to take the word in its rigorous sense would be to deprive the clause of real practical effect: "It is essential to the being of the National Government, that so erroneous a conception of the meaning of the word *necessary* should be exploded."[73]

In *McCulloch v. Maryland,* Marshall adopted the broad Hamiltonian approach. The case itself presented the same issue on which Jefferson and Hamilton had differed—the constitutionality of the Bank of the United States, established by Congress to serve as a depository for federal funds and to print bank notes. Under pressure from its state banks, Maryland imposed a tax upon the federal bank's Baltimore branch and then brought suit in a state court against James William McCulloch, the branch's cashier, when he refused to pay the Maryland tax. The state won its suit; but the Federal Government, facing similar taxes in other states, appealed to the Supreme Court.

To decide whether the Maryland tax law was constitutional the Court had to decide whether Congress had the power to charter the bank. In relying upon the Necessary-and-Proper Clause for an affirmative answer, Marshall relied directly upon the reasoning of Hamilton's *Bank Opinion*. If the establishment of a national bank would aid the government in the exercise of its granted powers, the authority to set one up would be implied. "Let the end be legitimate," reads the key sentence of the Marshall opinion, "let it be within the scope of the constitution; and all means which are appropriate, which are plainly adapted to that end, which are not prohibited, but consist with the letter and spirit of the constitution, are constitutional."[74]

This passage is essentially similar to the "criterion of what is constitutional" contained in Hamilton's *Bank Opinion*. Once again, however, it was Marshall, not Hamilton, who made the implied powers doctrine an accepted element of our constitutional law and finally put to rest the view that the Necessary-and-Proper Clause extended only to laws that were indispensably necessary.

Marshall himself, writing extrajudicially, stressed that if the rejected view "would not absolutely arrest the progress of the government, it would certainly deny to those who administer it the means of executing its acknowledged powers." Indeed, Marshall asserted, "[T]he principles maintained by the counsel for the state of Maryland . . . would essentially damage the constitution, render the government of the Union incompetent to the objects for which it was instituted, and place all powers under the control of the state legislatures."[75] Or, as it was put in a Marshall letter to Justice Story, "If the principles which have been advanced on this occasion were to prevail, the Constitution would be converted into the old confederation."[76]

Marshall used *McCulloch v. Maryland* not only to ensure that the nation had the powers needed to govern effectively; he used it also to cement the federal supremacy declared in article VI. Having decided, as just seen, that Congress had the power to charter the Bank of the United States, the Court then had to determine whether Maryland might tax the bank. The Marshall opinion answered the question of state power with a categorical negative. Since the bank was validly established by Congress, it followed logically that it could not be subjected to state taxation.

The national government, declared Marshall, "is supreme within its sphere of action. This would seem to result necessarily from its nature." National supremacy is utterly inconsistent with any state authority to tax a federal agency. "The question is, in truth, a question of supremacy; and if the right of the states to tax the means employed by the general government be conceded the declaration that the constitution, and the laws made in pursuance thereof, shall be the supreme law of the land, is empty and unmeaning declamation."[77]

Federal supremacy, to Marshall, meant "that the states have no power, by taxation or otherwise, to retard impede, burden, or in any manner control, the operations of the Federal Government, or its agencies and instrumentalities.[78] It also meant that federal action, if itself constitutional, must prevail over inconsistent state action. This second meaning was developed in *Gibbons v. Ogden* (1824).[79] The decision there held that New York statutes which had granted an exclusive license to use steam navigation on the waters of the state were invalid so far as they applied to vessels licensed under a federal statute to engage in coastwise trade. According to Marshall's opinion, "[T]he laws of New York . . . come into collision with an act of Congress, and deprived a citizen of a right to which that act entitles him." In such a case, "[T]he acts of New York must yield to the law of Congress; and the decision [below] sustaining the privilege they confer, against a right given by a law of the Union, must be erroneous. In every such case, the act of Congress . . . is supreme; and the law of the state, though enacted in the exercise of powers not controverted, must yield to it."[80]

Commerce Power

The same expansive approach to federal authority can be seen in the *Gibbons v. Ogden* opinion on the most important substantive power vested in the Federal Government in time of peace: the power "[t]o regulate commerce with foreign nations, and among the several States."[81] The need to federalize regulation of commerce was one of the principal needs that motivated the Constitutional Convention of 1787. Yet the delegates there were interested mainly in the negative aspects of such regulation, concerned as they were with curbing state restrictions that had oppressed and degraded the commerce of the nation. It was Marshall, in *Gibbons v. Ogden,* who first construed the commerce power in a positive manner, enabling it to be fashioned into a formidable federal regulatory tool.

Gibbons v. Ogden itself arose out of the invention of the steamboat by Robert Fulton. Fulton and Robert Livingston, American Minister in Paris when the inventor had demonstrated his steamboat in France in 1803, secured from the New York legislature a monopoly of steam navigation on the waters of that state. Under the monopoly, the partners licensed Aaron Ogden to operate ferryboats between New York and New Jersey. When Thomas Gibbons began to run steamboats in competition with Ogden and without New York permission (though he had a coasting license from the Federal Government), Ogden sued to stop Gibbons.

The case became a sensational battle between the two men and almost wrecked them both. However, the Supreme Court decision nullifying Ogden's monopoly was more than the settling of a quarrel between two combative men. Marshall seized the opportunity to deliver an opinion on the breadth of Congress's authority under the Commerce Clause. The clause vests in Congress the power "to regulate commerce." The noun "commerce" determines the subjects to which congressional power extends. The verb "regulate" determines the types of authority that Congress can exert. Both the noun and the verb were defined most broadly in Marshall's opinion.

"Commerce," in Marshall's view, covered all economic intercourse—a conception comprehensive enough to include within its scope all business dealings: "It describes the commercial intercourse between nations, and parts of nations, in all branches."[82]

Having given such a broad construction to the noun "commerce," Marshall proceeded to take an equally liberal view of the meaning of the verb "regulate." "What is this power?" he asked. "It is the power to regulate; that is, to prescribe the rule by which commerce is to be governed. This power, like all others vested in congress is complete in itself, may be exercised to its utmost extent."[83]

According to the most recent history of the Marshall Court, however, Marshall's *Gibbons* opinion was "highly inconclusive. . . . *Gibbons,* for all the fanfare with which it was received, settled very little and that in an awkward fashion."[84] This surely understates the seminal role of the *Gibbons* decision in the expansion of federal power. Justice William O. Douglas once stated that the Commerce Clause "is the fount and origin of vast power."[85] But that is true only because, in *Gibbons,* "Marshall described the federal commerce power with a breadth never yet exceeded."[86] So interpreted, the Commerce Clause was to become the source of the most important powers the Federal Government exercises in time of peace. If in recent years it has become trite to point out how regulation from Washington controls Americans from the cradle to the grave, that is true only because of the Marshall Court's emphasis at the outset on the embracing and penetrating nature of the federal commerce power.

Looking back, it is easy to conclude that the Marshall conception was demanded by the needs of the developing nation. To Americans today, the broad construction of the federal commerce power was plainly essential to the period of growth upon which the United States was entering. To the men of Marshall's day, the need was not nearly so obvious. To appreciate the very real contribution to national power made by *Gibbons v. Ogden,* we must contrast the opinion there with the restricted scope which President James Monroe had just given to the commerce power in his 1822 veto of the Cumberland Road Act (which provided for the building of a federal road to the West). According to Monroe, "A power . . . to impose . . . duties and imposts in regard to foreign nations and to prevent any on the trade between the States, was the only power granted."[87] Marshall's sweeping opinion ruthlessly brushes aside this narrow theory. That Marshall was able to mold his convictions on effective national power into positive law at the outset made a profound difference to the development of the American nation.

Contracts, Corporations, and Property

According to Vernon L. Parrington, "The two fixed conceptions which dominated Marshall during his long career on the bench were the sovereignty of the federal state and the sanctity of private property."[88] In the landmark cases just discussed, Marshall used constitutional law to establish federal sovereignty as the foundation of the polity. But he also employed the law to further the protection of property rights, which, to him as to other jurists of the day, was a primary end of law. Marshall subscribed completely to the then-prevailing conception of a natural right to acquire property and to use it as one saw fit.[89] He referred to "the right which every man retains to acquire property, to dispose of that property according to his own judgement, and to pledge himself for a future act. These rights are not given by society, but are brought into it."[90]

To Marshall, the natural right of property was one to be exercised free from governmental interference. "I consider," he once wrote, "the interference of the legislature in the management of our private affairs, whether those affairs are committed to a company or remain under individual direction, as equally dangerous and unwise. I have always thought so and still think so."[91]

However, the Marshall conception of property rights, like that of other early American jurists, differed essentially from that in England. American property law was expansive rather than defensive in character. We can see this in the changes already made in this country in the land law, which had freed real property from most of the restrictions that still prevailed in English law. Speaking of the English system, a New York court asserted, "This ancient, complicated and barbarous system . . . is entirely abrogated."[92] Real property in this country became allodial (i.e., unrestricted) with the freehold established as the normal type of land title.[93]

If land could now be dealt with according to the will of the owner, the same was soon to be true of other forms of property. But individual property rights alone, even liberated from common law archaisms, were scarcely enough for the needs of the expanding American economy. The industrial growth which so strikingly altered the nature of the society during the nineteenth century could scarcely have been possible had it depended solely upon the initiative and resources of the individual entrepreneur. It was the corporate device that enabled men to establish the pools of wealth and talent needed for the economic conquest of the continent.

The ability of American courts to adapt the common law to the nation's requirements is nowhere better seen than in the development of corporation law. The American law of corporations, more than most branches of our judge-made law, was an indigenous product.[94] The English courts had for centuries been deciding cases relating to corporate problems, but the law developed by them dealt almost entirely with nonprofit corporations and was of limited value in solving the problems confronting business enterprises in the United States. The development of the business corporation (formed to carry on business for profit) and resolution of the legal issues connected with it were almost entirely the handiwork of American law.

Corporation law itself well illustrates the developing conception of American law. From the beginning, American judges looked with favor upon the corporate device as a method of doing business. It was during the Marshall era that the first steps were taken in "[t]he constant tendency of judicial decisions in modern times . . . in the direction of putting corporations upon the same footing as natural persons."[95] Corporations may, in Coke's famous phrase, "have no souls,"[96] but they gained the essentials of legal personality by the decisions of the Marshall Court.

It was Marshall who laid down the first essential prerequisite to corporate expansion in the *Dartmouth College* case (1819).[97] The decision there vested the corporation with constitutionally protected contract rights by holding that a corporate charter was a contract within the protection of the Contract Clause of the Constitution. The corporate creature of the law— "invisible, intangible, and existing only in contemplation of law"[98]—was endowed with basic legal rights even against its creator.

Sir Henry Maine, writing in 1885, characterized the *Dartmouth College* decision as "the basis of the credit of many of the great American Railway Incorporations." It is, he went on, its principle "which has in reality secured full play to the economical forces by which the achievement of cultivating the soil of the North American Continent has been performed."[99] At a time when no other constitutional provision would serve the purpose, corporate property rights were brought under the fostering guardianship of the Contract Clause. Those who were called upon to pool their wealth and talents in the vast corporate enterprises needed for the nation's development were thus ensured that their contributions would not remain at the mercy of what Justice Story termed "the passions of the popular doctrines of the day."[100] Before *Dartmouth College,* there were still relatively few manufacturing corporations in the country. Under the confidence created by Marshall's decision, those corporations proliferated to such an extent that they soon transformed the face of the nation.[101]

A historian of the Marshall Court concludes that its decisions affecting property and business "facilitated commerce, shaped the law to conform to the dictates and practices of the market, and developed doctrinal rules that were consistent with dynamic and expansive uses of property and mechanisms of commercial exchange."[102] More than that, the justices were well aware of the social and economic ramifications of their decisions. That was particularly true of the man who sat in the Court's center chair. Here, too, Marshall looked at the law as a tool to enable the needs of the society to be served. In cases like *Dartmouth College,* he helped mold legal doctrine both to protect property rights and to further economic expansion.

Of course, Marshall made mistakes in using the law as a means to accomplish the ends he favored. His *Dartmouth College* decision may have fostered the corporate proliferation that soon distinguished American economic development. In Bank of the *United States v. Dandridge,*[103] however, Marshall refused to loosen the bonds of corporate formalism that had so restricted the use of the corporation in English law. At issue was what the Supreme Court historian termed "a vital question of corporation law—whether approval of acts of its agents by a corporation may be shown by presumptive testimony or only by written record and vote."[104] Marshall held on circuit that the record and vote were necessary. As he wrote to a colleague at the time, "I thought the assent of the Bank Directors indispensable . . . and that consent I thought could be given only at the board and could be proved only by the minutes of their proceedings."[105]

An "affirmance of this view by the Court would have retarded the commercial development of this country immeasurably,"[106] for it would have required corporate contracts to be cast in the elaborate forms of English law, with a record and vote required for each contract. Marshall himself recognized that his decision was contrary to corporate practice. "The case," he wrote to Justice Story, "goes to the Supreme Court & will probably be reversed. I suppose so, because I conjecture that the practice of banks has not conformed to my construction of the law." Marshall did, however, indicate, "I shall retain the opinion I have expressed."[107] When the Court, in an opinion by Story, did reverse his circuit decision, Marshall delivered a rare lengthy dissent.

Dandridge was the exception in the Marshall jurisprudence. Normally, Marshall spoke for the Court and his opinions used the law to lay the legal foundations of the political and economic order that he favored. Marshall is considered great because his conception coincides with what we now deem were the dominant needs of the new nation. This is all but self-evident to anyone familiar with our legal history, so far as Marshall's public-law opinions are concerned. They confirmed the expansive interpretation of the Constitution and helped to weave the legal fabric of Union in such a way that it was to prove strong enough to withstand even the shock of civil war.

But the same approach was generally used by Marshall in his opinions dealing with property and business. It should not be forgotten that, even in the Marshall era of burgeoning constitutional law, nonconstitutional cases still made up the bulk of the Court's docket.[108] The developing American common law was also shaped by Marshall and his colleagues to serve the needs of the expanding society and economy. Many of the cases involved adjudication of real property disputes, and the decisions furthered the change in the legal conception of land from a static locus to a commodity that could be bought and sold in a market economy.[109] Tocqueville contrasts the European expectation of passing on to sons land held in a long family line with his observation of the American practice, where the farmer "brings lands into tillage in order to sell it again, . . . on the speculation that, as the state of the country will soon be changed by the increase of population, a good price may be obtained for it."[110] The Marshall Court, like other courts of the day, fostered the change from the European to the American practice.

The same was true of the Court's commercial cases. The legal status of contracts and secured transactions produced a jurisprudence that would facilitate the operation of the developing commercial market.[111] Corporate growth was advanced by the treatment of corporations as property owners having protected constitutional rights. Commercial dealings were furthered by emphasis on the security of transactions freely entered into; the basic legal principle became that promises be kept and undertakings be carried out in good faith. When the Court held in *Coolidge v. Payson* (1817)[112] that a promise to accept a bill of exchange had the same effect as an acceptance, where a person had taken it on the credit of the promise, the Marshall opinion explained that the decision would promote commercial transactions based upon the bill: "The great motive for considering a promise to accept, as an acceptance, is, that it gives credit to the bill, and may induce a third person to take it." Marshall stressed that "[i]t is of much importance to merchants that the question should be at rest" and, according to a note by the reporter, the Marshall "decision may be considered as settling the law of the country on the subject."[113]

However, like Lord Mansfield, his great counterpart on the other side of the Atlantic, Marshall recognized that commercial law could not be based upon common law alone. "Bills of exchange," he affirmed on circuit, "are transferable . . . by the custom of merchants. Their transfer is regulated by usage and that usage is founded in convenience."[114] In the *Coolidge* case, Marshall refused to follow English decisions disapproving of "the doctrine of implied acceptance"[115] because he deemed them to be "anticommercial"[116] and unsuited to an expanding market economy. Instead, under the Marshall decision, a promise to accept a bill of exchange converted the bill into an instrument which could be negotiated by other, even unknown, parties. The original instrument had been turned into a negotiable instrument that could be circulated to third persons.[117]

To the Marshall Court, the key consideration was the need to further negotiability so that commercial paper could properly serve the needs of the developing economy. As Justice Story was later to put it, "It is for the benefit and convenience of the commercial world to give as wide an extent as practicable to the order and circulation of negotiable paper."[118] The result, a history of the Marshall Court concludes, was that "[t]he sanctioning of negotiability meant that commercial paper would be a commonplace of American business life."[119] Promissory notes and other negotiable instruments became an essential medium of commercial exchange.

The legal rules developed by Marshall and his colleagues reflected changing business practices and facilitated their spread. The Court "shaped the law to conform to the dictates and practices of the market, and developed doctrinal rules that were consistent with dynamic and expansive uses of property and mechanisms of commercial exchange."[120] The changes in the economy were paralleled by the rules affecting contracts, property, and negotiable instruments laid down by the Marshall Court.

Marshall's Own Defense

Though, as seen, public opinion at the time largely ignored the *Marbury v. Madison* holding on judicial review, Thomas Jefferson was well aware of its potential. In a letter to Judge Spencer Roane, Jefferson characterized Marshall's *Marbury* opinion as follows: the Constitution "has given, according to this opinion, to one of them alone the right to prescribe rules for the government of the others; and to that one too which is unelected by, and, independent of, the nation, for experience has already shewn that the impeachment it has provided is not even a scare crow. . . . The constitution, on this hypothesis is a mere thing of wax in the hands of the judiciary, which they may twist and shape into any form they please."[121]

Spencer Roane, to whom Jefferson thus wrote, was the President of the Virginia Court of Appeals, and head of the Republican party organization in the state. Jefferson had planned to appoint Roane as Chief Justice upon the death of Chief Justice Ellsworth; his plan had been thwarted when Ellsworth resigned in time to permit Adams to nominate Marshall as his successor. From then on, there was a bitter enmity between Marshall and Roane. In fact, according to Marshall's biographer, Roane was one of only two men who hated the Chief Justice personally (the other was Jefferson).[122]

But the antagonism between Marshall and Roane was based upon more than personal ill will. Their hostility was fueled by fundamental differences in constitutional philosophy and principle. Marshall was, of course, the great exponent of the Federalist conception of the Constitution, elevating that view to the supreme law of the land. Roane had a diametrically opposed view of the legitimate sphere of federal authority. He has been called "the most energetic states' rights ideologue of all."[123]

In 1819 Roane published four essays in the *Richmond Enquirer,* signed "Hampden," in which he bitterly attacked the nationalistic decisions of the

Marshall Court. The Chief Justice was greatly disturbed by the "Hampden" essays, which he likened to a "most furious hurricane" that had burst on the judges' heads. "I find myself," he stated, "more stimulated on this subject than on any other because I believe the design to be to injure the Judges & impair the constitution. I have therefore thoughts of answering these essays."[124]

Marshall published nine essays in the *Alexandria Gazette* in answer to Roane. They were signed "Friend of the Constitution," for the Chief Justice sought to keep his authorship secret and it was not until recently that it was made known that the essays were written by Marshall himself.

His extrajudicial excursus—so untypical of the judge, who otherwise let his opinions speak for themselves—showed how strongly Marshall felt about the principles laid down in his leading opinions. In addition, his "Friend of the Constitution" essays dramatically demonstrate how Marshall used our public law to give effect to the type of polity he deemed appropriate to the developing nation.

Roane's "Hampden" essays had attacked the Marshall decisions as "well calculated to aggrandize the general government, at the expense of the states; to work a consolidation of the confederacy."[125] Their result, Roane asserted, was "to give a Carte Blanche to our federal rulers, and to obliterate the state governments, forever, from our political system." In particular, the *McCulloch v. Maryland* interpretation of the Necessary-and-Proper Clause had been the object of the Roane censure. Under the clause, Hampden asserted, "the only enquiry is whether the power is properly an incident to an express power and necessary to its execution, and if it is not, congress cannot exercise it." Only "such means were implied, and such only, as were *essential* to effectuate the power."

Marshall's essays replied "that this charge of 'in effect expunging those words from the constitution,' exists only in the imagination of Hampden. It is the creature of his own mind." The Constitution as "expounded by its enemies" would "become totally inoperative." They "may pluck from it power after power in detail, or may sweep off the whole at once by declaring that it shall execute its acknowledged powers by those scanty and inconvenient means only which the states shall prescribe." The national government would then "become an inanimate corpse, incapable of effecting" the objects for which it was created.

Marshall strongly objected to Hampden's claim that the grant of implied powers "is limited to things strictly necessary, or without which the obligation could not be fulfilled." Instead, said Marshall, the grant to Congress "carried with it such additional powers as were *fairly incidental* to them."

Hampden had relied upon common-law authorities, particularly Coke. Marshall countered by expanding on his seminal *McCulloch* dictum.[126] The difference, he declared, between "the examples taken . . . from the books of the common law; and the constitution of a nation" are apparent. The Constitution is not a contract: "It is the act of a people, creating a government, without which they cannot exist as a people . . . it is impossible to construe such an instrument rightly, without adverting to its nature, and marking the points of difference which distinguish it from ordinary contracts." Such an instrument gives only the "great outlines" of governmental power and is not to be construed like an instrument with "a single [object] which can be minutely described."

As in his opinions, Marshall's essays stressed the Hamiltonian principle of liberal construction which must govern constitutional doctrine. Under it, the "means for the execution of powers should be proportioned to the powers themselves."

Roane had repudiated Marshall's famous dictum, that "it is a *constitution* we are expounding,[127] saying, "If it is a constitution, it is also a *compact* and a limited and defined compact." To this Marshall sarcastically noted, "[H]e is so very reasonable as not to deny that it is a constitution." All Marshall meant, he wrote, was "only that, in ascertaining the true extent of those powers, the constitution should be fairly construed." Under this approach, "the choice of these means devolve on the legislature, whose right, and whose duty it is, to adopt those which are most advantageous to the people, provided they be within the limits of the constitution."

In particular, Marshall rejected the notion that the Necessary-and-Proper Clause limited Congress "to such [laws] as are indispensable, and *without which* the power would be nugatory." Such a principle would be disastrous: "[T]his principle, if recognized, would prove many of those acts, the constitutionality of which, are universally acknowledged . . . to be usurpations."

Toward the end of his essays, Hampden had attacked the Court's jurisdiction to decide cases involving conflicts between federal and state power. Marshall realized that the core issue here between him and his adversary was that of the nature of the Constitution. "[T]he point to which all his arguments tend," Marshall stated, is "his idea that the ligament which binds the states together, is an alliance, or a league." To support this principle, "an unatural [*sic*] or restricted construction of the constitution is pressed upon us . . . which would reduce the constitution to a dead letter." The Roane attack upon the Court's jurisdiction was based upon what Marshall termed the "unaccountable delusion . . . that our constitution is . . . a compact, between the several state governments, and the general government."

As in his opinions, Marshall's essays completely rejected the compact theory upon which the position of states'-rights advocates such as Roane was based. "Our constitution," Marshall affirmed in his essays, "is not a compact. It is the act of a single party. It is the act of the people of the United States, assembling in their respective states, and adopting a government for the whole nation."

Marshall next went into the Court's constitutional role. "For what purpose," he asked, "was [the judicial] department created?" The answer was apparent to "any reasonable man . . . must it not have been the desire of having a tribunal for the decision of all national questions?" The Constitution clearly answered in the affirmative when it provided for federal judicial power over "cases . . . arising under the constitution, and under the laws and treaties of the U. States."

Roane had, however, urged that the Supreme Court could not decide such a case "without treading under foot the principle that forbids a man to decide his own cause." Marshall countered by asking, "To whom more safely than to the judges are judicial questions to be referred? . . . It is not then the party sitting in his own cause. It is the application to individuals by one department of the acts of another department of the government. The people are the authors of all; the departments are their agents; and if the judge be personally disinterested, he is as exempt from any political interest that might influence his opinion, as imperfect human institutions can make him."

Marshall asked what alternative there was to Supreme Court jurisdiction in cases arising under the Constitution. Roane had said, "[T]hey must of course be decided in the state courts." But see where that would leave us. "It follows then that great national questions are to be decided, not by the tribunal created for their decision by the people of the United States, but by the tribunal created by the state which contests the validity of the act of congress, or asserts the validity of its own act." The result was summed up in Marshall's concluding sentences: "Let Hampden succeed, and that instrument will be radically changed. The government of the whole will be prostrated at the feet of its members; and that grand effort of wisdom, virtue, and patriotism, which produced it, will be totally defeated."

The Roane-Marshall essays show how the opposing schools of constitutional construction used their jurisprudence to further the type of polity and society that they favored. Leader of the Republican Junto in Virginia, Roane shared the Jeffersonian vision of national development—emphasizing an idealistic agrarianism instead of the centralizing capitalism that was emerging. Jefferson had urged the danger of a consolidated government, which invariably tended toward self-aggrandizement—with the inevitable result a political Leviathan. The danger could be avoided by circumscribing central power and emphasizing states' rights.

Marshall's vision was an entirely different one. For him, what was required was a truly national government that would neet the needs of an expanding people and promote the physical and economic conquest of the continent. The sovereignty of the federal state was the fixed conception that dominated Marshall throughout his judicial tenure. His constitutional jurisprudence was consistently molded to give effect to this overriding conception.

If Roane and his fellow states' righters had obtained the palm, they would have used their victory to secure a polity and society very different from that which did evolve. The legal doctrines on which Roane rested his "Hampden" critique were employed to reach the constitutional results conducive to attainment of his political and social ends.

But the same was true of Marshall. His "Friend of the Constitution" essays, like his judicial opinions, were intended to supply the legal support for the values in which he believed. At the core of the Marshall conception was the supremacy of federal power, exercised by a government endowed with the means necessary to give effect to his vision of a strong nation. In the emerging struggle between the commercial and agrarian interests, Marshall's jurisprudence emphatically supported the former. If the compact theory meant keeping the Federal Government secondary in all but "indispensably requisite" powers to state sovereignties, it had to be repudiated. Instead of a rigid approach to national authority, constitutional doctrine must be the plastic one exemplified by *McCulloch*'s construction of the Necessary-and-Proper Clause.

Chase Impeachment

Marshall's work in strengthening the judicial department was strongly resisted by the Jeffersonian party, which was dominant in the other two departments. Jefferson was, indeed, Marshall's principal antagonist throughout his life. To the great democrat, control of the validity of governmental acts by nonelected judges "would place us under the despotism of an oligarchy."[128] He never really appreciated the need for judicial review as the true safeguard of constitutional rights against the power of government.

The Jeffersonians did not confine their opposition to the judges to verbal criticism such as that in Roane's "Hampden" essays. Instead, they sought to use the weapon of impeachment to bend the judicial department to their will. Their efforts in that direction culminated in the 1805 attempt to secure the removal by impeachment of Justice Samuel Chase, then a member of the Marshall Court. The charges against Chase were based on his acts while on the bench and were far removed from the "high Crimes and Misdemeanors" required by the Constitution. Rather, it was generally recognized that the impeachment was political in purpose. As Senator William Branch Giles, the Jeffersonian leader in the upper House, candidly expressed it to John Quincy Adams while the Chase trial was pending, "We want your offices, for the purpose of giving them to men who will fill them better."[129] It was widely believed that the Chase impeachment was to be but the first step in the Jeffersonian plan. "The assault upon Judge Chase," wrote John Quincy Adams to his father, "was unquestionably intended to pave the way for another prosecution, which would have swept the Supreme Judicial Bench clean at a stroke."[130]

The arrangements for the Chase trial were as dramatic as the event itself. The pomp of the Warren Hastings impeachment, when, says Macaulay, "The grey old walls were hung with scarlet," was still vivid in the minds of all, and perhaps in imitation, the Senate Chamber was, in the words of one Senator, "fitted up in a stile beyond anything which has ever appeared, in the Country." The Senate Chamber too was "aglow with theatrical color . . . [the] benches . . . covered with crimson cloth." As Henry Adams characterized it, "The arrangement was a mimic reproduction of the famous scene in Westminster Hall; and the little society of Washington went to the spectacle with the same interest and passion which had brought the larger society of London to hear the orations of Sheridan and Burke."[131]

The Chase trial itself resulted in an acquittal, for enough Senators of the Jeffersonian party were convinced by the argument of the defense—"Our property, our liberty, our lives, can only be protected and secured by [independent] judges"[132]—to make the vote for conviction fall short of the constitutional majority. "The significance of the outcome of the Chase trial," says Chief Justice William H. Rehnquist, "cannot be overstated."[133] Had Justice Chase been removed, it would have made impossible the independence of the judiciary upon which the constitutional structure rests. The Chase acquittal, as a matter of history, put an end to the danger of judicial removal on political grounds. Since 1805, though impeachment proceedings have been brought against other federal judges, in none of these cases was the effort to secure removal based upon political reasons.

The Chase acquittal meant that the Marshall Court could exercise the constitutional authority asserted by it without fear or favor. To Marshall, as has been stressed, judicial power was not an end in itself, but only a means to attain the end of a sound national structure. Once he had obtained for the Court the authority to enforce the Constitution, and once the independence had been secured that is the essential prerequisite for the fearless exercise of such authority, Marshall could turn the judicial instrument to the forging of the legal bonds of a strong Union. The nationalism nurtured at Valley Forge was to flower in the great decisions by which were hewn the high road of the nation's destiny.

Marshall's Colleagues

Describing her 1835 visit to the Supreme Court, the British writer Harriet Martineau told how she heard Chief Justice Marshall deliver an opinion in his "mild voice" and gave her impression of his colleagues on the bench: "[T]he three Judges on either hand gazing at him more like learners than associates."[134] Virtually every estimate of the Marshall Court agrees with the Martineau characterization. Though the Brethren on his bench were men of intellectual stature, they were overshadowed by the Chief Justice, who dominated his Court as few judges have ever done.

To be sure, during his first years on the bench, the Court was composed of Federalists who were expected to share Marshall's nationalistic views. However, in 1811, after Gabriel Duval and Joseph Story replaced Justices Chase and Cushing, the Court had a Republican majority. Yet, as his leading biographer tells us, "Marshall continued to dominate it as fully as when its members were of his own political faith and views of the government. In the whole history of courts there is no parallel to such supremacy."[135]

What gave Marshall his commanding influence? Certainly it was not his intellect and learning. Joseph Story was his equal in the first and by far his superior in the second and William Johnson had both a strong intellect and a far better education. Bushrod Washington would also have been a prominent judge on any other Court. All three Justices, however, stood in the Chief Justice's shadow throughout their judicial tenure.

In the end, Marshall's dominance over his associates rests upon two things. The first is the elusive quality we call leadership—to which we can apply Justice Potter Stewart's celebrated aphorism: "I could never succeed in [defining it]. But I know it when I see it."[136] It may be impossible to say what makes a great leader. But we know leadership when we see it; and we *know* that Marshall was *the* leader par excellence of the highest Court. Whatever the qualities of judicial leadership may be, Marshall plainly possessed them to the ultimate degree.

Just as important, however, was that the principal Marshall decisions corresponded to the "felt necessities"[137] of the developing nation. The Republican appointees came to see this as clearly as the Chief Justice himself. In a day when, to most Americans, one's state was still one's country, all the Justices understood the need to assert national power and the need for a powerful Union.

Even a strong Jeffersonian such as Justice William Johnson worked as constantly as Marshall for principles that would strengthen the bonds of union.[138] In *Gibbons v. Ogden*,[139] for example, Johnson delivered a concurrence which, according to Beveridge, was more nationalist than Marshall's opinion of the Court itself.[140] The adherence of the entire Court to the principles articulated by Marshall bears out the assertion once made by Johnson that the "pure" men of both parties were in basic agreement on fundamentals.[141]

Joseph Story

Of Marshall's associates, the most important was Justice Story. Joseph Story is, of course, one of the great names in American law; he was perhaps the outstanding Justice during the nineteenth century and stands high on every list of the greatest American judges. Story was the most learned scholar ever to sit on the Supreme Court and also the youngest person ever named to the Court. He was only thirty-two when President Madison appointed him in 1811. Yet he had already been a Congressman, Speaker of the Massachusetts House, a leader at the Bar, and author of two volumes on pleading as well as three American editions of standard English works. More than that, he enjoyed a reputation as a minor poet. While studying law, he composed a lengthy poem, *The Power of Solitude*, referring to it in a letter as "the sweet employment of my leisure hours."[142] Story rewrote the poem, with additions and alterations, and published it with other poems in 1804. One who reads the extracts contained in his son's biography quickly realizes that it was no great loss to literature when Story decided to devote his life to the law. Story himself apparently recognized this, for he later bought up and burned all copies of the work he could find.

When the Supreme Court vacancy filled by Story occurred in 1810, Jefferson gloated "old Cushing is dead. At length then, we have a chance of getting a Republican majority in the Supreme Judiciary." Yet the former President also predicted "it will be difficult to find a character of firmness enough to preserve his independence on the same Bench with Marshall."[143] Story was soon the Court's leading supporter of Marshall's nationalistic views and became a vital second to the Chief Justice in constitutional doctrine.

In his opinions supporting Marshall, Story supplied the one thing the Chief Justice lacked—legal scholarship. "Brother Story here . . . can give us the cases from the Twelve Tables down to the latest reports," Marshall is reputed to have said.[144] If Marshall disliked the labor of investigating legal authorities to support his decisions, Story reveled in legal research. His opinions were usually long and learned and relied heavily on prior cases and writers.

Story may have been appointed as a Republican. But it soon became apparent that he fully shared Marshall's nationalistic views. His opinion in *Martin v. Hunter's Lessee,*[145] discussed earlier in this chapter, contributed as much as any the Chief Justice delivered to laying the jurisprudential foundation of a strong nation. And its impact was as great as any Marshall opinion. After Story had delivered his opinion, there was no disputing the appellate power of the Supreme Court over state court decisions. Story had demonstrated conclusively that the Union could not continue if state courts were able to defy it.

But it was not as a junior Marshall that Story left his main imprint on American law. If Marshall was the prime molder of early American public law, Story was his Supreme Court counterpart so far as private law was concerned. Early American commercial and admiralty law were largely the creation of Story's decisions. Story's opinions strikingly exemplified the common law's capacity to reshape itself to meet changing needs and develop the legal framework of the new industrial order. Important Story decisions blended the law of trusts with the rudimentary law of corporations that had developed in England to produce the modern business corporation and enable it to conduct its affairs on the same basis as natural persons.

The key case here was the *Dandridge* case.[146] Our previous discussion of the case showed Marshall taking an unusual narrow view and refusing to allow approval of acts of its agents by a corporation to be shown by presumptive testimony, but only by written record and vote. The Marshall approach, we saw, would have required corporate contracts to be cast in the elaborate forms of English law, with a record and vote required for each contract. That would have substantially hindered the growth of the business corporation in this country.

In *Dandridge*, however, it was Story, not Marshall, who spoke for the Court. Story's opinion held that the fact of approval could be shown by presumptive evidence. It stated specifically that the common law governing corporations was irrelevant to an American corporation created by statute. Instead, the corporation was to be treated like a natural person: "[T]he acts of artificial persons afford the same presumptions as the acts of natural persons."[147]

The *Dandridge* decision played a vital part in the development of the business corporation, which (as Kent's *Commentaries* then noted) was beginning to "increase in a rapid manner and to a most astonishing extent."[148] By permitting corporations to operate as freely as individuals, Story played a crucial part in accommodating the corporate form to the demands of the expanding American economy. The ability of the American courts to adapt the common law to the new nation's requirements is nowhere better seen than in cases such as *Dandridge*.

In his classic constitutional commentaries Story pointed out that the American colonists did not adopt the whole body of the common law, but only those portions which their different circumstances did not require them to reject.[149] "The common law of England," he wrote in another opinion, "is not to be taken in all respects to be that of America. Our ancestors brought with them its general principles, and claimed it as their birthright; but they brought with them and adopted only that portion which was applicable to their situation."[150] Indeed, the principal contribution of judges such as Story was to remold the common law to fit the different situation that existed on the western side of the Atlantic.

The quotation in the preceding paragraph is from Story's 1829 opinion in *Van Ness v. Pacard*,[151] where the traditional land law was adapted to meet the needs of the new mobile business economy rather than a static agricultural one. The Story decision modified the rigid conception of property that underlay the common-law rule on ownership of fixtures, rejecting the rule that the landlord owned all fixtures which the tenant had annexed to the land. Story's opinion "broke new ground in treating fixtures in terms of an increasingly mobile, business-oriented economy rather than a static agricultural one."[152] In an 1833 article, the common-law rule on fixtures was denounced as one that "must operate as a restraint upon the improvement of real property; and have a general tendency to lessen the amount of its productions and profits."[153] The Story decision helped avoid that consequence in American law. Under it, as Story's opinion put it, the law provided "every motive to encourage the tenant to devote himself to agriculture, and to favor any erection which should aid this result." Otherwise, "what tenant could afford to erect fixtures of much expense or value, if he was to lose his whole interest therein by the very act of erection?"[154]

Story's contribution in helping lay the American legal foundation was not limited to his work as a judge. In 1829, while he was still on the Supreme Court, Story became the first Dane Professor of Law at Harvard. His appointment signaled the reorganization of Harvard Law School and its emergence as the first modern school of law in the country. Despite his heavy judicial duties, he taught two of the three yearly terms at the school. He also found time to publish an amazing number of significant works that constituted the first great specialized treatises on American law. "I have now published seven volumes," he wrote in 1836, "and, in five or six more, I can accomplish all I propose."[155] By the end of his career he had published nine treatises (in thirteen volumes) on subjects ranging from constitutional to commercial law. They confirmed the victory of the common law in the United States and presented judges with authoritative guides. As a judge, Story may have been overshadowed by Marshall; as a law teacher and writer, he had no peer.

Other Associates

The Associate Justices on the Court during Marshall's early years as Chief Justice were succinctly characterized in a letter from Justice William Johnson to Jefferson: "Cushing was incompetent. Chase could not be got to think or write—Paterson was a slow man and willingly declined the trouble, and the other two judges you know are commonly estimated as one judge."[156]

The last two Justices referred to by Johnson were John Marshall and Bushrod Washington. The latter would have been an outstanding judge on any other court. Story wrote about him, "[H]e is highly esteemed as a profound lawyer, and I believe not without reason. His written opinions are composed with ability."[157] On the Marshall Court, however, he was, as the Johnson estimate indicates, virtually considered the Chief Justice's alter ego; the two differed in opinion only three times in their twenty-nine years together on the Court.[158]

Yet, when he worked outside of Marshall's shadow, Justice Washington did make important contributions of his own. It was Washington's opinion on circuit in *Corfield v. Coryell* (1823)[159] that gave the definitive answer to the question of what specific privileges and immunities are protected by the Comity Clause of article IV, which entitles "[t]he Citizens of each State . . . to all Privileges and Immunities of Citizens in the several States." Under Washington's opinion, the constitutional provision does not create any rights; it only ensures that such rights, so far as they do exist within a state, will be afforded equally to citizens of the state and other states. The Washington approach has been uniformly followed in later cases; it also set the pattern for the restricted interpretation of the Fourteenth Amendment's Privileges and Immunities Clause that has prevailed.[160]

The Court described by Justice Johnson began to change when Johnson was appointed in 1804 in place of Justice Moore, who had resigned.

Moore was said to possess a mind of uncommon strength and great power in analysis. On the Court, nevertheless, he was a virtual nonentity, having delivered an opinion in only one reported case.[161] William Johnson was an entirely different judge. His leading biography is titled *Justice William Johnson: The First Dissenter*.[162] Technically the subtitle is inaccurate. The first dissenter in the Supreme Court was Justice Johnson; but it was Justice Thomas Johnson who, we saw in the last chapter, delivered a dissent in the very first opinion reported in the Court.

The first Justice Johnson is, however, remembered, if at all, only for that first opinion; he did nothing more of consequence on the Court. Justice William Johnson, on the other hand, stands as Marshall's most competent colleague, aside from Justice Story himself. More than that, the second Justice Johnson was the member of the Marshall Court who displayed the most independence from the Chief Justice. His, says Justice Frankfurter, was one of the strongest minds in the Court's history.[163]

Johnson was appointed at the age of thirty-three (the second youngest Justice after Story). He was a member of South Carolina's highest court and was one of the leading Republicans of his state, having served in the legislature and been speaker of its lower House. He was Jefferson's first appointee, and the President desired most of all a loyal Republican who would serve as a counterweight to the Chief Justice and his jurisprudence.

His nominee was, in a Senator's characterization, "a zealous democrat," but he did not wholly fulfill Jefferson's expectations even though he was, as stated, the most independent member of the Marshall Court—the Justice least under the Chief Justice's sway. He was the first to demonstrate the potential of the dissenting opinion; he delivered his first dissent in his third term and delivered many more separate opinions than any other Marshall colleague. There were thirty-five concurring opinions and seventy-four dissents while Johnson was on the Court; of these he wrote twenty-one concurrences and thirty-four disssents.[164]

Yet Johnson himself virtually acquiesced in Marshall's unanimity rule after his first decade and a half on the Court. As Johnson explained it in a noted 1822 letter to Jefferson, "I . . . was not a little surprised to find our Chief Justice in the Supreme Court delivering all the opinions in cases in which he sat, even in some instances when contrary to his own judgment and vote. But I remonstrated in vain; the answer was he is willing to take the trouble and it is a mark of respect to him." After trying to resist the Marshall practice, Johnson went on, "At length I found that I must either submit to circumstances or become such a cipher in our consultations as to effect no good at all. I therefore bent to the current."[165]

Jefferson, however, persisted in his opposition to what he termed, in reply to Johnson, "cooking up opinions in conclave, [which] begets suspicions that something passes which fears the public ear." Jefferson stressed "the importance and the duty of [the judges] giving their country the only evidence they can give of fidelity to its constitution and integrity in the administration of its laws; that is to say, by every one's giving his opinion seriatim and publicly on the cases he decides."[166]

Jefferson's letters led Justice Johnson to renew his practice of speaking out—alone if need be. During his last ten terms on the Court, Johnson issued nine concurring and eighteen dissenting opinions.[167] In the end, however, if Jefferson had hoped that Johnson would lead a Republican opposition on the Court that would curb the Marshall jurisprudence, it proved a false hope. Jefferson had warned Johnson to resist Marshall's centralization of power in Washington.[168] "[I]n truth," he wrote to Johnson in 1823, "there is no danger I apprehend so much as the consolidation of our government by the noiseless, and therefore unalarming, instrumentality of the Supreme Court. This is the form in which federalism now arrays itself, and consolidation is the present principle of distinction between Republicans and these pseudo-republicans but real federalists."[169]

Johnson on the bench, however, revealed himself as nationalistic as any of his associates. He remained silent in the face of the McCulloch v. Maryland opinion,[170] thus acquiescing in what Jeffersonians deemed the heresy of implied powers.[171] Two years later, in 1821, the Justice wrote an opinion strongly supporting the implied powers doctrine in language that could have been written by Marshall himself.[172] In addition, Johnson raised no objection to the Chief Justice's resounding affirmation of the Court's jurisdiction to hear appeals from state courts.

Though Justice Johnson was silent in McCulloch, he indicated soon thereafter that he fully agreed with Marshall's broad construction of federal power there. In 1822, he answered President Monroe's reliance upon a narrow theory of federal power in his veto of the Cumberland Road Act. Johnson sent a letter to the President in which he asserted the McCulloch principle "that the grant of the principal power carries with it the grant of all adequate and appropriate means of executing it. That the selection of those means must rest with the general government and as to that power and those means the Constitution makes the government of the U.S. supreme." Indeed, Johnson wrote, he considered the McCulloch opinion so sound that the President should have it "printed and dispersed through the Union."[173]

These views were enough to make Johnson a virtual traitor in the eyes of the Jeffersonians.[174] Johnson and the other apostate Republican Justices were denounced in another series of newspaper articles by Spencer Roane, under the pen name "Algernon Sidney." "How else is it," Roane asked, referring to the Republican Justices, "that they also go to all lengths with the ultra-federal leader who is at the head of their court? That leader is honorably distinguished from you messieurs judges. He is true to his former politics. . . . He must be equally delighted and surprised to find his Republican brothers going with him."[175]

President Jefferson and his successors may have expected the Justices they appointed to change the course of Supreme Court jurisprudence. But it did not work out that way. Roane, to be sure, exaggerated in his

"Sidney" articles when he asserted that the Chief Justice's sway over his Court "is the blind and absolute despotism which exists in an army, or is exercised by a tyrant over his slaves."[176] Yet it cannot be doubted that Marshall remained, in Beveridge's characterization, as much the master of the Supreme Court after it acquired a Republican majority as he had been before that time.

The other Justices appointed by Jefferson and his successors appear in the Court's history even more as mere appendages to the Chief Justice. Certainly none of them has attained anything like the stature associated with Marshall's most important colleagues, Justices Story and Johnson, and, to a lesser extent, Justice Washington. Three of them have been called "silent Justices" in the Holmes Devise study of the Marshall Court.[177] They were Brockholst Livingston (appointed from New York in 1806 to succeed Justice Paterson), Thomas Todd (a Kentuckian chosen in 1807 to fill an additional seat created by Congress), and Gabriel Duval (appointed from Maryland in 1811 to succeed Justice Chase). Todd is now best known for the large number of terms (five out of nineteen) that he missed, Duval for his deafness, and Livingston for the duels he fought, in one of which he killed his adversary. All three could be counted on, in Story's phrase, to "steadfastly support . . . the constitutional doctrines which Mr. Chief Justice Marshall promulgated, in the name of the court."[178]

Of the other Marshall Court Justices, the only one who served for some time was Smith Thompson, a New Yorker appointed in 1823 to Justice Livingston's seat, in which he sat for twenty years. He is largely known for his active participation in politics even after his appointment; he ran for Governor of New York in 1828, thus breaking the practice established by Marshall and his colleagues of withdrawal from political activities (except for Justice Chase, of course, whose blatant electioneering for Adams had been one of the factors that led to his impeachment). Next to Justice Johnson, Thompson was the Justice who wrote the most concurrences and dissents. But his views were not consistent and he tended to support Marshall in the Court's opposition to the Jeffersonian Virginia School, though he did recognize a greater concurrent state power to regulate commerce than did the Chief Justice.[179]

Robert Trimble, another Kentuckian selected in 1826 in place of Justice Todd, gave signs of a potentially distinguished Court career. However, the potential was never realized, since he died two years after his appointment. The Marshall Court in its last years also had three Justices appointed by Andrew Jackson: John McLean (1829), Henry Baldwin (1830), and James Wayne (1835). There are indications that they would have supplied the opposition that might have ended Marshall's monolithic tenure. But they served too briefly with the great Chief Justice for that to happen. Instead, they made their principal contributions under Marshall's successor, Roger B. Taney.

Marshall's Jurisprudence

More than any other jurist, Marshall employed the law as a means to attain the political and economic ends that he favored. In this sense, he was the very paradigm, during our law's formative era, of the result-oriented judge. More than that, the law which he thus used was, in major part, molded as well as utilized by him. That is all but self-evident as far as Marshall's public-law decisions are concerned. The constitutional principles Marshall proclaimed in his cathedral tones were, in large part, principles of his own creation.

Marshall was undoubtedly one of the greatest legal reasoners. But his ability in that respect only masked the fact that he was the author as well as the expounder of his legal doctrines. His public-law opinions were based on supposedly timeless first principles which, once accepted, led, by unassailable logic, to the conclusions that he favored. "The movement from premises to conclusion is put before the observer as something more impersonal than the working of the individual mind. It is the inevitable progress of an inexorable force."[180]

Even Marshall's strongest critics were affected by the illusion. "All wrong, all wrong," we are told was the despairing comment of one critic, "but no man in the United States can tell why or wherein."[181]

It is not generally realized that Marshall also followed his instrumentalist approach in nonconstitutional cases. The common assumption has been that the Marshall Court was not a great common-law court and that its head was anything but a master of the common law. Thus it has often been pointed out that, in the Marshall–Story correspondence, there are requests from the Chief Justice for advice on various nonconstitutional issues. Now it is certainly true that Marshall never approached such issues with the mastery he displayed in his public-law opinions. Yet it unduly denigrates Marshall's legal ability to assume that he was a mere slouch as far as private law was concerned.

Such denigration of Marshall's legal ability has unfortunately not been uncommon. But "the fact is that he was a brilliant attorney whose expertise extended to both domestic and international law."[182] Few men have come to the Supreme Court with Marshall's legal experience. His legal education may, we saw, have been limited, but his years of practice had made him a leader of the Virginia bar and his cases covered the whole gamut of private law, particularly property and commercial law. Marshall's conception of private law was, of course, based primarily upon the common law. The young Marshall had been given a copy of Blackstone by his father, one of the original subscribers to the American edition, and the common law became the basis of his jurisprudence. During his brief study at William and Mary under George Wythe, Marshall wrote almost two hundred pages of manuscript notes, which were intended as a summary of the common law as it was then practiced in Virginia.[183]

Marshall had no doubt that American law had a common-law foundation. "My own opinion," he wrote in 1800, "is that our ancestors brought with them the laws of England both statute and common law, so far as they were applicable to our situation." With the Revolution and adoption of the Federal Constitution, "the common and statute law of each state remained as before and . . . the principles of the common law of the state would apply themselves to magistrates."[184]

To Marshall as to other common lawyers, the law was essentially judge-made law. That was why he placed such stress upon the role of the judge and the need for judicial independence and prestige. "That in a free country," he declared to Story, "any intelligent man should wish a dependent judiciary, or should think that the constitution is not a law for the court . . . would astonish me." Much of his hostility toward Jefferson was based upon Marshall's belief that Jefferson "looks of course with ill will at an independent judiciary."[185] During the Chase impeachment proceedings, Marshall asserted to the beleaguered Justice, "The present doctrine seems to be that a Judge giving a legal opinion contrary to the opinion of the legislature is liable to impeachment."[186]

But the judicial role was to Marshall plainly a means, not an end. The judge was to use his independence and prestige to mold the law in accordance with the needs of American society. In public law, the goal was to lay down constitutional principles that would give effect to the Marshall nationalistic vision. In private law, the end was both the protection of property rights and their expansion to permit them to be used to foster the growing entrepreneurial economy. Common-law principles were to be adapted, not transported wholesale in their English form. Both property and commercial law began to receive their modern cast, as a common law appropriate to the new nation's situation was being developed.

Oliver Wolcott once described Marshall as "too much disposed to govern the world according to rules of logic."[187] Marshall the logician is, of course, best seen in his magisterial opinions, which, to an age still under the sway of the syllogism, built up in broad strokes a body so logical that it baffled criticism from contemporaries.[188] To Marshall, however, logic, like law, was only a tool. Indeed, the great Chief Justice's opinions may be taken as an early judicial example of the famous Holmes aphorism: "The life of the law has not been logic: it has been experience."[189] Marshall, more than any early judge, molded his decisions to accord with "the felt necessities of the time." If this was often intuitive rather than conscious on his part, the intuitions were those that best furthered his notion of the public interest.[190]

For Marshall, then, the Constitution was a tool, and the same was true of the common law. Both public law and private law were to be employed to lay down the doctrinal foundations of the polity and economy that served his nationalistic vision of the new nation. Compared to Jefferson, the Marshall vision may have been a conservative one. Yet though their visions may not have been the same, both the great Chief Justice and his lifelong antagonist looked at the law as an instrument to serve the needs of the new nation.

Jefferson could write of "the rancorous hatred which Marshall bears to the government of his country." The truth is that each man had a different conception of what the American polity should become. Marshall saw all too acutely that the Jeffersonian theme was sweeping all before it. "In democracies," he noted in 1815, "which all the world confirms to be the most perfect work of political wisdom, equality is the pivot on which the grand machine turns." As he grew older, Marshall fought the spread of the equality principle, notably in the Virginia Convention of 1829–1830. For, as he saw it, "equality demands that he who has a surplus of anything in general demand should parcel it out among his needy fellow citizens."[191]

Yet if Marshall's last effort against the triumph of Jacksonian democracy—was doomed to failure, his broader battle for his conception of law was triumphantly vindicated. One the least conversant with our public law knows that it is the Marshall conception of the Constitution that has dominated Supreme Court jurisprudence, particularly during the present century. But the same has also been true of the Marshall concept of private law. The Marshall Court decisions adapting the common law to the needs of the expanding market economy led the way to the remaking of private law in the entrepreneurial image. Free individual action and decision became the ultimate end of law, as it became that of the society itself. The law became a prime instrument for the conquest of a continent and the opening of the economy to men of all social strata. Paradoxically perhaps, it was Marshall, opponent of Jefferson–Jackson democracy though he may have been, whose conception of law furthered opportunity and equality in the marketplace to an extent never before seen.

3

Taney Court, 1837–1864

"Imagine a Court . . . conducting its business not in a massive building but in a basement room of an unfurnished Capitol."[1] One familiar with the marble temple in which the highest bench now sits will find it hard to picture the dingy quarters which that tribunal occupied during its early years. We saw in Chapter 2 that when the new capital was built, no chamber had been built for the Supreme Court. Instead, when the Government moved to Washington, the Court had to hold its sessions in a House committee room on the first floor of the Capitol. When the Capitol north wing was rebuilt in 1809, the Court moved to a new courtroom underneath the reconstructed Senate Chamber. After the British burned the Capitol in 1814, the Court moved to temporary quarters for five years. They were back in their basement courtroom for the 1819 Term.

That courtroom was almost as unimpressive as the committee room in which the Court first sat. In the first place, as a newspaper described it, "The apartment is not in a style which comports with the dignity of that body, or which wears a comparison with the other Halls of the Capitol . . . it is like going down cellar to reach it." Second, the paper complained, it was "a room which is hardly capacious enough for a ward justice." Hence it lacked the dignity appropriate for a puisne court, much less for the highest Court of the land. "Owing to the smallness of the room," the same article tells us, "the Judges are compelled to put on their robes in the presence of the spectators, which is an awkward ceremony, and destroys the effect intended to be produced by assuming the gown."[2]

Even the elevated bench that adds to a court's dignity was lacking.

"The part where the judges sit, is divided from the bar, by a neat railing; . . . beyond the railing, are the judges' seats, upon pretty nearly a level with the floor of the room, not elevated as are our judges' seats."[3]

Charles Sumner described the Court's basement chamber as "a dark room almost down cellar."[4] "A stranger," wrote a newspaper, "might traverse the dark avenues of the Capitol for a week, without finding the remote corner in which Justice is administered to the American Republic."[5] According to the sardonic comment of a contemporary, housing the Court underneath the Senate was "an arrangement wholly unjustifiable unless perhaps by the idea that Justice should underlie legislation."[6]

When Benjamin F. Butler visited a Supreme Court session with his son, the latter recalled that his "boyish attention was fastened upon the seven judges as they entered the room—seven being the number then composing the Court. It was a procession of old men—for so they seemed to me—who halted on their way to the bench, each of them taking from a peg hanging on the side of the wall near the entrance a black robe and donning it in full view of the assembled lawyers and other spectators."[7]

Marshall's Successor

It was just such a session over which Roger Brooke Taney first presided as Chief Justice at the beginning of 1837. The new Chief Justice was tall and impressive. He was, said an 1838 magazine article, "full six feet high: spare, but yet so dignified in deportment that you are at once impressed with an instinctive reverence and awe."[8] As he led the Supreme Court into its chamber on January 9, 1837, he looked the picture of a model judge. On that day Chief Justice Taney first took his seat in the Court's central chair[9] and began a new era in the constitutional history of the nation. Taney, of course, started with the handicap of having to fill the place of the greatest judge in our history.

The void created by Chief Justice Marshall's death can scarcely be overestimated. Wrote Joseph Story (who, as senior Associate Justice, had to "act as *locum tenens* of the Chief Justiceship"), "I miss the Chief Justice at every turn . . . the room which he was accustomed to occupy . . . wears an aspect of desolation."[10] The dejection of Marshall's admirers was compounded by apprehension with regard to his potential successor. "It is much to be feared," gloomily wrote John Quincy Adams, "that a successor will be appointed of a very different character. The President of the United States now in office . . . has not yet made one good appointment. His Chief Justice will be no better than the rest."[11]

Marshall's adherents had hoped against hope that Joseph Story would become the new Chief Justice. "The Supreme Court," Harvard President Josiah Quincy toasted, "may it be raised one Story higher."[12] President Andrew Jackson, however, could scarcely appoint one so opposed to his views. Instead, Story became a vigorous dissenter in the Taney Court, delivering caustic dissents like his opinion in the soon-to-be-discussed

Charles River Bridge case. Several weeks after it was delivered, he declared, "I am the last of the old race of Judges."[13]

Marshall himself toward the end of his life had expressed misgivings about the future of the Supreme Court. The advent of Jacksonian democracy, with its "enormous pretentions of the Executive," appeared but a portent of the fate that awaited both his constitutional labors and the strong national government which he sought to construct through them. "To men who think as you and I do," he wrote Story during the last year of his life, "the present is gloomy enough; and the future presents no cheery prospect."[14] Toward the end of his career, the great Chief Justice saw the Supreme Court defied, both by the State of Georgia and by the President himself. "Georgia," complained Adams, "has planted the Standard against the Supreme Court of the United States—and I hear the twenty-fifth Section of the Judiciary Law is to be repealed. To these proceedings there is an apparent acquiescence of the People in all Quarters."[15]

President Jackson, too, was the author of a vehement attack upon the very basis of the Supreme Court's review power in his famous 1832 message vetoing a bill to extend the charter of the Bank of the United States.[16] Well might Marshall feel that his long effort to construct judicial power as the cornerstone of an effective and enduring Union had been all but in vain.

Now it was Jackson who, on Marshall's death, was given the occasion to remold the Court in the feared radical image. He had an opportunity denied to most Presidents. He was able to place more men on the Supreme Court than any President before him except Washington or after him except Franklin D. Roosevelt. Not unnaturally, Jackson chose his six appointees from men of his own party, whom he felt he could trust. Not unnaturally, the Whigs attacked the packing of the Court with Democrats and Southerners (by 1837, soon after Jackson went out of office, a majority of the high tribunal, newly enlarged to nine, came from below the Mason-Dixon line). Such a bench, its opponents were convinced, would be all too ready to write the principles of Jacksonian democracy into the law. Above all, the opposition was apprehensive about Jackson's choice of a new Chief Justice. To Marshall's admirers, it must be admitted, no selection Jackson might have made, except perhaps Joseph Story, would have been satisfactory. Jackson's choice, asserted Story, "will follow a man who cannot be equalled and all the public will see . . . the difference."[17]

The apprehension of men like Story appeared justified when, on December 28, 1835, Jackson nominated Roger B. Taney as Chief Justice of the United States. It was Taney who had drafted the key portions of the 1832 Veto Message and who had been the instrument for carrying out the President's plan for the removal of Government deposits from the Bank of the United States. The veto had questioned the very review power of the Supreme Court, asserting that "the opinion of the judges has no more authority over Congress than the opinion of Congress has over the judges, and on that point the President is independent of both. The authority of the Supreme Court must not, therefore, be permitted to control the Congress or the Executive."[18] The choice of the author of these words to head a bench dominated by Jacksonian Democrats appeared to presage the virtual undoing of all that the Marshall Court had accomplished. Wrote Daniel Webster soon after the Taney nomination, "Judge Story . . . thinks the Supreme Court is *gone* and I think so too."[19]

Despite the bitterness of the opposition—"[T]he pure ermine of the Supreme Court," acidly affirmed one Whig newspaper, "is sullied by the appointment of that political hack"[20]—and the fact that Taney had, during the preceding two years, been turned down by the Senate as Secretary of the Treasury and as a Justice of the Supreme Court, this time his nomination was confirmed by the upper House, on March 15, 1836, by a nearly two-to-one majority. The majority in Taney's favor is somewhat surprising since the Jackson and anti-Jackson forces were equally divided in the forty-eight-member Senate. When John Tyler received his "walking papers from the [Virginia] Legislature"[21] and, the day before the vote, was replaced by a Democrat, the Jackson forces still had only the slimmest of majorities.

Apparently, what happened was that most of the Senate opposition abstained from the proceedings, largely because they felt that the Administration now had the votes necessary for the nomination. As Francis Scott Key tells it in a letter to his sister (Taney's wife), "Taney, Kendall & Barbour have all passed . . . those who did not choose to vote for them went off, knowing it was of no use to stay." Therefore, concluded Key, "I must greet you as Mrs. *Chief Justice Taney*."[22]

Taney and Jacksonian Democracy

Chief Justice Taney first sat with his Brethren when he was just under sixty years old. He was to serve until he was eighty-seven, a tenure as Chief Justice second only to that of Marshall. He was the first Chief Justice to wear trousers; his predecessors had always given judgment in knee breeches.[23] There was something of portent in his wearing democratic garb beneath the judicial robe,[24] for under Taney and the new majority appointed by Jackson, the Supreme Court for the first time mirrored the Jacksonian emphasis upon public power as a counterweight to the property rights stressed by the Federalists and then the Whigs.

Taney had been one of the foremost exponents of Jacksonian democracy; it has been asserted that the Jacksonian political theory is more completely developed and more logically stated in Taney's writings and speeches than anywhere else.[25] This assertion may be extreme, but it cannot be denied that Taney's years on the Court marked growing judicial concern for safeguarding of the rights of the community as opposed to property rights—of the public, as opposed to private welfare. "We believe property should be held subordinate to man, and not man to property," declared a leading Jacksonian editor, "and therefore that it is always lawful to make such modifications of its constitution as the good of Humanity requires."[26] The Taney Court was to elevate this concept to the constitutional plane.

Taney was well aware that his relationship to Jackson played a crucial part in his career. When the Senate approved his nomination, Taney wrote the President expressing warm gratitude, saying he would rather owe the honor to Jackson than to any other man in the world. It was a particular gratification, he declared, that "it will be the lot of one of the rejected of the panic Senate, as the highest judicial officer of the country to administer in your presence and in the view of the whole nation, the oath of office to another rejected of the same Senate, when he enters into the first office in the world."[27]

It is hard to understand Taney and his judicial work without awareness of his constant concern with the rejections that occurred during different stages of his career, from his early defeats in elections for Congress and the Maryland legislature[28] to the refusals of the Senate in 1834 and 1835 to confirm his nomination by Jackson as Secretary of the Treasury and then as Associate Justice of the Supreme Court. In this respect, Taney is one of the most difficult judicial historical subjects, much more so than Marshall, for his character was far more complex than that of his relatively straightforward predecessor. Like Marshall, he left an autobiographical sketch, but it is longer, rambling and abstruse, and unfinished.[29] It does clearly reveal his more complicated character—a constant emphasis on what he himself termed "morbid sensibility."[30] This sensibility, exaggerated perhaps by his delicate health and the fact that he was a Catholic in the Know-Nothing era, was to remain an essential part of the true Taney, beneath the stern facade shown to contemporaries. "I do not exactly understand why *Friday* has become the fashionable day for dinners here," he plaintively complained in an 1845 letter to his son-in-law, indicating his acute susceptibility to supposed slights at his religion.[31]

Taney was not only overly sensitive but had an exaggerated conception of himself as the very paragon of rectitude, an attitude that was to lead directly to the judicial fall that followed the *Dred Scott* decision. When he was first appointed to Jackson's Cabinet, he served briefly as both Attorney General and Acting Secretary of War. During that period he drew the salaries of both positions—something which strikes the observer as unethical. Yet he stoutly defended his action in an 1841 letter, declaring that "as I performed the duties of both offices, I received the salaries of both. I thought then and still think that it was right."[32]

Even at Marshall's death, it should have been evident that the doctrines of national power the great Chief Justice had espoused were bound to prevail. Contemporary admirers of the Marshall constitutional edifice might look upon Taney as the instrument chosen for its destruction, but Taney was not the man to preside at the liquidation of the tribunal he was called upon to head. On the contrary, the Supreme Court under him continued the essential thrust of constitutional development begun by Marshall and his colleagues.

In fact, if we look at Taney's constitutional work, avoiding the tendency to compare his accomplishments with the colossal structure erected by his predecessor, we find it far from a mean contribution. The shadow of the *Dred Scott* decision, it is now generally recognized, for too long cast an unfair pall over his judicial stature. To be sure, there was an inevitable reaction after Marshall's death, but it was not as great as has often been supposed. Chief Justice Taney may not have been as nationalistic in his beliefs as his predecessor, but his greater emphasis on states' rights should not obscure the continuing theme of his Court: that of formulating the principles needed to ensure effective operation of the Constitution.

In addition, it should be borne in mind that, however far-reaching Jacksonian democracy might have seemed to its contemporary opponents, it was, by present-day conceptions, quite limited. The Jacksonians did, it is true, go further than the Founders in the direction of both political and economic equality, but their notion of the democratic ideal as providing both liberty and equality for all must be sharply distinguished from the twentieth-century conception of the meaning of the word "all." The Jacksonians, like the Framers before them, did not understand the ideal of liberty and equality *for all men* to require the abolition of slavery, the emancipation of women from legal and political subjection, or the eradication of all constitutional discriminations based on wealth, race, or previous condition of servitude.[33] Yet, though the Jacksonian conception was limited, one should not underestimate its significance: it made substantial contributions to both the theory and practice of equality.

When the occasion demanded it, indeed, the Jacksonians could eloquently articulate the concept of equality and the premises upon which it was based. "In the full enjoyment of the gifts of Heaven and the fruits of superior industry, economy, and virtue," declared Jackson in his 1832 veto of the bill rechartering the Bank of the United States,

> every man is equally entitled to protection by law; but when the laws undertake to add to these natural and just advantages artificial distinctions, to grant titles, gratuities, and exclusive privileges, to make the rich richer and the potent more powerful, the humble members of society—the farmers, mechanics, the laborers—who have neither the time nor the means of securing like favors to themselves, have a right to complain of the injustice of their Government. . . . If it would confine itself to equal protection, and, as Heaven does its rains, shower its favors alike on the high and the low, the rich and the poor, it would be an unqualified blessing.[34]

The language quoted (which may have been written by Taney) is a statement, in positive terms, of the equal right of all persons to the equal protection of equal laws, comparable to the negative version in the Fourteenth Amendment, which was adopted thirty-six years later.[35]

Charles River Bridge Case

We need not, in Justice Frankfurter's phrase, subscribe to the hero theory of history to recognize that great men do make a difference, even in the law.[36] Certainly it made a difference that the 1837 Term of the Supreme Court was presided over by Taney instead of Marshall. In all likelihood Marshall would have decided differently in the three key decisions rendered in 1837.[37] The three cases had been argued while Marshall was still Chief Justice, but the Court had been unable to reach a workable decision. The cases were inherited by the Taney Court, and the new Chief Justice galvanized the Court into speedy action; the cases were all reargued and decided within less than a month after Taney first sat with his Brethren.

The Marshall Court had been concerned with strengthening the power of the fledgling nation so that it might realize its political and economic destiny. Like the Framers themselves, it stressed the need to protect property rights as the prerequisite to such realization. To Jacksonians like Taney, private property, no matter how important, was not the be-all and end-all of social existence. "While the rights of property are sacredly guarded," declared the new Chief Justice in his first important opinion, "we must not forget that the community also have rights, and that the happiness and well being of every citizen depends on their faithful preservation."[38] The opinion was delivered in *Charles River Bridge v. Warren Bridge*,[39] a case which was a cause célèbre in its day, both because it brought the Federalist and Jacksonian views on the place of property into sharp conflict and because stock in the corporation involved was held by Boston's leading citizens and Harvard College.

The Charles River Bridge had been operated as a toll bridge by a corporation set up under a charter obtained by John Hancock and others in 1785. Each year two hundred pounds was paid from its profits to Harvard. The bridge, opened on a day celebrated by Boston as a "day of rejoicing," proved so profitable that the value of its shares increased tenfold and its profits led to public outcry. The bridge became a popular symbol of monopoly, and, in 1828, the legislature incorporated the Warren Bridge Company to build and operate another bridge near the Charles River Bridge. The second charter provided that the new bridge would become a free bridge after a short period of time. This would, of course, destroy the business of the first bridge, and its corporate owner sued to enjoin construction, alleging that the contractual obligation contained in its charter had been impaired.

The case was elaborately argued on January 24, 1837, with Daniel Webster appearing for the Charles River Bridge, "and at an early hour all the seats within and without the bar . . . filled with ladies, whose beauty and splendid attire and waving plumes gave to the Court-room an animated and brilliant appearance such as it seldom wears."[40] Less than three weeks later, the Court was ready for decision. On February 11, Justice Story wrote to his Harvard colleague Professor Simon Greenleaf (who had argued in opposition to Webster), "[T]omorrow . . . the opinion of the Court will be delivered in the Bridge case. You have triumphed."[41]

The new Chief Justice delivered the opinion of the Court. Taney's opinion refused to hold that there had been an invalid infringement upon the first bridge company's charter rights. There was no express provision in the charter making the franchise granted exclusive or barring the construction of a competing bridge, and the basic principle is "that in grants by the public, nothing passes by implication."[42] Since there is no express obligation not to permit a competing bridge nearby, none may be read in.

In deciding as it did, the Taney Court laid down what has since become a legal truism: the rights of property must, where necessary, be subordinated to the needs of the community. The Taney opinion declined to rule that the charter to operate a toll bridge granted a monopoly in the area. Instead, the charter should be construed narrowly to preserve the rights of the community: where the rights of private property conflict with those of the community, the latter must be paramount. "The object and end of all government," Taney declared in words virtually setting forth the theme of Jacksonian democracy in the economic area, "is to promote the happiness and prosperity of the community by which it is established, and it can never be assumed that the government intended to diminish its power of accomplishing the end for which it was created." Governmental power in this respect may not be transferred, by mere implication, "to the hands of privileged corporations."[43]

Justice Story, who delivered a characteristically learned thirty-five-thousand-word dissent, bitterly attacked the majority decision, asserting in a letter to his wife that "a case of grosser injustice, or more oppressive legislation, never existed."[44] In his dissent, he declared that the Court, by impairing the sanctity of property rights, was acting "to alarm every stockholder in every public enterprise of this sort, throughout the whole country."[45] Yet, paradoxical though it may seem, it was actually the Taney decision, not the Story dissent, which ultimately was the more favorable to the owners of property, particularly those who invested in corporate enterprise.

Though in form the *Charles River Bridge* decision was a blow to economic rights, it actually facilitated economic development by providing the legal basis for public policy choices favoring technological innovation and economic change, even at the expense of some vested interests. The case arose when the corporate form was coming into widespread use as an instrument of capitalist expansion. In the famous *Dartmouth College* case,[46] the Marshall Court had ruled the grants of privileges in corporate charters to be contracts and, as such, beyond impairment by government. The Marshall approach here would have meant the upholding of the first bridge company's monopoly. Such a result would have had most undesirable consequences, for it would have meant that every bridge or turnpike company was given an exclusive franchise which might not be impaired by the newer forms of transportation being developed.

"Let it once be understood," declared Taney's *Charles River Bridge* opinion, "that such charters carry with them these implied contracts, and give this unknown and undefined property in a line of travelling; and you will soon find the old turnpike corporations awakening from their sleep, and calling upon this court to put down the improvements which have taken their place. The millions of property which have been invested in railroads and canals, upon lines of travel which had been before occupied by turnpike corporations, will be put in jeopardy."[47] To read monopoly rights into existing charters would be to place modern improvements at the mercy of existing corporations and defeat the right of the community to avail itself of the benefits of scientific progress.

"Taney's decision in the *Charles River Bridge* case," as Justice Frankfurter sums it up, "shows the statesman, Story's dissent proves that even vast erudition is no substitute for creative imagination."[48] Those who believed as Justice Story did, however, refused to see the beneficial implications of Chief Justice Taney's decision. Like all those wedded to the old order, they knew only that a change had been made in the status quo, and that was sufficient for their condemnation. "I stand upon the old law," plaintively affirmed the Story dissent, "upon law established more than three centuries ago . . . not . . . any speculative niceties or novelties."[49] In a letter written several weeks later, he dolefully declared, "I am the last of the old race of Judges."[50] To men like Story, Taney and the majority had virtually "overturned . . . one great provision of the Constitution."[51]

The truth, of course, is that the Taney Court had only interpreted the Contract Clause in a manner that coincided with the felt needs of the era of economic expansion upon which the nation was entering. Because of the Taney decision, that expansion could proceed unencumbered by inappropriate legal excrescences. By 1854, a member of the highest Court could confidently assert, with regard to the *Charles River Bridge* decision, "No opinion of the court more fully satisfied the legal judgment of the country, and consequently none has exerted more influence upon its legislation."[52]

State Power

Two other cases decided by the Taney Court during its first term received much public attention. They too had been inherited from the Marshall Court and were decided differently than they would have been before Taney's accession. Both *Briscoe v. Bank of Kentucky* and *New York v. Miln*[53] dealt with the question of reserved state power—an issue crucial in a federal system such as ours in which national and state governments coexist, each endowed with the complete accoutrements of government, including the full apparatus of law enforcement, both executive and judicial. Marshall, with his expansive nationalistic tenets, had perhaps tilted the scale unduly in favor of federal power. The Taney Court sought to redress the balance by shifting the emphasis to the reserved powers possessed by the states.

In the *Briscoe* case (1837), the Court held that the issuance by a state-owned bank of small-denomination notes which circulated as currency did not violate the constitutional prohibition against issuance by the states of bills of credit. According to the majority opinion of Justice John McLean, the notes were not bills of credit put out by the state since they were issued by the bank, not the state, even though the state owned the bank. Again Justice Story dissented. He tells us that Marshall himself—"a name never to be pronounced without reverence"—would not have been with the majority: "Had he been living, he would have spoken in the joint names of both of us."[54] As it was, Story was alone in his effort to preserve the reign of the dead hand.[55]

The *Briscoe* decision is today of purely historical significance since the problem of state power at issue there has long been academic. Yet the decision does show the willingness of the Taney Court to uphold state action if at all possible, even though it involved a refusal to look behind the form to the substance of the challenged action. Perhaps the best explanation of *Briscoe* is to be found in the Jacksonian fear of the growing power of finance, particularly as exemplified by "the power which the moneyed interest derives from a paper currency which they are able to control."[56] To avoid the evils of financial monopoly, the state was ruled able to regulate its circulating medium through the issue of notes by its own bank.[57]

More interesting to the present-day observer is *New York v. Miln* (1837), for it dealt with an aspect of state power that is still most pertinent, namely, the police power and its impact upon commerce. At issue in *Miln* was a New York law which required masters of vessels to report the names, places of birth, ages, health, occupations, and last legal residence of all passengers landing in New York City and to give security to the city against their becoming public charges. The city was seeking to collect the statutory penalty against the ship *Emily* because of its master's failure to file the report required by the statute. Defendant contended that the statute involved an invalid state regulation of foreign commerce since the power over such commerce was vested exclusively in Congress by the Constitution.

The opinion of the Court in *Miln* was written by Justice Philip P. Barbour (characterized by John Quincy Adams as that "shallow-pated wildcat . . . fit for nothing but to tear the Union to rags and tatters"),[58] who had been appointed to the Court at the same time as Taney. The Barbour opinion avoided the Commerce Clause issue, holding that the statute was valid as a matter of "internal police." The state's powers with regard to such "internal police" were not surrendered or restrained by the Constitution; on the contrary, "in relation to these, the authority of a state is complete, unqualified, and exclusive." The law at issue was passed by the state "to prevent her citizens from being oppressed by the support of multitudes of poor persons, who come from foreign countries, without possessing the means of supporting themselves. There can be no mode in which the power to regulate internal police could be more appropriately exercised."[59]

Perhaps the most significant aspect of *New York v. Miln* is its role in the development of the police power concept. That subject is so important that it deserves separate treatment. Here let us note another phase of the decision, which plainly appears anomalous today yet is useful to illustrate the restricted scope of the Jacksonian notions of freedom and equality. The *Miln* opinion asserts a general power in the states to exclude undesirables. "We think it," declared the opinion, "as competent and as necessary for a state to provide precautionary measures against the moral pestilence of paupers, vagabonds, and possibly convicts; as it is to guard against the physical pestilence, which may arise from unsound and infectious articles imported."[60] Similar language, it should be noted, was repeated in other decisions down to the turn of the century.[61]

Relying upon these Supreme Court dicta, many states enacted laws restricting the movement of indigent persons. Those laws were consistent with the historical common-law tradition of restricting the liberty of the pauper. To the judges of a century ago, to strike down such a restriction would be to include in citizenship "a right of the indigent person to live where he will although the crowding into one State may be a menace to society. No such right exists."[62] But this justification for a statutory restriction upon the poor person's freedom of movement is now considered wholly inconsistent with our concepts of personal liberty.

In 1941 the Supreme Court ruled that the power to restrict freedom of movement may never be based upon the economic status of those restricted. The Court then stated that it did not consider itself bound by the contrary language in the *Miln* case, emphasizing that *Miln* was decided over a century ago: "Whatever may have been the notion then prevailing, we do not think that it will now be seriously contended that because a person is without employment and without funds he constitutes a 'moral pestilence.'"[63]

Police Power

Taney's leading biographer asserts that more credit has been given Taney in recent years for the development of the police power than he is entitled to or than he himself would have been willing to accept.[64] This assertion unduly denigrates the contribution of Taney and his Brethren in the development of what has become so seminal a concept in our public law. It was the Taney Court which first gave to the notion of police power something like its modern connotation. In his opinion in the *Charles River Bridge* case, Chief Justice Taney affirmed the existence of police power in the states: "We cannot . . . by legal intendments and mere technical reasoning, take away from them any portion of that power over their own internal police and improvement, which is so necessary to their well-being and prosperity."[65] And, as noted previously, the decision in *New York v. Miln* turned expressly upon the police power concept.

In the 1847 *License Cases* Taney himself gave to the police power the broad connotation that has been of such influence in molding the development of constitutional law:

> But what are the police powers of a State? They are nothing more or less than the powers of government inherent in every sovereignty to the extent of its dominions. And whether a State passes a quarantine law, or a law to punish offenses, or to establish courts of justice, or requiring certain instruments to be recorded, or to regulate commerce within its own limits, in every case it exercises the same power; that is to say, the power of sovereignty, the power to govern men and things within the limits of its dominion.[66]

In the Taney conception, police powers and sovereign powers are the same.[67] In this sense, the states retain all powers necessary to their internal government which are not prohibited to them by the Federal Constitution. Of course, such a broad conception of state power over internal government may be inconsistent with the fullest exertion of individual rights. Taney saw the inconsistency as inherent in the very nature of the police power. Indeed, it was his chief contribution to recognize and articulate the superior claim, in appropriate cases, of public over private rights. The Taney Court developed the police power as the basic instrument through which property might be controlled in the public interest. Community rights were thus ruled "paramount to all private rights . . . , and these last are, by necessary implication, held in subordination to this power, and must yield in every instance to its proper exercise."[68]

It was the Taney opinion in the *License Cases* which gave currency to the phrase "police power." In 1851 was decided the first case in the state courts to speak of the police power, the now classic Massachusetts case of *Commonwealth v. Alger,*[69] with its oft-cited definition of the term by Chief Justice Lemuel Shaw. Only four years later, a Missouri court could say of this power that it was "known familiarly as the police power."[70] By the time of the Civil War, certainly, the term was in common use throughout the land.

The Taney Court's articulation of the police power concept was a necessary complement to the expansion of governmental power that was an outstanding feature of the Jacksonian period. During that period "the demand went forth for a large governmental programme: for the public construction of canals and railroads, for free schools, for laws regulating the professions, for anti-liquor legislation."[71] In the police power concept, the law developed the constitutional theory needed to enable the states to meet the public demand. The Taney Court could thus clothe the states with the authority to enact social legislation for the welfare of their citizens. Government was given the "power of accomplishing the end for which it was created."[72] Through the police power a state might, "for the safety or convenience of trade, or for the protection of the health of its citizens,"[73] regulate the rights of property and person. Thenceforth, a principal task of the Supreme Court was to be determination of the proper balance between individual rights and the police power.

Commerce Regulation

One of the most difficult tasks of the Taney Court was that of determining the reach of the Commerce Clause and the proper scope of concurrent state power over commerce. In *New York v. Miln,*[74] it will be recalled, the Justices had avoided direct resolution of the question of whether the commerce power was exclusively vested in the Federal Government. The question came before the Supreme Court with increasing frequency because of the growing resort by the states to regulatory legislation.

Taney and his colleagues vacillated on the commerce issue, confirming, in the 1847 *License Cases,*[75] the power of the states to regulate the sale of liquor which had been imported from abroad, and then, in the 1849 *Passenger Cases,*[76] striking down state laws imposing a tax on foreign passengers arriving in state ports. The confusion in the Court was shown by the plethora of judicial pronouncements to which this issue gave rise. Nine opinions were written in the first case and eight in the second; in neither was there an opinion of the Court in which a majority was willing to concur.

To understand the problem presented in these cases involving commerce regulation, we should bear in mind that the Commerce clause itself is, as Justice Wiley Rutledge tells us, a two-edged sword.[77] One edge is the positive affirmation of congressional authority; the other, not nearly so smooth or keen, cuts down state power by negative implication. By its very inferential character, the limitation is lacking in precise definition. The clause may be a two-edged blade, but the question really posed is the swath of the negative cutting edge.[78] To put it more specifically, did the Commerce Clause, of its own force, take from the states any and all authority over interstate and foreign commerce, so that state laws on the subject automatically dropped lifeless from the statute books for want of the sustaining power that had been wholly relinquished to Congress?[79] Or was the effect of the clause less sweeping, so that the states still retained at least a portion of their residual powers over commerce?

According to Justice Story's dissent in *New York v. Miln,* the Marshall Court had rejected the notion that the congressional power was only concurrent with that of the states. Marshall, said Story, held that the power given to Congress was full and exclusive: "Full power to regulate a particular subject implies the whole power, and leaves no residuum; and a grant of the whole to one, is incompatible with the grant to another of a part."[80]

In actuality, despite the Story statement to the contrary, the Marshall view of the commerce power was not that of unequivocal federal exclusiveness, as shown by his opinion in *Willson v. Black Bird Creek Marsh Co.*

(1829).[81] In that case, a state law had authorized the construction of a dam across a small navigable creek for the purpose of draining surrounding marshland. It was claimed that the law was repugnant to the federal commerce power. Chief Justice Marshall rejected this contention, emphasizing in his opinion the benefits to be derived from draining the marsh in enhanced land values and improved health. "Measures calculated to produce these objects," he said, "provided they do not come into collision with the powers of the general government, are undoubtedly within those which are reserved to the states."[82]

The *Willson* opinion indicates that Marshall's interpretation of the negative aspect of the Commerce Clause was not as far from that of Taney as is generally believed. "It appears to me to be very clear," declared Taney in an 1847 opinion, "that the mere grant of power to the general government cannot, upon any just principles of construction, be construed to be an absolute prohibition to the exercise of any power over the same subject by the States."[83] Yet the *Willson* case indicates that Marshall shared this view as far as the commerce power was concerned. Both Marshall and Taney, then, refused to follow the notion of complete exclusiveness of federal power under which the Commerce Clause, of its own force, removed from the states any and all power over interstate and foreign commerce.

Where Marshall and Taney differed was in their conception of just how much power over commerce remained in the states. Taney followed his rejection of the complete exclusiveness theory to the opposite extreme and asserted in the states a concurrent power over commerce limited only by the Supremacy Clause of the Constitution. The states, in his view, might make any regulations of commerce within their territory, subject only to the power of Congress to displace any state law by conflicting federal legislation.[84] His concurrent power theory (under which the states possess, concurrently with Congress, the full power to regulate commerce) is, however, incompatible with the basic purpose which underlies the Commerce Clause—that of promoting a system of free trade among the states protected from state legislation inimical to that free flow. For that goal to be achieved, the proper approach to the commerce power lies somewhere between the antagonistic poles of extreme exclusiveness and coextensive concurrent power.

Such an approach had been urged by William Wirt, the Attorney General, as cocounsel with Daniel Webster in *Gibbons v. Ogden*.[85] Webster, whose view of national power was similar to Marshall's, argued in the case for exclusive federal power, which would have barred all state economic regulation. Wirt was a Virginian whose views were closer to those of Jefferson and his followers. His argument for concurrent state power left an area open for state commercial regulation, consistent with the Jeffersonian view that the Constitution did not provide for a federal monopoly of the enumerated powers.

The potential in the Wirt approach may not have been immediately apparent. But it furnished the basis for state economic regulation during the years before Washington began to intervene actively in economic affairs. Wirt also set forth the theory upon which state regulation of commerce was to be sustained. In his *Gibbons* argument Wirt put forth the proposition, "not that all the commercial powers are exclusive, but that those powers being separated, there are some which are exclusive in their nature,"[86] while others might be left open to the states.

In addition, he set out a criterion by which to judge when the federal commerce power was exclusive—that of *uniformity*. In his argument, he said, "[L]et us suppose that the additional term, uniform, had been introduced into the constitution, so as to provide that Congress should have power to make uniform regulations of commerce throughout the United States." In his view, the express insertion was not necessary. Federal power under the Commerce Clause "necessarily implies uniformity, and the same result, therefore, follows as if the word had been inserted."[87] The implication was that where uniformity of regulation was required, only Congress might regulate; where it was not, the states had concurrent regulatory power—subject, of course, to federal supremacy where there were conflicting regulations.

What Wirt was urging in his *Gibbons v. Ogden* argument was that some, but not all areas of commercial regulation are absolutely foreclosed to the states by the Commerce Clause. Here was a doctrine of what might be termed "selective exclusiveness," with the Supreme Court determining, in specific cases, the areas in which Congress possessed exclusive authority over commerce. Its great advantage was that of flexibility. Since it neither permitted nor foreclosed state power in every instance in advance, it might serve as a supple instrument to meet the needs of the future.

Unfortunately, history has not given Wirt credit for this major creative accomplishment. Thus Justice Frankfurter refers to "Webster's doctrine of selective 'exclusiveness'" and states that in *Cooley,* "Webster's analysis became Supreme Court doctrine."[88] As already indicated, Webster's *Gibbons* argument was devoted entirely to the proposition that the federal power over commerce was exclusive. It was Wirt's alternative argument that ultimately became accepted doctrine and served as the basis for state regulatory power.

Cooley Case

It was not until *Cooley v. Board of Port Wardens* (1852)[89] that the Supreme Court was to adopt the middle approach urged by Wirt to the question of state power to regulate commerce. Before that case, as already indicated, the Taney Court had vacillated in its answer to that question. Taney had urged the existence of a commerce power in the states coextensive with that of Congress, to yield only where state regulation was in conflict with federal law, but he could not induce a majority to acquiesce in his view. A compromise was necessary if the question was to be resolved in a way that rejected the opposite extreme of exclusive congressional authority, urged by the "high-toned Federalists on the bench."[90]

The *Cooley* opinion was delivered by Justice Benjamin R. Curtis, who is remembered today almost entirely because of his dissent in the *Dred Scott* case.[91] Yet Curtis's contribution to American law was more significant than mere authorship of his now-classic dissent from the most discredited judicial decision in our history. Indeed, a 1972 evaluation by professors of law, history, and political science rates Curtis as a Supreme Court Justice higher than all the other members of the Taney Court except the Chief Justice.[92] "No one," says Justice Frankfurter, "can have seriously studied the United States Reports and not have felt the impact of Curtis' qualities—short as was the term of his office."[93]

Curtis had attended Harvard Law School, where he was one of Justice Story's outstanding students,[94] and then built up a reputation as leader of the Boston Bar, particularly in commerical law cases. His most noted argument while in practice defended the right of a slaveholder visiting Massachusetts to hold the slave and take her back to the owner's home in Louisiana[95]—arguing for the very principle that his *Dred Scott* dissent was to dispute so vigorously. Aside from brief service in the state legislature, Curtis's career was entirely in practice when he was appointed in 1851, largely through Webster's influence, to the New England seat on the Supreme Court.

As the Frankfurter quote indicates, Curtis's Court tenure was brief; he resigned after only six years, soon after the *Dred Scott* decision. During his short term, however, Curtis delivered opinions that indicated his judicial potential. Had he, as a laudatory article on his appointment put it, "consented to devote the rest of his days to dispensing justice on the highest tribunal in the world,"[96] he undoubtedly would have become one of the outstanding Supreme Court Justices.

The major Curtis contribution to our law came in the *Cooley* case, where his opinion resolved the issue of the reach of the Commerce Clause and the proper scope of concurrent state power over commerce. Before *Cooley*, we saw, the Justices had avoided direct resolution of that issue, with the Court divided between the view that the commerce power was exclusively vested in the Federal Government and the Taney view that the states possessed, concurrently with Congress, the full power to regulate commerce.

In *Cooley*, the Curtis opinion of the Court adopted the "selective exclusiveness" compromise that had been urged by William Wirt in his *Gibbons v. Ogden* argument. It is not known whether Justice Curtis was familiar with Wirt's argument. But he adopted the Wirt approach in his *Cooley* opinion as a necessary compromise to resolve the issue on which the Court had until then vacillated. Curtis had taken his seat only two months before *Cooley* was argued and was thus an ideal judge to write a compromise opinion between the extremes of exclusive congressional power advocated by Justices McLean and Wayne (who dissented in *Cooley*) and the Taney view of coextensive concurrent power.

Chief Justice Taney concurred silently in the Curtis *Cooley* opinion. Why he did so has always been a matter for speculation. As Chief Justice, he could, if he chose, make himself spokesman for the Court. That he did not do so shows that he could not carry a majority for his own approach.[97] If he did not accept the *Cooley* compromise, it would have meant the same fragmented resolution of the commerce issue that had occurred in the prior cases. Taney's concurrence in the *Cooley* compromise made it possible for the law at last to be settled with some certainty on the matter (it was only after *Cooley,* asserts the Court's historian, "that a lawyer could advise a client with any degree of safety as to the validity of a State law having any connection with commerce between the states").[98]

Taney's biographer asserts that the author of the *Cooley* opinion "brought to the Court no new ideas on the subject of the interpretation of the commerce power."[99] The assertion is unfair. Of course, Justice Curtis followed the time-honored judicial technique of pouring new wine into old bottles. He based his opinion on Wirt's "selective exclusiveness" doctrine, but he went beyond Wirt's argument to make a truly original contribution which has since controlled the law on the matter. Well could Curtis write, just before the *Cooley* decision was announced, "I expect my opinion will excite surprise. . . . But it rests on grounds perfectly satisfactory to myself . . . although for twenty years no majority has ever rested their decision on either view of this question, nor was it ever directly decided before."[100]

The *Cooley* case itself arose out of a Pennsylvania law requiring vessels using the port of Philadelphia to engage local pilots or pay a fine, amounting to half the pilotage fee, to go to the Society for the Relief of Distressed and Decayed Pilots. Since there was no federal statute on the subject, the question for the Supreme Court was that of the extent of state regulatory power over commerce where Congress was silent on the matter. It was contended that the pilotage law was repugnant to the Consitution because the Commerce Clause had vested the authority to enact such a commercial regulation exclusively in Congress. To the question whether the power of Congress was exclusive, Justice Curtis answered, "Yes and No"—or, to put it more accurately, "Sometimes Yes and sometimes No." There remained the further inquiry: "When and why, Yes? When and why, No?"[101]

In his *Gibbons v. Ogden* argument, Wirt's cocounsel, Daniel Webster, had said that "the power should be considered as exclusively vested in Congress, so far, and so far only, as the nature of the power requires."[102] *Cooley* followed the same basic approach. If the states are excluded from power over commerce, Curtis said, "it must be because the nature of the power, thus granted to Congress, requires that a similar authority should not exist in the states."[103] If that be true, the states must be excluded only to the extent that the nature of the commerce power requires. When, Curtis asked, does the nature of the commerce power require that it be considered exclusively vested in Congress? This depends not upon the abstract "nature" of the commerce power itself but upon the nature of the "subjects" over which the power is exercised, for "when the nature of a power like this is spoken of, when it is said that the nature of the power requires that it should be exercised exclusively by Congress, it must be intended to refer to the subjects of that power, and to say they are of such a nature as to require exclusive legislation by Congress."[104]

Having thus transferred the focus of inquiry from the commerce power in the abstract to the subjects of regulation in the concrete, Curtis then examined them pragmatically. If we look at the subjects of commercial regulation, he pointed out, we find that they are exceedingly various and quite unlike in their operation. Some imperatively demand a single uniform rule, operating equally on commerce throughout the United States; others as imperatively demand that diversity which alone can meet local necessities. "Either absolutely to affirm, or deny," said Curtis, "that the nature of this power requires exclusive legislation by Congress, is to lose sight of the nature of the subjects of this power, and to assert concerning all of them, what is really applicable but to a part."[105]

Whether the states may regulate depends upon whether it is imperative that the subjects of the regulation be governed by a uniform national system. As the *Cooley* opinion put it, "Whatever subjects of this power are in their nature national, or admit only of one uniform system, or plan of regulation, may justly be said to be of such a nature as to require exclusive legislation by Congress."[106] On the other hand, where national uniformity of regulation is not necessary, the subject concerned may be reached by state law. That is the case with a law for the regulation of pilots like that at issue in *Cooley*.

Almost two decades after the *Cooley* decision, Justice Samuel F. Miller, speaking for the Supreme Court, stated, "Perhaps no more satisfactory solution has ever been given of this vexed question than the one furnished by the court in that case."[107] Over a century later, much the same comment can be made, despite the attempts by the Court since *Cooley* to formulate other tests. Those tests have proved unsatisfactory, and the Court has basically continued to follow the *Cooley* approach in cases involving the validity of state regulations of commerce.

The Curtis approach in *Cooley* was a necessary modification of the developing conception of law. Judges like Marshall and Story had developed legal principles to accord with their vision of the emerging society and economy. In doing so, they had rejected the opposing vision of men like Jefferson and the legal doctrines of jurists like Spencer Roane, who sought to give effect to that vision. What was to happen, however, when neither vision was able to command majority support? That had become the situation with regard to the *Cooley* issue. The "high-toned Federalists on the bench"[108] refused to yield on the Marshall vision of a nation vested with exclusive power over commerce. Chief Justice Taney was equally unyielding on the opposite Jacksonian posture.

Ultimately, the difference on the matter came down to a difference in the protection of property rights. In particular, the principle of federal exclusiveness meant the virtual immunity of property from public power, since congressional power over commerce was to remain in repose during most of the century. What regulation of business there was occurred at the state level. Hence the Taney conception of concurrent state power gave effect to the Jacksonian emphasis upon public power as a counterweight to the property rights stressed by the Federalists and then the Whigs.

As it turned out, neither the Federalist nor the Jacksonian view could command the needed juristic support. More important, neither was appropriate to the nation's commercial needs. Federal exclusiveness would have led to a complete absence of control over business abuses for almost a century. Taney's opposite approach would have resulted in the crazy quilt of commercial regulations that had led to the Constitution and the Commerce Clause themselves.

What was needed was the *Cooley* compromise, which could both secure the necessary votes and further the needs of commerce in a federal system. The *Cooley* test was one that could be adjusted to the differing demands of a polity characterized at first by absense of federal regulation and later by one dominated by control from Washington. The *Cooley* approach neither permitted nor prohibited state power in advance. As such, it could be molded by future jurists to meet the "felt necessities" of their times. The same would not have been true if the simple universality of the rules[109] rejected by Curtis had been elevated to the plane of accepted jurisprudence.

Curtis did more in *Cooley* than resolve the commerce issue by compromise. He stated a balancing test which makes the validity of a state regulation depend upon a weighing of the national and local interests involved. "More accurately," the Court more recently informed us, "the question is whether the State interest is outweighed by a national interest in the unhampered operation of interstate commerce."[110] An affirmative answer must be given only when a case falls within an area of commerce thought to demand a uniform national rule. But in the absence of conflicting legislation by Congress, there is a residuum of power in the states to make laws governing matters of local concern which nevertheless affect, or even regulate, interstate commerce.[111]

In marking out the areas of permissible state regulation, *Cooley* makes the primary test not the mechanical one of whether the particular activity regulated is part of interstate commerce, but rather whether, in each case, the competing demands of the state and national interests involved can be accommodated.[112] State regulations are to be upheld where it appears that the matter involved is one which may appropriately be regulated in the interest of the safety, health, and well-being of local communities. *Cooley* recognizes that there are matters of local concern which may properly be subject to state regulation—matters which, because of their local character and the practical difficulties involved, may in fact never really be adequately dealt with by the Congress.[113]

Under *Cooley*, then, regulation depends upon balancing the circumstances of the locality which may tilt in favor of local regulation, on the one hand, and the national need for uniformity, on the other. As one commentator summarizes it,

> In his recognition of the complexity of commercial activity, his desire to strike a balance between upholding federal regulatory power while safeguarding local freedom of action, his indication to leave to the future and to the courts the job of drawing lines of responsibility in the gray areas of jurisdiction, his requirement that judges look hard at the specific facts on which a particular case turns and avoid Federalist or Jeffersonian dogmatizing, and his insistence upon results—the arrangement that works best—Curtis grafted onto the Constitution a flexible approach with a pragmatic method of analysis.[114]

In *Cooley*, Justice Curtis stated a new balancing approach to law that foreshadowed modern constitutional jurisprudence.

Corporate Expansion

Justice Frankfurter once said that the history of our constitutional law in no small measure is the history of the impact of the modern corporation upon the American scene.[115] While the Taney Court sat, new economic forces were bringing new issues for judicial resolution; the corporate device and the concentrations of economic power made possible by it began to come before the Justices with increasing frequency.

If there was one tenet common to advocates of Jacksonian democracy, it was that of opposition to what Jackson's Bank Veto Message termed "the rich and powerful [who] too often bend the acts of government to their selfish purposes."[116] They deeply distrusted corporations as aggregations of wealth and power—the "would-be lordlings of the Paper Dynasty"[117]— which posed a direct danger to the democratic system. In his 1837 Farewell address, Jackson had warned of the perils posed by "the great moneyed corporations": "[U]nless you become more watchful . . . and check this spirit of monopoly and thirst for exclusive privileges you will in the end find that the most important powers of Government have been given or bartered away, and the control over your dearest interests has passed into the hands of these corporations."[118]

The Jacksonian view of corporate power was shared by Chief Justice Taney and most of his colleagues on the bench. Taney himself had been a leader in the war against the Bank of the United States—the corporate monster, "citadel of the moneyed power,"[119] which the Jacksonians had finally overthrown. An 1834 Taney speech affirmed that "in every period of the world . . . history is full of examples of combinations among a few individuals, to grasp all power in their own hands, and wrest it from the hands of the many."[120] Certainly Taney subscribed to the view that "the extent of the wealth and power of corporations among us, demands that plain and clear laws should be declared for their regulation and restraint."[121]

In theory at least, the Jacksonians on the bench shared the agrarian persuasion of their most extreme member, Justice Peter V. Daniel, who wrote in 1841 that, though he perceived the spread of banks and corporations to every hamlet, he still hoped that they might be weeded completely out of society.[122] In practice, however, even the Jacksonian Justices had to recognize that the corporation had a proper place in the legal and economic systems. The result was that, as Jacksonians, men like Taney might fear its abuses, but as practical men of affairs they had to recognize its utility in an expanding nation. To the United States of the first half of the nineteenth century, the corporate device was an indispensable adjunct of the nation's growth. The corporation enabled men to establish the pools of wealth and talent needed for the economic conquest of a continent. Even these Jacksonian judges realized the relationship between the corporation and economic development and made decisions favorable to the corporate personality—notably the 1839 decision in *Bank of Augusta v. Earle*.[123]

The question presented in that case has been characterized by the Supreme Court's historian as "of immense consequence to the commercial development of the country—the power of a corporation to make a contract outside of the State in which it was chartered."[124] It should be borne in mind that the corporation is entirely a creation of law; its very existence and legal personality have their origin in some act of the law. Corporations, of course, appear at an early stage of American history, for chartered companies first settled the Colonies of Virginia and Massachussets Bay. Yet, though the corporation as a legal person was developed under English law and recognized from the beginning in American law (especially in the classic 1819 *Dartmouth College* case), it was not until the decision in *Bank of Augusta v. Earle* that it could really be made to serve the needs of the burgeoning American economy.

In the *Bank of Augusta* case two banks and a railroad, incorporated respectively in Georgia, Pennsylvania, and Louisiana, brought an action in the federal court in Alabama on bills of exchange purchased by them in that state; the makers had refused to pay on the ground that the corporations had no power to do business in Alabama, or, indeed, outside their own states. Their contention was upheld by Justice John McKinley, sitting in the circuit court. As explained in an oft-quoted letter of Justice Story to Charles Sumner, "He has held that a corporation created in one State has no power to contract (or, it would seem, even to act) in any other State, directly or by an agent."[125]

The McKinley ruling was characterized by Story as "a most sweeping decision . . . which has frightened half the lawyers and all the corporations of the country out of their proprieties."[126] Its practical effect was to limit corporate business to the states in which the corporations were chartered, which would have rendered all but impossible the growth of interstate enterprises of any consequence. Well might Webster, in his argument, characterize McKinley's decision as "anti-commercial and anti-social . . . and calculated to break up the harmony which has so long prevailed among the States and people of this Union."[127]

The Supreme Court opinion in the *Bank of Augusta* case was delivered by the Chief Justice. Taney rejected the notion that a corporation could have no existence beyond the limits of the state in which it was chartered. He held that a corporation, like a natural person, might act in states where it did not reside. Comity among the states provided a warrant for the operation throughout the Union of corporations chartered in any of the states: "We think it is well settled that by the law of comity among nations, a corporation created by one sovereignty is permitted to make contracts in another, and to sue in its courts; and that the same law of comity prevails among the several sovereignties of this Union."[128]

Chief Justice Taney did not go as far as Webster had urged in his argument. Though he upheld the power of corporations to act outside their domiciliary states, he also recognized the power of a state to legislate against the entrance of outside corporations. Corporations could operate nationwide, but each state was given the authority to regulate corporate activities within its own borders.[129]

In this respect, the *Bank of Augusta* opinion is a clear reflection of the mixed attitude of judges like Taney toward the corporation. Taney gave legal recognition to the fact that a corporation has the same practical capacity for doing business outside its home state as within its borders. But he refused to go further and adopt the Webster theory of citizenship for corporations within the protection of the Privileges and Immunities Clause of the Constitution. Instead, he carefully circumscribed the basis of their constitutional rights.[130]

Historically speaking, the most important aspect of the decision is the stimulus it provided to economic expansion. The view of the rising capitalist class was expressed by Story, when he wrote to Taney, "Your opinion in the corporation cases has given very general satisfaction to the public; . . . it does great honor to yourself as well as to the Court."[131] Because of the Taney decision, said Webster, "we breathe freer and deeper."[132] *Bank of Augusta v. Earle* was the first step in what the Supreme Court in 1898 was to term "the constant tendency of judicial decisions in modern times . . . in the direction of putting corporations upon the same footing as natural persons."[133] This tendency has been the essential jurisprudential counterpart of the economic unfolding of the nation. Looked at this way, the *Bank of Augusta* decision was as nationalistic as those rendered by Marshall himself.

Taney and Judicial Power

In 1842 John J. Crittenden, recently resigned as President Tyler's Attorney General, was commenting about a case he had just lost before the highest bench. "If it was not a decision of the Supreme Court," he declared, "I should say it was Supremely erronious [/*sic*]—It is thoroughly against us on all the questions of law and evidence. . . . Sic Transit &c."[134] The Crittenden complaint is one which has been directed against the Supreme Court throughout its history, and not only on behalf of disappointed litigants or their counsel. At times the propensity of the high tribunal toward error has been animadverted upon by Justices themselves. "There is no doubt," caustically commented Justice Robert H. Jackson over a century after the Crittenden reproof, "that if there were a super Supreme Court, a substantial proportion of our reversals . . . would also be reversed. We are not final because we are infallible, but we are infallible only because we are final."[135]

That the Taney Court was far from infallible is apparent to even a casual student of its work. Yet it is amazing to note how, once Taney had established his imprint upon the Court, the opposition that had greeted his appointment was quickly stilled. Even his bitterest enemies soon saw, from his work on the bench, that their partisan censures were unjustified. Until the *Dred Scott* case, the stature of the Supreme Court compared favorably with what it had been under Marshall, and, if anything, its decisions were more generally accepted. Criticisms by disappointed litigants and political opponents, of course, continued, but its prestige as an institution never stood higher than in Chief Justice Taney's first twenty years.

It was doubtless of Taney, who had been a Federalist before he became a supporter of Andrew Jackson,[136] that James K. Polk was thinking when, in 1845, he wrote in his diary, "I have never known an instance of a Federalist who had after arriving at the age of 30 professed to change his opinions, who was to be relied on in his constitutional opinions. All of them who have been appointed to the Supreme Court Bench, after having secured a place for life became very soon broadly Federal and latitudinarian in all their decisions involving questions of Constitutional power."[137]

To accuse Taney of a "relapse into the Broad Federal doctrines of Judge Marshall and Judge Story"[138] was unfair. The Taney Court did make important doctrinal changes, particularly in shifting the judicial emphasis from private to community rights and stressing the existence of power to deal with internal problems. That the Court's reaction after Marshall's death was not as great as has often been supposed does not alter the fact that there was a real change.

Even with the changes in constitutional law which it continuously made, however, the Taney Court did not (Justice Story to the contrary notwithstanding) seek to destroy the constitutional structure built by Marshall and his colleagues. Instead, it used that structure as the base for its own jurisprudence, making only such modifications as it deemed necessary to meet the needs of the day. In no respect was this more apparent than in its decisions on the place of judicial power in the governmental system.

In the 1832 Veto Message on the bill to recharter the Bank of the United States, President Jackson had denied the authority of the Supreme

Court to make decisions binding upon the political branches. The implication was that the Court's review power could not control the President. Jackson's opponents charged (as Taney put it years later) that he was, in effect, asserting "that he, as an executive officer, had a right to judge for himself whether an Act of Congress was constitutional or not, and was not bound to carry it into execution, even if the Supreme Court had decided otherwise."[139] Writing to Martin Van Buren in 1860, Taney denied that the Veto message meant any such thing: "[N]o intelligent man who reads the message can misunderstand the meaning of the President. He was speaking of his rights and duty when acting as part of the legislative power, and not his right or duty as an executive officer."[140] If all Jackson meant was that the President could veto bills on constitutional grounds despite Supreme Court decisions going the other way, the Veto Message was far from heretical doctrine, despite the contrary view of Jackson's Whig opponents.

Whether Taney's later justification of the words he wrote for Jackson in the heat of political battle was valid is not as relevant as the fact that almost three decades as Chief Justice gave ample proof of his full adherence to the notion of judicial power expounded by the Marshall Court. In the very first case in which he sat, even before he presided over a Supreme Court session, he declared (in an 1836 charge to a circuit court grand jury), "In a country like ours, blessed with free institutions, the safety of the community depends upon the vigilant and firm execution of the law; every one must be made to understand, and constantly to feel, that its supremacy will be steadily enforced by the constituted tribunals, and that liberty cannot exist under a feeble, relaxed or indolent administration of its power."[141]

The Taney Court was just as insistent as the tribunal headed by Marshall in vindicating the position of the Supreme Court as guardian of the Constitution and ultimate interpreter of its provisions. The judiciary, in the Taney view, was plainly the sine qua non of the constitutional machinery—draw out this particular bolt and the machinery falls to pieces: "For the articles which limit the powers of the Legislative and Executive branches of the Government, and those which provide safeguards for the protection of the citizen in his person and property, would be of little value without a Judiciary to uphold and maintain them which was free from every influence, direct or indirect, that might by possibility, in times of political excitement, warp their judgments."[142]

The point is illustrated most clearly by *Ableman v. Booth*[143]—a case which, during the 1850s, excited an interest comparable to that aroused by *Dred Scott* itself. The *Booth* case arose out of the prosecution of an abolitionist newspaper editor in Milwaukee for his part in rescuing a fugitive slave from federal custody. After his conviction in a federal court early in 1855 for violating the Fugitive Slave Act, Booth secured a writ of habeas corpus in the Wisconsin courts on the ground that the act was unconstitutional. A writ of error was taken to the United States Supreme Court, but the highest state court directed its clerk to make no return, declaring that its judgment in the matter was final and conclusive.

In effect, the Wisconsin judges were asserting a power to nullify action taken by the federal courts. In Taney's characterization, "[T]he supremacy of the State courts over the courts of the United States, in cases arising under the Constitution and laws of the United States, is now for the first time asserted and acted upon in the Supreme Court of a State." To uphold the power thus asserted would, he said, "subvert the very foundations of this Government."[144] If the state courts could suspend the operation of federal judicial power, "no one will suppose that a Government which has now lasted nearly seventy years enforcing its laws by its own tribunals, and preserving the union of States, could have lasted a single year, or fulfilled the high trusts committed to it." The Constitution, in its very terms, refutes the claimed state power; its language, in this respect, "is too plain to admit of doubt or to need comment."[145] The federal supremacy "so carefully provided in . . . the Constitution . . . could not possibly be maintained peacefully, unless it was associated with this paramount judicial authority." In affirming its authority to set federal judicial action at naught, Wisconsin really "has reversed and annulled the provisions of the Constitution itself . . . and made the superior and appellate tribunal the inferior and subordinate one."[146]

The Court's decision (correct though it was in law) was the subject of bitter political attack. To the public, the legal issues were inextricably interwined with the slavery controversy. More than a century later, we are scarcely concerned with the partisan censures of Taney's day, and *Ableman v. Booth* stands as a ringing affirmation of federal judicial power, as strong as any made by Marshall himself.

Judicial Self-Restraint

Just after Andrew Jackson took office Secretary of War J. H. Eaton informed him that "the Cherokees have filed here a protest against the laws of Georgia being extended over them. As it is a delicate matter will you think as to the course of the reply, to be given." Jackson took note of the problem thus presented and wrote on the address leaf of Eaton's letter, "[T]he answer to be well considered on constitutional grounds."[147] Despite his realization that Georgia was acting in violation of federal treaties, the President declined to support the Indians. Instead, he upheld Georgia and helped induce the "voluntary" removal of most of the Indians across the Mississippi.[148] The Cherokees then sought a judicial remedy, and the Supreme Court held that the Constitution barred Georgia from extending its laws over Indian lands and ruled invalid the arrest and imprisonment by the state of two missionaries working with the Cherokees.[149]

Georgia defied the Court's mandate and refused to release the imprisoned missionaries. "The Constitution, the laws and treaties of the United States," declared John Quincy Adams, "are prostrate in the State of

Georgia. Is there any remedy for this state of things? None. Because the Executive of the United States is in league with the State of Georgia."[150] Jackson is reported to have said that John Marshall had made his decision, now let him enforce it, but this may be only apocryphal.[151] Even so, it accurately describes Jackson's actions.[152] He did not seek in any way to enforce the judgment. Instead, he stated, "The decision of the supreme court has fell still born, and they find that it cannot coerce Georgia to yield to its mandate."[153]

This example of judicial impotence in the face of refusal by the political departments and the state to carry out the Supreme Court judgment is one that inevitably had great influence upon Chief Justice Taney, at least during most of his tenure on the bench. He developed a strong tendency to restrict the area of judicial discretion in constitutional decision.[154] Judicial self-restraint became for the first time an essential element of Supreme Court doctrine. With the *Cherokee Nation* example before him, Taney strove to steer the Court away from unduly political issues.

Speaking of Chief Justice Taney, Dean Acheson said that "judicial self-restraint . . . was his great contribution to the law and custom of the Constitution. . . . [T]he giant stature which Taney assumes in the history of the Supreme Court is due chiefly to his insistence that the judge, in applying constitutional limitations, must restrain himself and leave the maximum of freedom to those agencies of government whose actions he is called upon to weigh."[155] The concept of self-restraint cuts across the work of the Taney Court and distinguishes it most sharply from its predecessor. Where Marshall and his colleagues did not hesitate to involve themselves in issues that were essentially political in character, the Taney Court was more cautious. Until the *Dred Scott* case, Taney was largely successful in keeping the Court out of the "political thicket"[156] of party controversies. The basic Taney philosophy was to leave every opportunity for the solving of political problems elsewhere than in the courtroom. "In taking jurisdiction as the law now stands," he asserted in one case, "we must exercise a broad and indefinable discretion, without any certain and safe rule to guide us. . . . [S]uch a discretion appears to me much more appropriately to belong to the Legislature than the Judiciary."[157]

This statement was made in *Pennsylvania v. Wheeling & B. Bridge Co.* (1852),[158] a case that shows the Taney approach and the danger of departing from it. "The stupendous structure that spans the Ohio at Wheeling," wrote a contemporary of the bridge involved in the case, "strikes the eye of the traveller passing beneath it, as it looms above him in the darkness, as one of the great architectural wonders of the age."[159] At its dedication, Henry Clay had declaimed, "You might as well try to take down the rainbow."[160] But Pennsylvania sought to do just that by a suit in the Supreme Court for an injunction directing the removal of the bridge on the ground that it blocked river traffic.[161]

The majority of the Court was willing to order that the rainbow at least be raised to meet minimum ship clearances.[162] Chief Justice Taney dissented, urging (as the quote from his opinion already given indicates) that the matter was one for Congress, not the Court, to regulate under the commerce power. The Court's acceptance of jurisdiction was, however, short-lived. Congress passed a statute declaring the bridge to be a lawful structure and not an obstruction to navigation.[163] The Court then upheld the congressional power to enact such a law.[164] The ultimate result was thus precisely what Taney had urged in his original dissent—though only at the cost of congressional intervention to, in effect, reverse a Supreme Court decision.

Most of the time, Chief Justice Taney was able to carry the Court with him in adherence to the self-restraint doctrine, particularly in cases involving judicial attempts to dictate action by the other branches. "The interference of the courts with the performance of the ordinary duties of the executive departments of the government," he once affirmed, "would be productive of nothing but mischief."[165] In line with this view, he refused to order a state governor to extradite a fugitive from another state: "[I]f the governor of Ohio refuses to discharge this duty, there is no power delegated to . . . the judicial department . . . to use any coercive means to compel him."[166] At the back of Taney's mind must have been the need to avoid a clash such as that involved in the *Cherokee Nation* case.

The most famous case in which the Taney Court applied the self-restraint doctrine was *Luther v. Borden*.[167] It arose out of the only revolution that occurred in a state of the Union after the Revolutionary War itself—the so-called Dorr Rebellion in Rhode Island in 1841. That state was then still operating under the royal charter granted in 1663. It provided for a very limited suffrage and, worse still from the point of view of those who considered it completely out of date, no procedure by which amendments might be made. Popular dissatisfaction led to mass meetings in 1841, which resulted in the election of a convention to draft a new constitution. It was drawn up and provided for universal suffrage. Elections were held under it, and Thomas Wilson Dorr was elected Governor. All these acts were completely unauthorized by the existing charter government, which declared martial law and called out the militia to repel the threatened attack. In addition, it appealed to the Federal Government for aid, and President Tyler, expressly recognizing the charter government as the rightful government of the state, took steps to extend the necessary help, declaring that he would use armed force if that should prove necessary. The announcement of the President's determination caused Dorr's Rebellion to die out. *Luther v. Borden,* decided several years later, was left as its constitutional legacy.

The actual case arose out of the efforts of the charter government to suppress the Dorr Rebellion. When one of its agents broke into the house of a strong Dorr supporter and arrested him, the latter brought an action of trespass. Defendant justified his action by the plea that he was acting under the authority of the legal government of the state. Plaintiff countered with the contention that the charter government was not republican in form, as required by the Constitution. Therefore, he asserted, that government had no valid legal existence and the acts of its agents were not justified in law. Essentially, he was claiming that the action of the charter government violated his constitutional right to live under a republican government and that that claim was cognizable in a court.

The Supreme Court rejected the claim, denying that it was within judicial competence to apply the consitutional guaranty. On the contrary, the enforcement of the guaranty is solely for Congress. Under article IV, section 4, declares the opinion of Chief Justice Taney, "[I]t rests with Congress to decide what government is the established one in a State . . . as well as its republican character." Moreover, the congressional decision in the matter is not subject to any judicial scrutiny: "[I]ts decision is binding on every other department of the government, and could not be questioned in a judicial tribunal."[168]

Likewise, it is up to Congress "to determine upon the means proper to be adopted to fulfill this guaranty."[169] Under an Act of Congress that body had delegated to the President the responsibility of determining when the Federal Government should interfere to effectuate the constitutional guaranty,[170] and, in this case, as we saw, the President acted to support the charter government. After such action by the President, asked Taney, "[I]s a circuit court of the United States authorized to inquire whether his decision was right? Could the court, while the parties were actually contending in arms for the possession of the government, call witnesses before it and inquire which party represented a majority of the people? . . . If the judicial power extends so far, the guarantee contained in the Constitution of the United States is a guarantee of anarchy, and not of order."[171]

In *Luther v. Borden*, Taney refused to go into the issue of the legal authority of the government actually in power, holding that the questions involved were political and beyond the sphere of judicial compentence. The overriding consideration was to steer clear of political involvement; the question of governmental legitimacy was left exclusively to the political departments. The wisdom and authority of Taney's restraint in this respect has not been generally questioned.[172]

The judicial reluctance to approach too close to the founts of sovereignty was a dominant characteristic of the Taney Court. The soundness of such an attitude was amply demonstrated when the Court refused to follow the rule of abnegation and sought instead to resolve in the judicial forum the basic controversy over slavery which had come to tear the nation apart. Even masterful judges are not always restrained by the wisdom of self-denial: the *Dred Scott* case was the one occasion when Taney yielded to the temptation, always disastrous, to save the country, and put aside the judicial self-restraint which was one of his chief contributions to our constitutional law.

Taney's Associates

An 1859 article in the *New York Daily Tribune* described a visit to the Supreme Court:

> [Y]ou are ushered into a queer room of small dimensions, shaped over head like a quarter section of a pumpkin shell, the upper and broader rim crowning three windows, and the lower and narrower coming down garret-like to the floor; the windows being of ground glass, and the light trickling through them into the apartment. That which most arrests your attention is a long pew, just in front of these windows, slightly elevated above the floor, along which are ranged in a straight line nine ancient persons, clad in black-silk gowns.[173]

The "ancient persons" during the Taney tenure were, of course, different from those who had sat on the bench in Marshall's day. In 1836, just before Chief Justice Taney took his seat, Webster showed a visitor around the Capitol. At the Supreme Court, Webster referred to the great changes since he had first appeared there, saying, "No one of the Judges who were here then, remains."[174] When Story died in 1845, none of the Justices who had contributed to the work of the Marshall Court was on the bench.[175]

The supreme bench was completely remade by President Jackson, who, as already stated, appointed six Justices. Of the Justices who had sat sometime with Marshall, only Justices Story and Thompson served on the Taney Court and they realized that they were leftovers from another era— in Story's phrase, "in the predicament of the last survivor."[176] Justice Thompson had indicated a state's-rights leaning in Marshall's day, having differed from the great Chief Justice in cases on state power to enact bankruptcy laws, tax imports, and issue bank notes which circulated as money.[177] Now, however, he was as dismayed as Story at the tilt away from Marshall's nationalistic emphasis; John Quincy Adams in 1831 noted, "He is alarmed for the fate of the Judiciary," since "the leading system of the present Administration is to resolve the Government of the Union into the national imbecility of the old Confederation."[178]

It was that Jackson Administration that sought to remake the Court in its own image. Its first opportunity came when Justice Trimble died in 1828. In his place, President Jackson chose John McLean of Ohio, who had been on the highest court of his state and John Quincy Adams's Postmaster General. McLean served on the Court thirty-two years. Despite the many opinions he wrote, he is remembered today for his dissent in the *Dred Scott* case and, even more so, because he was the first Justice who, in Lincoln's phrase about Chief Justice Salmon P. Chase, "had the Presidential maggot in his brain."[179] In practically every election after his appointment, McLean was, actively or passively, a candidate for the Presidency.[180]

McLean's role as what a newspaper termed "a judicial politician"[181] could not help but have a harmful effect upon the Court's reputation—he was "dragging the ermine in the mire of politics," declaimed the *National Intelligencer*.[182] To others, McLean may, as Webster once said, have had "his head turned too much by politics."[183] McLean himself, however, indicated that he had no doubt about the propriety of a Justice being a candidate for the Presidency. "I did not suppose," he wrote in answer to a critic, "that you or any other person who had reflected upon the subject could entertain the least apprehension of any improper influence being used by a Judge who comes before the people in a popular election, and especially that it could lend [sic] to corrupt the Bench."[184]

McLean also did not hesitate to speak out publicly on controversial political issues. He published a letter strongly attacking the Mexican war and publicly expressed his views on slavery—most notably in an 1848 letter on the power of Congress over slavery in the territories. He thus undertook, in the words of another critic, "to adjudicate a question" that could come before the Court,[185] as it ultimately did in the *Dred Scott* case. Though we may have serious doubts about the propriety of such conduct by a Justice, here, too, McLean insisted, "As a citizen, I claim the right and shall exercise it, of forming and expressing my opinion on public measures."[186]

As a Justice, McLean disappointed the expectations of the President who had appointed him. During the years he served, McLean was one of the most nationalistic of the Taney Court Justices. In his brief tenure under Marshall, he was characterized in a newspaper "as sound as Marshall himself" on issues of federalism and property rights.[187] He continued to follow the same approach under Marshall's successor. Indeed, in an 1852 letter, Justice Curtis referred to "McLean & Wayne, who are the most high-toned Federalists on the bench."[188]

James M. Wayne, the third Justice appointed by Jackson, also was closer to Marshall's views than those of the President who chose him. Wayne was appointed in 1835 to succeed Justice Johnson, who had died the previous year. He had been active in Georgia politics and had supported Jackson as a Congressman in both the nullification controversy and the struggle over the Bank of the United States. These, more than Wayne's legal ability or his prior service as a judge in his state, led to his selection. Wayne, like McLean, continued to be a strong Unionist on the bench, as is shown by his statement of dissent in the *Cooley* case, which led to the quoted Curtis comment. Despite his role in the *Dred Scott* case, he remained an adherent of the Union to the end; during the Civil War, he abandoned his Savannah home for residence in Washington. Because of this, a Confederate court branded him an enemy alien and confiscated his Georgia property.[189]

When Wayne was appointed, James Buchanan wrote that he would "[n]ever make [an] able judge."[190] According to one commentator, "Buchanan's prophecy proved accurate. Wayne served on the Court for thirty-two years without making any conspicuous contribution."[191] On the other hand, it is said that Wayne was influential in the Court's internal deliberative process[192]—a conclusion apparently borne out by the part he played in steering the Court to its *Dred Scott* decision.

Between the appointments of McLean and Wayne, President Jackson was given the opportunity to select another Justice by the death in 1829 of Bushrod Washington. The President chose Henry Baldwin, who had been Jackson's outspoken defender while a Pennsylvania Congressman. Justice Baldwin was unhappy on the Marshall Court. Within a year, Martin Van Buren could write in his *Autobiography,* "Judge Baldwin is dissatisfied with his situation for reasons which . . . grow out of opposition to what he regards as an unwarrantable extension of its powers by the Court, and has given the President notice of his intention to resign."[193]

Jackson, however, prevailed on Baldwin not to leave the Court, where he remained a disturbing influence in part because, as Story wrote, "he is partially deranged."[194] His mental problems continued during most of his tenure, causing him to be erratic in his jurisprudence. Quick to concur or dissent, he followed no consistent constitutional approach. He was more of a jarring influence than a real contributor to the Taney Court.

President Jackson was, of course, also able to appoint Roger B. Taney as Marshall's successor, as well as to appoint two other Justices. The first was Philip P. Barbour, confirmed the same day as the new Chief Justice, who took the seat of Justice Duval, who had resigned in 1835. According to Senator Thomas Hart Benton, "Judge Barbour was a Virginia country gentleman, after the most perfect model of that class."[195] He had been a Congressman and a federal district judge. On his appointment, a Richmond newspaper wrote that he was "eminently fitted to adorn the Bench . . . and enlighten it with his inflexible and uncompromising State-Rights principles."[196] To Marshall's adherents, however, Barbour's appointment was an unhappy portent. John Quincy Adams referred to him as a "shallow-pated wild-cat, . . . fit for nothing but to tear the Union to rags and tatters."[197] Barbour did not, however, serve long enough (he died at the beginning of 1841) to tilt the Court toward the doctrines of the Virginia school.

President Jackson's last Court appointment filled one of two new seats created in 1837. "The Supreme Court," Justice Story wrote in that year, "now consists of nine Judges, two having been lately added by an act of Congress."[198] Jackson now had the opportunity to select two new Justices. However, one of his appointees, his lifelong friend William Smith, declined and Jackson's successor made the appointment. For the other new seat, Jackson chose John Catron of Tennessee, who met the key litmus requirements of Jacksonian loyalty, opposition to the Bank of the United States, and support of the President's stand against nullification.

Catron was not deterred from expressing fervent public support for Jackson's position by the fact that he was then Chief Justice of his state's highest court. In fact, Catron was another early Justice who never followed the traditional judicial ethic of divorcing himself from politics. He was a close adviser of Presidents Polk and Buchanan. His activities in this respect leave more recent Justices who have advised the White House in the shade. Catron's contacts with President Buchanan in the *Dred Scott* case (to be discussed in the next chapter) violated all notions of judicial propriety, even by the more relaxed standards of his day.

When we think of the Presidents between Jackson and Lincoln we must ask, with James Bryce, "who now knows or cares to know anything about the personality of James K. Polk or Franklin Pierce? The only thing remarkable about them is that being so commonplace they should have climbed so high."[199] The same is true of most of the Justices chosen by our pre-Civil War Presidents. Almost all of them, too, have been relegated to the obscurity reserved for the Tylers, Buchanans, and other lesser lights who failed to measure up to what those in their high positions should be.

The Presidents who succeeded Jackson added the following Justices to the Taney Court:

President Van Buren: John McKinley, a former Senator and loyal Jacksonian, appointed from Kentucky to fill the new ninth seat; Peter V. Daniel of Virginia, another ardent Jackson man, to replace the deceased Justice Barbour.

President Tyler: Samuel Nelson, a judge from New York, who was to serve for twenty-seven years, replacing Justice Thompson, who had died.

President Polk: Levi Woodbury of New Hampshire, a former judge, Governor, Senator, and Cabinet member, who could, of course, scarcely fill the seat left vacant by Justices Story's death in 1845; Robert C. Grier, a Pennsylvania judge appointed after Justice Baldwin's death.

President Fillmore: Benjamin R. Curtis, already discussed, who despite the shortness of his tenure, was the outstanding Associate Justice on the Taney Court.

President Pierce: John A. Campbell, a preeminent Alabama lawyer, whose appointment, Campbell himself informs us, was "one recommended by the Justices—Justices Catron and CURTIS bearing their recommendation to the President,"[200] who succeeded Justice McKinley on the latter's death.

President Buchanan: Nathan Clifford from Maine, a former Attorney General, to replace Justice Curtis, who resigned after the *Dred Scott* decision.

Writing about one of these Justices, Taney's biographer tells us that he was a "man of moderate ability who achieved neither distinction nor notoriety."[201] Except for Justice Curtis, the same can be said of the other Justices just listed. Attempts by revisionist biographers to change this conclusion can scarcely alter history's estimate. The only place in legal history attained by some of these Justices stems from their role in the *Dred Scott* case—which, of course, finally gave them the "notoriety" that they did not otherwise achieve.

The appointments by President Jackson and his successors did, however, have one important consequence for the Court. After Justice McKinley of Kentucky was appointed, a majority of the Justices were from below the Mason-Dixon Line. This was to prove of great significance, since it led directly to the Court's proslavery position, which reached its disastrous climax in the *Dred Scott* case. There is irony in the fact that the Southern Court majority was brought about by the appointment of Justice McKinley by President Van Buren, who was himself an opponent of slavery and ran as the candidate of the antislavery Free Soil Party in 1848.

Just before the end of the Taney tenure, at the beginning of the December 1860 Term, the Court moved into the old Senate Chamber in the Capitol. The Court was to occupy this as its chamber until the construction of the present Supreme Court building. In addition, twelve other rooms were provided for the use of the Court, its officers, and records—particularly a separate robing room, which enabled the Justices to make the dignified formal entry that had been impossible when they had donned their robes from pegs on the wall in the presence of the audience.

The new Court Chamber was certainly an improvement over the one previously used in the Capitol basement. The new courtroom was much larger and more elegant. Though it was still semicircular in shape, like the previous basement chamber, it was forty-five feet long and the same distance wide at its widest point. The ceiling was a low half-dome, with a suspended chandelier. As in the lower chamber, the bench was arranged with judicial backs to the wall, and it was now substantially elevated. Ionic marble columns formed a colonnade along one side of the room, while pilasters of marble decorated the circular wall. Marble busts of Chief Justices were arranged around the walls. The added dignity of the chamber was enhanced by soft brown carpeting and red velvet cushioning of the benches available to the public.[202]

Certainly this was an improvement over what a newspaper called the old "potato hole of a place"[203] in the Capitol basement. It was, however, still a far cry from the Court's present marble palace—the first setting that housed the court in a manner befitting its august constitutional role and its position as the highest court in the land.

Taney and His Court

It is customary to point to the drastic change that occurred in constitutional jurisprudence when Tanley succeeded Marshall. The traditional historical view was summarized over a generation ago by Justice Frankfurter: "[E]ven the most sober historians have conveyed Taney as the leader of a band of militant 'agrarian,' 'localist,' 'pro-slavery' judges, in a strategy of reaction against Marshall's doctrines. They stage a dramatic conflict between Darkness and Light: Marshall, the architect of a nation; Taney, the bigoted provincial and protector of slavery."[204]

Such an approach is based upon ignorance of the manner in which a tribunal like the Supreme Court functions. It is incorrect to suppose that Taney accomplished a wholesale reversal of Marshall's doctrines. He did not and could not do so: the institutional traditions of the Supreme Court have always exercised an overpowering influence. Even the Jacksonian neophytes on the bench were molded, more than is generally realized, into the Court's institutional pattern. To be sure, with Taney's accession, the supreme bench was now safely in the hands of the Democrats. That fact alone implies much.[205] The Justices appointed by Jackson and Van Buren inevitably had a different outlook than their predecessors, products of an earlier day. As already emphasized, Taney and his colleagues shared the Jacksonian belief that property rights must be subject to control by the community. Acting on that belief, they sought to redress the balance of constitutional protection which they felt the Marshall Court had thrown unfairly against the public interest in favor of property.

Yet, as indicated previously, it is an error to assume that the Taney Court translated wholesale the principles of Jacksonian democracy into constitutional law. The performance of the Jacksonian Justices shows, as well as anything, the peril of predicting in advance how new appointees to the Supreme Court will behave after they don the robe. "One of the things that laymen, even lawyers, do not always understand," Justice Frankfurter once stated, "is indicated by the question you hear so often: 'Does a man become any different when he puts on a gown?' I say, 'If he is any good, he does.'"[206] Certainly, Taney and his Brethren must have seemed in many cases altogether different men as judges than they had been off the bench. Paradoxically, perhaps, the erstwhile Jacksonian politicians did as much as Marshall and his colleagues to promote economic development and the concentrations of wealth and financial power that were its inevitable concomitants.

Chief Justice Taney may have had the strong Jacksonian bias against what Jackson called "the multitude of corporations with exclusive privileges which [the moneyed interest] have succeeded in obtaining in the different States,"[207] but it was the Taney opinions in cases like *Charles River Bridge v. Warren Bridge* and *Bank of Augusta v. Earle* which opened the door to the greatest period of corporate expansion in our history. The corporation first became common in the 1820s and 1830s[208]—stimulated both by the *Dartmouth College* case and by the decisions favorable to corporate personality rendered during the early years of the Taney Court. The statistics underline the stimulus given to economic expansion by the decisions of the high tribunal. In the 1830s and 1840s there was a sharp increase in the number of corporations, particularly those engaged in manufacturing.[209] Before Taney, only $50 million was invested in manufacturing; that figure had grown to $1 billion by 1860.[210]

Perhaps the major change in the jurisprudence of the Taney Court arose from its tendency, in doubtful cases, to give the benefit of the doubt to the existence of state power far more than had been the case in Marshall's day; but this is far from saying that Taney and his confreres were ready to overturn the edifice of effective national authority constructed so carefully by their predecessors. On the contrary, like Jackson himself, they were firm believers in national supremacy where there was a clear conflict between federal and state power. When state authorities acted to interfere with federal power, Chief Justice Taney and his colleagues were firm in upholding federal supremacy. Hence, despite its greater willingness to sustain state authority, it is unfair to characterize the Taney Court as concerned only with states' rights.

When the occasion demanded, Taney could assert federal power in terms characterized by Chief Justice Huges as "even more 'national' than Marshall himself."[211] This is shown dramatically by the 1852 case of *The Genesee Chief v. Fitzhugh*,[212] which arose out of a collision between two ships on Lake Ontario. A damage suit was brought in a federal court under an 1845 statute extending federal admiralty jurisdiction to the Great Lakes and connecting navigable waters. The constitutionality of this law was upheld in *The Genesee Chief*. In an earlier case,[213] the Supreme Court had confined the territorial extent of federal admiralty jurisdiction substantially to that followed under English doctrine, namely, to the high seas and to rivers only as far as the ebb and flow of the tide extended. In a small island like Britain, where practically all streams are tidal, such a limitation might be adequate, but it hardly proved so in a country of continental extent.

The Taney opinion in the *Genesee Chief* well illustrates the manner in which the law changes to meet changed external conditions. When the Constitution went into operation, the English "tidal flow" test of admiralty jurisdiction may well have sufficed. In the original thirteen states, as in England, almost all navigable waters were tidewaters. With the movement of the nation to the west and the consequent growth of commerce on the inland waterways, the English test became inadequate. "It is evident," says the Taney opinion, "that a definition that would at this day limit public rivers in this country to tide water rivers is utterly inadmissible. We have thousands of miles of public navigable waters, including lakes and rivers in which there is no tide. And certainly there can be no reason for admiralty power over a public tide water, which does not apply with equal force to any other public water used for commercial purposes."[214]

An inexorable advocate of states' rights would scarcely have written the *Genesee Chief* opinion. In fact, the extreme Jacksonian on the Court, Justice Daniel, flatly refused to countenance the revolutionary[215] enlargement of federal jurisdiction approved by the decision and delivered a stinging dissent. But Daniel's opinion was (as he himself conceded) "contracted and antiquated, unsuited to the day in which we live."[216] The Taney opinion was dictated by sound common sense; it was a legitimate nationalizing decision brought on by the changed conditions resulting from the geographic growth of the nation. As Ralph Waldo Emerson put it, in commenting on the case, "The commerce of rivers, the commerce of railroads, and who knows but the commerce of air balloons, must add an American extension to the pondhole of admiralty."[217]

A decision like the *Genesee Chief* shows how difficult it is to pigeonhole judges like Taney. His states'-rights heritage did not blind him to the need for effective governmental power. His distrust of corporations did not make him disregard the practical possibilities of the corporate device and its utility in an expanding economy. Indeed, it was Taney, Justice Frank-furter tells us, "who adapted the Constitution to the emerging forces of modern economic society."[218] Jacksonianism was at bottom only an ethical conception of the social responsibilities of private property.[219] To translate that conception into decisions like that in the *Charles River Bridge* case was the great constitutional contribution of the Taney Court.

Henry Clay, who had led the fight against Taney's confirmation, was later to tell the new Chief Justice that "no man in the United States could have been selected, more abundantly able to wear the ermine which Chief Justice Marshall honored."[220] The judgment of history has confirmed the Clay estimate. The pendulum has shifted from the post–*Dred Scott* censures by men like Charles Sumner to the more sober estimate of those who sat with Taney on the bench or argued before him at the Bar. According to a vituperative denunciation published at his death, Taney "was, next to Pon-tius Pilate, perhaps the worst that ever occupied the seat of judgment."[221] Today we reject such partisan bias and agree with the estimate of Justice Frankfurter: "The devastation of the Civil War for a long time obliterated the truth about Taney. And the blaze of Marshall's glory will permanently overshadow him. But the intellectual power of his opinions and their enduring contribution to a workable adjustment of the theoretical distri-bution of authority between two governments for a single people, place Taney second only to Marshall in the constitutional history of our coun-try."[222]

4

Watershed Cases:
Dred Scott v. Sandford, 1857

Supreme Court history is marked by landmark cases which have drastically affected both the country and the Court itself. These are watershed cases, which, in Holmes's words, "exercise a kind of hydraulic pressure which makes what previously was clear seem doubtful, and before which even well settled principles of law will bend."[1]

If any case deserves to be treated as such a case, it is the *Dred Scott* case.[2] Before the decision there, the prestige of the Supreme Court had never been greater. Taney was universally acclaimed worthy of his predecessor, destined to rank almost with Marshall himself in the judicial pantheon. After the *Dred Scott* decision all was changed. "The name of Taney," declared Charles Sumner early in 1865, "is to be hooted down the page of history. . . . The Senator says that he for twenty-five years administered justice. He administered justice, at last, wickedly, and degraded the Judiciary of the country and degraded the age."[3]

Soon after Taney died, an anonymous pamphlet was published entitled *The Unjust Judge.* In it, Taney, dead less than a year, was excoriated "with hatred so malignant that it seems obscene." Its vilification culuminated in the assertion that "as a jurist, or more strictly speaking as a Judge, . . . he was, next to Pontius Pilate, perhaps the worst that ever occupied the seat of judgment among men."[4]

To so many of his contemporaries, *Dred Scott* made Taney the very prototype of "the unjust judge." Conceding that the deceased Chief Justice may have had "good qualities and . . . ability," Gideon Welles wrote in his famous diary, "But the course pursued in the Dred Scott case . . . forfeited respect for him as a man or a judge."[5] For more than a century the case has stood as a monument of judicial indiscretion: as Justice Robert Jackson acidly commented: "One such precedent is enough!"[6]

Almost a century and a half later, however, we can say that *Dred Scott* was not so much a judicial crime as a judicial blunder—a blunder that resulted from the Taney Court's failure to follow the doctrine of judicial self-restraint that was one of Taney's great contributions to our law. In it, in Justice Frankfurter's phrase, "[T]he Court disregarded its settled tradition against needlessly pronouncing on constitutional issues."[7] The *Dred Scott* Court fell victim to its own success as a governmental institution. The power and prestige that had been built up under Marshall and continued under Taney had led men to expect too much of judicial power. The Justices themselves too readily accepted the notion that judicial power could succeed where political power had failed. From this point of view, Taney may be characterized not as an "unjust judge" but as an "unwise judge." His essential mistake was to imagine that a flaming political issue could be quenched by calling it a "legal" question and deciding it judicially.[8]

Slavery in the Territories

To understand the issues in the *Dred Scott* case, it is necessary to have some knowledge of what had by the 1850s become the thorniest aspect of the slavery controversy—the question of slavery in the territories. From the founding of the Republic, the question had been dealt with by Congress. When the Constitution went into effect, the United States possessed vast territories which had been ceded by Virginia and other states. The Confederation Congress had provided for the government of the territory northwest of the Ohio River by the famous Northwest Ordinance of 1787, which flatly prohibited slavery in the territory governed by it.

One of the earliest measures enacted by the first Congress that convened under the Constitution was a law providing that the Northwest Ordinance should "continue to have full effect."[9] In 1790, Congress passed an act accepting a deed of cession by North Carolina of the territory that later became the State of Tennessee. That statute declared that no regulations were to be made in the territory which "tend to emancipate slaves."[10] These early assertions of congressional power to govern slavery in the territories were reinforced in scores of later statutes, some of which contained the express prohibition of the Northwest Ordinance.

Then, in 1820, came the Missouri Compromise, by which, it was hoped, the question of slavery in the territories had finally been settled. It prohibited slavery in the remainder of the territory included in the Louisiana Purchase north of a prescribed line, 36° 30' of north latitude.[11] As it turned out, this provision did not really resolve the issue of the extension of slavery. All it did was establish a temporary armistice in the growing conflict between the pro- and antislavery forces. In this sense, John Quincy Adams was correct when he wrote in his diary at the time "that the present question is a mere preamble—a title-page to a great tragic volume."[12]

The question of slavery in the territories arose again at the end of the Mexican war, when large areas were acquired. Conflict over the extension of slavery into the new regions grew in intensity in the decade that followed and towered over other political issues; the crisis that sounded in Jefferson's ears "like a fire bell in the night"[13] in 1819 had become a primary cause of sectional animosity.

The slavery issue was brought to the fore by the so-called Wilmot Proviso. In the summer of 1846, President Polk asked for an appropriation to enable him to negotiate a cession of Mexican territory. On August 8, he wrote in his diary, "I learned that after an excited debate in the House a bill passed that body, but with a mischievous & foolish amendment to the effect that no territory which might be acquired by treaty from Mexico should ever be a slave-holding country. What connection slavery had with making peace with Mexico it is difficult to conceive."[14]

If the President, eager to vindicate his Mexican policy by expansion of the Union, could not see the intimate relationship between adding "to the U.S. an immense empire"[15] and the question of whether the new territories would be slave or free, others in the political arena did. The war on the battlefield was minor compared to the one that now arose. The Wilmot Proviso never became part of Polk's appropriation bill, but the issue it raised overshadowed all others. "The United States," Emerson foresaw in 1846, "will conquer Mexico, but it will be as the man who swallows the arsenic which brings him down in turn. Mexico will poison us."[16] The struggle over slavery in the new territories soon showed how valid this prophecy was.

Constitutional Theories

The controversy catalyzed by the Wilmot Proviso brought to the fore sharply opposed constitutional theories on the issue of slavery in the territories. The antislavery men relied upon the express congressional power to "make all needful Rules and Regulations respecting the Territory . . . belonging to the United States" and urged that it included the authority to deal with slavery in the territories. Such authority had been exercised by the national legislature from the beginning, and its constitutionality had not been questioned. From the Wilmot Proviso debates a new version of this theory emerged: Congress had the moral duty to prohibit slavery wherever its jurisdiction extended; freedom must be national, slavery only sectional.[17] This version, soon to be adopted by the Free Soil and Republican parties, also rested upon the constitutional power of Congress to regulate slavery in the territories.

The Southerners put forward an opposing constitutional theory denying that congress had any legitimate authority to exclude slavery from the territories. This rejection of congressional power represented a shift in the Southern position. At the time of the Missouri Compromise, John Quincy Adams could say that only some "zealots . . . on the slave side" argued "that Congress have not power by the Constitution to prohibit slavery . . . in any territory."[18] Responsible Southern leaders did not take any such extreme position. When President Monroe put the question to his Cabinet in March 1820, "it was unanimously agreed that Congress have the power to prohibit slavery in the Territories."[19] Among those who strongly argued in support of that authority was Secretary of War Calhoun.

However, Southerners came to believe that the Union itself depended upon an equal division between slave and free states. "Sir," Calhoun declared to the Senate in 1847, "the day that the balance between the two sections of the country—the slaveholding States and the nonslaveholding States—is destroyed, is a day that will not be far removed from political revolution, anarchy, civil war, and wide-spread disaster."[20] The controversy over the Wilmot Proviso made it plain that the delicate free–slave equilibrium would soon be upset. Calhoun sought to preserve the balance by having the Missouri Compromise line extended to the Pacific. His efforts proved futile: all proposals to extend the Missouri line were voted down.

The rejection of the Compromise approach led Calhoun to reexamine his constitutional position. Now he saw that the westward march of the nation meant the inevitable end of equality for the slave states. Senate protection had to be replaced by some other instrument to defend slaveholding interests. That need was met by a change in constitutional theory. The only hope now, declared Calhoun in an 1847 speech, lay in the basic document itself: "The constitution . . . is a rock. . . . Let us be done with compromises. Let us go back and stand upon the Constitution."[21]

It is usually said that Chief Justice Taney, in his *Dred Scott* opinion, was simply elevating to the constitutional plane the new Calhoun theory on slavery in the territories. This view, as we shall see, is an oversimplification. While Calhoun, like Taney in *Dred Scott,* denied the constitutional power of Congress to prohibit slavery in the territories, the Carolinian's approach was far more extreme in its rejection of federal power than that later adopted by the Supreme Court. The Calhoun theory was based upon the doctrine of state sovereignty pushed almost to absurdity. The territories, he argued, were "the common property of the States of this Union. They are called 'the territories of the United States,' and what are the 'United States' but the States united? Sir, these territories are the property of the States united; held jointly for their common use."[22] The Federal Government, as the agent of the sovereign states, held the territories in trust for their common benefit; consequently it could not prevent a citizen of any one state from carrying with him into the territories property whose legal status was recognized by his home state.[23]

In February 1847, Calhoun introduced resolutions before the Senate stating the essentials of his new position: the territories were the joint property of the states; Congress, as the states' agent, could not make any discriminations between states depriving anyone of them of its equal right in any territory; a law depriving citizens of any state of the right to emigrate into any territory with their property would violate the Constitution and the rights of the states.[24] These resolutions, adopted by many Southern legislatures, became the virtual platform of the South. Under the Constitution, wrote Jefferson Davis, there was an "obligation of the U.S. Govt. to recognize property in slaves, as denominated in the compact, . . . to enforce the rights of its citizens to equal enjoyment of the territorial property which had been acquired and held as a common possession."[25]

This constitutional issue gave rise to most of the increasingly bitter political dialogue after the Mexican war. To the South particularly, defense of the Calhoun theory was seen as a matter of life and death. Only by denying congressional authority to prohibit slavery in the territories could the South prevent itself from being swamped by a vast new free-soil area that would reduce the slave states to an ever-smaller minority. If the balance of power were altered, the very ability of the South to defend itself would be at an end. "The surrender of life," Calhoun warned in a famous 1847 speech, "is nothing to sinking down into acknowledged inferiority."[26]

Need for Judicial Resolution

Although the primary error of the Supreme Court in the *Dred Scott* case was its assumption that the issue of slavery in the territories could be resolved judicially, it is a mistake to picture the Justices as blithely rushing into the political arena, officiously seeking to save the nation. Perhaps Taney and his colleagues should never have tried to settle the slavery issue, particularly since the case before them could have been disposed of without consideration of the slavery question; yet it is fair to say that their action was a response to a widespread popular desire to have the issue decided by the highest Court.

The opposing constitutional theories on congressional power could scarcely be resolved through normal political processes. Upon the issue joined by those theories, Congress itself was largely helpless:[27] "[N]o Bill to establish a Territorial Government could be passed through the Ho. Repts. without having the Wilmot Proviso attached to it as a condition . . . with this provision the Bill would probably be rejected by the Senate, . . . and . . . the people of California would be left without a Government."[28] Settlers in the Far West had to do without government because Congress could not decide whether they should have slaves.[29]

In this situation, it was not unnatural to turn to the tribunal vested with the primary function of resolving disputed constitutional issues. The impasse between the Northern and Southern views led a Senate select committee to propose the so-called Clayton Compromise. Under it, Congress was to provide for governments in California and New Mexico, and "they should be restrained by Congress from Legislating on the subject of slavery, leaving that question, if it should arise, to be decided by the judiciary."[30] In this way, the right to introduce or prohibit slavery was to rest "on the Constitution, as the same should be expounded by the judges, with a right to appeal to the Supreme Court."[31]

With the support of Calhoun,[32] the Clayton attempt to have Congress "avoid the decision of this distracting question, leaving it to be settled by the silent operation of the Constitution itself"[33] passed the Senate, but it was defeated in the House. In his last Annual Message, Polk restated the essence of the Clayton proposal, "to leave the subject to the decision of the Judiciary,"[34] as a possible solution: "If the whole subject be submitted to the judiciary, all parts of the Union should cheerfully acquiesce in the final decision of the tribunal created by the Constitution for the settlement of all questions which may arise under the Constitution."[35]

Buchanan used strikingly similar language in his Inaugural Address, referring to the then-pending *Dred Scott* case,[36] and called down upon himself the vitriolic abuse of the antislavery press. By then, opponents of slavery feared an adverse decision, but almost a decade earlier the movement to have the Supreme Court resolve the issue was supported by political leaders on both sides. It was widely recognized, Jefferson Davis wrote later, that "it was necessary to settle finally the asserted right of the Southern people to migrate with their slaves to the territories and there to have for that property the protection which was given to other property of citizens by the U.S. Govt."[37]

The Compromise of 1850 itself was essentially based upon the need to have the key constitutional question settled judicially. On that point, Senator Davis could agree with Senator E. J. Phelps of Vermont: "The Constitution has provided its remedy . . . that tribunal which sits in the chamber below us, Mr. President . . . we are entitled to a decision of the Supreme Court."[38] The Compromise established territorial governments for Utah and New Mexico and provided that "the legislative power of the Territory shall extend to all rightful subjects of legislation consistent with the Constitution of the United States."[39] Provision was made for judicial settlement of the constitutional question by special provisions liberalizing federal court jurisdiction in slavery litigation. In "all cases involving title to slaves," appeals to the Supreme Court were to be allowed without regard to the jurisdictional amount normally required for such appeals.[40]

It has been questioned whether the framers of the Compromise really intended to turn over the constitutional issue to the highest tribunal.[41] During the debates, however, Henry Clay (the prime author of the 1850 measure) did indicate that this was his intent. What, he asked the Senate, could be "more satisfactory to both sides" than to have Congress keep its hands off the issue "and to leave the question of slavery or no slavery to be decided by the only competent authority that can definitely settle it forever, the authority of the Supreme Court?"[42] And the judicial review provisions of the Compromise are a virtual copy of the parts of the Clayton Compromise which proposed leaving the slavery question to the highest Court.[43]

The Kansas–Nebraska Act of 1854 followed the Compromise approach, containing, like the 1850 measure, provisions indicating congressional intent not to deal with slavery in the territory (this time in terms of Stephen A. Douglas's theory of popular sovereignty) and authorizing liberalized appeals to the Supreme Court in slavery cases. The purpose was to leave "the question where . . . it should be left—to the ultimate decision of the courts. It is purely a judicial question."[44] Douglas himself affirmed in 1856 that "I stated [in the Kansas–Nebraska debate] I would not discuss this legal question, for by the bill we referred it to the Courts."[45]

This widespread sentiment is plainly relevant to the charge that the Court's decision in the *Dred Scott* case amounted to mere judicial usurpation. It acted in response to congressional invitation[46] and did no more than yield to the prevalent public demand for judicial pronouncement on the matter. Even Lincoln, severe critic of the decision though he later showed himself, welcomed Supreme Court action in 1856. Noting the Democratic view that restrictions of slavery in the territories would be unconstitutional, he declared that he was not bound by such political construction of the Constitution: "The Supreme Court of the United States is the tribunal to decide such questions, and we will submit to its decisions."[47]

Facts and Issues

Dred Scott was originally called Sam and was so listed in the inventory of his first owner's estate. The name made so famous by the Supreme Court decision was acquired in Illinois or the Wisconsin Territory, where Sam was taken by his new owner, Dr. Emerson, an army surgeon. The case made the short, stubby slave "the hero of the day, if not of the age. He has thrown Anthony Burns, Bully Bowlegs, Uncle Tom and Fred Douglas into . . . oblivion."[48]

In 1846 Scott brought suit in a Missouri court for his freedom against Mrs. Emerson, who had acquired title to him on her husband's death. Scott's counsel argued that his service for Dr. Emerson in Illinois and in territory from which slavery had been excluded by the Missouri Compromise made him a free man. The jury returned a verdict in Scott's favor, but the Missouri Supreme Court reversed on the ground that Missouri law governed, and under it Scott was still a slave.

Scott's attorneys next maneuvered the case into the federal courts. Mrs. Emerson had remarried, and Scott found himself the purported property of her brother, John Sanford, of New York. Scott, claiming Missouri citizenship, could now sue in a federal court on the ground of diversity of citizenship. In 1853 an action was instituted in the United States Circuit Court for Missouri. Scott, as a citizen of Missouri, brought an action for damages, alleging that Sanford,[49] a citizen of New York, had assaulted him. Defendant filed a plea in abatement, alleging that plaintiff was not a citizen of Missouri "because he is a Negro of African descent; his ancestors . . . were brought into this country and sold as negro slaves." The court sustained a demurrer to this plea, and defendant then pleaded that Scott was his slave and that, therefore, no assault could have occurred. After a jury verdict, judgment was given for defendant on the ground that Scott was still Sanford's property. A writ of error was taken by Scott to the Supreme Court.

Until the high bench appeal, the *Dred Scott* case was like many others heard in the courts on behalf of slaves, scarcely noted except by the participants. But from the beginning it was really "enclosed in a tumultuous privacy of storm,"[50] for inherent in it was "the much vexed [question] whether the removal by the master of his slave to Illinois or Wisconsin marks an absolute emancipation."[51] And that, in turn, involved consideration of the effect of the provisions prohibiting slavery found in the Illinois Constitution and the Missouri Compromise. Necessarily included in that issue was the question of power over slavery in the territories.

When *Dred Scott* first instituted his suit, debate over the crucial constitutional issue had been relatively low-keyed. Between that time and the date of the Supreme Court decision, however, it intensified, and just before the case was appealed to the highest Court the whole question was brought to the boiling point by the Kansas–Nebraska Act and its repeal of the Missouri Compromise. The potential of the case for resolution of the issue of congressional power over slavery in the territories was now widely grasped. "This is a question of more importance, perhaps," Scott's attorney could say in his Supreme Court argument, "than any which was ever submitted to this court; and the decision of the court is looked for with a degree of interest by the country which seldom attends its proceedings. It is, indeed, the great question of our day."[52]

But there was more in the case than this: defendant's plea in abatement had posed the question of whether even a free black could be a citizen. In some ways, that question was more fundamental than that of congressional authority over slavery. Legislative power to eliminate slavery would be empty form if those freed could not attain citizenship. If even the free black would have to remain "like some dishonoured stranger"[53] in the community, the Northern majority who hoped that slavery would gradually disappear throughout the country was doomed to disappointment. Extralegal means would be needed to end the degraded status of the enslaved race. What had come to the Supreme Court as a question of law now became a matter of morality.

Maneuverings Toward Decision

The day after the first *Dred Scott* conference Justice Curtis wrote his uncle, "The court will not decide the question of the Missouri Compromise line—a majority of the judges being of the opinion that it is not necessary to do so."[54] At the conference, a majority were of the opinion that the case should be decided without consideration of the two crucial issues. They felt that the issue of citizenship was not properly before them and also took the position that they need not consider the Missouri Compromise because Scott's status was a matter for Missouri law and had already been determined against him by the state's highest court. Justice Nelson was selected to write an opinion disposing of the case in this manner.

Had the Nelson opinion (limiting itself to Scott's status under Missouri law after his return to that state) prevailed as the opinion of the Court, the *Dred Scott* case would scarcely be known today except to the curious student of high bench miscellany. Pressures were, however, building up which soon led the Justices to abandon their original intent.

Soon after his election to the Presidency, James Buchanan wrote to Justice Grier that "the great object of my administration will be, if possible to destroy the dangerous slavery agitation and thus restore peace to our distracted country."[55] The pending decision of the Supreme Court gave him hope that a major part of the problem could be solved at a single stroke.[56] On February 3, the President-elect wrote to Justice Catron, a close friend, asking him whether the case would be decided before March 4, the date of the inauguration. Catron replied that "it rests entirely with the Chief Justice to move in the matter" and that he had said nothing about it. Then, on February 10, Catron wrote Buchanan that the case would be decided four days later but that no opinion would be announced before the end of the month. The decision would not help Buchanan in his Inaugural Address, he said, since the question of congressional power over the territories would probably not be touched on in it.[57]

In the meantime, the Justices had been shaken in their initial resolve to decide the case without considering the issues of citizenship or slavery in the territories. Justice Curtis later said that the change was brought about by Justice Wayne, a Georgian who, while serving as a judge in Savannah, had sentenced an offender for "keeping a school for Negroes." Two years before *Dred Scott,* he had declared that there was no possibility that even free blacks "can be made partakers of the political and civil institutions of the states, or those of the United States."[58] As Curtis recalled it, "it was urged upon the court, by Judge Wayne, how very important it was to get rid of the question of slavery in the Territories, by a decision of the Supreme Court, and that this was a good opportunity of doing so."[59]

Wayne moved in conference that the decision deal with the two vital issues Justice Nelson was omitting. "My own and decided opinion," he said, "is that the Chief Justice should prepare the opinion on behalf of the Court upon all of the questions in the record."[60] The five who voted in favor of Wayne's motion were from slave states. Wayne himself told a Southern Senator that he had "gained a triumph for the Southern section of the country, by persuading the chief-justice that the court could put an end to all further agitation on the subject of slavery in the territories."[61]

The Chief Justice himself apparently did not play a major part in the conference that adopted Wayne's motion, though he clearly was in favor of it and undoubtedly spoke to that effect. On the other hand, according to Curtis's brother, the Justice "in the conferences of the court, explained in the strongest terms that such a result, instead of putting an end to the agitation in the North, would only increase it." In addition, Curtis stressed that it was "most unadvisable to have it understood that the decision of these very grave and serious constitutional questions had been influenced by considerations of expediency."[62] The fact that the five votes for the new decision were by Southerners would lead to anything but Wayne's conference prediction that "the settlement . . . by judicial decision" would result in "the peace and harmony of the country."[63] Instead, as Horace Greeley noted in the *New York Tribune,* settlement of the slavery issue by the Court meant submitting it to five slaveholders and "I would rather trust a dog with my dinner."[64]

After Wayne's motion had been adopted, two of the Justices—Catron and Grier—had written President-elect Buchanan that, in Catron's words, "[A] majority of my brethren will be forced up to this point [i.e., to rule on the constitutional issues of citizenship and slavery in the territories]."[65] These letters to Buchanan were intended to inform the President-elect of the Court's plan to have the Chief Justice write a broad majority opinion. Justice Catron urged Buchanan to write Justice Grier (a fellow Pennsylvanian), who hesitated to join the new majority, telling him "how necessary it is—and how good the opportunity is to settle the agitation by an affirmative decision of the Supreme Court." Buchanan did write to Grier, who showed the letter to Chief Justice Taney and Wayne and then wrote Buchanan that he fully concurred with the need for decision on "this troublesome question." He was afraid that the case would be decided on sectional lines; so "that it should not appear that the line of latitude should mark the line of division in the Court," he would concur with Taney. Both Justices wrote Buchanan that the Court's decision would not be announced until just after the inauguration because of the Chief Justice's poor health.[66]

By present-day standards, the correspondence between Buchanan and two members of the Court was improper. Even more so was Buchanan's pressure on Justice Grier, at the invitation of another Justice, to join the majority. To say, as the Supreme Court historian does,[67] that it was not infrequent at the time for Justices to tell a friend or relative the probable outcome of a pending case scarcely excuses Buchanan and the Justices concerned. Buchanan was not just a friend; he was the new President and was hoping to use the information and his influence over Grier for political purposes. Even given the more permissive standards of an earlier day, the propriety of their conduct cannot be defended.

Yet this is not to say, as was widely charged at the time, that the *Dred Scott* decision itself was the result of a conspiracy between Buchanan and the Southern members of the Court. Though Lincoln asserted, in his famous "House Divided" speech, that the decision was the product of an understanding between "Stephen, Franklin, Roger, and James" in which "all worked upon a common plan . . . drawn up before the first lick was struck,"[68] all we know about the case indicates that it did not happen that way.

Decision

Chief Justice Taney may not have played a key role in the Court's changed posture. However, once the conference voted to decide the merits of the two crucial issues, he became the principal protagonist of the majority view. It was Taney who wrote the opinion of the Court, which stated the polar view against Scott's case, just as Justice Curtis was to write the dissenting opinion that best set forth the opposite position.

On March 6, 1857, the nine Justices filed into their basement courtroom, led by the now-feeble Chief Justice, exhausted by age and illness—a mere shadow, save in intellect, of the man who first presided over the Court two decades earlier. Taney began the reading of the *Dred Scott* opinions in a voice so weak that, during much of the two hours in which he spoke, it sank to a whisper. Each of the majority Justices read his own opinion, and Justices McLean and Curtis read lengthy dissents.[69] The reading of the opinions took two days.

"No wonder," declaimed Greeley's *Tribune,* soon after the decision was announced, "that the Chief Justice should have sunk his voice to a whisper . . . knowing that he was engaged in a pitiful attempt to impose upon the public."[70] To Greeley and other abolitionist editors, the decision was a patent triumph for slavery—a view that was accepted by the South as well.

Chief Justice Taney's opinion for the Court contained three main points: (1) Negroes, even those who were free, were not and could not become citizens of the United States within the meaning of the Constitution; (2) Scott had not become a free man by virtue of residence in a territory from which slavery had been excluded by the Missouri Compromise because the Compromise provision excluding slavery was itself beyond the constitutional power of Congress; (3) Scott was not free by reason of his stay in Illinois because the law of Missouri alone governed his status once he returned to that state.

Only on the third point (which was the sole ground upon which the majority had originally agreed to decide)[71] was the Taney opinion relatively uncontroversial.[72] The seven majority Justices concurred on this point, and the Court's opinion was but a reaffirmation of the law laid down in earlier decisions.[73] What burst with such dramatic impact upon the nation was the fact that the highest Court in the land had denied both the right of blacks to be citizens and the power of Congress to interfere with slaveholding in the territories.

At any rate, it is clear that the effort to have the Court settle the troublesome constitutional issues once and for all failed dismally. In his concurring opinion, Justice Wayne stated that the issues involved had become so controversial "that the peace and harmony of the country required the settlement of them by judicial decision."[74] Seldom has wishful thinking been so spectacularly wrong.[75] Whatever *Dred Scott* brought about, it was anything but peace and harmony—either for the Court or for the country. Instead, as Justice Frankfurter tells us, "*Dred Scott* . . . probably helped to promote the Civil War, as it certainly required the Civil War to bury its dicta."[76]

Congressional Power

To the contemporary observer, the most important part of the opinion of the Court was its holding that the Missouri Compromise was unconstitutional. Five justices[77] concurred with Chief Justice Taney in this holding. This aspect of the opinion was also most strongly censured by critics. Speaking on the Court's view "on the question of the power of the Constitution to carry slavery" into the territories, a leading Northern Senator declared, "beyond all question, to any fair and unprejudiced mind, that the decision has nothing to stand upon except assumption, and bad logic from the assumptions made."[78]

The Taney holding on congressional power was deceptively simple. It began by recognizing congressional authority to acquire new territory and to determine what rules and regulations to make for any territory. That authority was, however, subject to the limitations imposed by the Constitution upon governmental power, including those designed to safeguard private property rights. In particular, property rights are protected by the Due Process Clause of the Fifth Amendment: "And an act of Congress which deprives a citizen of the United States of his liberty or property, merely because he came himself or brought his property into a particular Territory of the United States, and who had committed no offence against the laws, could hardly be dignified with the name of due process of law."[79] Hence the Missouri Compromise prohibition against the holding of property in slaves is unconstitutional and void.

Two aspects of the reasoning just summarized are of special significance. In the first place, Taney depends upon the assumption that congressional power over slavery in the territories is limited by the Constitution itself. This basic holding was sharply censured by former Senator Thomas H. Benton, who, though near death from cancer, published a lengthy attack on the decision soon after it was handed down: "The Court sets out with a fundamental mistake, which pervades its entire opinion, and is the parent of its portentous error. That mistake is the assumption, that the Constitution extends to Territories as well as to States."[80]

Though the law on the matter may not have been settled over a century ago, today we can see that Taney was correct in his approach to the question of the applicability of constitutional limitations in the territories.

The alternative is to hold that Congress may, "when it enters a Territory . . . , put off its character, and assume discretionary or despotic powers which the Constitution has denied to it."[81] Americans migrating to a territory would, if that were true, be mere colonists, dependent upon the will of the Federal Government.

Later decisions of the Supreme Court confirm the Taney reasoning. The landmark *Insular Cases*,[82] decided at the turn of the last century, held that a fundamental provision such as the Due Process Clause is definitely binding in all American territory, including conquered territory subject to military government. More recently, Justice Black used language recalling that of Taney himself; according to Black, whenever our government acts, regardless of locale, it can act only "in accordance with all the limitations imposed by the Constitution."[83]

Having held Congress bound by the requirements of due process in legislating for the territories, the Chief Justice next proceeded to hold that the prohibition of slavery violated due process. Here we come to the second significant aspect of his holding on congressional power. In his ruling that the Missouri Compromise was unconstitutional, Taney was, for the first time in Supreme Court jurisprudence, holding that the Due Process Clause has a substantive as well as a procedural aspect. It was as a violation of substantive due process that the congressional prohibition of slavery was stricken down; what Taney was saying was that a law which deprives a citizen of his property in slaves simply because he brings such property into a territory is arbitrary and unreasonable and hence violative of due process.

Although *Dred Scott* was the first case in which the Supreme Court used the Due Process Clause as a substantive restriction upon governmental power, the Taney approach was not something made up out of legal whole cloth. On the contrary, the development of substantive due process was one of the outstanding judicial achievements of the last century. It began in several state courts during the 1830s and 1840s and culminated in 1856 in *Wynehamer v. People*,[84] decided by the highest court of New York in the period between the first and second arguments in *Dred Scott*.[85] That decision (recognized as epoch-making almost as soon as it was rendered) may well have been the immediate source of Taney's opinion on due process.

Nor was the notion that congressional prohibition of slavery violated due process original with Taney. In the debates preceding the Missouri Compromise, several members of Congress expressed the view that prohibiting slavery in Missouri would violate the Due Process Clause.[86] In 1841 a Northern member of the Supreme Court declared, with regard to slaves, "Being property . . . , the owners are protected from any violations of the rights of property by Congress, under the fifth amendment."[87] Plainly, this was getting very close to Taney's approach in *Dred Scott*.

Even more relevant to the Taney treatment of due process as a substantive restraint was the fact that Justice Curtis, while on circuit in 1852, had stricken down a state liquor law on substantive due process grounds.[88] Particularly suggestive is the fact that Curtis discussed his approach in this case with Taney, who approved the reasoning employed.[89] Taney had only to change the word "liquor" in the Curtis opinion to "slave" and he had the substance of the reasoning by which he invalidated the Missouri Compromise.[90] In view of this, it is surprising that the Curtis dissent in *Dred Scott* emphasized the novel nature of the Taney approach on due process.

Today the Taney application of substantive due process may be considered unduly simplistic, if not naive. The mere fact that a law destroys property rights, we now know, does not necessarily mean that it violates due process. Governmental power does, in appropriate circumstances, include the power to prohibit as well as the power to regulate. It should, however, be borne in mind that Taney was speaking at the very infancy of substantive due process. If his approach was relatively unsophisticated, the same was true of the other early opinions that developed it.

In the era after the Civil War the Taney approach became established in the law. Toward the end of the century, substantive due process was to be used as the fundamental restriction upon govermental action interfering with property rights. The discrediting of the *Dred Scott* decision did not really affect the seminal nature of the concept invoked by Taney. Though the particular property interest which he sought to protect was soon to become anachronistic, the doctrine he articulated opened a new chapter in our constitutional law.

To opponents of slavery, however, the Taney denial of congressional power to interfere with slavery in the territories was a disaster. Acquiescence in the ruling was fatal to the Republicans and the advocates of popular sovereignty alike. It frustrated the hopes of those who sought to confine slavery to an area that would become an ever-smaller portion of an expanding nation. It meant instead that slavery was a national institution; there was now no legal way in which it could be excluded from any territory.

Black Citizenship

In 1834 the status of the free colored population in Pennsylvania was elaborately set forth in a pamphlet published by a member of the Bar of that state. It arrived at the conclusion that the free Negro was neither a citizen of the United States nor a citizen of Pennsylvania. A copy of the pamphlet was sent to Chief Justice Marshall, and he sent the author a letter expressly endorsing his conclusion on Negro citizenship.[91] Thus Marshall, not long before his death, came to the same conclusion as Taney with regard to Negro citizenship. This fact that (so far as the present writer could determine) has been unknown to previous commentators indicates that the Taney ruling may not have been as contrary to law as most of its critics have contended.

Despite this, without a doubt, the Chief Justice's categorical denial of black citizenship, even for free blacks, is the aspect of Taney's opinion that is most difficult to grasp. It seems completely out of line with constitutional conceptions to doom the members of a particular race to live in permanent limbo, forever barred from the dignity of citizenship. Yet that was exactly the result under Taney's holding. As *Harper's Weekly* summed it up, "[T]he Court has decided that free negroes are not citizens of the United States."[92]

Taney's answer to the question of black citizenship resulted from the manner in which he framed the question: "The question is simply this: can a negro, whose ancestors were imported into this country and sold as slaves, become a member of the political community formed and brought into existence by the Constitution of the United States, and as such become entitled to all the rights, and privileges, and immunities, guaranteed by that instrument to the citizen. One of these rights is the privilege of suing in a court of the United States in the cases specified in the Constitution."[93]

Taney's answer was based upon a distinction between "the rights of citizenship which a state may confer within its own limits, and the rights of citizenship as a member of the Union." Since adoption of the Constitution, national citizenship has been federal, not state, in origin. National citizenship was created by the Constitution and, under it, "every person, and every class and description of persons, who were at the time of the adoption of the constitution recognized as citizens in the several States, became also citizens of this new political body; but none other."[94]

Taney went into a lengthy analysis of the situation in this respect and concluded "that neither the class of persons who had been imported as slaves, nor their descendants, whether they had become free or not, were then acknowledged as a part of the people, nor intended to be included in the general words used in [the Declaration of Independence]."[95]

The Taney conclusion rested ultimately upon the concept of Negro inferiority, which was also the basis of the Southern slavery jurisprudence: "They had for more than a century before been regarded as beings of an inferior order; and altogether unfit to associate with the white race, either in social or political relations; and so far inferior, that they had no rights which the white man was bound to respect; and that the negro might justly and lawfully be reduced to slavery for his benefit. He was bought and sold, and treated as an ordinary article of merchandise and traffic."[96]

Legislation, as well as practice, Taney asserted, "shows, in a manner not to be mistaken, the inferior and subject condition of that race at the time the Constitution was adopted, and long afterwards." It can hardly "be supposed that they intended to secure to them rights, and privileges, and rank, in the new political body [when] they had deemed it just and necessary thus to stigmatize, and upon whom they had impressed such deep and enduring marks of inferiority and degradation." In consequence, "Dred Scott was not a citizen of Missouri within the meaning of the Constitution of the United States, and not entitled as such to sue in its courts."[97]

Curtis Dissent

Taney's *Dred Scott* opinion takes up fifty-fives pages of small print in Howard's *Reports,* with over four-fifths devoted to the issues of citizenship and congressional power to prohibit slavery in the territories. There were five concurring and two dissenting opinions. The principal dissent was by Justice Curtis, and his response to Taney is generally considered the most effective statement of the law the other way. The Curtis opinion was the longest of all in *Dred Scott,* covering seventy pages in the *Reports.*

The bulk of the Curtis dissent was devoted to answering the Taney opinion on its two principal rulings. Curtis argued that United States citizenship depended upon state actions. Citizenship within the Constitution for persons born within the United States was through the states and did not depend upon national authority: "[T]he citizens of the several States were citizens of the United States under the Confederation" and the same was true under the Constitution. Curtis cites both statutes and decisions to "show, in a manner which no argument can obscure, that in some of the original thirteen States, free colored persons, before and at the time of the formation of the Constitution, were citizens of those states."[98] That, in turn, under the Curtis approach, made them citizens of the United States.

Curtis dealt with the issue of the Missouri Compromise slavery prohibition by strongly reaffirming the congressional power over the territories. Taney's opinion had recognized congressional authority to acquire new territory and to determine what rules and regulations to make for any territory. But it did so in what we should now consider a peculiar way—recognizing it as an implied power rather than one expressly provided in article IV, section 3, giving Congress power to make rules and regulations for the territories. Curtis gave full effect to the Territories Clause, saying that the power "to make all needful rules and regulations respecting the Territory, is a power to pass all needful laws respecting it."[99]

To be sure, the power "finds limits in the express prohibitions on Congress not to do certain things." Thus it cannot pass an ex post facto law or bill of attainder for a territory any more than it can for any other part of the country. There is, however, no such prohibition for laws relating to slavery and none can be implied. "An enactment that slavery may or may not exist there, is a regulation respecting the Territory."[100] Hence it is within the power of Congress under the Territories Clause. Curtis here referred with particular effect to the Northwest Ordinance prohibition against slavery in the Northwest Territory and the enactment in the First Congress that it should "continue to have full effect."[101]

To Curtis, then, the Territories Clause plainly gave Congress the power to prohibit slavery. There is "no other clause of the Constitution . . . which requires the insertion of an exception respecting slavery" and nothing to indicate that such an exception was intended by the Framers. And "where the Constitution has said all needful rules and regulations, I must find something more than theoretical reasoning to induce me to say it did not mean all."[102]

To us today, the most important part of the Curtis dissent was its refutation of Taney on the citizenship issue. Commentators today assume that the materials relied on by Curtis showed conclusively that free blacks were citizens of at least some of the original thirteen states and hence were citizens of the United States for purposes of the case. And, as the issue was raised by the plea of abatement filed by defendant, "[I]t is only necessary to know whether any such persons were citizens of either of the States under the Confederation at the time of the adoption of the Constitution."[103]

Curtis relied upon constitutional and statutory provisions and decisions in five states[104] to show that "free persons of color"[105] had the right to vote and were consequently citizens of those states. In reality, the evidence in support of Curtis's position was stronger than he indicated. Taney had relied upon the Militia Law of 1792, which limited military service to white males, to show that blacks could not perform one of the essential duties of citizenship.[106] Yet, as pointed out by Judge John Appleton of Maine's highest court, who had once been Curtis's teacher, in an opinion issued only a few months after *Dred Scott,* "[T]here are no historic facts more completely established, than that during the revolution they were enlisted, and served as soldiers; that they were tendered and received as substitutes; that they were required to take, and took the oath of allegiance."[107]

"If these things be so," Appleton went on, "and that they are so cannot be denied or even doubted, and if they had been known to the learned Chief Justice, his conclusions would have been different, for he says, 'every person and every class and description of persons, who *were at the time of the adoption of the constitution recognized as citizens of the several states, became also citizens of this new political body.*" Appleton concluded that Taney's "published opinion, therefore, rests upon a remarkable and most unfortunate misapprehension of facts, and his real opinion upon the actual facts must be considered as in entire and cordial concurrence with that of his learned dissenting associates."[108]

The Appleton conclusion here was ingenuous. It is, to say the least, unlikely that Taney would have concurred with Curtis had the facts with regard to military service been pointed out to him. Moreover, it should be recognized that the case for black citizenship in the 1850s was not as conclusive as the Curtis presentation indicates. Before the Civil War the question of black citizenship was by no means settled clearly. Indeed, there was substantial authority that tended to support Taney rather than Curtis on the matter. Several attorneys general (including Taney himself in 1832)[109] and a number of state courts had concluded that free Negroes were not citizens.[110] Their decisions were based upon the many disabilities from which blacks suffered, which made it plain that they did not enjoy the full rights of citizens.

It is true that there were the state decisions cited by the Curtis dissent holding that free blacks were citizens. But those decisions use the notion of citizenship in a manner which now seems most peculiar. Thus *State v. Manuel*[111]—the case most relied on in the Curtis dissent—involved a North Carolina law providing that, where a free Negro had been convicted of a misdemeanor and could not pay the fine, his services could be sold for up to five years to the highest bidder. This statute (which applied only to blacks, not whites) was upheld by the state court, which stated in its opinion that what "citizenship" the Negro had was of a most restricted sort—on a lower level, as it were, than that possessed by other citizens. Taney could easily have used the *Manuel* case to support his basic thesis of inequality in the treatment of the races.

Curtis also used *State v. Newsom,*[112] a later North Carolina case, to support the *Manuel* citation, but *Newsom* sustained a law making it a crime for "any free Negro" to carry a gun or knife. Here again we have a disability which seems inconsistent with the rights of citizenship. The law was attacked on the ground that free blacks, as citizens, were entitled to the same rights as other citizens. The court stated that *Manuel* was a "controlling influence." Yet, in upholding the law, it went on to say, "[T]he free people of color cannot be considered as citizens, in the largest sense of the term, or if they are, they occupy such a position in society, as justifies the Legislature in adopting a course of policy in its acts peculiar to them."[113]

The truth seems to be that implied in the *Newsom* case: Negro citizenship was a legal euphemism. The current of judicial decisions was relegating the free black to a subordinate status, regardless of whether he was clothed with the formal title of citizen. Actually, a third class of free residents in this country was being created in the law: there were now citizens, free Negroes, and aliens.[114] In this sense, the *Dred Scott* decision was, despite the Curtis dissent, only confirming one line of pre–Civil War jurisprudence.

Yet if the Taney conclusion on citizenship had stronger support in the law than most commentators have recognized, it must still be conceded that the decision was little short of disastrous. It meant that, without constitutional amendment, the Negro was consigned to a permanent second-class status which could not be changed even if all the slaves were ultimately freed. More fundamentally, it gave the lie to the very basis of the American heritage: the notion of equality that was the central theme of the Declaration of Independence—in Lincoln's words, "the electric cord in that Declaration that links the hearts of patriotic and liberty-loving men together."[115] The ruling would have aborted the effort to give effect to the "progressive improvement in the condition of all men"[116] that had been a dominant force since the founding of the Republic.

Result-oriented Jurisprudence

The Taney and Curtis opinions in *Dred Scott* are prime illustrations of the result-oriented judge that is assumed by so many to be a unique characteristic of our own day. Both Justices were employing the legal materials used by them to reach the results they favored. Each was treating the law as an instrument to foster his own societal vision.

If the *Dred Scott* decision brought about anything but the peace and harmony intended by the majority Justices, it did result from the desire of Taney and his Southern colleagues to settle the slavery issue by authoritative judicial decision. The Taney opinion was written to support the Southern position, which in turn was deemed a sine qua non for the preservation of Southern society and its way of life. Only by denying congressional authority to prohibit slavery in the territories could the South prevent itself from being swamped by a vast new free-soil area that would reduce the slave states to an ever-smaller minority. If the balance of power were altered, the very ability of the South to defend itself would be at an end. "The surrender of life," Calhoun warned in an already-quoted speech, "is nothing to sinking down into acknowledged inferiority."[117]

To support his decision, Chief Justice Taney was ready not only to use but to make legal doctrine in a transforming manner that Marshall himself might have envied. To demonstrate that even free blacks were not citizens, Taney made a most selective use of the available materials. Despite Judge Appleton, Taney must have known about the black military experience during the Revolution. But his opinion refers only to the 1792 law which provides for militia service by every "free . . . white male citizen."[118] Yet Curtis also gave a partisan cast to the statutes and cases cited by him. This has been shown, for example, of the North Carolina cases relied upon by Curtis. He quoted the general language on citizenship in the opinions, but he ignored the facts and statements indicating that free blacks still had a subordinate status inconsistent with true citizenship.

With regard to congressional power to prohibit slavery in the territories, Taney went even further by using legal doctrine that may not have been made up out of whole cloth but was certainly new in Supreme Court jurisprudence. And he did so with the mere ipse dixit that a law which deprives a person of his property because he brought it into a particular territory violated due process.

The Supreme Court later pointed out that the Taney conclusion here depends upon the proposition that a slave is property just the way "an ordinary article of merchandise"[119] is property: "If the assumption be true, that slaves are indistinguishable from other property, the inference from the *Dred Scott Case* is irresistible that Congress had no power to prohibit their introduction into a territory."[120] But the crucial weakness of slavery law was that the slave was not ordinary property, the way a house or a horse was. "The difficulty with the *Dred Scott Case* was that the court refused to make a distinction between property in general, and a wholly exceptional class of property."[121]

Taney stretched the law to protect this exceptional property because, like other Southern judges, he was most concerned with preserving what he considered the indispensable foundation of his society and its economy.

Indeed, as the leading modern student of *Dred Scott* puts it, by the time of the case, Taney "had become as resolute in his determination to protect [slavery] as Garrison was in his determination to destroy it."[122]

Ultimately, however, *Dred Scott* stands as a monument of judicial hubris—with both Taney and Curtis assuming that they could resolve in the judicial forum the basic controversy that was tearing the country apart. By trying to act as the deus ex machina on the slavery issue, the Court was stretching judicial power to the breaking point. The case could have been disposed of without consideration of the slavery question and was thus one where the Justices should have adhered to the doctrine of judicial self-restraint that, we saw in Chapter 3, was one of Taney's great contributions to public-law jurisprudence.

On June 12, 1857, Stephen A. Douglas, the chief political victim of the *Dred Scott* decision, addressed a grand jury at Springfield, vigorously defending the Supreme Court and rejecting the charge that the Justices had gone out of their way to decide the crucial constitutional issues. According to Douglas, if the Court had relied on a technicality to avoid the main issues, the outcry against it would have been even worse: "If the case had been disposed of in that way, who can doubt . . . the character of the denunciations which would have been hurled upon the devoted heads of those illustrious judges, with much more plausibility and show of fairness than they are now denounced for having decided the case . . . upon its merits?"[123]

The Court might, as Douglas claimed, have disappointed some, but it could scarcely have tarnished its reputation to the extent that the actual decision did. As a general proposition, it may be said that the Supreme Court as an institution has never been harmed by abstention from political issues. On the contrary, most of the controversies in which it has been embroiled have been caused by failure to follow the doctrine of judicial self-restraint.

Regardless of legal logic, the opponents of slavery could not accept the Court's decision as final, particularly the Republican party, whose very raison d'être was undercut by it. This explains (though it may not justify) the vituperation which Republican orators directed against both the decision and the Court. Lincoln's repeated claim that there was a master conspiratorial plan which sought to use the Supreme Court to make the country "an entire slave nation"[124] by a decision "ere long . . . declaring that the Constitution . . . does not permit a *state* to exclude slavery"[125] must be laid to a lack of understanding of constitutional doctrine. *Dred Scott* could be based upon the Fifth Amendment, for it dealt with congressional authority; before the Fourteenth Amendment, there was no organic provision upon which the Court could base a comparable limitation upon state power.[126]

After the Civil War, Jefferson Davis prepared some notes for Major W. T. Walthall, who was helping him prepare his well-known history of the Confederacy, "on the assigned causes for the invasion of the South." In these notes he made the curious assertion that "the unjust and offensive denial of an equal right to occupy the territories with any species of property recognized by the laws of their states was one of the causes which provoked the Southern people to withdraw from an association in which the terms of the partnership were disregarded."[127]

Davis was confused in his recollection of what had happened. It was not until 1862, well after the Southern states had seceded, that Congress passed a law expressly prohibiting slavery in the territories[128] (thus legislatively denying the right in slave property in the territories which *Dred Scott* had recognized). Davis's recollection does, however, demonstrate the crucial importance of *Dred Scott* in the events leading to the Civil War. In his notes for Walthall, he stated flatly that "the territorial question . . . is another . . . pretext for the war waged against the Southern states."[129]

The *Dred Scott* decision was thus a major factor in precipitating the political polarization of the nation. It was actually the catalyst for the civil conflict that soon followed. With it collapsed the practical possibility of resolving by political and legal means the issues which divided the nation. Thenceforth, extremists dominated the scene. Bloodshed alone could settle the issue of slavery—and of the very nature of the Union, which that issue had placed in the balance.

5

War and Reconstruction, 1861–1877

In many ways the Civil War was the test of fire of the American constitutional system. In an 1862 article, Lord Acton referred to it as the Second American Revolution[1]—a characterization that has since been made often. Like the Revolution, the Civil War represented an extralegal appeal to force to settle the ultimate legal issue of the nature of the polity. And the issue itself was decided, not by the tribunal to which the resolution of such questions was confided by the Constitution, but by the victorious Union armies. When the Supreme Court in 1869 decided that secession was illegal, since "[t]he Consititution in all its provisions, looks to an indestructible Union,"[2] it was only confirming a decision already made at Appomattox Courthouse.

Yet if our law broke down in the face of the nation's most serious crisis, that was not so much the fault of the law itself. The men of the day expected too much of both the law and the courts. In particular, the power and prestige that had been built up under Marshall, and continued under Taney, had led to these too great expectations. And the Justices themselves had succumbed to the lure of seeking to save the country from the bench, losing sight of the limitations inherent in judicial power.

If the Civil War represented an appeal from law to the sword, that was true because the opposing extremes no longer accepted the underlying premises of the legal order. Americans too often forget that the rule of law draws only limited strength from judicial guaranties; it must have roots far deeper than a formal fundamental document and decisions of the judges enforcing it. Our public law depends for its efficacy on popular acceptance of its basic presuppositions. Acceptance, rather than formal legal machinery, is the decisive force in the law's implementation. With Learned Hand in a famous passage, we may "wonder whether we do not rest our hopes too much upon constitutions, upon laws and upon courts. These are false hopes, believe me, these are false hopes."[3]

Merryman and Military Power

"Determining the proper role to be assigned to the military in a democratic society," declared Chief Justice Earl Warren in his 1962 James Madison lecture, "has been a troublesome problem for every nation that has aspired to a free political life."[4] The claims of military power were first asserted in extreme form in the American constitutional system during the Civil War. It cannot be said that a proper balance between military power and law was achieved during that conflict. On the contrary, in the midst of civil strife most of all, as Burke pointed out in his *Reflections on the French Revolution,* "laws are commanded to hold their tongues amongst arms; and tribunals fall to the ground with the peace they are no longer able to uphold."

At the outset of the Civil War the extreme claims of both war and law were presented. The former was personified by President Lincoln, the latter by Chief Justice Taney. To deal with the life-and-death crisis facing the Government after Sumter, Lincoln assumed unprecedented powers. On his own authority he suspended the writ of habeas corpus and ordered wholesale arrests without warrants, detentions without trials, and imprisonments without judicial convictions. Newspapers were seized and their publication suppressed;[5] persons were arrested and held incommunicado by military officers acting under presidential authority. As Taney put it, the military had "thrust aside the judicial authorities and officers to whom the constitution has confided the power and duty of interpreting and administering the laws, and substituted a military government in its place, to be administered and executed by military officers."[6]

The passage quoted is from an opinion Taney delivered in May 1861, in the celebrated *Merryman* case.[7] On April 27 Lincoln authorized the Commanding General of the Army to suspend the right of habeas corpus along any military line between Philadelphia and Washington. A month later Taney, sitting in the federal circuit court in Baltimore, was petitioned for habeas corpus by John Merryman, who had been arrested by the Army and confined in Fort McHenry for his secessionist activities, particularly his participation in the attack upon the Sixth Massachusetts Militia while it was en route to Washington and the destruction of railroad bridges to prevent the passage of troops. Sitting in chambers, Taney granted a writ of habeas corpus directed to the general commanding the fort.

On the return date, an aide-de-camp (in full military uniform and wearing, appropriately, a sword and bright red sash) appeared in the court-room and declined obedience to the writ on the ground that it had been suspended by the Commanding General pursuant to the April 27 order of the President. Taney issued a writ of attachment for contempt against the general, but the marshal seeking to serve it was refused entry to the fort. Taney then delivered his *Merryman* opinion, in which he sharply con-demned as illegal the suspension of habeas corpus by the President and the arrest, without warrant and hearing, of a civilian by military order. But his attempt to uphold the letter of the law against military claims of emergency was fruitless. As he himself plaintively put it, "I have exercised all the power which the constitution and laws confer upon me, but that power has been resisted by a force too strong for me to overcome."[8]

Taney filed his opinion with the clerk of the circuit court, with the direction that a copy be sent to the President: "It will then remain for that high officer, in fulfillment of his constitutional obligation, to 'take care that the laws be faithfully executed,' to determine what measures he will take to cause the civil process of the United States to be respected and enforced."[9] We do not know what Lincoln did with his copy of the Taney opinion (or whether he ever received it), but we do know that he went right on exercising the power that Taney had branded unconstitutional. In addition to other limited suspensions, such as that in the *Merryman* case, he issued an order on September 24, 1862, suspending the writ throughout the country for all persons confined by military authority.[10] Despite the refusal of the military to obey Taney's writ, however, Merryman was released from military custody shortly afterward, and a subsequent indictment against him was never prosecuted.[11]

Over a century later, looking back at the conflict, we can see that neither the Lincoln nor the Taney philosophy alone is adequate. What is needed at such times is a reconciliation of the extreme demands of war and law, not exclusion of the one or the other. It was with keen perception that Justice Robert H. Jackson wrote, "Had Mr. Lincoln scrupulously observed the Taney policy, I do not know whether we would have had any liberty, and had the Chief Justice adopted Mr. Lincoln's philosophy as the philoso-phy of the law, I again do not know whether we would have had any liberty."[12]

When all is said and done, however, there remains something admi-rable in Taney's action in the *Merryman* case:

> There is no sublimer picture in our history than this of the aged Chief Justice— the fires of Civil War kindling around him . . . serene and unafraid, . . . interposing the shield of law in the defense of the liberty of the citizen. Chief Justice Coke when the question was put to him by the King as to what he would do in a case where the King believed his prerogative concerned, made the answer which has become immortal. "When the case happens, I shall do that which shall be fit for a judge to do." Chief Justice Taney when presented with a case of presidential prerogative did that which was fit for a judge to do.[13]

The Court and Civil Liberties

"In the interval between April 12 and July 4, 1861," says W. A. Dunning, "a new principle thus appeared in the constitutional system of the United States, namely, that of a temporary dictatorship. All the powers of government were virtually concentrated in a single department, and that the department whose energies were directed by the will of a single man."[14] According to Lincoln's critics, this situation did not really change even after Congress met, at the President's call, on July 4, 1861. Wendell Phillips continued to denounce Lincoln's government as a "fearful peril to democratic institutions,"[15] and a law professor at Harvard characterized Lincoln as a government in himself—"an absolute, . . . uncontrollable government; a perfect military despotism."[16]

In Lincoln's expansive view of presidential power in wartime, even constitutional doctrine might have to give way if it conflicted with the national necessity. "By general law," he asserted, at the height of what must still be considered our greatest national emergency, "life and limb must be protected, yet often a limb must be amputated to save a life; but a life is never wisely given to save a limb."[17] In assessing this philosophy, we should recognize the difficult choices which confronted the President when strong measures seemed the only alternative to disintegration and defeat. In a famous statement he posed the "grave question whether any government, not *too* strong for the liberties of its people, can be strong *enough* to maintain its own existence, in great emergencies."[18] If the war were lost, government, country, and Constitution itself would all fall together: "I felt that measures, otherwise unconstitutional, might become lawful, by becoming indispensable to the preservation of the constitution, through the preservation of the nation."[19]

It is true that throughout his Presidency Lincoln expressed his distaste for the extraconstitutional measures which he had taken. At the very outset of the conflict he told General Winfield Scott "how disagreeable it is to me to do a thing arbitrarily."[20] This theme he developed in both public and private utterances. When he was informed of military arrests of civilians in the District of Columbia, he wrote, "Unless the necessity for these arbitrary arrests is manifest and urgent, I prefer they should cease,"[21] and to Benjamin Butler, at the height of that officer's conflict with the "restored" Pierpoint government of Virginia, he declared, "Nothing justifies the suspending of the civil by the military authority, but military necessity."[22]

Perhaps the best statement of Lincoln's inner conflict is found in an 1862 letter: "I am a patient man—always willing to forgive on the Christian terms of repentance; and also to give ample *time* for repentance. Still I must save this government if possible."[23] If measures of dubious constitutionality were necessary to accomplish that end, that was, to paraphrase the just-quoted letter, a card that had to be played to prevent losing the game.[24]

It was a card that, despite the distaste expressed by him, Lincoln constantly played. In particular, arrests and suspensions of habeas corpus, such as that in the *Merryman* case, were carried out on a broad scale throughout the war. Nor did the President authorize these measures with the belief that they were unconstitutional. On the contrary, he sought to justify his "supposed unconstitutional action such as the making of military arrests" in a noted 1863 letter to Erastus Corning. Far from conceding that he had abused the power to make military arrests, the time would come, he asserted, "when I shall be blamed for having made too few arrests rather than too many."[25]

Lincoln went on in the Corning letter to note that the arrests which his critics attacked were preventive, rather than vindictive. Such preventive detention could scarcely be accomplished by the traditional processes of the ordinary law: "Nothing is better known to history than that courts of justice are utterly incompetent to try such cases."[26] At any rate, it is clear that, during the Civil War, the courts were not able to decide the legality of Lincoln's measures restricting personal liberty, particularly his suspensions of habeas corpus. It is true, as we saw, that Chief Justice Taney ruled against the presidential suspension in the *Merryman* case; true also that the consensus of learned opinion has agreed that Taney was right and Lincoln wrong on the question of presidential power to suspend the writ. But Taney's decision, as seen, had no practical effect because of the refusal of the military authorities to obey the *Merryman* writ.

Nor was the issue decided by the tribunal set up by the Constitution to resolve such matters. The legality of the habeas suspensions, as well as the other restrictions imposed by military authorities during the war, did not come to decision before the Supreme Court at all. The Court, to be sure, dealt with important aspects of the civil liberties issue in the soon-to-be-discussed *Milligan* case.[27] But *Milligan* was decided after the war and the restrictions laid down by the Court there had no practical effect upon the military violations committed during the conflict.

What was true of the wartime restrictions upon civil liberties was also true of other measures taken during the conflict. The Supreme Court did little more than passively confirm the measures taken by the government to cope with the Southern rebellion. During the whole period, the Court remained in the state of recession which its *Dred Scott* decision had induced. Unconstitutional though many of the wartime measures may have been (at least by present-day standards), the Court itself was unable to rule upon almost all of them. In the one case to reach it during the war involving a violation of civil liberties—*Ex parte Vallandigham,*[28] where the notorious Copperhead had been arrested and tried by the military—the Court avoided the issue by holding that, under the Judiciary Act, it had no appellate jurisdiction over a military commission.

Prize Cases

The Supreme Court did hand down one decision of consequence during the Civil War—that in the 1863 *Prize Cases*.[29] It arose out of one of the emergency measures taken by President Lincoln just after the fall of Fort Sumter, his April 1861 proclamation of a blockade of Southern ports. Four ships had been captured by Union naval vessels enforcing the blockade and had been brought into ports to be sold as prizes. Their owners contended that they had not been lawfully seized because a blockade was a belligerent act which could not be proclaimed in the absence of a state of war declared by Congress.

The formal proclamation of a blockade at the outset of the Civil War has been criticized as a tactical error.[30] In international law, a blockade implies a state of belligerency. In its neutrality proclamation of May 1861, Great Britain took note of such belligerency, and the British Foreign Secretary was able to state, in reply to the claim that the proclamation was "precipitate," "It was, on the contrary, your own Government which, in assuming the belligerent right of blockade, recognized the Southern States as belligerent."[31]

Legally speaking, the proclamation of a blockade, with its recognition of belligerency, constitutes an act of war. To the Supreme Court, indeed, it was Lincoln's blockade proclamation that constituted the beginning of the Civil War.[32] But could the President thus begin a war without violating the claimed "inexorable rule" that the country could be involved in war legally only by declaration of Congress?

The Court in the *Prize Cases* avoided a direct answer to this question by stating that the President did not, by his blockade proclamation or any other act, initiate the conflict. In his argument on behalf of the Government, William Evarts urged that "war is, emphatically, a question of actualities."[33] Whenever a situation assumes the proportions and pursues the methods of war, he said, the peace is driven out, and the President may assert the warlike strength of the nation. Evarts's approach was essentially that followed by the Court. The actuality of the situation confronting the President after Sumter was one of war; "However long may have been its previous conception, it nevertheless sprung forth from the parent brain, a Minerva in the full panoply of War." The President did not initiate such war, but he was bound to accept the challenge "in the shape it presented itself, without waiting for Congress to baptize it with a name; and no name given to it by him or them could change the fact."[34]

A commentary on the *Prize Cases* asserts that that case was as important as a case can be in shaping the contours of presidential power for future occasions when Presidents would wage war without congressional authorization.[35] The decision itself holds only that the President could deal with the situation presented after Sumter as a war and employ what belligerent measures he deemed necessary without waiting for Congress to declare war.[36] It would be absurd for the President to be required, simply because Congress had not declared its existence, "to affect a technical ignorance of the existence of a war, which all the world acknowledges to be the greatest civil war known in the history of the human race, and thus cripple the arms of the Government and paralyze its power by subtle definitions and ingenious sophisms."[37]

It is when we look beyond the bare holding to the language of the Court and its import that we can understand the wide implications of the *Prize Cases*. War, said the opinion of Justice Grier, is "that state in which a nation prosecutes its right by force."[38] Under such a definition, the President can in fact (if not in the technical contemplation of the Constitution) initiate a war. The *Prize Cases* constitute a rejection of the doctrine that only Congress can stamp a hostile situation with the character of war and thereby authorize the legal consequences which ensue from a state of war.[39] Rejection of the rule that only Congress can initiate a war has been of tremendous practical significance. If the President can initiate belligerent measures to cope with civil rebellion, why may he not do so to deal with hostile invasion? In such a case also he would be empowered to meet the challenge of war without waiting for Congress to act. It would be no less a war for the fact that it was begun not by formal declaration but by unilateral act.[40] Must the President take belligerent measures only after the first blow has been struck? Such a limitation on his powers could mean national annihilation in an age in which a nation has the absolute power to destroy an enemy. A constitution which did not permit the Commander in Chief to order belligerent acts whenever necessary to defend his country's interests would be little more than a suicide pact.[41]

On the other hand, as Lincoln himself noted when he was a Congressman during the Mexican war, "Allow the President to invade a neighboring nation, whenever *he* shall deem it necessary to repel an invasion, and you allow him to do so, whenever he may choose to say he deems it necessary for such purpose—and you allow him to make war at pleasure."[42] If we give the President the power to order the commission of belligerent acts whenever he deems necessary, we invest him with the power to make war without legal check. His authority is to act to defend the interests of the United States, but history shows that this is no real restraint, since even aggressive action can be framed in ostensibly defensive terms.

Nature of the Union

In an 1839 letter to Gerrit Smith, an abolitionist, John Quincy Adams predicted that the slavery conflict would ultimately lead to both secession and civil war:

> I believe that long before [emancipation] . . . the slave holding representation would secede in a mass, and that the States represented by them would secede from the Union. I know that among the abolitionists there are some leading and able men, who consider this a desirable event. I myself believe that it would

naturally and infallibly lead to the total abolition of Slavery but it would be through the ultimate operation of a War, more terrible than the thirty years war . . . and I shrink from it with horror."[43]

The conflict which Adams so graphically foresaw raised the overriding issue of the legal nature of the Union itself. That issue had been at the core of most of the pre–Civil War constitutional controversy. "That the Slave holders of the South," Adams went on in his letter to Smith, "should flatter themselves that by seceding from this Union they could establish their peculiar institutions in perpetuity, is in my judgment one of those absurd self-delusions which would be surprising if they did not compose the first chapter in the history of human nature." Yet, he accurately guessed, "the Slaveholders do so flatter themselves, and will act accordingly."[44]

This "delusion" was a natural consequence of the Southern conception of the Constitution. Secession was but the logical culmination of the doctrine of states' rights and state sovereignty which dominated thinking below the Mason-Dixon Line. That doctrine was so ingrained in the Southern mind that it enabled the movers of secession to (in Lincoln's phrase) "sugar-coat" their rebellion "by an insidious debauching of the public mind. They invented an ingenious sophism, which, if conceded, was followed by perfectly logical steps, through all the incidents, to the complete destruction of the Union. The sophism itself is, that any state of the Union may, consistently with the national Constitution, and therefore lawfully, and peacefully, withdraw from the Union, without the consent of the Union, or of any other state."[45]

The truth is that secession and union are constitutionally incompatible. If the Civil War accomplished anything in the constitutional sphere, it was to reject categorically "the position that secession is consistent with the Constitution—is lawful and peaceful."[46] That position was relegated to the realm of constitutional heresy along with the Calhoun doctrine of the states as separate sovereignties upon which it was based.

From a Southern point of view, the Civil War may be looked upon as an attempt to overrule the nationalistic conception of the Constitution which had prevailed since Marshall became Chief Justice. Virginian though he was, Marshall's dominant aim was to establish a strong nation, with the powers needed to govern a continent. The decisions of Marshall and his colleagues constructed federal supremacy upon so strong a base that it has never since been subjected to successful *legal* attack. The adherents of state sovereignty could hope to prevail only by resorting to methods outside the judicial arena. To render the Constitution workable, it had to incorporate "a coercive principle"—the question being, as one of the Framers put it, whether it should be "a coercion of law, or a coercion of arms."[47] With national supremacy so firmly established by the coercion of law, its opponents deemed themselves relegated to the coercion of arms if their view of the nature of the nation was to prevail.

The defeat of the South placed the imprimatur of arms upon both the intent of the Framers and the Marshall interpretation of federal power. The conduct of the war itself furnished ample proof of the soundness of the Marshall conception. "The Federal Government," Winston Churchill tells us, "gaining power steadily at the expense of the states, rapidly won unquestioned control over all the forces of the Union. The Southern 'Sovereign States,' on the other hand, were unable even under the stress of war to abandon the principle of decentralization for which they had been contending."[48] The kind of government Southerners wanted was not the type that could win a lengthy war; states' rights was a hopeless base for total conflict.

The war not only confirmed but accelerated the trend toward strong national government that has been the underlying theme of our constitutional development. "The South," says a Southern writer, "with whatever justification, tried in '61 to break the Union. She succeeded only in strengthening what she fought against."[49] Until the war the advocates of state sovereignty could, despite the uniform case law in opposition to their view, continue to assert the temporary contractual nature of the Union. The defeat of the South meant the final repudiation of such an assertion. In the law itself this repudiation was marked by *Texas v. White*,[50] decided by the Supreme Court shortly after the war ended.

In *Texas v. White*, the State of Texas brought an original action to enjoin the payment of certain United States bonds owned by the state before the war and negotiated by the Confederate state government to the defendants. The key issue presented was whether Texas was then a state of the Union and, as such, capable of bringing suit. Defendants contended that it was not—that having seceded and not yet being represented in Congress, it was still out of the Union. According to the Court's opinion, the ordinance of secession by Texas was a legal nullity. Texas consequently always remained a state within the purview of the Constitution: "When, therefore, Texas became one of the United States, she entered into an indissoluble relation. . . . The act which consummated her admission into the Union was something more than a compact; it was the incorporation of a new member into the political body. And it was final. . . . There was no place for reconsideration, or revocation."[51]

It is all too easy to dismiss the case as only the judicial ratification of the real decision on the validity of secession made at Appomattox Courthouse. To be sure, if the actual outcome of the conflict had been different, the Supreme Court decision could never have been made, but that is true because the constitutional nature of the Union would have been completely altered by military power. As a purely legal decision, under the Constitution as it is written, *Texas v. White* is sound. It is "self-evident that the Union could scarcely have had a valuable existence had it been judicially determined that powers of sovereignty were exclusively in the States":[52] the very language of the Constitution refutes the notion that the states have a sovereign right to secede at will. The Articles of Confederation declare the Union's character to be "perpetual." Says the Court,

"[W]hen these Articles were found to be inadequate to the exigencies of the country, the Constitution was ordained 'to form a more perfect Union.' It is difficult to convey the idea of indissoluble unity more clearly then by these words. What can be indissoluble if a perpetual Union made more perfect, is not?"[53]

The Constitution is thus a bond of national unity, not a mere league which may be dissolved at the pleasure of any party. "The Constitution of the United States," said a member of the highest Court in 1871, "established a government, and not a league, compact or partnership. . . . The doctrine so long contended for, that the Federal Union was a mere compact of States, and that the States, if they chose, might annul or disregard the acts of the National legislature, or might secede from the Union at their pleasure, and that the General Government had no power to coerce them into submission to the Constitution, should be regarded as definitely and forever overthrown."[54]

Reconstruction and the Constitution

When the Civil War ended, the "peace" that followed was anything but a return to the status quo ante—at least so far as the defeated South was concerned. In 1849 John C. Calhoun had evoked what must have seemed to his supporters an apocalyptic vision of the consequences of forcible emancipation. If emancipation ever should be effected, he asserted, "it will be through the agency of the Federal government, controlled by the dominant power of the Northern States." Emancipation itself would come "under the color of an amendment of the Constitution," forced through by the North. It "would lead to consequences unparalleled in history."

Nor, according to Calhoun, would the North stop at emancipation of the slaves: "Another step would be taken—to raise them to a political and social equality with their former owners, by giving them the right of voting and holding public offices under the Federal Government." The ex-slaves would become "the fast political associates of the North," cementing the political union by acting and voting with them. "The blacks, and the profligate whites that might unite with them, would become the principal recipients of federal offices and patronage, and would, in consequence, be raised above the whites of the South in the political and social scale."[55]

The Carolinian's forecast bears a striking resemblance to what used to be the accepted view of the constitutional history of the postbellum South. If, in the end, it did not turn out as Calhoun had predicted—Negro supremacy, he said in his 1849 address, would force the whites to flee the very homes of their ancestors and leave the South "to become the permanent abode of disorder, anarchy, poverty, misery and wretchedness"[56]—that was because of the extreme nature of the Radical Republican program. The measures taken during Reconstruction, in the traditional view, were bound to result in a reaction in the opposite direction once Southerners regained control over their own destiny.

Reconstruction was traditionally seen as an aberration in American constitutional history. It was, wrote Sir Henry Maine soon after it ended, "a Revolutionary period of several years, during which not only the institutions of the Southern States, but the greater part of the Federal institutions were more or less violently distorted to objects not contemplated by the framers of the Constitution."[57] This language has been echoed by more recent writers, even those who have contributed to the changed climate of opinion on Reconstruction. "Frankly revolutionary in mood," concedes C. Vann Woodward, "Thaddeus Stevens and his followers overrode constitutional restraints right and left."[58]

Reconstruction can be considered a patent violation of the Constitution only if we ignore the fact that it posed issues which the Framers had neither foreseen nor provided for in the document they drafted. To be sure, throughout our history "the Court has viewed the separation and subordination of the military establishment as a compelling principle."[59] Yet that is true only in states which are not in an actual theater of military operations and in whch the civil courts are open and functioning.[60] Ever since the Mexican war, a different rule had been applied to territory occupied by American forces; there the prevailing principle has been that of military conquest, with government set up by the occupying forces, though subject to ultimate congressional control.[61]

What happens, however, if the occupied territory consists of states which have sought to secede and have been prevented from doing so by federal force? Such a situation plainly was not considered by the Framers, who intended the Union to be perpetual and indissoluble. "The Constitution," declared the Supreme Court in *Texas v. White*, "in all its provisions, looks to an indestructible Union."[62] Nor were there constitutional provisions for the legal status of the defeated states after their attempt at secession had been suppressed.

How to deal with these unprecedented constitutional problems? The one thing clear to the Republican leaders was that the constitutional clock could not simply be turned back to 1860. That had, of course, become the "Southern" theory of Reconstruction—that with the end of the war, all affairs should revert to their previous condition. By 1865, however, the North had come to recognize the truth of Elizur Wright's statement that "the general facts . . . make a restoration of the state [of affairs] before the war equivalent to defeat."[63]

This meant that the congressional leaders could not agree with President Andrew Johnson's theory of Reconstruction, for it was essentially similar to the Southern position—based as it was upon the conception that the Southern states had only had "their life-breath . . . suspended:[64] and that it could be speedily restored by presidential action.

The congressional leaders could not accept the Johnson conception of the postwar task as that of bringing about a prompt restoration of the South to the Union. The President, said Thaddeus Stevens, "preferred 'restoration' to 'reconstruction.' He chooses that the slave States should remain as nearly as possible in their ancient position."[65] Though there were differences of detail and degree between the various theories advanced by different Radical spokesmen—from the extreme "conquered provinces" theory of Stevens to the somewhat more moderate ones of "state suicide" espoused by Charles Sumner or "forfeited rights" of Samuel Shellabarger—they all refused to accept the view that the Southern states needed only the restoration of "loyal" governments.

Instead, however they were phrased, the congressional Reconstruction theories meant in practice that the rebel states would be treated (in George W. Julian's phrase) "as outside of their constitutional relations to the Union, and as incapable of restoring themselves to it except in conditions to be prescribed by congress."[66] The Southern states could no longer be considered in the same relationship to the Union as other states. On the contrary, "[S]uch States and their people ceased to have any of the rights or powers of government as States of this Union."[67] Consequently, it was for Congress to decide the conditions upon which the Southern states were to be reconstructed as full states of the Union. "The Southern states have ceased to be states of the Union—their soil has become National territory"[68]—subject, as such, to congressional power.

Supreme Court Reconstruction Theory

In the already-discussed case of *Texas v. White*[69] the Supreme Court stated its position on the constitutional basis of Reconstruction. In that case, it will be recalled, the Court upheld, in strong language, the indissoluble nature of the Union. From a constitutional point of view, the attempted secession of a state like Texas was ruled "absolutely null . . . utterly without operation in law."[70] Texas remained a state, with its obligations as a member of the Union unimpaired.

The fact that secession was legally void did not mean that it had never happened, however, and that "the governmental relations of Texas to the Union remained unaltered."[71] There was a difference between the constitutional existence of a state itself and the existence within it of a government competent to represent it in its relations with the nation. When the war ended there was no such government in Texas, and it became the duty of the United States to provide for the reestablishment of such a government. The President had initial authority in the matter, since as Commander-in-Chief he could institute governments in areas occupied by federal forces. However, "the action of the President must . . . be considered as provisional";[72] presidential power was ruled subject to the overriding authority of Congress to provide for lawful governments in the Southern states.

The answer given to the question of Reconstruction in *Texas v. White* is one that has been repeated in more recent cases involving occupied territory, particularly those growing out of the war with Spain and World War II.[73] Those cases confirm the overriding congressional power to establish governments in areas occupied by American forces. Under them, too, the military power of the President to govern such areas continues only until it has been terminated by congressional action.[74]

Texas v. White supports both the claim of overriding Reconstruction authority in Congress and the constitutionality of the congressional Reconstruction measures. The Supreme Court recognized that it was for Congress to provide for governments in the defeated states to fill the vacuum that existed after the Southern defeat. Just as important was the source of the congressional power: "[A]uthority was derived from the obligation of the United States to guarantee to every state in the Union a republican form of government."[75] *Texas v. White* followed Chief Justice Taney in *Luther v. Borden* (1849)[76] in holding that the power to carry out the republican guaranty clause "resides in Congress."[77] Under *Luther v. Borden* and the later cases, legislative action to enforce the Guaranty Clause presents a political, rather than a judicial, question.

What this means is shown by *Georgia v. Stanton,*[78] where an action was brought to enjoin enforcement of the Reconstruction Acts. As more recently explained by Justice Brennan, "It seemed to the Court that the only constitutional claim that could be presented was under the Guaranty Clause, and Congress having determined that the effects of the recent hostilities required extraordinary measures to restore governments of a republican form, this Court refused to interfere with Congress' action at the behest of a claimant relying on that very guaranty."[79]

In substance, the Supreme Court adopted the constitutional position upon which congressional Reconstruction was based. The framers of the Wade-Davis bill had expressly relied on *Luther v. Borden*. According to Congressman H. W. Davis, that case meant that "it is the exclusive prerogative of Congress—of Congress, and not of the President—to determine what is and what is not the established government of the State."[80] In *Texas v. White* the Supreme Court placed its imprimatur upon this view. That one may disapprove of some or all of the Reconstruction measures shoud not obscure this fact. To characterize Reconstruction as a constitutional aberration is an exercise in rhetoric, not in law—certainly not in the law laid down by the Supreme Court.

Congressional Reconstruction

That the general theory of congressional Reconstruction was accepted by the Supreme Court does not mean that the details of Reconstruction in operation were approved by the Justices. The 1866 election had given the Republicans an overwhelming majority in both houses. This majority the congressional leaders used to remake the Reconstruction process in the legislative image. The governments instituted under the presidential plan of Reconstruction were swept aside, and Congress assumed control over the reestablishment of Southern governments. Most members of Congress were prepared to do so because they had come to feel that drastic measures were needed to deal with the results of President Johnson's laissez-faire Reconstruction program. Rather than permit an unreconstructed South "to substitute a degrading peonage for slavery and make a mockery of the moral fruits of northern victory,"[81] the congressional majority decided upon the drastic measure of military rule.

The basic statute in the congressional Reconstruction program was the First Reconstruction Act of March 2, 1867.[82] Its two principal features were the imposition of military rule and the complete reorganization of government. It declared that "no legal State governments or adequate protection for life or property" existed in the ten "rebel States." Those states were then divided into five military districts, each under the command of an army general. These commanders were given broad powers "to protect all persons in their rights of person and property, to suppress insurrection, disorder, and violence, and to punish . . . all disturbers of the public peace." To make such powers effective, they were authorized to make arrests, conduct trials in military courts,[83] and use federal troops to preserve order.

Writing of the Reconstruction Act in 1902, John W. Burgess asserted, "There was hardly a line in the entire bill which would stand the test of the Constitution." This assertion is wide of the legal mark. Burgess himself concedes, "There can be no question in the mind of any sound political scientist and constitutional lawyer that Congress was in the right, logically, morally, and legally, in insisting upon brushing aside the results of executive Reconstruction in the winter of 1867, and beginning the work itself from the bottom up." If Congress had the power to brush aside the governments set up during presidential Reconstruction, it surely had the power to set up governments in their place. Perhaps, as Burgess contends, Congress should have set up "regular Territorial civil governments."[84] The choice, however, was within the discretion of Congress, and that body could reasonably conclude that a probationary period under military rule was necessary. That an immediate transition to civil government might have been a wiser choice does not affect the legality of the congressional action.

The decision of the Supreme Court in *Ex parte Milligan*[85] does not alter the constitutional picture. The decision there was referred to by Chief Justice Warren as a "landmark," which "established firmly the principle that when civil courts are open and operating, resort to military tribunals for the prosecution of civilians is impermissible."[86] Yet vital though the *Milligan* case has been as the foundation of the wall of separation between the military and civil classes in the community, it had little immediate practical effect, since during the war the Supreme Court had refused to rule on the legality of military arrests, notably in the case of Clement Vallandigham. The holding of illegality in the similar *Milligan* fact pattern came over a year after the war was over. Milligan may have had the satisfaction of being immortalized in the *Supreme Court Reports*, but that hardly was an adequate substitute for the imprisonments suffered by Copperheads and others while the Court declined to come to grips with the constitutionality of military arrests and trials.

In *Milligan*, the Court went out of its way to lay down limitations upon resort to martial law and use of military tribunals to punish civilians. This led Thaddeus Stevens to assert that the *Milligan* decision, "although in terms perhaps not as infamous as the Dred Scott decision, is yet far more dangerous in its operation."[87] But it was the exercise of military jurisdiction in Indiana—a loyal state not in an actual theater of war, in which the civil courts were functioning—that called forth restrictive language from the Court. Military jurisdiction, it said, "can never by applied to citizens in states which have upheld the authority of the government, and where the courts are open."[88]

This *Milligan* reasoning did not necessarily apply to states whose attempt to secede had been overcome by force and which Congress had not yet provided with lawful governments, entitling them to resume their full place in the Union. Justice Davis, the author of the Court's opinion, indicated that *Milligan* did not necessarily imply the unconstitutionality of Reconstruction. In a letter early in 1867, he noted that there was "not a word said in the opinion about reconstruction, & the power is conceded in insurrectionary States."[89]

McCardle and Judicial Power

Despite what has just been said, it was widely assumed at the time that *Milligan*, in deciding against the military trial of civilians, had indicated that the Supreme Court would invalidate the military governments set up under the Reconstruction statutes. The occasion for doing so, it was believed, was furnished by *Ex parte McCardle*,[90] then on its way to the highest bench. McCardle was a Mississippi newspaper editor who had been arrested in 1867 and held for trial by a military commission. The charges were based upon editorials published by McCardle, particularly one which asserted that General Sheridan and the other generals commanding Southern military districts "are each and all infamous, cowardly, and abandoned villains, who, instead of wearing shoulder straps and ruling millions of people, should have their heads shaved, their ears cropped, their foreheads branded, and their precious persons lodged in a penitentiary."[91]

McCardle petitioned for a writ of habeas corpus in the federal circuit court, challenging the validity of the First Reconstruction Act's provision authorizing the military detention and trial of civilians. The writ was denied by the circuit court, and an appeal was taken to the Supreme Court under an 1867 statute authorizing appeals from circuit court decisions in all cases involving detentions in violation of the Constitution or federal laws.[92] The Supreme Court unaminously decided that it had jurisdiction to hear the appeal.[93] The case was thoroughly argued on the merits and taken under advisement by the Justices.

Congressional leaders feared that the Court would seize the opportunity presented by *McCardle* to invalidate the military governments authorized by the Reconstruction Act. "Should the Court in that case, as it is supposed they will," wrote Gideon Welles in his famous diary, "pronounce the Reconstruction laws unconstitutional, the military governments will fall and the whole Radical fabric will tumble with it."[94]

To avoid this danger, the congressional leaders considered various maneuvers. The most extreme was embodied in a bill passed by the House early in 1868,[95] which required a two-thirds vote of the Justices before any act of Congress could be ruled unconstitutional. That bill, said Gideon Welles, "is a scheme to change the character of the Supreme Court."[96] It ultimately died in the Senate, as did a bill introduced by Senator Lyman Trumbull forbidding the Court to take jurisdiction in any case arising out of the Reconstruction acts.[97] Congress then passed a law repealing the 1867 statute authorizing an appeal to the Supreme Court from circuit court judgments in habeas corpus cases and prohibiting the Court's exercise of any jurisdiction on appeals which had been or which might be taken.[98] The *McCardle* case was then reargued on the question of the authority of Congress to withdraw jurisdiction from the Supreme Court over a case which had already been argued on the merits.

The Court in its *McCardle* decision unanimously answered the question of congressional power over its appellate jurisdiction in the affirmative even in such a case. The effect of the repealing act, said the Court, upon the case before it was plain: to withdraw jurisdiction over the appeal. It is quite clear, therefore, the Court decided, "that this court cannot proceed to pronounce judgment in this case, for it has no longer jurisdiction of the appeal."[99]

If the Court had been able to decide the merits in *McCardle,* the decision might well have been in petitioner's favor—that, at any rate, was what Chief Justice Chase and Justice Stephen J. Field told two of their contemporaries.[100] But the point of *McCardle* is that Congress was able to prevent a decision on the merits. "The Judges of the Supreme Court," Gideon Welles plaintively wrote, "have caved in, fallen through, failed, in the McCardle case."[101] The *McCardle* law is the only instance in American history in which Congress rushed to withdraw the appellate jurisdiction of the Supreme Court for the purpose of preventing a decision on the constitutionality of a particular statute. That law, in the pithy phrase of a newspaper, "put a knife to the throat of the *McCardle* Case."[102] And the *McCardle* decision permitted Congress to do just that: "Congress," wrote former Justice Curtis, "with the acquiescence of the country, has subdued the Supreme Court."[103]

Commentators, both on and off the bench, have construed *McCardle* as the ultimate illustration of the unlimited legislative power over the appellate jurisdiction of the Supreme Court. The result of *McCardle,* we are told,[104] is to vest an unrestrained discretion in Congress to curtail and even abolish the appellate jurisdiction of the highest tribunal. After referring to *McCardle,* Justice Owen J. Roberts asked: "What is there to prevent taking away, bit by bit, all the appellate jurisdiction of the Supreme Court?"[105]

One seeking to understand the *McCardle* case should certainly not unduly minimize its impact. The repealing act there had as its aim the prevention of a decision by the Court on the constitutionality of the Reconstruction Acts. That was its sole purpose and end[106]—clearly understood as such by the Congress and the country, especially after President Johnson's veto message, which directly attacked such purpose as contrary to the spirit of the basic document.

Ex parte McCardle is, however, a case more celebrated than understood. Far-reaching though the *McCardle* decision may be, it cannot be taken as a judicial confirmation of congressional omnipotence with regard to the appellate jurisdiction of the highest Court. The organic position of the Supreme Court is specifically provided for in article III and its appellate jurisdiction is also given directly by that article. The appellate powers of the court flow, as a consequence, from the constitutional source.

The power given to Congress to prescribe exceptions and regulations to the appellate jurisdiction of the Supreme Court cannot be taken to include the authority to do away with such jurisdiction. Instead, the purpose of the Exceptions-and-Regulations Clause was to authorize exceptions and regulations by Congress not incompatible with the essential function of the Court as ultimate arbiter of the constitutional system.

The congressional power to prescribe exceptions to the Supreme Court's appellate jurisdiction may thus not be treated as authorizing exceptions which engulf the rule—even to the point of eliminating the appellate jurisdiction altogether. The Court affirmed that the congressional authority in this respect is limited by the fundamental purposes of the Constitution: "What such exceptions and regulations should be it is for Congress, in its wisdom, to establish, having, of course, due regard to all the provisions of the Constitution."[107] The exceptions and regulations laid down by Congress must not be such as will destroy the basic role of the Supreme Court in the constitutional scheme. Reasonably interpreted, the organic clause means: "With such exceptions and under such regulations as the Congress may prescribe, not inconsistent with the essential functions of the Supreme Court under the Constitution."[108]

But is not such an interpretation wholly contrary to *Ex parte McCardle,* where, as already seen, Congress was sustained in ousting the Court of competence over a case already at the bar, which was of such drastic import to the liberty of the individual concerned?

Those who would unqualifiedly assert that an affirmative response to this query is the only correct one overlook the real meaning of the *McCardle* case. Far-reaching though its decision there was, the Court in *McCardle* did not hold that the Congress could validly oust it of all appellate jurisdiction in habeas corpus cases. The repealing act at issue there did not have that extreme result. In the words of the *McCardle* opinion: "Counsel seem to have supposed, if effect be given to the repealing Act in question, that the whole appellate power of the court, in cases of habeas corpus, is denied. But this is an error. The Act of 1868 does not except from that jurisdiction any cases but appeals from circuit courts under the Act of 1867. It does not affect the jurisdiction which was previously exercised."[109]

Prior to the *McCardle* statute, the Supreme Court could review denials of habeas corpus by lower courts either on appeals[110] or on petitions to it for habeas corpus.[111] The *McCardle* statute did no more than eliminate the first of these methods for obtaining review of decisions denying the Great Writ. But, as the Supreme Court held in *Ex parte Yerger*,[112] only half a year after its *McCardle* decision, it left unimpaired the other method of invoking the Court's appellate jurisdiction in habeas corpus cases.

The *McCardle* case consequently did not really present the question of the congressional power to destroy the Supreme Court's appellate jurisdiction over denials of the Great Writ. The *McCardle* statute withdrawing jurisdiction, though successful to frustrate decision of the appeal in that case, left intact the power to review denials of the writ through a habeas petition in the Court itself. Indeed, under *Ex parte Yerger*, McCardle could presumably have petitioned the Supreme Court for a writ of habeas corpus to test the constitutionality of his military detention.

In *Yerger*, the same Court that decided *McCardle* strongly intimated that Congress lacked the power to deprive the high bench of all habeas corpus jurisdiction. "It would have been, indeed, a remarkable anomaly," declares the *Yerger* opinion, "if this court, ordained by the Constitution for the exercise, in the United States, of the most important powers in civil cases of all the highest courts of England, had been denied, under a constitution which absolutely prohibits the suspension of the writ, except under extraordinary exigencies, that power in cases of alleged unlawful restraint, which the Habeas Corpus Act of Charles II expressly declares those courts to possess."[113]

The implication is that, by virtue of the Habeas Corpus Clause, the jurisdiction of the Supreme Court to issue the writ, once conferred, may not be withdrawn by the legislature, except in cases of rebellion or invasion, despite its power to prescribe exceptions and regulations with regard to the high Court's appellate powers. As the *Yerger* Court put it: "[I]t is too plain for argument that the denial to this court of appellate jurisdiction in this class of cases must greatly weaken the efficacy of the writ, deprive the citizen in many cases of its benefits, and seriously hinder the establishment of that uniformity in deciding upon questions of personal rights which can only be attained through appellate jurisdiction."[114] To permit Congress to push its power over appellate jurisdiction to the extreme of abolishing the Supreme Court's competence in habeas corpus cases is to empower it, at will, to abrogate the guaranty of the Habeas Corpus Clause. For, in the language of the *Yerger* opinion, "[I]t is evident that the imprisoned citizen, however unlawful his imprisonment may be in fact, is wholly without remedy unless it be found in the appellate jurisdiction of this court."[115]

Despite *McCardle,* then, the Exceptions-and-Regulations Clause of article III does not vest Congress with unlimited power over the appellate jurisdiction of the Supreme Court. The clause does not permit Congress to negate the essential functions of a coordinate department. The power to make exceptions may not be pushed so far that those prescribed eliminate the appellate jurisdiction altogether or leave only a trifling residuum of jurisdiction—as by an exclusion of everything but patent cases.[116] The power to regulate is not the power to destroy where the subject of regulation is so essential to the existence of the Constitution itself. The congressional power is that to modify—not that to abolish.

Era of the Oath

To one who remembers all too vividly the "cold war" era of emphasis on individual loyalty, a particularly interesting aspect of the Civil War and postbellum period was the pervasive use of loyalty tests. Before Sumter, Americans took it for granted that public servants were loyal to the United States. As soon as hostilities began, that assumption gave way. Two weeks after Sumter fell, Lincoln's Attorney General recommended that "all the employees of the Departments—from the head secretary to the lowest messenger, be required to take anew the oath of allegiance."[117]

But the simple oath to defend the Constitution (which was contained in the first statute enacted by the first Congress)[118] was soon deemed inadequate to ensure loyalty. In August 1861, Congress passed a law prescribing a new and more elaborate oath for government employees. They were required to swear to "support, protect, and defend" the Constitution and the Federal Government and to declare their "loyalty to the same, any ordinance, resolution, or law of any State Convention or Legislature to the contrary notwithstanding."[119] The swearing process was duly repeated a second time in all federal offices.[120] This new loyalty oath was soon believed to be insufficient, and on July 2, 1862, Congress enacted into law the so-called ironclad oath of loyalty.[121]

That oath became the very backbone of the congressional system of disenfranchisement and disqualification for office during the war and in the Reconstruction period. All persons (except the President) "elected or appointed to any office . . . under the government of the United States, either in the civil, military, or naval departments" were required to take the ironclad oath. The oath was in two parts. The affiant had to swear that he had never voluntarily borne arms against the United States or given any voluntary aid to those engaged in armed hostilities against the Union, and that he had not held office under or yielded voluntary support to any government hostile to the United States. The second part of the oath was a pledge to support and defend the Constitution and bear true faith and allegiance to it in the future.

During Reconstruction, the congressional leaders insisted upon the ironclad oath as the fundamental test. "I have ceased to hope anything that justice or humanity demands," wrote Judah P. Benjamin in October 1866, "from the men who now seem to have uncontrolled power over public affairs in the U.S."[122] The inronclad oath had become the fulcrum upon which Reconstruction turned. The Supplemental Reconstruction Act (March 23, 1867)[123] prescribed an oath of past loyalty comparable to the ironclad oath for all who sought to register as voters; all registration officials were required to take the ironclad oath itself. The Third Reconstruction Act (July 19, 1867) required that "all persons hereafter elected or appointed to office in said military district" should take the ironclad oath.[124] The final step was a law of 1869 requiring the military commanders in Virginia, Texas, and Mississippi (which were still unreconstructed) to remove all officials who could not take the ironclad oath and to replace them with persons who could.[125]

The first people usually required to take loyalty oaths are public employees; concern with loyalty, however, soon extends to other areas. By mid-1862, oaths of loyalty to the Union were required of government contractors,[126] shipmasters,[127] claimants before federal agencies,[128] pensioners, telegraphers, and passport applicants.[129] Congress imposed the ironclad oath upon attorneys seeking to practice in the federal courts, [130] as well as a comparable oath upon federal jurors.[131] In addition, as we have seen, the Reconstruction laws required Southern voters to take such an oath.

"It is unfortunate," wrote Georges Clemenceau in 1867, "that the Republicans have not in all cases shown good judgment in their Reconstruction measures. One of the principal tests of loyalty . . . is the oath. But the Anglo-Saxons have always abused the oath. . . . It does not in the least hamper a rogue who becomes as accustomed to taking an oath as a dealer in church furniture to handling a pyx."[132] Even more important is the impact of the requirement upon honorable men. As Lincoln put it with regard to the Tennessee loyalty oath, "I have found that men who have not even been suspected of disloyalty, are very averse to taking an oath of any sort as a condition to exercising an ordinary right of citizenship."[133]

More fundamental is the question whether the oath technique can possibly attain its purpose of fostering loyalty. The observer who has lived through a second "era of the oath" has more than a modest doubt about what the oath technique accomplishes apart from indicating the malaise of the society in which it is employed. While the Decii are rushing with devoted bodies on the enemies of Rome, what need is there of preaching patriotism? When loyalty is made a principal object of the state's concern, it has already become less than all-transcendent.

The ironclad oath was put to the constitutional test and found wanting in *Ex parte Garland*[134] and *Cummings v. Missouri*[135]—two companion cases decided in 1867. In *Garland* the Court held invalid the ironclad oath which Congress had required for admission to practice in the Supreme Court. In *Cummings* the Missouri oath required to practice any profession (in this case, that of a Catholic priest) was ruled unconstitutional. In both cases, as the Court more recently explained, the oaths were ruled unconstitutional "as bills of attainder on the ground that they were legislative acts inflicting punishment on a specific group: clergymen and lawyers who had taken part in the rebellion and therefore could not truthfully take the oath."[136] In addition, since they imposed a penalty for an act not so punishable at the time it was committed, they also violated the prohibition against ex post facto laws.

Cummings and *Garland* may be leading cases on loyalty oaths. However, the post–*Dred Scott* shadow in which the Court still labored ensured that the decisions would have little immediate practical effect. Under *Cummings* and *Garland,* it is clear that much of the Reconstuction loyalty oath program was unconstitutional. The imposition of disqualifications upon those who could not swear to their past loyalty to the Union comes directly within the reach of the Supreme Court decisions. Yet only two monts after *Cummings* and *Garland,* Congress (as already seen) prescribed an oath of past loyalty for all voters in the reconstructed South and, a few months later, required the ironclad oath of all officeholders in the South. Despite the Supreme Court's categorical condemnation, these oath requirements were continued during the entire Reconstruction period. Nor did the Supreme Court's censure affect the use of the ironclad oath in the Federal Government, both for civil servants and in other cases. Four years after *Cummings* and *Garland,* Benjamin F. Butler declared, "I hope the iron-clad oath will never be repealed—ay, even after every disability is removed from every rebel. . . . I roll it as a sweet morsel under my tongue."[137] It was not, indeed, until 1884 that it was finally repealed.[138]

6

Chase and Waite Courts, 1864–1888

On June 26, 1857, Abraham Lincoln replied to the contention of Stephen A. Douglas that the Declaration of Independence, in declaring "that all men are created equal," was only "speaking of British subjects on this continent being equal to British subjects born and residing in Great Britain." Lincoln emphatically rejected this interpretation. The authors of the Declaration, he said, "intended to include all men. . . . They meant to set up a standard maxim for free society, which should be familiar to all, and revered by all; constantly . . . spreading and deepening its influence, and augmenting the happiness and value of life to all people of all colors everywhere."[1]

In emphasizing the concept of equality as a central theme of the Declaration of Independence Lincoln echoed what has always been a driving force in American history, despite the fact that the Framers of the Constitution did not repeat the unqualified assertion of the Declaration of Independence. Nowhere in the basic document is there any guaranty of equality or even any mention of that concept. Yet whatever may have been the Framers' intent, their work disseminated the ideals of Liberty and Equality throughout the world. "What Archimedes said of the mechanical powers," wrote Tom Paine in *Rights of Man*, "may be applied to Reason and Liberty. 'Had we,' said he, 'a place to stand upon, we might raise the world.' The revolution of America presented in politics what was only theory in mechanics."[2]

The concept of equality, however, could scarcely complete its triumphant march while slavery not only existed but was protected by the Constitution. "Liberty and Slavery," declared Frederick Douglass, "—opposite as Heaven and Hell—are both in the Constitution," and the Constitution itself was "a compromise with Slavery—a bargain between the North and the South."[3] While that bargain persisted, an express guaranty of equality would have only been hypocritical. With the Civil War, the situation completely changed. "The bond of Union being dissolved," Jefferson Davis conceded, "the obligation of the U.S. Govt. to recognize property in slaves, as denominated in the compact, might be recognized as thereby no longer binding."[4] William Lloyd Garrison, who had earlier committed the Constitution to the fire, could now fervently support the Union. When charged with inconsistency, he replied: "Well, ladies and gentlemen, when I said I would not sustain the Constitution, because it was a 'covenant with death and an agreement with hell,' I had no idea that I would live to see death and hell secede."[5]

When slavery was abolished and the American system repudiated the heresy that "all men are created equal, except Negroes,"[6] it was no longer inconsistent with reality for the Constitution to contain an express guaranty of equality. It came with ratification of the Fourteenth Amendment in 1868. That amendment and the other postbellum additions to the Constitution made equality regardless of race a fundamental constitutional principle.

The postbellum amendments constituted the first changes in the organic text in over sixty years. From a legal point of view, the changes were fundamental, for they made for a nationalization of individual rights that was completely to transform the constitutional system. The protection of life, liberty, and property now became a national responsibility—federalizing, as it were, the vindication of individual rights throughout the land.

One must, however, note a shift in constitutional emphasis as the post–Civil War period developed. The early Reconstruction concern with vindication of civil rights was soon replaced by primarily economic concerns. The headlong industrialization of the period inevitably raised new problems for the law, and the constitutional history of the nation after Appomattox must largely be written in terms of the reaction of the legal order to the new economy. If, before the Civil War, the major constitutional theme was the nation–state problem, in the period that followed the dominant concern became the government–business relationship.

The key constitutional provision of the new industrial era was the Fourteenth Amendment, which was the most significant of the legal changes imposed as part of the price of Southern defeat. Its Due Process Clause was to serve as the Great Charter for the protection of the private enterprise that was so transforming society. Due process as the great bulwark of private property did not, however, develop fully until the last decade of the century. During the period to which this chapter is devoted, it had not yet been converted into the cornerstone of American constitutionalism. The first decisions under the Fourteenth Amendment manifested a restrictive attitude toward its effect, but they were only the first steps in the interpretation of the new amendment. The dissents delivered in them ultimately served as the foundation upon which due process was to be elevated to the foremost place in the organic pantheon. Before dealing with the constitutional protection of property rights under the post–Civil War Constitution, however, we should take note of the personnel changes that took place as the Taney Court gave way to its successor.

Taney's Successor

During the Civil War and Reconstruction, the Supreme Court was anything but the master of the Constitution. In the main, control of the constitutional machine was concentrated in the legislative department, and the Court could play only a minor part. When Chief Justice Taney died in 1864, the age of giants on the bench ended. Now it was the turn of the political jobbers and manipulators. Not for more than half a century would a man of true stature again sit in the Court's central chair.

Lincoln was frank about the political considerations that governed his choice of Taney's successor. "We wish," he said, "for a Chief Justice who will sustain what has been done in regard to emancipation and the legal tenders. . . . Therefore, we must take a man whose opinions are known."[7] Such a man Lincoln thought he had found in Salmon P. Chase, his former Secretary of the Treasury and a leader of the Republican Radicals. Chase was appointed to Taney's vacant seat on December 6, 1864.

The Supreme Court historian declares, of Chase's appointment, that "it was of inestimable value to the country to have at the head of the Court not only a great lawyer, but a great statesman."[8] One familiar with Chase's legal career can only be amazed at this characterization. Regardless of what history may think of Chase as a statesman, he was anything but a "great lawyer." A leading biography concedes "his modest qualifications for the position of Chief Justice,"[9] and Chase himself tells us that when he applied in 1829 to Judge Cranch of the District of Columbia Circuit Court for admission to the Bar, Cranch was so skeptical of his professional attainments that he agreed to admit him only after Chase explained that he did not intend to practice in Washington but expected to go to the "western country."[10] He was able, after some years, to build up a practice at the Cincinnati Bar. A recent account terms his practice "a most distinguished and lucrative" one,[11] but an advertising circular sent out by Chase in 1839 indicates that it was largely that of a glorified collection agent,[12] and his political ambitions soon interfered even with that practice. Spending more and more time on politics, he all but gave up his legal work in the decade and a half before his appointment.

Noting Chase's probable appointment, Gideon Welles wrote, "The President sometimes does strange things, but this would be a singular mistake."[13] The Welles assessment proved accurate, and not primarily because of Chase's lack of learning. More important was the overriding fact that (as Lincoln is said to have put it) Chase "had the Presidential maggot in his brain, and he never knew anybody who once had it to get rid of it."[14] Certainly, Chase did not get rid of his ambition merely because of his appointment to the highest judicial position. As Chief Justice, says Henry Adams, "He loved power as though he were still a Senator"[15] and throughout his judicial career still nourished the hope that the presidential mantle would at last descend upon him. "In my judgment," wrote Morrison R. Waite (Chase's successor) in 1875, "my predecessor detracted from his fame by permitting himself to think he wanted the Presidency. Whether true or not it was said that he permitted his ambitions in that direction to influence his judicial opinions."[16] His confreres on the bench, like the rest of the country, felt that Chase's judicial actions were governed primarily by political considerations. The inevitable result was a decline in the leadership role of the Chief Justice.

Chase's Associates

In the Marshall and Taney Courts, the Chief Justice towered over his colleagues, both in leadership and in legal ability. That was clearly not the case after Chief Justice Chase took his place in the Court's center chair. The new Chief Justice was not the intellectual leader of the Court. In fact, in both leadership and intellect, he was inferior to several of his associates—particularly to Justices Miller and Field, two of the outstanding Justices in Supreme Court history.

Justice Miller described how Chase had to adapt to the new role of primus inter pares which was thenceforth to characterize the position of Chief Justice. "He liked to have his own way," Miller said about Chase, "but when he came upon the bench it was admirable to see how quietly and courteously the Court resisted his imperious will, never coming to direct conflict, and he finally had to take the position which he held, that he was the Moderator and presiding officer over the Supreme Court, and not possessed of any more authority than the rest of the Bench chose to give him."[17]

When Chief Justice Chase took his seat he joined a Court composed of four Justices appointed by Lincoln's Democratic predecessors (Justices Wayne, Catron, Nelson, and Grier) and four appointed by Lincoln himself. The first of the latter was Noah H. Swayne, a former Attorney General and leader of the Ohio Bar, who was chosen in January 1862 to succeed Justice McLean, who had died. On Taney's death, a majority of the Justices proposed Swayne as his successor. He was a learned and amiable colleague and presumably the Justices, particularly the Democratic half, preferred his appointment to the Republican Radical Lincoln might otherwise select.

Samuel Freeman Miller was Lincoln's second Court appointee, having been chosen in 1862 to replace Justice Daniel, who had died two years earlier. Miller had been the leader of the Iowa Bar and a leader among the state's Republicans. As already indicated, Miller is one of the great Justices in the Court's history. During Chase's tenure, he was the Court's intellectual leader. His constitutional posture became the Chase Court's doctrine—especially in the *Slaughter-House Cases,*[18] where that Court handed down its most important decision. Miller was the first Justice appointed from the new Northwest and his selection signaled the shift that was occurring in the national center of gravity.

The shift was also reflected in Lincoln's next two appointees, Justices Davis and Field. Justice Campbell had resigned to follow his State of Alabama out of the Union. To replace him, Lincoln chose his friend David Davis, an Illinois judge before whom the President had practiced and who had been one of those present on those fabulous nights on the Eighth Illinois Circuit when the elect gathered to hear Lincoln talk.

In 1863, Congress added a tenth seat to the Court and Lincoln appointed Stephen J. Field, then Chief Justice of the California Supreme Court. Field was one of the most colorful men appointed to the highest bench. He was the brother of David Dudley Field, the leader of the nineteenth-century codification movement, and Cyrus W. Field, who laid the Atlantic Cable. Justice Field lived a more flamboyant life than his brothers. In 1849 he joined the gold rush to California, becoming a frontier lawyer and carrying a pistol and bowie knife. He became involved in a quarrel with a judge, during which he was disbarred, sent to jail, fined, and embroiled in a duel. His lengthy feud with another judge, David Terry (Chief Justice of the California Supreme Court when Field was elected to that body in 1857), led to a threat to shoot Field. Years later, in 1889, when Field had long been Justice of the U.S. Supreme Court, Terry assaulted him in a restaurant and was shot by a federal marshal assigned to guard Field. The marshal was indicted for murder, but the Supreme Court held the killing justified.[19]

During Chief Justice Chase's tenure, Justice Miller was the intellectual leader of the Court, particularly in its narrow conception of due process. Then, under Chief Justices Morrison R. Waite and Melville W. Fuller, the leadership gradually shifted to Justice Field and his broad notion of substantive due process. Before his retirement, Field was to see the elevation of his earlier dissents on the matter into the law of the land. Ultimately, as Justice Frankfurter put it, the Justices "wrote Mr. Justice Field's dissents into the opinions of the Court."[20]

Field served on the Court for thirty-four years, eight months, and twenty days—the longest tenure save that of Justice William O. Douglas. Toward the end, Field's mind began to falter. In 1896, Justice John Marshall Harlan was deputized to suggest that Field resign. He reminded the aged Justice that Field had done the same years earlier in suggesting that another Justice step down. "Yes!" replied Field. "And a dirtier day's work I never did in my life!" In April 1897, however, he sent a letter of resignation to take effect December 1—the postponement enabling him to stretch the length of his tenure beyond that of John Marshall, the longest up to that time.

The Court in Operation

Toward the end of the Taney tenure, as we saw, the Supreme Court moved into a chamber more befitting its exalted constitutional status. When new wings were added to the Capitol for the Senate and the House, the former Senate Chamber was adapted for the high bench's use as its courtroom. At last, the Justices had a chamber comparable to those possessed by other courts—with a raised bench, marble pillars, and a separate robing room.

The Justices could thenceforth begin their sessions with the now-traditional formal entry, entering the chamber in their robes through parted curtains as the Marshal announced the Court. The order of seating was that which has since prevailed—the senior Associate Justice at the Chief Justice's right, the next at his left, and so on, in order of seniority. When the Justices were at their places, the Crier would proclaim the Court open: "God save the United States and this Honorable Court." The sessions lasted four hours and the Justices also met in conference on Saturdays to consider pending cases.[21]

By the end of Taney's Chief Justiceship, the Court had developed the internal process of decision that is still current. In particular, the opinion-writing process had evolved from the practice in John Marshall's day to that which has since been followed. When Chase became Taney's successor, the most important function of the Chief Justice was already that of assigning opinions. The power of the Chief Justice to assign the opinions probably goes back to Marshall's tenure. During Marshall's early years, it is probable that he delivered the opinion of the Court even in cases where he dissented. Apparently the practice then was to reserve delivery of the opinion of the Court to the Chief Justice or the senior Associate Justice present on the bench and participating in the decision.[22] But as time went on, other Justices also began to deliver opinions. By Taney's day, the Chief Justice assigned each opinion.

In the early years of opinion assignment by the Chief Justice, he may well have assigned all opinions. It was not very long, however, before the Chief Justice's assigning power was limited to cases where he had voted with the majority. It is probable that this practice developed under Chief Justice Taney. In his history of the Supreme Court under Chief Justice Chase, Charles Fairman describes the procedure at the beginning of Chase's tenure: "The writing of opinions was assigned by the Chief Justice—save that if he were dissenting, the Senior Justice in the majority would select the one to write."[23]

Writing in his diary, Chief Justice Chase noted, "Field intimated that Miller was displeased with my assignment of cases and after we adjourned I took occasion to speak to M. frankly on the subject."[24] Apparently the Justices were already starting to complain of the way in which the Chief

Justice assigned opinions—a complaint that has been a common theme in the Court since then.

There was, however, still one major difference between the work of the Justices in Chase's day and at the present time—the duty the Justices then had to make the rounds of their respective circuits. It was the duty of every Justice to sit in the circuit court once each year for each district within his circuit. In one sense, the burden had eased with the spread of the railroad—a definite improvement over having to ride thousands of miles "on the circuit" on horseback or even in carriages or coaches. As William Herndon, Lincoln's last law partner, put it with regard to riding the much smaller circuit in Illinois, "No human being would now endure what we used to do on the circuit . . . and oh—such victuals."[25]

An 1839 Senate report gave the following mileage summary for the Justices' circuit duties at the time:

Taney	458 Miles
Baldwin	2,000
Wayne	2,370
Barbour	1,498
Story	1,896
Thompson	2,590
McLean	2,500
Catron	3,464
McKinley	10,000[26]

Justices Catron and McKinley, assigned to the two Southern circuits, had the greatest distances to cover and the most backward travel conditions to endure.

A few years later, Justice Daniel, who had succeeded to a Southern circuit, wrote to Van Buren, who had appointed him, from Jackson, Mississippi, "I am here two thousand miles from home (calculating by the travelling route,) on the pilgrimage by an exposure to which, it was the calculation of federal malignity that I would be driven from the Bench. Justice to my friends, and a determination to defeat the machinations of mine and their enemies, have decided me to undergo the experiment, and I have done so at no small hazard, through yellow fever at Vicksburg and congestive and autumnal fevers in this place and vicinity."[27]

The circuit burden was particularly severe upon Justice Field during his first years on the Court. He had to follow the route he had used when he first went to California—by sail via the railroad at Panama—until the transcontinental railroad was opened in 1869.[28] Even with that railroad, travel to the Far West remained burdensome, particularly as Field grew older.

Throughout the tenure of Chief Justice Chase and his successor, complaints were constantly voiced by the Justices about their circuit obligation. One of the problems, as Charles Fairman pointed out, was that Congress had not appropriated funds for this travel. In their stead, the Justices apparently accepted passes from the railroads, which they used for both judicial and personal travel. The practice was basically improper; it made the Justices beholden to the railroads even though they were constantly deciding cases involving them.[29]

Despite the burden and the complaints, Congress did nothing to relieve the Justices of their circuit duties until almost the end of the century. During the period covered by this chapter, the circuit obligation remained the Justices' great albatross.

Judicial Nadir?

The traditional view of the Supreme Court during the Civil War and Reconstruction has been that it played a more subdued role than at any other time in its history—that it had been weakened, if not impotent, ever since the *Dred Scott* decision. "Never," states a leading history of the period, "has the Supreme Court been treated with such ineffable contempt, and never has that tribunal so often cringed before the clamor of the mob."[30] This view was challenged a quarter century ago by Stanley I. Kutler, who asserts that "the Court in this period was characterized by forcefulness and not timidity, . . . by boldness and defiance instead of cowardice and impotence, and by a creative and determinative role with no abdication of its rightful powers." Kutler's study is scholarly and full of suggestive insights. One may wonder, nevertheless, whether his attempt to change the accepted picture completely is justified. The postbellum Court may have played a more important role than the traditional view admitted; all the same, the historical evidence does not support the Kutler conclusion that "the Supreme Court under Salmon P. Chase was of only 'little less importance' than that under John Marshall."[31]

The Kutler case for judicial activism during Reconstruction is based upon the increasing use by the Chase Court of the power to hold laws of Congress unconstitutional. From 1865 to 1873 ten congressional acts were voided, a statistic which, Kutler points out, must be compared with two judicial vetoes in the previous seventy-six years.[32]

Two things should be noted before accepting his conclusion, however. First, the Chase Court was exercising a review power that had already been confirmed in both law and practice. By the postbellum period, there was no doubt of the legal power of the courts to review constitutionality. The Supreme Court may have exercised the power over congressional acts rarely before the Civil War, but it was exercised in many cases by state courts and was accepted without question by the leading text writers and other legal commentators. Even the critics of *Dred Scott* did not dispute the power of judicial review; their strictures were directed to the merits of the Court's decision.

In the second place, it should be recognized that, of the ten cases cited by Kutler, seven were of little practical importance and received scant notice either at the time or from constitutional historians since then.[33] This cannot be said of *Hepburn v. Griswold*,[34] where the Chase Court made its boldest assertion of review authority; yet even there the decision was limited in its effect. It applied only to contracts entered into before 1862, and, even more important, as we shall see, it was overruled by the Supreme Court the next year.[35] Reargument of the issue was granted only three months after the case had been decided. The promptness of the Court in allowing reargument "had the effect of apprising the country that the decision was not fully acquiesced in, and of obviating any injurious consequences to the business of the country by its reversal."[36] Certainly, *Hepburn v. Griswold* and the *Legal Tender Cases* focused attention upon the Court's review function, but their main immediate impact was in their demonstration of the manner in which the Court could be "packed" by new appointments to secure a desired decision.

The remaining two cases arose out of the congressional Reconstruction program. The significance of *United States v. Klein*[37] as a limitation upon congressional control over Supreme Court jurisdiction has been demonstrated by me in another book.[38] Its impact at the time was nevertheless highly limited; it invalidated a statute that had been scarcely noted when it was passed by Congress. In addition, its practical effect was largely nullified by a later decision.[39] The other case dealing with an aspect of Reconstruction was *Ex parte Garland*.[40] The decision there, as we saw in Chapter 5, held invalid the ironclad oath which Congress had required for admission to practice in the Supreme Court.

Under *Garland* and the companion decision in *Cummings v. Missouri*[41] it is clear that much of the loyalty oath program was unconstitutional. Yet even after those decisions, as seen in the last chapter, similar loyalty oath requirements were enacted and enforced. Here, too, the Supreme Court decisions, however important they may have been in constitutional jurisprudence, had no practical effect during the Reconstruction period.

Hepburn v. Griswold and Original Intention

Nothing illustrates the position of the Supreme Court during Chief Justice Chase's tenure better than its two legal tender decisions. In addition, nothing shows the inadequacy of "original intention" as the be-all-and-end-all of constitutional interpretation as well as those decisions.

During the early history of the United States, federal paper currency, with notes issued as legal tender, did not exist. Instead, as John Kenneth Galbraith points out, "[T]he money of the United States was precious metal. . . . The only paper currency was the notes of banks."[42] During the Civil War, however, Congess was forced to make subsantial changes in the currency system. In three Legal Tender Acts, it provided for the issuance of $450 million in United States notes not backed in specie (the so-called greenbacks) and provided that those notes were to be legal tender at face value in all transactions. A constitutional controversy soon arose over Congress's power to make its paper money legal tender.

During the Civil War the Supreme Court astutely avoided deciding a case challenging the validity of the greenback laws. After the war, the issue could not be evaded. In *Hepburn v. Griswold*,[43] a bare majority ruled the Legal Tender Acts invalid. One of the main reasons Lincoln had appointed Chase as Chief Justice was to ensure a favorable decision on the constitutionality of the legal tender laws, for Chase, as Secretary of the Treasury, had been their chief architect. But the new Chief Justice disappointed the presidential expectation. Writing of Chase's attitude toward legal tender, Henry Adams comments, "As Secretary of the Treasury he had been its author; as Chief Justice he became its enemy."[44] It was Chase who delivered the majority opinion in *Hepburn v. Griswold*.

What in another judge might have been considered high moral courage was in Chase condemned as but another example of political jobbery. His act was interpreted not as an indication of judicial independence but as a bid for the nomination for President.

The young Holmes pointed out, in a contemporary comment, that *Hepburn v. Griswold* "presented the curious spectacle of the Supreme Court reversing the determination of Congress on a point of political economy."[45] At the same time, it cannot be denied that the *Hepburn* decision was in exact accord with the original intention of the Framers of the Constitution. If there was one point on which the men of 1787 were agreed, it was the need to prevent a repetition of the paper money fiasco of the American Revolution, when the expression "not worth a Continental" was born. The Framers "had seen in the experience of the Revolutionary period the demoralizing tendency, the cruel injustice, and the intolerable oppression of a paper currency not convertible on demand into money, and forced into circulation by legal tender provisions and penal enactments."[46] They therefore determined to give the government they were establishing the power to issue only a metallic currency.

This can be seen from both the constitutional text and the Framers' debates. They gave Congress the power "to coin Money," which clearly indicates "their determination to sanction only a metallic currency."[47] As Chief Justice Chase put it, "The power conferred is the power to coin money, and these words must be understood as they were used at the time the Constitution was adopted. And we have been referrred to no authority which at that time defined coining otherwise than as minting or stamping metals for money; or money otherwise than as metal coined for the purposes of commerce."[48]

The accuracy of the Chase statement is confirmed by the only dictionary available to the Framers—the one compiled by Samuel Johnson. It defines the verb "coin" as "to mint or stamp metals for money" and the noun "money" as "metal coined for the purposes of commerce."[49]

The available records of the Philadelphia Convention also bear out Chase's view of the Framers' intent. The original constitutional draft gave Congress power to "emit Bills on the Credit of the United States."[50] Gouverneur Morris moved to strike out these words. Except for one delegate, who said that he "was a friend to paper money," those who spoke on the matter supported the motion, which carried, nine to two. Madison appended a note to the debate, explaining his affirmative vote by stating that he "became satisfied that striking out the words . . . would only cut off the pretext for a paper currency and particularly for making the bills a tender either for public or private debts."[51]

The Framers' intent with respect to paper money and making it legal tender is as clear as anything that we know about the Philadelphia convention. As Luther Martin, a delegate at Philadelphia, explained it in November 1787, a "majority of the convention, being wise beyond every event, and being willing to risk any political evil, rather than admit the idea of a paper emission, in any possible event, refused to trust this authority to [the federal] government."[52]

Nor can it be doubted that the decision in *Hepburn v. Griswold* was completely in accord with the original intention of the Framers on the matter. Yet if the *Hepburn* decision was thus categorically correct in terms of original intention, it was plainly wrong so far as the needs of the nation were concerned.

It is all but impossible to conceive of a functioning modern economy without paper money, in which the only currency is specie. Yet that is exactly what would have been required under *Hepburn v. Griswold*. Well might the Supreme Court later say that its decision on the matter would

> affect the entire business of the country, and take hold of the possible continued existence of the government. If it be held by this court that Congress has not constitutional power, under any circumstances, or in any emergency, to make Treasury notes a legal tender for the payment of all debts (a power confessedly possessed by every independent sovereignty other than the United States), the government is without those means of self-preservation which, all must admit, may, in certain contingencies, become indispensable.[53]

Hence, the *New York Herald* could assert, if *Hepburn v. Griswold* meant what it said, it "involved the whole country in financial chaos and the Government perhaps in bankruptcy and repudiation."[54]

Legal Tender Cases

Hepburn v. Griswold, however consistent with the Framers' original intention, was not destined to achieve this disastrous result. When the case was decided, the Supreme Court consisted of only seven members, who divided four to three on the ruling. To deprive President Andrew Johnson of the opportunity of filling expected vacancies, Congress had passed a law providing that no vacancy on the Court was to be filled until it was reduced to fewer than seven members.[55] With President Grant's election the situation was changed, and an 1869 statute raised the number of Justices to nine and authorized the President to make the necessary appointments.[56]

On the very day when the decision adverse to the government was announced in *Hepburn v. Griswold,* Grant appointed two new Justices (Strong and Bradley), who were known to support the constitutionality of the Legal Tender Acts. After they took their seats, the Court permitted argument again on the validity of the greenback laws. This time, in the *Legal Tender Cases*[57]—decided only a year after *Hepburn v. Griswold*— Justices Strong and Bradley, plus the Hepburn dissenters, made up a new majority. Finally putting to rest the controversy over congressional authority, the Court ruled that the nation's fiscal powers included the authority to issue paper money vested with the quality of legal tender.

Historians today reject the charge that Grant "packed the Court" for the deliberate purpose of obtaining a reversal of *Hepburn v. Griswold.*[58] At the same time, it is clear that the President chose the new Justices not only because he was convinced of their fitness but because he believed they would sustain the Legal Tender Acts. For years after the cases were decided there was strong criticism because of the coincidence of the change in constitutional interpretation with the change in Court personnel. The Court's action, a contemporary newspaper commented, "will greatly aggravate the growing contempt for what has long been the most respected . . . department of our government, its Judiciary."[59] From this point of view, Chief Justice Hughes writes, "the reopening of the case was a serious mistake and the overruling in such a short time, and by one vote, of the previous decision shook popular respect for the Court."[60]

The legal tender decisions demonstrate the congressional predominance over the Court in the post–Civil War period. Even if there was no specific intent to "pack" the Court to secure a favorable legal resolution of the greenback controversy, the eventual outcome was the same. Yet even here, the picture is not entirely one-sided. The very fact that the weighty issue of legal tender was accepted as a judicial issue to be resolved by the Supreme Court is ultimately more important than the political injury inflicted on the Court. As it turned out, the vote of one Justice (however the new majority was really secured) decided a matter crucial to the economic life of the nation.

Slaughter-House Cases

The history of the Supreme Court in the post-Reconstruction period can be written largely in terms of the Court's interpretation of the Fourteenth Amendment and its Due Process Clause. That clause was ultimately to serve as the legal foundation for the great era of economic expansion upon which the nation was entering. During the Chase tenure the amendment was construed most narrowly. The key Chase Court decision here was that rendered in the 1873 *Slaughter-House Cases.*[61]

The fundamental role of the Supreme Court in the constitutional system, even in a period when the judicial power is essentially in repose, was underscored by the *Slaughter-House* decision. Like so many landmark decisions rendered by the Court, its effect was scarcely noted at the time.

"The decision," wrote a newspaper reporter the day after it was announced, "was given to an almost empty Courtroom . . . and has as yet attracted little attention outside of legal circles, although the Judges of the Court regarded the case as the most important which has been before them since the *Dred Scott* decision."[62]

Section 1 of the Fourteenth Amendment defined United States citizenship so as to include the newly freed blacks, and it prohibited states from making laws abridging the "privileges or immunities" of that citizenship or denying "due process of law" or the equal protection of the laws. Yet though the *Slaughter-House Cases* were the first cases involving the interpretation of the Fourteenth Amendment, they had nothing to do with the rights of the freedmen. They arose out of an 1869 statute passed by the "carpetbag" legislature of Louisiana. The law, secured by widespread bribery (the governor, legislators, various state officials, and two newspapers had all been paid for their support), had incorporated the Crescent City Live Stock Landing and Slaughter House Company and had given it the exclusive right to slaughter livestock in New Orleans. It had driven from business all the other butchers in the city, and the Butchers' Benevolent Association had brought an action challenging "the Monopoly," as the new corporation was called, for operating in violation of the Fourteenth Amendment.

The case was argued by legal giants of the day: John A. Campbell (leader of the Southern Bar, who had resigned from the Supreme Court when his state had seceded) for the butchers, and former Senator Matthew H. Carpenter (who had helped draft the Fourteenth Amendment) for the Monopoly. The Court ruled for the Monopoly, adopting the view that the provisions of the Fourteenth Amendment were intended only to protect the Negro in his newly acquired freedom, and that the Due Process Clause of the amendment was irrelevant to the case.

"The banded butchers are busted," Carpenter announced exultingly after the decision.[63] But it was not only the plaintiff butchers who were "busted" by the decision. The *Slaughter-House* opinion virtually emasculated section 1 of the Fourteenth Amendment itself. Had the Court's restrictive interpretation not ultimately been relaxed, the amendment could scarcely have come to serve as the legal instrument for the protection of property rights, particularly those of corporations.

The congressional debates on the Fourteenth Amendment indicate that its framers (particularly Representative John Bingham, who drafted most of section 1, and Senator Jacob Howard, who opened the Senate debate) placed particular stress upon the clause prohibiting the states from abridging "the privileges and immunities of citizens of the United States." It is possible, indeed, that the privileges and immunities to be protected included all the rights covered in the first eight amendments, with the Privileges and Immunities Clause intended to make the Bill of Rights binding upon the states.

If that was the intent of the draftsmen, it was soon frustrated. The clause was all but read out of the amendment by the *Slaughter-House Cases,* where the Court found crucial decisional significance in the difference in language between its Citizenship Clause and its Privileges and Immunities Clause. The opinion of Justice Miller stressed the fact that, while the first sentence of the amendment makes all persons born or naturalized in this country both "citizens of the United States and of the State wherein they reside," the next sentence protects only "the privileges or immunities of citizens of the United States" from state abridgement. The distinction was intended to leave the fundamental rights of life and property untouched by the amendment; they remained, as always, with the states.

Under *Slaughter-House,* the Privileges and Immunities Clause did not transform the rights of citizens of each state into rights of national citizenship enforceable as such in the federal courts. It protected against state encroachment only those rights "which owe their existence to the federal Government, its national character, its Constitution, or its laws."[64] Rights which antedate and thus do not owe their existence to that government are privileges and immunities of state citizenship alone. Earning a living is such a right. Hence the Louisiana law in *Slaughter-House* was not violative of the clause.

If the *Slaughter-House* decision rendered the Privileges and Immunities Clause "a practical nullity"[65] within five years after it became part of the Constitution, what of the amendment's Due Process Clause, upon which the *Slaughter-House* butchers had also relied? The opinion adopted the limited view that the Fourteenth Amendment was intended only to protect blacks in their newly acquired freedom. That being the case, the Due Process Clause was all but irrelevant in considering the constitutionality of the law which conferred upon the Monopoly the exclusive right to slaughter livestock. Referring to the Due Process Clause, the Court declared that "under no construction of that provision that we have ever seen, or any that we deem admissible, can the restraint imposed by the State of Louisiana upon the exercise of their trade by the butchers of New Orleans be held to be a deprivation of property within the meaning of that provision."[66] With the Due Process Clause inapplicable, the states were left almost as free to regulate the rights of property as they had been before the Civil War.

The *Slaughter-House* Court was, however, sharply divided on this restrictive interpretation of due process. Four Justices strongly disputed the Court's casual dismissal of the Due Process Clause. Foremost among them were Justices Field and Bradley, who delivered vigorous dissents. In their view, the Fourteenth Amendment "was intended to give practical effect to the declaration of 1776 of inalienable rights, rights which are the gift of the Creator, which the law does not confer, but only recognizes."[67] From the rights guaranteed in the Declaration of Independence to due process was a natural transition in the Field-Bradley approach: "Rights to life, liberty, and the pursuit of happiness are equivalent to the rights of life, liberty and property. These are the fundamental rights which can only be taken away by due process of the law."[68] A law like that in *Slaughter-House*, in the dissenting view, did violate due process: "In my view a law which prohibits a large class of citizens from adopting a lawful employment, or following a lawful employment previously adopted, does deprive them of liberty as well as property, without due process of law."[69]

What the Field-Bradley dissents were doing was to urge adoption of a substantive due process approach similar to that used in Chief Justice Taney's ill-fated *Dred Scott* opinion.[70] Like Taney, the *Slaughter-House* dissenters rejected the limitation of due process to a procedural guaranty. They urged that it also contemplated judicial review of the substance of challenged state action. In their view a monopoly law which deprived the New Orleans butchers of their right to earn their living was an arbitrary violation of due process. Much of the substance of constitutional history in the quarter century following *Slaughter-House* involved the writing of the Field-Bradley dissents into the opinions of the Supreme Court;[71] but for over a decade after it was decided, *Slaughter-House* sharply restricted the reach of the Fourteenth Amendment and its Due Process Clause. "When this generation of mine opened the reports," says a federal judge who came to the bar at that time, "the chill of the Slaughter House decision was on the bar . . . the still continuing dissents of Judge Field seemed most unorthodox. The remark in another judgment,[72] that due process was usually what the state ordained, seemed to clinch the matter."[73]

Waite and His Associates

Three weeks after the *Slaughter-House* decision, Chief Justice Chase suddenly died. President Grant's attempts to find a successor were so ludicrous that they might be relegated to the realm of the comic but for the baneful effect they had on the Supreme Court's reputation. Charles Sumner is reported to have said, "We stand at an epoch in the country's life, in the midst of revolution in its constitutional progress . . . and I long for a Chief Justice like John Marshall, who shall pilot the country through the rocks and rapids in which we are."[74] Instead, Grant used the office as a political plum—a gift to be bestowed on those who had won his personal gratitude. Only after he had failed in his stumbling efforts to appoint various associates of his did Grant choose Morrison R. Waite, a little-known Ohio lawyer, who was accepted by the Senate and the country with a collective sigh of relief. "The President," declared *The Nation*, "has, with remarkable skill, avoided choosing any first-rate man. . . . [But], considering what the President might have done, and tried to do, we ought to be very thankful."[75]

Waite was a competent legal craftsman, though scarcely endowed with the personality or prestige usually associated with the highest judicial office. "The touch of the common-place about him was, indeed, the key to his appointment. . . . Grant doubtless felt confident that the relative obscurity of Waite was the best assurance for his confirmation."[76] Certainly,

Waite had nothing of the grand manner—the spark that made Marshall and Taney what they were. A humdrum, pedestrian lawyer, he remains a dim figure in our constitutional history. "I can't make a silk purse out of a sow's ear," wrote Justice Miller a year after Waite's appointment. "I can't make a great Chief Justice out of a small man."[77]

If Waite was not a great Chief Justice, he may have been just what the Supreme Court needed after the turbulence of *Dred Scott,* the war, Reconstruction, and the political maneuverings of Chase and some of his colleagues. The Court's tarnished reputation was largely refurbished during his tenure, and at his death in 1888, it was ready to take its place again as a fully coordinate department of government.

During the Waite tenure, the intellectual leadership in the Court remained with Justices Miller and Field, though an important role in this respect was also assumed by Justice Joseph P. Bradley. It was Bradley who, along with William Strong, had been appointed by President Grant in 1870 to ensure the overruling of *Hepburn v. Griswold.* Strong was a capable judge who had served with distinction on the Pennsylvania Supreme Court. He is largely forgotten today; his tenure was too short and most of his opinions dealt with matters of little current interest. The same is not true of Bradley, "whom I regard," Justice Frankfurter once wrote, "as one of the keenest, profoundest intellects that ever sat on that bench."[78]

Bradley was one of the very few men who became a Justice without having held prior public office (Justice Miller was the only other Justice in this category before the appointment of Justice Louis D. Brandeis in 1916).[79] Instead, Bradley's career had been entirely at the Bar; he had been an eminent railroad attorney in New Jersey for many years. Yet, Frankfurter tells us, though Bradley was thus "a corporation lawyer par excellence when he went on the Court . . . his decisions on matters affecting corporate control in the years following the Civil War were strikingly free of bias in favor of corporate power."[80]

Justice Bradley's importance on the Waite Court was greater than is apparent from only his reported opinions. Soon after Waite succeeded to his position, Bradley struck up a close relationship with him and the new Chief Justice relied on Bradley in his work. Waite once wrote that he respected Bradley's advice above all others and he was quite willing to acknowledge the Justice's help.[81] As he wrote to Bradley about an opinion he was working on, "I will take the credit, and you shall do the work, as usual."[82] Indeed, as we shall see, Bradley's help in the most important Waite opinion—that in the *Granger Cases*—was so extensive that he has been characterized as a virtual coauthor of the famous opinion there.[83]

Less needs to be said about the other Waite Court Justices. When the new Chief Justice was appointed, there were four other holdover Justices from the Chase Court: Justices Clifford, Swayne, Davis, and Hunt. The latter, lately Chief Judge of the New York Court of Appeals, had been appointed in 1872 on Justice Nelson's resignation. His tenure was brief and marred by illness. He suffered a stroke in 1878, but he held on until

1882 when Congress voted a special pension bill (he had been ineligible before) and Hunt finally resigned. In his place, President Arthur selected Circuit Judge Samuel Blatchford of New York, who turned out to be, in Waite's phrase, "a good worker,"[84] though hardly an outstanding jurist.

The year earlier, Justice Clifford had died and President Arthur appointed Horace Gray, Chief Justice of the Supreme Judicial Court of Massachusets, who had served on that bench since 1864. According to a letter by Justice Miller, "Gray . . . is the choice of our Court"[85] and his nomination was generally approved. Gray was to serve for twenty years and be succeeded by another Massachusets Chief Justice, Oliver Wendell Holmes.

Two other Waite Court appointees served even briefer terms than Justice Hunt. On Justice Strong's resignation in 1880, President Hayes appointed Circuit Judge William B. Woods of Georgia. Woods was the first judge from the South since the appointment of Justice Campbell twenty-eight years earlier. Woods was a hard worker, but a man of average capabilities, who served only seven years; his tenure was cut short by his death in 1887.

On Justice Swayne's retirement in 1881, his place was taken by Stanley Matthews, a railroad lawyer and former judge and Senator from Ohio. Matthews, too, served briefly (only eight years) and, as *The Nation* put it on his death, "[H]is service as judge has been without special distinction."[86]

Much more significant had been the appointment in 1877 of John Marshall Harlan to succeed Justice Davis, who had resigned after being elected to the Senate. Harlan was, in Justice Frankfurter's pithy description, a six-foot-three Kentuckian[87] who had been Attorney General of his state. In 1956, Frankfurter wrote to a close friend. "The present fashion to make old Harlan out a great judge is plumb silly."[88] Despite the Frankfurter disparagement, most students of the Court list Harlan as one of the most important Justices. He was certainly one of the great dissenters in Supreme Court history; his frequent challenges to the majority led his colleagues, as he once wrote to Chief Justice Waite, to suggest that he suffered from "dis-sent-ery."[89] Most important, Harlan's key dissents have generally been affirmed in the court of history. A century later, his rejection of the narrow view toward civil rights adopted by the Court majority has been generally approved.

On the bench, Harlan was the most serious of judges, who, Justice Frankfurter tells us, "wielded a battle-ax";[90] his opinions were vigorous, often impatient, sometimes bitter. With his colleagues, however, he was most sociable, being one of the leaders in the whist parties which, enlivened by the usual rounds of bourbon, were a traditional recreation of the Justices.[91] Harlan displayed a sense of humor that must have been a pleasant relief in a group of men who, from their photographs, were as somber, if not always as sober, "as a judge." When the Chief Justice sent Harlan a photograph, the Justice responded, "You look natural and life-like as you would look if I were to say that a gallon of old Bourbon was on the way from Kentucky for you."[92]

A few years later, a Harlan letter to the Chief Justice contained a witty sketch on the vacation activities of some of the Justices:

> The last I heard from Bro Woods he was at Newark. Bros Matthews and Blatchford will, I fear, get such lofty ideas in the Mountains that there will be no holding them down to mother Earth when they return to Washington. Bro Bradley, I take it, is somewhere studying the philosophy of the Northern Lights, while Gray is, at this time, examining into the Precedents in British Columbia. Field, I suppose has his face towards the setting sun, wondering, perhaps, whether the Munn case or the essential principles of right and justice will ultimately prevail.[93]

Granger Cases

The *Munn* case to which Justice Harlan referred was the principal case in a series of companion cases collectively known as the *Granger Cases*.[94] They were decided in 1877 and were the most important cases in the Waite Court. It was during Chief Justice Waite's term that the Supreme Court was first called upon to respond to the modern current of social legislation. His was the beginning of the epoch when due process served as the most fertile source of constitutional lawmaking. Before the trend toward due process as the basic restriction upon state power became established in the Supreme Court, the Court decided the *Granger Cases*. "Judged by any standards of ultimate importance," says Justice Frankfurter, Waite's ruling in the *Granger Cases* "places it among the dozen most important decisions in our constitutional law."[95] It upheld the power of the states to regulate the rates of railroads and other businesses—a holding, never since departed from, which has served as the basis upon which governmental regulation in this country has essentially rested.

The *Granger Cases* arose out of the abuses that accompanied the post/-Civil War growth of railroads. Highly speculative railroad building, irresponsible financial manipulation, and destructive competitive warfare resulted in monopolies, fluctuating and discriminatory rates, and inevitable public outcry. The grievances against the railroads were especially acute in the Midwest, where the farmer was dependent upon them for moving his crops, as well as on the grain elevators in which those crops were stored. The farmers' resentment led to the Granger movement, which swept through the Midwest in the early 1870s. The Grangers sought to correct these abuses through state regulation. They secured laws in Illinois, Wisconsin, Minnesota, and Iowa regulating railroads and grain elevators and limiting the prices they could charge. These were the laws at issue in the *Granger Cases*. In the principal case before the Court, an Illinois law fixed the maximum prices to be charged by grain elevators in Chicago; four companion cases involved state statutes regulating railroad rates.

The Court sustained all these laws against due process attacks on the ground that "property . . . become[s] clothed with a public interest when used in a manner to make it of public consequence, and affect the community at large. When, therefore, one devotes his property to a use in which the public has an interest, he, in effect, grants to the public an interest in that use, and must submit to be controlled by the public for the common good, to the extent of the interest he has thus created."[96]

Chief Justice Waite's opinion in the *Granger Cases* was greatly influenced by an outline prepared by the Court's leading legal scholar, Justice Bradley.[97] In particular, it was Bradley who called Waite's attention to the common law on the subject, especially Lord Hale's seventeenth-century statement that when private property is "affected with a publick interest, it ceases to be juris privati[98] only."[99] But the *Granger* opinion was more than a rehash of the Bradley outline. Waite articulated his opinion in language broad enough to transform the whole course of the law of business regulation. In the words of a contemporary, "Suffice it, that the decision itself in its general breadth and purpose has no precedent."[100]

Waite was only following the time-honored judicial technique of pouring new wine into old bottles. He read and expounded Lord Hale in the spirit of the industrial era. He tore a fragment from the annals of the law, stripped away its limited frame of reference, and re-created it in the image of the modern police power.[101] Under the *Granger* approach, for a business to be subject to regulation, it need only be one which affects the community. "Waite's reference to property 'clothed with a public interest' surely meant no more than that the Court must be able to attribute to the legislature the fulfillment of a public interest."[102] In this sense, a business affected with a public interest becomes nothing more than one in which the public has come to have an interest.[103] This rationale becomes a means of enabling governmental regulatory power to be asserted over business far beyond what was previously thought permissible. As a member of the highest bench once pointed out, "There is scarcely any property in whose use the public has no interest."[104] The public is concerned about all business because it contributes to the welfare of the community.[105]

Waite's rationale did not really reveal its potential until over half a century later. In the years immediately following *Granger*, it was virtually neutralized by judicial adoption of the Field-Bradley notion of due process. It was revived when the due process current was reversed, starting in 1934.[106] Since that time, it has been the doctrine that has furnished the constitutional foundation for the ever-broader schemes of business regulation that have become so prominent a feature of the present-day society.

Civil Rights Cases

The Reconstruction period saw not only the adoption of the postbellum amendments but also the enactment of significant civil rights statutes by Congress. The most important of these laws was the Civil Rights Act of 1875.[107] That statute constituted the culmination of the postbellum Republican program and a decade of efforts to place the ideal of racial equality upon the legal plane. One may go further and see in the 1875 law the last victory for the egalitarian ideal of the Reconstruction period. From 1875 to the middle of the next century, there were to be no further legal gains for racial equality. On the contrary, the civil rights legislation enacted during the Reconstruction decade was soon to be virtually emasculated by both Congress and the Supreme Court.

To the present-day observer, the Civil Rights Act of 1875 is of particular interest, for it provides the historical nexus between the Fourteenth Amendment and the Civil Rights Act of 1964. The goal of equality in public accommodations, which Congress sought to attain by enactment of the 1964 statute, was what had been intended by the 1875 law. The legislative history of the 1875 law demonstrates that the legislators of the post–Civil War period were intimately concerned with many of the key problems that are still with us in the field of civil rights: integration versus segregation (particularly in education), legal versus social equality, and the crucial question of whether an ideal such as racial equality can be achieved by legislative action, especially in a society opposed to practical implementation of that ideal.

The key figure in the enactment of the 1875 Civil Rights Act was Senator Charles Sumner. Whatever may be said against Sumner, he was, throughout his career, a sincere believer in the cause of equal rights. Well before emancipation, he gave substance to Whittier's economium, "He saw a brother in the slave, With man as equal man he dealt." His crucial position in the history of the act is not affected by the fact that he died in March 1874, a year before it became law. As the sponsor of the measure in the House pointed out, the bill was originated by Sumner and he regarded it as his main legacy to his country.[108] On his death bed, he is said to have told Judge Ebenezer R. Hoar, then a Congressman from Massachusetts, "You must take care of the civil-rights bill,—my bill, the civil rights bill,—don't let it fail!"[109]

Sumner's bill reached the statute book as the Civil Rights Act of 1875. It contained a prohibition against racial discrimination in inns, public conveyances, and places of amusement. The prohibition was, however, ruled invalid by the Waite Court in the 1883 *Civil Rights Cases*[110] on the ground that it sought to reach discriminatory action that was purely private in nature and consequently not within the scope of the Equal Protection Clause. "Can the act of a mere individual," asked Justice Bradley for the Court, "the owner of the inn, the public conveyance, or place of amusement, refusing the accommodation, be justly regarded as imposing any badge of slavery or servitude upon the applicant, or only as inflicting an ordinary civil injury, properly cognizable by the laws of the state, and presumably subject to redress by those laws until the contrary appears?" Answering this query in favor of the latter construction, the opinion asserted, "Individual invasion of individual rights is not the subject-matter of the amendment."[111]

Only Justice Harlan—a former slaveholder—dissented from this narrow construction of the Fourteenth Amendment. He declared that the majority's narrow concept of "state action" reduced the amendment to "splendid baubles, thrown out to delude those who deserved fair and generous treatment at the hands of the nation."[112] Similarly, Frederick Douglass attacked the decision as "a concession to prejudice" and contrary to Christianity, the Declaration of Independence, and the spirit of the age.[113]

Despite the attraction of the Harlan dissent for present-day jurists, the Court has continued to follow the rule laid down in the *Civil Rights Cases*. As stated in the leading modern case, "The principle has become firmly embedded in our constitutional law that the action inhibited by the first section of the Fourteenth Amendment is only such action as may fairly be said to be that of the States. That Amendment erects no shield against merely private conduct, however discriminatory or wrongful."[114]

Critics of the Court, especially in recent years, have contended that the decision in the *Civil Rights Cases* amounted to virtual judicial usurpation, that the Justices emasculated the post–Civil War amendments to nullify the broad remedial intent of their framers. The congressional debate on the 1875 civil rights law demonstrates that such a view is unfounded. There is ample indication in the debates that a substantial number of legislators considered the bill before them unconstitutional, many of them[115] for the very reason later stated by the Supreme Court—that is, that it sought to reach individual, rather than state, action.

The congressional discussions also bear directly upon more recent developments in the field of civil rights. In the Senate debate in February 1875, Senator Matthew H. Carpenter (one of the outstanding lawyers of the day) stated that Congress might try to accomplish the public accommodation purposes of the 1875 act under its commerce power. "Such provision in regard to theaters," he asserted, "would be somewhat fantastic as a regulation of commerce."[116] In 1964, the Congress did enact a civil rights act based upon the commerce power of the very type which Senator Carpenter had termed "fantastic" in 1875,[117] and, as Carpenter also prophesied,[118] such a statute was upheld by the Supreme Court.[119]

To the observer today, the congressional debate on the 1875 Act is also most pertinent for its discussion of discrimination in education. The very problems that have become so important since the landmark decision in *Brown v. Board of Education*[120]—integration versus segregation, the threat of the South to close down the public school system rather than have "mixed" schools, and the claim that all that is really needed is "separate but equal" facilities for the two races—appear here. The sharpest controversy arose over the original Sumner bill's prohibition of racial discrimination not only in public accommodations but also in all "common schools and public institutions of learning or benevolence supported in whole or part by general taxation." Though a strong effort was made to strike out this prohibition in the Senate, it was defeated, and the bill as passed by the upper chamber in 1874 contained the provision drafted by Sumner.

The situation was different when the House considered the bill a year later. Public opposition (as shown by the 1874 election results) led it to strike out the clause prohibiting racial discrimination in educational institutions, as well as one covering cemeteries. The actual vote on the amendment to strike out the school provision was overwhelmingly in favor. The consensus against the school prohibition was now so great that no effort was made in the Senate to reinsert it in the bill. Instead, that chamber speedily passed the House bill.

The debate on the proposed prohibition of racial discrimination in schools is directly relevant to the intent of those who wrote the Fourteenth Amendment with regard to segregation in education. One who has read it cannot help but conclude that the Congress that sat less than a decade after the Fourteenth Amendment was sent to the states for ratification did not think that the amendment had the effect of prohibiting school segregation. If it had, the whole debate would have been irrelevant, since integration would have been constitutionally required, regardless of any congressional provision in the matter. It is fair to say that no participant in the congressional debate took such a view (which was, of course, that ultimately taken by the Supreme Court in *Brown v. Board of Education*).

This does not, however, mean that the decision in *Brown* was wrong. The Court there was interpreting the Constitution to meet society's needs in 1954—needs which were not necessarily the same as those of 1875. Only those who would make the Constitution as inflexible as the laws of the Medes and Persians will object to such constitutional construction. Stability and change are the twin sisters of the law and together make the Constitution a document enduring through the ages.

Corporate Protection

The Waite Court's narrow construction of the Fourteenth Amendment in the *Civil Rights Cases* should be contrasted with its extension of constitutional protection to corporations.

One of the key questions for constitutional historians has been whether the framers of the Fourteenth Amendment intended to include corporations within the scope of its protection. A decade and a half after it was adopted, Roscoe Conkling, a former member of the committee which drafted it, implied, in argument before the Supreme Court, that he and his colleagues, in framing the Due Process and Equal Protection Clauses, had deliberately used the word "person" in order to include corporations.[121] "At the time the Fourteenth Amendment was ratified," he averred, "individuals and joint stock companies were appealing for congressional and administrative protection against invidious and discriminating State and local taxes."[122] The implication was that the committee had taken cognizance of such appeals and had drafted its text to extend the organic protection to corporations: "The men who framed . . . the Fourteenth Amendment must have known the meaning and force of the term 'persons.'"[123]

Most historians reject the Conkling insinuation.[124] From a purely historical point of view, it is clear that Conkling, influenced by the advocate's zeal, overstated his case. Yet even if his argument on the real intent of the draftsmen was correct, that alone would not justify the inclusion of corporations within the word "person." As Justice Hugo L. Black once put it, "a secret purpose on the part of the members of the committee, even if such be the fact, . . . would not be sufficient to justify any such construction."[125] After all, what was adopted was the Fourteenth Amendment and not what Roscoe Conkling or the other members of the draftng committee thought about it.[126]

What stands out to one concerned with the meaning of the amendment is the deliberate use in its Equal Protection and Due Process Clauses of the same language employed in the Fifth Amendment. It is surely reasonable to assume that, when Congressman John A. Bingham, "the Madison . . . of the Fourteenth Amendment,"[127] deliberately used that language,[128] he intended to follow the same approach as his predecessors with regard to the applicability of the new safeguard. By the middle of the nineteenth century, the corporate entity had become an established part of the economy. If corporate "persons" were to be excluded from the new constitutional protections, it is difficult to see why the unqualified generic term "persons"[129] was employed.

It must be emphasized that corporate personality antedated the Fourteenth Amendment. Its protection had, by the time of the postbellum amendments, become a vital concern of the law. The end of the Civil War saw a vast expansion in the role of the corporation in the economy,[130] but even before that conflict, the corporate device was recognized as an indispensable adjunct of the nation's growth. This realization had already led to decisions favorable to the corporate personality.[131] When the ultimate protection of person and property was transferred by the Fourteenth Amendment from the states to the nation, the judicial trend in favor of the corporation also became a national one. The role of the corporate person in the post/-Civil War economy made the use of the Fourteenth Amendment to safeguard such persons a natural development, whatever may have been the subjective goals of its framers.

At any rate, the Waite Court speedily gave corporate protection its imprimatur and it did so in a manner that indicated that it had no doubt on the matter. In 1877, in the *Granger Cases,*[132] the Court had ruled on the merits of state regulatory laws which were asserted to violate due process and equal protection without even considering whether plaintiff corporations were "persons" capable of invoking the organic guarantees. Nine years later, in *Santa Clara County v. Southern Pacific Railroad Company,*[133] the question of whether corporations were "persons" within the meaning of the Fourteenth Amendment was extensively briefed by counsel. At the beginning of oral argument in the case, however, Chief Justice Waite tersely announced: "The court does not wish to hear argument on the question whether the provision in the Fourteenth Amendment to the Constitution, which forbids a State to deny to any person within its jurisdiction the equal protection of the laws, applies to these corporations. We are all of opinion that it does."[134]

The Court in the *Santa Clara* case was apparently so sure of its ground that it wrote no opinion on the point.[135] Be that as it may, nevertheless, the Waite pronouncement definitively settled the law on the matter. In the words of Justice Douglas, "It has been implicit in all of our decisions since 1886 that a corporation is a 'person' within the meaning of the . . . Fourteenth Amendment."[136] Countless cases since *Santa Clara* have proceeded upon the assumption that the Fourteenth Amendment assures corporations, as well as individuals, both due process and equal protection.[137]

The Justices and the Election Crisis

Over a century later, the Waite Court may appear unduly restrictive in its interpretation of civil rights guaranties. To its contemporaries, however, the Court appeared as a prime instrument of the conciliation needed to signal the end of Reconstruction and a desired return to "normalcy." The Court composition itself reflected that changing era when, just a few months before Chief Justice Waite's death in 1888, President Cleveland appointed Lucius Quintus Cincinnatus Lamar of Mississippi to replace Justice Woods, who had died. Lamar, then Secretary of the Interior and a former Senator, was the first Democrat appointed since Justice Field in 1862 and, more important, the first Justice who had served in the Confederate Army. To have an ex-Confederate on the highest Court was, to most, a welcome symbol of the post-Reconstruction reconciliation. Now the Court, like the country itself, could return to "normalcy" and put the trauma of the war and Reconstruction behind it.

The movement for returning stability, both for the Court and the country, however, had been rudely interrupted by the election crisis of 1876–1877. The Supreme Court was involved in that crisis, not as an institution, but through the appointment of five Justices to the commission set up by Congress to resolve the dispute. "Divided seven to seven on recognized party lines, the decisive vote and opinion was that of the member appointed for judicial impartiality, Justice Joseph P. Bradley."[138]

Coming so soon after the traumatic experiences of civil conflict and Reconstruction, the disputed Hayes–Tilden election of 1876 might well have resulted in a permanent breakdown of the constitutional system— bringing about, in the contemporary terminology, the "Mexicanization" of American politics. A study published thirty years after the event asserts, "Few of the generation which has grown up since then will have any but the faintest conception of the gravity of the situation existing during the winter of 1876–1877."[139] Such a comment is, of course, even more true today. It is all but impossible now to appreciate the gravity of the crisis presented by the dispute. At the time, "[M]ore people dreaded an armed conflict than had anticipated a like outcome to the secession movement of 1860–1861."[140] This sentiment was expressed in a letter from Senator Sherman to Hayes himself: "The same influence now rules . . . as did in 1860–1861, and I feel that we are to encounter the same enemies that we did then."[141] Well might Chief Justice Waite, in a letter to a federal judge, characterize the situation as a "great trial."[142]

As so often in our history, an essentially political controversy was converted into a legal battle, with the disputed issues argued and resolved in constitutional terms. Perhaps, ultimately, that is why the crisis could be settled without bloodshed. Justice Jackson's striking claim—"struggles over power that in Europe call out regiments of troops, in America call out battalions of lawyers"[143]—was given dramatic corroboration in this peaceful resolution.

Legally speaking, the conflict arose because of a lacuna in the Constitution with regard to the process of electing the President. Article II provides for the selection of presidential electors under state laws, for the casting of their votes, and for the certification of the electors to the President of the Senate. It then goes on. "The President of the Senate shall, in the Presence of the Senate and House of Representatives, open all the Certificates, and the Votes shall then be counted." But counted by whom? The President of the Senate (who in 1876–1877 was Thomas W. Ferry, a leading Republican), the two Houses separately (leading to a deadlock, since the Senate had a Republican and the House a Democratic majority), or the Houses jointly (in which case the Democratic House would outvote the Republican Senate)?

The Constitution did not answer these questions, which assumed critical importance in the face of conflicting electoral certificates from four states. The returning boards in Florida, Louisiana, and South Carolina (solidly Republican) had certified the electors for Hayes, converting Tilden majorities by disallowing thousands of Democratic votes. The Democrats, claiming fraud, had conflicting certificates, certifying their electors, sent to Washington. In Oregon, where Hayes had received a clear majority, one of his electors was ineligible under the Constitution because he was a federal officer. The Governor certified the other two Republican electors and the Democrat who had lost to the ineligible official. The two Repulican electors chose a third Republican to fill the vacancy and sent a certificate, accompanied by a certification of the election results by the Oregon Secretary of State. In these circumstances, the crucial question was, of course, who counted the electoral votes, and it could not be decided by the normal political machinery. That the situation was finally resolved by extra-constitutional means may be attributed to the overwhelming popular desire, particularly in the South, for a peaceful solution.[144]

When the crisis was at its height, early in 1877, Chief Justice Waite wrote that "the good sense of the people is exerting its influence upon the leaders."[145] Two weeks later Congress set up an Electoral Commission to decide which of the disputed electoral votes to count.[146] It was to be composed of five Senators and five Congressmen, equally divided between the two parties, and four Supreme Court Justices, designated by circuits. These four (two from each party) were then to select a fifth member of the Court, who would be the commission's key man, if, as was expected, the other fourteen members divided evenly along party lines. It was hoped that the partisan element in the commission's work would be neutralized by the selection of David Davis as the fifth Justice (he was the only member of the Court not formally affiliated with either party). This expectation was frustrated by Davis's sudden resignation from the Court after his election to the Senate by the Illinois legislature. That left only Republican members of the Court to choose from, and Justice Bradley, supposedly the least partisan among them, was chosen.

When it came to decide the disputed returns, the Electoral Commission divided, in every instance, strictly along party lines. Justice Bradley's vote, added to those of the other Republicans, meant an eight-to-seven division in Hayes's favor on every disputed elector, and the Republican candidate was declared elected by the margin of one electoral vote. By then it was March 2, 1877—only two days before inauguration day.

The vital legal question before the Electoral Commission was that of whether it could properly go behind the returns certified by the relevant state officials. The Republican majority gave a negative answer on the disputed returns from Florida, Louisiana, and South Carolina. "It seems to me," declared Justice Bradley for the majority, "that the two Houses of Congress, in proceeding with the count, are bound to recognize the determination of the State board of canvassers as the act of the State, and as the most authentic evidence of the appointment made by the State."[147]

This position appears valid and was, in fact, the one ultimately adopted when Congress, a decade later, finally provided a permanent procedure for counting the electoral vote.[148] Any other rule leaves it open for a majority in Congress—even though repudiated at the polls—to perpetuate its candidate in the highest office. It has, however, been claimed that the commission did not follow its own ruling when, in Oregon, it refused to accept the Governor's certification of the one Tilden elector. Though a close question, it seems that the claim misconceives the nature of what the commission did in this case. Under the Oregon statutes it was the Secretary of State who had the authority to canvass the returns, and his certificate as to those chosen was accepted in view of his exclusive authority under state law.[149]

Legally justified or not, a storm of controversy resulted from the Electoral Commission's rulings. In particular, Justice Bradley was subjected to vituperative attacks for allegedly changing his original opinion in favor of the Democrats after pressure from leading Republicans and railroad interests, to which he was supposedly beholden. The charge against Bradley's integrity severely tarnished the remaining career of one who (from the point of view of legal ability) was one of the best men ever to sit on the high tribunal.

More important, as in every instance in which Justices have performed nonjudicial duties, the judicial descent into the political arena reflected unfavorably on the Supreme Court itself. According to James A. Garfield, "All the judges, save one, were very sorry to be called to this commission."[150] The spectacle of the Justices casting their votes on partisan lines cannot but have had a deleterious effect upon the Court's reputation. At the same time, it must be recognized that without them, it is doubtful that the Electoral Commission could ever have been approved—much less had its decision accepted by the country. Had they refused to serve, they would have upset the carefully worked-out compromise and plunged the country into a crisis which it might not have been possible to settle peacefully.

"Just at present," wrote Chief Justice Waite after the Electoral Commission had decided, "our judges are severely criticized, but I feel sure time will bring us out all right."[151] And so it turned out. With Henry Adams, the country "still clung to the Supreme Court, much as the churchman still clings to his last rag of Right. Between the Executive and the Legislature, citizens could have no Rights; they were at the mercy of Power. They had created the Court to protect them from unlimited Power."[152] The need for an impartial umpire in a working federation was too great. For the balance properly to be kept, judicial power could not long be kept in repose.

Resolution of the dispute took place soon after the centennial of the nation. Writing at the time, Henry Adams mourned that "the system of 1789 had broken down, and with it . . . the fabric of . . . moral principles. Politicians had tacitly given it up."[153] Adams was (as all too often) wide of the mark. The constitutional system set up a century earlier had endured the test of fire. Reconstruction and the bitterness it engendered was at last ended. For the first time since the war, it was governmental policy that "the flag should wave over states, not provinces, over freemen and not subjects."[154] The focus of the Court's concern could now shift from the great issues that had almost destroyed the nation to those more appropriate to a less troubled era.

7

Fuller Court, 1888–1910

The law is both a mirror and a motor. It is, as Holmes tells us, a mirror wherein we see reflected the society which it serves.[1] But the law also helps to move the society in the direction that is perceived to serve best the "felt necessities of the time."[2] The jurisprudence of the Supreme Court inevitably reflects both aspects of the law's role.

This was particularly true as the Supreme Court began its second century. Despite the celebrated Holmes animadversion, the law then did virtually "enact Mr. Herbert Spencer's *Social Statics.*"[3] The Court's decisions reflected the Spencerean laissez faire that had become dominant in the society as a whole at the time. However, the Court also helped to mold the society and economy in the Spencerean image. It furnished the legal tools to further the period's galloping industrialism and ensure that public power would give free play to the unrestrained capitalism of the era.

The end of the last century saw the beginning of a period of negative Supreme Court jurisprudence, when government was denied the essential powers which it was to assume during the next century. As the Court itself recently conceded, the Court then "imposed substantive limitations on legislation limiting economic autonomy . . . , adopting [instead] the theory of *laissez faire.*"[4] The Court became a primary pillar of the dominant jurisprudence of the day—its overriding theme that of the individualism of the law applied with mechanical rigor, with abstract freedom of the individual will as the crucial factor in social progress. This was the time when the Court apparently believed in everything we now find it impossible to believe in: the danger of any governmental interference with the economy, the danger of subjecting corporate power to public control, the danger of any restriction upon the rights of private property, the danger of disrupting the social and economic status quo—in short, the danger of making anything more, the danger of making anything less.

Chief Justice Fuller

In the Court's history, Melville Weston Fuller remains the prime example of that luckiest of all persons known to the law—the innocent third party without notice. Fuller was a little-known Chicago lawyer when the lightning struck. On Chief Justice Waite's death in March 1888, President Cleveland decided to appoint someone from Illinois in his place. His first choice, Judge John Shoffield of the state's Supreme Court, refused the appointment because he did not want to raise his nine children in Washington. Cleveland then chose Fuller, who had become a successful attorney—though, in his own phrase at the time, not someone "already in the public eye" or even "publicly known to a greater or less extent."[5]

Fuller was the first Chief Justice who had never held any federal office prior to his appointment. In fact, as his biographer concedes, his prior public service was "pitifully small,"[6] consisting only of brief membership in a constitutional convention and a state legislature. One newspaper called him the most obscure man ever appointed Chief Justice. Fuller's new colleagues apparently agreed. Writing to Justice Field, who had hoped for the appointment, Justice Bradley complained that though Fuller was "a very estimable man and a successful practitioner; [this] hardly fills the public expectation for the place of Chief Justice of the United States."[7]

Fuller was an extremely small man—so small, indeed, that it was necessary to elevate his chair on the bench and provide a hassock to prevent his feet from swinging in the air. As Justice Frankfurter tells it, "Fuller came to a Court that wondered what this little man was going to do. There were titans, giants on the bench. They were powerful men, both in experience and in force of conviction, and powrful in physique, as it happened." A number of the Justices were big men: Justices Miller, Harlan, and Gray were great, stocky men, over six feet; Justice Field was also well above average size. "Those were the big, powerful, self-assured men over whom Melville Fuller came to preside."[8]

"Oh, but there were Giants on the Court in those days," Fuller used to say of his early years as Chief Justice. Nor was he referring only to the great stature of his colleagues. The Court at the time contained some of the greatest Justices in its history; Justices Miller, Field, Bradley, and Harlan were among the Justices who have left an enduring mark on our law. Well could the new Chief Justice write soon after his appointment, "No rising sun for me with these old luminaries blazing away with all their ancient fires."[9]

As it turned out, Fuller was one of the most effective Chief Justices. His new colleagues, says Justice Frankfurter, "looked upon him . . . with doubt and suspicion, but he soon conquered them." Fuller had a remarkable capacity for leading the Court conferences. In Frankfurter's phrase, "He had gentle firmness, courtesy, and charm."[10] At the core of the Fuller success as Chief Justice was what his biographer calls his "remarkable capacity for mediation; he liked to 'tinker a compromise,' as Justice Holmes put it." Holmes himself used to say "that there never was a better presiding officer, or rather, and more important in some ways, a better moderator inside the conference chamber, than this quiet gentleman from Illinois."[11] Indeed, according to Holmes, "I think he was extraordinary. He had the business of court at his fingers' ends; he was perfectly courageous, prompt, decided. He turned off the matters that daily called for action easily, swiftly with the least possible friction, with imperturbable good humor, and with a humor that relieved any tension with a laugh."[12]

Humor, in fact—what Justice Frankfurter termed "lubricating humor"—was Fuller's secret weapon. Frankfurter gives an example that he heard from Justice Holmes:

> Justice Harlan, who was oratorical while Justice Holmes was pithy, said something during one of the Court's conferences that seemed to Holmes not ultimate wisdom. Justice Holmes said he then did something that ordinarily isn't done in the conference room of the Supreme Court. Each man speaks in order and there are no interruptions, because if you had that you would soon have a Donnybrook Fair instead of orderly discussion. But Holmes afterward said, "I did lose my temper at something that Harlan said and sharply remarked, 'That won't wash. That won't wash.'" Tempers flared and something might have happened. But when Holmes said, "That won't wash," the silver-haird, gentle little Chief Justice said, "Well, I'm scrubbing away. I'm scrubbing away."[13]

Fuller presided, in Frankfurter's phrase, "with great but gentle firmness."[14] After returning from a Saturday conference, Justice Gray, the first to hire a law clerk, used to tell Samuel Williston, his clerk when Fuller took his seat (and later the leading authority on the law of contracts), how the discussion had been heated but the Chief Justice had kept the Court together. It was Fuller who inaugurated the practice still followed of having each Justice greet and shake hands with every other Justice each morning. "This practice," wrote Fuller's biographer, "tends to prevent rifts from forming."[15]

The Court and the Justices

A former Fuller classmate at Bowdoin described the courtroom as the new Chief Justice prepared to take the oath: "A small white-walled room . . . a long massive desk, behind which, seated in their massive chairs ranged side by side, sit eight figures . . . clothed to their feet in flowing robes of 'solemn black,' apparently unmovable with stern fixed gaze, and seemingly almost as emotionless as effigies of departed greatness which are clustered in 'Statuary Hall' not far distant."[16]

The Fuller Court in operation fully followed the practice and traditions established by its predecessors, since, as Justice Holmes once put it, "Fuller hated to change anything—even to adjourn half an hour for luncheon instead of two."[17] One thing, however, was substantially changed during Fuller's tenure—the burden of circuit court duty that had been the bane of the Justices for a century.

A bill for the relief of the Supreme Court had been pending for some years in Congress. None had been passed and the Court's situation continued in its unsatisfactory state, because of both the circuit obligation and increasing docket congestion. Fuller's biographer tells how the aging Chief Justice was compelled to go on circuit to South Carolina in June in very hot weather. Though the burden may have been less great than it was before the railroad, it was still substantial. "I am so weary I can hardly sit up," wrote Fuller at the end of the 1889 Term.[18]

In 1881, former Justice Strong published an article which called attention to the unsatisfactory situation. He also urged "the only possible adequate remedy for the existing evil . . . the establishment of a court of appeals in each of the circuits into which the country is now divided—a court intermediate between the Supreme Court and the circuit courts."[19] Such a measure had been proposed in a bill introduced in the Senate by former Justice Davis after he had resigned to accept a seat in the upper House. It was also the solution preferred by the Justices themselves. As early as 1872, Justice Miller had written "of the plan which has always had my preference, an intermediate appellate court in each circuit, or such a number of intermediate courts of appeal as may be found useful."[20]

Now Chief Justice Fuller put the prestige of his office behind the proposal. But he did it informally at a dinner to which he invited the important members of the Senate Judiciary Committee and by cultivation of Senator George F. Edmunds, the key member of the committee. The Fuller effort was soon to bear fruit. The Senate Judiciary Committee wrote Fuller that it would "be agreeable to the Committee to receive . . . the views of the Justices."[21] The latter, in a report prepared by Justice Gray, recommended the establishment of circuit courts of appeal. Congress then set up the proposed courts in 1891, under a bill sponsored by Senator Edmunds. Though it did not specifically relieve the Justices of circuit duty, it did so in practice, since they were not expected to sit in the new courts. The old circuit courts were finally abolished by a 1911 statute.

During Chief Justice Fuller's tenure, there was an almost complete change in the Court's composition. Indeed, when the Chief Justice died in 1910, only Justice Harlan remained of those who had been on the bench when Fuller was appointed. The first of the new Justices was David J. Brewer, appointed in 1889 to fill the seat of Justice Matthews, who had died. Brewer, a former Kansas Supreme Court Justice and federal circuit judge, was Justice Field's nephew. On the Court, Brewer proved a strong supporter of his uncle's due process posture. Soon after his appointment, Brewer wrote an opinion in which he both attacked the *Granger Cases*[22] doctrine as "radically unsound" and issued the clarion of the coming era of

Court jurisprudence: "The paternal theory of government is to me odious."[23] Instead, the theme was to be that of Brewer's 1891 address at Yale Law School: "Protection to Private Property from Public Attack."[24]

Most of the other Justices appointed during the Fuller tenure can be dealt with more briefly. On Justice Miller's death in 1890, after twenty-eight years on the Court, Henry B. Brown of Michigan, a federal district judge for fifteen years, was chosen. He was to serve until 1906—an average Justice whose work on the bench is all but forgotten.

In the same mold was George Shiras, Jr., of Pennsylvania, appointed in 1892 in the place of Justice Bradley, upon the latter's death. Shiras had no previous judicial experience; he was a successful practitioner whose clients included large steel corporations and the Baltimore and Ohio Railroad. Shiras served only until 1903, when he retired. "His retirement," writes a biographer, "attracted little notice, and his death even less, for Shiras appeared to have been an undistinguished jurist."[25]

Other Justices on the Fuller Court who were buried in what a biographer of one of them terms "the shroud of anonymity"[26] were Howell E. Jackson of Tennessee, a former Senator and federal circuit judge—the first Democrat appointed by a Republican President since Justice Field in 1861—who died in 1895, only two years after he was chosen; Joseph McKenna of California, a former Congressman, circuit judge, and Attorney General, chosen to succeed Justice Field, who had resigned in 1897; William R. Day of Ohio, who had been Secretary of State and a circuit judge, when Justice Shiras resigned in 1903; William H. Moody of Massachusetts, a former Congressman, Secretary of the Navy, and Attorney General, chosen when Justice Brown resigned in 1910; and Horace H. Lurton, a circuit judge, appointed in place of Justice Rufus W. Peckham, who died in 1909 (and whose appointment will be discussed shortly).

Three Justices appointed during Fuller's term stand out from this group of less then mediocre Justices. They are Edward Douglass White, Rufus Wheeler Peckham, and Oliver Wendell Holmes. White was a Senator from Louisiana when he was appointed in 1894 to succeed Justice Blatchford, who had died. Owner of a large plantation, White had served in the Confederate Army and briefly in his state's highest court. White was a more than competent Justice, who served as an Associate for sixteen years, but he is remembered primarily as Fuller's successor as Chief Justice and will be discussed more fully in that position in Chapter 9. Justice Holmes also will be dealt with later (in Chapter 8), since his contribution to both the Court and the law was so important that it deserves separate treatment.

That leaves Justice Peckham, a member of New York's highest court, appointed in 1895 to the seat of Justice Jackson, who had died after serving only two years. Holmes wrote that his Supreme Court colleagues were "enthusiasts for liberty of contract."[27] Foremost among these liberty-of-contract enthusiasts was Justice Peckham, who was to be Holmes's principal antagonist in *Lochner v. New York*,[28] the leading case on the subject.

More than any other judge, Peckham was the exemplar of the conservative jurist early in this century. His decisions were prime applications of the dominant legal thought of the day—using the law as the barrier against interferences with the operation of the economic system. If laissez faire was read into the Due Process Clause, that was true in large part because of Justice Peckham's opinions.

Like so many of the Justices of his day, Peckham was a strong earthy character; Holmes termed him "a master of Anglo-Saxon monosyllabic interjections."[29] A young law clerk once asked Holmes, "What was Justice Peckham like, intellectually?" "Intellectually?" Holmes replied, puzzlement in his voice. "I never thought of him in that connection. His major premise was, 'God damn it!'"[30] A few years later, after making the same comment, Holmes explained that he meant "thereby that emotional predilections governed him on social themes."[31]

Peckham's opinions bear witness to the acuteness of the Holmes observation. The "emotional predilections" that governed Peckham's decisions were based upon the fear of changes in the existing order. "When socialism first began to be talked about," Holmes tells us, "the comfortable classes of the community were a good deal frightened. I suspect that this fear has influenced judicial action both here and in England."[32] It certainly influenced the Peckham jurisprudence.

At the same time, few can doubt Justice Peckham's importance in helping to translate the prevailing jurisprudence into the law of the land. It was Peckham who wrote the opinions in both the case in which liberty of contract was first relied upon by a majority of the Supreme Court[33] and the case where the liberty-of-contract tide reached its crest.[34] In both cases, Justice Frankfurter tells us, "Mr. Justice Peckham wrote Mr. Justice Field's dissents into the opinions of the Court."[35] It was because of the Peckham opinions that Holmes could say that the Fourteenth Amendment may have begun with "an unpretentious assertion of the liberty to follow the ordinary callings," but "[l]ater that innocuous generality was expanded into the dogma, Liberty of Contract."[36]

Due Process and Liberty of Contract

That "dogma" became the foundation of Fuller Court jurisprudence. Justice Frankfurter once said that, to judges like those on the Fuller Court, "Adam Smith was treated as though his generalizations had been imparted to him on Sinai."[37] Such judges were bound to look upon the law as though it were intended to suppy a legal sanction to those generalizations. To them, regulatory legislation presented itself as a clear infringement upon the economic laws posited by Adam Smith and Herbert Spencer, and the progressive evolution of the society which was supposed to be based upon them:[38] "[A]ny legislative encroachment upon the existing economic order [was] infected with unconstitutionality."[39]

The Fuller Court jurisprudence, Justice Frankfurter tells us, was ulti-

mately based upon "misapplication of the notions of the classic econo-
mists. . . . The result . . . was that economic views of confined validity
were treated by lawyers and judges as though the Framers had enshrined
them in the Constitution."[40]

To the Justices of the day as to most of their contemporaries, the law
existed above all to protect freedom of contract. Whatever the law might
do in other respects, it might not limit contractual capacity,[41] because that
capacity was an essential element of what a Peckham opinion termed "the
faculties with which [man] has been endowed by his Creator."[42] In
another opinion, Justice Peckham referred to "the general rule of absolute
liberty of the individual to contract" and urged that "no further violation"
of that rule "should be sustained by this court."[43] If a 1900 American Bar
Association paper could proclaim "there is . . . complete freedom of contract; competition is now universal, and as merciless as nature and natural
selection,"[44] that was true largely because of the Fuller Court opinions in
the matter.

It was Justice Peckham who spoke for the majority in the important
freedom-of-contract cases decided by the Fuller Court. In particular, he
wrote the landmark opinion in *Allgeyer v. Louisiana* (1897),[45] where freedom of contract was established as an essential element of the "liberty"
protected by due process. At issue in *Allgeyer* was a state law that prohibited an individual from contracting with an out-of-state insurance company for insurance of property within the state. Such a law was ruled
violative of the Due Process Clause, which protects liberty to contract:
"Has not a citizen of a State, under the provisions of the Federal Constitution above mentioned, a right to contract outside of the State for insurance
on his property—a right of which state legislation cannot deprive him?"[46]

The key passage of the Peckham opinion gave a broad construction to
the "liberty" protected by the Fourteenth Amendment. "The liberty mentioned in that amendment," Peckham wrote, "means not only the right of
the citizen to be free from the mere physical restraint of his person, as by
incarceration, but the term is deemed to embrace the right of the citizen to
be free in the enjoyment of all his faculties; to be free to use them in all
lawful ways; to live and work where he will; to earn his livelihood by any
lawful calling; to pursue any livelihood or avocation, and for that purpose
to enter into all contracts which may be proper, necessary and essential to
his carrying out to a successful conclusion the purposes above mentioned."[47]

Yet *Allgeyer* did more than enshrine liberty of contract in the constitutional pantheon. It made due process dominant as the doctrine virtually
immunizing economic activity from regulation deemed contrary to the
laissez-faire philosophy of the day. Justice Peckham once said that to uphold
government regulation of the *Granger Cases* or *Allgeyer* type "is to take a
long step backwards and to favor that class of paternal legislation,
which . . . interferes with the proper liberty of the citizen."[48] Economic
abuses should be dealt with not by a law which "will not, as seems to me

plain, even achieve the purposes of its authors," but by "the general laws of trade [and] the law of supply and demand."[49]

To the Fuller Court, a law which interfered with the free operation of the market was a violation of substantive due process. In this respect, *Allgeyer* marked the culmination of the trend away from the *Slaughter-House Cases,*[50] which marked Chief Justice Fuller's tenure. Indeed, much of the substance of Fuller Court jurisprudence involved the elevation of the dissents in *Slaughter-House* into the law of the land. The development starts with cases involving railroad regulation. In the *Granger Cases,*[51] we saw, the Court followed the strict *Slaughter-House* approach, ruling that the Due Process Clause did not subject the legislative judgment in fixing rates to judicial review: "For protection against abuses by Legislatures, the people must resort to the polls, not to the courts."[52]

The restrictive approach to due process was, however, abandoned during the Fuller Chief Justiceship. The Court soon held that the power to regulate was not the power to confiscate;[53] whether rates fixed were unreasonable "is eminently a question for judicial investigation, requiring due process of law."[54] The rule laid down was that the Due Process Clause permits the courts to review the substance of rate-fixing legislation—at least to determine whether particular rates are so low as to be confiscatory.[55]

During this period, the state courts were moving even faster in developing substantive due process. Even before Chief Justice Fuller took his seat, they had used substantive due process to strike down regulatory laws on the ground that such a law "arbitrarily deprives him of his property and some portion of his personal liberty."[56] In an 1885 decision, the New York court declared that the "liberty" protected by due process meant one's right to live and work where and how he will; laws that limit his choice or place of work "are infringements upon the fundamental rights of liberty, which are under constitutional protection."[57]

These state decisions directly anticipated the Supreme Court's adoption of the substantive due process concept: "[A]ll that happened," writes a federal judge who came to the Bar at the time, "was that the Supreme Court joined hands with most of the appellate tribunals of the older states."[58]

The joining of hands occurred in the *Allgeyer* case, where, Justice Frankfurter tells us, "Mr. Justice Field's [*Slaughter-House*] dissent in effect established itself as the prevailing opinion of the Supreme Court."[59] In *Allgeyer,* for the first time, a state law was set aside on the ground that it violated substantive due process. The "liberty" referred to in the Due Process Clause, said Justice Peckham's opinion, embraces property rights, including that to pursue any lawful calling. A state law that takes from its citizens the right to contract outside the state for insurance on their property deprives them of their "liberty" without due process.

Between the dictum of the *Granger Cases,* that for protection against legislative abuses "the people must resort to the polls, not to the courts," and *Allgeyer v. Louisiana* and its progeny lies the history of the emergence of modern large-scale industry, of the consequent public efforts at control of business, and of judicial review of such regulation.[60] Thenceforth, all governmental action—whether federal or state—would have to run the gantlet of substantive due process; the substantive as well as the procedural aspect of such action would be subject to the scrutiny of the highest Court: "[T]he legislatures had not only domestic censors, but another far away in Washington, to pass on their handiwork."[61]

The Court's utilization of substantive due process was not mere control of state legislation in the abstract. Court control was directed to a particular purpose, namely, the invalidation of state legislation that conflicted with the doctrine of laissez faire which dominated thinking at the turn of the century. What Justice Frankfurter termed "the shibboleths of a pre-machine age . . . were reflected in juridical assumptions that survived the facts on which they were based. . . . Basic human rights expressed by the constitutional conception of 'liberty' were equated with theories of *laissez-faire.*"[62] The result was that due process became the rallying point for judicial resistance to the efforts of the states to control the excesses and relieve the oppressions of the rising industrial economy.[63]

In the Fuller Court jurisprudence, the "liberty" protected by due process became synonymous with governmental hands-off in the field of private economic relations. "For years," Justice William O. Douglas tells us, "the Court struck down social legislation when a particular law did not fit the notions of a majority of Justices as to legislation appropriate for a free enterprise system."[64]

Substantive due process now became the businessman's first line of defense. Behind it, corporate power could operate free from legal interference. In the Fuller Court, the negative conception of law reached its judicial climax. The Court now saw its task as one not of further innovation but of stabilization and formalization. The law itself had become the great bulwark against economic and social change.

Shackling Federal Power

What the Fuller Court's interpretation of due process did to state regulatory power, its interpretation of the Commerce Clause did to federal regulatory power. Toward the end of the century, John Marshall's broad conception of the commerce power[65] gave way to a much more restricted view. To Marshall, the reach of the Commerce Clause extended to all commerce that concerned more states than one. Now this concept of "effect upon commerce" gave way to emphasis upon transportation across state lines. While commerce remained within the confines of a state, it did not come within federal regulatory power even though it had impacts which radiated beyond the state's borders.

This narrow conception of commerce subject to the Commerce Clause was adopted in *Kidd v. Pearson,*[66] decided a few months after Chief Justice

Fuller took office in 1888. At issue was a state statute which prohibited the manufacture of intoxicating liquors, even though they were made for sale outside the state. The law was upheld on the ground that it involved the regulation, not of commerce, but of manufacturing. The power to regulate commerce, according to the decision, does not include any authority over manufacturing, even though the products are the subject of commercial transactions in the future. To hold otherwise, the Court asserted, would be to vest in Congess control over all productive industries.

In *Kidd v. Pearson,* the challenged power was that of a state. What was said there about congressional authority was thus technically only obiter. But it soon became the basis of decision in *United States v. E. C. Knight Co.* (1895),[67] more popularly styled the *Sugar Trust Case.* That case arose out of the first important prosecution brought by the Government under the Sherman Anti-Trust Act. Defendant company had obtained a monopoly over the manufacture of refined sugar. The complaint charged that defendant had violated the Sherman Act by its acquisition of the stock of competing sugar refining companies. The Court, in an opinion by the Chief Justice, held that such an acquisition could not be reached by the federal commerce power. The monopolistic acts alleged related only to manufacturing, which was not within the scope of the Commerce Clause.

The *Knight* decision, like that in *Kidd v. Pearson* upon which it was based, was a logical consequence of the Court's changed approach to commerce. Once the Marshall conception of commerce as an organic whole gave way to the crossing of state lines as the criterion of congressional power, *Kidd-Knight* followed naturally. The result was the artificial and mechanical separation of "manufacturing" from "commerce," without regard to their economic continuity or the effects of the former upon the latter. Manufacture was treated as a "purely local" activity and hence beyond the compass of the Commerce Clause.

The motivating consideration that led the Court to this restricted conception of commerce was stated by Chief Justice Fuller in his *Knight* opinion: "Slight reflection will show that if the national power extends to all contracts and combinations in manufacture, agriculture, mining, and other productive industries, whose ultimate result may effect external commerce, comparatively little of busines operations and affairs would be left for state control."[68]

But the converse of this assertion was also true. If the commerce power did not extend to manufacture, agriculture, mining, and other productive industries, comparatively little of business operations and affairs in this country would really be subject to federal control.

Almost needless to say, the Fuller Court's restricted conception of the commerce subject to federal regulatory power fitted in perfectly with the laissez-faire theory of governmental function that dominated political and economic thinking at the time. To bar federal intervention, as the Court did in these cases, was all but to exclude the possibility of any effective regulation in them. This was, of course, exactly what was demanded by the advocates of laissez faire; to them, the economic system could function properly only if it was permitted to operate free from governmental interference.

The Constitution, states Justice Holmes in a celebrated passage, "is not intended to embody a particular economic theory, whether of paternalism and the organic relation of the citizen to the state or of laissez faire."[69] At the same time, it was most difficult for judges not to assume that the organic document was intended to embody the dominant economic beliefs of their own day. The Constitution may not, under the famous Holmes phrase, enact Mr. Herbert Spencer's *Social Statics*.[70] But the Court's narrow notion of commerce was a necessary complement to the translation of Spencerean economics into the keystone of the American polity.

Income Tax Case

Chief Justice Fuller's most famous and most criticized opinion[71] was that in the 1895 case of *Pollock v. Farmer's Loan & Trust Co.*[72]—usually known as the *Income Tax Case*—in which the Court ruled the Income Tax Act of 1894 unconstitutional. This was the case which demonstrated dramatically how the Court would use the Constitution to protect private property from governmental infringements.

The issue in the *Income Tax Case* was relatively simple: Was the income tax a "direct tax" which, under article I, section 2, "[s]hall be apportioned among the several States . . . according to their respective numbers"? If so, the 1894 statute was invalid, since it was levied on all persons who had incomes of over $4,000, with no provision for any apportionment. Both counsel and the Justices, however, did not limit themselves to the relatively uncomplicated issue before them. Instead, the case was used as the vehicle for a broadside attack upon governmental interferences with private property.

The attack began when former Senator Edmunds warned the court that such a tax "imposed by those who pay nothing, upon a very small minority" would lead to "communism, anarchy, and then, the ever following despotism."[73] Then Joseph Choate, considered the leading advocate of the day, declared that the challenged tax "is communistic in its purposes and tendencies, and is defended here upon principles as communistic, socialistic—what shall I call them—populistic as ever have been addressed to any political assembly in the world."[74]

Addressing the Justices directly, Choate warned, "If you approve this law . . . and this communistic march goes on," the law would thenceforth be helpless: "There is protection now or never." The Court "will have nothing to say about it if it now lets go its hold upon this law."[75]

To uphold the tax, Choate argued, would be "to enunciate . . . a doctrine worthy of a Jacobin Club . . . of a Czar of Russia," the "new doctrine of this army of 60,000,000—this triumphant and tyrannical majority—who want to punish men who are rich and confiscate their property."[76]

The Court rendered two decisions in the *Income Tax Case*. In the first, it held that the tax on income from land was invalid, but it was evenly divided (four-to-four) on the tax on other income. After reargument, the Court, in a five-to-four decision, decided that the entire income tax law was invalid. Chief Justice Fuller's opinions were largely technical in seeking to show that the income tax was a "direct tax" within the meaning of the Constitution. The constitutional provision, according to Fuller, was "put in antithesis to . . . duties, imposts, and excises,"[77] which were to be the principal source of federal revenue. Reliance was placed upon a work by Albert Gallatin to show that direct taxes were "those which are raised on the capital or revenue of the people; . . . indirect such as are raised on their expense."[78] The income tax was a tax on the capital or revenue of the people rather than on their expense. Hence it was a direct tax and invalid because not apportioned among the states in proportion to their population, as required by the Constitution.

The decisions in the *Income Tax Case* were severely criticized because they appeared contrary to earlier decisions which the Chief Justice failed to distinguish adequately. In addition, it was widely reported that the second decision resulted from a switched vote by one of the Justices, who had been in favor of sustaining the tax on nonrent income at the time of the first decision, to the antitax side, which gave the latter its bare majority. At the time it was believed that it was Justice Shiras who had changed his mind, and he was widely blamed for wrecking the income tax. More recent commentators have questioned whether it was Justice Shiras who had switched, or even whether there was any switch at all.[79] At any rate, if there was what has been termed "The Mystery of the Vacillating Jurist,"[80] it remains to this day essentially unsolved.

Instead, the *Income Tax Case* remains as the Fuller Court's response to warnings such as those raised in the Choate argument. Justice Harlan delivered an impassioned dissent rejecting what he called the argument urging "this court . . . to stand in the breach for the protection of the just rights of property against the advancing hosts of socialism." Instead, Harlan declared that the decisions were "a disaster to the country" because their "interpretation of the Constitution . . . impairs and cripples the just powers of the National Government." The Court's action, Harlan asserted, invests property owners "with power and influence that may be perilous to that portion of the American people upon whom rests the large part of the burdens of the government, and who ought not to be subjected to the dominion of aggregated wealth."[81]

Justice Holmes called Justice Harlan "the last of the tobacco-spittin' judges."[82] As Harlan delivered his *Income Tax* dissent, his face grew visibly redder, and his fist banged the bench as he glared defiantly at the Chief Justice. *The Nation* called Harlan's dissent "the most violent political tirade ever heard in a court of last resort."[83]

But the fervent rhetoric was not all on one side. Choate's ardent oratory found a receptive ear in the *Income Tax* majority. This may be seen from the concurring opinion of Justice Field, whose due process philosophy was now to be dominant in the Fuller Court. "The present assault upon capital," declared Justice Field, "is but the beginning. It will be but the stepping-stone to others, larger and more sweeping, till our political contests will become a war of the poor against the rich; a war constantly growing in intensity and bitterness." If the Court were to sanction the income tax law, "it will mark the hour when the sure decadence of our present government will commence."[84]

The judges who felt this way about a tax of 2 percent on annual incomes above $4,000 now had at their disposal the newly fashioned tool of substantive due process. How they would use it became clear in the *Lochner* case, to be discussed in Chapter 8.

Insular Cases

The so-called *Insular Cases,*[85] decided in 1901 by the Fuller Court, are remembered today largely because of Mr. Dooley's famous aphorism that the Supreme Court follows the election returns.[86] All but forgotten is the fact that the *Insular Cases* were great cases at the time which decided one of the crucial constitutional issues of the day. That issue was also well stated in Mr. Dooley's summary of the Court's holding: "I see," said Mr. Dooley, "Th' supreme court has decided th' constitution don't follow th' flag."[87]

The question of whether the Constitution follows the flag was an issue of the relationship between the organic instrument and conquered territory. The problem was posed in acute form by the war with Spain and the territorial acquisitions that were its outcome. Soon after the war ended, the question of whether government in the new territories was subject to those constitutional limitations which apply in the continental United States came before the Supreme Court in the series of 1901 decisions that have come to be known as the *Insular Cases.*

They arose out of the 1900 statute providing a government for conquered Puerto Rico. Among that law's provisions were sections requiring customs duties to be paid upon goods imported into the United States from the island. It was contended that such a provision was invalid, since Puerto Rico had become a part of the United States within the constitutional requirement that "all Duties, Imposts and Excises shall be uniform thoughout the United States." This, in turn, said the Court, posed the broader question of whether the provisions "of the Constitution extend of their own force to our new acquired territories."[88]

According to the *Insular Cases,* whether the Constitution follows the flag depends, in the particular case, upon the type of territory that is involved. The Court drew a distinction between "incorporated" and "unincorporated" territories. The former are those territories which Congress has incorporated into and made an integral part of the United States.

Without express provision by Congress, territory acquired by the nation remains unincorporated. Applying the distinction between incorporated and unincorporated territories to Puerto Rico, the Court found that that island belonged to the latter category: "[W]hilst in an international sense Porto Rico was not a foreign country, since it was subject to the sovereignty of and was owned by the United States, it was foreign to the United States in a domestic sense, because the island had not been incorporated into the United States, but was merely appurtenant thereto as a possession."[89]

Justice Frankfurter tells us that the "over two hundred pages of opinions . . . were illuminatingly summarized by that great philosopher, Mr. Dooley, when he said that so far as he could make out, 'the Supreme Court decided that the Constitoosh'n follows the flag on Mondays, Wednesdays, and Fridays.'"[90] In other words, the Constitution sometimes follows the flag and sometimes does not. Whether it does depends on whether the territory concerned is incorporated or unincorporated. In the former, all the constitutional rights and privileges must be accorded. But the same is not true in unincorporated territory like Puerto Rico. In them, a constitutional provision like that governing duties and imposts does not restrict governmental authority.

Chief Justice Fuller, joined by Justices Harlan, Brewer, and Peckham, delivered what his biographer calls a "calm and restrained" dissent.[91] Justice Harlan also delivered his more typical impassioned dissent, in which he urged, "The idea that this country may acquire territores anywhere upon the earth, by conquest or treaty, and hold them as mere colonies or provinces—the people inhabiting them to enjoy only such rights as Congress chooses to accord to them—is wholly inconsistent with the spirit and genius as well as with the words of the Constitution."[92]

Three years after the *Insular Cases,* its holding was applied in *Dorr v. United States.*[93] The question there was whether trial by jury became a necessary incident of justice in the Philippine Islands when they became American territory. The Supreme Court held that it did not. Since the Philippines had not been incorporated into the United States, the jury-trial requirement of the Sixth Amendment was not a limitation upon the power to provide a government for that territory.

Mr. Dooley may have satirized the Court that decided the *Insular Cases.* But that holding has remained the basic principle in dealing with the relationship of the Constitution to overseas territories. It was to be of particular pertinence in a later age when the United States was to become a leader of the international community. What the Supreme Court said in those cases on the government provided in territories acquired as a result of the Spanish War was to apply as well to the military governments set up in conquered territory almost half a century later.

At the same time, there is an anomaly in the holding that our Government may act in violation of constitutional guarantees. Justice Harlan indicated how troubling such a result was in a letter he sent to the Chief

Justice. "The more I think of these questions," Harlan wrote, "the more alarmed I am at the effect upon our institutions of the doctrine that this country may acquire territory inhabited by human beings anywhere upon the earth and govern it at the will of Congress and without regard to the restraints imposed by the Constitution upon governmental authority. There is a danger that commercialism will sweep away the safeguards of real freedom."[94]

Separate but Equal

Chief Justice Fuller's biography does not even mention the 1896 case of *Plessy v. Ferguson*.[95] Yet the decision there is now one of the most criticized decisions of the Fuller Court. It was the seminal decision which, for more than half a century, made equal protection no more than a hortatory slogan for African-Americans. While the Fuller Court developed the Fourteenth Amendment's Due Process Clause as the principal safeguard of property rights, its *Plessy* decision ensured that the amendment was of little value to the blacks for whose benefit it had primarily been adopted.

Homer Plessy, a Louisiana resident, was one-eighth black. In 1892, while riding on a train out of New Orleans, he was ejected by the conductor from a car for whites and directed to a coach assigned to nonwhites. The conductor acted under a Louisiana statute that provided for "equal but separate [railroad] accommodations for the white and colored races."

Plessy claimed that the statute was contrary to the Fourteenth Amendment's requirement of equal protection of the laws and took his case to court. As recently summarized by the Court, *Plessy* held that "racial segregation . . . works no denial of equal protection, rejecting the argument that racial separation enforced by the legal machinery of American society treats the black race as inferior."[96] Instead, the *Plessy* Court stated, "Laws permitting, and even requiring their separation in places where they are liable to be brought into contact do not necessarily imply the inferiority of either race to the other."[97]

The *Plessy* decision gave rise to what has been termed one of the most vigorous dissents in Supreme Court history[98]—certainly the greatest delivered by Justice Harlan. The dissent attacked the very basis of the Court's decision, that is, that segregation alone was not discriminatory. To anyone familiar with the techniques of racial discrimination, the Court's view is completely out of line with reality. The device of holding a group of people separate—whether by confinement of Jews to the Ghetto, by exclusion of untouchables from the temple, or by segregation of the black—is a basic tool of discrimination. "The thin disguise of 'equal' accommodations for passengers in railroad coaches," movingly declared the Harlan dissent, "will not mislead anyone, nor atone for the wrong this day done."[99]

Plessy v. Ferguson gave the lie to the American ideal, so eloquently stated in the Harlan dissent: "Our Constitution is color-blind, and neither knows nor tolerates classes among citizens."[100] Upon the "separate but equal" doctrine approved by the Court was built a whole structure of racial discrimination. Jim Crow replaced equal protection, and legally enforced segregation became the dominant fact in Southern life.

To the present-day observer, the merits of the case are all with Justice Harlan's dissent. All the same, perhaps, one should not be too harsh in judging the Fuller Court for a decision that mirrored its own time and place. Living in an era that has witnessed a virtual egalitarian revolution, we find it all too easy to censure the Fuller Court for its reliance upon doctrine that we now deem outmoded. But that Court—a reflection of the less tolerant society in which it sat—could hardly hope to lift itself (by its own bootstraps as it were) above the ingrained prejudices of its day.

In addition, we should recognize that, inadequate though the *Plessy* decision may have been in its failure to implement the guaranty of equality, it was the language in *Plessy* requiring equality of treatment for the separate races that was to prove decisive in the movement for legal equality in the racial field. Indeed, it was to be precisely the requirement of equality of treatment articulated in the *Plessy* opinion that was half a century later to provide the opening wedge for the ultimate overruling of the *Plessy* holding itself.

8

Watershed Cases:
Lochner v. New York, 1905

Aside from *Dred Scott* itself, *Lochner v. New York*[1] is now considered the most discredited decision in Supreme Court history. When commentators discuss the case at all, they use it as a vehicle to illustrate the drastic change in jurisprudence during the twentieth century, which has seen the Holmes dissent in *Lochner* elevated to established doctrine.

Yankee from Olympus

The paradigmatic early twentieth-century conflict over constitutional construction was that in the *Lochner* case between Justice Rufus W. Peckham and Justice Oliver Wendell Holmes. The appointment of Holmes was a capital event in the history of the Supreme Court. Our discussion of John Marshall quoted Holmes: "[I]f American law were to be represented by a single figure, skeptic and worshipper alike would agree without dispute that the figure could be one alone, and that one, John Marshall."[2] If American law were to be represented by a second figure, most jurists would say that it should be Holmes himself. For it was Holmes, more than any other legal thinker, who set the agenda for modern Supreme Court jurisprudence. In doing so, he became as much a part of American legend as law: the Yankee from Olympus[3]—the patrician from Boston who made his mark on his own age and on ages still unborn as few have done. To summarize Holmes's work is to trace the development from nineteenth-century law to that of the present day. The younger Holmes came from what his father, the famous New England writer, termed "the Brahmin caste of New England"—the "untitled aristocracy" of early America.[4] After graduation from Harvard and Civil War service in the Union Army, Holmes decided to study law. He told his father that he was going to Harvard Law School, and Dr. Holmes is said to have asked, "What is the use of that? A lawyer can't be a great man."[5] Holmes's career showed how mistaken his father was.

After his graduation from law school, Holmes was admitted to the Bar, joined a law firm, and became a part-time lecturer at Harvard. He wrote articles for legal periodicals and edited the twelfth edition of Kent's *Commentaries*. Then, in 1880, came the invitation to deliver a series of lectures. He chose as his topic *The Common Law* and the lectures were published in a book of that name in 1881. This book was to change both Holmes's life and the course of American law.

As a state judge tells us, "The book propounds an idea audacious and even revolutionary for the time."[6] The Holmes theme has become so settled in our thinking that we forget how radical it was when it was announced over a century ago. The very words used must have appeared strange to the contemporary reader: "experience," "expediency," "necessity," "life." Law books at the time used far different words: "rule," "precedent," "logic," "syllogism."[7] As Holmes's biographer tells us, "The time-honored way was to deduce the *corpus* from *a priori* postulates, fit part to part in beautiful, neat logical cohesion."[8] Holmes rejected "the notion that a given [legal] system, ours, for instance, can be worked out like mathematics."[9] Instead, he declared, "The law embodies the story of a nation's development through many centuries, and it cannot be dealt with as if it contained the axioms and corollaries of a book of mathematics."[10]

But the great Holmes theme was stated at the very outset of *The Common Law:* "The life of the law has not been logic: it has been experience. The felt necessities of the time, the prevalent moral and political theories, intuitions of public policy, avowed or unconscious, even the prejudices which judges share with their fellow-men, have had a good deal more to do than the syllogism in determining the rules by which men should be governed."[11]

When Holmes wrote these words, he was pointing the way to a new era of jurisprudence that would, in former Attorney General Francis Biddle's words, "break down the walls of formalism and empty traditionalism which had grown up around the inner life of the law in America."[12] The courts, Holmes urged, should recognize that they must perform a legislative function, in its deeper sense. The secret root from which the law draws its life is consideration of "what is expedient for the community." The "felt necessities of the time," intuitions of what best serve the public interest, "even the prejudices which judges share with their fellow-men"—all have much more to do than logic in determining the legal rules that govern the society.

The Holmes lectures purported to be only a descriptive statement of what the law was and how, historically, it came to be that way. In fact, however, Holmes was making a prescriptive statement of what the law ought to be—a statement that was ultimately to set the theme for the jurisprudence of the coming century. The success of *The Common Law* led to a Harvard law professorship in 1882. But Holmes taught there only a term, for he was appointed in December 1882 to the Supreme Judicial Court of Massachusetts. He served on that tribunal for twenty years (from 1899 as Chief Justice), when he was elevated to the U.S. Supreme Court. Though he was already sixty-one when he took his seat on that Court, he still had his greatest judicial years to serve. He did not leave the Supreme Court until his retirement in January 1932. During the thirty years he spent in Washington, he made the greatest contribution since Marshall to American constitutional law.

Peckham Precursor

Holmes's great antagonist in the *Lochner* case was Justice Peckham, who had already been discussed as the exemplar of the conservative Justice at the turn of the century.[13] To us today, Peckham's *Lochner* opinion of the Court is a prime example of the reactionary jurisprudence of the day. We should, however, realize that Peckham himself saw his opinion quite differently. To him it was the culmination of the progressive trend away from the paternalistic theory of the state that was as "odious" to him as it was in Justice Brewer's already quoted statement.[14]

Justice Peckham best explained his posture in this respect in *People v. Budd,*[15] decided in 1889, while Peckham was still on the highest New York court. At issue was a state law fixing maximum rates for grain elevators. The New York court followed the *Granger Cases*[16] and upheld the law. Judge Peckham delivered a vigorous dissent, which exemplifies the conception of law that he was soon to elevate to Supreme Court doctrine.

In his dissent, Peckham flatly rejected the businesses-affected-with-a-public-interest doctrine adopted in the *Granger Cases,* which had been established as the common-law rule by Lord Hale in the seventeenth century. Lord Hale, Peckham stressed, had written "when views of governmental interference with the private concerns of individuals were carried to the greatest extent." Indeed, "in those days the theory of a paternal government . . . was to watch over and protect the individual at every moment, to dictate the quality of his food and the character of his clothes, his hours of labor, the amount of his wages, his attendance upon church, and generally to care for him in his private life."[17]

Two centuries later, Peckham went on, a different view prevailed "as to how far it is proper to interfere in the general industrial department of the country." There was now "no reason [to] go back to the seventeenth or eighteenth century ideas of paternal government." "State interference in matters of private concern" was no longer considered proper, since it was contrary to "the later and, as I firmly believe, the more correct ideas which an increase of civilization and a fuller knowledge of the fundamental laws of political economy, and a truer conception of the proper functions of government have given us at the present day."[18]

The economic orthodoxy of the day told Judge Peckham that such legislative attempts "to interfere with what seems to me the most sacred rights of property and the individual liberty of contract" were bound to be ineffective. Such a law "will result either in its evasion or else the work will not be done, and the capital employed will seek other channels where such [unregulated] rate can be realized, or the property will become of little or no value." In the latter case, the law "may ruin or very greatly impair the value of the property of wholly innocent persons." To Peckham, it was clear that such a law was "wholly useless for any good effect, and only powerful for evil."[19] Instead, the New York law was an unjustified interference with "the law of supply and demand."

Illustrating the Holmes comment quoted in the last chapter on the fear of socialism and judicial action, Peckham warned that "[t]o uphold legislation of this character is to provide the most frequent opportunity for arraying class against class." The challenged law was not only, "in my belief, wholly inefficient to permanently obtain the result aimed at," but it was "vicious in its nature, communistic in its tendency."[20]

The Peckham jurisprudence was, of course, to attain its apogee in the *Lochner* case. However, "The Peckham of *Lochner v. New York* surely needs no introduction after *People v. Budd*."[21] The Peckham concept of law was fully developed in his *Budd* dissent. His important Supreme Court opinions, particularly that in *Lochner*, were foreshadowed by what he wrote in *Budd*.

Facts and Opinion

Joseph Lochner had been convicted for violating a New York law by requiring a worker in his bakery to work more than sixty hours in one week. The statute prohibited bakery employees from working more than ten hours a day, or sixty hours a week. The law was challenged as a violation of due process: "The Statute in Question is Not a Reasonable Exercise of the Police Power."[22]

The case gave the Supreme Court great difficulty. The Justices first voted by a bare majority to uphold the law. The case was assigned to Justice Harlan, who wrote a draft opinion of the Court. Justice Peckham wrote a strong draft dissent. Before the case came down, however, there was a vote switch. The Peckham dissent became the opinion of the Court and the Harlan opinion a dissent.[23] It is not known who changed his vote, though the probability is that it was Chief Justice Fuller. Though Fuller had voted to uphold other maximum-hour laws,[24] his biographer tells us that "the ten-hour law for bakers seemed to him to be 'featherbedding,' paternalistic, and depriving both the worker and employer of fundamental liberties."[25]

The other cases in which laws regulating hours of labor had been sustained were treated by the Court as health measures. In *Lochner,* it has been suggested, Justice McKenna, whose father had owned a bakery, may have persuaded Fuller and others in the majority that bakery work was not dangerous and that the health rationale was a sham.[26] Justice Peckham himself needed no persuading. His *Lochner* opinion of the Court was a natural product of the judge who had elevated liberty of contract to the constitutional plane in *Allgeyer v. Louisiana,*[27] ruled against interferences with the operation of the market in his *Budd* opinion, and even voted against a maximum-hours law for miners.[28] If Justice Peckham refused to consider the law protecting miners a legitimate health measure, it was obvious that he would not accept the health justification for a similar law regulating bakery work.

For Justice Peckham, *Lochner* was essentially a reprise of *Allgeyer* and *Budd.* Here, too, the crucial factor was the violation of freedom of contract which *Allgeyer* had ruled "part of the liberty of the individual." The *Lochner* "statute necessarily interferes with the right of contract between the employer and employees, concerning the number of hours in which the latter may labor in the bakery of the employer."[29]

In this case, the state has clearly limited "the right of the individual to labor for such time as he may choose." It then becomes "a question of which of two powers or rights shall prevail—the power of the State to legislate or the right of the individual to liberty of person and freedom of contract." To answer that question, the Court must answer the further Peckham query: "Is this a fair, reasonable and appropriate exercise of the police power of the State, or is it an unreasonable, unnecessary and arbitrary interference with the right of the individual to his personal liberty or to enter into those contracts in relation to labor which may seem to him appropriate or necessary for the support of himself and his family?"[30]

The Peckham opinion had no doubt about the answer. In the first place, Justice Peckham asserted, the argument that "this act is valid as a labor law, pure and simple, may be dismissed in a few words." There is no reason for treating bakers differently from other employees and "the interest of the public is not in the slightest degree affected by such an act." Hence, "There is no reasonable ground for interfering with the liberty of person or the right of free contract, by determining the course of labor, in the occupation of a baker."[31]

In consequence, said Justice Peckham, if the law is to be upheld, it "must be . . . as a law pertaining to the health of the individual engaged in the occupation of a baker."[32] But the mere assertion that the subject relates to health is not enough. The relationship to public health must be direct enough for the Court to deem it reasonable.

The Peckham opinion found the required relationship to be lacking.

The trade of baker, in the Court's view, was not an unhealthy one, which would justify legislative interference with the right of contract. Of course, "almost all occupations more or less affect the health." Yet that alone does not mean that such occupations must be subject to any police power regulation on public health grounds. "There must be more than the mere fact of the possible existence of some small amount of unhealthiness to warrant legislative interference with liberty." Labor, in and of itself, may carry with it the seeds of unhealthiness. "But are we all, on that account, at the mercy of legislative majorities?"[33]

The Peckham conclusion is that the *Lochner* law "is not, within any fair meaning of the term, a health law, but is an illegal interference with the rights of individuals, both employers and employees, to make contracts regarding labor upon such terms as they may think best." Its real purpose was, not to protect health, but to have the state again assume "the position of a supervisor, or *pater familias,* over every act of the individual."[34]

To Peckham, the *Lochner* law was a reversion to the paternal role of government which he had condemned in his *Budd* opinion. "Statutes of the nature of that under review," he declared, "limiting the hours in which grown and intelligent men may labor to earn their living, are mere meddlesome interferences with the rights of the individual."[35]

Unfortunately, "This interference on the part of the legislatures of the several States with the ordinary trades and occupations of the people seems to be on the increase." Under the Peckham jurisprudence, however, these interferences cannot pass muster. Such attempts "simply to regulate the hours of labor between the master and his employees (all being men, *sui juris*), in a private business" must give way before "the right of free contract and the right to purchase and sell labor upon such terms as the parties may agree to." Hence the *Lochner* law must fall: "[T]he freedom of master and employee to contract with each other in relation to their employment, and in defining the same, cannot be prohibited or interfered with, without violating the Federal Constitution."[36]

Holmes Dissent

Aside from its use as the horrible example of what we now consider the wrong kind of judicial activism, *Lochner* is remembered today for its now-classic dissent by Justice Holmes, celebrated for its oft-quoted aphorisms. Indeed, the Holmes *Lochner* opinion is probably the most famous dissent ever written. "There is a famous passage," Justice Cardozo tells us, "where Matthew Arnold tells us how to separate the gold from the alloy in the coinage of the poets by the test of a few lines which we are to carry in our thoughts."[37] The flashing epigrams[38] in Holmes's *Lochner* dissent do the like for those who would apply the same test to law.

The *Lochner* dissent contains one of Justice Holmes's most famous statements: "General propositions do not decide concrete cases." Yet the Holmes dissent is based more upon general propositions than upon concrete rules or precedents. Indeed, Holmes begins with a broad proposition: "This case is decided upon an economic theory which a large part of the country does not entertain."[39] Holmes neither explains nor elaborates the charge.[40] Instead, he goes on to point out that the decision on economic grounds is not consistent with his conception of the judicial function. "If it were a question whether I agreed with that theory, I should desire to study it further and long before making up my mind. But I do not conceive that to be my duty, because I strongly believe that my agreement or disagreement has nothing to do with the right of a majority to embody their opinions in law."[41]

The dissent then strikes directly at the dominant conception, which equated the law with laissez faire. That conception is stated by Holmes as a paraphrase of Herbert Spencer's first principle:[42] "The liberty of the citizen to do as he likes so long as he does not interfere with the liberty of others to do the same." That may have been "a shibboleth for some well-known writers," but it "is interfered with by school laws, by the Post Office, by every state or municipal institution which takes his money . . . whether he likes it or not." Indeed, it is settled that "laws may regulate life in many ways which we as legislators might think as injudicious . . . as this, and which equally with this interfere with the liberty to contract."[43]

This leads Holmes to his best-known aphorism: "The Fourteenth Amendment does not enact Mr. Herbert Spencer's Social Statics."[44] This "general proposition" is supported by the "decisions cutting down the liberty to contract." Cited without discussion are the cases upholding a maximum-hours law for miners and prohibiting sales of stock on margin, as well as compulsory vaccination laws.[45] The lack of discussion is explained by the Holmes conviction that it is irrelevant whether the judges share the "convictions or prejudices" embodied in these laws:

> [A] constitution is not intended to embody a particular economic theory, whether of paternalism and the organic relation of the citizen to the State or of *laissez faire*. It is made for people of fundamentally differing views, and the accident of our finding certain opinions natural and familiar or novel and even shocking ought not to conclude our judgment upon the question whether statutes embodying them conflict with the Constitution of the United States.[46]

This proposition, Holmes indicates, may be an exception to his warning against "general propositions." As such, it supports the general Holmes approach to judicial review. "I think that the word liberty in the Fourteenth Amendment is perverted when it is held to prevent the natural outcome of a dominant opinion, unless it can be said that a rational and fair man necessarily would admit that the statute proposed would infringe fundamental principles as they have been understood by the traditions of our people and our law."[47]

A law such as that at issue is not be be invalidated unless it fails to meet this standard. "No such sweeping condemnation can be passed upon" the *Lochner* law. On the contrary, "A reasonable man might think it a proper measure on the score of health." That is all that is necessary for the conclusion that the law should be sustained. "Men whom I certainly could not pronounce unreasonable would uphold it."[48]

Judge Richard Posner asserts that the Holmes *Lochner* dissent would not have received a high grade in a law school examination: "It is not logically organized, does not join issue sharply with the majority, is not scrupulous in its treatment of the majority opinion or of precedent, is not thoroughly researched, does not exploit the factual record."[49] Certainly, the Holmes opinion is utterly unlike the present-day judicial product—all too often the work of law clerks for whom the acme of literary style is the law review article. The standard opinion style has become that of the reviews: colorless, prolix, platitudinous, always erring on the side of inclusion, full of lengthy citations and footnotes—and above all dull.[50]

The Holmes dissent is, of course, anything but dull. In fact, as Posner sums it up, it may not be "a *good* judicial opinion. It is merely the greatest judicial opinion of the last hundred years. To judge it by [the usual] standards is to miss the point. It is a rhetorical masterpiece."[51]

Scope of Review

There are indications that Justices Holmes and Peckham did not have high opinions of each other. Reference has been made to Holmes's deprecating comment when asked what Peckham was like intellectually.[52] On his side, Peckham was once asked by Chief Justice Fuller whether he was "willing to part with" the opinion in a case[53] to Holmes. Peckham answered, "I will part with it in spite of _____ _____ as Brother Harlan would say!" Harlan's well-known vituperation usually had a subject, and that of Peckham's blanks was undoubtedly Holmes.[54]

The difference between the two Justices in *Lochner* was, however, based on more than their possible personal antagonism. The Peckham and Holmes *Lochner* opinions represent two opposed conceptions of jurisprudence—the one that of the late nineteenth century, the other that of the coming legal era. In this respect there were two essential differences between the two antithetic approaches: (1) on the proper scope of judicial review; and (2) on the reliance upon economic theory by the reviewing court.

According to Justice Peckham, the question to be determined in cases involving challenges to *Lochner*-like legislation is: "Is this . . . fair, reasonable and appropriate . . . or is it an unreasonable, unnecessary and arbitrary interference with the right of the individual?"[55] Judge Posner asserts that the Holmes dissent does not really "take issue with the fundamental premise of the majority opinion, which is that unreasonable statutes violate the due process clause of the Fourteenth Amendment."[56] Instead, by his conclusion that a "reasonable man might think it a proper measure,"[57] Posner asserts, "Holmes seems to concede the majority's conclusion that the due process clause outlaws unreasonable legislation."[58]

Though Justices Peckham and Holmes both state a test of reasonableness, there is all the difference in the world between the Peckham and Holmes manner of applying the reasonableness test. The Peckham opinion indicated that the reasonableness of the challenged statute must be determined as an objective fact by the judge upon his own independent judgment. In holding the *Lochner* law invalid, the Court in effect substituted its judgment for that of the legislator and decided for itself that the statute was not reasonably related to any of the social ends for which the police power might validly be exercised. This interpretation of reasonableness, as an objective criterion to be determined by the judge himself, permeates the *Lochner* opinion.

The *Lochner* Court, in striking down a law whose reasonableness was, at a minimum, open to debate, in effect determined upon its own judgment whether such legislation was desirable. Such an approach was utterly inconsistent with the basic Holmes doctrine, which was one of judicial restraint. Justice Holmes himself once wrote: "On the economic side, I am mighty skeptical of hours of labor . . . regulation."[59] His personal opinion about the desirability of the law was, however, irrelevant under his theory of review. The "criterion," Holmes stated in a 1923 case, "is not whether we believe the law to be for the public good," but whether "a reasonable man reasonably might have that belief."[60] If the "character or effect" of a law "be debatable, the legislature is entitled to its own judgment, and that judgment is not to be superseded . . . by the personal opinion of judges, 'upon the issue which the legislature has decided.'"[61]

Under the Peckham approach, the desirability of a statute was determined as an objective fact by the Court on its own independent judgment. For Justice Holmes, a more subjective test was appropriate: Could rational legislators have regarded the statute as a reasonable method of reaching the desired result?[62] In the words of Holmes's leading judicial disciple, "It can never be emphasized too much that one's own opinion about the wisdom or evil of a law should be excluded altogether when one is doing one's duty on the bench. The only opinion of our own even looking in that direction that is material is our opinion whether legislators could in reason have enacted such a law."[63]

Reliance on Economic Theory

The other fundamental Peckham–Holmes difference was on the reliance on economic theory by the Court in its review of the *Lochner* law. The Holmes assertion that the case was "decided upon an economic theory" was the opening salvo in the twentieth-century approach to review of regulatory action. According to Sir Frederick Pollock, what Holmes was saying here was "that it is no business of the Supreme Court of the United States to dogmatize on social or economic theories."[64] The *Lochner* Court struck down the statute as unreasonable because a majority of the Justices disagreed with the economic theory on which the state legislature had acted. This was precisely the approach to judicial review that Justice Holmes rejected. There may, in the given case, be economic arguments against a challenged regulatory law. To Holmes, however, such arguments were properly addressed to the legislature, not to the judges.

As the Court put it half a century later, after the Holmes posture had become the accepted one, it is improper for the courts "to strike down state laws, regulatory of business and industrial conditions, because they may be unwise, improvident, or out of harmony with a particular school of thought."[65] It is not for the judge to intervene because he disagrees with the economic theory upon which a law is based. "Whether the legislature takes for its textbook Adam Smith, Herbert Spencer, Lord Keynes, or some other is no concern of ours."[66]

According to Justice Peckham, however, that is exactly what should be the concern of a reviewing court. If a law is based upon what the judge considers an unsound economic theory, the judge should hold the law invalid. And there is no doubt that Peckham considered the *Lochner*-type law to be, at the least, unsound.

Lochner has become so discredited that we forget that, in his own day, Justice Peckham was considered a good judge (he had been recommended for Chief Justice in a letter to President Cleveland by Melville W. Fuller, before the latter was appointed to the position).[67] In addition Peckham was representative of the dominant legal thought at the beginning of the century. To such a jurist, *Lochner* was correct both in its rationale and result, since the statute violated the fundamental proposition upon which his jurisprudence was grounded: that of law designed to ensure the unfettered operation of the market and the freedom of contract that was its foundation.

The law to Peckham was based upon what the New York court had stressed as "the unceasing struggle for success and existence which pervades all societies of men." But the operation of the evolutionary struggle must not be interfered with by government. "Such governmental interferences disturb the normal adjustments of the social fabric, and usually derange the delicate and complicated machinery of industry and cause a score of ills while attempting the removal of one."[68]

Justice Peckham followed a similar approach. As he saw it, the "liberty" protected by the law "is deemed to embrace the right of man to be free in the enjoyment of the faculties with which he has been endowed by his Creator, subject only to such restraints as are necessary"—here, too, a paraphrase of Herbert Spencer's first principle.[69] This principle was plainly violated by the *Lochner* law.

To Justice Peckham, the regulation of bakery hours was a deviation from the evolutionary progress that underlay his conception of law. It was a reversion to the paternalism of an earlier day. "The paternal theory of government" was as odious to the *Lochner* majority as it was to Justice Brewer.[70] "The utmost possible liberty to the individual, and the fullest possible protection to him and his property, is both the limitation and duty of government."[71] To judges who adopted this philosophy, the "liberty" protected by law became synonymous with no interference with economic activities. "For years," Justice Douglas was later to explain, "the Court struck down social legislation when a particular law did not fit the notions of a majority of Justices as to legislation appropriate for a free enterprise system."[72] Any other posture, to judges like Justice Peckham, would have meant a reversion to the paternalistic theory of government that had been repudiated by "the more correct ideas [of] the present day."[73]

Rehabilitating *Lochner?*

A word remains to be said about a surprising sequel to the *Lochner* story that, not too long ago, few would have anticipated. Those who were to change the course of jurisprudence as the twentieth century went on "repeated to one another, as creed, . . . Justice Holmes's dissenting opinion in *Lochner.*"[74] By midcentury, the once-heretic creed had become accepted doctrine; *Lochner* appeared to be as repudiated as *Dred Scott.* Indeed, not long ago, Justice John Paul Stevens declared, "When the Court repudiated the line of cases that is often identified with *Lochner v. New York,* it did so in strong language that . . . seemed to foreclose forever any suggestion that the due process clause of the fourteenth amendment gave any power to federal judges to pass on the substance of the work product of state legislatures."[75]

To Stevens, as to other commentators, the post-*Lochner* jurisprudence "seemed to foreclose" any possible *Lochner* revival. And so it appeared until recently, when a number of jurists have sought to accomplish the result stated in the title of a 1985 article: "Rehabilitating Lochner."[76] They argue that even if Justice Holmes was correct in his claim that *Lochner* was decided upon the Court's own economic theory, that need not mean that the decision was wrong. On the contrary, these jurists urge, the *Lochner* Justices were doing only what judicial review requires when they invalidated the law because it was based upon what they considered an incorrect economic theory.

Perhaps the most influential writer to support the economic theory behind *Lochner* is Judge Posner. He notes that the prevailing view in recent years has been that *Lochner* and similar decisions earlier in the century "reflected a weak grasp of economics."[77] According to Posner, however, it is the economic analysis that led to the *Lochner* statute that was seriously flawed.

To Judge Posner, laws like that in *Lochner* "were attempts to suppress competition under the guise of promoting the general welfare."[78] Such attempts are all but heresy to advocates of present-day Chicago School economics, which Posner himself has done so much to translate into legal doctrine. That school has never reconciled itself to the fact that, in this century, the "invisible hand" of Adam Smith has increasingly been replaced by the "public interest" as defined in regulatory legislation and administration. To the Chicago School, the overriding goal of law, as of economics, should be that of efficiency. The law should intervene "to reprehend only that which is inefficient," and even then the law's role should be limited, since the "market punishes inefficiency faster and better than the machinery of the law."[79]

Such an approach would turn the legal clock back to *Lochner*. The primary criterion for those, like Judge Posner, who see economics as the foundation of law is efficiency and to them efficiency is best promoted by the free operation of the market. Thus they are drawn inevitably to the *Lochner* rationale—that governmental interference with the market promotes inefficiency and must normally be considered arbitrary. We are thus brought back to the law at the turn of the century, when cases like *Lochner* set the pattern for judicial reception of laws that attempted to curb the excesses and abuses of a completely unrestrained market.

Judge Posner writes that he "was the first to suggest that the discredited 'liberty of contract' doctrine could be given a solid economic foundation and as good a jurisprudential basis as the Supreme Court's aggressive modern decisions protecting civil liberties." Nevertheless, Posner denies advocating the *Lochner* approach, declaring, "I have never believed, however, that such a restoration of the '*Lochner* era' . . . would be, on balance, sound constitutional law."[80] The denial is disingenuous. The Posner approach lends direct support to the effort to take our public law back to *Lochner*. With efficiency and wealth maximization as its end and the market as the instrument through which it is achieved, Posnerian jurisprudence leads to what Posner himself terms the constitutionalization of laissez faire.[81]

Though it was uniformly thought that the verdict of history was resoundingly against *Lochner*, it thus now appears that the jury may still be out. Yet the accepted judgment on the Peckham–Holmes disagreement has surely been correct. The primary effect of the Peckham approach was to immunize the economy from interference by the machinery of law. To a judge like Peckham, *Lochner* did not involve control of legislation in the abstract. Court control was directed to a particular purpose—the invalidation of legislation that conflicted with the doctrine of laissez faire that dominated thinking at the turn of the century.[82] What Justice Frankfurter termed "the shibboleths of a pre-machine age . . . were reflected in juridical assumptions that survived the facts on which they were based. . . . Basic human rights expressed by the constitutional conception of 'liberty' were equated with theories of *laissez-faire*."[83] The result was that the law became the rallying point for judicial resistance to the efforts to control the excesses and relieve the oppressions of the rising industrial economy.[84]

Almost a century later, we tend to forget how inadequate the law was at the time of *Lochner*. To return to the Peckham conception of law is to return to a time when "it was unconstitutional to intrude upon the inalienable right of employees to make contracts containing terms unfavorable to themselves, in bargains with their employers." In those days, "[a]n ordinary worker was told, if he sought to avoid harsh contracts made with his employer . . . that he had acted with his eyes open, had only himself to blame, must stand on his own feet, must take the consequences of his own folly."[85] And if, as in *Lochner,* a law sought to equalize the situation, it was ruled an invalid interference with freedom of contract. To return to *Lochner* is to return to the abuses that inevitably accompany unrestricted laissez faire. Few today will agree that such a return is desirable.

From a broader point of view, Justice Holmes was surely correct in repudiating the Peckham concept that the judge should decide on the basis of the economic theory that he deems correct. The judge qua economist will inevitably write his own economic views into the Constitution, and, as Holmes once put it, all too often on the basis "of the economic doctrines which prevailed about fifty years ago."[86]

If we have learned anything in this century, however, it is that judges should not substitute their economic judgments for those of the legislature. What Justice Holmes told his fellow judges is still as valid as it ever was—that the Constitution was not "intended to give us *carte blanche* to embody our economic . . . beliefs in its prohibitions."[87] "Otherwise," as Holmes put it in his first Supreme Court opinion, "a constitution, instead of embodying only relatively fundamental rules of right, . . . would become the partisan of a particular set of . . . economical opinions, which by no means are held *semper ubique et ab omnibus.*"[88] The economic theory behind a law should continue to be primarily a question for the legislator, not the judge. Provided that they have a rational basis, it is the judge's duty to enforce even "laws that I believe to embody economic mistakes."[89]

"Judges," reads another famous Holmes passage, "are apt to be Naif, simpleminded men."[90] This was particularly true of a judge like Justice Peckham when he used his conception of economics as his legal compass. The result in *Lochner* was that the Constitution was virtually treated as a legal sanction of the Survival of the Fittest.

That result will be avoided only if the courts follow the Holmes approach and reject the view that their notions of economics should override the economic theory upon which the legislature acted. Today, as in Holmes's day, the proper posture is for the judge to say that even though "speaking as a political economist, I should agree in condemning the law, still I should not be willing to think myself authorized to overturn legislation on that ground, unless I thought that an honest difference of opinion was impossible, or pretty nearly so."[91]

9

White and Taft Courts, 1910–1930

William Howard Taft, the only man who was both President and Chief Justice, once said that the Supreme Court was his notion of what heaven must be like. This led Justice Frankfurter to say that "he had a very different notion of heaven than any I know anything about."[1]

If the Supreme Court early in this century was not "heaven," it certainly had attained a preeminent rank in the American polity. In this respect, there was a quantum difference between the Supreme Court and all other courts in the country. Before his elevation to the supreme bench, Benjamin N. Cardozo was for many years a distinguished member and chief of New York's highest tribunal. With the perspective gained from judicial service in both Albany and Washington, he could note acutely a basic difference between the highest courts of state and nation. The New York Court of Appeals, he said, "is a great common law court; its problems are lawyer's problems. But the Supreme Court is occupied chiefly with statutory construction—which no man can make interesting—and with politics."[2] Of course, as Justice Robert H. Jackson pointed out, in this statement, the word "politics" is used in no sense of partisanship but in the sense of policy-making.[3]

The transition from a state court, eminent though it may be, to the supreme tribunal in Washington is more than mere promotion to a higher judicial body. When Cardozo came to Washington, he left what was, without a doubt, the greatest common-law court in the land; it dealt essentially with the questions of private law that are the preoccupation and delectation of most lawyers. The Court to which he came was not, and has not been, since the time of John Marshall, the usual type of law court. Public, not private, law is the stuff of Supreme Court litigation. Elevation to that tribunal requires the judge to make the adjustment from preoccupation with the restricted, however novel, problems of private litigation to the most exacting demands of judicial statesmanship.

It is the fact that the Supreme Court is more than the usual law court that makes its work of vital significance to more than a relatively small number of jurists. The Court is primarily a political institution, in whose keeping lies the destiny of a mighty nation. Its decrees mark the boundaries between the great departments of government; upon its action depend the proper functioning of federalism and the scope to be given to the rights of the individual.

A judge on such a tribunal has an opportunity to leave his imprint upon the life of the nation as no mere master of the common law possibly could. Only a handful of men in all our history have made so manifest a mark on their own age and on ages still to come as did Justice Holmes.[4] The same cannot be said of even the greatest of modern English judges. To be a judge, endowed with all the omnipotence of justice, is certainly among life's noblest callings; but the mere common-law judge, even in a preeminently legal polity like that in Britain, cannot begin to compare in power and prestige with a Justice of our Supreme Court. A judge who is regent over what is done in the legislative and executive branches—the deus ex machina who has the final word in the constitutional system—has attained one of the ultimates of human authority.

"Mr. Taft Has Rehabilitated the Supreme Court"

President Taft devoted more attention to the choice of Justices than any other President. Taft had been Solicitor General and a circuit judge and was fully aware of the importance of judicial appointments. He himself appreciated the need for changes in the now-aged Fuller Court. "The condition of the Supreme Court is pitiable," Taft wrote soon after his election, "and yet those old fools hold on with a tenacity that is most discouraging."[5]

The new President was soon given the opportunity virtually to remake the Court. He was given his first chance a half year after he took office in 1909 when Justice Peckham died. Taft chose his old friend and former circuit court colleague, Horace H. Lurton of Tennessee. It is, as Taft's biographer points out, illogical that, having deplored the senility of the highest Court only four months earlier, the President should have appointed a judge who was almost sixty-six.[6] But the friendship, born of years of service together on the circuit court, overrode the fact that Lurton was the oldest ever to ascend to the Court. Taft himself wrote that "there was nothing that I had so much at heart in my whole administration as

Lurton's appointment."[7] Lurton was a mediocre judge who turned out to be a mediocre Justice. He served only five years and contributed little to Supreme Court jurisprudence.

The same was not true of Taft's second appointee, Charles Evans Hughes. His is, of course, one of the great names in Supreme Court history, for he was to preside over the Court during one of its most crucial periods. That was, however, to be two decades later, when he was to be appointed a second time to fill the Court's center chair. In 1910, when he took the place of Justice Brewer on the latter's death, Hughes was Governor of New York. He had gone into politics after a successful career at the Bar and as a legislative investigator. He had been a possible presidential candidate and had declined the vice presidential nomination in 1908. Hughes resigned from the Court in 1916 to accept the Republican nomination for the Presidency.

When he appointed Hughes, President Taft indicated in a letter to his nominee that he would choose him as Chief Justice should that position become vacant. The vacancy occurred only two months later, when Chief Justice Fuller died even before Hughes had taken his seat on the bench. But Hughes was not to receive the appointment. Taft gave "prayerful consideration" to the matter for months and then, swayed in part by the preference of the Justices as reported to him by the Attorney General, promoted Justice Edward D. White to the Chief Justiceship.[8] "Hughes is young enough to wait," said the President, "and if he makes good on the bench I may yet be able to appoint him.[9]

The new Chief Justice had been a more than competent Justice for sixteen years. As Justice Frankfurter later recalled, White "looked the way a Justice of the Supreme Court should look. . . . He was tall and powerful. I think a jowl also helps a Justice of the Supreme Court, and White had an impressive jowl."[10]

White had served on the Southern side in the Civil War. Frankfurter tells us that this was a factor in his appointment: "Taft was glad to appoint . . . White as Chief Justice because White had been a Confederate . . . to make a Confederate, an ex-Confederate—are Confederates ever 'ex'?—Chief Justice was something that could contribute much, even then, so Taft thought, and I believe rightly, to the cohesion of our national life."[11]

Despite the Frankfurter aside, White was an "ex-Confederate" who had completely changed his views during what he was to call "the anguish, more appalling than the calamity of the war"[12] of the Reconstruction period. "My God," he later said in horror-stricken tones of the Confederate cause, "my God, if we had succeeded."[13] At any rate, it was Chief Justice White, the ex-Confederate plantation owner from the Deep South, who was to write the first opinions vindicating the black right to vote and to live in predominantly white areas.[14]

After he had been in office a year and a half, President Taft wrote with satisfaction to his half-brother, "I shall have the appointment of probably a majority of the Supreme Court before the end of my term, which, in view of the present agitation in respect to the Constitution, is very important."[15] As it turned out, Taft was able to appoint five Justices and the new Chief Justice.

When Chief Justice White's nomination went to the Senate it was accompanied by two nominations for Associate Justice: Willis Van Devanter of Wyoming and Joseph R. Lamar of Georgia, chosen to succeed White as a Justice and Justice Moody, whom ill health forced to resign in 1910. Van Devanter had been the first Chief Justice of his state's highest court, though he soon resigned to return to a lucrative practice. He later served as Assistant Attorney General and a circuit judge. Van Devanter was to be on the Court for twenty-six years. He is remembered now primarily for his role as one of the "Nine Old Men" who struck down much of Franklin D. Roosevelt's New Deal legislation. To his associates in the White and Taft Courts, however, he was a most valuable colleague. Chief Justice Taft was later to say his "mainstay in the court is Van Devanter."[16]

Van Devanter illustrates how a Justice can play an important role in the Court, belying a poor public reputation. "Mr. Justice Van Devanter," says Justice Frankfurter, "is a man who plays an important role in the history of the Court, though you cannot find it adequately reflected in the opinions written by him because he wrote so few."[17] Van Devanter was afflicted with what one of his colleagues describes as "pen paralysis." On the other hand, Chief Justice Hughes was to recall years later, "his careful and elaborate statements in conference . . . were of the greatest value. If these statements had been taken down stenographically, they would have served with little editing as excellent opinions. His perspicacity and common sense made him a trusted advisor in all sorts of matters. Chief Justice White leaned heavily upon him and so did Chief Justice Taft."[18]

Justice Lamar, appointed at the same time as White and Van Devanter, had been a successful corporation lawyer and member of Georgia's highest court. A tall Southern patrician with silver hair, Lamar was said by the *New York Times* to look both the scholar and the judge.[19] He died in 1916; his tenure of less than five terms was too short to make a mark. Today, in Supreme Court history, Lamar remains a cipher who, according to one commentator, "is remembered, if at all, only by his grandchildren."[20]

The last of the Taft appointees was Mahlon Pitney, then Chancellor of New Jersey, chosen in 1912 on the death of Justice Harlan. His appointment was opposed in the Senate because of allegedly antilabor decisions in the state court. Justice Pitney served until 1922, when a stroke forced him to retire. On the Court, Pitney was, according to one summary, "a respectable judge . . . without sign or promise of distinction."[21] As Holmes later put it, "He had not wings and was not a thunderbolt, but he was a very honest hard working Judge."[22]

President Taft expected his appointments to confirm the Court's conservative balance. His new Court majority consoled him with the realization that the six staunch conservatives would protect the Constitution from the attacks leveled by Theodore Roosevelt and his new Progressive party. The duty of the Court, Taft had written to Justice Moody, was to "preserve the fundamental structure of our government as our fathers gave it to us."[23] The sound men he had appointed would ensure the needed preservation. Well might Joseph H. Choate, the leading conservative lawyer of the day, boast at a dinner in the President's honor, "Mr. Taft has rehabilitated the Supreme Court."[24]

That it did not quite work out as the President had planned was due in large part to circumstances beyond anyone's control. Speaking of his Court appointees, Taft told reporters, "I have said to them, 'Damn you, if any of you die, I'll disown you.'"[25] But die or retire most of them did. Except for Justice Van Devanter, Taft's appointees as Justices served only four, six, and ten years and Chief Justice White sat for only ten years.

Under the new Chief Justice, the atmosphere within the Court became noticeably less rigid. Before his Court appointment, White's career had been more in politics than law and he remained, in Holmes's phrase, "naturally a politician and a speaker."[26] Chief Justice Hughes later recalled that White "was most considerate and gracious in his dealings with every member of the Court, plainly anxious to create an atmosphere of friendliness and to promote agreement in the disposition of cases."[27] In particular, the new Chief Justice, perhaps influenced by his senatorial experience, conducted conferences with much less restraint—allowing freer discussion and being, as Holmes was to note, less inclined "to stop the other side when the matter seems clear to all of us."[28] The result was a more relaxed Court, which was greatly appreciated by its members, who, as Hughes put it, "became a reasonably happy family."[29]

However, the family's material condition continued to be that of genteel poverty. The Court continued to sit in the old Senate Chamber that had been its home since 1860. As time went on, it became ever more apparent that the courtroom was scarcely suitable for the highest bench in the land. First of all, as Justice Frankfurter once said, "It was a small room, you know,"[30] badly ventilated and poorly lighted. The conference room in the Capitol basement was even worse. As Chief Justice Hughes remembered it. "[T]he room became overheated and the air foul . . . not conducive to good humor." Hughes complained, "I suppose that no high court in the country had fewer conveniences."[31]

Yet many of the Justices were attached to the old courtroom and deemed its location in the Capitol an important plus. The Court may have been barren in physical facilities, but its atmosphere was rich in dignity and tradition. President Taft wanted to initiate construction of a Supreme Court building. Chief Justice White resisted the idea; he feared that the public would lose interest in the Court if it left the Capitol.[32] Indeed, after the Court finally moved out of its cramped Capitol quarters in 1935 to the marble temple in which it now sits, a Justice was to refer longingly to "that wonderful old courtroom in the Capitol, which I think it was almost a desecration of tradition to leave."[33]

At the time of the White Court, no office space was provided for the Justices. They all had to write their opinions and do their research at home, providing their own working space for themselves and their secretaries. Since 1886, the Justices had been provided with $2,000 a year to pay a secretary or clerk. Most of the Justices hired stenographer-typists. Thus Justice Hughes hired three young lawyers during his first brief Court tenure. He later recalled, "I kept them busy with dictation, hating to write in longhand," and, referring to research, "whatever was necessary in that line I did myself." In a prescient passage, Hughes also noted "that if we had experienced law clerks, it might be thought that they were writing our opinions."[34] Though some Justices, notably Gray and his successor Holmes, hired law clerks rather than stenographers, it was not until 1919 that Congress provided specifically for law clerks in addition to secretarial assistance.

The improved atmosphere in the White Court could not lighten what Chief Justice Taft was to call the "exhausting character"[35] of the ever-growing docket. The cases docketed showed a steady augmentation, and each term ended with the Court increasingly in arrears. Justice Louis D. Brandeis asked former Justice Hughes, who had returned to practice, whether he did not envy Brandeis's coming summer vacation. "Not at the price you have to pay for it," was Hughes's answer.[36]

Rule of Reason

When Chief Justice White took his seat, there was the usual mass of matters on the docket. Among them were cases on what a commentator called "the main question of the day"—"the regulation by law of corporate activity in its relation to the country at large."[37] To the public and the profession, the greatest of these were the landmark Sherman Act cases.

Harper's noted that a number of Supreme Court decisions had "been awaited with country-wide suspense and attention." Nevertheless, none of them had "caused the market and the whole industrial and commercial world to pause more perceptibly than have the cases of the Government against the Standard Oil Company and the American Tobacco Company. They came to be known simply as the Trust Cases. For months the financial markets have virtually stood still awaiting their settlement."[38]

The key decision in the *Trust Cases*[39] arose out of the Government's prosecution of the Standard Oil Company under the Sherman Act. The lower court had found the great oil monopoly in violation of the Act and had ordered its dissolution. A unanimous Supreme Court upheld the dissolution ruling. Yet, ironically, though the Government won the case, it had to accept an interpretation of the Sherman Act which greatly reduced that law's effectiveness. The Court ruled that Standard Oil's practices constituted "unreasonable" restraint of trade prohibited by the Sherman Act, rather than the type of "reasonable" restraint which the Act permitted. Thus was born "the most curious *obiter dictum* ever indulged in by the

Supreme Court"[40]—the so-called *rule of reason* in antitrust cases: "[I]n every case where it is claimed that an act or acts are in violation of the statute the rule of reason . . . must be applied."[41]

The rule of reason was almost entirely the handiwork of Chief Justice White; Justice Holmes called White's "invention of the rule of reason . . . [t]he Chief Justice's greatest dialectical coup."[42] Certainly it was the principal legal legacy of White's Court tenure. In practice, it greatly restricted the scope of the Sherman Act and made prosecutions under it more difficult. At the same time, it greatly increased the judicial role in Sherman Act cases and ensured that our antitrust law, based though it might be on enactments by Congress, would still be primarily judge-made law.

Justice Harlan delivered a typically strong dissent, which Chief Justice Hughes later recalled as "a passionate outburst seldom if ever equaled in the annals of the Court."[43] To Harlan, the Court's action was an example of "the tendency to judicial legislation . . . [t]he most alarming tendency of this day, in my judgment, so far as the safety and integrity of our institutions are concerned." Here, the Court was led "to so construe the Constitution or the statutes as to mean what they want it to mean." The result was "that the courts may by mere judicial construction amend the Constitution . . . or an Act of Congress."[44]

All the same it was difficult to disagree with a decision that asserted that it was only interpreting a law "by the light of reason."[45] Justice Holmes pointed this out in his comment to a law clerk about the White *Standard Oil* opinion: "The moment I saw that in the circulated draft, I knew he had us. How could you be against that without being for a rule of unreason?"[46]

A Progressive Court?

Writing in 1912, Felix Frankfurter asserted that "the fate of social legislation in this country rests ultimately with our judges."[47] In the White Court there were conflicting currents in the judicial attitude to what a magazine termed "the main question" of the day—"the regulation by law of corporate activity."[48] To supporters of the laissez-faire jurisprudence of the Fuller Court, there were disturbing tendencies in some of its successor's decisions. In a 1913 article, "The Progressiveness of the United States Supreme Court,"[49] Charles Warren noted that few recent social and economic laws had been invalidated by the Court. Instead, the Court upheld laws drastically changing the rules governing employer liability as well as wage and hour laws.[50]

By the beginning of this century, the failure of the common law to provide adequately for workers' injuries had made reform efforts inevitable. In 1908, a federal statute abolished the fellow-servant rule and restricted the defenses of contributory negligence and assumption of risk. An opinion by Justice Van Devanter for a unanimous Court upheld the statute[51]—though, as a Van Devanter letter informs us, "there had there-tofore been pronounced differences of opinion" among the Justices.[52]

The 1908 statute, however, was at most a partial remedy. As Justice Brandeis later wrote, "[N]o system of indemnity dependent upon fault on the employers' part could meet the situation."[53] What was needed was a complete transformation of tort law, with its essential element the elimina-tion of the rule "that fault is requisite to liability."[54] The needed reform was provided by workmen's compensation laws, enacted in almost half the states by the time White became Chief Justice. Workmen's compensation involved a rejection of fault as the basis for liability; instead, liability was based on the concept of protection of individuals from the consequences of industrial accidents, regardless of culpability on their part. The fundamen-tal principle is that of liability without fault, with recovery provided for all injuries arising out of and in the course of employment. The result, as Justice Holmes pointed out, is that the pain and mutilation incident to production is thrown upon the employer in the first instance and the public in the long run.[55]

The Court, most of whose members were still set in conservative laissez-faire beliefs, found the *Arizona Employers' Liability Cases (1919)*,[56] in which a state workmen's compensation law was challenged, difficult to decide. Liability without fault by legislative decree was something the Chief Justice along with Justices McKenna, Van Devanter, and McReynolds could not accept. In the words of the latter Justice's dissent, "As a measure to stifle enterprise, produce discontent, strife, idleness, and pauperism, the outlook for the enactment seems much too good."[57]

Nevertheless, a bare majority voted to uphold the law. The opinion was assigned to Justice Holmes, but he wrote one of such "sweeping generality"[58] that he lost the majority. According to Holmes, Justices Pitney and Day "thought there was danger in this op. and P wrote what none of his majority could disagree with."[59] Pitney's draft became the opinion of the Court and Holmes's, which "was thought too strong by some of the majority,"[60] became a concurrence.

Despite his famous aphorism against general propositions,[61] the Holmes opinion was based upon the "general proposition that immunity from liability when not in fault is [not] a right inherent in free govern-ment."[62] The Pitney opinion of the Court was more pedestrian, stressing the limitations of review power: the courts should not consider the wisdom of legislation, and the novelty of the statutory scheme "is not a constitutional objection."[63] The important thing, however, is not the lack of sparkle in the Pitney opinion but the fact that the Court upheld a law which sought to protect labor by making such drastic inroads into the principle that was still widely seen as "of the very foundation of right—of the essence of liberty as it is of morals—to be free from liability if one is free from fault."[64]

Even more significant in the White Court's "progressive" decisions were decisions upholding maximum-hour laws. First came a 1917 decision on the Adamson Act, which Congress had enacted to avert a railroad strike. Among its provisions was the requirement of an eight-hour day for railroad workers. The provision was sustained in an opinion by Chief Justice White that stressed the plenary congressional power over interstate commerce—particularly its power to deal with a strike that would interrupt commerce.[65] As Justice Holmes summarized it, the Court "went the whole unicorn as to the power of Congress."[66] The case was thus one on the commerce power, not the police power to regulate hours. "I think," Holmes wrote explaining the decision, "if Congress can weave the cloth it can spin the thread."[67]

Bunting v. Oregon,[68] decided later the same year, did decide the police power issue, for it involved the constitutionality of an Oregon law limiting the hours of work in manufacturing establishments to ten hours a day. Felix Frankfurter, who presented the case for the law, later recalled a dramatic moment in the argument: "During the course of the argument McReynolds said to me, 'Ten hours! Ten hours! Ten! Why not four?' . . . in his snarling, sneering way. . . . I moved down towards him and said, 'Your honor, if by chance I may make such a hypothesis, if your physician should find that you're eating too much meat, it isn't necessary for him to urge you to become a vegetarian.'"

According to Frankfurter, "Holmes said, 'Good for you!' very embarrassingly right from the bench. He loathed these arguments that if you go this far you must go further. 'Good for you!' Loud. Embarrassingly."[69]

To the Court that had decided *Lochner, Bunting* would have been an even easier case. But two things had happened since *Lochner* was decided. In 1908, *Muller v. Oregon*[70] had upheld a maximum-hours law for women. The Justices had been persuaded by Louis D. Brandeis's famous argument and even-more-famous brief that, unlike the situation in *Lochner,* there was a direct correlation between hours worked by women and their health. Hence a law limiting the hours worked by women was valid, even though, under *Lochner,* a maximum-hours law for all bakery employees was not. Yet, though *Muller* was thus based upon the need to protect women, it was but a short step for its reasoning to be used to justify similar laws to protect all workers.

In addition, the personnel of the Court had changed substantially since *Lochner.* Only the Chief Justice and Justices McKenna, Holmes, and Day remained, and all but McKenna had been dissenters in *Lochner.* As it turned out, McKenna was the key Justice in *Bunting.* It has been said that McKenna was all but "mesmerized" by the brilliant Brandeis presentation in *Muller v. Oregon.*[71] Though, as seen,[72] he had played a key role in the *Lochner* decision process, Justice McKenna now voted to uphold maximum-hours regulation under the Adamson Act and in *Bunting.* More than that, he delivered the opinion of the court upholding the Oregon law.

The *Bunting* opinion ignored *Lochner.* It did not cite the case or even refer to the freedom of contract issue that had been so crucial to the *Lochner* decision. Instead, the opinion assumed the correctness of the *Muller* finding that a law regulating the hours of service was a health law, since "it is injurious to their health for them to work . . . more than ten hours in any one day." The argument the other way was summarily rejected: "The record contains no facts to support the contention."[73]

Bunting in effect overruled *Lochner,* though sub silentio. Why it did so was intimated in the only pregnant portion of the otherwise pedestrian McKenna opinion: "New policies are usually tentative in their beginnings, advance in firmness as they advance in acceptance. . . . Time may be necessary to fashion them to precedent customs and conditions, and as they justify themselves or otherwise they pass from militancy to triumph."[74] Maximum-hour laws had gone through this process; the "new policies" upon which they were based had gone from the *Lochner* rejection to the *Bunting* triumph.

Child Labor Case

The decisions just discussed may have demonstrated, as Charles Warren called it in his already-mentioned article, the "progressiveness" of the White Court. But they were more than balanced by decisions restricting the rights of labor[75] and, most of all, by that in *Hammer v. Dagenhart* (1918),[76] usually known as the *Child Labor Case.* Most commentators today place that case with *Lochner* on the list of discredited Supreme Court decisions.

In the *Child Labor Case,* a federal statute prohibited transportation in interstate commerce of goods made in factories that employed children. Though the statute did not in terms interfere with local production or manufacturing, its real purpose was to suppress child labor. With goods produced by children denied their interstate market, child labor could not continue upon a widespread scale. To the majority of the Court, the congressional purpose rendered the law invalid. Congress was seeking primarily to regulate the manner in which manufacturing was carried on; such manufacturing under the restrictive meaning of the Court in cases like the already-discussed *Sugar Trust Case*[77] was not commerce which could be reached by federal authority. Congress could not, even by an act whose terms were specifically limited to regulation of commerce, use its commerce power to exert authority over matters like manufacturing, which were not, within the Court's restricted notion, commerce.

Justice Holmes wrote just after the decision that he thought it "ill timed and regrettable."[78] This led him to deliver a dissent that stands second only to that delivered by him in *Lochner.* Holmes explained his dissent in a letter: "I said that as the law unquestionably regulated interstate commerce it was within the power of Congress no matter what its indirect effect on matters within the regulation of the states, or how obviously that effect was intended."[79]

The Holmes dissent emphasized the distressing effect of the Court's decision. "If there is any matter," asserted Holmes, "upon which civilized countries have agreed . . . it is the evil of premature and excessive child labor."[80] Yet the practical result of the decision was to render effective regulation of child labor all but impossible. In a country like the United States, if a practice like child labor is to be dealt with effectually, it must be by national regulation. By rigidly excluding Congress from exercising regulatory authority, the *Child Labor Case* virtually decreed that child labor should be left only to whatever controls were afforded by the workings of an unrestrained system of laissez faire. The United States alone, among nations, was precluded from taking effective action against an evil so widely censured by civilized opinion.

Chief Justice Taft and His Court

"There is nothing I would have loved more than being chief justice of the United States," President Taft told his Attorney General as he signed Chief Justice White's commission. "I cannot help seeing the irony in the fact that I, who desired that office so much, should now be signing the commission of another man."[81]

However, Chief Justice White died in May 1921. A month later, President Harding appointed Taft to what he had called only two months earlier "the position, which I would rather have than any other in the world."[82] Taft began his new judicial career at an age when most men are about to retire; he was sixty-four when he was appointed. "I am older and slower and less acute," Taft wrote.[83] Despite this, he was an effective Chief Justice. Even those who criticize the conservatism that permeated his jurisprudence concede that he brought a needed leadership to the highest Court.

Felix Frankfurter tells how Justice Brandeis once said to him, "It's very difficult for me to understand why a man who is so good a Chief Justice . . . could have been so bad as President. How do you explain that?" Frankfurter replied, "The explanation is very simple. He loathed being President and being Chief Justice was all happiness for him."[84]

There is no doubt that Taft was, in his biographer's phrase, "a happy man" as Chief Justice.[85] The Chief Justiceship was to him the ultimate compensation for the unhappiness of his years in the White House. Of course, Taft was the very paradigm of the genial politician—in Frankfurter's phrase, "instinctively genial, with great warmth, and a capacity to inspire feelings of camaraderie about him."[86] More than that, he proved in the Court what he had failed to be in the White House—a strong leader. As Chief Justice, Taft wielded greater authority than any of his predecessors since Taney. He met the criterion for a Chief Justice stated in one of his letters of "leadership in the Conferences, in the statement of the cases, and especially with respect to applications for certiorari."[87]

Justice Holmes summed up the situation under the new Chief Justice: [W]ith the present C.J. things go as smoothly as possible." That was particularly true of the Court conferences. According to Holmes, "The meetings are perhaps pleasanter than I have ever known them—thanks largely to the C.J." Before, Holmes wrote, the Justices at conference "regarded a difference of opinion as a cockfight," but now "the Chief's way of conducting business" results in "keeping things moving."[88] Taft was stricter than his predecessors in controlling the conference discussion. As Holmes said, "[T]he C.J. inclines more than Fuller or White to stop the other side when the matter seems clear . . . , which I think is a good thing."[89] At any rate, Holmes wrote to Taft in 1925, "never before . . . have we gotten along with so little jangling and dissension."[90]

A large part of the Chief Justice's success in this respect was due to the fact that he had colleagues on the Court who were congenial to his conservative views. The majority who had decided the *Child Labor Case* were still on the bench, except for Chief Justice White, whom Taft himself had succeeded. It is true that Justices Day, Pitney, and Clarke were soon replaced, since they resigned or retired from the Court in 1922. But they were replaced by men who were, if anything, even more conservative. Day's seat was taken by Pierce Butler of Minnesota, Pitney's by Edward T. Sanford of Tennessee, and Clarke's by Senator George Sutherland of Utah.

Justice Sanford was, in the characterization of a biographer, an undistinguished conservative Justice who generally followed the lead of the Chief Justice.[91] To such an extent was this carried that Sanford died on the same day as Taft. Justice Sutherland replaced the more liberal Justice Clarke, who had dissented in the *Child Labor Case*. After Sutherland's appointment, Woodrow Wilson wrote to Clarke about his successor, "In my few dealings with Mr. Justice Sutherland I have seen no reason to suspect him of either principles or brains."[92] This was not entirely fair. Sutherland was a better than average spokesman for his conservative views. Both he and Justice Butler are today remembered primarily as two of the four Justices who opposed the New Deal measures during the 1930s.

The other members of what Justice Frankfurter called the "Four Horsemen,"[93] Justices Van Devanter and McReynolds, also sat on the Taft Court. James C. McReynolds of Kentucky had been Wilson's Attorney General; he had been appointed to the Court in 1914 to succeed Justice Lurton, who had died. McReyonlds was perhaps the least lovable person ever to sit on the Court. *Time* called him "intolerably rude," "savagely sarcastic," "incredibly reactionary," and "anti-Semitic."[94] The latter characteristic was as pronounced as it has been in any American public figure. McReynolds once refused to accompany the Court on a ceremonial occasion because Justice Brandeis would be there. "As you know," McReynolds wrote to the Chief Justice, "I am not always to be found when there is a Hebrew abroad."[95] Taft wrote that McReynolds was "fuller of prejudice than any man I have ever known."[96] Harold J. Laski summed him up: "McReynolds and the theory of a beneficent deity are quite incompatible."[97]

McReynolds's bête noire, Louis D. Brandeis, was the first Jewish Justice on the Supreme Court. Brandeis is, of course, another of the great names in the Court's history. Brought up in Louisville, he attended Harvard Law School and became a successful attorney in Boston. Brandeis soon became active as a reformer; he became known as the "People's Attorney," since he worked without fee for a great number of public causes. Brandeis was not, however, the typical turn-of-the-century progressive—content only to expose and deplore. While the muckrakers of the day dealt in invective and generalities, he sought remedies achieved through social legislation, particularly in his reforms of gas rates, insurance, and railroads.

When Justice Joseph Lamar died in 1916, President Wilson chose Brandeis in his place. The nomination led to a bitter confirmation battle (Brandeis himself wrote that "[t]he dominant reasons for the opposition . . . are that he is considered a radical and is a jew").[98] Brandeis was confirmed despite the unprecedented opposition of the American Bar Association and ex-President Taft, who asserted in a letter, "Mr. Louis D. Brandeis . . . is not a fit person to be a member of the Supreme Court."[99]

Brandeis at the Bar is best remembered for the new dimension that he added to legal thought—one that emphasized the facts to which the law applied. The Brandeis method was inaugurated by the brief submitted by him in *Muller v. Oregon*[100]—the generic type of a new form of legal argument, ever since referred to as the "Brandeis Brief." To persuade the Court to uphold an Oregon law prohibiting women from working in factories more than ten hours a day, Brandeis marshaled an impressive mass of statistics to demonstrate "that there is reasonable ground for holding that to permit women in Oregon to work . . . more than ten hours in one day is dangerous to the public health, safety, morals, or welfare."[101] The Brandeis Brief and argument in *Muller* were devoted almost entirely to the facts—and to facts not in the record, but which the Court was asked to accept as "facts of common knowledge." The *Muller* brief contains 113 pages. Only two of them are devoted to argument on the law.

The *Muller* Court upheld the Oregon law and it did so by relying upon the Brandeis approach, expressly noting in its opinion how the Brandeis Brief had supplied the factual basis for its decision. *Muller* thus was, as Justice Frankfurter termed it, "'epoch making,' . . . because of the authoriative recognition by the Supreme Court that the way in which Mr. Brandeis presented the case—the support of legislation by an array of facts which established the *reasonableness* of the legislative action, however it may be with its wisdom—laid down a new technique for counsel."[102] The Brandeis Brief still remains the model for constitutional cases.

Brandeis on the bench was only a more exalted version of Brandeis in the forum. If the Brandeis Brief replaced the black-letter judge with the man of statistics and master of economics,[103] Justice Brandeis himself was the prime exemplar of the new jurist in action. Above all, as in his brief, the Justice was a master of the facts in his opinions. For him the search of the legal authorities was the beginning, not the end, of research. He saw that the issues which came to the Court were framed by social and economic conditions unimagined even a generation before. Hence "the judicial weighing of the interests involved should, he believed, be made in the light of facts, sociologically determined and more contemporary than those which underlay the judicial approach to labor questions at the time."[104] When Brandeis marshaled his usual mass of facts in one of his opinions, Holmes characterized a Justice who had written the other way: "I should think [he] would feel as if a steam roller had gone over him."[105]

The Brandeis method on the bench was used for a particular purpose: to reject the prevailing notion that the law was to be "equated with theories of *laissez faire.*"[106] If twentieth-century law has enabled the society to move from laissez faire to the welfare state, that has been true in large part because it has accepted Justice Brandeis's approach.

The Brandeis technique helped persuade jurists that the legal conception of "liberty" should no longer be "synonymous with the laissez faire of Herbert Spencer."[107] Instead, the law has come to believe with Brandeis that "[r]egulation . . . is necessary to the preservation and best development of liberty."[108] This in turn has led to acceptance of the Brandeis rejection of laissez faire as the foundation of our jurisprudence.

It was the Brandeis fact-emphasis technique as much as anything that heralded the end of the turn-of-the century concept of law. Compare the Brandeis opinion in a case involving a regulatory law, with its emphasis throughout on the economic and social conditions that called forth the challenged statute, with that in *Lochner,* where those factors were all but ignored. The difference is as marked as that between the poetry of T. S. Eliot and Alfred Austin.

There was another appointment to the Taft Court that should be mentioned. In 1925, Justice McKenna retired and Attorney General Harlan F. Stone of New York recieved his seat. Stone had been a professor and dean at the Columbia Law School and had indicated adherence to the laissez-faire economics that still dominated jurisprudence. On the Court, however, Chief Justice Taft complained in a letter, Stone became "subservient to Holmes and Brandeis. I am very much disappointed in him; he hungers for the applause of the law-school professors and the admirers of Holmes."[109]

Despite Taft's disappointment with Stone (he had urged his appointment to President Coolidge), the majority continued to follow the Chief Justice's conservative lead in most cases. He led the Court to decisions defending private property and laissez faire that reaffirmed the trend established by the Fuller Court. On the whole, he was one of the most successful Chief Justices—if success is measured by the extent to which his Court mirrored his own juristic philosophy.

The frustration that had encumbered Taft in the White House was now largely forgotten. "The truth is," the Chief Justice wrote in 1925, "that in my present life I don't remember that I ever was President."[110]

Taft has been called "the most 'political' of Chief Justices in American history."[111] He never hesitated to "lobby" Presidents and Congress to secure judicial appointments and legislative action. It was Taft's "politicking" that led to the legislation that finally allowed the Supreme Court, in Justice Frankfurter's phrase, "to be master in its own household."[112] The Judges Bill of 1925, which gave the Court virtual control over its own docket, was largely the result of the Chief Justice's own lobbying on Capitol Hill. "Van Devanter, McReynolds and I," he wrote, "spent two full days at the Capitol, and Van and I one full day more to get the bill through."[113]

The 1925 law's remedy for Court congestion was increased resort to certiorari, which was to be granted or denied in the Court's discretion. Henceforth, as Chief Justice Taft wrote, it was to "be reserved to the discretion of the Supreme Court to say whether the issue between [litigants] is of sufficient importance to justify a hearing of it in the Supreme Court."[114] The result is, Justice Frankfurter tells us, "that the business which comes to the Supreme Court is the business which the Supreme Court allows to come to it. Very few cases can come up without getting its prior permission."[115] The Court was thus now able "to confine its adjudication to issues of constitutionality and other matters of essentially national importance."[116]

Labor and the Court

"The only class which is arrayed against the court . . . is organized labor," wrote Chief Justice Taft to his brother in 1922.[117] Labor had good cause for complaint against the Court, for the Justices continued to serve as the censors of legislative attempts to enact regulatory laws, particularly those protecting the rights of labor.

The Taft Court's antilabor jurisprudence began soon after the Chief Justice took his seat with the 1921 decision in *Truax v. Corrigan*.[118] The Court there struck down an Arizona law barring courts from issuing injunctions in most cases growing out of a labor dispute. The union in *Truax* had picketed a restaurant, which caused its business to fall dramatically. This, said Taft for the majority, was an intentional injury that constituted a tort. A statute which made such a legal wrong remediless deprived the person suffering the loss of due process.

To Chief Justice Taft, the case was an example of how "we have to hit [organized labor] every little while, because they are continually violating the law and depending on threats and violence to accomplish their purpose."[119] But the practical result of a decision such as *Truax* was clear—in the phrase of Justice Holmes's dissent, "to prevent the making of social experiments that an important part of the community desires."[120]

Chief Justice Taft also delivered the opinion in the 1922 *Child Labor Tax Case*[121]—a sequel to the White Court's most controversial decision. That decision had invalidated a direct congressional prohibition of child labor on the ground that the national commerce power did not extend so far.[122] Congress then enacted a law imposing a 10 percent tax upon the profits of all persons employing children. The purpose of the law was, of course, to achieve precisely the result aimed at by the statute previously held unconstitutional, that is, to eliminate child labor. This motive, said the Taft opinion of the Court, rendered the exercise of the taxing power invalid. Congress was trying to suppress an activity that, under the *Child Labor Case,* could be controlled only by the states. When the taxing power is utilized for regulatory purposes in an area where Congress has no direct regulatory power, the tax itself must be invalidated because of its improper underlying purpose.

In his opinion, the Chief Justice conceded that the law at issue was "legislation designed to promote the highest good."[123] To his brother he wrote that the statute was an "effort of good people, who wish children protected." Nevertheless, he went on, "Unfortunately we cannot strain the Constitution . . . to meet the wishes of good people."[124] At the same time, the decision was ruinous in its impact on child labor regulation. In effect, in the words of a biographer, "Taft's opinion had effectively driven a second spike into congressional efforts to regulate child labor."[125]

The *Truax* and *Child Labor Tax* decisions were, however, only the beginning in the Taft Court's attack on regulatory legislation. "Since 1920," Professor Frankfurter noted in 1930, "the Court had invalidated more legislation than in fifty years preceding. Views that were antiquated twenty-five years ago have been resurrected in decisions nullifying minimum-wage laws for women in industry, a standard-weight-bread law to protect buyers from short weights and honest bakers from unfair competition, a law fixing the resale price of theater tickets by ticket scalpers in New York, laws controlling exploitation of the unemployed by employment agencies, and many tax laws."[126]

Of these decisions, the most extreme was that in the 1923 minimum-wage case—*Adkins v. Children's Hospital.*[127] So extreme was it, indeed, that Chief Justice Taft himself, despite his frequently expressed aversion toward dissents, could not go along with the majority and issued a dissenting opinion. The majority opinion was by Justice Sutherland, who thus began to assume the intellectual leadership of the most conservative Justices— soon to become the "Four Horsemen" in the Court that invalidated New Deal legislation.

In *Adkins* itself, as the Court recently summarized, "this Court held it to be an infringement of constitutionally protected liberty of contract to require the employers of adult women to satisfy minimum wage standards."[128] The *Adkins* opinion, like that in *Lochner,* was based upon extreme reliance upon the doctrine of freedom of contract. The law in question, said the Court, "forbids two parties having lawful capacity . . . to freely contract with one another in respect of the price for which one shall render service to the other in a purely private employment where both are willing, perhaps anxious, to agree." Nor did the economic inequality of women make them a proper subject for such protective legislation. In the

Court's view, such inequality did not justify the added burden imposed upon employers: "[T]o the extent that the sum fixed exceeds the fair value of the services rendered, it amounts to a compulsory exaction from the employer for the support of a partially indigent person, for whose condition there rests upon him no peculiar responsibility, and therefore, in effect, arbitrarily shifts to his shoulders a burden which, if it belongs to anybody, belongs to society as a whole."[129]

In *Adkins* freedom of contract reached its apogee. As stated by Justice Sutherland: "[F]reedom of contract is, nevertheless, the general rule and restraint the exception; and the exercise of legislative authority to abridge it can be justified only by the existence of exceptional circumstances."[130]

This, said Justice Frankfurter years later, was "the most doctrinaire view about 'liberty of contract.'" What it meant was "that presumptively every encroachment on 'liberty of contract' is unconstitutional, and you had to show some very good reason why there should be a curtailment of the freedom of contract—freedom of contract between a great, big laundry and Bridget McGinty. They were at arm's length, etcetera, and therefore you shouldn't interfere with their contracting equality."[131]

The effect of *Adkins* on social legislation was even more devastating than that of *Lochner*. The decision, Frankfurter tells us, "struck the death knell not only of this legislation, but of kindred social legislation because it laid down as a constitutional principle that any kind of change by statute has to justify itself, not the other way around." As such, *Adkins* had a serious inhibiting effect on legislative action. "It prevented legislation from being introduced, and it made still-born legislation which was by way of being introduced."[132]

Holmes and Judicial Restraint

In *Adkins,* Justice Holmes delivered another now-classic dissent. A Holmes letter states that his dissent "was intended . . . to dethrone Liberty of Contract from its ascendancy into the Liberty business."[133] But his *Adkins* dissent also sounded the theme that was most prominent in the Holmes jurisprudence. His English correspondent, Sir Frederick Pollock, summarized Holmes's dissent in a letter to the Justice: "The wisdom of the Act of Congress may well be open to grave doubt: but that, as you have said, was not the question before the Court."[134]

This was a pithy summary of the doctrine of judicial restraint that was Justice Holmes's great contribution to Supreme Court jurisprudence. Holmes was led to the doctrine by his innate skepticism, which made him dubious of dogma and decisions based upon dogmatic clichés. "Lincoln for government and Holmes for law," Justice Frankfurter once wrote, "have taught me that the absolutists are the enemies of reason— that . . . the dogmatists in law, however sincere, are the mischief-makers."[135] For Holmes, the only absolute was that there were no absolutes in law. His philosopher's stone was "the conviction that our . . . system rests upon tolerance and that its greatest enemy is the Absolute."[136] It was not at all the judicial function to strike down laws with which the judge disagreed. "There is nothing I more deprecate than the use of the Fourteenth Amendment . . . to prevent the making of social experiments that an important part of the community desires . . . even though the experiments may seem futile or even noxious to me."[137] Not the judge but the legislator was to have the primary say on the policy considerations behind a regulatory measure. The judge's business was to enforce even "laws that I believe to embody economic mistakes."[138]

The same theme was to be repeated many times by Justice Holmes. He continually reiterated that, as a judge, he was not concerned with the wisdom of the social policy behind a challenged legislative act. The responsibility for determining what measures were necessary to deal with economic and other problems lay with the people and their elected representatives, not the judges. The Constitution, Holmes declared, was not "intended to give us *carte blanche* to embody our economic or moral beliefs in its prohibitions."[139] The Constitution was never intended to embody absolutes. Instead, "Some play must be allowed for the joints of the machine, and it must be remembered that legislatures are ultimate guardians of the liberties and welfare of the people in quite as great a degree as the courts."[140]

Justice Holmes recognized, with the majority in cases such as *Lochner v. New York,* that the question at issue was whether the challenged law was a *reasonable* exercise of the police power of the state. But if Holmes, too, started with the test of reasonableness, he applied it in a manner very different from the *Lochner* majority. The Holmes approach was based upon the conviction that it was an awesome thing to strike down an act of the elected representatives of the people, and that the power to do so should not be exercised save where the occasion was clear beyond fair debate.[141] The Constitution was not to be treated "as prohibiting what 5 out of 9 old gentlemen don't think about right."[142]

In the Holmes view, the test to be applied was whether a reasonable legislator—the legislative version of the "reasonable man"—could have adopted a law like that at issue. Was the statute as applied so clearly arbitrary that legislators acting reasonably could not have believed it necessary or appropriate for public health, safety, morals, or welfare?[143]

In the individual case, to be sure, the legislative judgment might well be debatable. But that was the whole point about the Holmes approach. Under it, the opposed views of public policy, as respects business, economic, and social affairs, were considerations for the legislative choice,[144] to which the courts must defer unless it was demonstrably arbitrary or irrational.[145] "In short, the judiciary may not sit as a super-legislature to judge the wisdom or desirability of legislative policy determinations . . . in the local economic sphere, it is only the . . . wholly arbitrary act which cannot stand."[146]

In his *Lochner* dissent, as we saw, Holmes asserted, "This case is decided upon an economic theory which a large part of the country does not entertain." It may now be fairly said that both the economic and the legal theories upon which *Lochner* rested have been repudiated. While the Supreme Court at the beginning of this century was increasingly equating the law with laissez faire, men turned to Holmes's dissents as the precursors of a new era. The at-first-lonely voice soon became that of a new dispensation which wrote itself into American public law.[147]

This was true because the Holmes doctrine of judicial restraint was the necessary legal foundation for the soon-to-emerge welfare state. The Holmes approach meant that the courts would uphold laws that coincided with changing views on the proper scope of governmental regulation. American judges were soon to follow Holmes when he rejected legal shibboleths that equated "the constitutional conception of 'liberty' . . . with theories of *laissez faire*."[148] They came to recognize that the rule of restraint was essential if the law was to enable the society to make the necessary transition from laissez faire to the welfare state.

Holmes and Free Speech

The theme of judicial restraint was, however, overridden by another Holmes theme in cases involving the freedom of expression guaranteed by the First Amendment. Restraint may have been the proper posture for the Justice in cases like *Lochner v. New York,* where economic regulation was an issue. But a different situation was presented in First Amendment cases. Here, says Justice Frankfurter, history had taught Holmes that "the free play of the human mind was an indispensable prerequisite"[149] of social development.

More than that, the Bill of Rights itself, as Holmes recognized, specifically enshrines freedom of speech as its core principle. "If there is any principle of the Constitution that more imperatively calls for attachment than any other it is the principle of free thought," he asserted in a 1928 dissent.[150] Because freedom of speech was basic to any notion of liberty, "Mr. Justice Holmes was far more ready to find legislative invasion in this field than in the area of debatable economic reform."[151]

The Holmes concept of freedom of speech is a direct descendant of John Milton and John Stuart Mill. It found its fullest expression in the Justice's dissent in the 1919 case of *Abrams v. United States,*[152] which has been termed "the greatest utterance on intellectual freedom by an American."[153] Milton's *Areopagitica* argues for "a free and open encounter" in which "[Truth] and Falsehood grapple."[154] The *Abrams* dissent sets forth the foundation of the First Amendment as "free trade in ideas,"[155] which through competition for their acceptance by the people would provide the best test of truth. Or as Holmes put it in a letter, "I am for aeration of all effervescing convictions—there is no way so quick for letting them get flat."[156]

Like Milton and Mills, Justice Holmes stressed the ability of truth to win out in the intellectual marketplace. For this to happen, the indispensable sine qua non was the free interchange of ideas.[157] In the crucial passage of his *Abrams* dissent, Holmes tells us that those who govern too often seek to "express [their] wishes in law and sweep away all opposition," including "opposition by speech." They forget that time may also upset their "fighting faiths" and that government itself is an experimental process. The Constitution also "is an experiment, as all life is an experiment." To make the experiment successful, room must be found for new ideas which will challenge the old, for "the ultimate good desired is better reached by free trade in ideas." And "the best test of truth is the power of the thought to get itself accepted in the competition of the market, and that truth is the only ground upon which their wishes safely can be carried out."[158]

In *Abrams* defendants had been convicted under the Espionage Act of 1917 for the publishing of leaflets which incited resistance to the American war effort by encouraging "curtailment to cripple or hinder the United States in the prosecution of the war." Written in lurid language, the leaflets contained a bitter attack against the sending of American soldiers to Siberia and urged a workers' general strike in support of the Russian Revolution. The Supreme Court affirmed the convictions, holding that, even though the defendants' primary intent had been to aid the Russian Revolution, their plan of action had necessarily involved obstruction of the American war effort against Germany.

As already noted, Justice Holmes issued a strong dissent in *Abrams,* setting forth his conception of the "free trade in ideas" as the foundation of the right of expression. The Holmes dissent argued that the "silly" leaflets thrown by obscure individuals from a loft window presented no danger to the American war effort. Not enough, he said, "can be squeezed from these poor and puny anonymities to turn the color of legal litmus paper."[159]

According to Justice Holmes, "Only the emergency that makes it immediately dangerous to leave the correction of evil counsels to time warrants making any exception to the sweeping command, 'Congress shall make no law . . . abridging the freedom of speech.'"[160] But when does such an "emergency" arise? Holmes himself had provided the answer a few months earlier in another case: when "the words used are used in such circumstances and are of such a nature as to create a clear and present danger that they will bring about the substantive evils that Congress has a right to prevent."[161]

Under this Clear and Present Danger Test, speech may be restricted only if there is a real threat—a danger, both clear and present, that the speech will lead to an evil that the legislature has the power to prevent. In the *Abrams* case, the legislature had the right to pass a law to prevent curtailment of war production; but, said Holmes, there was no danger, clear and present, or even remote, that the leaflets would have had any effect on production.

Justice Brandeis tells us that the Clear and Present Danger Test, as stated by Justice Holmes, "is a rule of reason. Correctly applied, it will preserve the right of free speech both from suppression by tyrannous, well-meaning majorities and from abuse by irresponsible, fanatical minorities."[162]

The Holmes test is above all a test of degree. "Clear and present" danger is a standard, not a mathematical absolute. "It is a question of proximity and degree," said Holmes, after the passage stating the test quoted above.[163] As such, its application will vary from case to case and will depend upon the particular circumstances presented.

That the Holmes test is sound can be seen from the analogy of the law of criminal attempts. Just as a criminal attempt must come sufficiently near completion to be of public concern, so there must be an actual danger that inciting speech will bring about an unlawful act before it can be restrained.

Thus, if I gather sticks and buy some gasoline to start a fire in a house miles away and do nothing more, I cannot be punished for attempting to commit arson. However, if I put the sticks against the house and pour on some gasoline and am caught before striking a match, I am guilty of a criminal attempt. The fire is the main thing, but when no fire has occurred, it is a question of the nearness of my behavior to the outbreak of a fire. So under the Constitution, lawless acts are the main thing. Speech is not punishable as such, but only because of its connection to lawless acts.

But more than a remote connection is necessary, just as with the attempted fire. The fire must be close to the house; the speech must be close to the lawless acts. So long as the speech is remote from action, it is protected by the Constitution.[164] But if the speech will result in action that government can prohibit, then the speech itself can constitutionally be reached by governmental power, provided there is a clear and present danger that the action will result from the speech.

It is true that the Holmes doctrines discussed—both that of judicial restraint and that of Clear and Present Danger—were stated almost entirely in dissents. But those dissents were prime examples of Chief Justice Hughes's characterization of a dissent as "an appeal to . . . the intelligence of a future day."[165] When Harold J. Laski was told by an English lawyer that he was amazed that Holmes was not speaking for the Court in *Abrams,* he wrote to the Justice, "I explained that you were speaking for the Court of the next decade."[166] And so it turned out (though Laski was overoptimistic on the time it would take for the Holmes approach to become accepted doctrine).

Today, more than ever, we can see that it was Justice Holmes who set Supreme Court jurisprudence on its coming course. When Holmes asserted in his *Common Law,* "The life of the law has not been logic: it has been experience," and that the law finds its philosophy in "consideration of what is expedient for the community concerned," he was sounding the clarion of twentieth-century law. If the law reflected the "felt necessities of the time,"[167] then those needs rather than any theory should determine what the law should be. These were not, to be sure, the views followed by American judges and lawyers at the beginning of this century—or even by the majority of the Supreme Court during Holmes's tenure. But the good that men do also lives after them. If the late nineteenth century was dominated by the passive jurisprudence of the Fuller Court, the twentieth was, ultimately, to be that of Mr. Justice Holmes.

10

Hughes Court, 1930–1941

In 1935 the Supreme Court moved into its new building across the plaza from the Capitol. For the first time in its history, the Court had a home of its own—a magnificent Marble Palace symbolizing its role as the ultimate embodiment of Equal Justice Under Law—the motto inscribed on the frieze above the front entrance.

The new building at last presented the Court with a physical setting that matches the splendor of its constitutional role. Whatever purely architectural criticisms may be directed at the Court building, it cannot be denied that it is one of the most imposing structures in Washington. Its design is modeled on a classic Greek temple and is intended as a shrine to the majesty of the law. Its physical scale is truly impressive. Both longer and wider than a football field, it is four stories high and is constructed almost entirely of marble. At the main entrance are sixteen huge Corinthian columns, topped by a pediment; in its center, Liberty Enthroned, holding the scales of justice, guarded by Order on one side and Authority on the other.

The interior of the Court building is as impressive as its exterior. As a Smithsonian pamphlet describes it, "Six kinds of marble, three domestic and three foreign, along with thousands of feet of clear-grained white oak, give the building a feeling of polished, dust-free smoothness. Openwork gates, elevator doors, even the firehose cupboards are of gleaming bronze. Two spiral marble staircases, self-supporting marvels of engineering, soar from garage to the top floor, five levels up. For security's sake, these are unused—but only the Vatican and the Paris Opera can boast similar ones."

The building also has abundant office space, both for Justices' chambers and Court staff, and a magnificent courtroom—as well as ample amenities, including a minigymnasium and basketball court on the top floor, which Court personnel like to call "the highest court in the land."

When Justice Harlan F. Stone visited the new Court building, he wrote to his sons, "The place is almost bombastically pretentious, and thus it seems to me wholly inappropriate for a quiet group of old boys such as the Supreme Court of the United States."[1] When the Court was preparing to move into the new edifice, one of the Justices sardonically asked, "What are we supposed to do, ride in on nine elephants?"

But traditions give way slowly at the Supreme Court. There are still spittoons behind the bench for each Justice, pewter julep cups (now used for their drinking water), and, not long ago, there were quill pens at counsel tables. After the Court formally moved from the cramped quarters in the old Senate Chamber into the new building, most of the Justices resented the change and declined to use the handsome new suites provided for them. With Chief Justice Hughes, they continued to work in their homes, as they had been accustomed to do. One result of this was that Hugo L. Black, the first "new" Justice to occupy chambers in the building, and at that time the junior member of the Court, got his pick and was able to choose a splendid corner suite, which he kept for the remaining thirty-four years of his life (instead of the least desirable space normally left to the junior Justice).

Chief Justice Hughes and His Court

The new Court building was actually the result of Chief Justice Taft's efforts. "We ought to have a building by ourselves . . . as the chief body at the head of the judiciary," Taft told a key Senator and his efforts bore fruit when Senator Reed Smoot wrote to him that the Court would be included in an appropriation for new buildings.[2] Taft's lobbying ultimately ensured funding both for a building site and the new Court building itself. At the 1932 cornerstone ceremony, Chief Justice Hughes declared that the building was "the result of his [predecessor's] intelligent persistence."[3]

"My prayer," Taft wrote to his nephew in 1927, "is that I may stay long enough on the Court to see that building constructed."[4] Taft was not to be granted his wish. A complete breakdown in health forced his resignation on February 3, 1930, and he died a month later.

On the day Chief Justice Taft resigned, President Hoover nominated Charles Evans Hughes to succeed him. Hoover later wrote, "It was the obvious appointment."[5] Despite Hughes's eminent qualifications, his nomination led to the bitterest confirmation fight over a Court head since Chief Justice Taney was named a century earlier. The chief opponent was Senator George Norris, who asserted, "No man in public life so exemplifies the influence of powerful combinations in the political and financial world as does Mr. Hughes."[6] Despite the opposition, Hughes was confirmed by fifty-two to twenty-six.

Chief Justice Hughes was sixty-eight when he was appointed—the oldest man chosen to head the Court. However, he undertook his new duties with the vigor of a much younger person. In addition, his more than distinguished career endowed him with prestige which few in the highest judicial office have had. "He took his seat at the center of the Court," Justice Frankfurter was to write, "with a mastery, I suspect, unparalleled in the history of the court."[7]

As a leader of the Court, Hughes must be ranked with Marshall and Taney. Whatever the test of leadership, in Frankfurter's words, "Chief Justice Hughes possessed it to a conspicuous degree. In open court he exerted this authority by the mastery and distinction with which he presided. He radiated this authority in the conference room."[8]

The Hughes manner of conducting the Court's business has been described by Frankfurter, who had served as a Justice under him. "In Court and in conference he struck the pitch, as it were, for the orchestra. He guided discussion by opening up the lines for it to travel, focusing on essentials, evoking candid exchange on subtle and complex issues, and avoiding redundant talk. He never checked free debate, but the atmosphere which he created, the moral authority which he exerted, inhibited irrelevance, repetition, and fruitless discussion."[9]

In another passage Frankfurter writes that the "word which for me best expresses the atmosphere that Hughes generated . . . was taut. Everything was taut. He infected and affected counsel that way. Everybody was better because of Hughes, the leader of the orchestra."[10]

The Hughes conferences were militarylike models of efficiency. According to Justice Brandeis these "lasted for six hours and the Chief Justice did virtually all the speaking."[11] This was an exaggeration, but Hughes is still noted for his tight control over the conference discussion. Rarely did any Justice speak out of turn and Hughes made sure that the discussion did not stray from the issues he had stated in his incisive presentation. For him, Justice Frankfurter later told an interviewer, "the conference was not a debating society."[12] Frankfurter concludes, "To see [Hughes] preside was like witnessing Toscanini lead an orchestra."

The new Chief Justice's leadership abilities were precisely what the Court needed to enable it to confront its most serious crisis in almost a century. Some years earlier, Justice Holmes had written that, while things at the Court were quiet then, it was really only "the quiet of a storm centre."[13] The same could be said of the Court when Hughes took its center chair.

From outward appearances, the Hughes Court also seemed quiet—ready to continue along the conservative path taken by its predecessors. Yet from almost the beginning of the new Chief Justice's tenure, it was "enclosed in a tumultuous privacy of storm."[14] In decisions like that in the

Adkins case,[15] the Court's conservative core had carried their laissez-faire interpretation of the Constitution to the point where there was, in Holmes's phrase, "hardly any limit but the sky to the invalidating of [laws] if they happen to strike a majority of the Court as for any reason undesirable."[16] But changing conditions in the society itself were about to render the jurisprudence of the day obsolete.

When Chief Justice Hughes ascended the bench early in 1930, the country was already deep in the most serious economic crisis in our history. The crisis only became worse as the Hughes term went on—putting the entire leadership of the country, and not least the Court itself, to perhaps its most severe test.

The new Chief Justice had to meet that test with a Court composed almost entirely of Justices who had served under his predecessor. Four of the five Justices who had made up the *Adkins* majority (Van Devanter, McReynolds, Sutherland, and Butler) were still on the bench, serving as the nucleus for decisions extending the Taft Court's laissez-faire jurisprudence. It is true that the Court also contained Justices Holmes, Brandeis, and Stone as its liberal bloc. They could act as a brake upon the tendency to further treat the Constitution as a legal sanction for laissez faire—particularly if they were joined by the new Chief Justice and Justice Roberts, who came to the Court at the same time as Chief Justice Hughes.

Owen J. Roberts had been a successful practicing lawyer in Philadelphia who attracted national attention as prosecutor in the Teapot Dome scandal. Roberts had been appointed to fill Justice Sanford's seat upon the latter's death in 1930, after the Senate had turned down Circuit Judge John J. Parker's nomination. Roberts was a better than average Justice—but one who, as he himself recognized, would never be placed in the judicial pantheon. "Who am I," he wrote after leaving the bench, "to revile the good God that he did not make me a Marshall, a Taney, a Bradley, a Holmes, a Brandeis or a Cardozo."[17]

Justice Roberts was nevertheless to play a crucial role as the "swing vote" in the Hughes Court. It was his key vote that enabled the conservative bloc to prevail in the decisions striking down the important New Deal measures during the first part of Chief Justice Hughes's tenure. It was Justice Roberts's vote as well that enabled the Chief Justice to bring about the great jurisprudential reversal that took place in 1937.

Before we discuss the Hughes Court's jurisprudence, a word should be said about another personnel change, for it involved two of the outstanding Justices in the Court's history. On January 3, 1932, after the Justices had heard oral arguments, Justice Holmes casually announced, "I won't be here tomorrow," and he submitted his resignation later that day. On that day coincidentally, Earl Warren, then a California district attorney, had argued his first case before the Court. Warren used to say that his friends accused him of driving Holmes from the bench. They used to tease him— "one look at you and he said, 'I quit.'"

The departure of Holmes meant that the Court had lost one of its giants—the Justice who more than any other had set the theme for twentieth-century jurisprudence. Then a most unusual thing happened. The all but unanimous national consensus was that only one man deserved the succession to Holmes—Benjamin Nathan Cardozo. From a political point of view, his appointment seemed impossible. Cardozo was a New Yorker and there were already two on the Court from New York (Hughes and Stone); he was a Jew and there was already a Jewish Justice (Brandeis); and a conservative Republican President could scarcely name a liberal not a member of his party.

The sentiment in Cardozo's favor overrode these objections. Justice Stone told President Hoover that he was willing to resign to overcome the geographical objection and the powerful Senator from Idaho, William E. Borah, told the President that Cardozo belonged as much to Idaho as to New York. Borah went on, "Just as John Adams is best remembered for his appointment of John Marshall to the Supreme Court, so you, Mr. President, have the opportunity of being best remembered for putting Cardozo there."[18] And so it turned out. One of the few positive things for which President Hoover is remembered is his appointment of Cardozo to fill the Holmes seat.

Except for Holmes himself, Justice Cardozo was the preeminent judge of the first half of the twentieth century. Indeed, Cardozo was the outstanding common-law jurist of the twentieth century. It was he who led the way in adapting the common law to the requirements of the postindustrial society. Cardozo showed how traditional principles and techniques could be used to effect a complete change in the relationship between the law and individual rights of substance.

In American law, Cardozo remains the consummate legal craftsman, the master of the principles, ideals, and techniques of Anglo-American law. More than any other judge, Roscoe Pound once pointed out, "he has known the tools of his craft and his known how to use them."[19]

There was little drama in Cardozo's life. He was born in New York City, the son of a judge who was besmirched by his association with the notorious Tweed Ring. During his youth, he had a number of tutors, including Horatio Alger. After study at Columbia College and Law School and admission to the New York Bar in 1891, Cardozo became a lawyer's lawyer, to whom other attorneys referred difficult cases. He became a judge in 1914, serving eighteen years (five of them as chief judge) on the New York Court of Appeals and then six years on the United States Supreme Court. Though he was to be granted less than six full terms on the highest bench, Cardozo was able to play an important role as a member of the liberal wing which first resisted the Hughes Court's early reactionary decisions and then led the great changeover in the Court's constitutional jurisprudence.

Cardozo's major contribution to our law was his use of traditional judicial techniques to adapt the law to society's changing requirements. To Cardozo, the job of the judge was to adapt the experience of the past so that it would best serve the needs of the present. More than any judge, he showed how the common-law technique could be adapted for contemporary use. Reasoning by analogy, he showed how existing doctrines could be adapted to new needs. His mastery of judicial technique made the emerging law appear to be the logical product of established doctrines; in his hands the changing common law was made a blend of both continuity and creativeness.[20]

It was Cardozo who, next to Holmes, most marked the transition from the concept of law that prevailed a century ago. Cardozo was the first judge who explained systematically how judges reason and who made the first serious effort to articulate a judicial philosophy.[21] But he was not just an academic legal theorist; his judicial tenure gave him ample opportunity to apply his philosophy to the needs of the changing law.

Cardozo did more than demonstrate that law was Heraclitean rather than Newtonian in nature. To him, the law was neither an *is* nor an *ought;* it was also an endless *becoming.* Far from being the static system posited by turn-of-the-century jurists, "even now there is change from decade to decade." Since Cardozo, we have not doubted that "the end of the law" should "determin[e] the direction of its growth."[22] Cardozo showed how the common law could be freed to serve present needs—how the judge could be truly innovative while remaining true to the experience of the past. By doing so, he helped to move the law closer to the goal of making the law an effective instrument of social welfare.[23]

First Hughes Court

Justice Frankfurter once said that Chief Justice Hughes "was, in fact, the head of two courts, so different . . . was the supreme bench in the two periods of the decade during which Hughes presided over it."[24] The first Hughes Court sat from the Chief Justice's appointment in 1930 until 1937. The period was dominated by the decisions which both nullified the most important New Deal legislation and restricted state regulatory power. In both respects, the Court confirmed the laissez-faire jurisprudence of its predecessors. But the Court was sharply divided in its controversial decisions.

Just before Hughes's appointment, Chief Justice Taft, failing in health, gave voice to his concerns about the continued conservatism of the Court. The most that could be hoped for, he wrote Justice Butler, "is continued life of the present membership . . . to prevent disastrous reversals of our present attitude. With Van [Van Devanter] and Mac [McReynolds] and Sutherland and you and Sanford, there will be five to steady the boat . . . we must not give up at once."[25] But Chief Justice Taft and Justice Sanford both died a few months later. Now the Court's conservative majority itself might be in danger.

Taft's stricture about President Hoover—"that it is just as well for him to remember the warning in the Scriptures about removing landmarks"[26]—appeared borne out by some of the early Hughes Court decisions. The first of them, *Home Building & Loan Association v. Blaisdell* (1934),[27] upheld the governmental power to enact moratory laws for the relief of debtors during the Great Depression. The Hughes opinion found that the economic emergency furnished legitimate occasion for the exercise of the police power to protect both debtors and the community against the collapse of values that had occurred. To the four dissenters, the law was a patent violation of the categorical prohibition against "impairing the obligation of contracts."[28] Yet, as Justice Cardozo put it in an undelivered concurrence, while the moratory law "may be inconsistent with things" which the Framers believed, "their beliefs to be significant must be adjusted to the world they knew. It is not . . . inconsistent with what they would say today."[29]

Another case in which the early Hughes Court adjusted the intent of the Framers to contemporary needs was *Nebbia v. New York* (1934),[30] where a New York law fixing milk prices was ruled valid. In his opinion of the Court, Justice Roberts transformed the Court's attitude toward the legality of price regulation by doing away with the limited category of "businesses affected with a public interest" upon which the price-fixing power had until then been based. In doing so, Justice Frankfurter tells us, "Roberts wrote the epitaph on the misconception, which had gained respect from repetition, that legislative price-fixing as such was at least presumptively unconstitutional."[31] Instead, price fixing, like other types of business regulation, was to be sustained when there was a reasonable relationship between it and the social interests which may be vindicated by the police power.

In the *Blaisdell* and *Nebbia* cases, Chief Justice Hughes and Justice Roberts had joined with Justices Brandeis, Stone, and Cardozo. Liberal commentators expressed hope that the constitutional tide had now turned in their direction. That hope, however, proved short-lived when Justice Roberts joined the four *Blaisdell-Nebbia* dissenters in striking down a federal law requiring railroads to contribute to a pension fund for aged employees.[32] The decision was based upon a restricted conception of the commerce power that would also form the basis for the invalidation in the next two years of the most important New Deal measures—particularly when the Chief Justice joined Justice Roberts in his shift to the conservative wing of the Court.

New Deal Cases

"During the past half century," asserted President Franklin D. Roosevelt in 1937, "the balance of power between the three great branches of the Federal Government, has been tipped out of balance by the Courts in direct contradiction of the high purposes of the framers of the Constitution."[33] What has been called government by judiciary was dramatically illustrated by the Supreme Court reception of the early New Deal laws.

Based on the need to resuscitate the depressed economy by extended governmental intervention, the New Deal program involved the negation of laissez faire; it meant a degree of economic regulation far greater than any previously attempted. If the country was to go forward, said President Roosevelt in his First Inaugural Address, "we must move as a trained and loyal army willing to sacrifice for the good of a common discipline, because without such discipline no progress is made, no leadership becomes effective."[34]

The effort to move the nation forward came up against the restricted view of governmental power still held by the Supreme Court. The result was a series of decisions that invalidated most of the important New Deal legislation. In 1935 and 1936 cases, the Supreme Court struck down the two key New Deal antidepression measures, the National Industrial Recovery Act and the Agricultural Adjustment Act.[35] Both measures were held beyond the reach of the federal commerce power.

The NIRA was ruled invalid as applied to small wholesale poultry dealers in Brooklyn. The business done by them was purely local in character, even though the poultry handled by them came from outside the state. And, under the Court's approach, it did not make any difference that there was some effect upon interstate commerce by the business being regulated. Similarly, in holding the AAA unconstitutional, the Court replied upon the proposition that agriculture, like manufacturing, is not commerce and hence is immune from federal control.

Nor were these decisions all. Still other cases struck down measures providing for regulation of the bituminous coal industry, municipal bankruptcy relief, and farm debtors' relief.[36]

The decisions alone were bad enough. Even worse, however, was the manner in which the decrees of invalidity were delivered. Speaking in 1928 of Supreme Court decisions setting aside statutes enacted by Congress, Chief Justice Hughes had asserted that few of these cases had been of great importance in shaping the course of the nation.[37] The same could not be said of the decisions nullifying the New Deal measures. As far as the measures themselves were concerned, even their proponents had to concede that many of them were imperfectly conceived and crudely executed.[38] There is little doubt that they were subject to legitimate constitutional attack. Had the Court in its decisions confined itself to these limited constitutional issues, at the same time leaving the way open for Congress to remedy the defects by tighter draftsmanship, it would hardly have been subjected to such bitter controversy.

But the Court deliberately did not choose the more prudent course. To paraphrase Justice Robert H. Jackson,[39] in striking at the New Deal legislation, the Court allowed its language to run riot. It sought to engraft its own nineteenth-century laissez-faire philosophy into the Constitution. In invalidating the National Industrial Recovery Act, the Court did not limit itself to criticism of the obviously objectionable features of that law; the rationale of its decision was, instead, so broad that it struck at all national efforts to maintain fair industrial and labor standards. Similarly, in overthrowing the Agricultural Adjustment Act, the Court cast doubt upon all federal aid to agriculture, as well as upon any extensive use of the congressional power to tax and spend in order to promote the general welfare.

The Court's action in this respect came to its culmination just before the 1936 election, when it followed *Adkins* and ruled that there was no power in either states or nation to enact a minimum-wage law.[40] In the words of a contemporary critic, "The Court not merely challenged the policies of the New Deal but erected judicial barriers to the reasonable exercise of legislative powers, both state and national, to meet the urgent needs of the twentieth-century community."[41]

The narrow interpretation of governmental power in these decisions was catastrophic. "We have . . . reached the point as a Nation," President Roosevelt declared, "where we must take action to save the Constitution from the Court."[42] Elimination of manufacturing, mining, and agriculture from the reach of federal power had rendered Congress powerless to deal with problems in those fields, however pressing they might become.

Obviously the rejection of governmental power in the New Deal decisions fitted perfectly with the restricted theory of governmental function that had dominated American thinking for the previous half century. The Constitution, stated Justice Holmes in a noted passage, "is not intended to embody a particular economic theory, whether of paternalism and the organic relation of the citizen to the state or of laissez faire."[43] But it was most difficult for judges not to assume that the basic document was intended to embody the dominant economic beliefs on which they had been nurtured.

The grim economic background behind the New Deal measures, however, indicated how totally unrealistic was reliance on laissez faire. Giant industries prostrate, nationwide crises in production and consumption, the economy in a state of virtual collapse—if ever there was a need for exertion of federal power, it was after 1929. The market and the states had found the crisis beyond their competence. The choice was between federal action and chaos. A system of constitutional law that required the latter could hardly endure. The New Deal decisions, the Supreme Court was later to concede, "produced a series of consequences for the exercise of national power over industry conducted on a national scale which the evolving nature of our industrialism foredoomed to reversal."[44]

Constitutional Revolution, Ltd.

President Roosevelt's answer to the judicial decisions was his "Court-packing" plan of February 5, 1937. Under it, the President could appoint another judge for every federal judge who was over seventy and had not retired. This would have given the President the power to appoint six new Supreme Court Justices.

After lengthy hearings and public discussion, the Senate Judiciary Committee rejected the plan. Yet, if the President lost the Court-packing battle, he was ultimately to win the constitutional war, for the Supreme Court itself was soon to abandon its restrictive approach to the proper scope of governmental power. Hence, in Justice Jackson's summary of the Court-packing fight, "Each side of the controversy has comforted itself with a claim of victory. The President's enemies defeated the court reform bill—the President achieved court reform."[45]

A remarkable reversal in the Supreme Court's attitude toward the New Deal program took place early in 1937. From 1934 through 1936, the Court rendered twelve decisions declaring New Deal measures invalid; starting in April 1937, that tribunal upheld every New Deal law presented to it, including some that were basically similar to earlier nullified statutes. It is, in truth, not too far-fetched to assert that in 1937 there was a veritable revolution in the Court's jurisprudence, which one commentator characterized as "Constitutional Revolution, Ltd."[46]

It is too facile to state that the 1937 change was merely a protective response to the Court-packing plan, to assert, as did so many contemporary wags, that "a switch in time saved Nine." The furor over the President's proposal obviously had repercussions within the Court's marble halls. As FDR himself expressed it, "It would be a little naive to refuse to recognize some connection between these decisions and the Supreme Court fight."[47] At the same time, it misconceives the nature of the Supreme Court and its manner of operation as a judicial tribunal to assume that the 1937 change in jurisprudence was solely the result of the Court-packing plan. The 1937 reversal reflected changes in legal ideology common to the entire legal profession. The extreme individualistic philosophy upon which the Justices had been nurtured had been shaken to its foundations. If laissez-faire jurisprudence gave way to judicial pragmatism, it simply reflected a similar movement that had taken place in the country as a whole.

In an unpublished 1934 draft opinion, Justice Cardozo had asserted, "A gospel of laissez faire . . . may be inadequate in the great society that we live in to point the way to salvation, at least for economic life."[48] The conception of the proper role of government upon which the 1934–1936 decisions were based was utterly inconsistent with an era which demanded ever-expanding governmental authority. "Leviathan hath two swords: war and justice," states Thomas Hobbes in a famous passage. The need effectively to deal with the great economic crisis of the 1930s had, nevertheless, made it plain that the armory of the state had to include much more than these two elementary weapons. Before the New Deal, government was chiefly negative; its main task, apart from defense, was to support the status quo and maintain some semblance of fair play while private interests asserted themselves freely. Under the Roosevelt Administration, government became positive in a new sense.

For the Supreme Court, Canute-like, to attempt to hold back indefinitely the waves of ever-increasing governmental authority was to set itself an impossible task. "Looking back," declared Justice Roberts (the man whose switch is, more than anything else, said to have "saved the Nine" in 1937) in 1951, "it is difficult to see how the court could have resisted the popular urge for uniform standards throughout the country—for what in effect was a unified economy."[49] The laissez-faire doctrine, upon which the operation of American government had been essentially based since the founding of the Republic, had by then proved inadequate to meet pressing economic problems. As the Court recently put it, "the Depression had come and with it the lesson that seemed unmistakable to most people by 1937, that the interpretation of contractual freedom protected in *Adkins* rested on fundamentally false factual assumptions about the capacity of a relatively unregulated market to satisfy minimum levels of human welfare."[50]

The national economy could be resuscitated only by extended federal intervention. For the Government in Washington to be able to exercise regulatory authority upon the necessary national scale, it was essential that the Supreme Court liberalize its construction of the Constitution. To quote Justice Roberts again, "An insistence by the court on holding federal power to what seemed its appropriate orbit when the Constitution was adopted might have resulted in even more radical changes in our dual structure than those which have been gradually accomplished through the extension of the limited jurisdiction conferred on the federal government."[51]

In any event, there *was* a real conversion in a majority of the Supreme Court and its effects do justify the "constitutional revolution" characterization. And it is usually overlooked that the decision first signaling the reversal in jurisprudence was reached before the President introduced his Court-packing plan. On March 29, 1937, Chief Justice Hughes announced a decision upholding a state minimum-wage law, basically similar to one the Court had held to be beyond the power of both states and nation to enact only nine months previously.[52] The Court's confession of error was announced a month after the President's proposal, but the case itself was decided in conference among the Justices about a month before the publication of the Court-packing plan. This circumstantial evidence strongly bears out the statement made some years later by Chief Justice Hughes to his authorized biographer: "The President's proposal had not the slightest effect on our decision."[53]

It should, however, be noted that, even with the majority change in jurisprudence, a hard core of the 1934–1936 majority utterly refused to alter its views—which shows how narrow the actual margin of change was in the Court. In reality, it was the recognition by two Justices (primarily Justice Roberts and, to a lesser extent, Chief Justice Hughes) of the need for increased national governmental power that made for the switchover in the high tribunal. "Years ago," wrote an eminent professor of constitutional law of the Court in the mid-thirties, "that learned lawyer John

Selden in talking of 'Council' observed: They talk (but blasphemously enough) that the Holy Ghost is President of their General Councils when the truth is, the odd Man is still the Holy Ghost.'"[54] It was the conversion of "odd men" Roberts and Hughes that made the constitutional revolution of 1937 possible.

301 U.S.

Narrow though the margin for change may have been, there is little doubt that there was a real conversion among the new majority of the Supreme Court. On March 29, 1937, the Chief Justice announced the opinion upholding a state minimum-wage law,[55] in the process overruling both *Adkins* and a decision following that case made only nine months earlier.[56] According to one who sat at the Government counsel table that day, "[T]he spectacle of the Court that day frankly and completely reversing itself and striking down its opinion but a few months old was a moment never to be forgotten."[57]

March 29, 1937, as already indicated, saw the upholding of a state minimum-wage law. Though not directly concerned with national power, the Court did expressly overrule *Adkins,* which had denied congressional authority to fix wages; hence the decision was a substantial step forward in the movement toward increased national power. On the same day, the Court dealt squarely with federal statutes similar to several annulled in the 1934–1936 period. This time the Court upheld laws providing for farm debtors' relief, collective bargaining in the nation's railroads, and a penalizing tax on firearms analogous to that which it had struck down under the Agricultural Adjustment Act.[58] Well could a leading New Dealer chortle, "What a day! To labor, minimum-wage laws and collective bargaining; to farmers, relief in bankruptcy; to law enforcement, the firearms control. The Court was on the march!"[59]

These cases, in Volume 300 of the *Supreme Court Reports,* were to prove but the prelude to an even more drastic revolution in consitutional jurisprudence. To demonstrate the extent of the judicial revolution, one has, to use the method stated by Edward S. Corwin, only to "turn to Volume 301 of the *United States Supreme Court Reports,* a volume which has a single counterpart in the Court's annals. I mean Volume 11 of Peters's *Reports,* wherein is recorded the somewhat lesser revolution in our constitutional law precisely 100 years earlier, which followed upon Taney's succession to Marshall."[60]

On page 1 of 301 U.S., there is printed the April 12, 1937, decision of the Court in *National Labor Relations Board v. Jones & Laughlin Steel Corp.*[61] In it, the constitutionality of the National Labor Relations Act of 1935 was upheld. Robert H. Jackson termed the decision there the most far-reaching victory ever won on behalf of labor in the Supreme Court.[62] This was no overstatement, for the 1935 act was the Magna Carta of the American labor movement. It guaranteed the right of employees to organize collectively in unions and made it an unfair labor practice prohibited by law for employers to interfere with that right or to refuse to bargain collectively with the representatives chosen by their employees.

The Labor Act was intended to apply to industries throughout the nation, to those engaged in production and manufacture as well as to those engaged in commerce, literally speaking. But this appeared to bring it directly in conflict with the decisions drastically limiting the scope of the Federal Government's authority over interstate commerce, including some of the decisions of the 1934–1936 period on which the ink was scarcely dry. This was particularly true of the Court's decision nullifying the National Industrial Recovery Act, which had denied power in Congress to regulate local business activities, even though they affected interstate commerce. In the *Jones & Laughlin* case, these precedents were not followed: "These cases," laconically stated the Court, "are not controlling here."[63]

Instead, the Court gave the federal power over interstate commerce its maximum sweep. Mines, mills, and factories, whose activities had formerly been decided to be "local" and hence immune from federal regulation, were now held to affect interstate commerce directly enough to justify congressional control. There is little doubt that, as the dissenting *Jones & Laughlin* Justices protested, Congress in the Labor Act exercised a power of control over purely local industry beyond anything theretofore deemed permissible.

The *Jones & Laughlin* case was followed six weeks later by three equally significant decisions, also printed in Volume 301 of the *Supreme Court Reports,* upholding the constitutionally of one of the most important of the New Deal innovations, the Social Security Act of 1935. That law, which for the first time brought the Federal Government extensively into the field of social insurance, had been held unconstitutional by the lower court. The Supreme Court, however, in a precedent-making opinion by Justice Cardozo, reversed, holding that the scheme of old-age benefits provided for by the federal law did not contravene any constitutional prohibition.[64] In so doing, the Court gave the broadest possible scope to the congressional power to tax and spend for the general welfare, even though its reasoning on this point was inconsistent with its 1936 decision invalidating the Agricultural Adjustment Act.

In addition, the Court upheld the unemployment compensation schemes established under the Social Security Act.[65] The decisions sustaining that law put an end to fears that unemployment insurance and old-age benefit laws might prove beyond the power of either states or nation, as minimum-wage regulation had been held to be under the pre-1937 Court. Henceforth the United States was not to be the one great nation powerless to adopt such measures.

These decisions in 301 U.S. formed the heart of the constitutional revolution of 1937. Breaking with its previous jurisprudence, the Supreme Court upheld the authority of the Federal Government to regulate the entire economy under its commerce power and to use its power to tax and spend to set up comprehensive schemes of social insurance. And, it should be noted in light of later criticisms of the Court whose members were subsequently appointed by President Roosevelt, because of its claimed cavalier discard of established precedents, the cases in 301 U.S. were decided before a single Roosevelt-appointed Justice took his seat upon the bench. The most important of the old precedents which so restricted the scope of governmental authority were repudiated by the identical Court that had previously invoked them. There was no change in the Court's personnel until after it provided new precedents that served as a basis for much that the new judges were later to decide.

Second Hughes Court

The 1937 reversal marked the accession of what may be considered the second Hughes Court—so different was its jurisprudence from that of the Hughes Court that had preceded it. As just stressed, the new decisions were the product of the same Justices who had sat in the first Hughes Court. But the composition of the Court was now to change drastically as President Roosevelt was given the opportunity to "pack" the Court through the retirement or death of most of its members. Among the new Roosevelt-appointed Justices were some of the greatest names in modern Supreme Court history.

The first of them was Hugo L. Black of Alabama, a leading New Deal Senator, who was chosen to fill the first vacancy in five years, after Justice Van Devanter retired after the 1936 Term. The Black appointment was a controversial one because he had been a member of the Ku Klux Klan. In a short time, however, the furor over the disclosure that he had once been a member of the Ku Klux Klan seemed an echo from another world. "At every session of the Court," a *New York Times* editorial thundered, after Black's Klan membership had been revealed, "the presence on the bench of a justice who has worn the white robe of the Ku Klux Klan will stand as a living symbol of the fact that here the cause of liberalism is unwittingly betrayed." Within a few years, Justice Black became a leader of the Court's liberal wing.

Justice Black never forgot his origins in a backward Alabama rural county. But his Alabama drawl and his gentle manners masked an inner firmness found in few men. "Many who know him," wrote Anthony Lewis when Black turned seventy-five, "would agree with the one-time law clerk who called him 'the most powerful man I have ever met.'"[66] Though of only slight build, Black always amazed people by his physical vitality. He is quoted in *The Dictionary of Biographical Quotation* as saying, "When I was forty my doctor advised me that a man in his forties shouldn't play tennis. I heeded his advice carefully and could hardly wait until I reached fifty to start again."

Black's competitive devotion to tennis became legend. Until he was eighty-three, he continued to play several sets every day on the private court of his landmark federal house in the Old Town section of the Washington suburb of Alexandria. He brought the same competitive intensity to his judicial work. According to his closest colleague, Justice William O. Douglas, "Hugo Black was fiercely intent on every point of law he presented."[67] Black was as much a compulsive winner in the courtroom as on the tennis court. "You can't just disagree with him," acidly commented his great Court rival, Justice Jackson, to a columnist. "You must go to war with him if you disagree."[68] Black would fight bitterly on the issues that concerned him, such as the First Amendment.

If impact on the law is a hallmark of the outstanding judge, few occupants of the bench have been more outstanding than Black. It was Justice Black who fought for years to have the Court tilt the Constitution in favor of individual rights and liberties and who was a leader in what Justice Fortas once termed "the most profound and pervasive revolution ever achieved by substantially peaceful means."[69] Even where Justice Black's views have not been adopted literally, they have tended to prevail in a more general, modified form. Nor has his impact been limited to the Black positions that the Court has accepted. It is found in the totality of today's judicial awareness of the Bill of Rights and the law's newly intensified sensitivity to the need to apply its protection to all.

More than anything, Justice Black brought to the Supreme Court a moral fervor rarely seen on the bench. A famous passage by Justice Holmes has it that the black-letter judge will be replaced by the man of statistics and the master of economics.[70] Justice Black was emphatically a judge who still followed the black-letter approach in dealing with the constitutional text. "That Constitution," he said, "is my legal bible. . . . I cherish every word of it from the first to the last."[71] The eminent jurist with a dog-eared copy of the Constitution in his right coat pocket became a part of contemporary folklore. In protecting the sanctity of the organic word, Justice Black displayed all the passion of the Old Testament prophet in the face of graven idols. His ardor may have detracted from the image of the "judicial," but if the Justice did not bring to constitutional issues that "cold neutrality" of which Edmund Burke speaks,[72] his zeal may have been precisely what was needed in the Supreme Court. Anything less might have been inadequate to make the Bill of Rights the vital center of our constitutional law.

Justice Black's principal supporter on the Court was William O. Douglas, who succeeded Justice Brandeis, forced to retire in 1939 after a heart attack. To outside observers, Justice Douglas seemed the personification of the last frontier—the down-to-earth Westerner whose granite-hewed physique always seemed out of place in Parnassus. More than that, Douglas was the Court's Horatio Alger, whose early life was a struggle against polio and poverty. Told that he would never walk, he became a noted sportsman. He came east on a freight car to enroll at Columbia Law School, with six cents in his pocket, and went on to become an eminent law professor, chairman of the Securities and Exchange Commission, and at the age of forty a Supreme Court Justice—the youngest Supreme Court appointee in over a century.

On the bench, Justice Douglas was known as Justice Black's chief ally. "If any student of the modern Supreme Court took an association test," wrote Hugo Black, Jr., in his book about his father, "the word 'Black' would probably evoke the response 'Douglas' and vice versa."[73] Justice Black himself recognized this. Declining a 1958 invitation to write an article about Justice Douglas, Justice Black wrote, "our views are so nearly the same that it would be almost like self praise for me to write what I feel about his judicial career."[74]

Yet, even though he was normally to be found in the Black column, on the bench, as in his personal life, Justice Douglas always was a maverick, who went his own way regardless of the feelings of the other Justices. Justice Douglas would stick to his own views, and he was quick to use his own method of deciding in concurrence or dissent. It made little difference whether he carried a majority or stood alone. He would rarely stoop to lobbying for his position and seemed more interested in making his own stand public than in working to get it accepted. As a law clerk once put it to me, "Douglas was just as happy signing a one-man dissent as picking up four more votes."

If Justice Douglas was the strongest Black supporter, Justice Black's greatest intellectual adversary on the Court was Felix Frankfurter, who became a member of the Court just before Douglas did in 1939, replacing Justice Cardozo. Few members of the Supreme Court have been of greater interest than Frankfurter both to the public and to Court specialists. In large measure, this has been true because his career poses something of a puzzle. Before his appointment to the bench, he was known for his interest in libertarian causes. He was also closely connected in the public mind with the New Deal, and it was generally expected that, once on the Court, he would continue along a liberal path. Yet if one thing is certain, it is that it is risky to make predictions of how appointees will behave after they don the robe. "One of the things," Frankfurter once said, "that laymen, even lawyers, do not always understand is indicated by the question you hear so often: 'Does a man become any different when he puts on a gown?' I say, 'If he is any good, he does.'"[75] Frankfurter himself seemed an altogether different man as a Justice than he had been off the bench. From academic eminence behind the New Deal to leader of the conservative court cabal— thus did press and public tend to tag Justice Frankfurter.

Frankfurter's career was another legal version of the Horatio Alger success story. He arrived at Ellis Island as a twelve-year-old immigrant from Vienna in 1894, had outstanding records at City College in New York and Harvard Law School, and then divided his time between private practice and government work. In 1914, he was appointed to the Harvard law faculty. He became one of the best-known law professors in the country, specializing in the emerging field of administrative law. His primary contribution was not, however, academic, but his work in defense of liberal causes (he argued successfully in defense of maximum-hour and minimum-wage laws and was a leader in the opposition to the Sacco-Vanzetti convictions) and as governmental adviser. He was the intellectual force behind much of the New Deal program and many of its most effective administrators were recruited by him. The pervasiveness of Frankfurter's "Happy Hot Dogs," as his protégés in Washington were called, led the National Recovery Administration's director to label Frankfurter "the most influential individual in the United States."[76]

His friendship with Franklin D. Roosevelt and his role as an intimate adviser to the President led to Frankfurter's 1939 Supreme Court appointment. News of the appointment led to a champagne celebration in Harold Ickes's Department of the Interior office, attended by leading New Deal liberals. "We were all very happy," Ickes wrote, "there will be on the bench of the Supreme Court a group of liberals under aggressive, forthright, and intelligent leadership."[77]

It did not turn out that way. There would be a cohesive liberal majority on the Court, but it would not be led by Frankfurter. Instead, the liberal leadership was assumed by Frankfurter's two judicial rivals, Justice Black and later by Chief Justice Earl Warren. Frankfurter became the leader of the Court's conservative core, particularly during the Vinson and early Warren years.

Mention should also be made of two lesser appointees to the Hughes Court. The first was Stanley Reed of Kentucky, then Solicitor General, who was appointed in 1938 upon Justice Sutherland's retirement. Justice Reed was the most conservative of the Roosevelt-appointed Justices as well as the least intellectually gifted of them. He was a solid, plodding worker, who considered law in the traditional terms that had prevailed before the Court was recast by eight Roosevelt appointments. More than any other of the New Deal Brethren, Reed voted to uphold federal power, whether directed against property or personal rights. "How sure I was," reads a handwritten note from Reed to Frankfurter, "in the innocent days when law to a country lawyer seemed automatic—no two sides to any legal issue."[78] Reed tended throughout his judicial tenure to view often complex issues in simplistic terms.

Altogether different was Frank Murphy of Michigan, who was President's Roosevelt's Attorney General when he was appointed in 1940 in place of Justice Butler, who had died. Justice Murphy turned out to be one of the most liberal Justices on the modern Court—noted for voting with his heart rather than his head in cases involving racial minorities and the poor. To many his overriding emphasis on reaching the *right* result regardless of technicalities smacked of cant or sanctimony. "Justice tempered by Murphy" was the way wags described his record on the Court. Justice Frankfurter sarcastically called Murphy "St. Frank" in his correspondence. "The short of the matter," he once wrote Justice Reed, "is that today you would no more heed Murphy's tripe than you would be seen naked at Dupont Circle at high noon tomorrow."[79]

National Power Extended

The second Hughes Court contained some of the most eminent Justices in Supreme Court history: the Chief Justice himself and Justices Stone, Black, Frankfurter, and Douglas. The latter three did their most important work under Hughes's successors. In the later Hughes Court, they and their Roosevelt-appointed colleagues confirmed and extended the "constitutional revolution" that had taken place just before their appointment.

The *Jones & Laughlin* decision marked a definite break with the restricted view that productive industries are beyond the federal commerce power. *Jones & Laughlin* removed the immunity from the commerce power that manufacturing had come to enjoy. But the Court soon extended the *Jones & Laughlin* approach to other productive industries. *Sunshine Anthracite Coal Co. v. Adkins*[80] upheld a 1937 congressional act regulating the coal industry, similar in many ways to that which had been annulled in 1936. *Mulford v. Smith*[81] sustained the Agricultural Adjustment Act of 1938, whose basic features were not unlike those of the law of the same name that had previously been condemned.

It is true that *Mulford* did not expressly hold that agriculture came within the definition of commerce. This omission led a lower court as late as 1954 to assert that agriculture is not commerce and, hence, "Federal regulation of agriculture invades the reserved rights of the states."[82] The Supreme Court quickly laid to rest this ghost, declaring categorically, in reversing the lower-court decision, that regulation of agriculture was within the commerce power.[83]

Since *Jones & Laughlin,* productive industries have no longer been removed from the commerce power. No longer must production be treated as purely "local" activity, immune from congressional control regardless of the impact that it may have. The law has come back to the Marshall conception of commerce as an organic whole, with the Commerce Clause embracing all commerce that concerns more than one state. Under the conception, federal power is not limited to commerce that actually moves across state lines. It includes all activities that affect interstate commerce, though such activities, taken alone, might be considered "local." The whole point about the post-1937 law is that these activities can no longer be considered alone. If they have an effect upon interstate commerce, they concern more than one state and come within the Commerce Clause.

The key question thus becomes: Does the subject of regulation affect interstate commerce? An affirmative answer compels the conclusion that it is within federal power. Mines and mills, factories and farms—all engaged in production, rather than commerce in the literal sense—are brought within the sweep of the Commerce Clause, provided only that they exert some effect upon interstate commerce.

"Almost anything," caustically declared the *Jones & Laughlin* dissent "—marriage, birth, death—may in some fashion affect commerce."[84] Under contemporary conditions, the economic system has become so interconnected that there are few local business activities that may not have at least some repercussions upon commerce that extends beyond state lines. If centripetal forces are elevated, to the exclusion of the forces that counteract them, there is practically no economic activity that is immune from congressional control. If effect upon commerce is the test, irrespective of degree, the radius of federal power becomes as broad as the economic life of the nation.

In addition, reference should be made to *United States v. Darby* (1941),[85] one of the last cases in the Hughes Court. The decision there removed another pre-1937 limitation upon federal power when it overruled the *Child Labor Case*.[86] At issue in *Darby* was the Fair Labor Standards Act, which provides for the fixing of minimum wages and maximum hours by a federal agency. It goes on to prohibit the shipment in interstate commerce of goods manufactured by employees whose wages are less than the prescribed minimum or whose hours of work are more than the prescribed maximum. The Act was attacked on the ground that, while the prohibition was nominally a regulation of commerce, its motive was really regulation of wages and hours.

The Court candidly recognized that that was in fact the case. But the whole point about *Darby* is that, under it, the end toward which a congressional exercise of power over commerce is directed is irrelevant. This is, of course, contrary to the *Child Labor Case* thesis that the motive of the prohibition or its effect to control production within the states could operate to deprive the congressional regulation of its constitutional validity. The Court in *Darby* expressly disowned the *Child Labor Case* approach. The *Child Labor Case*, the *Darby* opinion declared, "should be and now is overruled."[87]

The overruling of the *Child Labor Case* returned the Court to Marshall's view of the federal power to regulate under the Commerce Clause as a complete one. In *Darby*, the Court relied directly upon Marshall's definition of the power to regulate commerce as the power "to prescribe the rule by which commerce is governed."[88] Under *Darby*, once again, the sole question is whether a challenged law does prescribe a governing rule for commerce. If it does, it is valid, regardless of the ends that may have induced its enactment.

The *Darby* decision marks the culmination in the development of the Commerce Clause as the source of a natural police power. The *Child Labor* decision constituted a significant rebuff to that development. *Darby* removed whatever limitation it imposed. Under *Darby*, Congress can utilize its commerce power to suppress any commerce contrary to its broad conception of public interest. The national police power (as this aspect of the commerce power may be termed) is the plenary power to secure any social, economic, or moral ends, so far as they may be obtained by the regulation of commerce.

Due Process and Judicial Restraint

The decisions of the second Hughes Court signaled a significant change in the Supreme Court's role in the constitutional structure. Where the Court had previously set itself up as virtual supreme censor of the wisdom of challenged legislation, it now adopted the view formerly expressed in dissent by Justice Holmes. Under the earlier approach, the desirability of a statute was determined as an objective fact on the Court's independent judgment. Now the more subjective Holmes test was applied: Could rational legislators have regarded the statute as a reasonable method of reaching the desired result?[89]

The change in the Court's approach had a seismic impact on the doctrine of substantive due process. Few today doubt that the high tribunal went too far before 1937 in its application of the doctrine or that the Court after that time was correct in deliberately discarding the extreme due process philosophy. The Due Process Clause was not intended to prevent legislatures from choosing whether to regulate or leave their economies to the blind operation of uncontrolled economic forces, futile or even noxious though the choice might seem to the judges. Economic views of confined validity are not to be treated as though the Framers had enshrined them in the constitution.[90]

In his dissent in *Lochner,* Justice Holmes had asserted, "This case is decided upon an economic theory which a large part of the country does not entertain."[91] After 1937, both the economic and legal theories on which *Lochner* rested were repudiated by the Supreme Court. In the 1937 decision overruling its earlier holding that a minimum-wage law violated due process by impairing freedom of contract between employers and employees, the Court asked: "What is this freedom? The Constitution does not speak of freedom of contract."[92] The liberty safeguarded by the Constitution is liberty in a society that requires the protection of law against evils which menace the health, safety, morals, or welfare of the people. Regulation adopted in the interests of the community, the Court concluded, is due process.

After 1937, the Hughes Court had only one occasion directly to overrule other due process decisions of its predecessors. That occurred in 1941, when a 1928 decision voiding a state statute regulating the fees charged by employment agencies as inconsistent with due process had been relied on by a lower court to invalidate a similar Nebraska law; the Supreme Court speedily reversed, holding that the earlier case could no longer be deemed controlling authority.[93]

Although the Hughes Court had no occasion directly to repudiate other specific due process decisions of the pre-1937 period, its later decisions were clearly inconsistent with the earlier due process philosophy. From 1890 to 1937 the high bench used the Due Process Clause as a device to enable it to review the desirability of regulatory legislation. Since that time, "The day is gone when this Court uses the Due Process Clause of the

Fourteenth Amendment to strike down state laws, regulatory of business and industrial conditions, because they may be unwise, improvident, or out of harmony with a particular school of thought."[94]

The view that due process authorized judges to hold laws unconstitutional because they believe the legislature has acted unwisely was definitely discarded. Instead, under the post-1937 jurisprudence, it is not for courts to judge the correctness of the economic theory behind a regulatory law. Not only was the Holmes view that the Constitution does not enact Spencer's *Social Statics* emphatically adopted; in the Court's more recent words, "Whether the legislature takes for its textbook Adam Smith, Herbert Spencer, Lord Keynes, or some other is no concern of ours."[95]

The decline of substantive due process was now firmly ingrained in our public law. And, the Court would say, such rejection is entirely consistent with the role of the judiciary in a representative democracy. To draw the pre-1937 due process line as a limit to regulatory action is, in Holmes's phrase, to make the criterion of constitutionality only what the judges believe to be for the public good.[96]

From this point of view, the decisions of the second Hughes Court can be characterized as constituting a constitutional revolution not just because they recognized significant governmental powers that had theretofore been denied. They also inaugurated a drastic shift in the balance that had previously existed between the Court and the other branches. The pre-1937 interpretation of the doctrine of judicial supremacy had been dominated by the primacy of the Supreme Court, culminating in the Court's review of the desirability of the early New Deal legislation. After 1937, the Court receded to a much more subdued position.

The new restrained posture was, nevertheless, one that was ultimately to give way to a more activist role. Writing as a contemporary who participated at the Government counsel table in the 1937 cases that have been discussed, Robert H. Jackson noted acutely that the new decisions of the Court did not necessarily establish immutably the constitutional law of the future: "No doubt another day will find one of its tasks to be correction of mistakes that time will reveal in this structure in which we now take pride. As one who knows well the workmen and the work of this generation, I bespeak the right of the future to undo our work when it no longer serves acceptably."[97]

The future was to do exactly what Justice Jackson had predicted. Judical restraint was to prove inadequate to meet the needs of the society during the second half of the century. Starting with the accession of Chief Justice Warren, the Court was once again to assume a primary role in the constitutional structure. That was to occur, however, only after the more subdued interlude of the Stone and Vinson Courts.

11

Stone and Vinson Courts, 1941–1953

While it may be the custom to designate the Supreme Court by the name of its head, one who looks only to the bare legal powers of the Chief Justice will find it hard to understand this underscoring of his preeminence. Aside from his designation as Chief of the Court and the attribution of a slightly higher salary, his position is not superior to that of his colleagues—and certainly is not legally superior. In Justice Tom C. Clark's words, "The Chief Justice has no more authority than other members of the court."[1]

The Chief Justiceship should not, however, be approached only in a formalistic sense. Starting with Marshall, the greatest of the Chief Justices have known how to make the most of the extralegal potential inherent in their position. Although perhaps only primus inter pares, the Chief Justice is *primus*. Somebody has to preside over a body of nine, and it is the Chief Justice who directs the business of the Court.

Charles Evans Hughes is the prime modern example of an effective Chief Justice. As Justice Frankfurter once put it, "Chief Justice Hughes radiated authority, not through any other quality than the intrinsic moral power that was his. He was master of the business."[2] The same was not true of Hughes's two successors. In terms of their leadership abilities, in fact, Chief Justices Harlan F. Stone and Fred M. Vinson were the least effective Court heads during the present century.

Chief Justice Stone and His Colleagues

Harlan Fiske Stone on Olympus shows that the qualities that make for an outstanding Justice are not necessarily the qualities that make for a good Chief Justice. There is no doubt that, since his appointment to the Court in 1925, Stone had made his mark as a superior Justice. He had been a leader in the fight against equating the Constitution with laissez faire, as well as in the movement to conform the Court's jurisprudence to the "felt necessities" of the changing times. By the time of Chief Justice Hughes's retirement in June 1941, Stone was recognized as the intellectual leader of the Court. He was, therefore, the natural choice to succeed to the Chief Justiceship—acknowledged as such by both his colleagues and the country. Hughes himself told President Roosevelt that Stone's record gave him first claim upon the honor.[3]

Time wrote that "it liked the idea of a solid man as Chief Justice to follow Charles Evans Hughes. And solid is the word for Chief Justice Stone—200 lb., with heavy, good-natured features and a benign judicial air."[4] Yet, impressive though the new Chief Justice may have been as a figure of justice, he proved anything but a leader in the Hughes mold. Indeed, Stone at the head of the Court was the very antithesis of the Hughes model of dynamism and efficiency. According to Stone's biographer, indeed, "Stone's techniques stood in bold contrast with those of his predecessor."[5]

Justice Frankfurter recalls that while the Hughes passion for efficiency made everything in his Court "taut . . . Stone was an 'easy boss.'"[6] After he had attended the new Chief Justice's first conference, Frankfurter wrote to Stone about "the relaxed atmosphere and your evident desire to have our conferences an exchange of . . . views of nine men."[7]

Chief Justice Hughes had conducted the conferences in the manner of a strict teacher in the classroom. The Hughes conference was normally a four-hour affair;[8] discussion was brief and to the point and woe to the Justice who spoke out of turn. In the Stone conferences, on the other hand, Frankfurter could write about "the deviations from the tradition against speaking out of turn."[9] Like the law professor that he once was, Stone was slow to cut off debate in his eagerness to have all issues thoroughly explored. The result was a freewheeling discussion in which the Chief Justice was more a participant than a leader. "The Chief Justice," commented Justice Reed, "delighted to take on all comers around the conference table and . . . to battle . . . for his views."[10] Stone, says Frankfurter, had "the habit . . . of carrying on a running debate with any justice who expresses views different from his."[11]

Justice Potter Stewart confirmed to me that he heard that "Stone's problem was that, at a conference, he himself always insisted upon having the last word, and that's not the way you preside—always arguing with the person that had spoken." Discussion became wrangling and the Justices emerged from these interminable meetings irritated and exhausted, their differences inflamed from excessive argument.[12] The Stone method only exacerbated the personal and professional differences in what soon became one of the most divided Courts in our history.

The fragmentation in the Stone Court was, in part at least, caused by personal antipathy among the Justices. That, in turn, was aggravated by the appointment to the Stone Court of Robert H. Jackson. But first, a brief word about two other appointments to that Court.

Just before the Stone nomination to head the Court, President Roosevelt selected Senator James F. Byrnes of South Carolina for the vacancy created by Justice McReynolds's retirement. The new Justice contributed little to the Court, since he resigned in 1942, only a year after he had taken his seat, to become, in Roosevelt's own term, "Assistant President"—in charge of domestic policies during the war.

To fill the Byrnes seat, the President selected Wiley B. Rutledge, a former dean of the Iowa and Washington University (St. Louis) Law Schools—at the time a judge on the Court of Appeals for the District of Columbia. Justice Rutledge became a member of the Court's liberal bloc and is noted for his opinions in the field of civil liberties, though he was to serve only six years until his death in 1949.

Between the Byrnes and Rutledge appointments, there was the selection of Robert H. Jackson, then Attorney General, to the seat held by Stone as a Justice. Jackson had been a successful practitioner in upstate New York and had gone to Washington to hold various legal positions in the Roosevelt Administration.

A book on the differences between Justices Black and Frankfurter is titled *The Antagonists*.[13] Yet the differences between the two were primarily intellectual. Those between Justices Black and Jackson were intensely personal. In fact, the two became as bitter personal antagonists as ever sat together on the Supreme Court.

Justice Harold H. Burton noted in his diary his surprise that Justices Black and Jackson exhanged "Good mornings" and even "joined in a brief discussion" at that morning's conference. "I mention this," he wrote, "because of the popular idea . . . that they could not speak to each other." Burton did, however, observe, "These were the first instances of their speaking to each other that I have seen this fall."[14]

The Black–Jackson feud racked both the Stone and Vinson Courts and contributed to the ineffectiveness of both Chief Justices. It also played a major part in Jackson's personal failure as a Justice. One of the most gifted men ever to serve on the Court, Jackson harbored ambitions to be President or, at the least, to occupy the Court's central chair. His lack of success in this regard poisoned his outlook and made him, in his last years on the bench, increasingly embittered.

Justice Jackson was termed by his closest colleague, Justice Frankfurter, "by long odds the most literarily gifted member on the Court."[15] As a stylist and phrase-maker, Jackson can be compared only with Justice Holmes. It was Justice Jackson who aphorized the reality of the Supreme

Court's position: "There is no doubt that if there were a super-Supreme Court, a substantial proportion of our reversals of state courts would also be reversed. We are not final because we are infallible, but we are infallible only because we are final."[16]

The Court and the Law of War

During Chief Justice Stone's tenure, the change from judicial supremacy to the judicial restraint of the post-1937 period gained added emphasis from American participation in World War II. To the Holmes restraint canon was added the truth contained in a striking passage from Burke's *Reflections on the Revolution in France:* "Laws are commanded to hold their tongues amongst arms; and tribunals fall to the ground with the peace they are no longer able to uphold." One familiar with the practical working of a constitutional system realizes that Burke's dictum all too often accords with the realities of wartime.

During the second global conflict, as during the Civil War period, the Supreme Court did little more than confirm the action taken by the Government to deal with the war emergency. Executive primacy is an inevitable concomitant of full-scale war, and it is perhaps unfair to expect the Justices to do more than stamp with their imprimatur measures deemed necessary by those wielding the force of the nation. In practice the Court could do no more than ratify the plenary power vested in government to meet the needs of global war.

In many ways the most dramatic of the Court's war decisions was rendered in the case of the eight German saboteurs who had been landed on our shores from submarines in June 1942. The eight had been arrested by FBI agents soon after their landings and tried by a military commission specially appointed by President Roosevelt for offenses against the law of war and the Articles of War. The commission had found them guilty of violating the law of war by attempting sabotage of our war facilities and had ordered death sentences for six of them and prison terms for the other two. The officers who had been appointed to defend the saboteurs before the military tribunal then sought habeas corpus.

To deal with the cases "without any avoidable delay," after the lower courts had refused relief, the Supreme Court convened in June 1942, in special term. After hearing argument for two days, it handed down a brief per curiam opinion denying habeas corpus. A formal opinion by Chief Justice Stone, setting forth the reasoning of the Court, was not filed until three months later[17]—weeks after the death sentences ordered by the military commission had been carried out.

Before the Supreme Court, the German saboteurs had contended that they could not validly be tried by a military tribunal, asserting that they were entitled to be tried in the civil courts with the safeguards, including trial by jury, which the Fifth and Sixth Amendments guarantee to all persons tried in such courts for criminal offenses. The Court rejected their contention, holding that the consitutional safeguards did not apply to offenses against the law of war.

Japanese Evacuation

Few, it is believed, will take issue with the Court's decision in the case of the German saboteurs. But the same is scarcely true of the high bench's handling of what a *Harper's* article was to term "America's Greatest Wartime Mistake"—the evacuation of those of Japanese ancestry from the West Coast.

Acting upon their belief that those of Japanese heritage posed a security threat after Pearl Harbor, the military moved to eliminate the danger by a number of restrictive measures. The most important of them was a series of Civilian Exclusion Orders, issued early in 1942, excluding "all persons of Japanese ancestry, both alien and non-alien," from the westernmost part of the country. Those so excluded were gathered together in so-called assembly centers and then evacuated to what were euphemistically termed Relocation Centers in interior states, where they were detained until almost the end of the war. Under this evacuation program, over 112,000 persons of Japanese ancestry were herded from their homes on the West Coast into the relocation centers, which, had they been set up in any other country, we would not hesitate to call by their true name— concentration camps.

The record of his government in dealing with the West Coast Japanese during the war is hardly one that an American can contemplate with satisfaction. As the Court eloquently declared in 1943, "Distinctions between citizens solely because of their ancestry are by their very nature odious to a free people whose institutions are founded upon the doctrine of equality."[18] Despite this, the Court did uphold the evacuation of the Japanese in *Korematsu v. United States* (1944).[19]

Korematsu had been convicted for remaining in a military area contrary to the Civilian Exclusion Order of the military commander. Such an order, said the Court, could validly be issued by the military authorities in light of the particular situation confronting them on the West Coast after Pearl Harbor. In the face of a threatened Japanese attack, citizens of Japanese ancestry could rationally be set apart from those who had no particular associations with Japan; in time of war residents having ethnic affiliations with an invading enemy may be a greater source of danger than those of a different ancestry. That being the case, it could not be said that the exclusion order bore no reasonable relation to the demands of military necessity.

In *Ex parte Endo* (1944),[20] it is true, the Court did order the release of the Japanese-Americans from the Relocation Centers, on the ground that, though the original evacuations might have been justified by necessity, such necessity did not exist three years after Pearl Harbor, during which time the Government had had ample opportunity to separate the loyal

from the disloyal among those detained. There was no evidence of disloyalty against Miss Endo. In her case, the authority to detain her as part of a
program against espionage or sabotage was exhausted as soon as her loyalty was conceded. Consequently, said the Court, "Mitsuye Endo is entitled to an unconditional release by the War Relocation Authority."[21]

The *Endo* decision demonstrates both the strength and weakness of
judicial review of exercises of the war power. Certainly, the Court's grant
of habeas corpus to Miss Endo vindicates the rule of law even in wartime.
It shows that, even though military authorities can take whatever measures
may be demanded by the exigencies of war, the military's ipse dixit is not of
itself conclusive of the necessity for the measures taken. The test of necessity is, with us, a judicial question, and the *Endo* case illustrates how it can
be applied by the Court to condemn measures that bear no reasonable
relation to military needs.

At the same time, the *Endo* case shows the limitations of judicial power
as a practical check on military arbitrariness. By its very nature, judicial
justice is dispensed slowly, though it may be dispensed exceedingly well.
Mitsuye Endo was evacuated from her home and placed in a Relocation
Center early in 1942. In July 1942, she filed a petition for a writ of habeas
corpus in a federal district court; yet it was not until December 1944 that
she was ordered released by the Supreme Court. But the Court's decision
did not and could not affect her three-year deprivation of liberty, illegal
though such deprivation might have been.

Despite the Supreme Court's decision, to quote from the concurring
opinion of Justice Roberts, "An admittedly loyal citizen has been deprived
of her liberty for a period of years. Under the Constitution she should be
free to come and go as she pleases. Instead, her liberty of motion and other
innocent activities have been prohibited and conditioned."[22] Mitsuye
Endo may have had the satisfaction of being immortalized in the *Supreme
Court Reports;* but she was most unlikely to consider that an adequate
substitute for her loss of liberty during her illegal confinement in the
Relocation Center.

Property Rights

The Stone Court also did little to restrain the drastic restrictions upon
property rights that took place during World War II. The war power has,
of course, always had a drastic impact upon property as well as persons.
Nor is it surprising that this should be so. At a time when it is the un-
doubted law of the land that citizens may by conscription be compelled to
give up their life for their country's cause, it should occasion no astonishment that they may similarly be required to yield their earthly possessions,
if that be demanded. We may resist a planned economy and the coming of
the omnipotent state in peacetime; at the same time, complete control of
both person and property (what Justice Jackson once termed "military
socialization")[23] is accepted by all as a patriotic necessity in time of war.

Total mobilization of both the work force and the economy reached its peak during World War II. Indeed, under the war statutes delegating authority to him, President Franklin D. Roosevelt can be said to have been vested with more arbitrary power over persons and property than any English-speaking statesman since Oliver Cromwell. But such total power in the Executive was deemed necessary to meet the demands of global war. And the Supreme Court was in the forefront of those recognizing this necessity.

The power fully to mobilize workers had been recognized in the Government during World War I;[24] thus, as the Court put it, "The constitutionality of the conscription of manpower for military service is beyond question."[25] The Court's decisions arising out of World War II recognized governmental authority over property rights as extensive as that over the work force. Said the Court, in the case just quoted, on the impact of "total global warfare" upon our system: "With the advent of such warfare, mobilized property in the form of equipment and supplies became as essential as mobilized manpower. Mobilization of effort extended not only to the uniformed armed services but to the entire population. . . . The language of the Constitution authorizing such measures is broad rather than restrictive."[26] Congress can, of course, clearly draft men for battle service. According to a 1942 opinion, "Its power to draft business organizations to support the fighting men who risk their lives can be no less."[27]

The most important World War II decision upholding governmental authority over property rights was *Yakus v. United States* (1944),[28] which involved the validity of price control. It was contended that the Emergency Price Control Act of 1942 unconstitutionally delegated the authority to control prices to the Price Administrator. Under the Act, the Administrator was empowered to fix maximum prices for all commodities. Under this law the most extensive scheme of price-fixing ever attempted in our system was carried out. The prices of almost all goods and services were directly controlled from Washington in a manner which was unprecedented. Yet the Court had no difficulty in sustaining the congressional assertion of such broad authority under the war power. Under that power governmental authority was upheld over the most important property right, namely, the right to dispose of property at the highest obtainable price.

In the realities of a war economy, the sanctions available to the government through its power over priorities and allocations are even more important as a means of securing obedience to its orders than the traditional methods of judicial enforcement provided for in the Price Control Act. Thus the power given to the President to allocate materials during World War II was used extensively to withhold materials from those who disobeyed the economic control orders of governmental agencies. This was true even though there was no statutory authority for such coercive use of the allocation power.

A good example of the manner in which the power was used is found in a 1944 case.[29] A retail fuel oil dealer had been found by the Office of

Price Administration to have violated its rationing order by obtaining large quantities of fuel oil without surrendering ration coupons and by delivering thousands of gallons of fuel oil to consumers without receiving ration coupons. As a punishment, the OPA suspended the right of the dealer to receive any fuel oil for resale for a year. This suspension order was upheld by the Supreme Court as against the claim that it imposed a penalty not provided for by Congress. The President's statutory power to allocate materials, said the Court, included the power to issue suspension orders against retailers and to withhold rationed materials from them where it was established they had violated the ration regulations.

The extreme sanction utilized by the OPA (which amounted, in effect, to an economic death sentence against the dealer concerned, at least for the period of the suspension order) was sustained, although the power to impose such a sanction was nowhere conferred by Congress. The normal reluctance of our courts to imply penal powers in the administration gave way in the face of what the Court felt to be the necessities inherent in a scheme of effective wartime rationing.

The Least Effective Chief

Fred M. Vinson may have been the least effective Court head in the Supreme Court's history. Appointed in 1946 after Chief Justice Stone's sudden death, the Kentuckian had been a Congressman and circuit judge, and had served in high executive positions, ending in his pre-Court tenure as Secretary of the Treasury. His appointment was due primarily to his close friendship with President Truman, who hoped that his skill at getting along with people would enable him to restore peace to a Court that had become splintered under Chief Justice Stone.

The new Chief Justice was (as his predecessor had been) a large man— in the Frankfurter phrase, "tall and broad and [with] a little bit of a bay window."[30] Throughout his career, Vinson had been known for his skill at smoothing ruffled feathers. But his hearty bonhomie was not enough to enable him to lead the Court effectively. The Justices looked down on the new Chief as the possessor of a second-class mind. Even Justice Reed, the least intellectually gifted of the Roosevelt appointees, could dismiss the dour-faced Chief, in a comment to Justice Frankfurter, as "just like me, except that he is less well-educated."[31] Frankfurter himself could characterize Vinson in his diary as "confident and easy-going and sure and shallow . . . he seems to me to have the confident air of a man who does not see the complexities of problems and blithely hits the obvious points."[32]

Phillip Elman, who had clerked for Frankfurter and was one of the most knowledgeable Court watchers, wrote to the Justice about "the C.J." from the Solicitor General's Office: "What a mean little despot he is. Has there ever been a member of the Court who was deficient in so many respects as a man and as a judge. Even that s.o.b. McReynolds, despite his defects of character, stands by comparison as a towering figure and powerful intellect . . . this man is a pygmy, morally and mentally. And so uncouth."[33]

The new Chief Justice was even more inept than his predecessor in leading the conference. According to Frankfurter's diary, Chief Justice Vinson presented cases in a shallow way. He "blithely hits the obvious points . . . disposing of each case rather briefly, by choosing, as it were, to float merely on the surface of the problems raised by the cases."[34] Certainly, the Vinson conference management was anything but masterful.

When Vinson supported Justice Tom Clark's appointment, Washington wags said it was because he wanted someone on his Court who knew less law than he did.[35] Throughout his tenure, the Justices were openly to display their contempt for their Chief. As a law clerk recalls it, several of Vinson's colleagues "would discuss in his presence the view that the Chief's job should rotate annually and . . . made no bones about regarding him—correctly—as their intellectual inferior."[36]

Such a Chief Justice could scarcely be expected to lead the gifted prima donnas who then sat on the Court. If anything the division among the Justices intensified and, all too often, degenerated into personal animosity during Vinson's service.

As it turned out, the Vinson Court was the most fragmented in the Court's history. During the last Vinson term, only 19 percent of the cases were decided unanimously—a record low. The situation was worsened by the fact that the antagonism between Justices Black and Jackson became even more bitter in the Vinson Court. The rancor between the two was exacerbated by the Jackson belief that Justice Black had frustrated his long ambition to become Chief Justice by intervening with President Truman after Chief Justice Stone's death in 1946. A widely circulated column quoted the President as saying, "Black says he will resign if I make Jackson Chief Justice and tell the reasons why. Jackson says the same about Black."[37] Some time later Justice Frankfurter wrote to a close friend, quoting "a most reliable witness," that Truman had planned to appoint Jackson until he was "threatened with resignations" from the Court.[38] Jackson, then chief American prosecutor at the Nuremberg war crimes trials, held a well-publicized press conference, in which he ventilated his dispute with Black. Then he wrote bitterly to Frankfurter, "Black is now rid of the Chief. . . . Now if he can have it understood that he has a veto over the promotion of any Associate, he would have things about where he wants them."[39]

The bitterness between these two Justices continued until Jackson's death in 1954. Not long before, Jackson sent Frankfurter a note in which, referring to Black, he declared, "I simply give up understanding our colleague and begin to think he is a case for a psychiatrist."[40] Black, on the other side, wrote a former law clerk that a copy of the *Macon Telegraph* had been sent him that contained an editorial entitled "Jackson Is an Unmitigated Ass." On the same page, Black went on, "appeared an article by John

Temple Graves on the same subject. I have nothing but sympathy for John Temple."[41]

Vinson Court Appointments

During the early Vinson years, the Court was sharply divided between two blocs. The first, led by Justice Frankfurter, joined by the new Chief Justice and Justices Jackson and Reed, urged judicial restraint as the only criterion of constitutional adjudication. The other, led by Justice Black, joined by Justices Douglas, Murphy, and Rutledge, asserted that restraint was not the judicial be-all-and-end-all and that it should give way in cases involving civil liberties.

The rather even division between the two blocs was changed dramatically by the three Court appointments made by President Truman. The first was made just before Chief Justice Vinson was chosen, when Justice Roberts left the Court in 1945. The Truman appointee was Harold H. Burton, a Senator from Ohio, who had become a friend of the President as a member of the famous Truman Committee which investigated defense contracts during World War II. Burton's path to the high bench had followed the traditional pattern of practice as a local leader of the Bar, a political career (state legislator, Mayor of Cleveland, U.S. Senator), then elevation to the Court. In appearance, he has been compared to a small, neat version of a village storekeeper.[42] His biographer concedes that "Burton, an average justice, was not a bright, witty intellectual like a Frankfurter or a Black."[43] Yet, if he was quiet and unassuming, he was also hardworking. Frankfurter wrote Burton in 1947 that he had known every Justice since 1906, and "it is on that basis that I can say to you what I have said behind your back, that this court never had a Justice who was harder working or more conscientious."[44]

Burton, like the other Truman-appointed Justices, was usually to be found in the Frankfurter wing of the Court. Fully appreciative of his modest abilities, Burton was most deferential toward the former professor. Praise from the celebrated Harvard scholar led Burton to write, "I feel as though you have awarded me a mythical grade 'A' in your course on Consitutional Law, of which I may be proud."[45]

Truman's second Court appointee was Tom C. Clark, chosen to fill the seat of Justice Murphy, who died in 1949. Clark had started his legal career as a prosecutor, moved on to the Department of Justice, and then been raised to Attorney General when Truman became President. Clark remained the glad-handing politician, whose flamboyant bow tie (worn even under the judicial robe) gave him a perpetual sophomoric appearance. Clark continued to flaunt his Texas background—his normal way of signifying agreement to an opinion was to write "Okey." "The duck was delicious," Clark wrote to Chief Justice Earl Warren in 1955. "It was big enough to be from Texas."[46]

The Justices, on their side, constantly teased Clark about his state. In

1959, Justice John M. Harlan sent Clark a postcard from Australia: "Some of their sheep stations are nearly the size of the Sovereign State of Texas."[47] President Truman himself was quoted as saying that "Tom Clark was my biggest mistake. No question about it." According to the former President, "[I]t isn't so much that he's a bad man. It's just that he's such a dumb son of a bitch. He's about the dumbest man I think I've ever run across."[48]

To one familiar with Justice Clark's work, the Truman comment is ludicrous. Clark may not have been the intellectual equal of his more brilliant Brethren, but he developed into a more competent judge than any of the other Truman appointees. In fact, Clark has been the most under-rated Justice in recent Supreme Court history.

Under Chief Justice Vinson, Justice Clark almost always followed the conservative pro-Government Vinson position. The same was true of Sherman Minton, the last Truman-appointed Justice, who succeeded Justice Rutledge upon the latter's death in 1949. Like President Truman and Justice Burton, Minton had been a midwestern Senator, elected from Indiana. During his one term, he was a strong Roosevelt supporter and served as Democratic whip. This probably cost him reelection, but FDR consoled him with a seat on the U.S. Court of Appeals for the Seventh Circuit, where he served without distinction for eight years before being named to the high bench.

Minton was square-faced, with the build of a heavyweight boxer, and characterized by the saltiness of his tongue. He may have been the last Justice to use the spittoon provided for him behind the bench, which always upset the fastidious Justice Burton next to him. Minton, the worst of the Truman appointees, ranks by any standard near the botton on a list of Justices. Yet his fellows considered the earthy Hoosier most congenial to work with. "Minton," wrote Justice Frankfurter to a close friend, "will not go down as a great jurist, but he was a delightful colleague." Then he plaintively asked, "Why are most lawyers dull company?"[49]

The Court and the Cold War

The appointment of Chief Justice Vinson and Justices Burton, Clark, and Minton drastically tilted the Court balance in favor of the Frankfurter bloc. To Frankfurter, the judge who tried most to be a conscious Holmes disciple, the Holmes canon had become the only orthodox doctrine. For Justice Black, the restraint doctrine may no longer have been an appropriate response to the new constitutional issues presented to the Court. Frankfurter, on the contrary, whose attitude toward Holmes smacked as much of veneration as agreement, remained wholly true to the approach of the mentor whom he called "My Master." To Frankfurter, the Holmes canon remained the judicial polestar throughout his career on the Court. Judicial restraint became the established order so long as the Frankfurter bloc constituted the Court majority.

To Justice Frankfurter and his followers, restraint was the proper posture for a nonrepresentative judiciary, regardless of the nature of the asserted interest in particular cases. To refuse to defer to the legislative judgment did violence to the basic presuppositions of representative democracy.

Adherence to the restraint doctrine was carried to its logical extreme in the Stone and Vinson Court decisions deferring to the Government demand for security. It may be unfair to expect the Justices to have done more than confirm measures deemed necessary by those wielding the force of the nation. But the same was surely not true of the "cold war" period that followed the cessation of hostilities. Doubtless some of the excesses committed during the postwar years are still too close in time to be able to deal impartially with them. These excesses did, however, reveal that security, like the patriotism of which Dr. Johnson speaks, might also come to be the last refuge of a scoundrel: many of the things done in the postwar era in security's name would not have been tolerated in less tense times.

A basic problem for the American system of law is that of reconciling the antinomy between liberty and security. Both have, to be sure, always been essential elements in the polity, whose coexistence has had to be reconciled by the law. In the postwar period, nevertheless, security tended to dominate. The response to the tensions of the cold war made American law security-conscious as it had never been before.

The governmental demand for security was articulated in laws and other measures restricting rights normally deemed fundamental. For the first time since the notorious Alien and Sedition Acts of 1798, a peacetime sedition law (making subversive speech criminal) put people in prison. The law in question—the Smith Act—was enacted in 1940; but the first significant prosecutions, those brought in 1948 against the leaders of the American Communist party, were a direct fruit of the postwar confrontation with the Soviet Union. The Communist prosecutions were upheld in *Dennis v. United States* (1951)[50] with the decision turning on the "clear and present danger" presented by Communist advocacy during the tense postwar period.

The *Dennis* decision, however, involved a clear watering-down of the Clear and Present Danger Test as it was stated by Justice Holmes. According to Chief Justice Vinson's opinion of the Court, the correct interpretation of the test was: "In each case [courts] must ask whether the gravity of the 'evil,' discounted by its improbability, justifies such invasion of free speech as is necessary to avoid the danger."[51]

No substantive "evil" is as grave as the forcible overthrow of government; hence the danger that that will occur need not be nearly as "clear and present" as would be required if a lesser "evil" was involved. To the Court, the "evil" in *Dennis* was so overwhelming that it had to defer to Congress on whether any nexus between defendants' teaching and advocacy and that "evil" did exist.

Restraint and deference were, indeed, carried to their extreme in *Dennis*. Of course, as Justice Douglas pointed out in dissent, Communists in this country were miserable merchants of unwanted ideas, whose wares remained unsold.[52] To the majority, however, that did not justify a judicial tribunal in substituting its judgment for that of the elected representatives of the people that the Communist party constituted a "clear and present" danger to national security. In a democratic system, under the restraint canon, the primary responsibility for determining when there is danger that speech will induce the substantive evil that the Government has a right to prevent—in this case, attempts to overthrow government by force and violence—must lie with the elected representatives of the people. In this, as in other fields of judicial review, the Vinson Court saw its function as one to serve as a brake upon arbitrary extremes. But its task was exhausted when there was found to be a rational basis for the particular exercise of congressional judgment.

Dennis was not the only decision sustaining cold war restrictions under the restraint doctrine. In addition, the Court upheld other significant restrictions, ranging from drastic restraints upon aliens to the loyalty–security programs instituted by governments in this country. The restrictions on Communist aliens were ruled within the plenary power of Congress over citizens of other lands,[53] and the federal loyalty program was upheld under the settled principle that "[t]he Constitution does not guarantee public employment."[54] In addition, the Court refused to strike down restrictions on the procedural rights of notice and full hearing in cases where national security was involved.[55]

These decisions, occurring during the immediate postwar period, may be understandable as a continued reaction from the excesses of pre-1937 judicial supremacy. Justices who had repudiated those excesses continued to display the same Holmes-like approach of deference to the legislator. Nevertheless, one may wonder whether the Supreme Court did not go too far in standing aside in the face of the extreme restrictions imposed in security's name.

A Court overimbued with the dominant demand for security may tend to accede to that demand, even if the cost be distortion of accepted principles of constitutional law. Yet this can hardly be done without important effects on general jurisprudence. A supreme tribunal that molds its law only to fit immediate demands of public sentiment is hardly fulfilling its proper role. As Justice Frankfurter once put it, "The Court has no reason for existence if it merely reflects the pressures of the day."[56] The doctrine of deference to the legislature may require abnegation on the part of the Court but hardly abdication by it of the judicial function. Whatever may be said about the strains and stresses of the cold war period, the enemy was not so near the gates that the nation had to abandon respect for the organic traditions that had theretofore prevailed in the American system.

Decisions against Government

The ledger was not, however, all in favor of governmental power during the Stone and Vinson years. There were also significant cases in which the Court refused to accept claims of public authority vis-à-vis individual rights. The most important of them was the *Steel Seizure Case* (1952),[57] in which the Court (over Chief Justice Vinson's dissent) invalidated President Truman's seizure of the nation's steel mills during the Korean War. According to the Government, a strike disrupting steel production for even a brief period would have so endangered the well-being and safety of the nation that the President had "inherent power" to do what he had done.

The Court denied that the President had any such prerogative to exercise what amounted to lawmaking authority: "In the framework of our Constitution, the President's power to see that the laws are faithfully executed refutes the idea that he is to be a lawmaker. . . . The Founders of this Nation entrusted the lawmaking power to the Congress alone in both good and bad times." The President, in Justice Black's opinion, had no authority, either as Chief Executive or as Commander in Chief, to take possession of private property in order to keep labor disputes from stopping production: "This is a job for the Nation's lawmakers."[58]

If, at first glance, the *Steel Seizure* decision seems inconsistent with the judicial restraint doctrine, the inconsistency is more apparent than real. The case was not one involving only the question of whether the Court should defer to the President's action. On the contrary, the Court here, in Justice Frankfurter's phrase, had "to intervene in determining where authority lies as between the democratic forces in our scheme of government."[59] In the *Steel* case, the Court was acting not as overseer of the Chief Executive but as holder of the constitutional balance between the two political branches of government, to both of which the Court, under its post-1937 doctrine, owed deference.

In such a situation, to which branch should the Court yield? Where power to seize private property for public use (clearly within legislative authority) is involved, the supremacy of the congressional policy is the only principle consistent with a polity in which "[a]ll legislative powers herein Granted" have been vested in Congress.

There were also Stone and Vinson Court decisions that were favorable to the protection of civil liberties. The most dramatic of them well demonstrated the emotional trials presented by a rigorous employment of the Frankfurter judicial restraint technique. At issue was the constitutionality of a state law making it compulsory for school children to salute the flag. In *Minersville School District v. Gobitis,*[60] decided in 1940, Justice Frankfurter had delivered the opinion of the Court sustaining the flag-salute requirement, with Justice Stone alone dissenting. In a letter to Stone explaining his opinion, Frankfurter claimed that "nothing has weighed as much on my conscience, since I have come to this Court, as has this case."[61] Then, only three years later, in *West Virginia Board of Education v. Barnette*,[62] the Court reversed itself and ruled the compulsory salute unconstitutional.

In *Barnette*, Justice Jackson delivered perhaps his best opinion for the Court. "The Bill of Rights," he declared, "denies those in power any legal opportunity to coerce" allegiance. "Authority here is to be controlled by public opinion, not public opinion by authority."[63] Justice Frankfurter stood his original ground and delivered a sharp *Barnette* dissent, which emphasized the need for judicial restraint even in such a case. As the Justice wrote to Chief Justice Stone explaining his opinion upholding the flag salute, "What weighs with me strongly in this case is my anxiety that, while we lean in the direction of the libertarian aspect, we do not exercise our judicial power unduly, and as though we ourselves were legislators by holding with too tight a rein the organs of popular government."[64]

The *Barnette* case well illustrates that no matter how he tried to clothe his opinions with the Holmes mantle, there was an element of shabbiness in the results reached by Justice Frankfurter in too many cases. After Frankfurter delivered his opinion upholding the compulsory flag salute, he was talking about the opinion over cocktails at Hyde Park. Eleanor Roosevelt impulsively declared that regardless of the Justice's learning and legal skills, there was something wrong with an opinion that forced little children to salute a flag when such a ceremony was repugnant to their conscience.[65]

In *Barnette*, the Court also stated the preferred-position doctrine that was to prove seminal in First Amendment cases. The Jackson opinion emphasized the difference in approach which must be followed as between First Amendment cases and other cases: "The right of a State to regulate, for example, a public utility may well include, so far as the due process test is concerned, power to impose all of the restrictions which a legislature may have a 'rational basis' for adopting. But freedoms of speech and of press, of assembly, and of worship may not be infringed on such slender grounds."[66]

In later Courts, the view that the First Amendment freedoms are in a preferred position led to renewed emphasis upon the need to protect personal rights in preference to those rights primarily economic in nature. Certainly, as Justice Frankfurter stated it, "those liberties of the individual which history has attested as the indispensable conditions of an open as against a closed society come to this Court with a momentum for respect lacking when appeal is made to liberties which derive merely from shifting economic arrangements."[67]

The judicial tendency to find legislative invasion more readily where personal rights are involved than in the sphere of economics[68] began in the Stone and Vinson Courts. According to its proponents, this approach was not really inconsistent with the Holmes restraint canon. This was pointed out by Justice Stone in a letter just before he became Chief Justice: "Justice Holmes' opinions indicate that he thought that the judge should not be too rigidly bound to the tenet of judicial self-restraint in cases involving civil liberties, although so far as I know he never formulated the distinction. You will find my formulation of it in a footnote in *United States v. Carolene Products Company.*"[69]

In his *Carolene Products* footnote[70]—the second most famous footnote in Supreme Court history[71]—Justice Stone also asked whether legislation aimed at "discrete and insular minorities" should not be subject to "more searching judicial inquiry."[72] Then in the *Korematsu* case, the Stone Court stated that "all legal restrictions which curtail the civil rights of a single racial group are immediately suspect . . . courts must subject them to the most rigid scrutiny."[73] These statements by Stone and his Court were to be the foundation of the "suspect class" concept that was to prove of such significance in the Warren and Burger Courts.

Perhaps the most important Stone and Vinson Court decisions protecting individual rights were those involving racial discrimination. It was those Courts that began to make equal protection more than a mere slogan for minority groups. For virtually the first time since their adoption, the gulf between the letter of the Fourteenth and Fifteenth Amendments and their practical effect began to be significantly narrowed. In its decisions the Stone-Vinson Court removed the legal prop from some of the most important manifestations of racial discrimination in this country. In a 1944 case, the so-called white primary, upon which Southern efforts to disfranchise blacks were based, was ruled unconstitutional.[74] In 1948 the enforcement of racial restrictive covenants was stricken down.[75]

It is true that neither the Stone nor the Vinson Court questioned the "separate but equal" doctrine of *Plessy v. Ferguson,*[76] which served as the legal foundation for racial segregation—particularly in the field of education. But those Courts were, nevertheless, able to make important progress by placing increasing emphasis upon judicial implementation of the requirement of equality in facilities. Their decisions were aimed at ensuring that the separate facilities provided for blacks were in fact substantially equal to those afforded to whites.

In 1948, the Court held that black applicants must be admitted to law schools reserved to whites unless equivalent facilities were provided for them.[77] In Texas, a separate black law school was, indeed, opened. A first-rate law school cannot, however, come into being full-grown, like Minerva from the head of Jove. The facilities afforded by the newly opened black law school could not, in fact, equal those available to white students at the University of Texas. Under these circumstances, the Court ruled that blacks in Texas had been denied a legal education equivalent to that offered to students of other races: "We hold that the Equal Protection Clause of the Fourteenth Amendment requires that petitioner be admitted to the University of Texas Law School."[78]

The Court, to be sure, did not directly overrule *Plessy* during the Stone and Vinson years. But its decisions came very close to holding that segregation as such, at least in higher education, was contrary to the Constitution. What was said of the University of Texas Law School applied with equal force to all long-established white educational institutions. Though *Plessy* permitted segregation, provided the requirement of equality in facilities was met, the Court's approach meant, in practice, that that requirement could never be met in the field of higher education.

But what is true of segregation in higher education is, in reality, also true of segregation as such. There can never be equality in separated facilities, for the mere fact of segregation makes for discrimination. The arbitrary separation of African-Americans solely on the basis of race is a "badge of servitude"[79] that must generate in them a feeling of inferior social status, regardless of the formal equality of the facilities provided for them.

In effect, then, the Stone and Vinson Courts were not far from the holding that segregation as such was discriminatory and hence a denial of equal protection—a holding but a step away from the decision in the Texas law school case. As we shall see, however, Chief Justice Vinson strongly opposed taking that step and it was left to the Court under his successor to do so in the *Brown* case, to be discussed in Chapter 13.

But it was not only the *Brown* decision that was to signal the arrival of a Court head so different from Chief Justice Vinson himself. The cases discussed in this section, in which the claims of the individual vis-à-vis government were upheld, were but a small part of the work of the Stone and Vinson Courts. Apart from them, those Courts, and particularly that under Chief Justice Vinson, were most receptive to claims of governmental authority as against claims of individual right. Judicial restraint and deference to the legislature had carried the day in the Supreme Court.

All this was, however, soon to change. A new Chief Justice was to turn the Court in a new direction—one which adapted Supreme Court jurisprudence to the changing needs of the second half of the twentieth century.

12

Warren Court, 1953–1969

There have been two great creative periods in American public law. The first was the formative era, when the Marshall Court laid down the foundations of American constitutional law, giving specific content to the broad general terms in which the Constitution is written. The judicial task at that time was to work out from the constitutional text a body of legal doctrines adapted to the needs of the new nation and the new era into which it was entering.

The second great creative period was the Warren Court era. The judicial task then was to keep step with the twentieth century's frenetic pace of societal change. To do this, the Warren Court had to perform a transforming role, usually thought of as more appropriate to the legislator than the judge. In the process it rewrote much of the corpus of American constitutional law. Indeed, in terms of creative impact on the law, the Warren Court's tenure can be compared only with that of the Marshall Court.

Chief Justice Warren and His Background

Of course, the Supreme Court is a collegiate institution whose collegiate nature is underscored by the custom the Justices have had of calling each other "Brethren." But each of the Brethren can only be guided, not directed. As Justice Frankfurter once stated in a letter to Chief Justice Vinson, "[G]ood feeling in the court, as in a family, is produced by accommodation, not by authority—whether the authority of a parent or a vote."[1]

The Court "family" is composed of nine individuals, who have borne out James Bryce's truism that "judges are only men."[2] "To be sure," Frank-furter once wrote Justice Reed, "the Court is an institution, but individ-uals, with all their diversities of endowment, experience and outlook deter-mine its actions. The history of the Supreme Court is not the history of an abstraction, but the analysis of individuals acting as a Court who make decisions and lay down doctrines."[3]

Foremost among the individuals who made up the Warren Court was, of course, the Chief Justice. In many respects Earl Warren could have been a character out of Sinclair Lewis. Except for his unique leadership abilities, he was a rather typical representative of the Middle America of his day, with his bluff masculine bonhomie, his love of sports and the outdoors, and his lack of intellectual interests or pretensions.

In an interview Justice Potter Stewart, a member of the Warren Court, told me that the Chief Justice had a "simple belief in the things we now laugh at: motherhood, marriage, family, flag, and the like." These fur-nished the foundation for Warren's scale of values throughout his profes-sional life. If there was something of the Babbitt in this, it was also, as Justice Stewart put it to me, "a great source of strength, that he did have these foundations on which his thinking rested."

The early Warren was a direct product of his upbringing and sur-roundings. Born and raised in California, he grew up in a small town that was a microcosm of the burgeoning West. From a last vestige of the American frontier—with cowboys on horses, saloons, and gunfights—the town and state quickly came to be the paradigm of twentieth-century America. "All changed, changed utterly,"[4] as growth became the prime element of California life.

Like his state, Warren displayed a capacity for growth throughout his career. The popular conception of Warren's judicial career has, indeed, been one of a virtual metamorphosis—with the political grub suddenly transformed into the judicial lepidopteran. Certainly, Warren as Chief Justice appeared an entirely different person than he had been before his elevation to the Court. As his state's leading law-enforcement officer, War-ren had been perhaps the foremost advocate of the forced evacuation of persons of Japanese ancestry from the West Coast after the Japanese attack on Pearl Harbor in December 1941. As Chief Justice, Warren was the foremost proponent of racial equality. From his crucial role in the *Brown* segregation case[5] to the end of his Court tenure, he did more than any other judge in American history to ensure that the law, in W. H. Auden's phrase, "found the notion of equality."

As Governor, Warren strongly opposed reapportionment of the Cali-fornia legislature, even though, as he later conceded, "My own state was one of the most malapportioned in the nation." As Chief Justice, Warren led the movement to bring the apportionment process within the equal protection guaranty, a movement that culminated in the Chief Justice's own opinion laying down the "one person, one vote" principle.[6]

Like John Marshall, Earl Warren had a politicl background. Soon after he had obtained his law degree from the University of California, Warren worked in the office of the District Attorney of Alameda County, across the bay from San Francisco. Five years later, in 1925, he was elected District Attorney, serving in that position until 1938. A 1931 survey of American district attorneys by Raymond Moley (later famous as a member of President Franklin D. Roosevelt's so-called Brain Trust) "declared without hesitation that Warren was the best district attorney in the United States."[7]

In 1938 Warren was elected Attorney General of California and became Governor in 1942. He was a most effective chief executive; he reorganized the state government and secured major reforming legislation—notably measures for a modern hospital system, improving the state's prisons and its correction system, providing an extensive highway program, and improving old-age and unemployment benefits. Warren proved an able administrator and was the only Governor of his state to be elected to three terms.

On September 8, 1953, Chief Justice Vinson suddenly died. President Eisenhower appointed Warren to the seat. The California Governor resigned his position and took up his new duties as Chief Justice at the beginning of the 1953 Term.

Leadership Not Scholarship

According to a famous Macaulay statement: "There were gentlemen and there were seamen in the navy of Charles II. But the seamen were not gentlemen, and the gentlemen were not seamen." There have been scholars and there have been great Justices on the Supreme Court. But the scholars have not always been great Justices, and the great Justices have not always been scholars.

To be sure, outstanding scholars did sit on the Warren Court; among them, Felix Frankfurter stands out. Frankfurter was as learned a Justice as ever sat on the Court. His scholarship far exceeded the bounds of legal arcana, unlike so many juristic scholars. The range of the Justice's scholarly interests is illustrated not only in his opinions and published writings, but also in his amazingly varied correspondence with the leading intellectual figures of the day—ranging from Alfred North Whitehead to John Dewey to Albert Einstein. Publication of Frankfurter's best letters would serve not only law, but scholarship and literature as well.

Yet Frankfurter may have been a better letter writer than he was a judge. With all his intellect and scholarly talents, Frankfurter's judicial career remained essentially a lost opportunity. As far as public law was concerned, he may well have had more influence as a law professor than as a Supreme Court Justice. Although Frankfurter may have expected to be the intellectual leader of the Court, as he had been of the Harvard law faculty, the Chief Justice himself performed the true leadership role in the Warren Court.

But Warren was never a legal scholar in the Frankfurter sense. "I wish that I could speak to you in the words of a scholar," the Chief Justice once told an audience, "but it has not fallen to my lot to be a scholar in life."[8] The Justices who sat with him all stressed that Warren may not have been an intellectual like Frankfurter, but then, as Justice Stewart observed to me, "he never pretended to be one."

In assessing the importance of scholarship as a judicial attribute, one should distinguish sharply between a member of the Supreme Court and its Chief Justice. Without a doubt, Justice Story was the greatest legal scholar ever to sit on the Court. His scholarship enabled him to make his outstanding judicial record, and his legal expertise supplied the one thing that Chief Justice Marshall lacked. Indeed, Marshall is reputed to have once said: "Brother Story here . . . can give us the cases from the Twelve Tables down to the latest reports."[9] It is safe to assume that Story's learning often fleshed out the Chief Justice's reasoning with the scholarly foundation needed to support some Marshall opinions.

Still, no one conversant with American law will conclude that Story was a greater judge than Marshall. Story's scholarship could scarcely have produced the constitutional landmarks of the Marshall Court. When Marshall died, Story's admirers hoped that he would become the new Chief Justice. "The Supreme Court," Harvard President Josiah Quincy toasted, "may it be raised one Story higher."[10] But Story's appointment could have been a disaster; the scholar on the bench would have been a misfit in the Court's center chair.

This hypothesis is not mere conjecture. It is supported by the Court's experience under Chief Justice Stone, who, like Frankfurter, had been a noted law professor. From an intellectual viewpoint, Stone was an outstanding judge. Yet, as we saw, he failed as Chief Justice; his lack of administrative ability nearly destroyed the Court's effectiveness. The Stone Court presented a spectacle of unedifying atomization wholly at variance with its functioning as a collegiate tribunal.

Warren clearly did not equal Stone as a legal scholar. But his leadership abilities and skill as a statesman enabled him to be the most effective Chief Justice since Hughes. Those Justices who served with him stressed Warren's leadership abilities, particularly his skill in conducting the conference. "It was incredible," said Justice Brennan just after Warren's death, "how efficiently the Chief would conduct the Friday conferences, leading the discussion of every case on the agenda, with a knowledge of each case at his fingertips."[11]

A legal scholar such as Stone treated the conference as a law school seminar, "carrying on a running debate with any justice who expresse[d] views different from his."[12] At conference, Chief Justice Warren rarely contradicted the others and made sure that each of them had his full say. Above all, he stated the issues in a deceptively simple way, reaching the heart of the matter while stripping it of legal technicalities. As the *Wash-*

ington Post noted, "Warren helped steer cases from the moment they were first discussed simply by the way he framed the issues."[13]

In his first conference on *Brown v. Board of Education,*[14] Warren presented the question before the Court in terms of racial inferiority. He told the Justices that segregation could be justified only by belief in the inherent inferiority of blacks and, if *Plessy v. Ferguson*[15] was followed, it had to be upon that basis. A scholar such as Frankfurter certainly would not have presented the case that way. But Warren's "simplistic" words went straight to the ultimate human values involved. In the face of such an approach, arguments based on legal scholarship would have seemed inappropriate, almost pettifoggery.

The work of a Chief Justice differs greatly from that of other members of the Court as far as legal scholarship is concerned. A person without scholarly interest would find the work of an Associate Justice most unrewarding, since an Associate Justice spends time in Court only hearing and voting on cases and writing opinions. Thus, while considering the appointment of a successor to Chief Justice Vinson, President Eisenhower asked a member of Governor Warren's staff whether Warren would really want to be on the Court after his years in high political office: "Wouldn't it be pretty rarified for him?" "Yes," came back the answer, "I frankly think he'd be very likely to be bored to death [as an Associate Justice]." But, the response went on: "My answer would be emphatically different if we were talking about the Chief Justiceship. He could run the place."[16]

The staff member's answer gets to the heart of the matter. The essential attribute of a Chief Justice is not scholarship but leadership. One who can "run the place" and induce the Justices to follow will effectively head the Court.

The Chief Justice must still write opinions backed by the traditional indicia of legal scholarship: discussion of complicated technical issues, citation and consideration of precedents, and learned-looking footnotes. But a lack of scholarly attainments does not necessarily preclude the production of learned opinions. The necessary scholarship can be supplied by the bright, young, ex-law review editors who serve as the Justices' law clerks. It did not take *The Brethren*[17] to make students of the Court aware of how much of the opinion-writing process has been delegated to the clerks. "As the years passed," wrote Justice Douglas of his own Court years, "it became more and more evident that the law clerks were drafting opinions."[18] The first drafts of the opinions that Chief Justice Warren assigned to himself were almost all prepared by his law clerks.

The Chief Justice would outline the way he wanted the opinion drafted, leaving the clerk with a great deal of discretion to flesh out the details of the opinion. Warren never pretended to be a scholar interested in research and legal minutiae. He left the reasoning and research supporting the decision to his clerks, as well as the task of compiling extensive footnotes, an indispensable component of the well-crafted judicial opinion.

Perhaps the most famous footnote in any Supreme Court opinion appeared in *Brown v. Board of Education*.[19] Noted footnote 11 listed seven works by social scientists to support the statement that segregation meant black inferiority. Yet one of Warren's law clerks inserted the footnote into the opinion, and, as will be seen, neither the Chief Justice nor the Associate Justices paid much attention to it at the time.

It *Was* the *Warren* Court

There are those who claim that although Chief Justice Warren may have been the nominal head of the Court that bears his name, the actual leadership was furnished by other Justices. Thus a biography of Justice Black is based on the proposition that the Alabaman was responsible for the "judicial revolution" that occurred during the Warren years.[20] More recently, one review of my biography of the Chief Justice asserts that, more than anything, it shows that the proper title of the Court while Chief Justice Warren sat in its center chair would be the *Brennan* Court.[21]

Justice Black himself always believed that he had led the judicial revolution that rewrote so much of the corpus of our constitutional law. Black resented the acclaim the Chief Justice received for leading what everyone looked on as the Warren Court. As Justice Black saw it, the Court under Chief Justice Warren had only written into law the constitutional principles that Justice Black had been advocating for so many years. When Warren retired as Chief Justice, the Justices prepared the traditional letter of farewell. The draft letter read, "For us it is a source of pride that we have had the opportunity to be members of the Warren Court." Justice Black changed this to "the Court over which you have presided."[22]

Nevertheless, the other Justices who served with Chief Justice Warren all recognized his leadership role. Justice Douglas, closest to Justice Black in his views, ranks Warren with Marshall and Hughes "as our three greatest Chief Justices."[23] Another member of the Warren Court told me that it was the Chief Justice who was personally responsible for the key decisions during his tenure. The Justices who sat with him have all stressed to me that Chief Justice Warren may not have been an intellectual like Justice Frankfurter, but then, to quote Justice Stewart again, "he never pretended to be one." More important, says Stewart, he possessed "instinctive qualities of leadership." When I asked Stewart about claims that Justice Black was the intellectual leader of the Court, he replied, "If Black was the intellectual leader, Warren was the *leader* leader."

Chief Justice Warren brought more authority to the Chief Justiceship than had been the case for years. The most important work of the Supreme Court, of course, occurs behind the scenes, particularly at the conferences where the Justices discuss and vote on cases. The Chief Justice controls the conference discussion, his is the prerogative to call and discuss cases before the other Justices speak. All those who served with him stressed Chief Justice Warren's ability to lead the conference.

Justice Stewart told me that at the conferences, "after stating the case, [Warren] would very clearly and unambiguously state his position." The Chief Justice rarely had difficulty in reaching a decision, and once his mind was made up, he would stick tenaciously to his decision. As Justice White expressed it to me in an interview, Warren "was quite willing to listen to people at length . . . but, when he made up his mind, it was like the sun went down, and he was very firm, very firm about it." The others never had any doubt about who was the head of the Warren Court.

A reading of the conference notes of Justices on the Warren Court reveals that the Chief Justice was as strong a leader as the Court has ever had. As the *Washington Post* summarized my Warren biography, it "shows Warren as even more a guiding force in the landmark opinions of his court than some have previously believed. Chief Justice Warren helped steer cases from the moment they were first discussed simply by the way he framed the issues."[24] In almost all the important cases, the Chief Justice led the discussion toward the decision he favored. If any Court can properly be identified by the name of one of its members, this Court was emphatically the *Warren* Court and, without arrogance, he, as well as the country, knew it. After an inevitable initial period of feeling his way, Chief Justice Warren led the Supreme Court as effectively as any Chief Justice in our history. When we consider the work of the Warren Court, we are considering a constitutional corpus that was directly a product of the Chief Justice's leadership.

The Other Justices

Of course, the Supreme Court is inevitably more than the judge who sits in its center chair. In many ways, the individual Justices operate, as some of them have said, like "nine separate law firms." Plainly, Chief Justice Warren was not going to be able to deal with the Justices in the way he had directed matters as Governor of California. "I think," Justice Stewart affirmed to me, "he came to realize very early, certainly long before I came here [1958], that this group of nine rather prima donnaish people could not be led, could not be told, in the way the Governor of California can tell a subordinate, do this or do that."

What Justice Stewart says is true of any Supreme Court, but it was particularly true of the Justices on the Warren Court. The Court in the mid-1940s was characterized by Yale law professor Fred Rodell as "the most brilliant and able collection of Justices who ever graced the high bench together."[25] The stars of that Court were Justices Black, Frankfurter, Douglas, and Jackson—four of the greatest judges ever to serve on the highest bench, brilliant jurists, each possessed of a peculiarly forceful personality. In addition, Justices Black and Douglas, on the one side, and Justices Frankfurter and Jackson, on the other, represented polar views on the proper role of the Court in interpreting the Constitution. Their doctrinal differences, fueled by increasing personal animosity, erupted into the most bitter feud in Supreme Court history. All four were still serving when Warren was appointed, though Jackson died before he could play an important role in the development of the Warren Court's jurisprudence.

Justices Black and Douglas were the leading advocates among the Justices of the activist approach that became the Warren Court's trademark. But the Chief Justice's principal ally was Justice William J. Brennan, Jr., appointed in 1956 on Justice Minton's retirement. Before then, Brennan had been a judge in New Jersey for seven years, rising from the state trial court to its highest bench. He was the only Warren Court Justice to have served as a state judge.

"One of the things," Justice Frankfurter once said, "that laymen, even lawyers, do not always understand is indicated by the question you hear so often: 'Does a man become any different when he puts on a gown?' I say, 'If he is any good, he does.'"[26] Certainly Justice Brennan on the supreme bench proved a complete surprise to those who saw him as a middle-of-the-road moderate. He quickly became a firm adherent of the activist philosophy and a principal architect of the Warren Court's jurisprudence. Brennan had been Frankfurter's student at Harvard Law School; yet if Frankfurter expected the new Justice to continue his pupilage, he was soon disillusioned. After Brennan had joined the Warren Court's activist wing, Frankfurter supposedly quipped, "I always encourage my students to think for themselves, but Brennan goes too far!"

Justice Brennan soon became Chief Justice Warren's closest colleague. The Chief Justice would turn to Brennan when he wanted to discuss a case or some other matter on which he wanted an exchange of views. The two would usually meet on Thursdays, when the Chief Justice would come to the Brennan chambers to go over the cases that were to be discussed at the Court's Friday conference.

Justice Brennan's unassuming appearance and manner mask a keen intelligence. He was perhaps the hardest worker on the Warren Court. Unlike some others (notably Justice Douglas), Brennan was always willing to mold his language to meet the objections of some of his colleagues, a talent that would become his hallmark on the Court and one on which the Chief Justice would rely frequently. It was Justice Brennan to whom the Chief Justice was to assign the opinion in some of the most important cases to be decided by the Warren Court.

A year before the Brennan appointment, in 1955, Justice John Marshall Harlan was chosen to fill the vacancy created by Justice Jackson's death. Harlan was the grandson of the Justice with the same name who had written the dissent in *Plessy v. Ferguson*.[27] As soon as he took his place on the bench, Harlan had taken a place in the Court's history, as the only descendant of a Justice to become one. The first Harlan had been a judicial maverick, who had been an outspoken dissenter. The second Harlan took a more cautious approach to the judicial function that reflected his background. Educated at Princeton, he had been a Rhodes Scholar and had had a successful career with a leading Wall Street law firm prior to his appointment in 1954 to the U.S. Court of Appeals for the Second Circuit.

On the Supreme Court, Harlan, like Justice Jackson before him, became a firm adherent of Justice Frankfurter's judicial restraint philosophy. After Frankfurter's retirement, it was Harlan who came to be looked on as the conservative conscience of an ever-more-activist Court. But Harlan had none of the acerbity that made Frankfurter distasteful to some of his colleagues.

Harlan looked like the contemporary vision of a Supreme Court Justice. Tall and erect, with sparse white hair, conservatively dressed in his London-tailored suits, with his grandfather's gold watch chain across the vest under his robe, he exuded the dignity associated with high judicial office. Yet underneath was a warm nature that enabled him to be close friends with those with whom he disagreed intellectually, notably Justice Black. Visitors could often see the two Justices waiting patiently in line in the Court cafeteria. The two were a study in contrasts: the ramrod-straight patrician with his commanding presence and his slight, almost wispy colleague who always looked like the lively old Southern farmer.

If Harlan at the Bar had been known as a "lawyer's lawyer," on the Court he soon acquired the reputation of a "lawyer's judge." Soon after Justice Harlan took his seat (he was confirmed by the Senate on March 17, 1955), Justice Frankfurter wrote a friend that "Harlan both on the bench and in the Conference is as to the manner born."[28] The new Justice was plainly one of the best, if not the best, lawyer on the Court and, next to Frankfurter, the Justice most interested in the technical aspects of the Court's work. He became a sound, rather than brilliant, Justice who could be relied on for learned opinions that thoroughly covered the subjects dealt with, though they degenerated at times into law review articles of the type Frankfurter too often wrote.

The term most frequently used to describe Justice Harlan by those who knew him is "gentleman"—though some say that beneath the veneer was a bland grayness that permeated both his life and his work. To the other Justices, Harlan always appeared the quintessential patrician, with his privileged upbringing and Wall Street background. "I hear 'mi lord,'" reads a note from Justice Clark to Harlan, "that you have been under the weather. . . . Your Lordship should be more careful of your whiskey and your habits."[29]

Soon after Justice Brennan's appointment, President Eisenhower selected Charles E. Whittaker in place of Justice Reed, who retired in 1957. The new Justice had grown up on a small farm in Kansas. He had quit high school at sixteen and had never gone to college. He began work in a Kansas City law firm as a messenger, office boy, and "bottle washer," going to an unaccredited law school at night. He eventually became a prosperous lawyer and was appointed a district judge and then promoted to the U.S. Court of Appeals for the Eighth Circuit.

Whittaker may have been the least talented Justice appointed during this century. Justice Whittaker, a member of the Warren Court told me, "used to come out of our conference literally crying. You know Charlie had gone to night law school, and he began as an office boy and he'd been a farm boy and he had inside him an inferiority complex, which . . . showed and he'd say, 'Felix used words in there that I'd never heard of.'"

A more important Warren Court member was Potter Stewart of Ohio, a federal circuit judge, appointed in 1958 after Justice Burton retired. Stewart was one of the youngest Justices (only forty-three when selected by President Eisenhower); at sixty-six he also was one of the youngest to retire. When he first took his seat, Stewart's youth and handsome appearance added an unusual touch to the highest bench, showing that it need not always be composed of nine old men. To those who knew him in those days, it was painful to see his physical decline before he died in 1985.

Before then, people who met Justice Stewart were surprised by his vigor and clearly expressed views, which contrasted sharply with his public image as an indecisive centrist without clearly defined conceptions. Unlike Justices Black and Frankfurter, Stewart never acted on the basis of a deepseated philosophy regarding the proper relationship between the state and its citizens. When asked if he was a liberal or a conservative, he answered, "I am a lawyer," and went on to say, "I have some difficulty understanding what those terms mean even in the field of political life. . . . And I find it impossible to know what they mean when they are carried over to judicial work."[30]

Stewart was a moderate with a pragmatic approach to issues that polarized others. In his early years on the Court, he tended to be the "swing man" between the activist and judicial restraint blocs. During that time, the two blocs were evenly divided and Stewart cast the key vote in many cases, voting now with the one and now with the other group. With Justice Frankfurter's 1962 retirement, Chief Justice Warren and his activist supporters gained the upper hand. Justice Stewart remained in the center as the Court moved increasingly to the left. At the end of Warren's tenure, he continued as the Court's leading moderate—though, according to Justice Douglas, by that time "Stewart and Harlan were the nucleus of the new conservatism on the Court."[31]

Justice Stewart was best known for his comment in a 1964 obscenity case, "I know it when I see it"[32]—a phrase that he later lamented might well become his epitaph. Stewart's aptness for the pungent phrase helped make him the press's favorite Justice, and he was more accessible to reporters than any of his colleagues.

Another moderate on the Warren Court was Byron R. White of Colorado, who was Deputy Attorney General when chosen in 1962 after Justice Whittaker was forced to retire because of ill health. On graduation from Yale Law School after the war, White had clerked for Chief Justice Vinson; he was the first former law clerk to become a Justice.

Justice White was certainly not the typical Supreme Court appointee. He was known to most Americans as "Whizzer" White—the all-American back who became the National Football League rookie of the year in 1938. Physically, White is most impressive. At six feet two and a muscular 190 pounds, he has maintained the constitution that made him a star football player. Even as a Justice, White retained his athletic competitiveness, never hesitating to take part in the clerks' basketball games in the gymnasium at the top of the Court building.

On the Supreme Court, White, like Stewart, defied classification. He, too, tended to take a lawyerlike approach to individual cases, without trying to fit them into any overall judicial philosophy. He did tend to be one of the more conservative Justices in the Court's center, particularly in criminal cases. "In the criminal field," as Justice Harry Blackmun has said, "I think Byron White is distinctly a conservative."[33] After his appointment to the Court, White was never close to Chief Justice Warren. "I wasn't exactly in his circle," White told me. Certainly White never became a member of the Warren Court's inner circle. He went his own way, voting against the Chief Justice as often as not.

During the first part of Chief Justice Warren's tenure, the Court was split between the activist wing led by Warren and the advocates of judicial restraint led by Frankfurter. With the 1962 retirement of Justice Frankfurter and his acolyte, Justice Whittaker, the Court balance was completely altered. For the remainder of his tenure the Chief Justice had a solid majority. The Warren majority was secured when Arthur J. Goldberg succeeded Justice Frankfurter, who wrote to the President in 1962 that he was "left with no choice but to" retire because of severe heart attacks.

A newspaper once characterized Justice Goldberg's success story as "almost too corny."[34] The last of eleven children of an immigrant Russian fruit peddler, Goldberg rose from one of the poorest sections of Chicago. He worked his way through Northwestern Law School, where he graduated first in his class. He developed a labor practice and became counsel to the AFL-CIO. He became a Kennedy supporter in early 1960 and was appointed Secretary of Labor when the new Administration took office. In that position, he became the Kennedy Administration's troubleshooter. In fact, as Robert Kennedy wrote about his discussions with the President on the Court vacancy, "[T]he only reservation about Arthur Goldberg was the fact that he was so valuable to the Administration and could handle labor and management in a way that could hardly be equalled by anyone else."[35]

Physically and emotionally Goldberg was the antithesis of the first Kennedy appointee. Where White was dispassionate and reserved, Goldberg was warm and ebullient. He was of average build, with wavy grey hair, and none of the athletic propensities of his colleague. Goldberg noted the contrast in a speech the winter after his appointment. "As a new brother," he said, "I think I should tell you some of the innermost secrets of the Supreme Court. The Court is sorely divided. There is one group that believes in an active judicial philosophy; Justices Black, Douglas, and White are addicted to physical exercise. The middle wing, which believes in moderate exercise, consists of the Chief Justice and Justices Clark and

Brennan. And then there's the third group—Justices Harlan and Stewart and myself."[36]

Goldberg soon became Warren's firm ally on the Court. "There is nobody," Goldberg told me, "I felt closer to than Warren." In fact, states the former Justice, "if you look at the *Harvard Law Review* annual rack-up of how we voted during my tenure, he and I voted together more than any other Justice, as I recall it." In some ways, indeed, Goldberg was even more activist than the Chief Justice. Wrote former Justice Minton to retired Justice Frankfurter in 1964, "Mr. J. Goldberg is a walking Constitutional Convention. Wow what an activist he is!"[37]

Justice Goldberg, however, served only three years; he resigned in 1965 to become Ambassador to the United Nations. His place was taken by Abe Fortas, who proved to be an equally firm Warren supporter. Fortas was no ordinary junior Justice. He was one of the few Court appointees who had to be virtually drafted for his seat. He also had one of the best minds of anyone appointed to the Supreme Court. Justice Harlan, himself an outstanding legal craftsman, told his law clerks that he considered Fortas the most brilliant advocate to appear in his time.

Before his appointment, Fortas listed his business address in *Who's Who in the South and Southwest* as "c/o White House, 1600 Pennsylvania Avenue, Washington, D.C." He came to the Court with the celebrity and status of the President's close adviser. After John F. Kennedy's assassination, the first telephone call the new President made in Dallas was to Fortas.

The Warren majority on the Court was strengthened toward the end of the Chief Justice's tenure when the seat of Justice Clark, who retired in 1967, was taken by Thurgood Marshall. Though Clark had backed the Chief Justice in important cases, he could not be counted on as a consistent Warren supporter. On the other hand, from the time he took his seat, Justice Marshall became a firm vote for Warren. Marshall gave an equal protection dimension to the Horatio Alger legend. Great-grandson of a slave and son of a Pullman car steward, Marshall was the first black appointed to the highest Court. Solicitor General at the time of his appointment, he had headed the N.A.A.C.P. Legal Defense Fund's staff for over twenty years and had been chief counsel in the *Brown* segregation case.

The appointments of Justices Goldberg, Fortas, and Marshall gave the Chief Justice a firm majority that enabled him to lead the Justices in what became the key decisions of the Warren Court jurisprudence. Of course, there were still opposing views among the Justices, but the principal Warren opponent had become the courtly Justice Harlan, who had neither Justice Frankfurter's abrasive personality nor his leadership abilities. Harlan's voice calling for judicial restraint was but a faint echo of that of his mentor and, in one reporter's phrase, "was now heard in a symbolic wilderness without the assured support of Frankfurter."[38] The balance of power had definitely shifted to the Chief Justice. Now the Warren Court jurisprudence could accelerate the onward rush of the "constitutional revolution" for which the Chief Justice, more than any person, was responsible.

Activism versus Judicial Restraint

There is an antinomy inherent in every system of law: the law must be stable and yet it cannot stand still.[39] It is the task of the judge to reconcile these two conflicting elements. In doing so, jurists tend to stress one principle or the other. Indeed, few judges can keep an equipoise between stability and change.

Chief Justice Warren never pretended to try to maintain the balance. As soon as he had become established on the Court, he came down firmly on the side of change, leading the Supreme Court's effort to enable our public law to cope with rapid societal change. Warren strongly believed that the law must draw its vitality from life rather than precedent. What Justice Holmes termed "intuitions" of what best served the public interest[40] played the major part in Warren's jurisprudence. He did not sacrifice good sense for the syllogism. Nor was he one of "those who think more of symmetry and logic in the development of legal rules than of practical adaptation to the attainment of a just result."[41] When symmetry and logic were balanced against considerations of equity and fairness, he normally found the latter to be weightier.[42] In the Warren hierarchy of social values, the moral outweighed the material.[43]

Throughout his tenure on the Court, the Chief Justice tended to use "fairness" as the polestar of his judicial approach. Every so often in criminal cases, when counsel defending a conviction would cite legal precedents, Warren would bend his bulk over the bench to ask, "Yes, yes—but were you fair?"[44] The fairness to which the Chief Justice referred was no jurisprudential abstraction. It related to such things as methods of arrest, questioning of suspects, and police conduct—matters that Warren understood well from his earlier years as District Attorney in Alameda County, California. Decisions like *Miranda v. Arizona*[45] were based directly upon the Warren fairness approach.

The Chief Justice's emphasis upon fairness and just results led him to join hands with Justices Black and Douglas and their activist approach to constitutional law. Their activism led to Warren's break with Justice Frankfurter—the foremost advocate on the Court of the Holmes doctrine of judicial restraint. To Justice Holmes, as we saw, the legislator was to have the primary say on the considerations behind laws; the judge's duty was to enforce "even laws that I believe to embody economic mistakes."[46] Justice Frankfurter remained true to the Holmes approach, insisting that self-restraint was the proper posture of a nonrepresentative judiciary, regardless of the nature of the asserted interests in particular cases. Warren followed the canon of judicial restraint in the economic area, but he felt that the Bill of Rights provisions protecting personal liberties imposed more active enforcement obligations on judges. When a law allegedly infringed upon personal rights guaranteed by the Bill of Rights, the Chief Justice refused to defer to the legislative judgment that had considered the law necessary.

Warren rejected the Frankfurter philosophy of judicial restraint because he believed that it thwarted effective performance of the Court's constitutional role. Judicial restraint, in the Chief Justice's view, all too often meant judicial abdication of the duty to enforce constitutional guarantees. "I believe," Warren declared in an interview on his retirement, "that this Court or any court should exercise the functions of the office to the limit of its responsibilities." Judicial restraint meant that "for a long, long time we have been sweeping under the rug a great many problems basic to American life. We have failed to face up to them, and they have piled up on us, and now they are causing a great deal of dissension and controversy of all kinds." To Warren, it was the Court's job "to remedy those things eventually," regardless of the controversy involved.[47]

The Warren approach in this respect left little room for deference to the legislature, the core of the restraint canon. Warren never considered constitutional issues in the light of any desired deference to the legislature. Instead, he decided those issues based on his own independent judgment, normally giving little weight to the fact that a reasonable legislator might have voted for the challenged law.

For Chief Justice Warren, the issue on judicial review was not *reasonableness* but *rightness*. If the law was contrary to his own conception of what the Constitution demanded, it did not matter that a reasonable legislator might reach the opposite conclusion. When Warren decided that the Constitution required an equal population apportionment standard for all legislative chambers except the United States Senate, the fact that no American legislature had followed the new requirement did not deter him from uniformly applying the standard.[48] Justice Harlan's dissent may have demonstrated that the consistent state practice was, at the least, reasonable. For the Chief Justice, however, legislative reasonableness was irrelevant when the practice conflicted with his own interpretation of the Constitution.

The Court and Civil Rights

Not too long ago, legal observers expected the post-1937 "constitutional revolution" to signal a permanent decline in the Supreme Court's position. The subdued role played by the Court in the later New Deal period, during World War II, and in the postwar years led many to expect the Court to wither away, much as the state was supposed to do in Marxist theory. Yet one thing is clear: the Marxist state may have disappeared, but America's high tribunal has anything but withered away in the second half of the century.

Still, the work of the Supreme Court under Chief Justice Warren differed from earlier periods. In the Warren Court, the emphasis in the

Court completed the shift from the safeguarding of property rights to the protection of personal rights. In enforcing the liberties guaranteed by the Bill of Rights, the Supreme Court forged a new and vital place for itself in the constitutional structure. More and more the Court came to display its solicitude for individual rights. Freedom of speech, press, and religion, the rights of minorities and those accused of crime, those of individuals subjected to legislative and administrative inquisitions—all came under the Warren Court's fostering guardianship.

Foremost in the Warren Court's catalogue of individual rights was that to racial equality. The landmark decision here was, of course, that in the *Brown* school segregation case, to which the next chapter is devoted. As we shall see there, *Brown* not only outlawed school segregation but also served as the foundation for a series of decisions outlawing racial segregation in all public institutions. By 1963, the Court could declare categorically, "It is no longer open to question that a State may not constitutionally require segregation of public facilities."[49]

In its *Brown* decision, the Court had held that school segregation was unconstitutional, and a year later, in its second *Brown* decision, the Court ordered the district courts to take such action as was necessary and proper to ensure the nondiscriminatory admission of plaintiffs to schools "with all deliberate speed."[50] The enforcement of *Brown* was left to the lower courts, which met massive resistance in many Southern school districts. The Warren Court intervened in several cases to force desegregation, particularly in *Griffin v. County Board of Prince Edward County* (1964),[51] in which a Virginia county had closed down its school system rather than have blacks attend schools with whites. Then, in *Green v. County School Board* (1968),[52] the Court invalidated "freedom of choice" plans, under which most Southern school districts then operated. The Court held that a school board had a duty to come forward with a desegregation plan that "promises realistically to work now." If the board did not do so, the federal court had authority to issue any order deemed necessary to achieve immediate desegregation.

The Warren Court decisions furthering racial equality were an important catalyst for the civil rights protests of the 1960s and congressional action to protect civil rights. Both developments received support from the Warren Court decisions. Convictions of civil rights demonstrators in public places and at sit-in demonstrations at restaurants, lunch counters, and libraries were reversed in a number of cases.[53] Other cases established the right to use the streets and other public places as "public forums" for the dissemination of even unpopular views.[54]

Soon after the Court decided the last of the important sit-in cases, the Civil Rights Act of 1964 became law—the first time since Reconstruction that Congress had passed an important statute to protect civil rights. The 1964 law prohibited racial discrimination in hotels, restaurants, and other public accommodations. The decision in the *Civil Rights Cases*[55] of 1883 had invalidated a similar law (the Civil Rights Act of 1875) on the ground that the Fourteenth Amendment's guaranty of equal protection was limited to "state action" and did not reach the discrimination of private hotel and restaurant owners, but the Warren Court upheld the 1964 Act.

The Court ruled in *Heart of Atlanta Motel v. United States* (1964)[56] that Congress could pass the law under its commerce power and a law under that power was not subject to the "state action" limitation. The Court also upheld the Voting Rights Act of 1965, which contained far-reaching provisions protecting the right of blacks to vote. Though the Act provides for the supplanting of state election machinery by federal law and federal officials, the opinion of Chief Justice Warren found it a valid congressional measure to enforce the Fifteenth Amendment.[57]

Reapportionment

The *Brown* decision signaled the expansive attitude of the Warren Court toward the constitutional guaranty of equality. From the field of racial equality involved in *Brown,* the Court spread the equal protection mantle over an increasingly broad area, notably in the field of political rights. The key decision here was *Baker v. Carr* (1962),[58] in which the federal courts were ruled competent to entertain an action challenging legislative apportionments as contrary to equal protection. The problem arose from the fact that though American legislative districts had originally been apportioned on an equal population basis, over the years population shifts had made for extreme malapportionment. Thus the seats in the Tennessee legislature, where *Baker* arose, had last been apportioned in 1901. By the time the case was brought, a vote from the most populous country had only a fraction of the weight of one from the least populous: the population ratio of the most and least populous districts was then greater than nineteen to one.

Before *Baker,* the Supreme Court had held that the federal courts had no jurisdiction in such cases. The question of legislative apportionment was ruled a "political question" and therefore beyond judicial competence. The leading pre-*Baker* apportionment decision had declared, "Courts ought not to enter this political thicket."[59] In *Baker,* Chief Justice Warren and his colleagues overruled the earlier cases and held that attacks on legislative apportionments on equal protection grounds could be heard and decided by the federal courts.

Then, in *Reynolds v. Sims* (1964),[60] the Chief Justice's own opinion ruled that the Constitution lays down an "equal population" principle for legislative apportionment. Under this principle, substantially equal representation is demanded for all citizens. According to the most noted passage in the Warren opinion, "Legislators are elected by voters, not farms or cities or economic interests." It follows, Warren said, that "the Equal Protection Clause requires that the seats in both houses of a bicameral state legislature must be apportioned on a population basis."[61] Legislative districts must represent substantially equal populations, which means that the "one person, one vote" principle is now enshrined in the United States

Constitution: equal numbers of people are entitled to equal representation in their government.

Chief Justice Warren himself characterized the reapportionment cases as the most important cases decided by the Court during his tenure. In those cases, the Warren Court worked an electoral reform comparable to that achieved by the nineteenth-century Parliament in translating the program of the English Reform Movement into the statute book. The result has been a virtual transformation of the political landscape, with voting power shifted from rural areas to the urban and suburban areas in which most Americans have come to live.

The Chief Justice never had doubts about the correctness of the reapportionment decisions. He maintained that if the "one person, one vote" principle had been laid down years earlier, many of the nation's legal sores would never have festered. According to Warren, "Many of our problems would have been solved a long time ago if everyone had the right to vote, and his vote counted the same as everybody else's. Most of these problems could have been solved through the political process rather than through the courts. But as it was, the Court had to decide."[62]

Equality and Criminal Justice

If one great theme recurred in the jurisprudence of the Warren Court, it was that of equality before the law—equality of races, of citizens, of rich and poor, of prosecutor and defendant. The result was what Justice Fortas termed "the most profound and pervasive revolution ever achieved by substantially peaceful means."[63] More than that, it was the rarest of all political animals: a judicially inspired and led revolution. Without the Warren Court decisions giving ever-wider effect to the right to equality before the law, most of the movements for equality that have permeated American society would have encountered even greater difficulties.

In addition to racial and political equality, the Warren Court moved to ensure equality in criminal justice. The landmark case was *Griffin v. Illinois* (1956).[64] Griffin had been convicted of armed robbery in a state court. He filed a motion for a free transcript of the trial record, alleging that he was indigent and could not get adequate appellate review without the transcript. The motion was denied. In the Supreme Court's conference on the case, Chief Justice Warren pointed out that the state had provided for full appellate review in such a case. A defendant who could pay for a transcript should not be given an advantage over one who could not. "We cannot," declared the Chief Justice, "have one rule for the rich and one for the poor." Hence he would require the state to furnish the transcript.

The Court followed the Warren lead and held that it violates the Constitution for a state to deny to defendants alleging poverty free transcripts of trial proceedings, which would enable them adequately to prosecute appeals from criminal convictions. According to Justice Black's opinion, "There can be no equal justice where the kind of trial a man gets depends on the amount of money he has. Destitute defendants must be afforded as adequate appellate review as defendants who have money enough to buy transcripts."[65]

As it turned out, *Griffin* was a watershed in the Warren Court's jurisprudence. In it the Court made its first broad pronouncement of economic equality in the criminal process. After *Griffin* the Warren Court appeared to agree with Bernard Shaw that "the worst of crimes is poverty," as it tried to equalize criminal law between those possessed of means and the less affluent. It was the *Griffin* approach that was the foundation of the landmark decision in *Gideon v. Wainwright* (1963),[66] which required counsel to be appointed for indigent defendants.

The *Gideon* case was one of the most famous decided by the Warren Court. Indeed, Clarence Gideon and his case have become part of American folklore. In *Gideon* the Court overruled an earlier case that had refused to hold that the right to counsel was so fundamental as to be included in the due process guaranty. Again following the Chief Justice's lead, the Court reversed Gideon's conviction, because his request to the trial judge to have a court-appointed lawyer to assist him was denied. "[R]eason and reflection," declares the *Gideon* opinion, "require us to recognize that in our adversary system of criminal justice, any person haled into court, who is too poor to hire a lawyer, cannot be assured a fair trial unless counsel is provided for him. This seems to us to be an obvious truth."[67]

Criminal Procedure

Gideon made plain that the Constitution requires public provision of counsel for criminal defendants who cannot afford to hire their own attorneys. The need for the assistance of counsel is not, however, limited to the courtroom. *Gideon* was based on the express constitutional guaranty of the right to counsel in "all criminal prosecutions." But the case only raised another critical question: When does the right to counsel begin?

The Warren Court answered this question in *Miranda v. Arizona* (1966).[68] Miranda had been convicted in a state court of kidnapping and rape. He had been arrested and taken to an interrogation room, where he was questioned without being advised that he had a right to have an attorney present. After two hours, the police secured a confession, which was admitted into evidence over Miranda's objection.

The state's highest court affirmed the conviction, but the Warren Court reversed. The majority agreed with Chief Justice Warren that for the police to be able to use any confession, they must show that they gave full effect to the defendant's right to remain silent and to the presence of an attorney, either retained or appointed. Warren had no doubt that the right to counsel began as soon as there was what his opinion termed "custodial interrogation"—that is, interrogation while an individual is in police custody. To the Chief Justice, the constitutional right came into play when Miranda was arrested. "I didn't know," he commented during the argument before the Court, "that we could arrest people in this country for investigation. Wouldn't you say it was accusatory when a man was locked in jail?"

The *Miranda* decision worked a drastic change in American criminal law and its application by police officers, prosecutors, and judges. The Warren Court in effect laid down the rule that an accused who wants a counsel should have one at any time after being taken into custody. Under Warren's decision, the police must give so-called *Miranda* warnings: that the person arrested has a right to remain silent, that anything he says may be used against him, that he can have a lawyer present, and that he can have counsel appointed if he cannot afford one.

Protection of the rights of criminal defendants had become a primary concern of the Warren Court. The *Miranda* decision, as much as anything, exemplified Warren's own concern in such cases. Indeed, *Miranda* was the ultimate embodiment of the Warren approach in criminal cases.

That approach was also illustrated by *Mapp v. Ohio* (1961),[69] where the Warren Court adopted the exclusionary rule, which bars the admission of illegally seized evidence, in state criminal cases. The Supreme Court had refused to follow that rule before *Mapp,* holding that the exclusionary rule was not required by the Constitution in state criminal cases. Now, under Chief Justice Warren, the *Mapp* state conviction was reversed because illegally seized evidence had been admitted at the trial. Such a holding, the Warren Court affirmed, closes "the only courtroom door remaining open to evidence secured by official lawlessness" in violation of the Constitution's guaranty against unreasonable searches and seizures.

From Property to Personal Rights

The dominant trend in the Court during the Warren tenure was a shift in emphasis from property rights to personal rights. "When the generation of 1980 receives from us the Bill of Rights," Chief Justice Warren declared in a 1955 article, "the document will not have exactly the same meaning it had when we received it from our fathers."[70] The Bill of Rights as interpreted by the Warren Court had a meaning much different from that handed down by its predecessors.

There were three principal developments in the Warren Court regarding the protection of personal rights: (1) acceptance of the preferred-position doctrine, (2) extension of the trend toward holding Bill of Rights guaranties binding on the states, and (3) broading of the substantive content of the rights themselves.

The preferred-position theory, we saw in Chapter 11, was first stated in *United States v. Carolene Products Co.,*[71] though only tentatively in a footnote. Under Chief Justice Warren it became accepted doctrine. The theory is based on the view that the Constitution gives a preferred status to personal, as opposed to property rights. The result is a double standard in the exercise by the Supreme Court of its review function. The tenet of judicial restraint does not rigidly bind the judge in cases involving civil liberties and other personal rights.[72] The presumption of validity for laws gives way far more readily in cases where life and liberty are restrained. In those cases, the legislative judgment must be scrutinized with much greater care.

Critics say that the preferred-position approach, with its elevation of personal rights, creates a hierarchy of rights not provided for in the Constitution. It should, however, be recognized that each generation must necessarily have its own scale of values. In nineteenth-century America, concerned as it was with the economic conquest of a continent, property rights occupied the dominant place. A century later, in a world in which individuality was dwarfed by concentrations of power, concern with the maintenance of personal rights had become more important. With the focus of concern on the need to preserve an area for the development of individuality, judges were naturally more ready to find legislative invasion when personal rights were involved than in the sphere of economics.[73]

One of the last decisions of the Marshall Court had ruled the Federal Bill of Rights binding only on the Federal Government, not on the states.[74] It has been urged that the Fourteenth Amendment changed that result, incorporating the entire Bill of Rights in the Fourteenth Amendment's due process clause.[75] The Court has never accepted this view, adopting instead a selective approach, under which only those rights deemed "fundamental" are included in due process. Yet if advocates of full incorporation seemingly lost the incorporation battle, after midcentury they came close to winning the due process war; for the Warren Court, without formally abandoning its selective incorporation approach, held almost all the Bill of Rights guaranties to be fundamental and hence absorbed by due process.

The key decisions were *Mapp* and *Gideon,* which reversed earlier refusals to hold the right against the use of illegally secured evidence and the right to counsel to be so fundamental as to be included in due process. Both *Mapp* and *Gideon* spoke in broad terms of the need to protect individual rights; they signaled a trend to include ever more of the Bill of Rights guaranties in the Fourteenth Amendment. In the following decade the Warren Court held these rights fundamental and hence binding upon the states: rights against double jeopardy[76] and self-incrimination[77] and rights to jury trial in criminal cases,[78] to a speedy trial,[79] and to confrontation.[80] Add to these rights those that had been held binding on the states before midcentury,[81] and they include all the rights guaranteed by the Federal Bill of Rights except the rights to a grand jury indictment and to a jury in civil cases involving more than twenty dollars. The two exclusions hardly alter the overriding tendency to make the Due Process Clause ever more inclusive.

The Warren Court did more than merely apply the Bill of Rights to the states: it also broadened the substantive content of the rights guaranteed, giving virtually all personal rights a wider meaning than they had theretofore had in American law. This was particularly true in two crucial areas: criminal justice and freedom of expression. The former has already been discussed, but it remains to say a word about the latter.

Two members of the Warren Court, Justices Black and Douglas, consistently urged an absolutist view of the freedom of speech guaranty.[82] Their view was based upon the unqualified language of the First Amendment, which says that "Congress shall make no law . . . abridging the freedom of speech." In the Black-Douglas view, when the amendment says that no laws abridging speech shall be made, it means flatly that *no* laws of that type shall, under any circumstances, be made. Under the Black-Douglas approach, no speech may ever be restricted by government action, even speech which is libelous, obscene, or subversive.

The Warren Court did not adopt the Black-Douglas absolutist view, but it did place increasing emphasis on freedom of expression as a preferred right. The primacy of the First Amendment was firmly established. The right to use the streets and other public forums was extended to those using them for civil rights protests and demonstrations.[83] Most criticisms of conduct by public officials and public figures were exempted from the law of libel.[84] Freedom of the press was broadened; censorship laws were struck down,[85] and the power to restrain publication on grounds of obscenity was drastically limited.[86]

In addition, the Warren Court began to recognize new personal rights not specifically guranteed in the Federal Bill of Rights. Foremost among these was a constitutional right of privacy. Justice Douglas urged the existence of such a right in a 1961 dissent: "This notion of privacy is not drawn from the blue. It emanates from the totality of the constitutional scheme under which we live."[87] The Douglas notion of a right to privacy as part of the area of personal rights protected by the Constitution was accepted by the Warren Court only four years later.

In *Griswold v. Connecticut* (1965),[88] defendants had been convicted of violating a state law prohibiting the use of contraceptive devices and the giving of medical advice in their use. In reversing the conviction the Supreme Court held that the law violated the right of privacy. The opinion expressly recognized the existence of a constitutionally protected right of privacy—a right said to be within the protected scope of specific Bill of Rights guaranties.

During Chief Justice Warren's tenure, protection of personal rights and liberties became the very focus of the Court's enforcement of the contemporary Constitution. With property rights constitutionally curtailed, compensatory scope had to be given to personal rights if the ultimate social interest—the individual life—was not to be lost sight of.

The need to broaden the constitutional protection of personal rights received added emphasis from the growth and misuse of governmental power in the twentieth century. Totalitarian systems showed dramatically what it meant for the individual to live in a society in which Leviathan had become a reality. The "Blessings of Liberty," which the Constitution's

Framers had taken such pains to safeguard, were placed in even sharper relief in a world that had seen so clearly the consequences of their denial.

Warren in the Pantheon

In 1966, Vice President Hubert Humphrey declared that if President Eisenhower "had done nothing else other than appoint Warren Chief Justice, he would have earned a very important place in the history of the United States."[89] By then, it was widely recognized that Earl Warren had earned a place in the front rank of the American judicial pantheon. That is true even though Chief Justice Warren will never rank with the consummate legal craftsmen who have fashioned the structure of Anglo-American law over the generations—each professing to be a pupil, yet each a builder who added his few bricks.[90] But Warren was never content to deem himself a mere vicar of the common-law tradition. Instead he was the paradigm of the "result-oriented" judge, who used his power to secure the result he deemed right in the cases that came before his Court.

In reaching what he considered the just result, the Chief Justice was not deterred by the demands of stare decisis. For Warren, principle was more compelling than precedent. The key decisions of the Warren Court overruled decisions of earlier Courts. Those precedents had left the enforcement of constitutional rights to the political branches. Yet the latter had failed to act. In Warren's view, this situation left the Court with the choice either to follow the precedent or to vindicate the right. For the Chief Justice, there was never any question as to which was the correct alternative.

Warren cannot be deemed a great juristic technician, noted for his mastery of the common law. But he never pretended to be a legal scholar or to profess interest in legal philosophy or reasoning. To him, the outcome of a case mattered more than the reasoning behind the decision.

The result may have been a deficiency in judicial craftsmanship that subjected Warren to constant academic criticism, both during and after his tenure on the bench. Without a doubt, Warren does not rank with Holmes or Cardozo as a master of the opinion, but his opinions have a simple power of their own; if they do not resound with the cathedral tones of a Marshall, they speak with the moral decency of a modern Micah. Perhaps the *Brown* opinion did not articulate the juristic bases of its decision in as erudite a manner as it could have. But the decision in *Brown* emerged from a typical Warren judgment, with which few today would disagree. The Warren opinion was so *right* in that judgment that one wonders whether additional learned labor in spelling out the obvious was really necessary.

When all is said and done, Warren's place in the judicial pantheon rests, not upon his opinions, but upon his decisions. If impact on the law is the hallmark of the outstanding judge, few occupants of the bench have been more outstanding than Chief Justice Warren.

Employing the authority of the ermine to the utmost, he never hesitated to do whatever he thought necessary to translate his own conceptions of fairness and justice into the law of the land. His Court's principal decisions have taken their place in the forefront of historic judicial decisions. Their impact on a whole society's way of life can be compared only with that caused by political revolution or military conflict.

"It is a delicious irony," reads a famous passage by Anthony Lewis, "that a President who raised inactivity to a principle of government . . . should have appointed a Chief Justice for whom action was all."[91] President Eisenhower said that one of the reasons he chose Warren was because he felt that Warren did not "hold extreme legal or philosophical views." Yet this criterion of moderation in legal and philosophical views is not necessarily valid as a measure by which to judge greatness on the bench. When people object to extremism in legal and philosophical views, they are really objecting to judicial activism. The judge who holds strong views is bound to take a more expansive view of the judicial function.

Perhaps the period of judicial activism that took place under the Warren Court was unprecedented in legal history. But almost all the outstanding judges in American law have been characterized by a more affirmative approach to the judicial role than that taken by their lesser colleagues. The great American judges have been jurists who used the power of the bench to the full. This was particularly true of Chief Justice Warren. The Marshall Court and the Warren Court have now become major parts of American legal history. The two men who sat at the center of those Courts were strong leaders who acquired their influence by the force of their character and their integrity.

We need not, in Justice Frankfurter's phrase, subscribe to the "hero theory of history" to recognize that great judges make a profound difference in the law. It did make a vast difference that Earl Warren and his colleagues rather than some other judges sat when they did. If Warren could not have made his judicial reputation without the opportunity that his position afforded him, it is also true that he forced the opportunity to make the creative contributions that escaped lesser Chief Justices. This, after all, has been the common characteristic of the greatest judges. Not all of them were masters of the common law or consummate craftsmen of judicial techniques. But all seized the occasion to make the creative contributions that eluded their lesser brethren.

13

Watershed Cases:
Brown v. Board of Education,
1954

"This is the first indication that I have ever had that there is a God." This caustic comment to two former law clerks was Justice Frankfurter's reaction to Chief Justice Vinson's death in September 1953, just before reargument was scheduled in the *Brown* school segregation case.[1] Had Vinson presided over the Court that decided *Brown,* the result would have been a divided decision. In a May 20, 1954, letter to his colleague Stanley Reed, three days after the unanimous *Brown* decision was announced, Frankfurter wrote, "I have no doubt that if the *Segregation* cases had reached decision last Term there would have been four dissenters—Vinson, Reed, Jackson and Clark—and certainly several opinions for the majority view. That would have been catastrophic."[2]

Instead, *Brown v. Board of Education* stands at the head of the cases decided by the Warren Court. In many ways, *Brown* was the watershed constitutional case of this century. Justice Reed told one of his clerks that "if it was not the most important decision in the history of the Court, it was very close."[3] When *Brown* struck down school segregation, it signaled the beginning of effective enforcement of civil rights in American law.

First *Brown* Conference

Chief Justice Vinson, notably gregarious and good natured, had grown increasingly irritable during his last Court term. According to a close associate, "[H]e was distressed over the Court's inability to find a strong, unified position on such an important case."[4] But Vinson was as much a cause as a critic of the *Brown* fragmentation. So ineffective a Chief Justice could scarcely be expected to lead the gifted prima donnas who then sat on the court. If anything, we saw, the division among the Justices intensified and, all too often, degenerated into personal animosity during Vinson's tenure. The first *Brown* conference, presided over by Vinson, saw the Court as divided as at any time during the Vinson tenure.

At that conference, on December 13, 1952, Chief Justice Vinson sounded what can most charitably be described as an uncertain trumpet, instead of the clarion needed to deal with the issue that had become an incubus on American society. His conference presentation totally ignored the fact that the "separate but equal" doctrine approved in *Plessy v. Ferguson*[5] had been the foundation of a whole structure of racial discrimination. Jim Crow replaced equal protection, and legally enforced segregation had become the dominant feature in Southern life.

Instead, at the *Brown* conference, Vinson's opening words indicated that he was not ready to overrule *Plessy v. Ferguson*. There was a whole "body of law back of us on separate but equal," he declared. Nor had the accepted law been questioned by Congress. "However [we] construe it," he said, "Congress did not pass a statute deterring and ordering no segregation." On the contrary, Congress itself had provided for segregation in the nation's capital. Since segregation in the District of Columbia had been imposed by a Congress including "men . . . who passed [the] amendments," he found it "hard to get away [from] that interpretation," particularly in light of the "long continued acceptance" of segregation in the District.[6]

On the other side, Justice Black asserted categorically that segregation rested on the idea of Negro inferiority; one did "not need books" or other sociological evidence "to say that." To Black, the "basic purpose" of the Fourteenth Amendment was "to protect [against] discrimination" and to abolish "such castes." For Justice Douglas also, the merits were "not in [the] realm of argument." The Constitution barred "classification on the basis of race." This principle was simple, "though the application of it may present difficulties." A similar view on the merits was stated by Justices Burton and Minton. As the latter stated it, "[C]lassification by race is not reasonable [and] segregation [is] per se unconstitutional."

The others, however, were closer to the Vinson position. The remaining Southerners on the Court, Justices Clark and Reed, indicated that they were following the Chief Justice's lead. Clark said that if the Court tried to impose desegregation immediately, "he would say we had led the states on to think segregation is OK and we should let them work it out."

Justice Reed went further, stating that he "approach[ed the case] from [a] different view," and would uphold the "separate but equal doctrine." In his view, the "states should be left to work out the problems for themselves."

Justices Frankfurter and Jackson were ambivalent. Frankfurter said that it was "intolerable" to have segregation in the District of Columbia. He found it difficult, however, to rule that segregation in the states was unconstitutional. He said that "he want[ed] to know why what has gone before is wrong." He could not accept a broad rule that "it's unconstitutional to treat a negro differently than a white."

Justice Jackson was also somewhat negative, though not as much as Justice Reed. Jackson declared that a decision to override *Plessy* could not be based on law as traditionally conceived. He said that he found nothing in the text, the opinions of the courts, or the history of the Fourteenth Amendment "that says [segregation] is unconstitutional," and asserted that "[Thurgood] Marshall's brief starts and ends with sociology." Yet that did not, as we shall see, mean that Justice Jackson would have voted in favor of segregation.

With the conference thus divided, any decision would have been sharply split. According to Justice Frankfurter, in his already-quoted letter to Justice Reed, there would have been only a bare majority in favor of striking down segregation. Justice Douglas read the conference consensus differently. In a *Memorandum for the File* on the day the *Brown* decision was delivered, Douglas wrote that if the cases had been decided during the 1952 Term, "there would probably have been many opinions and a wide divergence of views and a result that would have sustained, so far as the States were concerned, segregation of students."[7] Either way, such a fragmented decision would have been, in Frankfurter's phrase in his letter to Reed, "catastrophic."

Reargument Ordered

Fabian tactics are used as frequently in the Supreme Court as on the battleground. Justice Frankfurter, we have seen, made an ambiguous statement at the 1952 *Brown* conference. The Justice was not, however, entirely candid in his conference comments. Far from being in doubt about segregation in the states, he had concluded early in his consideration of the *Brown* case that segregation should now be stricken down. According to William R. Coleman, who had been the first black clerk at the Supreme Court when he clerked for Frankfurter during the 1948 Term, there was never any doubt about the Justice's *Brown* vote. "From the day the cases were taken," Coleman told an interviewer, "it was clear how he was going to vote. . . . I know . . . that he was for ending segregation from the start."[8]

More than any other Justice, Frankfurter was of the opinion that the close vote that would have resulted after the 1952 conference would, as he indicated in his letter to Reed, have been disastrous. With the Court as divided as it was, the only tactic that appeared at all promising was delay. The longer the Court's decision could be postponed, the more chance there was that the majority to end segregation could be increased. At the

December 1952 conference Frankfurter urged that the case be set for reargument. During the weeks that followed, the Justice sought to have reargument ordered for the next term, which would begin in October 1953.

To secure so long a postponement Justice Frankfurter would have to devise a plausible pretext, which would convince both the Court and the country that more than stalling for time was involved. Two factors made it easier to persuade the Justices. The first was that the conference had not taken any vote on the segregation issue. Justice Burton's diary entry on the 1952 conference records, "We discussed the segregation cases thus disclosing the trend but no even tentative vote was taken."[9] The same was true in the later conferences discussing the matter.

Just as important was the fact that, in Frankfurter's words at the time, "no one on the Court was pushing it."[10] Certainly Chief Justice Vinson was not eager to force a vote that he was going to lose; nor were the other Justices satisfied with the divided decision that would have come in the spring of 1953. According to Alexander Bickel, one of his 1952–1953 clerks, Justice Frankfurter returned from a conference toward the end of May 1953 in a euphoric state: "He said it looked as if we could hold off a decision that term . . . and that if we could get together some questions for discussion at a reargument, the case would be held over until the new term."[11]

With Bickel's help, Frankfurter formulated five questions "to which the attention of counsel on the reargument of the cases should be directed." At a conference on May 29, a majority agreed to put all the questions, with only minor changes from the Frankfurter draft. On June 8, the Court ordered the segregation cases restored to the docket for reargument in the next term, and the parties were asked to discuss the questions Frankfurter had drawn up, which related to the intent of the framers of the Fourteenth Amendment, as well as the remedial aspect of the case.[12]

Justice Jackson and Chief Justice Rehnquist

During the 1952 Term, one of Justice Jackson's law clerks was William H. Rehnquist, who was to become Chief Justice in 1986. Just before the 1952 conference Rehnquist wrote a memorandum on *Brown* which was headed *A Random Thought on the Segregation Case* and signed "whr."[13] It compared judicial action to invalidate segregation to the Court's "reading its own economic views into the Constitution" in cases such as *Lochner v. New York*[14]—"the high water mark in protecting corporations against legislative influence." According to the memo: "In these cases now before the Court, the Court is . . . being asked to read its own sociological views into the Constitution." For the Court to hold segregation invalid here, the memo asserted, would be for it to repeat the error of the *Lochner* Court. "If this Court, because its members individually are 'liberal' and dislike segregation, now chooses to strike it down, it differs from the McReynolds court only in the kinds of litigants it favors and the kinds of special claims it protects."

Rehnquist concluded his memo: "I think *Plessy v. Ferguson* was right and should be re-affirmed. If the Fourteenth Amendment did not enact Spencer's *Social Statics,*[15] it just as surely did not enact Myrdahl's [*sic*] *American Dilemma.*"[16]

The Rehnquist memo became an important factor in the Senate debate on the nominations of Rehnquist both to the Supreme Court and as Chief Justice. Justice Rehnquist himself maintained that his *Brown* memo "was prepared by me at Justice Jackson's request; it was intended as a rough draft of a statement of *his* views at the conference of the justices, rather than as a statement of my views."[17] The Rehnquist explanation has been challenged, particularly during the hearings on his judicial nominations.[18] It is hard not to conclude, as Richard Kluger did in his monumental book on the *Brown* case, that "one finds a preponderance of evidence to suggest that the memorandum in question—the one that threatened to deprive William Rehnquist of his place on the Supreme Court—was an accurate statement of his own views on segregation, not those of Robert Jackson."[19]

To the evidence so convincingly summarized in the Kluger book,[20] one must add the draft concurrence which Justice Jackson prepared, but never issued, in *Brown.* It has long been known that Jackson worked on a draft which he intended as the basis for a concurring *Brown* opinion. That draft, which has become available in the Jackson papers at the Library of Congress,[21] appears inconsistent with Rehnquist's assertion that his memo was intended to state Jackson's rather than Rehnquist's view on the constitutionality of segregation.

The key sentence in the Jackson draft states categorically, "I am convinced that present-day conditions require us to strike from our books the doctrine of separate-but-equal facilities and to hold invalid provisions of state constitutions or statutes which classify persons for separate treatment in matters of education based solely on possession of colored blood." At the end of his draft, Justice Jackson repeated this conclusion, stating, "I favor enter[ing] a decree that the state constitutions and statutes relied upon as requiring or authorizing segregation merely on account of race or color, are unconstitutional."

The Jackson draft shows clearly that the Justice held the view that school segregation was unconstitutional. He may, as the other Justices did, have recognized that before *Brown* the law had been the other way. He also had no illusions about the difficulties involved in enforcing a desegregation decision. Still, his draft expressed no doubt on the correctness of the *Brown* decision. By the time of the case, he was plainly ready to announce the principle that segregation was unconstitutional. And he did so in the draft prepared but never issued by him.

It is hard to believe that the man who wrote the sentences holding segregation invalid in his draft held the view only a few months earlier attributed to him in the Rehnquist memo—that *"Plessy v. Ferguson* was right and should be re-affirmed." So inconsistent, indeed, is this view with the Jackson draft that one is tempted to ask what might have happened had Justice Jackson's unequivocal draft statements on the invalidity of segregation been available when the Senate voted on the Rehnquist nomination to the Supreme Court or his later nomination as Chief Justice.

Warren's *Brown* Conference

By the time the *Brown* case was reargued in December 1953, Chief Justice Vinson's seat had been taken by Warren. Neophyte though he was, the new Chief Justice was to play the crucial role in fashioning the unanimous *Brown* decision. It is not too much to say, indeed, that Frankfurter's Fabian strategy was ultimately justified by Warren's leadership in disposing of the segregation issue. As Justice Burton wrote in his diary just before the Court handed down its unanimous *Brown* decision, "This would have been impossible a year ago. . . . However the postponement then was with the hope of a better result later."

The Warren leadership became apparent when the Justices met December 12, 1953, for their first conference on the case under the new Chief Justice. Until then, his Brethren had found a bluff, convivial colleague, who disarmed them with his friendliness and lack of pretension. Now they were to learn that he was a born leader, whose political talents were to prove as useful in the Judicial Palace as they had been in the State House.

The Warren *Brown* conference set the tone both for disposition of the segregation issue and for the entire tenure of the Warren Court. All the Justices were present except Black, who had to be away because his sister-in-law was near death in Alabama. The Chief Justice opened the conference by proposing that the Justices discuss the cases informally without taking any votes. The others agreed.

Warren's plan to talk about the issues as long as necessary without any vote led to what Justice Frankfurter called "a reconnoitering discussion, without thought of a vote."[22] That discussion, at the December 12 conference, was made easier by a step that Frankfurter had taken after the *Brown* case had come to the Court. Early in the previous term, the Justice had given Alexander Bickel, then one of his law clerks, the job of doing intensive research on the original intent of the framers of the Fourteenth Amendment. Bickel's work, based on months of plowing through the musty, near century-old folio volumes of the *Congressional Globe,* was finished late in the summer of 1953. His lengthy memorandum, carefully revised by both the Justice and Bickel himself, was printed and sent to the other Justices just before the *Brown* reargument in early December. Frankfurter's covering *Memorandum for the Conference* summarized the result of Bickel's labors: "The [Bickel] memorandum indicates that the legislative history of the Amendment is, in a word, inconclusive."[23] The Thirty-ninth Congress, which voted to submit the amendment, with its guaranty of equal protection, to the states for ratification, did not indicate an intent to have it either outlaw or not outlaw segregation in public schools.

The conclusion that the legislative history of the Fourteenth Amendment was "inconclusive" on school segregation was significant enough to be repeated as the first important point in the *Brown* opinion.[24] It meant that those who argued that the framers of the amendment had intended not to abolish segregation had misread the legislative history. At the beginning of the December 1952 conference, Chief Justice Vinson had asserted that it was "hard to get away from that contemporary interpretation of the amendments." If there was no such clear interpretation, the Justices were not foreclosed by any supposed intent in favor of segregation by those who wrote the amendment.

At the December 12 conference, the new Chief Justice set a completely different tone from that of his predecessor. His first words revealed his position and furnished a clear lead for the Court.

"I can't escape the feeling," Warren declared, "that no matter how much the Court wants to avoid it, it must now face the issue. The Court has finally arrived at the place where it *must* determine whether segregation is allowable in public schools." To be sure, there was legitimate concern over whether the Court was called upon to reverse the older cases and lines of reasoning. "But the more I've read and heard and thought, the more I've come to conclude that the basis of segregation and 'separate but equal' rests upon a concept of the inherent inferiority of the colored race. I don't see how *Plessy* and the cases following it can be sustained on any other theory. If we are to sustain segregation, we also must do it upon that basis."

Warren then asserted that "if the argument proved anything, it proved that that basis was not justified." More than that, he went on, "I don't see how in this day and age we can set any group apart from the rest and say that they are not entitled to exactly the same treatment as all others. To do so would be contrary to the Thirteenth, Fourteenth, and Fifteenth Amendments. They were intended to make the slaves equal with all others. Personally, I can't see how today we can justify segregation based solely on race."

Having indicated his opinion on the constitutional issue, Warren interposed some cautionary words. "It would be unfortunate," he said, "if we had to take precipitous action that would inflame more than necessary. The condition in the different states should be carefully considered by the Court." Referring to "the Deep South," he said, "[I]t will take all the wisdom of this Court to dispose of the matter with a minimum of emotion and strife. How we do it is important."

To sum up, the Chief Justice concluded his presentation, "[M]y instincts and feelings lead me to say that, in these cases we should abolish the practice of segregation in the public schools—but in a tolerant way."

His opening statement was a masterly illustration of the Warren method of leading the conference. Justice Abe Fortas told me that "it was

Warren's great gift that in presenting the case and discussing the case, he proceeded immediately and very calmly and graciously, to the ultimate values involved—the ultimate constitutional values, the ultimate human values." Warren's *Brown* presentation clearly stated the question before the Court in terms of the moral issue of racial inferiority. Segregation, he told the Justices, could be justified only by belief in the inherent inferiority of blacks and, if we follow *Plessy,* we have to do it upon that basis. Warren's words went straight to the ultimate human values involved. In the face of such an approach, traditional legal arguments seemed inappropriate, almost pettifoggery. To quote Fortas again, "[O]pposition based on the hemstitching and embroidery of the law appeared petty in terms of Warren's basic value approach."

Warren's presentation put the proponents of *Plessy* in the awkward position of appearing to subscribe to racist doctrine. Justice Reed, who spoke most strongly in support of *Plessy,* felt compelled to assert that he was not making "the argument that the Negro is an inferior race. Of course there is no inferior race, though they may be handicapped by lack of opportunity." Reed did not, however, suggest any other ground upon which the Court might rely to justify segregation now. The gap here was particularly apparent, since Reed went out of his way to "recognize that this is a dynamic Constitution and what was correct in *Plessy* might not be correct now." He also conceded that, under *Plessy,* "equal protection has not been satisfactory. The result has been less facilities for Negroes."

But Warren was not engaged in gaining debating points against Justice Reed and any of the others who might still oppose the overruling of *Plessy.* Warren knew that with the four Justices—Black, Douglas, Burton, and Minton—who had indicated at the conference a year earlier that they were in favor of striking down school segregation, he had at least five votes. But for him to gain only a sharply split decision would scarcely be a ringing victory. He tailored his presentation to mollify those who might be persuaded to join the evolving majority. By stating the matter in terms of the moral issue of racial inferiority, he placed those who might still lean toward *Plessy* on the defensive. Then he reached out to them by his stress on the need to proceed "in a tolerant way."

He recognized and regretted that precedents would have to be overturned but noted that this was necessary if the Court was not to rely on outdated racist theory. His moral tone did not contain any accusations against the South (that would certainly have raised the hackles of Justices Reed and Clark, the two Southern members present), but said only that segregation was no longer justifiable "in this day and age."

Warren also sought to assuage Southern sensibilities by stressing the need for caution in effectuating the Court's decision. Wisdom and understanding were called for if the decision was to produce "a minimum of emotion and strife." Warren was firm in his position that the Court should abolish school segregation. His clear lead on the overriding issue set the theme for the Court's decision—a matter of crucial importance given the uncertainties with which some of the Justices may have still been plagued. But the Chief Justice indicated that the ultimate decision should take account of conditions in different states. The Court should be flexible in how it framed its decree.

When Warren completed his opening statement, he probably supposed that he had five, or at most six, votes to abolish segregation. That, at any rate, was the reasonable assumption, based upon the Court's discussion the year before. Yet the views expressed after Warren spoke indicated that there had been some movement among the Justices. Justices Douglas, Burton, and Minton repeated their strong views against segregation. Justice Frankfurter again delivered an ambiguous statement, yet from all we know the Justice had concluded the year before to vote against segregation. But Justices Clark and Jackson, who had expressed reluctance the previous year, now suggested that they might be willing to support the new Chief Justice's position.

Justice Clark, who had supported Chief Justice Vinson at the December 1952 conference, pointed out how difficult the issue was for one who was closer to the race problem than anyone on the Court except Justice Black. Nevertheless, Clark said he was willing to agree to a decision against segregation, but "it must be done carefully or it will do more harm than good." Above all, there "must be no fiat or anything that looks like a fiat." Justice Clark indicated that he was not enthusiastic about an antisegregation decision, "but will go along as said before, provided relief is carefully worked out . . . in such a way that will permit different handling in different places."

Justice Jackson stated that the segregation issue was largely "a question of politics." This "for me personally is not a problem, but it is difficult to make it other than a political decision. . . . Our problem is to make a judicial decision out of a political conclusion"—to find "a judicial basis for a congenial political conclusion." The implication was that he would support a properly written decision striking down segregation. "As a political decision, I can go along with it."

The conference discussion showed Warren that he could count on five, and probably six, solid votes to end segregation, and could secure two more votes if an opinion could be written that would satisfy Justices Clark and Jackson. That left Justice Reed, who alone still supported the *Plessy* doctrine. But even Reed had conceded that *Plessy* should not be followed merely because it was a precedent. He had also recognized that, in practice, *Plessy* had not produced anything like equal facilities for blacks and had had difficulty in meeting Warren's claim that to affirm *Plessy* meant to affirm black inferiority.

Chief Justice Warren now devoted all his efforts to eliminating the danger of dissenting and concurring opinions. The main thing, he knew, was to avoid polarizing those who had not indicated wholehearted agreement with his own forthright view. The last thing he wanted was a candid concurrence by Justice Jackson, a learned separate opinion by Justice

Frankfurter—much less the Southern breach in Court unity that would be worked by a dissent by Justice Reed.

The Chief Justice's instinct for effective leadership was demonstrated by the way in which he acted after the December 12 conference. Warren moved on two levels to secure agreement to a single, unanimous opinion: the personal level and the conference level. During the months following the December conference, Warren had frequent lunches with several of his colleagues. Most often, the luncheon group consisted of the Chief Justice and Justices Reed, Burton, and Minton. The three worked on Reed to induce him to go along with the majority. Among those who strongly favored striking down segregation, Burton and Minton were the two most congenial to Reed and the most likely to influence his vote, particularly by stressing the baneful effects of a split decision.

Warren also had many individual meetings with his colleagues. Justice Burton's diary notes several such sessions at which he discussed the segregation case with the Chief Justice. From all we know about Warren, he was most effective when he was able to operate in a one-on-one setting. That was the way he had been able to accomplish things back in California. The result in *Brown* showed that he had not lost any of his persuasive powers in the Marble Palace.

Second *Brown* Conference

On January 16, 1954, Warren presided over his second *Brown* conference. For the January conference the Chief Justice had developed the second prong of his *Brown* strategy, which he had revealed to Justice Burton a month earlier. It was, in Burton's words, a "plan to try [to] direct discussion of segregation cases toward the decree—as providing now the best chance of unanimity in that phase."[25]

S. Sidney Ulmer, a political scientist who also used Justice Burton's diary in writing about the *Brown* decision, concluded that the conference plan disclosed to Burton "reveals poor judgment on Warren's part since the subsequent processes by which a decree was produced proved to be much more complicated and difficult than the processes leading to the initial decision."[26] This comment misconceives the Warren strategy. Far from revealing poor judgment, the plan remains a striking illustration of the instinctive leadership that Warren displayed throughout his career. Continued discussion of the decision itself would only polarize potential concurrers and dissenters, solidifying their intention to write separate opinions. By concentrating instead on the remedy, all the Justices would work on the assumption that the decision itself would strike down segregation. They would endeavor jointly to work out a decree that would best effectuate such a decision. Those who, like Justice Reed, found it most difficult to accept a decision abolishing segregation would grow accustomed to what might at first have seemed too radical a step.

At any rate, the second *Brown* conference under Warren was devoted to the question of remedy. The Chief Justice led off the session along the lines he had indicated to Justice Burton. And he did so by setting the remedial theme in the manner most calculated to appeal to Justices Reed, Clark, and even Black, who feared the effects of ordering the South to admit the black plaintiffs immediately into white schools. Above all, the Southerners wanted a flexible decree that, as Justice Clark had stated at the December 12 conference, "will permit different handling in different places."

In addition the Chief Justice sought to reassure Justice Frankfurter and, to a lesser extent, Justice Jackson, who feared that for the Supreme Court to order relief in the individual school districts would bog the Justices in a political quagmire. On the day before the January 16 conference, Frankfurter had circulated a five-page memorandum devoted to "considerations [which] have arisen within me in regard to the fashioning of a decree." In it, he categorically asserted, "The one thing one can feel confidently is that this Court cannot do it directly."[27]

The Chief Justice's opening statement at the January 16 conference was aimed, first of all, at Justice Frankfurter. The Court, Warren said, should be "as little involved in administration as we can. We should turn to the district courts for enforcement. But we ought not to turn them loose without guidance of what paths are open to them." Warren then addressed himself to the Southerners' concern. The Chief Justice stressed that the enforcement problem was not the same in different states. Kansas would present no difficulty, he said. In Delaware, there would likewise be no trouble and, in the District of Columbia, it could also be done quickly. The South was another matter. As Justice Frankfurter's notes tell us, Warren expressed "lot of concern for S.C. and Va."

Justice Black, who had been absent at the conference a month earlier, spoke next. The Alabaman wanted the Court to do as little as possible in enforcement. "Leave it to the district courts," he urged, "let them work it out." "Would you give them any framework?" Warren interjected. "I don't see how you could do it," came back the reply, "we should leave it up to the district courts."

Justice Reed also felt that the Court should lay down only general enforcement principles. But, unlike Justice Black, he thought the Court must say a few things. Above all, it must ensure that enforcement was "not a rush job. The time they give, the opportunities to adjust, these are the greatest palliative to an awful thing that you can do." By his remarks, Reed indicated that he was beginning to feel that the "awful thing" of desegregation was becoming palatable, if enough time for adjustment was given.

The notes we have of the January 16 conference were taken by Justice Frankfurter.[28] They do not contain any summary of his own statement. Presumably, he repeated the position taken in his January 15 memorandum that the Court should not enforce desegregation directly. He may also have repeated a suggestion that he made in the memorandum—that a master should be appointed, either by the Supreme Court or the district court, to determine the facts and propose decrees in each of the cases before the Court. Justice Douglas agreed that the use of a master was a possible solution, since it would be difficult for the Court to decide anything concrete on enforcement. Douglas stressed that any decree should reflect generosity, as well as flexibility.

Justice Jackson said that if it was only a matter of personal right, there was no answer to the N.A.A.C.P. claim that the black plaintiffs were entitled to immediate admission to desegregated schools. "If what we're doing is to uproot social policy, what business is it of ours?" Jackson did not attempt to resolve the dilemma. Instead, he suggested that the Court needed more time to consider the remedial issue. As Frankfurter's notes quoted him, "let's have a reargument on terms of a decree!!"

Jackson's suggestion for reargument on the terms of the decree was supported by Justices Clark and Black, and ultimately adopted by the Court. Justices Burton and Minton restated the need for the Court itself not to perform the enforcement function. Burton said that "our contribution is to decentralize" enforcement and Minton that he was "not given to throwing the Court's weight around."

The conference closed with a strong statement by Justice Black on the need for flexibility in enforcement. The worst thing would be for the Court to try to resolve everything at once by its decree. "If necessary, let us have 700 suits" to work out the process. "Vagueness is not going to hurt." What was most needed was time. That was why Black had no objection to reargument. "Let it simmer. . . . Let it take time. It can't take too long." In the Deep South "any man who would come in [in support] would be dead politically forever. . . . In Alabama most liberals are praying for delay." Justice Black concluded the conference by warning that enforcement would give rise to a "storm over this Court."

Unanimity Secured

At his second *Brown* conference, Warren had stated his basic approach in the manner calculated to appeal to those in doubt: delegation of the decree power (to meet Justice Frankfurter's fear of embroiling the Court directly in the enforcement process) and flexibility (to meet the fears of the Southerners over immediate desegregation). The discussion indicated a consensus that was in accord with the Chief Justice's own position. The Southerners' alarm at precipitate action had led even the strongest proponents of overruling *Plessy* to concede the need for flexibility and time to work out the desegregation process.

The general agreement on Justice Jackson's suggestion for a reargument on the terms of the decree now made the Chief Justice's task of securing a unanimous opinion outlawing segregation less difficult. Justices Frankfurter and Clark would find it easier to agree, once it was clear that the Court itself would not immediately decree an end to segregation. Justice Reed might, it is true, prove more difficult to convince. But he, too, could be persuaded more readily, now that all had agreed to flexibility in enforcement and postponed the specifics on the remedial question to a later day.

After the January 16 session, there was one other conference discussion, several weeks later, before the Court took a vote on the matter. We do not know any details about the later conference or when the vote was taken. In his posthumously published memoirs, the Chief Justice stated that the Court voted in February and that the vote was unanimous against the separate-but-equal doctrine.[29] In later interviews Warren indicated that the vote came in March. The question of the exact date is less important than that of how the vote went. Despite Warren's statement in his memoirs, it is probable that the vote was eight to one, with Justice Reed voting to follow the *Plessy* case.

That Reed did vote to uphold segregation is indicated by his working on the draft of a dissent during February, asserting that segregation by itself did not violate equal protection.[30] In addition, there are indications that the Justice persisted in standing alone until the end of April. Warren continued to work on him to change his vote, both at luncheon meetings and in private sessions. Then, toward the end, the Chief Justice put it to Justice Reed directly: "Stan, you're all by yourself on this now. You've got to decide whether it's really the best thing for the country."[31] As described by Reed's law clerk, who was present at the meeting, Warren was typically restrained in his approach. "Throughout the Chief Justice was quite low-key and very sensitive to the problems that the decision would present to the South. He empathized with Justice Reed's concern. But he was quite firm on the Court's need for unanimity on a matter of this sensitivity."[32]

Ultimately Justice Reed agreed to the unanimous decision. He still thought, as he wrote to Justice Frankfurter, that "there were many considerations that pointed to a dissent." But, he went on, "they did not add up to a balance against the Court's opinion . . . the factors looking toward a fair treatment for Negroes are more important than the weight of history."[33]

Drafting the Opinion

At the conference that took the vote to strike down segregation, it was agreed that the opinion should be written by the Chief Justice. The writing of the *Brown* opinion was done under conditions of even greater secrecy than usual. The extreme secrecy was extended to the entire deliberative process in the segregation case. Thus the covering note to a Frankfurter memorandum on the fashioning of a decree in the case stated at the end: "I need hardly add that the typewriting was done under conditions of strictest security."[34]

The Justices also took steps to ensure that the way they voted would not leak out. No record of action taken in *Brown* was written in the docket book that was kept by each Justice and was available to his clerks. Warren tells us that, at the conference at which the opinion was assigned, "the importance of secrecy was discussed. We agreed that only my law clerks should be involved, and that any writing between my office and those of the other Justices would be delivered to the Justices personally. This practice was followed throughout and this was the only time it was required in my years on the Court."[35]

Toward the end of April, after he had secured Justice Reed's vote, the Chief Justice was ready to begin the drafting process. Warren's normal practice was to leave the actual drafting of opinions to his law clerks. He would usually outline verbally the way he wanted the opinion drafted. The outline would summarize the facts and how the main issues should be decided. The Chief Justice would rarely go into particulars on the details involved in the case. That was for the clerk drafting the opinion, who was left with a great deal of discretion, particularly on the reasoning and research supporting the decision.

It has been assumed that this procedure was also followed in the *Brown* drafting process. However, it was Warren himself who wrote the first *Brown* draft. Headed simply "Memorandum" and undated, the original draft, in Warren's handwriting, is in pencil on nine yellow legal-size pages.

Certain things about Warren's first *Brown* draft stand out. First, it definitely set the tone of the final opinion. It was written in the typical Warren style: short, nontechnical, well within the grasp of the average reader. The language is direct and straightforward, illustrating the point once made to me by one of his law clerks: "He had a penchant for Anglo-Saxon words over Latin words and he didn't like foreign phrases thrown in if there was a good American word that would do."

Warren's own draft was based on the two things he later stressed to Earl Pollock, the clerk primarily responsible for helping on the *Brown* opinion: the opinion should be as brief as possible, and it was to be written in understandable English, avoiding legalisms. This was repeated in Warren's May 7 memorandum transmitting the draft opinion to the Justices. The draft, wrote the Chief Justice, was "prepared on the theory that the opinions should be short, readable by the lay public, non-rhetorical, unemotional and, above all, non-accusatory."[36]

Even more important is the fact that the Warren draft is basically similar to the final *Brown* opinion. Changes were, to be sure, made in the draft—both by the Chief Justice and his clerks as well as by other Justices. In particular, the clerks supplied supporting authority in the text and in fleshing out the opinion with footnotes. But the essentials of the *Brown* opinion (and most of its language) were contained in the draft Warren wrote out in his own forcefully legible hand at the end of April 1954.

The Warren draft contains two of the three most famous passages in the *Brown* opinion. First, after referring to the decision facing the Court, the draft states, "In approaching it, we cannot turn the clock of education back to 1868, when the Amendment was adopted, or even to 1895 [*sic*] when *Plessy v. Ferguson* was decided."

The Warren draft also contains *Brown*'s striking passage on the baneful effect of segregation on black children: "To separate them from others of their age in school solely because of their color puts the mark of inferiority not only upon their status in the community but also upon their little hearts and minds in a form that is unlikely ever to be erased."

In addition, it was the Warren draft that stressed the changed role of education in the contemporary society, as contrasted with the situation when the Fourteenth Amendment was adopted ("No child can reasonably be expected to succeed in life today if he is deprived of the opportunity of an education"). And it posed the critical question presented to the Court— "Does segregation of school children solely on the basis of color, even though the physical facilities may be equal, deprive the minority group of equal opportunities in the educational system?"—as well as its answer— "We believe that it does."

An early draft of the memorandum transmitting the *Brown* draft to the Justices declared, "On the question of segregation in education, this should be the end of the line."[37] If that was true, it was mainly the Chief Justice's doing—even more than commentators on *Brown* have realized. The Warren *Brown* draft shows us that the Chief Justice was primarily responsible not only for the unanimous decision, but also for the opinion in the case. This was one case where the drafting was not delegated.[38] The opinion delivered was essentially the opinion produced when Warren himself sat down and put pencil to paper.

Final Opinion

"An opinion in a touchy and explosive litigation . . . is like a souffle—it should be served at once after it has reached completion." The *Brown* drafting process, after Warren had penciled his draft opinion, showed that the Chief Justice agreed with this sentiment contained in a May 15, 1954, note from Justice Frankfurter.

As soon as Warren had finished his *Brown* draft and had it typed, he called in his three law clerks and told them that the decision of the Court was to overturn *Plessy,* and that the decision was unanimous. He enjoined them to the strictest secrecy, saying that he had not told anyone outside the Justices what the decision was—not even his wife. The Chief Justice asked all three clerks to write drafts based on his own draft opinion. It was now the end of April, and the clerks worked the entire weekend in order to have their drafts ready on Monday, May 3. Earl Pollock, in particular, recalls working on his draft straight through the weekend, virtually without sleep. Pollock was the clerk with primary responsibility for the case, since he had written the *Brown* bench memo. Such a memo is prepared for each Justice after the Court votes to hear a case.

Of the three clerks' drafts, Pollock's was the most important, for he made the only significant changes in the Chief Justice's draft. The most important change was the separation of the companion case of *Bolling v.*

Sharpe[39] from the *Brown* case itself. The segregation cases presented to the Court involved schools in four states and the District of Columbia. Warren's *Brown* draft had dealt with all these cases together, as shown by its opening sentence: "These cases come to us from the States of Delaware, Virginia, Kansas and South Carolina and from the District of Columbia." The Warren draft went on to say that, though they were separate cases, "the basic law involved in their decision is identical to the point that they can on principle properly be considered together in this opinion."

In treating the state and D.C. cases together, the Warren draft was making a legal mistake. The rationale for striking down segregation in the states cannot be used to reach that result in Washington, D.C. The state action in *Brown* was invalidated under the Equal Protection Clause of the Fourteenth Amendment. Yet that amendment is binding only on the states, not the Federal Government. The latter is bound by the Fifth Amendment, which contains a Due Process Clause but no requirement of equal protection. Obviously, the Court would not decide that the states could not have segregated schools while the District of Columbia could. But the result had to be reached in terms of due process, rather than equal protection, analysis.

Following the example set in Warren's draft, the three law clerks dealt with the state and D.C. cases together in their drafts. However, in the May 3 covering memorandum attached to his draft, Pollock indicated that this was not the proper approach. Pollock stated that his draft was "along the lines of your memo of last week. Like the memo, this draft covers all five cases in one consolidated opinion." Pollock then wrote, "I am inclined to think, however, that the District of Columbia case should be treated independently in a short, separate opinion accompanying the other one. . . . The material relating to the equal protection clause of the 14th Amendment has no direct relevance to the District of Columbia case, which, of course, is based primarily on the due process clause of the 5th Amendment."

Warren accepted Pollock's suggestion and the details of the legal theory underlying the D.C. case were worked out by the other two Warren clerks. They also drafted the separate short opinion delivered in the case.

In addition to the May 3 drafts of the clerks, there were further *Brown* drafts on May 5 and 7, before the draft opinion was ready to be circulated to the Justices, together with the draft in the D.C. case. This typed *Brown* draft, composed of nine legal size pages, was titled "MEMORANDUM ON THE STATE CASES." The draft in *Bolling v. Sharpe*, four typed pages, was titled "MEMORANDUM ON THE DISTRICT OF COLUMBIA CASE." The draft opinions were then delivered personally to the Justices on Saturday, May 8. Justice Burton's diary entry for that date notes: "In AM the Chief Justice brought his draft of the segregation cases memoranda. These were in accord with our conversations."[40] Warren himself took the printed drafts to the Justices who were in their chambers. His clerks delivered copies to the others. Justice Black's copy was brought to him on the tennis court at his home in Alexandria, Justice Minton's at his Washington apartment.

As already indicated, a few significant alterations were made in the Warren draft. The Justices themselves made only minor stylistic changes.[41] In the Warren chambers, the further drafts were prepared by Pollock, who also made numerous cosmetic alterations in the Chief Justice's draft. There were only two important changes. The first was a discussion of the post–*Plessy v. Ferguson* education cases. This added some legal meat to the opinion, but did not really add anything of substance to it.

The second change was more significant, particularly when we add the contribution made to it by a second clerk. After Warren's "hearts and minds" sentence on the baneful effect of segregation, Pollock's first draft of May 3 added the passage from the opinion of the lower court in the Kansas case that now appears in the *Brown* opinion. The Pollock draft then asserted, "Whatever may have been the state of psychological knowledge when *Plessy v. Ferguson* was decided, this finding is amply supported by modern authority. To the extent that there is language in *Plessy v. Ferguson* to the contrary, and to the extent that other decisions of this Court have been read as applying the 'separate but equal' doctrine to education, those cases are overruled."

This statement was accepted by the Chief Justice and repeated in the drafts of May 5, 7, and 8. The passage was put into its final form by written corrections in Pollock's writing in the draft of May 12, the final draft in the case.

In an interview Pollock told me that he had been greatly troubled by the *Plessy v. Ferguson* opinion. "It seemed to me," he went on, "that the most noxious part of *Plessy* was the notion that, if Negroes found segregation a 'badge of inferiority,' that was sort of in the eye of the beholder. I was looking for a way to part company and to say that, whatever the situation was in the 1890's, we know a lot more about law in society than we did then."

It was this approach that was responsible for the most controversial part of the *Brown* opinion—that relying not on law but "psychological knowledge." In the *New York Times* of May 18, 1954, James Reston analyzed *Brown* in a column headed "A Sociological Decision." According to Reston, the Court had relied "more on the social scientists than on legal precedents. . . . The Court's opinion read more like an expert paper on sociology than a Supreme court opinion."[42]

The Reston characterization was based on the assertion that the *Brown* opinion rested less on legal reasoning than on the Pollock statement on "psychological knowledge . . . amply supported by modern authority." Even more suggestive to commentators was the fact that the statement was backed by a footnote—the celebrated footnote 11, which soon became the most controversial note in Supreme Court history.

Footnote 11 listed seven works by social scientists, starting with an article by Kenneth B. Clark and concluding with the massive two-volume study by Gunnar Myrdal, *An American Dilemma.*[43] Both supporters and critics of the Court have assumed, like Reston, that footnote 11 means that the *Brown* decision was based on the work of the social scientists cited. As Kenneth Clark, the first mentioned in the footnote, summarized it, "[T]he Court . . . appeared to rely on the findings of social scientists in the 1954 decision."[44] A plethora of learned commentary followed, analyzing in amazing detail the works cited, the significance of the order of citation, and the fact that other relevant writings were not cited—as well as the whole subject of using the methods and products of social science in deciding controversial legal issues. Even supporters of the decision have shown how vulnerable the studies and tests relied on in most of the cited works really were.

Those who have focused intensively on the controversial footnote have acted out of ignorance of the manner in which Supreme Court opinions are prepared. Warren himself stressed that it was the decision, not the citations, that were important. "It was only a note, after all," he declared to an interviewer.[45] The Chief Justice normally left the citations in opinions to his law clerks. He considered them among the minutiae of legal scholarship, which could in the main be left to others.

In the *Brown* case, the fleshing out of the opinion with footnotes was left primarily to one of Warren's clerks, Richard Flynn. As he recalls it, there was no specific method in the organization of footnote 11. When it came time to cite supporting authority, the works listed (particularly those by Myrdal and Clark) were, to Flynn, the "obvious" things to list. When asked by me if there was any method in the way he organized the note, he answered, "I don't recall any, that's just the way it fell."

It has been said that footnote 11 provoked concern among several Justices, particularly in the gratuitous citation of the Myrdal work, which had in the decade since its publication become a red flag to the white South. In 1971, Justice Clark, then retired from the Court, told an interviewer, "I questioned the Chief's going with Myrdal in that opinion. I told him—and Hugo Black did, too—that it wouldn't go down well in the South. And he didn't need it."[46]

Clark's recollection appears inaccurate. Over the years, he may have come to feel that, in view of the storm in the South caused by the Myrdal citation, he should have said something at the time, which may, years later, have become a blurred recollection that he and Black had expressed concern. But in all likelihood, if Justices Black and Clark had objected, the Myrdal reference would have been taken out. The citation was just not important enough to Warren to withstand even a mild expression of concern by any of the Justices.

Justice Clark did suggest one correction in footnote 11 that was speedily accepted by the Chief Justice—which indicates that the same thing might well have happened if Clark had asked for the Myrdal work to be removed. In the draft of the *Brown* opinion originally delivered to the Justices, the footnote began with the citation "Clark, Effect of Prejudice and Discrimination on Personality Development (Midcentury White House Conference on Children and Youth, 1950)." Justice Clark objected that this did not sufficiently identify the Clark who had written the article cited. He did not want people, particularly in his own South, to think that the Court was citing an antisegregation article that he—Tom Clark—had authored. He therefore asked that the citation be changed to "K. B. Clark," so that no one would confuse the Justice with the author. In the final opinion, as Justice Clark had suggested, the name of the first author cited appears with initials, the only author in the footnote not identified solely by last name.

There was thus no controversy over footnote 11 in the Court itself. So far as we know, the draft *Brown* opinion was speedily approved by the Justices—and without significant changes. The general attitude among Warren's colleagues was expressed in a handwritten note by Justice Douglas: "I do not think I would change a single word. . . . You have done a beautiful job."[47]

The final *Brown* draft was circulated on May 13 in printed form. The next day, Saturday, May 15, was a conference day. At lunch, the Justices were entertained by Justice Burton, with a large salmon provided by Secretary of the Interior Douglas McKay. Just before, Burton wrote in his diary, the "conference finally approved Segregation opinions and instructions for delivery Monday—no previous notice being given to office staffs etc so as to avoid leaks. Most of us—including me—handed back the circulated print to C.J. to avoid possible leaks."[48]

Decision Day

Monday, May 17, 1954, Supreme Court Chamber. At noon precisely, the curtain behind the bench parted and, led by the Chief Justice, the Justices filed to their places. "As we Justices marched into the courtroom on that day," Warren later recalled, "there was a tenseness that I have not seen equaled before or since."[49] For weeks before the *Brown* decision was announced, the courtroom had been jammed; anticipation mounted as the weeks passed. Now, to the acute Court watcher, there were definite signs that the day would not be a quiet one. For one thing, several of the Justices' wives were present, something that rarely happened except on historic Court occasions. Even more significant was Justice Jackson's presence. Early that morning Warren had gone to the hospital, where Jackson was critically ill, to show him a copy of the final opinion. Then, says Warren, the ailing Justice "to my alarm insisted on attending the Court that day in order to demonstrate our solidarity."[50]

Warren had advised his law clerks to be in the courtroom that morning. They had also realized from the intensive work on the final proofs that weekend that announcement of the decision was imminent. Justice Frankfurter had also told his clerks that *Brown* was coming down. The other Justices' clerks had not been informed in advance, but they all sensed that this was to be more than the usual decision day. On his way to the robing room, Justice Clark had stopped to say to the clerks, "I think you boys ought to be in the courtroom today."[51]

Surprisingly, the air of expectancy was absent from the Supreme Court press room. The reporters were told before the Court convened that it looked like a quiet day. Their expectation appeared borne out by the routine business that occupied the first part of the Court session. First there was the admission of 118 attorneys to the Supreme Court Bar. Then three unimportant opinions were read by Justices Clark and Douglas.

By now, fifty minutes of the Court session had passed. The reporters did not bother going upstairs to hear the routine opinions being delivered. But then, as they sat in the press room over their coffee, Banning E. Whittington, the Court's press officer, started putting on his coat and announced, "Reading of the segregation decisions is about to begin in the courtroom." Whittington led a fast-moving exodus as the reporters dashed up the long flight of marble steps just as the Chief Justice began reading in his booming bass. It was then 12:52 P.M.

"I have for announcement" said Warren, "the judgment and opinion of the Court in No. I—Oliver Brown et al. v. Board of Education of Topeka." Then, in a firm, colorless tone, he read the opinion in the state segregation case. First, the background of the case was given. Plaintiff Negroes sought admission to public schools on a nonsegregated basis. They had been denied relief on the basis of the *Plessy* "separate but equal" doctrine. They contended that segregated schools were not "equal" and could not be made "equal" and, by their very nature, deprived plaintiffs of the equal protection of the laws. The Chief Justice then summarized the reargument and concluded (following the Bickel-Frankfurter memorandum) that the legislative history of the Fourteenth Amendment was, at best, inconclusive. He also stressed the changed position in the society of both public education and the Negro.

The opinion next went into the origin of the separate-but-equal doctrine and the cases which had applied it. Here, unlike those cases, the lower courts had found that the Negro and white schools had been or were being equalized as to buildings, curricula, teacher qualifications, and other "tangible" factors. The decision therefore could not turn on comparing merely these tangible factors: "We must look instead to the effect of segregation itself on public education."[52]

In approaching this problem, the Court could not "turn the clock back to 1868 when the Amendment was adopted, or even to 1896 when *Plessy v. Ferguson* was written. We must consider public education in light of its full development and its present place in American life throughout the Nation." Then, in what for him was eloquent language, the Chief Justice affirmed that "[t]oday, education is perhaps the most important function of state and local governments. . . . In these days, it is doubtful that any child may reasonably be expected to succeed in life if he is denied the opportunity of an education. Such an opportunity, where the state has undertaken to provide it, is a right which must be made available to all on equal terms."

This brought the opinion to the crucial question: "Does segregation of children in public schools solely on the basis of race, even though the physical facilities and other 'tangible' factors may be equal, deprive the children of the minority group of equal educational opportunities?"

Until then, with the opinion two-thirds finished, the Chief Justice had not indicated the outcome of the decision. Now, in the next sentence, he did. Answering the critical question, he asserted: "We believe that it does."

The opinion reviewed earlier cases which had held that, in colleges and universities, segregated schools could not provide equal educational opportunities. The same was true for children in public schools. "To separate them from others of similar age and qualifications solely because of their race generates a feeling of inferiority as to their status in the community that may affect their hearts and minds in a way unlikely ever to be undone." This was the final version of the soaring sentence Warren had put in his original outline; it stated the baneful impact of segregation on black children better than a whole shelf of learned sociological tomes.

Plessy v. Ferguson had said that the assumption that segregation supposed colored inferiority was fallacious. Warren now declared that segregation did mean the inferiority of the Negro group. "Whatever may have been the extent of psychological knowledge at the time of *Plessy v. Ferguson,* this finding is amply supported by modern authority. Any language in *Plessy v. Ferguson* contrary to this finding is rejected." This statement was supported by footnote 11 of the opinion, which listed the seven works by social scientists and was to become the most famous note in a Supreme Court opinion.

The Chief Justice then stated the Court's far-reaching conclusion: "We conclude"—here Warren departed from the printed text to insert the word "unanimously"—"that in the field of public education the doctrine of 'separate but equal' has no place. Separate educational facilities are inherently unequal." Warren later recalled: "When the word 'unanimously' was spoken a wave of emotion swept the room; no words or intentional movement, yet a distinct emotional manifestation that defies description."[53] Other observers agree that, as Warren pronounced the word, barely suppressed astonishment swept around the courtroom. Until then, neither the press nor the public had any idea that the man from California had achieved a unanimous decision.

The *Brown* opinion concluded with the holding that plaintiffs "and others similarly situated" had been deprived of equal protection by the segregation complained of. But it did not decree any relief. Instead, the Jackson suggestion at the January 16 conference was followed. "Because these are class actions, because of the wide applicability of this decision, the formulation of decrees in these cases presents problems of considerable complexity." This decision dealt only with "the constitutionality of segregation in public education. We have now announced that such segregation is a denial of the equal protection of the laws." The question of appropriate relief was still before the Court. "In order that we may have the full assistance of the parties in formulating decrees," the Court was scheduling further argument on the matter for the next Court term, beginning in October 1954. The U.S. Attorney General was invited to participate. So were the Attorneys General of states with segregated schools.

Almost never before, wrote Arthur Krock the next day in the *New York Times,* had the "high tribunal disposed so simply and briefly of an issue of such magnitude."[54] The *Brown* opinion was strikingly short for an opinion of such consequence: only ten pages in the *United States Reports,* in which Supreme Court opinions are printed. The second segregation opinion, that in *Bolling v. Sharpe,* was even shorter, disposing of District of Columbia segregation in six paragraphs.

When Warren concluded the *Bolling* opinion, it was 1:20 P.M.; it had taken only twenty-eight minutes for the Chief Justice to read both opinions. After Warren finished, everyone in the courtroom looked to Justice Reed to see what the courtly Southerner was going to do. Reed, who had had tears in his eyes during the opinion reading, now filed out silently with the Justices. Despite Warren's use of the word "unanimously," it was hard for many to grasp that neither Reed nor any of the other Justices had filed a separate opinion. For weeks thereafter people would call the clerk's office and ask to see the dissenting opinion.

Discussing the *Brown* unanimity later, Warren said with a characteristic generosity of spirit that the real credit should go to the three Southern Justices. "Don't thank me," he said to a California friend who visited him in his chambers, "I'm not the one. You should see what those . . . fellows from the southern states had to take from their constituencies. It was absolutely slaughter. They stood right up and did it anyway because they thought it was right."[55] Justice Reed, in particular, came to believe that the *Brown* decision was wholly right. He told one of his clerks that "if it was not the most important decision in the history of the Court, it was very close."[56]

The other Justices, too, were well aware that they had participated in what Justice Frankfurter termed "a day that will live in glory."[57] A few days earlier, in a note to Warren joining the opinion, Frankfurter wrote: "When—I no longer say 'if'—you bring this cargo of unanimity safely to port it will be a memorable day no less in the history of the Nation than in that of the Court. You have, if I may say so, been wisely at the helm throughout this year's journey of this litigation. Finis coronat omnia."[58]

Other Segregation Cases

Chief Justice Warren had been careful to limit the *Brown* opinion to desegregation in schools. But the decision necessarily had a broader impact. In *Bolling v. Sharpe,* the District of Columbia companion case, the Court had declared, "In view of our decision that the Constitution prohibits the states from maintaining racially segregated schools, it would be unthinkable that the same Constitution would impose a lesser duty on the Federal Government."[59] It would similarly be unthinkable that the same Constitution would prohibit segregation in schools and impose a lesser duty on other public institutions.

Soon after the first *Brown* decision, the U.S. Court of Appeals for the Fourth Circuit was presented with the question of whether Baltimore could continue to segregate its public beaches. The court held that *Brown* required a negative answer. If segregation in schools generates a feeling of inferiority in Negroes, the same must be true, said the court, of segregation in recreational facilities.[60] In November 1955, the Supreme Court unanimously affirmed this decision without opinion.[61] At the same time, it unanimously reversed a decision upholding a segregated municipal golf course in Atlanta, citing in support only its decision in the Baltimore case.[62]

In 1956, the Court affirmed a decision striking down the segregated bus system in Montgomery, Alabama.[63] After the conference, Chief Justice Warren told his law clerks that they were going to affirm summarily, without hearing oral argument. He said they were going to cite three cases: *Brown* and the Baltimore and Atlanta cases of the previous year. The clerk who drafted the opinion told me that, since he had no further guidance, he took the prudent course and simply followed the Chief Justice literally. That is the way the per curiam opinion in the Montgomery bus case appears in the *United States Reports*—stating merely that the decision below is affirmed and citing only the three cases, without explaining what the Court was doing and the reasoning behind its decision.

The clerk involved says, "I thought at the time that it was a pretty casual way for the Court to advance a major proposition of constitutional law and still do." Legal scholars have voiced a similar criticism of the Court's failure to explain its extension of *Brown* to public facilities outside the field of education. The criticisms, however, are beside the point. Was there a need for explanation once the *Brown* opinion—with the broad sweep of its language striking down separation of the races—had been written?

In the years after *Brown,* the Court ruled segregation invalid in all public buildings,[64] housing,[65] transportation,[66] and recreational[67] and eating facilities.[68] The Court, following Warren's lead, said as little as possible but continued to strike down every segregation law challenged before it. By 1963, an opinion could declare categorically: "[I]t is no longer open to question that a State may not constitutionally require segregation of public facilities."[69]

Chief Justice Warren used to recall that, when he first arrived, the Supreme Court had a separate washroom for Negroes. One of the first things he did was to end the discrimination taking place in the Court building itself. By the end of Warren's tenure, as the cases just discussed show, the Court had virtually rooted out racial discrimination from American law.

Brown in Perspective

An undated note, written on a Supreme Court memo pad in Justice Frankfurter's handwriting, reads: "It is not fair to say that the South has always denied Negroes 'this constitutional right.' It was NOT a constitutional right till May 17/54."[70] The more restrained critics of the *Brown* decision have been disturbed by what they claim is its inadequacy in explaining its vindication of the new right. They allege a lack of legal craftsmanship in the Warren opinion that has tended to deprive it of the respect to which it would otherwise be entitled. They point to the opinion's laconic nature, its failure to rely upon legal precedent, and its literary weakness, as compared with those produced by past masters of the judicial art, such as Marshall, Holmes, and Cardozo.

It may be unfortunate that the *Brown* opinion was not written by a John Marshall or a Benjamin Cardozo. Great cases deserve nothing less than opinions by the consummate giants of legal craftsmanship. But the criticism brings to mind a comment of Warren E. Burger, shortly after he succeeded Warren as Chief Justice. Seated before the fire at the elegant Elizabethan manor where international conferences are held in Ditchley, Oxfordshire, swirling the fine liqueur in a glass in his hand, the new Chief Justice was distressed by critics who contended that he did not have the qualifications of a Cardozo. "Who is there today who does?" he wryly asked.

The same can be asked of those who have urged that *Brown* deserved a Holmes or a Cardozo for its creator. One can go further and wonder whether those virtuosos of the opinion could possibly have secured the unanimous decision that was the Warren forte. If we take the *Brown* opinion as it is written, it certainly ranks as one of the great opinions of judicial history—plainly in the tradition of Chief Justice Marshall's seminal dictum that the Court must never forget that it is a *Constitution* it is expounding.[71] Perhaps the *Brown* opinion did not demonstrate as well as it might have that the mere fact of segregation denies educational equality. But *Brown* is so clearly right in its conclusion in this respect that one wonders whether additional labor in spelling out the obvious would really have been worthwhile. Considerations of *elegantia juris* and judicial craftsmanship are largely irrelevant to the truism that segregation was intended to keep blacks in a status of inferiority.

Four decades after the *Brown* case, it has become apparent that the criticisms of the Court's performance there have lost their relevancy. What is plain is that *Brown* has taken its place in the very forefront of the pantheon of historic decisions. In the light of what Justice Goldberg once termed the American commitment to equality[72] and its part in helping to fulfill the commitment, *Brown* will occupy a paramount position long after the contemporary criticisms will have ceased to have any more continuing significance than those voiced against the great decisions of the Marshall Court at the very outset of the nation's constitutional development.

14

Burger Court, 1969–1986

Before Warren E. Burger became Chief Justice, all Supreme Court documents were typed with as many carbon copies as needed. Thus the memoranda on in forma pauperis (or Miscellaneous Docket) petitions sent to each Justice required many copies. Because it was necessary to use very thin paper, these memoranda were called flimsies. The junior Justices, who received the last copies, often had difficulty reading them.

This was changed when Chief Justice Burger sent around an August 7, 1969, memorandum: "The necessary steps are now being taken toward acquiring a Xerox machine in the building." The new copiers "will be utilized primarily in preparation and distribution of the Miscellaneous Docket memoranda ('flimsies' as they are commonly called.)" Since that time, ample copiers have been provided for the Justices and Court staff, and word processors and computers have been introduced.

But the availability of copiers and the other communications devices had a baneful, though unintended, effect upon the operation of the Burger Court. One privy to the working of the Warren Court quickly notes the crucial importance of personal exchanges among the Justices—both in conference discussions and, even more so, in the postargument decision process. Such exchanges became less significant in the Burger Court. Conference notes during the Burger years show less an interchange of views than flat statements of each Justice's position in the case. "Not much conferencing goes on" at the conference, a Justice recently confirmed. "In fact, to call our discussion of a case a conference is really something of a misnomer, it's much more a statement of the views of each of the nine Justices, after which the totals are added and the case is assigned."[1]

"When I first went on the Court," writes Chief Justice Rehnquist, "I was both surprised and dismayed at how little interplay there was between the various justices."[2] Rehnquist, too, was referring to the conference, but his remark is equally applicable to the entire decision process. The constant personal exchanges in the Warren Court (much of it one-on-one lobbying by the Chief Justice and his allies or by opponents intended to influence votes) gave way to mostly written contacts through notes and memoranda. It is after all so much easier to make copies and send them around than to engage in protracted personal efforts to persuade others to change their positions. In the Court, as in other institutions, technology intended to facilitate communication has made for less personal interchange.

It was, however, more than the photocopier that made for the difference between the Burger and Warren Courts. A few years ago, the present Chief Justice compared the two tribunals. Rehnquist stated that the impact of the Court had been diminished under Chief Justice Burger. "I don't think that the Burger Court has as wide a sense of mission. Perhaps it doesn't have any sense of mission at all."[3]

In large part, this was true because of the differences in the leadership role assumed by the two Chief Justices. Warren brought more authority to the position of Chief Justice than had been the case for years, and the Warren Court bore his image as unmistakably as the earlier Courts of John Marshall and Roger B. Taney. This was plainly not as true while Chief Justice Burger occupied the Court's central chair. To be sure, Chief Justice Warren was inevitably a tough act to follow. But even on its own terms, the Burger tenure was not marked by strong leadership in molding Supreme Court jurisprudence.

Burger on Olympus

Warren E. Burger was cast from a different mold than Earl Warren. Burger's background was mostly in a law firm in St. Paul. He had nothing like Warren's spectacular career and broad political experience, although he had been active in the Republican party. He worked in Harold E. Stassen's successful campaign for Governor, and in 1952 he was Stassen's floor manager at the Republican national convention when Minnesota's switch supplied the necessary votes for Dwight Eisenhower's nomination.

After the election, Burger was appointed Assistant Attoney General in charge of the Claims Division of the Department of Justice. This experience led directly to one of his most noted opinions as an appellate judge.[4] It held that a government contractor might not be debarred from further government contracts without notice and hearing. Burger told me that the ruling was directly influenced by the many debarment orders that had come across his desk in the Justice Department—"issued in the name of the

Secretary of the Navy; but the actual decision was made by some Lieutenant, J.G., way down the line."

In 1956, Burger was named to the U.S. Court of Appeals in Washington, D.C., where he developed a reputation as a conservative, particularly
in criminal cases. Then, in 1969, came what Justice John M. Harlan once
called his "ascendancy to the Jupitership of Mount Olympus."[5] Burger was
sworn in as Chief Justice when Chief Justice Warren retired in 1969 and
headed the Court until his own 1986 retirement.

Burger, a reporter recently wrote, "looked as though he had been cast
by Hollywood for the part of chief justice."[6] With his snow-white hair and
broad shoulders, Burger was an almost too-perfect symbol of the law's
dignity. His critics contended that he stood too much on the dignity of his
office and was, more often than not, aloof and unfeeling. Intimates, however, stress his courtesy and kindness and assert that it was the office, not
the man, that may have suggested a different impression. "The Chief," says
Justice Harry A. Blackmun, who knew Burger far longer than anyone else
on the Court, "has a great heart in him, and he's a very fine human being
when you get to know him, when the tensions are off. One has to remember, too, that he's under strain almost constantly."[7]

Burger was not a person to develop intimate relationships with those
with whom he worked; yet he was as close to his clerks as to anyone in the
Marble Palace. A novel tells of a "tiny kitchen installed in his office by
Warren E. Burger who loved to cook and often prepared lunch for himself
or an occasional guest."[8] Every Saturday at noon, Burger made soup in his
kitchen for his clerks. They never knew what was in it, one of them told me,
but they ate it without question or complaint. Then Burger would sit and
talk informally with them for hours, usually with colorful reminiscences
about his career. The one rule at these sessions was that no one would talk
about the cases before the Court on which they were currently working.

Others picture the Chief Justice as a petty pedant, not up to the
demands of his position and most concerned with minor details and the
formal dignity of his office. Burger himself undertook the redecoration of
the Supreme Court cafeteria and personally helped choose the glassware
and china. He also redesigned the Court bench, changing it from a traditional straight bench to a "winged," or half-hexagon shape.

Burger was always sensitive to what he perceived to be slights to his
office and to himself; throughout his tenure he had an almost adversarial
relationship with the press. According to one reporter, "He fostered an
atmosphere of secrecy around the court that left some employees terrified
of being caught chatting with us."[9] When a network asked permission to
carry live radio coverage of the arguments at the Court, Burger replied
with a one-sentence letter: "It is not possible to arrange for any broadcast
of any Supreme Court proceeding." Handwritten at the bottom was a
postscript: "When you get the Cabinet meetings on the air, call me!"[10]

The Chief Justice was deeply hurt by derogatory accounts about his performance, particularly in the best seller *The Brethren,* and was gleeful when he told me that copies of the book were remaindered at ninety-eight cents in a Washington bookstore. But all the Justices were sensitive to the effect of *The Brethren* on the public perception of the Court. In a memorandum to the others, Rehnquist urged that it would be unwise for the Court to take certain action, "especially . . . in light of the microscopic scrutiny which our actions are apt to receive for a while."[11]

From his "Middle Temple" cheddar, made according to his own recipe, to the finest clarets, Burger was somewhat of an epicure. One of the social high points of a 1969 British-American conference at Ditchley, Oxfordshire, was the learned discussion about vintage Bordeaux between Burger and Sir George Coldstream, head of the Lord Chancellor's office and overseer of the wine cellar at his Inn of Court. The Chief Justice was particularly proud of his coup in snaring some cases of a rare Lafite in an obscure Washington wine shop.

The effectiveness of a Chief Justice is, of course, not shown by his epicurean tastes. Certainly, Burger in action cannot be compared with past virtuosos of the Court's center chair, such as Chief Justices Hughes and Warren. Burger came to the Court with an agenda that included a dismantling of the jurisprudential edifice erected by the Warren Court, particularly in the field of criminal justice. In large part, Burger owed his elevation to the highest judicial office to his reputation as a tough "law and order" judge. He had commented disparagingly on the Warren Court decisions on the rights of criminal defendants. As Chief Justice, he believed that he now had the opportunity to transform his more restrictive views into positive public law.

Burger expressed opposition during most of his tenure to *Mapp* and *Miranda*[12]—the two landmark criminal procedure decisions of the Warren Court—but he was never able to persuade a majority to cast those cases into constitutional limbo. The same was true of other aspects of Burger's anti-Warren agenda. No important Warren Court decision was overturned by the Burger Court. If Burger hoped that he would be able to undo much of the Warren "constitutional revolution," he was clearly to be disappointed.

Warren Court Holdovers

The Court that Chief Justice Burger was called upon to lead contained some of the most noted Justices in Supreme Court history. Two of them— Justices Black and Harlan—retired after the second Burger term. But they both played important parts in major cases before then.

The Black who sat on the Burger Court was no longer the leading liberal. The Alabaman's fundamentalist approach to the Constitution did not permit him to adopt an expansive approach toward individual rights. Justice Black stood his constitutional ground where the rights asserted rested on specific provisions, such as the First Amendment or the Fifth

Amendment privilege against self-incrimination; but when he could not find an express constitutional base, Black was unwilling to create one. Justice Black's opposition to busing at the conference on the *Swann* school busing case[13] was, Justice Brennan remarked, because the word bus is not found in the Constitution.

The Court's leading conservative was now Justice Harlan, a position he had held since Justice Frankfurter's retirement in 1962. When Burger took his seat, Harlan's was the Court's principal voice calling for judicial restraint, and the new Chief Justice had reason to expect support from him. He shared Burger's concern over "the 'horse and buggy' conditions under which the federal judiciary, and particularly this Court, are now operating"[14] and he had been the leading conservative in the last years of the Warren Court.

Justice Harlan's conservative philosophy did not, however, permit him to go along with the Chief Justice's agenda vis-à-vis the Warren Court decisions. "Respect for the Courts," Harlan once wrote, "is not something that can be achieved by fiat."[15] He applied this principle to reflexive refusal to follow prior decisions with which he disagreed. The true conservative, Harlan believed, adhered to stare decisis, normally following even precedents against which he had originally voted.

Harlan's antithesis in many respects was Justice Douglas, who never allowed jurisprudence the other way to deter him from reaching the liberal results that he favored. After Justices Black and Harlan retired in 1971, Douglas was the senior Associate Justice on the Burger Court, yet though the public considered him the leader of its liberal wing he was not the one to play the leadership role. He was a maverick, an idiosyncratic loner who was least effective in the give-and-take required in a collegial institution.

Instead, the leader of the Burger Court's liberal bloc was Justice Brennan, who had served as the catalyst for some of the most important decisions of the Warren Court. After Warren's retirement, Brennan was no longer the trusted insider. Instead, he became the Justice who tried above all to keep the Warren flame burning and, as a consequence, Burger's leading opponent on the Court. Both Brennan and the Chief Justice accepted this over the years the two sat together. One year the Brennan law clerks were guests at a convivial Burger luncheon. The Chief Justice telephoned Brennan to tell him what fine gentlemen his clerks were. When they returned, the Justice reproved them. "You turncoats," he said, "what did you do over there?"

The third member of the liberal bloc in the Burger Court was Justice Marshall. In the Burger Court he served as a virtual judicial adjunct to Justice Brennan. The law clerks, it is said, took to calling Marshall "Mr. Justice Brennan-Marshall."

The leading role in the Burger Court was not, however, assumed by its conservative or liberal wing. Instead, the most influential part was played by those Justices who were characterized by Justice Harry A. Blackmun as "in the middle." According to Blackmun, "Five of us" were in that position—Justices Stewart, White, Powell, Stevens, and himself.[16] Of these, Justices Stewart and White were holdovers from the Warren Court.

Justice Stewart continued as a moderate with a pragmatic approach to issues that polarized others. Under Chief Justice Warren, Stewart had remained in the center as the Court moved to the left. In the Burger Court he continued as the leading moderate. His center position enabled him to play a pivotal role. The others tended to turn to Justice Stewart because they trusted his judgment as a lawyer. Thus in the *Swann* school busing case,[17] where he was the senior Justice in the conference majority, Justice Douglas wrote at the time, "The case was obviously for me to assign, and I would have assigned it to Stewart."[18]

The other centrist Warren holdover, Justice White, did not play as influential a role in the Burger Court. As a Justice, White, like Stewart, has defied classification. He has tended to take a lawyerlike approach to individual cases without trying to fit them into any overall judicial philosophy, and he was considered one of the more conservative Justices in the Burger Court's center, particularly in criminal cases. "In the criminal field," as Justice Blackmun sees it, "I think Byron White is distinctly a conservative."[19]

It is fair to say that Justice White has been more respected among his colleagues than outside the Court—in part because of his gruff bluntness and no-nonsense manner. When loyalty-oath cases were still part of the Court's agenda, he curtly told a conference, these oath cases are a "pain in the neck."[20] When he did not think much of a case, he termed it "this pipsqueak of a case."[21] And when an attorney was doing a particularly bad job in oral argument, White was heard in a stage whisper, "This is unbelievable."[22]

Burger Court Appointments

Harry A. Blackmun, the first new Justice to be apppointed to the Burger Court, took his seat in 1970, replacing Justice Fortas, who had been forced to resign a year earlier. Blackmun had served eleven years on the U.S. Court of Appeals for the Eighth Circuit. He went to grade school with Warren Burger, and the two remained close friends thereafter. After graduation from Harvard Law School, Blackmun served as law clerk in the court of appeals, practiced with a Minneapolis law firm, and was counsel to the Mayo Clinic.

In his early years on the Court few expected Blackmun to be more than an appendage of the Chief Justice. He was then virtually Burger's disciple; they were on the same side in almost all cases. The press had typecast Blackmun as the subordinate half of the "Minnesota Twins," after the baseball team.

All this was to change and by the later years of the Burger tenure, Blackmun was completely his own man. His opinions became increasingly as liberal as any that Justices Brennan and Marshall might have written.

One can also see an improvement in Blackmun's work. If we compare his hesitant first draft in *Roe v. Wade*[23] with his more self-assured opinions in later cases, we see how the Justice grew with increasing experience and self-confidence. As a 1983 *New York Times* article put it, "Justice Blackmun's evolution as a jurist and prominence on the Court represent one of the most important developments in the judiciary's recent history."[24]

At the end of 1971, Lewis F. Powell and William H. Rehnquist were appointed to succeed Justices Black and Harlan, who had retired. Powell was, in many ways, the paradigm of the lawyer turned Justice. He came to the Court after private practice with one of Virginia's most prestigious law firms, a career that was capped by his term as President of the American Bar Association. Surprisingly few Supreme Court Justices have been drawn directly from the practicing bar. Indeed, during the past half century, only Powell and Justice Abe Fortas were in private practice when they were appointed.

On the bench, Powell was "a lawyer's Justice" and a pragmatic centrist who followed the measured approach developed by his thirty-five years of practice. He avoided doctrinaire positions and hard-edged ideological decisions and gained a reputation as a moderate, though he voted more often with Chief Justice Burger than some of the others in the center bloc. His quest for the middle ground is best illustrated by his most famous opinion—that in the *Bakke* case[25]—where he cast the deciding vote. Though the Powell *Bakke* opinion was joined by no other Justice, it is considered by most commentators as the authoritative statement of law.

Powell was essentially a conservative whose judicial approach was reminiscent of that followed by Justice Harlan during the early Burger years. Like Harlan, Powell believed in following precedents of which he may have disapproved until they were overruled. Thus he voted to decide cases in accordance with the *Mapp* and *Miranda* decisions,[26] even though he might well have voted against those decisions had he been on the Court. In the conference on a 1983 case,[27] Powell said, about a prior decision, "It's bad law. I would want to limit it to its own facts, without overruling it in so many words."[28]

Justice Rehnquist was, of course, the Burger Court's most conservative member—dubbed by *Newsweek* "The Court's Mr. Right."[29] During his early years on the Court, the majority remained largely unsympathetic to the Rehnquist entreaties from the right. It was then that he received a Lone Ranger doll as a gift from his law clerks, who called him the "lone dissenter" during that period. During his fourteen years as an Associate Justice, Rehnquist dissented alone fifty-four times—a Court record. By the time of his nomination as Chief Justice, however, Rehnquist had become the most influential Associate Justice in the Burger Court—anticipating the paramount role he was to assume when he was elevated to the Court's center chair.

The next appointment to the Burger Court was that of John Paul Stevens, a judge on the U.S. court of appeals when he was chosen to fill the vacancy created by Justice Douglas's retirement in 1975. Stevens was appointed as a moderate. It is, however, even harder to classify Stevens than the others on the Burger Court. As the *New York Times* wrote about him, "On a Court that everyone likes to divide into liberal and conservative, Justice Stevens has a list of labels all his own: enigmatic, unpredictable, maverick, a wild card, a loner."[30]

Statistically, Stevens was the Justice nearest the Burger Court's center, disagreeing equally with the Justices at the poles. Thus in the 1981 term, Stevens disagreed with Justice Rehnquist in 35 percent of the cases and with Justice Brennan 33 percent of the time.

Stevens as a loner reminds one of Justice Douglas, to whose seat Stevens was appointed. Like his predecessor, Stevens makes little effort to win over other members of the Court. What a law clerk once told me about Douglas applies equally to Stevens: "Douglas was just as happy signing a one-man dissent as picking up four more votes." Justice Stevens wrote more dissents than any other member of the Court; he was often a lone dissenter. A book on the Burger Court concludes that, while Justice Stevens was once viewed as a potential leader of the Court, "the effect of his independence of mind often has been to fragment potential majorities and leave the state of the law indeterminate."[31]

Over the years, Justice Stevens has acquired something of the reputation of an iconoclast—albeit an idiosyncratic one. Stevens is idiosyncratic in more than his decisions. He hires only two law clerks instead of the usual four and drafts more of his own opinions than any of the others. He also deviates from the Court's unwritten conservative dress code; his constant bow tie (worn under the judicial robe) gives him a perpetual sophomoric appearance. In 1986, the Justices were hearing argument on whether Orthodox Jews, with their religious duty to wear yarmulkes, should be exempt from the military dress code's ban on hats indoors. Counsel for the government told the Justices, "It's only human nature to resent being told what to wear, when to wear it, what to eat."

"Or whether you can wear a bow tie?" chimed in Justice Stevens.[32]

The First Sister

When the Supreme Court was first established, the author of an opinion was designated, "Cushing, Justice." In 1820, the form was replaced by "Mr. Justice Johnson" as opinion author. This style lasted over a century and a half. Then, in 1980, Justice White suggested to the conference that, since a woman Justice was bound to be appointed soon, they should avoid the embarrassment of changing the style again at that time. All the others agreed, and the manner of designating the author of an opinion became, simply, "Justice Brennan."[33]

Justice White's prescience was borne out the next year when Sandra Day O'Connor was appointed as what *Time* called "the Brethren's first sister."[34] Her career dramatically illustrates the changed place of women in the law. Though O'Connor graduated third in her class at Stanford Law School (Rhenquist had been first), only one California law firm would hire her; a Los Angeles firm offered her a job as a legal secretary. Ironically, Attorney General William French Smith, one of the partners in the firm that had refused to hire her as an associate, recommended O'Connor for the Supreme Court.

After law school, O'Connor returned to Arizona, where she combined legal work with political activity. She became assistant attorney general and then a member, and ultimately majority leader, of the state senate. She was elected to the Arizona Superior Court, where she served for five years. In 1979, she was appointed to the Arizona Court of Appeals. O'Connor was the second Burger Court member (after Justice Brennan) to have served as a state judge.

The Justices used to jest among themselves about the effect a woman Justice would have. Tradition says that the junior Justice answers the conference door (one of them used to quip that he was the highest-paid doorman in the world). As rumors of a female appointment gained ground, the Justices joked, first to Justice Rehnquist and then to the new junior Justice, Stevens, that when a woman came to the Court, he should be a gentleman and continue to answer the door. In the event, when O'Connor became the newest Justice, she assumed the doorkeeper's task without question. And the Justices continued to be called the Brethren even though a woman had joined their ranks.

Soon after O'Connor took her seat, a *Time* headline read "And Now the Arizona Twins; Justice O'Connor Teams Up with Court Conservative Rehnquist."[35] There is no doubt that Justice O'Connor has been more conservative than her predecessor, Justice Stewart. "I think it is fairly clear," said Justice Blackmun during the last Burger term, that O'Connor "is on the right."[36] She typically voted opposite Justice Rehnquist only about 10 percent of the time, while disagreeing with Justices Brennan and Marshall in over 45 percent of cases.

It is, however, not accurate to picture Justice O'Connor as only a Rehnquist clone on the Burger Court. She tended to be as conservative as the latter in criminal cases and was, in fact, the author of opinions limiting *Miranda* during the last two Burger terms.[37] She also sided with her fellow Arizonian on the importance of recognizing state powers[38] and the need for judicial restraint vis-à-vis the legislature.[39] But she was more moderate in a few areas—most notably (in view of her own experience with sex discrimination) in cases involving sexual bias,[40] but also in cases involving affirmative action[41] and the First Amendment.[42]

Even those who disagree with her recognize that O'Connor has been an above-average Justice, who has become an effective conservative voice. She has not been hesitant in expressing her views both in conference and from the bench. Her opinions have been characterized by clear analysis and focus upon the points at issue. But they have at times been lightened by a little-credited gift for language. In a case involving the right of a defendant to represent himself, the O'Connor opinion noted, "We recognize that a . . . defendant may wish to dance a solo, not a pas de deux."[43]

The Changed Judicial Agenda

Chief Justice Taft, we saw,[44] once said that the Supreme Court was his idea of what heaven must be like. More recently, however, Justice Blackmun said of being a Justice, "It's a rotten way to earn a living."[45]

In large part, the change in the judicial attitude is a reflection of the Court's ever-increasing caseload. In its early years, the Court had relatively few cases on its docket: in 1803, there were only 51 cases; seven years later, the number was 98. The numbers increased as the years went on—but not by much. There were 723 cases on the Court's docket in 1900 and 1,039 when Chief Justice Taft died. In recent years, however, the caseload increased dramatically. In the 1953 Term, Chief Justice Warren's first, 1,293 cases were disposed of; in the 1968 Term, Warren's last, 3,117 cases were disposed of.

The increase continued during Chief Justice Burger's tenure: the cases disposed of increased from 3,357 in the 1969 Term to 4,289 in the 1985 Term. The Court's caseload has more than tripled during the past four decades. The burgeoning workload has been responsible for advancing the Court's first conference from early October to the last week in September, for the inclusion of Wednesdays in the conference schedule, and for increasing the number of staff members. In the Warren Court, each Justice had two law clerks; in the Burger Court, the number was increased to four.

Chief Justice Burger warned repeatedly that unless the workload was curbed it would soon be "impossible" for the Justices "to perform [their] duties well and survive very long." Not all the Justices agreed. But the pressures of the docket certainly changed the Court atmosphere from what it was in Chief Justice Taft's day. In a speech, Justice Blackmun described the Court as weary and overworked. He asserted that he was "never so tired" as he was at the end of the 1984 Court Term.[46]

It is, however, not only the volume of cases that has changed in recent years. There has been an even-more-dramatic change in the quality of the cases decided in the Marble Palace. The Court has, of course, always played a pivotal role in the American polity—a role encapsulated in Tocqueville's famous statement that "scarcely any political question arises in the United States that is not resolved sooner or later into a judicial question."[47] From this point of view, the Supreme Court is primarily a political institution. Because its decrees mark the boundaries between the great departments of government and because on its actions depend the proper functioning of federalism and the scope to be given to the rights of the individual, a judge on such a tribunal has an opportunity to leave an imprint on the life of the nation as no mere master of the common law possibly could. Certainly, as an English writer noted not long ago, "In America, the Supreme Court is supreme. In no other democratic country do nine judges, none of them elected, tell the president and the legislature what each may or may not do."[48]

Yet that is precisely what the Burger Court did. In the *Nixon* case,[49] the Court not only told the President what he must do; its decision led directly to his forced departure from the White House. In *Roe v. Wade*,[50] the Justices not only told the legislatures they might not restrict the right to abortions; their decision caused a social schism that has remained a major divisive factor in our society. The Court's other decisions may not be as dramatic, yet each illustrates some facet of the Court's crucial place in the polity.

It may be said that the Court has decided landmark cases throughout its history. Here, too, there has been a difference. In the past, a *Dred Scott* case[51] or an *Income Tax* case[52] would come up every quarter century or so, but the time of the Court would be occupied mainly with lesser cases. During this century, however, the pace of landmark decision making has increased tremendously. This has been particularly true of decision making since Chief Justice Warren took his seat. From the *Brown* case[53] at the beginning of the Chief Justice's tenure to the *Powell* case[54] at its end, the Warren years saw a judicial revolution that transformed both the law and the society that it served. Leading case after leading case was decided at a pace that would have astounded Court observers in an earlier day.

The pace did not decrease under Warren's successor. Scarcely a term passed in the Burger Court without decisions that would be landmarks in all but a jaded age. Certainly, the Burger Court was as much in the spotlight of press attention as its precedent-shattering predecessor.

Since Chief Justice Warren's day, there has been a substantial change not only in the volume of leading cases, but also in their quality. In earlier Courts, the important cases involved property rights. In the first part of the century, the Justices used the Due Process Clause to strike down laws regulating economic activity. More recently, the Court came to accept governmental restrictions on the free exercise of property rights to an extent never before permitted in American law. But this has not led to a lessening of the Court's role in the constitutional system. Instead, there has been a shift in judicial emphasis from the protection of property rights to protection of personal rights. Such protection has, indeed, been elevated to the top of the judicial agenda during the past quarter century.

The development in this respect has been accompanied by a continuing rights explosion; as never before, new interests have pressed upon the law to seek recognition in the form of legal rights. The Burger Court recognized rights that had previously scarcely even pressed for recognition, raising ever more rights to the legally protected plane. The rights in question cut across the entire legal spectrum, ranging from extensions of traditional rights, such as those to freedom of expression and equal protection, to newly emerging rights not previously vindicated by law.

The Burger Court cases well illustrate the changed nature of the rights asserted before the Court. Among these rights are those to sexual equality,[55] to bodily autonomy and privacy,[56] to treatment by committed persons,[57] to access to news,[58] to notice and hearing before even a "privilege" may be taken away,[59] and to access to court proceedings.[60] The judicial agenda was more and more concerned with the new personal rights that increasingly pressed for legal recognition.

The shift in judicial emphasis to protection of personal rights reflected the Justices' concern with the changing nature of our society. With property rights constitutionally curtailed, compensatory scope had to be given to personal rights if the ultimate social interest—that in the individual life—was not to be lost sight of. The Justices, like the rest of us, were disturbed by the growth of governmental authority and sought to preserve a sphere for individuality even in a society in which individuals stand dwarfed by the power concentrations that confront them.

Desegregation and Racial Discrimination

Brown v. Board of Education[61] was, of course, the seminal case in ensuring that the Equal Protection Clause became more than a paper protection against racial discrimination. A second *Brown* decision ruled that the transition to desegregated schools should take place "with all deliberate speed."[62] The result was a gap in the *Brown* enforcement process; deliberate speed too often meant indefinite delay in vindicating the right to attend desegregated schools.

It was the Burger Court which laid to rest the "all deliberate speed" formula in *Alexander v. Holmes County Board of Education* (1969),[63] the first school desegregation case decided under the new Chief Justice. As explained in a letter by Justice White, what *Alexander* held was "that the deliberate speed formula has been abandoned . . . and that as soon as possible is [its] substitute."[64] Under *Alexander*, "[T]he obligation of every school district is to [desegregate] at once . . . and immediately to operate as unitary school systems."[65]

After abandoning the deliberate speed formula, the Burger Court dealt with the extent of remedial power possessed by the federal courts in desegregation cases. The key case here was *Swann v. Charlotte-Mecklenburg Board of Education* (1971).[66] The Court upheld the far-reaching desegregation order issued by the district court, which included what amounted to racial quotas (at least as starting points) in the schools and provision for extensive busing to help achieve integration. The case gave rise to a serious conflict between the new Chief Justice and the majority. The latter was ultimately able to frustrate the Burger effort to weaken the remedial power of the federal courts in desegregation cases.

The key issue in *Swann* was that of the remedial power of the courts in desegregation cases. As Justice Douglas stated at the conference: "The problem is what is the power of the court without the help of Congress to correct a violation of the Constitution." He pointed to the broad remedial powers of the courts in other areas. "If there is an antitrust violation, we give a broad discretion." The same should be true here.

Even though the Douglas view on remedial power was supported by the conference majority, the Chief Justice circulated a draft *Swann* opinion[67] that stated a most restricted view of remedial power, which the draft contrasted with what it termed "a classical equity case," for example, removal of an illegal dam or divestiture of an illegal corporate acquisition. Here, the situation was said to be different. Under the Burger draft, the implication was that federal courts could act only to bring about the situation that would have existed had there never been state-enforced segregation.

Chief Justice Burger's efforts to limit the remedial power of the district courts were frustrated by the other Justices. Their pressure led the Chief Justice to modify his restricted approach, and the final *Swann* opinion adopted a very broad conception of remedial power.

The final *Swann* opinion specifically rejected the view stated in the Burger draft that the remedial power in this type of case was somehow less than that in the classical equity case. According to it, "[O]nce a right and a violation have been shown, the scope of a district court's equitable powers to remedy past wrongs is broad, for breadth and flexibility are inherent in equitable remedies." Remedial discretion includes the power to reach a goal of racial distribution in schools comparable to that in the community and to order extensive busing if that is deemed appropriate to "produce an effective dismantling of the dual system."[68]

The most important thing about the *Swann* decision was its recognition of broadside remedial power. *Swann* goes far beyond the no-segregation principle laid down in *Brown*. Under *Swann* the federal courts have the power to issue whatever orders may be necessary to bring about an integrated school system—the broad and flexible power traditionally exercised by courts of equity. This includes extensive busing appropriate to attain the goal "of insuring the achievement of complete integration at the earliest practicable date."[69]

The Burger Court, however, made a sharp distinction between segregation required by law and that brought about by other factors, such as racially separate housing patterns. The de jure–de facto distinction continued as the dividing line in desegregation jurisprudence.[70] The mere fact that segregated schools exist in a district is not enough. Only where de jure segregation is shown may the *Swann* remedial power be used to do away with a dual school system.

In addition, the Court drew the line at interdistrict remedies. In *Milliken v. Bradley* (1974),[71] it refused to recognize a power in the federal courts to order the amalgamation of urban and suburban school districts to obtain a desirable racial mixture in the schools, where de jure segregation existed only in the urban district. As it was put by the Chief Justice in a *Milliken* draft, "Federal authority to impose cross-district remedies presupposes a fair and reasoned determination that there has been a constitutional violation by all of the districts affected by the remedy."[72]

In *Washington v. Davis* (1976),[73] the Court ruled that proof that a government act has a disproportionate impact upon racial minorities is not enough to show a violation of equal protection. A discriminatory racial purpose must be shown. Though criticized, this holding follows logically from the de jure–de facto distinction. A de facto segregation situation is not enough to make for a constitutional violation. In the absence of racially discriminatory intent or purpose, the mere fact that black and white children are treated differently does not prove a denial of equal protection. The same approach is the basis of the *Washington v. Davis* rule.

Affirmative Action

The Warren Court had it relatively easy in *Brown* and its progeny. The blatant discrimination involved in segregation made it a simple matter for the Warren Justices to decide the cases that came before them. Moreover, in *Brown* and the later desegregation cases, judicial enforcement did not deprive anyone else of the right to an equal education. Yet such a result was precisely that with which the decision in the *Bakke* case (1978)[74] had to deal. The special admissions program in *Bakke* provided both for admitting a specified number of minority students and for excluding others who might have been admitted had there been no special program. During the oral argument, Justice Marshall put his finger on the case's dilemma in this respect, when he told Bakke's counsel, "You are arguing about keeping somebody out and the other side is arguing about getting somebody in."[75] A decision for the university would keep Bakke and others like him out of the Davis Medical School; a decision for Bakke would prevent minority applicants from "getting in" under the special program.

The decision in the *Bakke* case and the process by which it was reached well illustrates the manner in which the Burger Court operated. Instead of a flat decision upholding or striking down racially preferential programs, the Court handed down a fragmented decision that mirrored the internal atomization of the Court. *Bakke* points up the essential failure of Chief Justice Burger to assume an effective leadership role in molding his Court's jurisprudence. In *Bakke*, the lead in the decision process was assumed by other members of the Court—notably by Justices Brennan and Powell.

The *Bakke* decision was two decisions, each decided by a five-to-four vote. The first decision was that the Davis special admissions program was invalid and that Bakke should be admitted to the Davis Medical School. Justice Powell joined the Chief Justice and Justices Stevens, Stewart, and Rehnquist to make up the majority. The second decision was that race was a factor that might be considered in an admissions policy without violating the Constitution. Justice Powell joined Justices Brennan, White, Marshall, and Blackmun to make up the bare majority here.

The unifying factor behind both *Bakke* decisions was Justice Powell's vote, which—though it was fully endorsed by no other Justice—spoke for the bare majorities on each of the major issues. The result has been that commentators, courts, and admissions officers have treated Justice Powell's opinion as the authoritative opinion in the *Bakke* case. The Davis program was invalidated, but admissions officers are permitted to operate programs that grant racial preferences—provided that they do not do so as blatantly as was done under the sixteen-seat "quota" provided at Davis.

Justice Powell's crucial part in the *Bakke* decision process began with his circulation of a draft opinion.[76] It rejected the view that allotting places for preferred racial groups was the only effective means to secure diversity in the student body. But the draft went on to show how an admissions program that considered race among other factors might be "designed to achieve meaningful diversity in the broad sense of this term." Such a program permits race to be considered but, at the same time, "specifically eschews quotas."

The Powell draft ended with a categorical rejection of the Davis program as contrary to equal protection. At the *Bakke* conference on the merits, Justice Powell repeated the views expressed in his draft and said that he would vote to affirm the California decision in Bakke's favor. Justice Brennan interjected that he thought that, under the approach to the case he had stated, Powell should vote to affirm in part and reverse in part. The judgment of the lower court had required that Davis adopt a color-blind admissions system for the future. Justice Powell went along with the Brennan approach, telling the conference, "I agree that the judgment must be reversed insofar as it enjoins Davis from taking race into account."

The Powell concession was the key that led to the ultimate compromise resolution of the *Bakke* case. Under the Court's decision, the Davis program was ruled violative of equal protection; but the decision specifically held that race might be considered as a factor in admissions programs. This has permitted the use of race in a flexible admissions policy designed to produce diversity in a student body. Minority students may be admitted even though they may not fully measure up to the academic criteria.

Bakke has consequently meant anything but the end of programs providing for racial preferences. On the contrary, the later Burger Court decisions built upon *Bakke* in dealing with such programs. Unless there was proof of purposeful discrimination or a legislative or administrative finding to that effect, race as the sole determining factor in employment decisions was ruled invalid, as it was in *Bakke* itself. But properly tailored affirmative action programs were upheld. The *Bakke* decision that race may be considered as a factor has permitted the widespread use of affirmative action programs to be continued.

Other Equal Protection Cases

The Burger Court confirmed the trend toward applying judicial restraint in cases involving economic regulation. Thus Justice Marshall could refer to the "minimal standards of rationality that we use to test economic legislation that discriminates against business interests."[77] The Court did, however, expand the use of a stricter level of scrutiny in certain cases, such as the racial discrimination cases just discussed. All the Burger Court Justices agreed that racial classifications are suspect and must be subject to strict scrutiny under which the classification will be held to deny equal protection unless justified by a "compelling" governmental interest.

In particular, the Burger Court held that gender classifications were subject to stricter scrutiny than the rational-basis test governing economic classifications. While the Justices did not go as far as Justice Brennan urged and make sex a wholly suspect classification,[78] they did make it what has been called a "quasi-suspect" classification, subject to an intermediate review standard: "To withstand constitutional challenge, classifications by gender must serve important governmental objectives and must be substantially related to attainment of those objectives."[79]

Under this standard, the Court struck down discriminatory classifications in education,[80] dependent benefits,[81] clubs,[82] alimony,[83] estate administration,[84] and jury selection.[85] Indeed, it can be said that the removal of sexual disabilities in our constitutional law was almost entirely the handiwork of the Burger Court.

The same is true of the removal of disabilities for aliens and illegitimates. Classifications based upon alienage and illegitimacy were also treated as more suspect than economic classifications and hence also subject to stricter review. Laws restricting public employment or welfare benefits to citizens[86] or prohibiting illegitimate children from inheriting from their fathers[87] were ruled invalid under the stricter scrutiny standard.

The Court did, however, reject attempts to have classifications based upon wealth treated as suspect classifications—or at least as semisuspect. In *San Antonio Independent School District v. Rodriguez* (1973)[88] a challenge to the financing of public school education by the property tax claimed that equal protection was denied to children in poorer districts that had a low tax base. The lower court had held the rational-basis standard inappropriate because "lines drawn on wealth are suspect." The Supreme Court reversed; the fact that the law burdened poor persons in the allocation of educational benefits was held not enough to make the classification a suspect one.

In other cases, the Court refused to rule that classifications based upon age[89] or mental retardation[90] should be treated as suspect. The Court had, in effect, decided to draw the line and refused to create other classifications subject to broader review. There would be no further classifications to which heightened scrutiny would be applied.

The Burger Court also applied the strict-scrutiny standard in cases affecting fundamental rights. This meant broader review in cases involving the right to travel,[91] the right to vote,[92] the right of access to the judicial process,[93] and rights growing out of the marital relationship.[94] However, in the previously mentioned *San Antonio* case, the Court refused to hold that the right to education was a fundamental right. According to *San Antonio,* only rights protected by the Constitution are subject to strict-scrutiny review. Since no one has a constitutional right to education, infringements upon that right are reviewable only under "the usual standard for reviewing a State's usual social and economic legislation"[95]—that is, the rational-basis test.

First Amendment

During the Warren years, the preferred-position theory—that the Constitution gives a preferred status to personal, as opposed to property, rights—became accepted doctrine. Early in Chief Justice Burger's tenure, the Court stated "that the dichotomy between personal liberties and property rights is a false one. . . . In fact, a fundamental interdependence exists between the personal right to liberty and the personal right to property. Neither could have meaning without the other."[96]

But the Burger Court did not abandon the preferred-position approach; on the contrary, like its predecessor, it recognized that each generation must necessarily have its own scale of values. Both the Warren Court and the Burger Court were especially willing to recognize First Amendment rights as peculiarly suitable for inclusion in the preferred-position theory. Countless cases have recognized the special constitutional function of the First Amendment—a function both explicit and indispensable.[97] The free society itself is inconceivable without what Justice Holmes called "free trade in ideas."[98] In the Burger Court, as in the Warren Court, governmental power over First Amendment freedoms was narrower than that permitted over property rights.

However, the Burger Court did more than confirm its predecessor's general approach in First Amendment cases. It also extended constitutional protection to types of speech previously held beyond the Amendment's reach—in particular, commercial speech, which had previously been held beyond the scope of the First Amendment guaranty.[99] In *Virginia State Board of Pharmacy v. Virginia Consumer Council* (1976),[100] the Court held squarely that commercial speech came within the protection of the First Amendment. A state statute barring a pharmacist from advertising prescription drug prices was ruled invalid. Speech "which does 'no more than propose a commercial transaction'"[101] was ruled squarely within the protection of the First Amendment. The same approach was followed in cases involving the barring of advertising by attorneys and other professionals.[102] The states may not prohibit truthful advertisements concerning the availability and terms of routine legal and other professional services.

The Burger Court also broadened the protection given to political speech. It struck down limitations on direct expenditures by political candidates, treating such expenditures as a form of political expression protected by the First Amendment.[103] The notion of nonverbal speech had, however, been used to protect symbolic speech well before the Burger

Court. Over half a century ago, the Court ruled that display of a red flag as a symbol of opposition to organized government is covered by First Amendment protection.[104]

In *Spence v. Washington* (1974),[105] the Burger Court held that the same is true of a display of the flag upside down with a peace symbol affixed. The Court reversed a conviction under a state law forbidding the exhibition of the U.S. flag with figures, symbols, or other extraneous material attached.

The symbolic speech concept was also applied to a case involving a New Hampshire law that required motor vehicles to bear license plates embossed with the state motto, "Live Free or Die," and made it a misdemeanor to obscure the motto. Two Jehovah's Witnesses viewed the motto as repugnant to their moral, religious, and political beliefs and covered it up with tape. They were found guilty of violating the statute, but the Court reversed their convictions.[106]

Well before the Burger Court, the cases had developed the concept of the "public forum," giving a right of access to public places for First Amendment purposes. That concept was both applied and expanded during Chief Justice Burger's tenure. The earlier cases had upheld the right of individuals to use public places as forums for expression.[107] The Burger Court also recognized, in *Kleindienst v. Mandel* (1972),[108] a First Amendment right "to receive information and ideas," and that freedom of speech "'necessarily protects the right to receive.'"[109]

The public forum concept was applied to a municipal theater which refused to allow its facilities to be used for a controversial production.[110] The theater was ruled a public forum dedicated to expressive activities, in which content-based regulation was not permissible. For First Amendment purposes, the public auditorium was equated with streets, parks, and other public places that come within the public forum concept.

On the other hand, the public forum concept was ruled inapplicable to privately owned shopping centers. The Warren Court had held that such a center was the functional equivalent of the business district of a town.[111] The Burger Court rejected this view and categorically ruled that the First Amendment does not apply to privately owned shopping centers.[112]

Freedom of the Press

The Burger Court's most celebrated First Amendment decision was that in *New York Times Co. v. United States* (1971)[113]—usually known as the *Pentagon Papers Case*. The Court there struck down an attempt by the government, for the first time, to use the courts to censor news before it was printed. The decision was based upon the basic principle that, except in cases where "disclosure . . . will surely result in direct, immediate, and irreparable damage to the Nation or its people,"[114] there may be no prior restraint upon publication.

The *Pentagon Papers* decision marks the most dramatic assertion of the principle against prior restraint of the press in American jurisprudence. The rule against prior restraints led the Court to invalidate so-called gag orders—judicial attempts to censor the press by forbidding news media from publishing material that could impair the right to a fair trial.[115] The Court also ruled that the press had a right of access to the courtroom, reversing the order of a trial court that had closed a criminal proceeding to the public and the press.[116] However, it refused to decide that the press had a First Amendment right of access to news which gave a television station a right to conduct interviews in a prison.[117] The press was held to have only the same right of access as the general public. Nor did the Court accept the claim that the press right to gather news implies, in turn, a right to a confidential relationship between a reporter and his source.[118] Reporters had argued that to gather news, they had to protect their sources; otherwise, the sources would not furnish information, to the detriment of the free flow of information protected by the First Amendment. The argument was rejected: reporters have the same obligation as other citizens to respond to grand jury subpoenas. The press does not have any immunity from grand jury subpoenas beyond that possessed by other citizens.

The Burger Court displayed a more favorable attitude toward television in the courtroom than did its predecessor. The Warren Court had decided that televising a notorious trial over defendant's objections was inconsistent with the fair trial guaranteed by due process.[119] The Burger Court, on the contrary, upheld a Florida rule permitting television coverage of criminal trials, notwithstanding the objections of the accused.[120] The result has been a proliferation of televised trials that would have been impossible had the Warren Court jurisprudence remained unchanged.

Criminal Procedure

During the 1968 presidential election, Richard M. Nixon had run against Chief Justice Warren and his Court as much as he had run against his Democratic opponent, Hubert H. Humphrey. He accused the Court of "seriously weakening the peace forces and strengthening the criminal forces in our society."[121] Nixon pledged that his Court appointees would be different.

When Nixon's appointee, Warren E. Burger, took his place in the Court's center chair, it was widely expected that he would implement what Warren had called Nixon's "law and order" issue.[122] Many feared that the Burger Court would soon relegate the criminal-law landmarks of the Warren Court's constitutional-law "revolution" to legal limbo. But the anticipated reversals of the key Warren Court precedents did not materialize. Instead, the essentials of the Warren jurisprudential edifice were preserved. *Gideon, Mapp,* and *Miranda*[123]—the great Warren Court trilogy on the procedural rights of criminal-law defendants—all survived. To be sure, they were modified, even narrowed and blunted in some ways.

In many respects, indeed, the Burger Court expanded the rights of criminal defendants. The Warren Court's landmark *Gideon* decision had established the indigent defendant's right to an appointed attorney. But the *Gideon* Court, following the conference suggestion of Chief Justice Warren, limited the decision to the felony case at hand, without addressing the question of how far the new right to assigned counsel extended. That question was presented to the Burger Court in *Argersinger v. Hamlin* (1972).[124] The Court there held that the right extended to misdemeanors as well as felonies. In fact, *Argersinger* ruled "that absent a knowing and intelligent waiver, no person may be imprisoned for any offense, whether classified as petty, misdemeanor, or felony, unless he was represented by counsel at his trial."[125] As it was put in a letter by Justice Stewart, no person may be "sentenced to imprisonment unless he had a lawyer at his trial."[126]

In addition, the Burger Court extended the requirement of free transcripts to indigents seeking to appeal misdemeanor cases, even those involving only fines, not imprisonments.[127] The Court also expanded the *Gideon* requirement to include the assistance of a psychiatrist at state expense and even other expert witnesses where they were necessary for the defense.[128]

The Court also held that the Equal Protection Clause prohibits a prosecutor from using peremptory challenges to exclude blacks from the jury.[129] Racial equal protection claims in the jury context were treated in basically the same way as other kinds of racial discrimination claims.

But there were also decisions more restrictive than those of the Warren Court. Most important in this respect were the Burger Court decisions narrowing *Mapp* and *Miranda*—the Warren Court's paradigmatic criminal procedure decisions. A majority of the Burger Court was dissatisfied with what the Chief Justice termed "the monstrous price we pay for the exclusionary rule in which we seem to have imprisoned ourselves."[130] This led them to adopt a good-faith exception to the rule under which illegally seized evidence may be admitted where the police "officer conducting the search acted in objectively reasonable reliance on a warrant issued by a detached and neutral magistrate that subsequently is determined to be invalid."[131] Where officers had acted in good-faith reliance upon search warrants, the convictions were upheld.[132]

Miranda was treated the same way by the Burger Court. As the Chief Justice himself said, "I would neither overrule *Miranda,* disparage it, nor extend it at this late date."[133] *Miranda,* like *Mapp,* was narrowed but not overruled during the Burger years.

The Burger Court's blunting of *Miranda* included a decision holding that a statement obtained in violation of *Miranda* could be used to impeach petitioner's testimony at trial.[134] Thus at least some use could be made of statements inadmissible under *Miranda* as part of the state's direct case. In another case, the Court laid down a "public safety" exception to *Miranda.* According to the Court there, *Miranda* should not "be applied in all its rigor to a situation in which police officers ask questions reasonably prompted by a concern for the public safety."[135]

Oregon v. Elstad (1985)[136] was more far-reaching in its implications for *Miranda*. The Court there held that a voluntary confession obtained in violation of *Miranda* did not taint a later confession secured after proper *Miranda* warnings had been given. For the first time the Court indicated that the *Miranda* safeguards are not themselves rights guaranteed by the Fifth Amendment: "The *Miranda* exclusionary rule . . . sweeps more broadly than the Fifth Amendment itself. . . . [A] simple failure to administer Miranda warnings is not in itself a violation of the Fifth Amendment."[137]

Perhaps the most important thing, however, about *Mapp* and *Miranda* in Burger Court jurisprudence is not that they were narrowed, but that they were not overruled. Both *Mapp* and *Miranda* were among the most criticized cases decided by the Warren Court, and it was widely expected that they would be among the jurisprudential casualties of the Burger Court. Yet, while their rules were narrowed in significant respects by the Burger jurisprudence, they continued as foundations of the law of criminal procedure. Indeed, at the end of the Burger tenure, the Court declared that *Miranda* struck the proper balance between the competing interests of society and those accused of crime.[138]

"The Counter-Revolution that Wasn't"

In 1983, a book was published entitled *The Burger Court: The Counter-Revolution That Wasn't*.[139] The subtitle is a succinct summary of the Burger Court in operation.

There is no doubt that Chief Justice Burger came to the Court with an agenda that included some dismantling of the jurisprudential structure erected under his predecessor, particularly in the field of criminal justice. Similarly, Burger's strongest supporter, Justice Rehnquist, took his seat with a desire to correct some of the "excesses" of the Warren Court[140]—to, as he put it, see that the "Court has called a halt to a number of the sweeping rulings that were made in the days of the Warren Court."[141]

The Burger-Rehnquist agenda was not carried out in the Burger years. Instead, the intended counterrevolution served only as a confirmation of most of the Warren Court jurisprudence. It can, indeed, be said that no important Warren Court decision was overruled during the Burger tenure. Some of them were narrowed by Burger Court decisions; others, however, were not only fully applied but even expanded.

We have seen this even in the field of criminal justice, where Burger and Rehnquist were most eager to disown the Warren heritage—in Rehnquist's phrase, to make "the law dealing with the constitutional rights of accused criminal defendants . . . more even-handed now than it was when I came on the Court." It was, after all, to "the area of the constitutional rights of accused criminal defendants" that Rehnquist primarily referred when he referred to the "sweeping rulings of the Warren Court."[142]

Though the Warren criminal cases became a major issue of Richard Nixon's presidential campaign, the Justices appointed by Nixon did not tilt the Court to the point of repudiating them. In fact, we saw, one of the Warren criminal trilogy was even substantially expanded by the Burger Court. *Gideon v. Wainwright*[143] was extended to every case in which imprisonment may be imposed as a penalty, regardless of whether the crime involved is classified as a felony, misdemeanor, or even petty offense.[144] *Gideon* also upheld the right to counsel only at the criminal trial. The Burger Court extended the right to counsel to preliminary hearings[145]—that is, before any formal accusation and trial—and gave practical effect to the right of the accused to represent himself if he so chose and knowingly and intelligently waived the right to counsel.[146]

Other Warren Court landmarks also served as foundations of the Burger Court jurisprudence. *Griffin v. Illinois*[147]—in many ways the Warren watershed case in the Court's effort to ensure economic equality in the legal process—was extended to include the right of an indigent defendant to the psychiatric assistance needed for an effective defense[148] and even, outside the criminal law field, to invalidate court fees that prevented indigents from bringing divorce proceedings.[149]

A similar picture was presented in other areas. *Brown v. Board of Education*[150] and its Warren Court progeny were applied in the *Swann* case[151] and held to vest broad remedial power in the courts to ensure desegregation, including extensive busing. The *Brown* principle was expanded to uphold affirmative action programs to aid minorities.[152] No Justice, not even Justice Rehnquist, who may once have taken a different view,[153] questioned the antidiscrimination premise that underlay *Brown*. In fact, the most important thing about the Burger Court decisions in this area was that, as Justice O'Connor was to conclude in the last Burger Term, "[W]e have reached a common destination in sustaining affirmative action against constitutional attack."[154]

The same was true in the other areas of Warren Court jurisprudence, including the First Amendment, reapportionment, other aspects of equal protection, and judicial review in operation. In all these areas, the central premises of the Warren Court decisions were not really challenged by its successor. The core principles laid down in the Warren years remained rooted in our public law as they had been when Chief Justice Burger first took his seat.

We Are All Activists Now

According to one commentator, "The entire record of the Burger Court . . . is one of activism."[155] Yet the Justices now "decide without much self-conscious concern for whether this is a proper role for the Court.

We are all activists now."[156] At least so the history of the Burger Court tells us. One thing to be learned from the Burger years "is that the great conflict between judicial 'restraint' and 'activism' is history now."[157]

The statistics bear out the conclusion that the Burger Court record was, indeed, one of judicial activism. One measure was its willingness to strike down legislative acts. The Warren Court invalidated 21 federal and 150 state statutes; the Burger Court struck down 31 federal and 288 state laws. The laws invalidated were at least as significant as those ruled unconstitutional by the Warren Court. The federal statutes that failed to pass constitutional muster in the Burger years included laws governing election financing and judicial salaries,[158] granting eighteen-year-olds the vote in state elections,[159] establishing bankruptcy courts,[160] as well as laws based on gender classifications in the military[161] and in various social security programs.[162] In addition, the Burger Court struck down the legislative veto, a method used by Congress to control executive action in nearly 200 statutes,[163] and a law designed to deal with the endemic budget deficit.[164] "If deference to Congress be the acid test of judicial restraint, the litmus of the Burger Court comes out much the same color as that of its predecessor."[165]

But it is not numbers alone that mark the Burger Court as an activist one. More important than quantity was the quality of the decisions rendered. The Burger Court was as ready as its predecessor to resolve crucial constitutional issues and to do so in accordance with its own conceptions of what the law should be. *United States v. Nixon*[166] brought the Court into the center of the Watergate vortex and its decision led directly to the first resignation of a President. Nor was there any doubt among the Justices on the propriety of their exercise of power to resolve the crisis. *Nixon* demonstrates the willingness of the Justices to mold crucial constitutional principles to accord with their individual policy perceptions. The impact of judicial review was definitely broadened by *Nixon* and the Burger Court's other separation-of-powers decisions.

The Warren Court's activism was manifested in the number of new rights recognized by it, but the "rights explosion" was more than equaled by that under its successor. Few decisions were more far-reaching in their recognition of new rights than *Roe v. Wade,* to be discussed in the next chapter. The *Roe* decision may indeed be taken as the very paradigm of the activist decision: the decision was based not upon principles worked out in earlier cases but upon "policy judgments" made upon an ad hoc basis which led to recognition of a new right. Even here the Justices were influenced more by pragmatism than principle. "Too many wealthy women were flouting the law to get abortions from respected physicians. Too many poor women were being injured by inadequately trained mass purveyors of illegal abortions. Concerns of that sort, rather than issues of high principle, are what appeal to the centrist activists of the Burger Court."[167]

The hallmark of the activist Court is the *Roe*-type decision that creates a new right not previously recognized in law. The Burger Court recognized new rights for women and those dependent on public largess. During the Burger years the law on sexual classifications was completely changed. Though the Court did not go as far as some had wished, virtually all legal disabilities based upon sex were placed beyond the legal pale.[168]

It should, however, be stressed that there was a fundamental difference between the activism of the Burger Court and that of its predecessor. Chief Justice Warren and his supporters acted on the basis of overriding principles derived from their vision of the society the Constitution was intended to secure.

In particular the Warren Court acted on the basis of two broad principles: nationalism and egalitarianism. It preferred national solutions to what it deemed national problems and, to secure such solutions, was willing to countenance substantial growth in federal power. Even more important was the Warren Court's commitment to equality. If one great theme recurred in its jurisprudence, it was that of equality before the law—equality of races, of citizens, of rich and poor, of prosecutor and defendant. The result was what Justice Fortas termed "the most profound and pervasive revolution ever achieved by substantially peaceful means."[169] More than that, it was the rarest of all political animals: a judicially inspired and led revolution. Without the Warren Court decisions giving ever-wider effect to the right to equality before the law, most of the movements for equality that have permeated American society would never have gotten off the ground.

Yet the Warren Court was more than the judicial counterpart of Plato's philosopher-king. To Warren and his supporters, the Supreme Court was a modern Court of Chancery—a residual "fountain of justice" to rectify individual instances of injustice, particularly where the victims suffered from racial, economic, or similar disabilities. The Warren Justices saw themselves as present-day Chancellors, who secured fairness and equity in individual cases, fired above all by a vision of equal dignity, to be furthered by the Court's value-laden decisions.

No similar vision inspired the activism of the Burger Court. Instead of consciously using the law to change the society and its values, it rode the wave, letting itself be swept along by the consensus it perceived in the social arena—moving, for example, on gender discrimination when it became "fashionable" to be for women's rights. From this point of view, the Burger Court's activism has been well termed a "rootless activism," which dealt with cases on an essentially ad hoc basis, inspired less by moral vision than by pragmatic considerations.[170]

The rootless activism of the Burger Court was a direct consequence of the divisions between the Justices. Because of it, "[T]he hallmark of the Burger Court has been strength in the center and weakness on the wings."[171] The balance of power was held by the Justices "in the middle." In the last Burger terms, however, the center's grip started to weaken. As

Justice Blackmun put it just after Chief Justice Burger retired, "I think the center held generally . . . [but] it bled a lot, and it needs more troops. Where it's going to get them, I don't know."[172]

The shift toward the right did not occur until the end of the Burger years. Before that, the balance was with the pragmatic Justices who did not decide cases in accordance with a preconceived ethical philosophy. This was particularly true when Justices Stewart and Powell were the key swing votes. The Stewart reply, when he was asked whether he was a "liberal" or a "conservative," bears repeating. "I am a lawyer," Stewart answered. "I have some difficulty understanding what those terms mean even in the field of political life. . . . And I find it impossible to know what they mean when they are carried over to judicial work."[173]

Justices who felt this way had the lawyer's aversion to making fundamental value choices. Judicial policy-making was as frequent a feature during the Burger years as in the Warren years. But the policy choices were, in the main, made by Justices who, as relatively moderate pragmatists, were motivated by case-by-case judgments on how to make a workable judicial accommodation that would resolve a divisive public controversy. Inevitably, their decisions did not make for a logically consistent corpus such as that constructed by the Warren Court. In most areas of the law, the Burger Court decisions reflected less an overriding calculus of fundamental values than lawyerlike attempts to resolve the given controversy as a practical compromise between both sides of the issues involved.[174]

In the Warren Court, the leadership had come from the left; constitutional doctrine was, in the important cases, made by Chief Justice Warren and his liberal supporters, notably Justice Brennan. Under Warren's successor, Justice Brennan was shunted to one of the extremes that now more often played a lesser role. The Burger Court's activism was molded more by the moderate Justices "in the middle." As such, it was "inspired not by a commitment to fundamental constitutional principles or noble political ideals, but rather by the belief that modest injections of logic and compassion by disinterested, sensible judges can serve as a counterforce to some of the excesses and irrationalities of contemporary governmental decision-making."[175]

Thus judicial activism itself became a centrist philosophy, primarily practical in nature, without an agenda or overriding philosophy. Its essential approach was to adapt the answer of Diogenes, Solvitur gubernando,[176] and more or less on a case-by-case basis. Fundamental value choices were more often avoided than made. In its operation, "[T]he Burger Court has exhibited a notable determination to fashion tenuous doctrines that offer both sides of a social controversy something important."[177]

The Burger years appear to have marked a legal watershed. After the Warren Court's rewriting of so much of our public law, the Burger Court was bound to be primarily a Court of consolidation. Transforming innovation, in the law as elsewhere, can take place only for so long. In historical terms, indeed, the Burger Court's main significance was its consolidation and continuation of the Warren heritage. Its role in this respect seems all the more important now that the Burger Court has given way to the Rehnquist Court.

15

Watershed Cases: *Roe v. Wade,* 1973

Roe v. Wade[1] was in many ways the paradigmatic Burger Court case. It was clearly the most controversial decision rendered by that Court, and no Court decision has been more bitterly attacked. "It is hard to think of any decision in the two hundred years of our history," declared Cardinal Krol, the President of the National Conference of Catholic Bishops, "which has had more disastrous implications for our stability as a civilized society."[2] Condemnatory letters were sent to the Justices in unprecedented volume, particularly to Justice Blackmun, the author of the opinion. Antiabortion pickets still show up at his speeches.

Griswold and Privacy

The right of privacy is the fundamental right upon which the *Roe* decision was based. It is most unlikely that the men who drew up the Constitution and the Bill of Rights intended to confer, as against government, a right of privacy in the sense in which that term is used today. But there are indications that the Founders did intend to include within the sphere of constitutional protection matters that the present-day observer would classify as coming under an overall right of privacy in the Fourth Amendment's prohibition against unreasonable searches and seizures.

The Fourth Amendment conception of privacy was, nevertheless, rudimentary compared to the right of privacy recognized in our law during the past quarter century. The Framers could think of a sphere peculiar to the individual in his home, his papers, his effects—a sphere that the Bill of Rights rendered immune from governmental encroachment. But the right to privacy in its present-day constitutional connotations is nothing less than the right of individuals to be protected from any wrongful intrusion into their private life.[3] "Liberty in the constitutional sense must mean more than freedom from unlawful governmental restraint; it must include privacy as well, if it is to be a repository of freedom. The right to be let alone is indeed the beginning of all freedoms."[4]

Griswold v. Connecticut,[5] decided in 1965, was the first case confirming the existence of a broad constitutional right of privacy "no less important than any other right . . . reserved to the people."[6] As Justice Black put it, *Griswold* elevated "a phrase which Warren and Brandeis used in discussing grounds for tort relief,[7] to the level of a constitutional rule which prevents state legislatures from passing any law deemed by this Court to interfere with 'privacy.'"[8]

A Connecticut law prohibited the use of contraceptive devices and the giving of medical advice on their use. Griswold and a doctor gave advice to married persons on preventing conception and prescribed contraceptive devices for the wives. They were convicted of violating the birth control law, and their conviction was affirmed by the state's highest court.

The *Griswold* conference found a seven-to-two majority in favor of striking down the Connecticut law, but the majority Justices did not articulate a clear theory on which to base the decision. Justice Douglas stated the simplest rationale. The law violated the defendant's First Amendment right of association, which was more than a right of assembly. Thus, he reasoned, the right to send a child to a religious school was "on the periphery" of the right of association.[9] He also used the analogy of the right to travel, which the Court had said "is in radiation of First Amendment and so is this right." There was nothing more personal than this right and it too was "on the periphery" and within First Amendment protection.

Justice Black was the strongest conference opponent of this Douglas approach. "The right of association is for me a right of assembly and the right of the husband and wife to assemble in bed is a new right of assembly for me."

Only Justice Stewart supported Justice Black's view. He stated that he could not "find anything [against this law] in the First, Second, Fourth, Fifth, Ninth or other Amendments. So I'd have to affirm." The others agreed that the law should be ruled unconstitutional, but differed in their reasoning.

Chief Justice Warren assigned the opinion to Justice Douglas, who had expressed the clearest theory upon which the Connecticut law might be invalidated. Douglas quickly prepared a draft opinion. The draft based the decision on the First Amendment, likening the husband-wife relationship to the forms of association given First Amendment protection. The draft did not mention, much less rely upon, a constitutional right of privacy, and had the draft come down as the *Griswold* opinion, the right of privacy might never have been recognized as a constitutional right by the Warren Court.

The Douglas draft was changed because of an April 24, 1965, letter to Justice Douglas from Justice Brennan. He wrote that the "association" of married couples had little to do with the advocacy protected by the First Amendment and urged that the *Griswold* decision be based upon the right of privacy. He suggested that the expansion of the First Amendment to include freedom of association be used as an analogy to justify a similar approach in the areas of privacy.

The final *Griswold* opinion of the Court stated that the "specific guarantees in the Bill of Rights have penumbras, formed by emanations from those guarantees that help give them life and substance." A constitutional right of privacy was included in these penumbras. The right of marital privacy—"older than our school system"[10]—was violated by the Connecticut law.

Griswold holds squarely that the Bill of Rights does establish a constitutionally protected zone of privacy. The *Griswold*-created right served as the foundation for some of the most controversial Burger Court decisions. By 1977, the Court could state, *"Griswold* may no longer be read as holding only that a State may not prohibit a married couple's use of contraceptives."[11] The right of privacy recognized in *Griswold* is not one that inheres only in the marital relationship. Instead, "If the right of privacy means anything, it is the right of the individual, married or single, to be free from unwarranted governmental intrusion into matters so fundamentally affecting a person."[12]

Conference and Assignment

During the *Griswold* conference Chief Justice Warren had stated that he could not say that the state had no legitimate interest, noting that that could apply to abortion laws—implying that he thought such laws were valid. Those who expected the Burger Court to be less activist than its predecessor relied upon false hopes. It was under Chief Justice Burger that the right of privacy was extended to include the right to an abortion. As Burger put it, in a "Memorandum to the Conference," "This is as sensitive and difficult an issue as any in this Court in my time."[13]

Roe v. Wade came before the Court together with a companion case, *Doe v. Bolton.* In both cases, pregnant women sought relief against state abortion laws, contending they were unconstitutional. At issue in *Roe* was a Texas statute that prohibited abortions except for the purpose of saving the mother's life. The statute in *Doe* was a Georgia law that proscribed an abortion except as performed by a physician who felt, in "his best clinical judgment," that continued pregnancy would endanger a woman's life or injure her health; the fetus would likely be born with a serious defect; or the pregnancy resulted from rape. In addition, the Georgia statutory

scheme posed three procedural conditions: (1) that the abortion be performed in an accredited hospital; (2) that the procedure be approved by
the hospital staff abortion committee; and (3) that the performing physician's judgment be confirmed by independent examinations by two other
physicians.

The final *Roe v. Wade* opinion contrasted the Texas and Georgia statutes as follows: "The Texas statutes under attack here are typical of those
that have been in effect in many States for approximately a century. The
Georgia statutes, in contrast, have a modern cast and are a legislative
product that, to an extent at least, obviously reflects the influences of recent
attitudinal change, of advancing medical knowledge and techniques, and
of new thinking about an old issue."[14]

Nevertheless, the lower court had held both laws invalid—in *Roe* because the statute infringed upon the plaintiff's "fundamental right . . . to
choose whether to have children [which] is protected by the Ninth
Amendment" and in *Doe* because the reasons listed in the statute improp-
erly restricted plaintiff's right of privacy and of personal liberty.

Roe v. Wade and *Doe v. Bolton* were both discussed at the same postargument conference in December 1971. The Chief Justice devoted much
of his *Roe v. Wade* discussion to the question of standing. Referring to the
lead plaintiff, he said, "Jane Roe is unmarried and pregnant. She doesn't
claim health; just doesn't want the baby." In the Burger view, "The unmarried girl has standing. She didn't lose standing through mootness." This
meant, the Chief Justice went on, that "she's entitled to an injunction if the
statute is [un]constitutional." On the merits, Burger said, "The balance
here is between the state's interest in protecting fetal life and the woman's
interest in not having children." In weighing these interests, the Chief
Justice concluded, "I can't find the Texas statute unconstitutional, although it's certainly archaic and obsolete."

Justice Douglas, who spoke next, declared categorically, "The abortion statute is unconstitutional. This is basically a medical and psychiatric
problem" and not one to be dealt with by prohibitory legislation. Douglas
also criticized the statute's failure to give "a licensed physician an immunity
for good faith abortions." Justice Brennan, who followed, expressed a
similar view, though he stressed more strongly than any of the others that
the right to an abortion should be given a constitutional basis by the
Court's decision.

Justice Stewart, next in order of seniority, also spoke in favor of standing. On the merits, Stewart stated, "I agree with Bill Douglas." Stewart
did, however, indicate that there might be some state power in the matter.
"The state," he said, "can legislate, to the extent of requiring a doctor and
that, after a certain period of pregnancy, [she] can't have an abortion."

Justice White began his presentation, "I agree with Potter on all pre-
liminaries, but on the merits I am on the other side. They want us to say
that women have a choice under the Ninth Amendment." But White said
that he refused to accept this "privacy argument."

Justice Marshall, on the other hand, declared, "I go with Bill Douglas, but the time problem concerns me." He thought that the state could not prevent abortions "in the early stage [of pregnancy]. But why can't the state prohibit after a certain stage?" In addition, Marshall said that he would use "'liberty' under the Fourteenth Amendment as the constitutional base."

Justice Blackmun, then the junior Justice, spoke last. He agreed that "the girl has standing." On the merits, Blackmun's presentation displayed an ambivalence that was to be reflected in his draft *Roe v. Wade* opinion. "Can a state properly outlaw all abortions?" he asked. "If we accept fetal life, there's a strong argument that it can. But there are opposing interests: the right of the mother to life and mental and physical health, the right of parents in case of rape, the right of the state in case of incest. I don't think there's an absolute right to do what you will with [your] body." Blackmun did, however, say flatly, "this statute is a poor statute that . . . impinges too far on her."

The discussion of *Doe v. Bolton* paralleled that in *Roe v. Wade*. The Chief Justice asserted, "I do not agree with this carving up of the statute by the three-judge court." As Burger saw it, "The state has a duty to protect fetal life at some stage, but we are not confronted with that question here . . . I would hold this statute constitutional."

The Georgia statute received a more favorable review than its Texas counterpart from Justice Douglas. "This is a much better statute than Texas," he declared. But Douglas had doubts on the statute's practical effects. "We don't know," he stated, "how this statute operates. Is it weighted on the side of only those who can afford this? What about the poor?" Douglas said that he was inclined "to remand to the district court to find out."

Justice Brennan had no doubts. He said that he would affirm the decision below "as far as it goes" but would also "go further to strike down the three-doctor thing as too restrictive." Justice Stewart agreed with the last point. But Justice White again spoke in favor of the state. As he saw it, "The state has power to protect the unborn child. This plaintiff didn't have trouble [taking][15] advantage of procedures. I think the state has struck the right balance here."

Once again, Justice Blackmun's position was ambivalent. "Medically," he pointed out, "this statute is perfectly workable." Blackmun emphasized the competing interests at stake. "I would like," he said, "to see an opinion that recognizes the opposing interests in fetal life and the mother's interest in health and happiness." Blackmun indicated interest in the approach stated by Justice Douglas earlier in the conference. "I would be perfectly willing," he stated, "to paint some standards and remand for findings as to how it operates: does it operate to deny equal protection by discriminating against the poor?"

The conference outcome was not entirely clear; the tally sheets of different Justices do not coincide on the votes.[16] What was clear, however, was that a majority were in favor of invalidating the laws: in *Roe v. Wade,* five (Justices Douglas, Brennan, Stewart, Marshall, and Blackmun) to two (the Chief Justice and Justice White) in the tally sheet made available to me—but four to three (with Blackmun added to the dissenters) according to a Douglas "Dear Chief" letter to Burger.

Despite the fact that he was not part of the majority, the Chief Justice assigned the opinions in the two abortion cases to Justice Blackmun. On December 18, 1971, two days after the conference, Justice Douglas (whose tally sheet showed four votes for invalidating the laws, with himself as senior Justice in the majority) sent his "Dear Chief" missive: "As respects your assignment in this case, my notes show there were four votes to hold parts of the . . . Act unconstitutional. . . . There were three to sustain the law as written." Douglas concluded, "I would think, therefore, that to save future time and trouble, one of the four rather than one of the three, should write the opinion."

The Chief Justice replied with a December 20 "Dear Bill" letter. "At the close of discussion of this case, I remarked to the Conference that there were, literally, not enough columns to mark up an accurate reflection of the voting in either the Georgia or the Texas cases. I therefore marked down no votes and said this was a case that would have to stand or fall on the writing, when it was done."

According to the Burger letter, "That is still my view of how to handle these two . . . sensitive cases, which I might add, are quite probable candidates for reargument."

A few months later, the *Washington Post* reported the Burger–Douglas exchange. According to the *Post* story, Douglas sent his letter "asserting his prerogative to assign the case, but Burger held fast to his position."[17] Justices Douglas and Brennan, who had led the proabortion bloc at the conference, then decided to wait to see the Blackmun drafts before doing anything further in the matter. Though Douglas had, as seen, tallied Blackmun with the minority, others had noted his vote as one with the majority. This might well mean Blackmun opinions agreeable to Douglas and Brennan.

Douglas Draft

That Justices Douglas and Brennan did reach the conclusion just indicated is shown by a letter sent by Brennan to Douglas on December 30: "I gathered from our conversation yesterday that you too think we might better await Harry Blackmun's circulation in the *Texas* abortion case before circulating one." After all, when Justice Blackmun did circulate, it might make either a confrontation with the Chief Justice or a separate majority draft unnecessary.

The Brennan letter was called forth by an uncirculated Douglas draft in the Georgia case, which its author had sent to Justice Brennan soon after the assignment to Justice Blackmun. This draft is presumably what Justice

Douglas would have circulated as his draft opinion of the Court had he been able to assign the abortion opinions.

The Douglas draft, headed "Memorandum from MR. JUSTICE DOUGLAS,"[18] was a typical Douglas product. Written personally at break-neck speed—almost six months before the Blackmun first draft was circulated—it was finished before the others had even had a chance to reflect seriously on what had happened at the argument and conference. Unlike the situation with other Douglas drafts, however, this first effort was not to be the only or final Douglas product. The Justice spent consid-erable effort in refining his opinion; there would be seven drafts of the Douglas opinion (the last on May 22, 1972) before it was replaced by Justice Blackmun's draft opinions in the two abortion cases. Probably, up until the Blackmun drafts were circulated, Justice Douglas still hoped that he would be able to write the Court's abortion opinions—which would explain the unusual Douglas effort to improve his opinion through so many separate drafts. Ultimately, the Douglas seventh draft became the concurrence that the Justice issued in *Roe v. Wade*.

The Douglas draft was an opinion in the Georgia case, *Doe v. Bolton*. But its broad reasoning on the merits—grounding the right to an abortion on the constitutional right of privacy—was equally applicable to the Texas case, *Roe v. Wade*. "The right of privacy," Douglas declared "is a species of 'liberty' of the person as that word is used in the Fourteenth Amendment. It is a concept that acquires substance, not from the predilections of judges, but from the emanations of the various provisions of the Bill of Rights, including the Ninth Amendment."

The heart of the Douglas draft was its holding that the abortion right was protected by the right of privacy. That right, wrote Douglas, "covers a wide range" and is "broad enough to encompass the right of a woman to terminate an unwanted pregnancy in its early stages, by obtaining an abor-tion." This does not mean that "the 'liberty' of the mother, though rooted as it is in the Constitution, may [not] be qualified by the State." But where fundamental rights are involved, "this Court has required that the statute be narrowly and precisely drawn and that a 'compelling state interest' be shown in support of the limitation." This requirement is of cardinal signifi-cance. "Unless regulatory measures are so confined and are addressed to the specific areas of compelling legislative concern, the police-power would become the great leveller of constitutional rights and liberties."

As the Douglas draft saw it, the statute at issue failed the constitutional test. That was true because, as Justice Brennan summarized the draft in his December 30 letter, "The statute infringes the right of privacy by refusing abortions where the mother's mental, but not physical health is in jeop-ardy." The Douglas draft noted that "the vicissitudes of life produce preg-nancies which may be unwanted or which may impair the 'health' in the broad . . . sense of the term or which may imperil the life of the mother or which in the full setting of the case may create such suffering, disloca-tions, misery, or tragedy as to make an early abortion the only civilized step to take. The suffering, dislocation, misery or tragedy just mentioned may be properly embraced in the 'health' factor of the mother as appraised by a person of insight." But the abortion statute did not embrace other than physical health and was therefore too narrow to meet constitutional requirements.

Justice Brennan sent his December 30 letter after reading the Douglas draft. The letter consisted of a ten-page analysis of the draft and suggestions for improvements. Brennan wrote, "I guess my most significant departure from your approach is in the development of the right-of-privacy argument." Brennan noted his agreement "that the right is a species of 'liberty' (although, as I mentioned yesterday, I think the Ninth Amendment . . . should be brought into this problem at greater length)."

The Brennan letter stressed that "[t]he decision whether to abort a pregnancy obviously fits directly within . . . the categories of fundamental freedoms . . . and, therefore, should be held to involve a basic individual right." This meant "that the crucial question is whether the State has a compelling interest in regulating abortion that is achieved without unnecessarily intruding upon the individual's right."

Justice Brennan wrote that, "although I would, of course, find a compelling State interest in requiring abortions to be performed by doctors, I would deny any such interest in the life of the fetus in the early stages of pregnancy." It follows "there is a right to an abortion in the early part of the term," and that the right of privacy in the matter of abortions means that the decision is that of the woman and her alone.

"In sum," the Brennan letter concluded, "I would affirm the district court's conclusion that the reason for an abortion may not be prescribed. I would further hold that the only restraint a State may constitutionally impose upon the women's individual decision is that the abortion must be performed by a licensed physician."

The later Douglas drafts as well as the ultimate Douglas concurrence adopted many of the Brennan suggestions. The Douglas draft also had an influence on Justice Blackmun's drafting process. There is a note in Justice Douglas's hand, dated March 6, 1972, indicating that a copy of the Douglas draft has been "sent . . . to HB several weeks ago."

Blackmun Drafts

In his December 30 letter, Justice Brennan had written, "I appreciate that some time may pass before we hear from Harry." Justice Blackmun was known as the slowest worker on the Court. The abortion cases were his first major assignment, and he worked at them during the next few months, mostly alone and unassisted in the Court library; he was still working on his draft as the Court term wore on. The opinions had been assigned in December 1971. However, it was mid-May before the Justice felt able to circulate anything.

Finally, on May 18, 1972, Justice Blackmun sent around his draft *Roe v. Wade* opinion.[19] "Herewith," began the covering memo, "is a first and tentative draft for this case." Blackmun wrote that "it may be somewhat difficult to obtain a consensus on all aspects. My notes indicate, however, that we were generally in agreement to affirm on the merits. That is where I come out on the theory that the Texas statute, despite its narrowness, is unconstitutionally vague."

The memo went on, "I think that this would be all that is necessary for disposition of the case, and that we need not get into the more complex Ninth Amendment issue. This may or may not appeal to you."

However, the Justice informed his colleagues, "I am still flexible as to results, and I shall do my best to arrive at something which would command a court."

As the covering memo explained, Blackmun's *Roe* draft avoided the broader constitutional issue and struck down the Texas statute on the ground of vagueness. The draft started by dealing with the issues of standing and mootness. It found that Roe had standing and that the termination of her pregnancy did not render the case moot.

On the merits, the Blackmun draft held the Texas statute unconstitutionally vague. The difficulty here was that, in *United States v. Vuitch*,[20] decided the year before, the Court had upheld a similar District of Columbia abortion law against a vagueness attack. The Blackmun draft distinguished *Vuitch* on the ground that the statute there prohibited abortion unless "necessary for the preservation of the mother's life or health," whereas the Texas statute permitted abortions only "for the purpose of saving the life of the mother." Consequently, the draft concluded, *Vuitch* "provides no answer to the constitutional challenge to the Texas statute."

In the Texas statute, "Saving the mother's life is the sole standard." According to the Blackmun draft, this standard was too vague to guide physicians' conduct in abortion cases. "Does it mean that he may procure an abortion only when, without it, the patient will surely die? Or only when the odds are greater than ever that she will die? Or when there is a mere possibility that she will not survive?"

In consequence, the draft declared, "We conclude that Art 1196, with its sole criterion for exemption as 'saving the life of the mother,' is insufficiently informative to the physician to whom it purports to afford a measure of professional protection but who must measure its indefinite meaning at the risk of his liberty, and that the statute cannot withstand constitutional challenge on vagueness grounds."

The Blackmun draft's vagueness analysis was extremely weak. If anything, the "life-saving" standard in the *Roe v. Wade* statute was more definite than the "health" standard upheld in *Vuitch*. But the draft's disposition of the case on the vagueness ground enabled the draft to avoid addressing what Justice Brennan, in a May 18 "Dear Harry" letter—after he had read the draft—called "the core constitutional question." As the Blackmun draft stated, "There is no need in Roe's case to pass upon her contention that under the Ninth Amendment a pregnant woman has an absolute right to an abortion, or even to consider the opposing rights of the embryo or fetus during the respective prenatal trimesters."

Indeed, so far as the draft contained intimations on the matter, they tended to support state substantive power over abortions. "Our holding today," the draft was careful to note, "does not imply that a State has no legitimate interest in the subject of abortions or that abortion procedures may not be subjected to control by the State." On the contrary, "We do not accept the argument of the appellants and of some of the *Amici* that a pregnant woman has an unlimited right to do with her body as she pleases. The long acceptance of statutes regulating the possession of certain drugs and other harmful substances, and making criminal indecent exposure in public, or an attempt at suicide, clearly indicate the contrary." This was, of course, completely different from the approach ultimately followed in the *Roe v. Wade* opinion of the Court.

In his covering memo transmitting his *Roe v. Wade* draft, Justice Blackmun also referred to the companion case, *Doe v. Bolton*. "The Georgia case, yet to come," he wrote, "is more complex. I am still tentatively of the view, as I have been all along, that the Georgia case merits reargument before a full bench. I shall try to produce something, however, so that we may look at it before any decision as to that is made."

On May 25, a week after he had sent around his *Roe v. Wade* draft, Justice Blackmun circulated his draft *Doe v. Bolton* opinion.[21] "Here, for your consideration," the covering memo began, "is a memorandum on the second abortion case." As summarized in the memo, his opinion "would accomplish . . . the striking of the Georgia statutory requirements as to (1) residence, (2) confirmation by two physicians, (3) advance approval by the hospital abortion committee, and (4) performance of the procedure only in [an] accredited hospital."

The *Roe v. Wade* draft did not deal at all with the right of privacy. It was, however, discussed in Justice Blackmun's *Doe* draft. Though it struck down the Georgia statute on the grounds noted in the covering memo, it also dealt with the claim that the law is an "invalid restriction of absolute fundamental right to personal and marital privacy." Here Justice Blackmun was substantially influenced by the treatment in the Douglas draft, particularly the later redrafts, which Justice Douglas noted in a May 19 letter, "I believe I gave you, some time back."

Blackmun's *Doe* draft dealt specifically with the claim that the law was an "invalid restriction of an absolute fundamental right to personal and marital privacy. . . . The Court, in varying contexts, has recognized a right of personal privacy and has rooted it in the Fourteenth Amendment, or in the Bill of Rights, or in the latter's penumbras." The draft flatly rejected the assertion "that the scope of this right of personal privacy includes, for a woman, the right to decide unilaterally to terminate an existing but *unwanted* pregnancy without any state interference or control whatsoever." As the draft put it, "Appellants' contention, however, that the woman's right to make the decision is absolute—that Georgia has either no valid interest in regulating it, or no interest strong enough to support any limitation upon the woman's sole determination—is unpersuasive."

The draft rejected as "unfair and illogical" the argument that "the State's present professed interest in the protection of embryonic and fetal 'life' is somehow to be downgraded. That argument condemns the State for past wrongs and also denies it the right to readjust its views and emphases in the light of the more advanced knowledge and techniques of today."

The *Doe* draft, utterly unlike the final Blackmun opinions, stressed the countervailing interest in fetal life. "The heart of the matter is that somewhere, either forthwith at conception, or at 'quickening,' or at birth, or at some other point in between, another being becomes involved and the privacy the woman possessed has become dual rather than sole. The woman's right of privacy must be measured accordingly." That being the case, "The woman's personal right . . . is not unlimited. It must be balanced against the State's interest." Hence "we cannot automatically strike down the remaining features of the Georgia statute simply because they restrict any right on the part of the woman to have an abortion at will."

The remainder of the *Doe* draft balanced "the impact of the statute upon the right, as it relates to the state interest being asserted." The balancing process led, as the covering memo summarized it, to invalidation of the residence, accreditation, approval, and confirmation requirements.

The Blackmun *Doe* draft was certainly an improvement over his first *Roe v. Wade* effort. Like the latter, however, it did not deal directly with Justice Brennan's "core constitutional question." Indeed, the implication here, too, was that substantial state power over abortion did exist. Under the *Doe* draft, as the Blackmun covering memo pointed out, the state may provide "that an abortion may be performed only if the attending physician deems it necessary 'based upon his best clinical judgment,' if his judgment is reduced to writing, and if the abortion is performed in a hospital licensed by the State through its Board of Health." This was, of course, wholly inconsistent with the Court's final decision in *Roe v. Wade*.

Justice Blackmun ended his *Doe* covering memo by again explaining his approach in the *Roe v. Wade* draft. "I should observe," he pointed out, "that, according to information contained in some of the briefs, knocking out the Texas statute in *Roe v. Wade* will invalidate the abortion laws in a *majority* of our States. Most States focus only on the preservation of the life of the mother. *Vuitch,* of course, is on the books, and I had assumed that the Conference, at this point, has no intention to overrule it. It is because of *Vuitch*'s vagueness emphasis and a hope, perhaps forlorn, that we might have a unanimous court in the Texas case, that I took the vagueness route."

Reargument and Second Conference

Had the Blackmun drafts in the abortion cases come down as the final decisions, the last twenty years in American life and politics might have been quite different. It soon became apparent, however, that the Blackmun drafts were not going to receive the majority imprimatur needed to transform them into Court opinions.

First came indications that the drafts were not satisfactory to the leaders of the conference majority. On May 18, soon after he had received the drafts, Justice Brennan sent a "Dear Harry" letter. "My recollection of the voting on this and the *Georgia* case," Brennan wrote, "was that a majority of us felt that the Constitution required the invalidation of abortion statutes save to the extent they required that an abortion be performed by a licensed physician within some limited time after conception. I think essentially this was the view shared by Bill, Potter, Thurgood and me. My notes also indicate that you might support this view at least in this *Texas* case."

This led Justice Brennan to urge a decision on the constitutional merits. "In the circumstances, I would prefer a disposition of the core constitutional question. Your circulation, however, invalidates the Texas statute only on the vagueness ground. . . . I think we should dispose of both cases on the ground supported by the majority."

The Brennan letter closed with an attempt to mollify Blackmun, who was, after all, the least firm of those willing to invalidate the laws. "This does not mean, however, that I disagree with your conclusion as to the vagueness of the Texas statute." But such deference did not indicate a Brennan inclination to allow the case to be decided narrowly. "I only feel that there is no point in delaying longer our confrontation with the core issue on which there appears to be a majority and which would make reaching the vagueness issue unnecessary."

The next day Justice Douglas wrote to Blackmun, "My notes confirm what Bill Brennan wrote yesterday in his memo to you—that abortion statutes were invalid save as they required that an abortion be performed by a licensed physician within a limited time after conception." That, according to Douglas, "was the clear view of the majority of the seven who heard the argument. . . . So I think we should meet what Bill Brennan calls the 'core issue.'" Justice Douglas also referred to the fact that, at the conference, "the chief had the opposed view, which made it puzzling as to why he made the assignment at all."

The Brennan and Douglas letters indicated opposition to the Blackmun attempt to avoid the "core [constitutional] issue" in *Roe v. Wade*. But now the conference minority sought to delay—and perhaps reverse—the abortion decision. *Roe* and *Doe* had come before a seven-Justice Court. The two vacancies were not filled until Justices Powell and Rehnquist took their seats in January 1972. After the Blackmun drafts were circulated in May, the Chief Justice directed his efforts to securing a reargument in the cases, arguing that the decisions in such important cases should be made by a full Court.

At this point Justice White sent around a brief draft dissent.[22] It effectively demonstrated the weakness of the Blackmun vagueness approach in striking down the Texas law. Referring to the *Vuitch* decision that a statute that permitted abortion on "health" grounds was not constitutionally vague,[23] the White draft declared, "If a standard which refers to the 'health' of the mother, a referent which necessarily entails the resolution of perplexing questions about the interrelationship of physical, emotional, and mental well-being, is not impermissibly vague, a statutory standard which focuses only on 'saving the life' of the mother would appear to be *a fortiori* acceptable. . . . [T]he relevant factors in the latter situation are less numerous and are primarily physiological."

On May 31, Chief Justice Burger sent around a Memorandum to the conference favoring reargument. The Chief Justice wrote, "[T]hese cases . . . are not as simple for me as they appear to be for others. The states have, I should think, as much concern in this area as in any within their province; federal power has only that which can be traced to a specific provision of the constitution." Moreover, the Burger memo went on, "This is as sensitive and difficult an issue as any in this Court in my time and I want to hear more and think more when I am not trying to sort out several dozen other difficult cases." Because of these factors, the memo concluded, "I vote to reargue early in the next Term."

The Burger move to secure reargument was opposed by the Justices in favor of striking down the abortion laws. They feared that, after the reargument, the two new Justices would vote for the laws. In addition the White draft dissent might lead another Justice to withdraw his support from the Blackmun *Roe* draft—maybe even Blackmun himself, whose position had been none too firm in the matter. At the least, the draft was subject to further erosion simply because it was based on the vulnerable vagueness argument.

On May 31, Justice Brennan wrote to Justice Blackmun, "I see no reason to put these cases over for reargument. I say that since, as I understand it, there are five of us (Bill Douglas, Potter, Thurgood, you and I) in substantial agreement with both opinions and in that circumstance I question that reargument would change things." Later that day, Justice Blackmun received a similar note from Justice Marshall: "Like Bill Brennan, I too, am opposed to reargument of these cases."

By now, however, Justice Blackmun was ready to break the five-man majority for immediate issuance of his opinions. He himself had become convinced that the cases should be reargued and circulated a "May 31 Memorandum to the Conference" to that effect: "Although it would prove costly to me personally, in the light of energy and hours expended, I have now concluded, somewhat reluctantly, that reargument in *both* cases at an early date in the next term, would perhaps be advisable." He gave two reasons for his position:

1. I believe on an issue so sensitive and so emotional as this one, the country deserves the conclusion of a nine-man, not a seven-man court, whatever the ultimate decision may be.

2. Although I have worked on these cases with some concentration, I am not yet certain about all the details. Should we make the *Georgia* case the primary opinion and recast Texas in its light? Should we refrain from emasculation of the Georgia statute and, instead, hold it unconstitutional in its entirety and let the state legislature reconstruct from the beginning? Should we spell out—although it would then necessarily be largely dictum—just what aspects are controllable by the State and to what extent? For example, it has been suggested that . . . Georgia's provision as to a licensed hospital should be held unconstitutional, and the Court should approve performance of an abortion in a "licensed medical facility." These are some of the suggestions that have been made and that prompt me to think about a summer's delay.

The Blackmun memo concluded with a vote supporting the Chief Justice: "I therefore conclude, and move, that both cases go over the Term."

Justice Douglas replied to Justice Blackmun with a letter that same day. "I feel quite strongly," Douglas wrote, "that they should not be reargued." He also had two reasons. "In the first place, these cases which were argued last October have been as thoroughly worked over and considered as any cases ever before the court in my time." The second reason was that reargument was not proper where an opinion was supported by a majority of the full Court. "I have a feeling," Douglas wrote, "that where the Court is split 4–4 or 4–2–1 or even in an important constitutional case 4–3, reargument may be desirable. But you have a firm 5 and the firm 5 will be behind you in these two opinions until they come down. It is a difficult field and a difficult subject. But where there is that solid agreement of the majority I think it is important to announce the cases, and let the result be known so that the legislatures can go to work and draft their new laws.

The Douglas letter concluded with a kudo to Justice Blackmun: "Again, congratulations on a fine job. I hope the 5 can agree to get the cases down this Term, so that we can spend our energies next Term on other matters."

The next day, June 1, an angry Douglas letter was sent to the Chief Justice:

Dear Chief:

I have your memo to the Conference dated May 31, 1972 re: *Abortion Cases*.

If the vote of the Conference is to reargue, then I will file a statement telling what is happening to us and the tragedy it entails.

The threatened Douglas statement was never issued, even though the Justices did vote to have the abortion cases reargued. The Douglas attempt to defeat reargument was doomed when the two new Justices voted in favor of reargument. On June 1, Justice Powell circulated a "Memorandum to the Conference" which began: "The question is whether the abortion

cases should be reargued." Powell noted that he had not until then participated in the vote on reargument motions. This case, he wrote, was different. "I have been on the Court for more than half a term. It may be that I
now have a duty to participate in this decision, although from a purely
personal viewpoint I would be more than happy to leave this one to
others."

The Powell memo went on: "I have concluded that it is appropriate for
me to participate in the pending question. . . . I am persuaded to favor
reargument primarily by the fact that Harry Blackmun, the author of the
opinions, thinks the cases should be carried over and reargued next fall. His
position, based on months of study, suggests enough doubt on an issue of
large national importance to justify the few months delay."

Justice Rehnquist also sent around a June 1 memo voting in favor of
reargument, as did Justice White on June 5. That gave the motion for
reargument five votes. When, on June 29, the last day of the 1971 term, the
Court issued its order setting the abortion cases for reargument, only
Justice Douglas was listed as dissenting.[24]

In one of those tricks legal history sometimes plays, it was Justice
Douglas and the others who favored invalidating the abortion laws who
gained the most from the order for reargument. Had Douglas won his
battle to prevent reargument, the original Blackmun drafts would have
remained the final *Roe* and *Doe* opinions. They would have dealt narrowly
with the issues before the Court and, as he predicted in his note to Blackmun, sent legislatures to work drafting new abortion laws, for these opinions were clearly not ringing affirmations of the right to abortion.

By moving for reargument, Chief Justice Burger hoped to secure the
votes of the two new Justices and then persuade Justice Blackmun himself
to switch to an opinion upholding the abortion laws. From his point of
view, the Chief Justice would have been better off had the weak original
Roe draft come down. As it turned out, he got a split vote from the new
Justices and a vastly improved *Roe* opinion, with its broadside confirmation of the constitutional right to an abortion.

The abortion cases were reargued on October 11, 1972. At the conference following reargument, the Justices who had participated in the earlier
conference took the same positions as before. The two new Justices took
opposing positions. Justice Powell said that he was "basically in accord
with Harry's position," whereas Justice Rehnquist stated, "I agree with
Byron [White]"—who had declared "I'm not going to second guess state
legislatures in striking the balance in favor of abortion laws."

Several Justices expressed dissatisfaction with the approach of the
Blackmun *Roe* draft, agreeing with Justice Stewart's statement that "I can't
join in holding that the Texas statute is vague." Stewart was for striking
that law but urged a different approach. He said that he would "follow
John Harlan's reasoning in the Connecticut case[25] and can't rest there on
the Ninth Amendment. It's a Fourteenth Amendment right, as John Harlan said in *Griswold*."[26]

Second Draft and Final Opinion

The most significant part of Justice Blackmun's postreargument conference presentation was his announcement, "I am where I was last Spring." However, he made a much firmer statement this time in favor of invalidating the abortion laws. He also said, "I'd make Georgia the lead case," but he was opposed on this by several others, particularly Justice Powell, who felt that "Texas should be the lead case."

Most important of all, Justice Blackmun announced to the conference, "I've revised both the Texas and Georgia opinions of the last term." During the past summer, Blackmun had devoted his time to the abortion opinions and had completely rewritten them. On November 22, he circulated a completely revised draft of his *Roe v. Wade* opinion. "Herewith," began the covering memo, "is a memorandum (1972 fall edition) on the Texas abortion case."

Justice Blackmun's second *Roe* draft expressly abandoned the vagueness holding on which his first draft had turned. The holding on the constitutional merits, the new draft stated, "makes it unnecessary for us to consider the attack made on the Texas statute on grounds of vagueness." The covering memo explained, "I have attempted to preserve *Vuitch* in its entirety. You will recall that the attack on the Vuitch statute was restricted to the issue of vagueness. 420 U.S. at 73. I would dislike to have to undergo another assault on the District of Columbia statute based, this time, on privacy grounds."

The new Blackmun draft contained the essentials of the final *Roe v. Wade* opinion, including its lengthy historical analysis. Instead of the earlier "vagueness" approach, Justice Blackmun now grounded his decision upon *Griswold v. Connecticut*. According to Blackmun, "[T]he right of privacy, however based, is broad enough to cover the abortion decision." In addition, since the right at issue was a "fundamental" one, the law at issue was subject to strict-scrutiny review: the state regulation of the fundamental right of privacy "may be justified only by a 'compelling state interest.'"[27]

At the postargument conference, the Chief Justice had asked, "Is there a fetal life that's entitled to protection?" Justice Stewart said that the Court should deal specifically with this issue, saying, "[I]t seems essential that we deal with the claim that the fetus is not a person under the fourteenth Amendment." The *Roe v. Wade* opinion met this Stewart demand with a statement that the word "person" in the Fourteenth Amendment does not include a fetus[28]—a point that was specifically added at Justice Stewart's insistence.[29]

The second draft also adopted the time approach followed in the final opinion. However, it used the first trimester of pregnancy alone as the line between invalid and valid state power. "You will observe," Justice Blackmun explained in his covering memo, "that I have concluded that the end of the first trimester is critical. This is arbitrary, but perhaps any other selected point, such as quickening or viability, is equally arbitrary."

The draft stated that before the end of the first trimester, the state "must do no more than to leave the abortion decision to the best medical judgment of the pregnant woman's attending physician." However, "for the stage subsequent to the first trimester, the State may, if it chooses, determine a point beyond which it restricts legal abortions to stated reasonable therapeutic categories."

Later drafts refined this two-pronged time test to the tripartite approach followed in the final *Roe* opinion. In large part, this was in response to the suggestion in a December 12 letter from Justice Marshall: "I am inclined to agree that drawing the line at viability accommodates the interests at stake better than drawing it at the end of the first trimester. Given the difficulties which many women may have in believing that they are pregnant and in deciding to seek an abortion, I fear that the earlier date may not in practice serve the interests of those women, which your opinion does seek to serve."

The Marshall letter stated that his concern would be met "[i]f the opinion stated explicitly that, between the end of the first trimester and viability, state regulations directed at health and safety alone were permissible."

Marshall recognized "that at some point the State's interest in preserving the potential life of the unborn child overrides any individual interests of the woman." However, he concluded, "I would be disturbed if that point were set before viability, and I am afraid that the opinion's present focus on the end of the first trimester would lead states to prohibit abortions completely at any later date."

Justice Blackmun adopted the Marshall suggestion, even though Justice Douglas sent him a letter: "I favor the first trimester, rather than viability."

In addition, Justice Brennan sent a "Dear Harry" letter. "While as you know," the letter began, "I am in basic agreement with your opinions in these cases, I too welcome your giving second thoughts to the choice of the end of the first trimester as the point beyond which a state may appropriately regulate abortion practices." The Justice, however, questioned whether "viability" was the appropriate point.

Justice Brennan summarized the latest Blackmun drafts: "I read your proposed opinions as saying, and I agree, that a woman's right of personal privacy includes the abortion decision, subject only to limited regulation necessitated by the compelling state interests you identify. Moreover, I read the opinions to say that the state's initial interest (at least in point of time if not also in terms of importance) are in safeguarding the health of the woman and in maintaining medical standards."

The Brennan letter then asked, "[I]s the choice of 'viability' as the point where a state may begin to regulate abortions appropriate? For if we identify the state's initial interests as the health of the woman and the maintenance of medical standards, the selection of 'viability' (i.e., the point in time where the fetus is capable of living outside of the woman) as the point where a state may begin to regulate in consequence of these interests seems to me to be technically inconsistent."

As Justice Brennan saw it, "'Viability,' I have thought, is a concept that focuses upon the fetus rather than the woman." Brennan preferred an approach that he said corresponded more with the medical factors that give rise to the "cut-off" point. "For example," Brennan wrote, "rather than using a somewhat arbitrary point such as the end of the first trimester or a somewhat imprecise and technically inconsistent point such as 'viability,' could we not simply say that at that point in time where abortions become medically more complex, state regulation—reasonably calculated to protect the asserted state interests of safeguarding the health of the woman and of maintaining medical standards—becomes permissible[?]"

Despite the Douglas and Brennan letters, Justice Blackmun continued to use the "viability" approach, though he did modify it in later drafts to meet the Marshall suggestion. At this point, Justice Stewart delivered a more fundamental criticism of the Blackmun approach in a December 14 letter. "One of my concerns with your opinion as presently written is the specificity of its dictum—particularly in its fixing of the end of the first trimester as the critical point for valid state action. I appreciate the inevitability and indeed wisdom of dicta in the Court's opinion, but I wonder about the desirability of the dicta being quite so inflexibly 'legislative.'"

This is, of course, the common criticism that has since been directed at *Roe v. Wade*—that the Court was acting more like a legislature than a court; its drawing of lines at trimesters and viability was, in the Stewart letter's phrase, "to make policy judgements" that were more "legislative" than "judicial." Justice Stewart worked on a lengthy opinion giving voice to this criticism. In a December 27 letter, however, he informed Justice Blackmun, "I have now decided to discard the rather lengthy concurring opinion on which I have been working, and to file instead a brief monograph on substantive due process, joining your opinions."

In early December, Justice Blackmun had sent around a revised draft of his *Doe v. Bolton* opinion as well. This was substantially very close to the final opinion in the Georgia case. On December 21, the Justice circulated further drafts and then, on January 17, 1973, the final versions that came down as the Court opinions in the two cases on January 22.

Compelling Interest and Due Process

According to Justice Blackmun's November 22, 1972, covering memorandum transmitting his second *Roe v. Wade* draft, "As I stated in conference, the decision, however made, will probably result in the court's being severely criticized." Just before he circulated the final *Roe v. Wade* draft, Blackmun sent around a January 16, 1973, "Memorandum to the Conference," which began, "I anticipate the headlines . . . when the abortion decisions are announced." Because of this, the Justice was enclosing the announcement from the bench that he proposed to read when the two cases were made public. With this announcement, the memo expressed the hope that "there should be at least some reason for the press not going all the way off the deep end."

The Blackmun announcement did not, of course, have the calming effect for which its author hoped. If anything, indeed, the Justice had understated the outcry. The scare headlines and controversy were far greater than anything anticipated by the Court. Almost all the criticism was directed to the question of whether abortion should be permitted or prohibited. To one interested in Supreme Court jurisprudence, of even greater interest is the constitutional approach followed in striking down the state abortion laws.

The Blackmun *Roe* opinon was based upon two essential holdings: (1) "[T]he right of privacy, however based, is broad enough to cover the abortion decision." It follows from this that there is a "fundamental right" to an abortion; and (2) "Where certain 'fundamental rights' are involved, the court has held that regulation limiting these rights may be justified only by a 'compelling state interest.'"[30]

The state interest in protecting the health of the woman does not become "compelling" until the end of the first trimester of pregnancy. The interest in protecting "the potentiality of human life[31] becomes "compelling" only after viability. Hence state laws restricting the "fundamental right" to an abortion before that time are invalid.

Justice Rehnquist, in his dissent, points out what the Court had done in its *Roe* opinion. *Roe* was a due process, not an equal protection case. "The test traditionally applied in the area of social and economic legislation is whether or not a law such as that challenged has a rational relation to a valid state objective."[32] But that was not the review standard applied in *Roe*. The abortion laws were subjected to strict scrutiny under the compelling-interest test.

According to Justice Rehnquist, "The court eschews the history of the Fourteenth Amendment in its reliance on the 'compelling state interest' test."[33] The strict-scrutiny–compelling-interest approach had been developed to deal with equal protection claims. When the Court applied the test that had been used in suspect-classification cases to cases involving fundamental rights, those cases were also equal protection cases. Now, in *Roe*, the Court held that the compelling-interest test should be used when a statute that infringed upon fundamental rights was challenged on due process grounds. As Justice Rehnquist put it in *Roe*, "The court adds a new wrinkle to this test by transposing it from the legal considerations associated with the Equal Protection Clause of the Fourteenth Amendment to this case arising under the Due Process Clause of the Fourteenth Amendment."[34]

In Justice Rehnquist's view, "[T]he court's sweeping invalidation of any restriction on abortion during the first trimester is impossible to justify under that standard, and the conscious weighing of competing factors that the Court's opinion apparently substitutes for the established test is far more appropriate to a legislative judgment than to a judicial one."[35]

Certainly, there is danger that the importation of the compelling-interest standard into the Due Process Clause will lead to a revival of the substantive due process approach that prevailed in what Justice Stewart termed "the heyday of the Nine Old Men, who felt that the Constitution enabled them to invalidate almost any state laws they thought were unwise."[36]

From this point of view, there is validity to the Rehnquist charge that *Roe* marked a return to the substantive due process approach followed in cases such as *Lochner v. New York*,[37] "when courts used the Due Process Clause 'to strike down state laws . . . because they may be unwise, improvident, or out of harmony with a particular school of thought.'"[38] According to Justice Rehnquist, the *Roe* adoption of the compelling-interest standard in due process cases will inevitably require the Court once again to pass on the wisdom of legislative policies in deciding whether the particular interest put forward is or is not "compelling." As Rehnquist put it in a 1977 memorandum, "[T]he phrase 'compelling state interest' really asks the question rather than answers it, unless we are to revert simply to what Holmes called our own 'can't helps.'"[39] Just as important, the determination of what are and what are not "fundamental rights" is also left to the unfettered discretion of the individual Justice.[40]

It should, however, be noted that the Rehnquist animadversion is not as valid today as it may have been when *Roe* was decided. The Burger Court later drew the line at what rights may be considered "fundamental" for the purposes of strict scrutiny under the Due Process Clause.[41] This substantially narrowed the scope of its revival of substantive due process.

It should also be borne in mind that there are due process cases where review less flaccid than that under the rational-basis standard is plainly appropriate. The rights guaranteed by the First Amendment are fundamental rights, made applicable to the states by the Due Process Clause of the Fourteenth Amendment.[42] When a state burdens the exercise of First Amendment rights there is a violation of due process, and most observers would agree that the state law should be subjected to strict scrutiny under the compelling-interest test. The entire Burger Court expressly stated that that is the case.[43]

Presumably even Chief Justice Rehnquist would agree with this strict-scrutiny posture in cases involving the fundamental rights guaranteed under the First Amendment. His criticism of the *Roe v. Wade* approach was thus more a criticism of degree than one of kind and was presumably answered by the later cases which limit the applicability of the strict-scrutiny approach by restricting the rights deemed fundamental for purposes of the more exacting review standard. Those cases prevented the *Roe* approach from being extended much beyond the abortion cases themselves. For those favoring an even broader judicial role in protecting privacy, the *Roe* substantive due process revival was to become essentially a lost opportunity.

Nonenumerated Rights

Critics of *Roe* have also attacked the decision as one that departs drastically from the constitutional canon of "textual fidelity."[44] Where in the Constitution, they ask, is there any guaranty of the right to an abortion or of the right of privacy upon which it is based?

The view that the *Roe*-type protection of rights not specified in the Constitution is illegitimate has been stated forcefully by Judge Robert H. Bork. Referring specifically to the right of privacy, Bork points out that *Griswold* and *Roe* created "an overall right of privacy that applies even where no provision of the Bill of Rights does." Under this approach, Bork asserts, "the Bill of Rights was expanded beyond the known intentions of the Framers. Since there is no constitutional text or history to define the right, privacy becomes an unstructured source of judicial power."[45]

As Judge Bork sees it, the *Griswold-Roe* approach "requires the Court to say, without guidance from the Constitution, which liberties or gratifications may be infringed by majorities and which may not."[46] Since the judge is given no guide other than the constitutional text, which, of course, does not cover a case such as *Griswold,* the question of what nontextual rights should be protected depends completely on the judge's own discretion. Once we depart from the text of the Constitution," asks Justice Scalia, "just where . . . do we stop?"[47] Or as a much-quoted Bork aphorism has it, "The truth is that the judge who looks outside the historic Constitution always looks inside himself and nowhere else."[48]

It is, however, erroneous to assume that only those rights specifically mentioned are given constitutional protection. As Justice Brennan once put it, "[T]he protection of the Bill of Rights goes beyond the specific guarantees to protect from congressional abridgement those equally fundamental personal rights necessary to make the express guarantees fully meaningful."[49] The reason why was best stated in Justice Goldberg's *Griswold* concurrence: "To hold that a right so basic and fundamental and so deep-rooted in our society as the right of privacy in marriage may be infringed because that right is not guaranteed in so many words by the first eight amendments to the Constitution is to ignore the Ninth Amendment and to give it no effect whatsoever."[50] In Goldberg's words, "[T]he Ninth Amendment shows a belief of the Constitution's authors that fundamental rights exist that are not expressly enumerated in the first eight amendments and an intent that the list of rights included there not be deemed exhaustive."[51]

The Ninth Amendment shows that there are basic rights not specifically mentioned in the Bill of Rights that are nevertheless protected from governmental infringement. "In sum," Justice Goldberg concludes, "I believe that the right of privacy in the marital relation is fundamental and basic—a personal right 'retained by the people' within the meaning of the Ninth Amendment."[52]

Of course, the most controversial application of the *Griswold*-created right was in *Roe v. Wade,* where the Court decided that the state law proscribing most abortions was violative of the right to privacy. That right was held to include the right to terminate pregnancies. The right of privacy was ruled broad enough to encompass the abortion decision.

In his *Roe v. Wade* concurrence Justice Douglas stressed the role of the Ninth Amendment as a source of the right protected by the *Roe* decision. As Douglas saw it, this right is one of personal autonomy that "includes customary, traditional, and time-honored rights, amenities, privileges, and immunities that come within the sweep of 'the Blessings of Liberty' mentioned in the preamble to the Constitution." The Douglas concurrence then listed three groups of rights that "come within the meaning of the term 'liberty' as used in the Fourteenth Amendment."[53] The Douglas list was based upon a suggestion contained in the December 30, 1971, letter that had been sent to him by Justice Brennan after the latter had read the Douglas draft concurrence. The letter consisted of a ten-page analysis of the draft and suggestions for improvements. The Douglas draft had found the abortion law violative of the right of privacy. Brennan suggested a broader approach to the privacy concept.

The Brennan letter noted his agreement

> that the right [of privacy] is a species of "liberty" (although, as I mentioned yesterday, I think the Ninth Amendment . . . should be brought into this problem at greater length), but I would identify three groups of fundamental freedoms that "liberty" encompasses: first, freedom from bodily restraint or inspection, freedom to do with one's body as one likes, and freedom to care for one's health and person; second, freedom of choice in the basic decisions of life, such as marriage, divorce, procreation, contraception and the education and upbringing of children; and, third, autonomous control over the development and expression of one's intellect and personality.

The Brennan list, as adopted by Justice Douglas in his concurring opinion,[54] is the most comprehensive judicial statement of what is included in the right of personal autonomy protected, under *Griswold* and *Roe,* by the Constitution. To be sure, none of the liberties in the Brennan-Douglas list is mentioned in the Constitution. Yet all involve freedoms that most Americans rightly believe are protected against governmental intrusion.

The right of personal autonomy comes down to what was stated in classic language by Justice Brandeis: "The makers of our Constitution conferred, as against the Government, the right to be let alone—the most comprehensive right and the right most valued by civilized men. To protect that right, every unjustifiable intrusion by the Government upon the privacy of the individual, whatever the means employed, must be deemed a violation of the [Constitution]."[55]

If the individual is not to be overwhelmed by the state, equipped as it is with all the resources of modern science and technology, he or she must be permitted to retain the essential attributes of individuality—that intrinsic element of life that distinguishes not only our species from all others, but all of us within the human community from each other.[56] Above all, in a society where science offers governments a continually refined set of tools for intrusion and surveillance, it is essential that there remain an area of apartness in which the individual may live as Walt Whitman's "simple separate person"—one that is immune from intervention by the community itself. When man stands in constant danger of being overwhelmed by the machine, he can retain his individuality only if there is preserved for him "a privacy, an obscure nook"[57]—"A liberty of choice as to his manner of life, and neither an individual nor the public has a right to arbitrarily take away from him this liberty."[58]

Even though they are not specifically mentioned in the Constitution, few people would deny that the aspects of autonomy in the Brennan-Douglas list are entitled to constitutional protection. For example, there is what Justice Douglas calls the "freedom from bodily restraint or compulsion, freedom to walk, stroll, or loaf."[59] During a Court conference on a case involving freedom of religion,[60] Douglas stated, "I think we're entitled to our religious scruples, but I don't see how we can make everyone attune to them. I can't be required to goose-step because eight or ninety percent goose-step."

More recently, Justice John P. Stevens (at the time a circuit judge) gave the example of "a case in which the sovereign insists that every citizen must wear a brown shirt to demonstrate his patriotism."[61] Would any American judge, no matter how opposed in theory to nonenumerated rights, uphold a law requiring people to goose-step or wear a brown shirt?

A comparable illustration is given in Justice Goldberg's *Griswold* concurrence. "Surely," Goldberg writes, "the Government . . . could not decree that all husbands and wives must be sterilized after two children have been born to them."[62] Would even opponents of nontextual rights say that such a law "would not be subject to constitutional challenge because . . . no provision of the Constitution specifically prevents the Government from curtailing the marital right to bear children and raise a family?"[63] Clearly, as Justice Goldberg puts it, Americans would find it "shocking to believe that the personal liberty guaranteed by the Constitution does not include protection against such totalitarian limitation of family size, which is at complete variance with our constitutional concepts."[64]

In view of the recent attacks on the *Griswold-Roe* concept of nontextual rights, it is significant that the concept was vigorously supported by Justice Harlan, now considered the very paradigm of the true conservative judge. A few years before *Griswold,* Harlan anticipated the decision there. Speaking of the contraceptive ban in conference, Harlan asserted, "This is more offensive to the right to be let alone than anything possibly can be."[65]

In a 1961 dissent, Justice Harlan indicated why the right to be let alone was guaranteed even though it was not mentioned in the constitutional text. The Court, said Harlan, must approach "the text which is the only commission for our power not in any literalistic way, as if we had a tax statute before us, but as the basic charter of our society, setting out in spare but meaningful terms the principles of government." For Harlan, "[I]t is not the particular enumeration of rights . . . which spells out the reach of" constitutional protection. On the contrary, the "character of Constitutional provisions . . . must be discerned from a particular provision's larger context. And . . . this context is one not of words, but of history and purposes."[66]

Because of this, Justice Harlan went on,

> the full scope of the liberty guaranteed by the Due Process Clause cannot be found in or limited by the precise terms of the specific guarantees elsewhere provided in the Constitution. This "liberty" is not a series of isolated points pricked out in terms of the taking of property; the freedom of speech, press, and religion; the right to keep and bear arms; the freedom from unreasonable searches and seizures; and so on. It is a rational continuum which, broadly speaking, includes a freedom from all substantial arbitrary impositions and purposeless restraints . . . and which also recognizes . . . that certain interests require particularly careful scrutiny of the state needs asserted to justify their abridgment.[67]

It is true that the Harlan recognition of nonenumerated rights was based upon the Due Process Clause rather than the Ninth Amendment. Thus, in a 1970 case,[68] Justice Harlan agreed that the reasonable-doubt standard in criminal trials was mandated by the Constitution. But his recognition of the nontextual right was explained on due process grounds: "I view the requirement of proof beyond a reasonable doubt in a criminal case as bottomed on a fundamental value determination of our society that it is far worse to convict an innocent man than to let a guilty man go free." Under this approach, "due process, as an expression of fundamental procedural fairness, requires a more stringent standard for criminal trials than for ordinary civil litigation."[69]

That Justice Harlan relied upon due process rather than the Ninth Amendment did not detract from his full acceptance of the concept of nonenumerated rights. As Harlan saw it, due process "is a discrete concept which subsists as an independent guaranty of liberty and procedural fairness, more general and inclusive than the specific prohibitions."[70] Except for its terminology, the Harlan approach is essentially similar to the approach that relies on the Ninth Amendment. If the right is a basic right "which [is] fundamental; which belong[s] . . . to the citizens of all free governments,"[71] it is one retained by the people under the Ninth Amendment or, in the Harlan view, included in the "liberty" protected by due process.

To be sure, the fact that Justice Harlan and other conservative judges, such as Chief Justice Burger himself, have supported the *Griswold-Roe* position that "fundamental rights even though not expressly guaranteed, have been recognized by the Court as indispensable to the enjoyment of rights explicitly defined,"[72] will scarcely change the bitter opposition to the Supreme Court jurisprudence on the matter—particularly that to *Roe v. Wade* itself. The controversy over that decision continues unabated to this day, to an extent far greater than anything anticipated by Justice Blackmun and his colleagues. All that would have been avoided had the original Blackmun *Roe v. Wade* draft come down as the final Court opinion. Instead of a *cause célèbre, Roe* might then have been a mere constitutional footnote used by law professors to illustrate how the Court can evade important legal issues.

16

Rehnquist Court, 1986–

The history of an institution such as the Supreme Court, like a tapestry, is made up of many strands that, interwoven, make a pattern; to separate a single one and look at it alone not only defaces the whole but gives the strand itself a false value.[1] All too many studies of the Supreme Court, or of its individual members, concentrate upon single strands of the Court's work, emphasizing, more often than not, those aspects that diverge most sharply from the overall pattern.

Such an approach is bound to give a distorted picture. Not infrequently, in truth, the reaction of commentators about the Court is akin to that of the blind man from Hindustan when first confronted with an elephant. The aspect of the Court's work emphasized by the particular observer tends to dominate his conception of the Court as a whole; yet he almost never comes to picture the Court as the institutional entity that it is. Small wonder, then, that the public, both legal and lay, has no clear picture of the working of our unique judicial organ and its proper place in a constitutional democracy.

Not long ago Chief Justice Rehnquist recalled his first visit to the Court after his appointment as a Justice: "We came over here, and it was kind of a grey afternoon. . . . And I just felt, literally, like I'd entered a monastery when I came over."[2] Neophytes on the high bench—even the strongest of them—are immediately aware of the overpowering institutional traditions. Such awareness continues throughout the Justices' tenure and, more than is generally realized, weaves into the Court's pattern all but the most eccentric of its members.

It has been said of one of the greatest Justices, Louis D. Brandeis, that he had an almost mystic reverence for the Court, whose tradition seemed to him not only to consecrate its own members, but to impress its sacred mission upon all who shared in any measure in its work.[3] Few members of the high tribunal may be capable of penetrating into its mystique with the perception of a Brandeis; still, says Chief Justice Rehnquist, "Everybody who comes here probably feels the constraints of the place."[4]

This history has been written upon the assumption that the pattern of the tapestry is more important than the single strands. Similarly, the Supreme Court as an institution is more significant than the individual Justices who make up its membership.

To be sure, to treat the Court as an institutional entity may seem outdated in an age when even the law has succumbed to our society's preoccupation with the behavioral sciences. Judges are only men, we were told[5]—which was, of course, an indisputable observation. All the same, it hardly follows from this that only study of the psychological makeup of the individual Justices is now worthwhile. The state of a man's mind is as much a fact as the state of his digestion, according to a nineteenth-century English judge. Now, however, we are told that the two are intimately related and that the state of a judge's mind can hardly be known without some knowledge of the state of his stomach.

To advocates of this sort of gastrological jurisprudence, all attempts to describe the Court as an institutional entity are fundamentally naive, and this is particularly true when the institutional ethos of the Court has seemed at a low ebb. At such a time, it is said, it is only the makeup of the individual Justice that is important if we are to understand the decisions of a fragmented Court.

No one not blind to the facts of legal life can deny that the Supreme Court has too often presented a far from edifying spectacle of internal atomization. But even that did not prevent that tribunal from functioning as an institutional entity. Even when the Court has been splintered, its work as a governmental organ had to go on. This is, in fact, a basic difference between an ultimate judicial tribunal and commentaries upon its work. The Court cannot adopt an either–or approach. It must decide the case before it, even though the decision requires it to choose between two conflicting truths. The theorist need wholly reject neither, where neither states an exclusive verity; the Court must choose between them. Yet it is a mistake to assume that because, in such cases, the individual members of the tribunal are sharply divided, the Court has ceased to function as an institution.

On the contrary, even amid a plethora of such cases, the institutional pattern continues to be woven. It may be harder to determine the boundary at which some Courts have balanced conflicting interests. Still, the Court is always engaged in drawing the line between conflicting interests. While we may not be able to determine it by a general formula, points in the line have been fixed by decisions that this or that concrete case fell on the nearer or farther side.

Mr. Right as Chief Justice

Drawing the line has, however, been easier since Chief Justice Burger retired in 1986 and was succeeded in the Court's center chair by Justice William H. Rehnquist. Nor can it be doubted that the line is being drawn farther to the right by the Rehnquist Court than it was by its immediate predecessors. The new Chief Justice was well characterized by a *Newsweek* article as "The Court's Mr. Right."[6] According to the *New York Times,* "William H. Rehnquist is a symbol. People who have trouble naming all nine Supreme Court Justices quickly identify him as its doctrinaire, right-wing anchor. . . . Justice Rehnquist is the Court's most predictable conservative member, using his considerable intelligence, energy and verbal facility to shape the law to his vision."[7]

The Rehnquist vision in this respect has always been a clear one. In a 1985 interview, he noted that he joined the Court with a desire to counteract the Warren Court decisions.[8] "I came to the court," Rehnquist said, "sensing . . . that there were some excesses in terms of constitutional adjudication during the era of the so-called Warren Court." Some of that Court's decisions, the Justice went on, "seemed to me hard to justify. . . . So I felt that at the time I came on the Court, the boat was kind of keeling over in one direction. Interpreting my oath as I saw it, I felt that my job was . . . to kind of lean the other way."[9]

By the time of his nomination as Chief Justice, Rehnquist had become the most influential member of the Burger Court, both because he stood out in a Court of generally bland personalities, which lacked a firm sense of direction, and because he was closely allied with the Chief Justice. During his early Court years, however, the majority remained largely unsympathetic to the Rehnquist entreaties from the right. It was then that he received a Lone Ranger doll as a gift from his law clerks, who called him the "lone dissenter" during that period. During his fourteen years as an Associate Justice, Rehnquist dissented alone fifty-four times—a Court record.

When asked about the origins of his conservatism, Rehnquist replied, "It may have something to do with my childhood."[10] He was raised in a modest house in a middle-class Milwaukee suburb. After World War II service in North Africa, he attended Stanford and its law school. He then served as a Supreme Court clerk to Justice Robert H. Jackson. Rehnquist wrote a memo on the *Brown* segregation case,[11] urging that the separate-but-equal doctrine, under which segregation had been upheld,[12] was "right and should be affirmed."[13]

Justice Rehnquist later stated that his views had changed and that he accepted *Brown* as the law of the land.[14] But his votes in cases involving racial issues clearly placed him at the opposite extreme from the Brennan wing of the Court. On most other issues, too, Rehnquist has reflected his conservative Republican background, with years of private practice and active involvement in the Goldwater wing of the party in Arizona and a position as Assistant Attorney General in the Nixon Department of Justice. Before his elevation to the Court's center chair, Rehnquist had anything but the appearance of a Justice; he still had the look of an overage college student—lumbering around the Court in his thick brown glasses, mismatched outfits, and Hush Puppies. As Chief Justice, however, he has trimmed his sideburns, begun to wear conservative suits and ties, and drives to work in a black limousine.

Despite his robust appearance and weekly tennis with his law clerks, Rehnquist has had health problems. In 1982, he was hospitalized because of his back and underwent withdrawal symptoms, with a period of mental confusion and slurred speech, when the heavy dosage of a powerful sedative, Placidyl, was reduced. In 1977, Rehnquist had written in reply to a letter comment on his draft opinion in a case: "It may be that my adverse reactions to your letter of March are partially induced by my doctor's insistence that I take valium four times a day. . . ."[15]

Time once called Justice Rehnquist the Court's "most self-consciously literate opinion writer."[16] He is arguably the best legal stylist and phrasemaker on the Court, though too much of his literary ability tends to be overshadowed by the extreme position which it supports. Rehnquist's literary talents are not limited to his opinion writing. A typical example is contained in a 1980 memo on a case involving a mandatory life sentence under a recidivist statute. The defendant had obtained $229 by fraud and forgery through his three criminal acts.[17] Rehnquist's draft opinion holding that the sentence did not constitute cruel and unusual punishment was disputed by a Powell draft dissent. Rehnquist took issue with the Powell view that, since the crimes were "properly related" and did not involve "violence," the sentence was unconstitutionally harsh. "The notions embodied in the dissent," Rehnquist wrote in his memo,

> that if the crime involved "violence," . . . a more severe penalty is warranted under objective standards simply will not wash, whether it be taken as a matter of morals, history, or law. Caesar's death at the hands of Brutus and his fellow conspirators was undoubtedly violent; the death of Hamlet's father at the hands of his brother, Claudius, by poison, was not. Yet there are few, if any states which do not punish just as severely murder by poison (or attempted murder by poison) as they do murder or attempted murder by stabbing. The highly placed executive who embezzles hugh sums from a state savings and loan association, causing many shareholders of limited means to lose substantial parts of their savings, has committed a crime very different from a man who takes a smaller amount of money from the same savings and loan at the point of a gun. Yet rational people could disagree as to which criminal merits harsher punishment. . . . In short, the "seriousness" of an offense or a pattern of offenses in modern society is not a line, but a plane.[18]

His extreme views have not prevented Rehnquist from being on good terms with the other Justices. Even his ideological opposites like Justice Brennan have commented on their cordial relations with the categorical conservative. To his colleagues, Rehnquist has been as well known for his good nature as for his rightist acumen. On a Court where, as Justice Blackmun once lamented, "[t]here is very little humor,"[19] Rehnquist stood out because of his impish irreverence and wit. When the Burger Court sat, one of Rehnquist's clerks would every now and then pass notes to the Justice. These were not legal memos but Trivial Pursuit-style questions. Rehnquist would answer them and then hand them to Justice Blackmun for that Justice to try his hand.[20]

Another illustration may also be seen in a 1973 Rehnquist memorandum: "In going over some material which had been stored for a long period of time in my present Chambers, I came across a manuscript poem entitled 'To a Law Clerk Dying Young,' written by someone named A. E. Schmaussman, or Schmousman[21] (the handwriting is not too good), who was apparently a law clerk here at one time." Rehnquist wrote, "I found the poem very moving and emotional, and thought that a public reading of it would be a suitable occasion for a gathering of present and retired members of the Court and their law clerks to toast a departing Term with sherry."

The Rehnquist memo concluded with what some considered a satiric allusion to Chief Justice Burger's constant emphasis on Court secrecy: "P.S. I debated circulating the actual text of the poem with this invitation, but decided that there was too great a chance that it mght be leaked to the newspapers before the party."[22]

The Rehnquist sense of humor sometimes degenerated into practical jokes. On April Fool's Day 1985, the Chief Justice was the Rehnquist victim. Rehnquist had a life-size photo cutout of Burger produced and sent a street photographer to a corner outside the Court with a sign: "Have your picture taken with the chief justice, $1." To make sure he wouldn't miss Burger's reaction, the Justice called him at home, saying he needed a ride to Court on April 1. Rehnquist "was laughing like crazy" when he drove past the scene that day with the overdignified Chief Justice.[23]

When all is said and done, however, the most important thing about Rehnquist is that he has proved to be a strong Chief Justice, more in the Warren than the Burger mold. It was said that Chief Justice Burger's discussion of cases at conference left the Justices with the feeling that he was "the least prepared member of the Court."[24] In a comment on Chief Justice Rehnquist, Justice Marshall said, "He has no problems, wishy-washy, back and forth. He knows exactly what he wants to do, and that's very important as a chief justice."[25] There is little doubt that Marshall was contrasting the Rehnquist performance with that of his predecessor.

Some years ago, the present Chief Justice compared the Burger and Warren Courts. Rehnquist stated that the impact of the Court had been diminished under Chief Justice Burger. "I don't think that the Burger Court has as wide a sense of mission. Perhaps it doesn't have any sense of mission at all."[26]

Certainly the Warren Court did have Rehnquist's "sense of mission" when it virtually rewrote the corpus of our constitutional law; concepts and principles that had appeared unduly radical became accepted rules of law. From this point of view, the Warren Court was the paradigm of the "result-oriented" Court, which used its power to secure the result it deemed right in the cases that came before it. Employing the authority of the ermine to the utmost, Warren and his colleagues never hesitated to do whatever they thought necessary to translate their own conceptions of fairness and justice into the law of the land. The same was plainly not true of the Burger Court; it did not have any "sense of mission" comparable to its predecessor.

Rehnquist himself has said, "I don't know that a court should really have a sense of mission."[27] Yet Rehnquist clearly is a judge who does have a sense of mission. From his first appointment to the Court Rehnquist has sought what he called "a halt to . . . the sweeping rules made in the days of the Warren Court"[28]—and not only a halt, but a rollback of much of the Warren jurisprudence. The Rehnquist conservative program has included enlargement of government authority over individuals, a check to the expansion of criminal defendants' rights, limitations on access to federal courts, and increased emphasis on protection of property rights. As Chief Justice, he has finally been in a position to advance his conservative agenda.

The Conservative Majority

Chief Justice Rehnquist has started to move the Justices in his desired direction because, for the first time in half a century, the Court had a conservative majority willing to support the shift to the right. This marked a definite change from prior Courts. Under Chief Justice Warren, the Court's liberal wing was dominant. In the Burger Court, the balance of power was held by the Justices who were, in Justice Blackmun's phrase, "in the middle."[29] In Chief Justice Burger's last terms, however, the center's grip started to weaken. As Justice Blackmun put it just after Burger retired, "I think the center held generally . . . [but] it bled a lot. And it needs more troops. Where it's going to get them, I don't know."[30]

As it turned out, it was not the center but the right which received the additional troops. The first of them, Antonin Scalia, was appointed in 1986 to fill the vacancy created by Chief Justice Rehnquist's elevation to the Court's center chair. Scalia had been a law professor (primarily at the University of Chicago), a government official, and a judge of the D.C. Circuit Court of Appeals. As a Justice, Scalia has been a doctrinaire conservative—even more extreme in his rightist views than the Chief Justice himself—though he has, as will be noted, also exhibited a libertarian streak that has led him to resist some governmental intrusions.

It was expected by many that Justice Scalia's intellectual brilliance would enable him to perform a leadership role on the Rehnquist Court. So far, it has not worked out that way. Instead, the Justice has persisted in extreme positions that have not been accepted even by a conservative majority that might be willing to accept a properly tempered Scalia posture.

Justice Scalia is the first noted law professor to be elevated to Olympus since Felix Frankfurter. Scalia has not, however, confined himself to the relatively restrained judicial role assumed by his predecessor. Instead, Scalia has been a judicial activist, not hesitating to import his own academic theories into our public law. But if Justice Scalia seems unduly rigid in his approach, at least he is always interesting in his opinions. This should make him the professoriate's favorite Justice. Both for those who agree and those who disagree with them, the Scalia opinions should provide grist for the academic mills for years to come.

Another vacancy occurred on the Rehnquist Court when Justice Powell retired in 1987. Anthony M. Kennedy, then a circuit judge, was chosen in Powell's place. After graduation from Harvard Law School, Kennedy was in private practice for fifteen years (six of those as a sole practitioner) and also taught part-time at the McGeorge School of Law in Sacramento. Justice Powell had been a leader in the Burger Court's centrist core. Justice Kennedy has, more often than not, been a vote for the Rehnquist Court's growing conservative majority. He has, however, been anything but a doctrinaire conservative in the Scalia sense. He has displayed a willingness to listen to opposing views and an openness to dialogue that contrast with Justice Scalia's often inflexible posture.

Perhaps the most notable thing about Justice Kennedy is the number of opinions he has written, particularly in critical cases. The unusually high number by a junior Justice indicates the Chief Justice's immediate confidence in the newest member of his Court. The confidence has been justified by Justice Kennedy's general adherence to the Rehnquist jurisprudence.

The Kennedy appointment meant that Chief Justice Rehnquist now had a five-Justice conservative core (the Chief Justice and Justices White, O'Connor, Scalia, and Kennedy). But the conservative majority was still a fragile one, which often saw defections by one or more members. That situation changed when President Bush was able to select replacements for Justices Brennan and Marshall, the last liberal holdovers from the Warren Court, who retired in 1990 and 1991.

To succeed Justice Brennan, the President nomimated David H. Souter, a former Attorney General and Supreme Court Justice in New Hampshire, who had been appointed a federal appeals judge just before his elevation to the highest Court. The most striking thing about the Souter pre-Court record is its skeletonlike nature. For a man who had held eminent state positions, including seven years on his state's highest court, Justice Souter left practically no "paper trail." He was not informative about his views in professional writings or speeches and wrote no significant opinions. This record was continued during his early Court tenure; by June 1991, near the end of his first term, Justice Souter had written only three opinions and no dissents—the lowest number of any Justice appointed in the previous two decades. Still, he has been called a "polite and professional" Justice[31] whose questions have played a prominent part in oral argument—though he has been far less abrasive than Justice Scalia, the

Rehnquist Court's most active questioner. Recently, indeed, Justice Souter has taken a more active part in the Court's decision process; it was he who was most responsible for the eloquent 1992 opinion refusing to overrule *Roe v. Wade*.[32]

To replace Justice Marshall, the first black Justice, President Bush selected Clarence Thomas, another black, who had recently been appointed to the D.C. Circuit Court. Thomas was only forty-three when appointed—the youngest Justice since Justice Stewart had gone on the Court at the same age. Thomas also had less experience in the law than any Justice appointed in this century; his pre-Court career had been almost entirely in the field of civil-rights enforcement, primarily as Chairman of the Equal Employment Opportunity Commission—which, however important, is scarcely the type of legal work that provides the legal background that one desires in a Supreme Court appointee.

The Thomas confirmation was marred by charges of sexual harassment, which led to controversial televised hearings on the matter. More important was the Justice's refusal to give specific answers to questions on his jurisprudential posture, even when not framed in terms of specific cases. On the Court, however, Justice Thomas has already indicated that he is a doctrinaire conservative in the Scalia mold; he has, in fact, voted more with Justice Scalia than any other member of the Court.

Junior Supreme Court

Before we discuss the emerging jurisprudence of the Rehnquist Court, a word should be said about an important development during the present century that is changing the very nature of the Supreme Court—the expanding role of the law clerks.

In a congratulatory letter to Justice Rehnquist upon his court appointment, Justice Douglas wrote, "I realize that you were here before as a member of the so-called Junior Supreme Court."[33] Douglas was referring to Rehnquist's service as a law clerk to Justice Jackson. Once upon a time, the Douglas characterization of the clerk corps might have been taken as one made wholly in jest, but that was no longer the case.

Over half a century ago, Justice Brandeis stated, "The reason the public thinks so much of the Justices of the Supreme Court is that they are almost the only people in Washington who do their own work."[34] The legend that this remains true is still prevalent, and in his book on the Court, even Chief Justice Rehnquist tells us that "the individual justices still continue to do a great deal more of their 'own work' than do their counterparts in other branches of the federal government."[35]

The Rehnquist-type account has been accepted by both the press and the public. "Alone among Government agencies," Anthony Lewis wrote in the *New York Times*, "the court seems to have escaped Parkinson's Law. The work is still done by nine men, assisted by eighteen young law clerks. Nothing is delegated to committees or ghostwriters or task forces."[36] We saw in Chapter 9 how the Justices were provided with funds to pay secretaries or clerks in 1886, with provision for law clerks rather than stenographers in 1919. At that time, the law clerk would perform only the functions of an associate in a law firm, that is, research for senior members and assistance generally in the firm's work. It may be doubted that Justices such as Holmes or Brandeis used their clerks as more than research assistants. In fact, as we saw, Justice Hughes worried at the time that if the clerks were used too much, "it might be thought that they were writing our opinions."[37] That, indeed, is what happened. In recent years the Justices have given their clerks an ever-larger share of responsibility, including even the writing of opinions.

Complaints against the clerks' role have been common, including a noted 1957 article in *U.S. News & World Report* by William H. Rehnquist himself.[38] Rehnquist stated that the Justices were delegating substantial responsibility to their clerks, who "unconsciously" slanted materials to accord with their own views. The result was that the liberal point of view of the vast majority of the clerks had become the philosophy espoused by the Warren Court.

The situation has, if anything, gotten worse in recent years. "In the United States," notes a 1986 *London Times* article, "judges have 'clerks', i.e., assistants who prepare and frequently write judgments which their masters often merely adopt and which a qualified observer can easily recognize as the work of a beginner."[39]

An even harsher view of the clerk system was expressed by Professor Philip B. Kurland, a leading constitutional scholar, a year after Chief Justice Rehnquist was appointed. As he notes, the law clerks now exercise a major role in the two most important functions of the Justices: (1) the screening of cases to determine which the Court will hear and decide; and (2) the drafting of opinions. "I think Brandeis would be aghast."[40]

In a public lecture, Justice Stevens conceded that he did not read 80 percent of the certiorari petitions presented to the Court.[41] Instead his clerks prepare memoranda summarizing those cases and issues and recommending whether or not certiorari should be granted. The Justice reads only those where the granting of certiorari is recommended. The only member of the Burger and Rehnquist Courts who personally went over petitions for review was Justice Brennan, who customarily shared the work with his law clerks. In a letter to Brennan, who was temporarily away from the Court, his clerks stated, "We are all fascinated by the certs and shudder to think that when you get back you may take some of them away from us. But if you're very nice we won't fight too hard."[42]

In the 1972 Term, Justice Powell urged that the Justices combine their efforts in the screening process by having their clerks work together in one "cert pool."[43] The petitions would be divided equally among all the clerks in the pool, and the cert memos prepared by them would be circulated to each of the Justices participating. The Chief Justice and Justices White, Blackmun, Powell, and Rehnquist agreed to join in the cert pool. Justices

Douglas, Brennan, Stewart, and Marshall declined to participate. In the present Court, only Justice Stevens is not a member of the pool.

While the Justices make the final decision on what certiorari petitions to grant, *the* work on the petitions is done by the law clerks. In the vast majority of cases, the Justices' knowledge of the petitions and the issues they present is based on the clerks' cert memos, and they normally follow the recommendations in their memos. Sheer volume, if nothing else, has made this the prevailing practice.

The Justices themselves have expressed qualms about this delegation of the screening task. In declining to join the cert pool, Justice Douglas wrote to the Chief Justice: "The law clerks are fine. Most of them are sharp and able. But after all, they have never been confirmed by the Senate."[44]

An even more important delegation to the clerks involves the opinion-writing process. "As the years passed," says Justice Douglas in his *Autobiography,* "it became more evident that the law clerks were drafting opinions."[45] Almost all the Justices have made more extensive use of their clerks in the drafting process than outside observers have realized. In recent Courts, indeed, the routine procedure has been for the clerks to draft virtually all opinions.

Chief Justice Rehnquist has candidly described the opinion-writing process. "In my case," Rehnquist said, "the clerks do the first draft of almost all cases to which I have been assigned to write the Court's opinion." Only "when the case-load is heavy" does Rehnquist sometimes "help by doing the first draft of a case myself."[46] Rehnquist concedes that the "practice . . . may undoubtedly . . . cause raised eyebrows." Still, the Chief Justice asserts, "I think the practice is entirely proper: The Justice must retain for himself control not merely of the outcome of the case, but of the explanation of the outcome, and I do not believe this practice sacrifices either."[47]

It is, of course, true that the decisions are made by the Justices— though, even with regard to them, the weaker Justices have abdicated much of their authority to their clerks. In most chambers, the clerks are, to use a favorite expression of Chief Justice Warren, not "unguided missiles." The Justices normally outline the way they want opinions drafted. But the drafting clerk is left with a great deal of discretion. The Justices may "convey the broad outlines," but they "do not invariably settle exactly how the opinion will be reasoned through."[48] The details of the opinions are left to the clerk, in particular the specific reasoning and research supporting the decision. The technical minutiae and footnotes, so dear to the law professor, are left almost completely to the clerks. Thus footnote 11 of the *Brown* school segregation opinion[49]—perhaps the most famous footnote in Supreme Court history—was entirely the product of a Warren law clerk.

To be sure, the Justices themselves go over the drafts, and, said Chief Justice Rehnquist, "I may revise it in toto." But, he also admits, "I may leave it relatively unchanged."[50] Too many of the Justices circulate drafts that are almost wholly the work of their clerks.

The growing number of law clerks has naturally led to an increase in the length, though plainly not the quality, of opinions. What Justice Douglas once wrote about Court opinions has become increasingly true: "We have tended more and more to write a law-review-type of opinion. They plague the Bar and the Bench. They are so long they are meaningless. They are filled with trivia and nonessentials."[51]

Law clerks have a similar academic background and little other experience. For three years they have had drummed into them that the acme of literary style is the law review article. It is scarcely surprising that the standard opinion style has become that of the student-run reviews: colorless, prolix, platitudinous, always error on the side of inclusion, full of lengthy citations and footnotes—and above all dull.[52]

The individual flair that makes the opinions of a Holmes or a Cardozo literary as well as legal gems has become a thing of the past. There is all the difference in the world between writing one's own opinions and reviewing opinions written by someone else. It is hard to see how an editor can be a great judge. Can we really visualize a Holmes coordinating a team of law clerks and editing their drafts?[53]

According to a federal appellate judge, "We need to reduce our dependence on the system of judicial apprenticeships and on a mass production model that will soon swallow us up."[54] In the Supreme Court, as in most institutions, the balance of power has shifted increasingly to the bureaucrats and away from the nominal heads. The Justices have become the managers of a growing corps of law clerks, who increasingly write the opinions even in the most important cases. The swelling system of judicial apprenticeships threatens to repeat the story of the *Sorcerer's Apprentice*.

Rehnquist Jurisprudence

The outstanding point to bear in mind about the Rehnquist Court is that it is a Court that has reflected the general tilt toward the right that characterized American politics before the 1992 election. More than that, under the leadership of the conservative activist who now sits in the center chair, it has begun to shape a new constitutional case law that has already undone some of the work of its predecessors.

The decisions rendered by the Rehnquist Court through 1992 enable us to note a definite change in direction in its jurisprudence. The change has been manifested in the Court's decisions on civil rights and criminal law. In 1989, the Court struck down a Richmond affirmative action plan under which prime contractors awarded city contracts were required to subcontract at least 30 percent of each contract to minority business enterprises. Similar plans had been upheld by the Burger Court, but its successor ruled that, in the absence of proof of intentional discrimination by the city, the Richmond plan might not be upheld. The argument that the city was attempting to remedy societal discrimination, as shown by the disparity between contracts awarded in the past to minority businesses and the city's minority population, was rejected.[55]

Other decisions shifted the burden of proof in civil rights cases, holding that plaintiffs, not employers, had the burden of proving that a job requirement that was shown statistically to screen out minorities was not a "business necessity" and permitted employers to show by only a preponderance of the evidence rather than by clear and convincing evidence (a higher burden of proof) that their refusal to hire someone was based on legitimate and not discriminatory reasons.[56]

The Rehnquist Court also refused to invalidate a death sentence imposed upon a black defendant despite a detailed statistical study which showed that black defendants who killed white victims were far more likely to receive the death penalty than white defendants. The Court stressed that there was no proof "that the decisionmakers in *his* case acted with discriminatory purpose."[57]

Perhaps even more indicative of the changing emphasis of the Rehnquist Court are its decisions which may mark the beginning of a trend in favor of property rights. For the first time in years, the Court relied upon the constitutional prohibition against takings of property without compensation to invalidate governmental action that did not involve public acquisition of property.[58] Noteworthy in those cases was the Court's use of heightened scrutiny to review the merits of land-use regulations in order to decide whether a challenged regulation required judicial invalidation in the absence of compensation. Indeed, the Court implied that claims of unconstitutional takings (whether by acquisition or regulation) now fall into a particularly sensitive constitutional category comparable to that in which freedom of speech claims fall.

Its decisions on takings without compensation may signal a fundamental shift in Bill-of-Rights jurisprudence, with a tilt by the Rehnquist Court in favor of protection of property rights and away from the strong preference given to personal rights by the Warren and Burger Courts. Yet, though there has been a definite tilt to the right since Chief Justice Rehnquist was appointed, the change until now has not led to the overruling of any of the important decisions of the Warren and Burger Courts.

Most important in this respect was the Rehnquist Court's refusal to overrule *Roe v. Wade*—the Burger Court's landmark decision that the constitutionally protected right of privacy includes a woman's decision to have an abortion. Few Supreme Court decisions have been as controversial as that in *Roe v. Wade;* and the Rehnquist Court was strongly urged by the Bush Administration to overrule that decision. The Court, however, expressly declined to do so, though it did narrow its ruling to a limited extent.[59]

The significant Warren Court criminal procedure decisions have also thus far remained a part of the Rehnquist Court jurisprudence. The key Warren Court criminal trilogy—*Gideon, Mapp,* and *Miranda*[60]—are still followed by the Court, though some of their doctrines have been narrowed under Rehnquist's lead. When the Court struck down the legislative apportionment for New York City's Board of Estimate, it did so on the basis of the one-person, one-vote principle laid down in one of the Warren Court's most important decisions.[61]

It would be erroneous to assume, however, that the Rehnquist Court will follow the Burger Court in consolidating and continuing the essential Warren Court heritage. Chief Justice Rehnquist, as indicated, is a conservative activist who gives every indication of being a strong Chief Justice. Like Chief Justice Warren, he proceeded cautiously in his early years as head of the Court. After all, the Supreme Court is not normally the place for innovation. If the Warren Court was an exception to this, that was true primarily in Warren's later years after personnel changes gave him a strong majority willing to follow his lead in remolding so much of the corpus of our constitutional law.

The conservative combination in the Rehnquist Court's early years was a fragile one. Though usually enough to give the Chief Justice a scant majority, it could not be pushed too fast or too far. When the Chief Justice tried too hard to correct what he termed the "excesses" of the Warren Court, his coalition often would splinter and Rehnquist would wind up in disssent.

This has, however, changed with the appointments of Justices Scalia, Kennedy, Souter, and Thomas. They have reinforced the Court's conservative bloc—a change that has given Chief Justice Rehnquist the majority that may enable him to translate his constitutional vision into accepted jurisprudence. It may, indeed, be true that, as the *New York Times* stated in 1991, "[T]he Supreme Court is no longer in transition. It has become the Court it will most likely be for the next generation."[62] The 1991 and 1992 cases indicate that the conservative wing was substantially strengthened by the replacement of Justices Brennan and Marshall by Justices Souter and Thomas.

Particularly significant in this respect were 1991 and 1992 decisions limiting the use of habeas corpus by prisoners,[63] broadening the power of the police to search automobiles,[64] applying the harmless-error doctrine to a constitutional error committed at the trial,[65] and upholding regulations prohibiting abortion counseling, referrals, or advocacy by federally funded clinics.[66] The latter decision, one of the most controversial by the Rehnquist Court, ruled for the first time that the government spending power might be used to restrict First Amendment rights.

In addition, the Court has ruled that the First Amendment's Free Exercise Clause no longer requires that action that burdens a religious practice must be justified by a compelling governmental interest.[67] Burdens on religious practices are now not to be subject to the strict scrutiny that has governed judicial review in other First Amendment cases.

If Chief Justice Rehnquist continues to have a majority that will translate his conservative views into Supreme Court jurisprudence, the history of the Rehnquist Court may turn out to be the reverse image of the Warren Court. The law, like other institutions, has its epochs of ebb and flow.[68] In the face of the probable Rehnquist flood tide, critics of the Burger Court may come to look back upon its receding period with more than a little nostalgia.

A Moderate Core?

It would, nonetheless, be a mistake to think of the Rehnquist Court as a monolithic tribunal inexorably following the Chief Justice in the conservative cast of his jurisprudence. It should, in the first place, be noted that even the most conservative judge may resist governmental intrusions upon the right of privacy—what Justice Brandeis once called "the right to be let alone—the . . . right most valued by civilized men."[69] The Senate hearings on the nominations of Judge Robert Bork and Justice Clarence Thomas to the Supreme Court revealed a remarkable consensus among Americans that there is a constitutionally protected right of privacy, even though it is not enumerated in the rights safeguarded in the Bill of Rights. Justice Antonin Scalia, the most conservative member of the Rehnquist Court, has given indications (for example, in his dissent from a 1989 decision upholding a drug-testing program for customs employees)[70] that he still places the right to privacy in a preferred position.

It was also Justice Scalia and Justice Kennedy (both conservative Reagan appointees), who cast the decisive votes in the 1989 and 1990 decisions ruling that flag burning as a political protest was a protected form of individual expression guaranteed by the Constitution, as well as the 1992 decision striking down a law criminalizing "hate speech" as violative of the First Amendment.[71] It should not be forgotten that conservative thought encompasses a libertarian strain that resists intrusions upon the area of what William Faulkner termed "individual privacy lacking which [one] cannot be an individual and lacking which individuality [one] is not anything at all worth the having or keeping."[72]

More important perhaps is the fact that, during 1992, the conservative Justices in the Rehnquist Court itself divided into two blocs—one composed of the Chief Justice and Justices Scalia and Thomas and the other made up of Justices O'Connor, Kennedy, and Souter. The Justices in the first tend to follow faithfully the Rehnquist agenda of correcting the "excesses" of the Warren and Burger Courts, ultimately leading to overruling of the key decisions of those Courts—particularly that in *Roe v. Wade* and those protecting criminal defendants.

The other group of Justices is more moderate and seems to have taken as their model the second Justice Harlan, now usually seen as the very paradigm of the true conservative judge. Harlan had been the leading conservative in the last years of the Warren Court and he dissented from some of its most important decisions. Harlan's conservative philosophy did not, however, permit him to go along with those who urged the cavalier overruling of those decisions. "Respect for the Courts," Harlan once wrote to another Justice, "is not something that can be achieved by fiat."[73] He applied this principle to refusals to follow prior decisions with which he disagreed. The true conservative, Harlan believed, adhered to stare decisis, normally following even precedents against which he had originally voted.

The Harlan posture in this respect can be best seen in the 1970 case of *Coleman v. Alabama*.[74] At issue was the right to counsel at a preliminary hearing, where the defendants were bound over to the grand jury. At the conference there were seven votes to affirm the conviction, with only Harlan voting the other way. The Justice had dissented from the Warren Court's landmark *Miranda* decision.[75] Despite this, Harlan said at the *Coleman* conference that *Miranda* was "still on the books" and it should be followed here since the preliminary examination was as critical a stage as the custodial interrogation involved in *Miranda*. Ultimately, the Court agreed with Justice Harlan, holding that the conviction had to be reversed because the defendants had not been assigned counsel.

Coleman shows better than anything the Harlan conception of a conservative judge. Such a judge is not to use "judicial fiat" to disregard a precedent any more than he is to establish the precedent by fiat in the first place. While the precedent is "still on the books," it is to be followed in cases to which it logically applies.

This is precisely the approach followed by Justices O'Connor, Kennedy, and Souter in their 1992 refusal to follow the Rehnquist bloc in voting to overrule *Roe v. Wade*.[76] The three Justices wrote a joint opinion that might have been written by Justice Harlan himself. According to them, the rule of law itself requires a respect for precedent. As they see it, the only time stare decisis should not be followed is when the precedent's rule has been found unworkable or the facts have so changed "as to have robbed the old rule of significant application or justification."[77] Only two cases are said to have met these criteria during the past century: *Lochner v. New York*[78] and *Plessy v. Ferguson*.[79] The same was not true of *Roe v. Wade;* it meets none of the criteria and a decision to overrule it would be based only on "a present doctrinal disposition to come out differently from the Court of 1973."[80] To the more moderate conservative, that is not enough to justify failure to follow stare decisis: "[A] decision to overrule should rest on some special reason over and above the belief that a prior case was wrongly decided."[81] Justice Harlan could not have said it better than this quote from the 1992 opinion refusing to overrule *Roe v. Wade*.

It should, however, be recognized that the centrist bloc in the Rehnquist Court is still composed of Justices who are more conservative than their predecessors. The joint opinion may have been unwilling to overrule *Roe,* but it did interpret it more narrowly; indeed, according to the Chief Justice, under its interpretation *"Roe v. Wade* stands as a sort of judicial Potemkin Village . . . a mere facade to give the illusion of reality."[82] Justices O'Connor, Kennedy, and Souter have joined most of the Rehnquist Court decisions that have meant a change in direction in our constitutional law—particularly those involving civil rights, property, and criminal law. If the three Justices have been classified as moderates by Court commentators,[83] that is true only in comparison with the tendency to reweigh first principles of Chief Justice Rehnquist and his adherents.

In his separate opinon in the 1992 abortion case, Justice Blackmun concluded with a poignant observation: "I am 83 years old. I cannot remain on this Court forever, and when I do step down . . . the choice between the two worlds will be made."[84] The Justice was referring to the possible overruling of *Roe v. Wade*. But what he said is also true from a broader perspective. In this sense, the Supreme Court is always at a turning point. The direction it will take—the world it will choose—will depend most of all upon the new Justices who will assume their seats upon the bench. That will be as true of the Rehnquist Court and its successors as it has been of the prior Courts discussed in this volume.

Epilogue

Not long ago, the attitude of Americans to their constitutional system was that described by Burke: "We ought to understand it according to our measure; and to venerate where we are not able presently to comprehend."[1] As the nation begins its third century, Burke's attitude appears as quaint as the costume of his time. During the present century, veneration has too often given way to vituperation, as we have begun to doubt much that had always been taken for granted in the polity. At a minimum, we no longer assume that, with the contemporary constitutional system, the ultimate stage of organic evolution has been reached. We know that the system is continuing to evolve beyond the "perfection" that Americans at the turn of the century assumed it had attained.

American constitutional law in operation has directly reflected the needs of the nation. At the outset, the primary needs of establishing national power on a firm basis and vindicating property rights against excesses of state power were met in the now-classic decisions of the Marshall Court. A generation later, the needs of the society had changed. If the Taney Court was to translate the doctrines of Jacksonian Democracy, and particularly its emphasis on society's rights, into constitutional law, that was true because such doctrines were deemed necessary to the proper development of the polity. In addition, they furthered the growth of corporate enterprise and prevented its restriction by the deadening hand of established monopoly.

If in the latter part of the nineteenth century the Court was to elevate the rights of property to the plane of constitutional immunity, its due process decisions were the necessary legal accompaniment of the industrial conquest of a continent. The excesses of a laissez-faire–stimulated industrialism should not lead us to overlook the vital part it played in American development. Nor should it be forgotten that the decisions exalting property rights may have been a necessary accompaniment of the post–Civil War economic expansion.

The picture has been completely altered during the present century. The Court came to recognize that property rights must be restricted to an extent never before permitted in American law. At the same time, unless the rights of the person are correlatively expanded, the individual will virtually be shorn of constitutional protection—hence the Court's shift in emphasis to the protection of personal rights. The Justices, like the rest of us, were disturbed by the growth of governmental authority and sought to preserve a sphere for individuality even in a society in which the individual stands dwarfed by power concentrations.

One must, however, concede that, despite the Court's efforts, the concentration of governmental power has continued unabated. The second half of the century has, if anything, seen an acceleration in the growth of such power. Indeed, the outstanding feature of the late twentieth century is the power concentrations that increasingly confront the individual. Even a more conservative Court may find it necessary to preserve a sphere for individuality in such a society.

Yeats tells us that "[a]ll states depend for their health upon a right balance between the One, the Few and the Many."[2] The maintenance of that balance is peculiarly the task of the Supreme Court since, following the famous Hughes aphorism, the Constitution is essentially what the judges say it is.[3] It is their unique function to serve as guardians of the organic ark. To enable them to do so effectively, they are armed with the awesome authority to nullify any governmental act deemed by them in conflict with any provisions of the basic document.

The historian who looks at the Supreme Court is struck with the generally successful way in which it has exercised this awesome authority. The Court's jurisprudence has illustrated the antinomy inherent in every system of law: the law must be stable and yet it cannot stand still.[4] The essential outlines of the constitutional system are still those laid down at the beginning in 1787; there is here a continuity in governmental structure that is all but unique in an ever-changing world. But the system still proves workable only because it has been continually reshaped to meet two centuries' changing needs.

There have been aberrations, but in the main the Supreme Court in operation has reflected the history of the nation: the main thrust has been to meet the "felt necessities"[5] of each period in the nation's history.

Now it is for the Rehnquist Court and its successors to construe the Constitution during the next stage of American development. Regardless of the Court's tilt, history gives confidence that, by and large at least, it will do the job so as to remain true to John Marshall's polestar—that we must never forget "it is a *constitution* we are expounding,"[6] a living instrument that must be construed to meet the practical necessities of the contemporary society.

Appendix: The Justices of the Supreme Court

Appointed by President Washington

JAY, JOHN*	1789†–1795	Resigned
Rutledge, John	1789–1791	Resigned
Cushing, William	1789–1810	Died
Wilson, James	1789–1798	Died
Blair, John	1789–1796	Resigned
Iredell, James	1790–1799	Died
Johnson, Thomas	1791–1793	Resigned
Paterson, William	1793–1806	Died
RUTLEDGE, JOHN	1795	Recess appointment; not confirmed
Chase, Samuel	1796–1811	Died
ELLSWORTH, OLIVER	1796–1800	Resigned

Appointed by President John Adams

Washington, Bushrod	1798–1829	Died
Moore, Alfred	1799–1804	Resigned
MARSHALL, JOHN	1801–1835	Died

---

*Block letters designate Chief Justices.

†Date of appointment.

Appointed by President Jefferson

Johnson, William	1804–1834	Died
Livingston, Brockholst	1806–1823	Died
Todd, Thomas	1807–1826	Died

Appointed by President Madison

Duval, Gabriel	1811–1835	Resigned
Story, Joseph	1811–1845	Died

Appointed by President Monroe

Thompson, Smith	1823–1843	Died

Appointed by President John Quincy Adams

Trimble, Robert	1826–1828	Died

Appointed by President Jackson

McLean, John	1829–1861	Died
Baldwin, Henry	1830–1844	Died
Wayne, James M.	1835–1867	Died
TANEY, ROGER B.	1835–1864	Died
Barbour, Philip P.	1835–1841	Died

Appointed by President Van Buren

Catron, John	1837–1865	Died
McKinley, John	1837–1852	Died
Daniel, Peter V.	1841–1860	Died

Appointed by President Tyler

Nelson, Samuel	1845–1872	Resigned

Appointed by President Polk

Woodbury, Levi	1845–1851	Died
Grier, Robert C.	1846–1870	Resigned

Appointed by President Fillmore

Curtis, Benjamin R.	1851–1857	Resigned

Appointed by President Pierce

Campbell, John A.	1853–1861	Resigned

Appointed by President Buchanan

Clifford, Nathan	1858–1881	Died

Appointed by President Lincoln

Swayne, Noah H.	1862–1881	Resigned
Miller, Samuel F.	1862–1890	Died
Davis, David	1862–1877	Resigned
Field, Stephen J.	1863–1897	Resigned
CHASE, SALMON P.	1864–1873	Died

Appointed by President Grant

Strong, William	1870–1880	Resigned
Bradley, Joseph P.	1870–1892	Died
Hunt, Ward	1872–1882	Resigned
WAITE, MORRISON R.	1874–1888	Died

Appointed by President Hayes

Harlan, John Marshall	1877–1911	Died
Woods, William B.	1880–1887	Died

Appointed by President Garfield

Matthews, Stanley	1881–1889	Died

Appointed by President Arthur

Gray, Horace	1881–1902	Died
Blatchford, Samuel	1882–1893	Died

Appointed by President Cleveland

Lamar, Lucius Q. C.	1887–1893	Died
FULLER, MELVILLE W.	1888–1910	Died

Appointed by President Harrison

Brewer, David J.	1889–1910	Died
Brown, Henry B.	1890–1906	Resigned
Shiras, George, Jr.	1892–1903	Resigned
Jackson, Howell E.	1893–1895	Died

Appointed by President Cleveland

White, Edward D.	1894–1910	Appointed Chief Justice
Peckham, Rufus W.	1895–1909	Died

Appointed by President McKinley

McKenna, Joseph	1897–1925	Resigned

Appointed by President Theodore Roosevelt

Holmes, Oliver Wendell	1902–1932	Resigned
Day, William R.	1903–1922	Resigned
Moody, William H.	1906–1910	Resigned

Appointed by President Taft

Lurton, Horace H.	1909–1914	Died
Hughes, Charles E.	1910–1916	Resigned
WHITE, EDWARD D.	1910–1921	Died
Van Devanter, Willis	1910–1937	Retired
Lamar, Joseph R.	1910–1916	Died
Pitney, Mahlon	1912–1922	Retired

Appointed by President Wilson

McReynolds, James C.	1914–1941	Retired
Brandeis, Louis D.	1916–1939	Retired
Clarke, John H.	1916–1922	Resigned

Appointed by President Harding

TAFT, WILLIAM H.	1921–1930	Resigned
Sutherland, George	1922–1938	Retired
Butler, Pierce	1922–1939	Died
Sanford, Edward T.	1923–1930	Died

Appointed by President Coolidge

Stone, Harlan F.	1925–1941	Appointed Chief Justice

Appointed by President Hoover

HUGHES, CHARLES E.	1930–1941	Retired
Roberts, Owen J.	1930–1945	Resigned
Cardozo, Benjamin N.	1932–1938	Died

Appointed by President Franklin D. Roosevelt

Black, Hugo, L.	1937–1971	Retired
Reed, Stanley F.	1938–1957	Retired
Frankfurter, Felix	1939–1962	Retired
Douglas, William O.	1939–1975	Retired
Murphy, Frank	1940–1949	Died
Byrnes, James F.	1941–1942	Resigned
STONE, HARLAN F.	1941–1946	Died

| Jackson, Robert H. | 1941–1954 | Died |
| Rutledge, Wiley B. | 1943–1949 | Died |

Appointed by President Truman

Burton, Harold H.	1945–1958	Retired
VINSON, FRED M.	1946–1953	Died
Clark, Tom C.	1949–1967	Retired
Minton, Sherman	1949–1956	Retired

Appointed by President Eisenhower

WARREN, EARL	1953–1969	Retired
Harlan, John Marshall	1955–1971	Retired
Brennan, William J., Jr.	1956–1990	Retired
Whittaker, Charles E.	1957–1962	Retired
Stewart, Potter	1958–1981	Retired

Appointed by President Kennedy

| White, Byron R. | 1962–1993 | Retired |
| Goldberg, Arthur J. | 1962–1965 | Resigned |

Appointed by President Lyndon B. Johnson

| Fortas, Abe | 1965–1969 | Resigned |
| Marshall, Thurgood | 1967–1991 | Retired |

Appointed by President Nixon

BURGER, WARREN E.	1969–1986	Retired
Blackmun, Harry A.	1970–	
Powell, Lewis F., Jr.	1971–1987	Retired
Rehnquist, William H.	1971–1986	Appointed Chief Justice

Appointed by President Ford

| Stevens, John Paul | 1975– |

Appointed by President Reagan

O'Connor, Sandra Day	1981–
REHNQUIST, WILLIAM H.	1986–
Scalia, Antonin E.	1986–
Kennedy, Anthony M.	1987–

Appointed by President Bush

| Souter, David H. | 1990– |
| Thomas, Clarence | 1991– |

Notes

Introduction

1. *Bartlett's Familiar Quotations* 720 (15th ed. 1980).

2. *Marbury v. Madison,* 1 Cranch 137 (U.S. 1803).

3. Coke himself gives the date as November 10. *Prohibitions del Roy,* 12 Co. Rep. 63 (1608). The correct date, however, seems to have been November 14. See 5 Holdsworth, *A History of English Law* 430 (2d ed. 1937).

4. Holdsworth, op. cit. supra note 3, at 428.

5. *Prohibitions del Roy,* 12 Co. Rep. at 65.

6. Holdsworth, op. cit. supra note 3, at 431.

7. Ibid.

8. 8 Co. Rep. 113b (1610).

9. Id. at 118a.

10. Bowen, *The Lion and the Throne: The Life and Times of Sir Edward Coke* 514 (1956).

11. Schwartz, *The Law in America: A History* 14 (1974).

12. Bowen, op. cit. supra note 10, at 514.

13. Id. at 291.

14. 10 *Works of John Admas* 244–245 (C. F. Adams ed. 1856).

15. Quincy Reports 51 (Mass. 1761). The best account of the case is in 2 *Legal Papers of John Adams* 123 et seq. (Wroth and Zobel eds. 1965).

16. Id. at 141.

17. Qiuncy Reports, Appendix 520–521 (Mass.).

18. Adams, op. cit. supra note 15, at 127–128.

19. Bowen, *John Adams and the American Revolution* 217 (1950).

20. Loc. cit. supra note 17.

21. Bowen, op. cit. supra note 10, at 316.

22. Id. at 520.

23. 2 Farrand, *The Records of the Federal Convention of 1787,* 73 (1937).

24. Wood, *The Creation of the American Republic* 538 (1969).

25. The case was unreported and the best account of it is in Scott, *Holmes vs. Walton:* The New Jersey Precedent: A Chapter in the History of Judicial Power and Unconstitutional Legislation, 4 *American Historical Review* 456 (1899).

26. Id. at 459–460; Goebel, *History of the Supreme Court of the United States: Antecedents and Beginnings to 1801,* 124 (1971).

27. Scott, op. cit. supra note 25, at 459, 464.

28. *State v. Parkhurst,* 9 N.J.L. 427, 444 (1802).

29. 4 Call 5 (Va. 1782).

30. Id. at 20.

31. Id. at 8. Pendleton's notes were sketchy on Wythe's opinion, but they confirm the essentials of the Call account. 2 *The Letters and Papers of Edmund Pendleton* 426 (Mays ed. 1961). See Goebel, op. cit. supra note 26, at 127–128.

32. Pendleton, op. cit. supra note 31, at 422. See 2 Mays, *Edmund Pendleton 1721–1803: A Biography* 200 (1952).

33. Edmund Pendleton to James Madison, Nov. 8, 1782. Mays, op. cit. supra note 32, at 201.

34. Id. at 202.

35. So characterized in Goebel, op. cit. supra note 26, at 131.

36. The best account is in 1 *The Law Practice of Alexander Hamilton* 282–419 (Goebel ed. 1964).

37. Id. at 305.

38. Morris, *Witnesses at the Creation* 45 (1985).

39. Varnum, *The Case, Trevett against Weeden* (Providence 1787).

40. So characterized in Wood, op. cit. supra note 24, at 460.

41. Quoted ibid.

42. *Newport Mercury,* Oct. 6, 1786.

43. 1 N.C. 42 (1787).

44. Id. at 45.

45. 2 McRee, *Life and Correspondence of James Iredell* 169, 172–173 (1858).

46. Op. cit. supra note 36, at 312.

47. Id. at 314.

48. Goebel, op. cit. supra note 26, at 140.

49. Farrand, op. cit. supra note 23, at 28. Madison's account was not completely acccurate. See Goebel, op. cit. supra note 26, at 141.

50. 3 Farrand, op. cit. supra note 23, at 13.

51. *Penhallow v. Doane,* 3 Dall. 54, 80 (U.S. 1795).

52. 1 Farrand, op. cit. supra note 23, at 34.

53. Id. at 30.

54. Id. at 21.

55. Farrand, *The Framing of the Constitution* 154 (1913).

56. Id. at 80.

57. 1 Farrand, op. cit. supra note 23, at 21; 2 id at 298.

58. 1 id. at 97.

59. 2 id. at 73.

60. Infra note 65.

61. Farrand, op. cit. supra note 23, at 78.

62. Id. at 76. See also 1 id. at 109 (Rufus King); 2 id. at 28 (Gouverneur Morris); id. at 27 (Roger Sherman).

63. Id. at 299.

64. Wood, op. cit. supra note 24, at 304.

65. 2 Farrand, op. cit. supra note 23, at 93.

66. Goebel, op. cit. supra note 26, at 388.

67. Id. at 310.

68. 4 *Documentary History of the Supreme Court of the United States, 1789–1800,* 11 (1992).

69. Goebel, op. cit. supra note 26, at 311.

70. *The Federalist,* No. 78.

71. Ibid.

72. 1 Cranch 137 (U.S. 1803).

73. Op. cit. supra note 68, at 427.

74. Id. at 474.

75. Frankfurter and Landis, *The Business of the Supreme Court* 189 (1927).

76. 1 Warren, *The Supreme Court in United States History* 449 (1924).

77. Op. cit. supra note 68, at 417.

Chapter 1

1. Caplan, *The Tenth Justice* 162 (1987).

2. 1 Warren, *The Supreme Court in United States History* 48 (1924) [hereinafter cited as Warren].

3. 3 *Dictionary of American Biography* 635 (1930).

4. 1 Warren 48.

5. No. 78.

6. *Felix Frankfurter on the Supreme Court* 472 (Kurland ed. 1970).

7. 1 *The Documentary History of the Supreme Court of the United States, 1789–1800,* 688 (1985) [hereinafter cited as *Documentary*].

8. 10 *The Writings of George Washington* 34–36 (Sparks ed. 1847).

9. 1 *Documentary* 619.

10. Id. at 661.

11. Id. at 9.

12. Id. at 712.

13. Id. at 700–701.

14. Id. at 706.

15. Id. at 692.

16. Ibid.

17. Id. at 700.

18. Id. at 731.

19. 3 id. at 240.

20. 2 id. at 132.

21. 1 id. at 732.

22. 2 id. at 126.

23. Id. at 344.

24. Id. at 288.

25. Id. at 289–290.

26. Id. at 290.

27. Ibid.

28. Goebel, *History of the Supreme Court of the United States: Antecedents and Beginnings to 1801,* 567 (1971).

29. 2 *Documentary* 345.

30. 1 id. at 875.

31. 2 Dall. 402 (U.S. 1792).

32. Conway, *Omitted Chapters of History Disclosed in the Life and Papers of Edmund Randolph* 168 (1889).

33. 2 Dall. 419 (U.S. 1793).

34. Id. at 429.

35. Id. at 456.

36. Id. at 453, 457.

37. Id. at 466.

38. 1 Warren 496.

39. 1 Cranch 137 (U.S. 1803).

40. See Schwartz, *The Great Rights of Mankind: A History of the American Bill of Rights* 95–100 (expanded ed. 1992).

41. Infra.

42. 3 Dall. 199 (U.S. 1796).

43. 1 *Documentary* 754.

44. 3 Dall. at 201.

45. 2 Beveridge, *The Life of John Marshall* 187 (1916).

46. 3 Dall. at 236–237.

47. 3 Dall. 386 (U.S. 1798).

48. Id. at 399.

49. Id. at 387–388.

50. Id. at 392.

51. 3 Dall. 171 (U.S. 1796).

52. Quoted in Corwin, *The Constitution of the United States of America: Analysis and Interpretation* 318 (1953).

53. 3 Dall. at 181.

54. Id. at 171.

55. Id. at 175.

56. Ibid.

57. Id. at 172.

58. Compare Bickel, *The Least Dangerous Branch* 71 (1986).

59. Jackson, *The Supreme Court in the American System of Government* 11 (1955).

60. *Muskrat v. United States,* 219 U.S. 346, 361 (1911).

61. Hughes, *The Supreme Court of the United States* 30 (1936).

62. See *United States v. Congress of Industrial Organizations,* 335 U.S. 106, 124 (1948).

63. 3 *The Correspondence and Public Papers of John Jay* 487–489 (Johnston ed. 1891).

64. Hughes, loc. cit. supra note 61.

65. *Alabama Federation of Labor v. McAdory,* 325 U.S. 450, 451 (1945).

66. *Giles v. Harris,* 189 U.S. 475, 486 (1903).

67. *United States v. Congress of Industrial Organizations,* 335 U.S. at 125.

68. 2 Dall. 409 (U.S. 1792).

69. See id. at 409–410.

70. *United States v. Ferreira,* 13 How. 40, 50 (U.S. 1851).

71. 1 Warren 71.
72. 2 Dall. at 411.
73. Id. at 411–412.
74. 1 Warren 72. See Goebel, op. cit. supra note 28, at 561.
75. *United States v. Ferreira,* 13 How. at 53.
76. 1 Warren 71.
77. Id. at 72.
78. Id. at 73.
79. Goebel, op. cit. supra note 28, at 562.
80. Conway, op. cit. supra note 32, at 145.
81. 1 *Documentary* 913–914.
82. Id. at 759.
83. Id. at 816.
84. Id. at 834.
85. Id. at 840.
86. Id. at 847, 842.
87. Id. at 842.
88. Goebel, op. cit. supra note 28, at 777, 849.
89. Id. at 778.
90. 3 Dall. 321 (U.S. 1796).
91. Id. at 327.
92. Id. at 326.
93. *Barry v. Mercein,* 5 How. 103, 119 (U.S. 1847).
94. *Daniels v. Railroad Co.,* 3 Wall. 250, 254 (U.S. 1866).
95. 1 *Documentary* 857.
96. Id. at 895.
97. Id. at 894.
98. Id. at 900.
99. 1 Warren 208–209.
100. 1 Cranch 299 (U.S. 1803).
101. Id. at 309.

Chapter 2

1. Haskins and Johnson, *History of the Supreme Court of the United States: Foundations of Power: John Marshall, 1801–1815,* 75 (1981).
2. 2 Beveridge, *The Life of John Marshall* 121 (1919).
3. Haskins and Johnson, op. cit. supra note 1, at 79.
4. *Selected Writings of Benjamin Nathan Cardozo* 179 (Hall ed. 1947).
5. 9 *Memoirs of John Quincy Adams* 243 (C. F. Adams ed. 1876).
6. 1 *The Documentary History of the Supreme Court of the United States, 1789–1800,* 147 (1985).
7. John Marshall's Autobiographical Letter, 1827, reprinted in Schwartz, *A Basic History of the U.S. Supreme Court* 102 (1968).
8. Ibid.
9. Op. cit. supra note 6, at 903.
10. Loc. cit. supra note 7.
11. Op. cit. supra note 6, at 918.
12. Ibid.
13. Id. at 920–921.

14. Id. at 925. The letter has apparently been lost.

15. Schwartz, op. cit. supra note 7, at 103.

16. Op. cit. supra note 6, at 929–930.

17. Hooker, John Marshall on the Judiciary, the Republicans, and Jefferson, March 4, 1801, 53 *American Historical Review* 518, 519 (1948).

18. 1 Warren, *The Supreme Court in United States History* 178 (1924).

19. *The Mind and Faith of Justice Holmes* 385 (Lerner ed. 1943).

20. Warren, *A History of the American Bar* 402 (1913).

21. 1 Story, *Commentaries on the Constitution of the United States* v (1833).

22. Schwartz, op. cit. supra note 7, at 99.

23. Id. at 100.

24. 1 *The Papers of John Marshall* 41 (Johnson ed. 1974).

25. 1 Beveridge, op. cit. supra note 2, at 154.

26. Id. at 159–160.

27. *Felix Frankfurter on the Supreme Court* 536 (Kurland ed. 1970).

28. Frank, *Marble Palace: The Supreme Court in American Life* 62 (1958).

29. 1 Beveridge, op. cit. supra note 2, at 119.

30. *An Autobiographical Sketch by John Marshall* 9 (Adams ed. 1973).

31. Corwin, *John Marshall and the Constitution* (1919).

32. Haskins and Johnson, op. cit. supra note 1, at 82.

33. Warren, op. cit. supra note 18, at 185.

34. Haskins and Johnson, op. cit. supra note 1, at 80.

35. Id. at 82.

36. Ibid.

37. Id. at 104–105.

38. *The Miscellaneous Writings of Joseph Story* 692 (W. W. Story ed. 1852).

39. Quoted in Warren, op. cit. supra note 20, at 421.

40. *McCulloch v. Maryland,* 4 Wheat. 316, 407 (U.S. 1819).

41. *Felix Frankfurter Reminisces* 166 (Phillips ed. 1960) (emphasis omitted).

42. Op. cit. supra note 6, at 926.

43. Beveridge, op. cit. supra note 2, at 16.

44. Ibid.

45. Haskins and Johnson, op. cit. supra note 1, at 382.

46. Morgan, *Justice William Johnson: The First Dissenter* 182 (1954).

47. Thayer, Holmes, and Frankfurter, *John Marshall* 142 (1967).

48. 1 Cranch 137 (U.S. 1803).

49. Schwartz, *The Unpublished Opinions of the Burger Court* 219 (1988).

50. Id. at 279.

51. 1 Adams, *History of the United States of America during the First Administration of Thomas Jefferson* 275 (1903).

52. Warren, op. cit. supra note 18, at 232.

53. *Dred Scott v. Sanford,* 19 How. 393 (U.S. 1857). It is true that a section of the Judiciary Act was declared unconstitutional in *Hodgson v. Bowerbank,* 5 Cranch 303 (U.S. 1800). But the opinion there was essentially unreasoned, attracted no notice at the time, and has been virtually ignored by commentators.

54. See supra p. 6.

55. See Gipson, *The Coming of the Revolution* 53–54 (1954).

56. See supra pp. 7–10.

57. 1 Cranch at 180.

58. Supra p. 23.

59. Beveridge, op. cit. supra note 2, at 118.

60. Corwin, *John Marshall and the Constitution* 70, 67 (1919).

61. 1 Cranch at 177–178.

62. 3 *Howell's State Trials* 45 (1627).

63. Holmes, *Collected Legal Papers* 295–296 (1920).

64. 6 Cranch 87 (U.S. 1810).

65. Id. at 136.

66. 1 Wheat. 304 (U.S. 1816).

67. 4 Beveridge, op. cit. supra note 2, at 164.

68. 6 Wheat. 264 (U.S. 1821).

69. Id. at 415.

70. 4 Beveridge, op. cit. supra note 2, at 343.

71. Corwin, op. cit. supra note 60, at 225.

72. 4 Wheat. 316 (U.S. 1819).

73. 8 *The Papers of Alexander Hamilton* 102 (Syrett ed. 1965).

74. 4 Wheat. at 421.

75. *John Marshall's Defense of* McCulloch v. Maryland 93, 99 (Gunther ed. 1969).

76. Warren, *The Story–Marshall Correspondence (1810–1831)* 3 (1942).

77. 4 Wheat. at 436, 433.

78. Id. at 436.

79. 9 Wheat. 1 (U.S. 1824).

80. Id. at 210–211.

81. Article I, section 8.

82. 9 Wheat. at 189–190.

83. Id. at 196.

84. White, *History of the Supreme Court of the United States: The Marshall Court and Cultural Change, 1815–35,* 578–579 (1988).

85. Douglas, *We the Judges* 192 (1956).

86. Wickard v. Filburn, 317 U.S. 111, 120 (1941).

87. 39 *Annals of Congress* 1833 (1822). There had been a similar veto by President Madison in 1817. 8 *The Writings of James Madison* 386 (Hunt ed. 1908).

88. 2 Parrington, *Main Currents in American Thought: The Romantic Revolution in America* 22 (1954).

89. See White, op. cit. supra note 84, at 597.

90. *Ogden v. Saunders,* 12 Wheat. 213, 346 (U.S. 1827).

91. 4 Beveridge, op. cit. supra note 2, at 479.

92. *Coster v. Lorillard,* 14 Wend. 265, 374–375 (N.Y. 1835).

93. See 4 Kent, *Commentaries on American Law* 3 (1830).

94. Dodd, *American Business Corporations until 1860,* 13 (1954).

95. *Barrow Steamship Co. v. Kane,* 170 U.S. 103, 106 (1898).

96. *Sutton's Hospital Case,* 10 Co. Rep. 1a, 23a, 32b (1612).

97. *Dartmouth College v. Woodward,* 4 Wheat. 518 (U.S. 1819).

98. Id. at 636.

99. Maine, *Popular Government* 248 (1886).

100. 1 *Life and Letters of Joseph Story* 331 (W. W. Story ed. 1851).

101. According to Wright, *Economic History of the United States* 388 (1941), the first frequent use of the corporation in this country came in the 1820s and 1830s—i.e., after the Dartmouth College decision.

102. White, op. cit. supra note 84, at 828.

103. 12 Wheat. 64 (U.S. 1827).

104. 2 Warren, op. cit. supra note 18, at 156–157.

105. Marshall to Bushrod Washington, July 12, 1823, Marshall Papers, Library of Congress. Marshall's circuit court decision is not reported. See 2 *The Papers of John Marshall: A Descriptive Calendar* (Rhodes ed. 1969).

106. 2 Warren, op. cit. supra note 18, at 157.

107. Warren, op. cit. supra note 76, at 20.

108. White, op. cit. supra note 84, at 791.

109. Id. at 751.

110. 2 Tocqueville, *Democracy in America* 166 (Bradley ed. 1954).

111. Compare White, op. cit. supra note 84, at 751.

112. 2 Wheat. 66 (U.S. 1817).

113. Id. at 72, 75, 76.

114. *Hopkirk v. Page,* 2 Brockenburgh 20, 41 (Cir. Ct. 1822).

115. 2 Wheat. at 74.

116. Loc. cit. supra note 114.

117. Compare White, op. cit. supra note 84, at 798.

118. *Swift v. Tyson,* 16 Pet. 1, 20 (U.S. 1842).

119. White, op. cit. supra note 84, at 813.

120. Id. at 828.

121. 10 *The Writings of Thomas Jefferson* 140 (Ford ed. 1899).

122. Beveridge, op. cit. supra note 2, at 78.

123. Supra note 75, at 1.

124. Id. at 16.

125. The quotes from the Roane and Marshall essays are taken from op. cit. supra note 75.

126. Supra p. 38.

127. Ibid.

128. Beveridge, op. cit. supra note 2, at 144.

129. Id. at 157 (italics omitted).

130. Warren, op. cit. supra note 18, at 294–295.

131. Elsmere, *Justice Samuel Chase* 225 (1980); 2 Adams, op. cit. supra note 51, at 227.

132. Beveridge, op. cit. supra note 51, at 227.

133. *N.Y. Times,* Dec. 16, 1991, at B11.

134. Warren, op. cit. supra note 18, at 250.

135. 4 Beveridge, op. cit. supra note 2, at 60.

136. *Jacobellis v. Ohio,* 378 U.S. 184, 197 (1964).

137. Holmes, *The Common Law* 1 (1881).

138. Morgan, op. cit. supra note 46, at 289.

139. Supra note 79.

140. 4 Beveridge, op. cit. supra note 2, at 443.

141. Morgan, op. cit. supra note 46, at 288.

142. Op. cit. supra note 100, at 84.

143. Quoted in Dunne, *Justice Joseph Story and the Rise of the Supreme Court* 77 (1970).

144. Quoted id. at 91.

145. Supra note 66.

146. Supra note 103.

147. Id. at 70.

148. Quoted in 2 Warren, op. cit. supra note 18, at 157.

149. Story, *Commentaries on the Constitution* § 148.

150. *Van Ness v. Pacard,* 2 Pet. 137, 144 (U.S. 1829).

151. 2 Pet. 137 (U.S. 1829).

152. Dunne, op. cit. supra note 143, at 283.

153. Fixtures, 10 *The American Jurist and Law Magazine* 53 (1833).

154. 2 Pet. at 145.

155. 2 Story, op. cit. supra note 142, at 318.

156. Morgan, op. cit. supra note 46, at 182.

157. Warren, op. cit. supra note 18, at 464.

158. Haskins and Johnson, op. cit. supra note 1, at 99.

159. 6 Fed. Cas. 546 (C.C.E.D. Pa. 1823).

160. Particularly in the *Slaughter-House Cases,* 16 Wall. 36 (U.S. 1873).

161. Haskins and Johnson, op. cit. supra note 1, at 101.

162. Morgan, op. cit. supra note 46.

163. Op. cit. supra note 27, at 540.

164. Morgan, op. cit. supra note 46, at 178, 189.

165. Id. at 181–182.

166. Id. at 183.

167. Id. at 185.

168. Id. at 190.

169. Id. at 157.

170. Supra note 72.

171. Morgan, op. cit. supra note 46, Chapter VII.

172. *Anderson v. Dunn,* 6 Wheat. 204 (U.S. 1821).

173. Morgan, op. cit. supra note 46, at 123–124.

174. Id. at 125.

175. 4 Beveridge, op. cit. supra note 2, at 359.

176. Ibid.

177. White, op. cit. supra note 84, at 327.

178. Op. cit. supra note 100, at 499.

179. See White, op. cit. supra note 84, at 316.

180. Op. cit. supra note 4, at 342–343.

181. Corwin, op. cit. supra note 60, at 124.

182. Baker, *John Marshall: A Life in Law* 353 (1974).

183. Id. at 65.

184. Marshall, letter headed "Washington, November 27, 1800," no addressee, Marshall Papers, Library of Congress.

185. Warren, op. cit. supra note 18, at 15.

186. Marshall to Samuel Chase, Jan. 23, 1804, Marshall Papers, Library of Congress.

187. 2 Beveridge, op. cit. supra note 2, at 437.

188. Compare Corwin, op. cit. supra ntoe 60, at 123–124.

189. Holmes, *The Common Law* 1.

190. Compare ibid.

191. Marshall to Richard Peters, July 21, 1815, Marshall Papers, Library of Congress.

Chapter 3

1. White, *History of the Supreme Court of the United States: The Marshall Court and Cultural Change, 1815–35,* 157 (1988).

2. 1 Warren, *The Supreme Court in United States History* 460 (1924).

3. 2 *American Law Register* 750, 706 (1954).

4. 2 Warren, op. cit. supra note 2, at 252.

5. Id. at 461.

6. Butler, *A Century at the Bar of the Supreme Court of the United States* 29 (1942).

7. Id. at 29–30.

8. Quoted in Lewis, *Without Fear or Favor: A Biography of Chief Justice Roger Brooke Taney* 250 (1965).

9. Actually, Taney presided over the Court on August 1, 1836, but no other Justice was present and the Court was adjourned until the January Term. See Frankfurter, *The Commerce Clause under Marshall, Taney and Waite* 46 (1964).

10. 2 *Life and Letters of Joseph Story* 227, 226 (W. W. Story ed. 1851).

11. 9 *Memoirs of John Quincy Adams* 243–244 (C. F. Adams ed. 1876).

12. Quoted in Schwartz, *The American Heritage History of the Law in America* 111 (1974).

13. Op. cit. supra note 10, at 277.

14. Id. at 173.

15. Letter from J. Q. Adams to General P. Porter, Jan. 11, 1831, Parke-Bernet Galleries, Sale No. 3103, Item 3 (1970).

16. 2 Richardson, *A Compilation of the Messages and Papers of the Presidents 1789–1897,* 576–591 (1896).

17. Letter from Joseph Story to Richard Peters, July 24, 1835, op. cit. supra note 10, at 202.

18. Richardson, op. cit. supra note 16, at 582.

19. Quoted in Warren, op. cit. supra note 2 at 284.

20. Id. at 290.

21. Letter from John Tyler to Mrs. Mary Jones, Jan. 20, 1836, Charles Hamilton, Auction No. 12, Item 190 (1966).

22. Letter from Francis Scott Key to Mrs. R. B. Taney, Mar. 15, 1836, Charles Hamilton, Auction No. 24, Item 183 (1968). Amos Kendall was nominated as Postmaster General and Phillip P. Barbour as a Supreme Court Justice.

23. See 2 Poore *Perley's Reminiscences of Sixty Years in the National Metropolis* 85 (1886).

24. See Swisher, *Roger B. Taney* 359 (1935).

25. Smith, *Roger B. Taney: Jacksonian Jurist* 3 (1936).

26. Orestes A. Brownson, quoted in Schlesinger, *The Age of Jackson* 312 (1945).

27. Letter from Roger B. Taney to Andrew Jackson, Mar. 17, 1836, in 5 Bassett, *Correspondence of Andrew Jackson* 390 (1933). The reference at the end of the letter is to Martin Van Buren, whom the Senate had refused to confirm as Minister to England in 1831.

28. Taney states that he was "mortified" by one of these early defeats. Lewis, supra note 8, at 38.

29. His autobiography is contained in Tyler, *Memoir of Roger Brooke Taney, LL.D.* 17–95 (1872).

30. Id. at 78, 79.

31. Letter from Roger B. Taney to James M. Campbell, Dec. 21, 1845, Parke-Bernet Galleries, Sale No. 2310, Item 125 (1964).

32. Letter from Roger B. Taney to James M. Campbell, Jan. 18, 1841, Parke-Bernet Galleries, Sale No. 2310, Item 125 (1964).

33. Compare Adler, *The Great Ideas: A Syntopicon, 2 Great Books of the Western World* 305, 221 (1952).

34. Richardson, op. cit. supra note 16, at 590.

35. Compare Harris, *The Quest for Equality* 17 (1960).

36. Frankfurter, op. cit. supra note 9, at 4.

37. See Story, J., dissenting, in *New York v. Miln,* 11 Pet. 102, 161 (U.S. 1837); *Briscoe v. Bank of Kentucky,* 11 Pet. 257, 328, 350 (U.S. 1837). It is probable that Marshall, after the first argument, had opted in favor of constitutionality in the *Charles River Bridge* case, the third of the key 1837 decisions. Kutler, *Privilege and Creative Destruction: The Charles River Bridge Case* 172–179 (1971); Dunne, *Justice Joseph Story and the Rise of the Supreme Court* 364 (1970).

38. *Charles River Bridge v. Warren Bridge,* 11 Pet. 420, 548 (U.S. 1837).

39. 11 Pet. 420 (U.S. 1837).

40. 2 Warren, op. cit. supra note 2, at 295–296.

41. Op. cit. supra note 11, at 267.

42. 11 Pet. at 546.

43. Id. at 547, 548.

44. Letter from Joseph Story to Mrs. Joseph Story, Feb. 14, 1837, op. cit. supra note 10, at 268.

45. 11 Pet. at 608.

46. *Dartmouth College v. Woodward,* 4 Wheat. 518 (U.S. 1819).

47. 11 Pet. at 552–553, per Taney, C. J.

48. Id. at 598.

49. *Felix Frankfurter on the Supreme Court* 121 (Kurland ed. 1970).

50. Letter from Joseph Story to Harriet Martineau, Apr. 7, 1837, op. cit. supra note 10, at 277.

51. Letter from Daniel Webster to Joseph Story, n.d., id. at 269.

52. Campbell, J., dissenting, in *Piqua Branch v. Knoop,* 16 How. 369, 409 (U.S. 1853).

53. 11 Pet. 257 (U.S. 1837); 11 Pet. 102 (U.S. 1837).

54. *Briscoe v. Bank of Kentucky,* 11 Pet. at 328, 350.

55. Compare Swisher, op. cit. supra note 24, at 375.

56. Jackson, Farewell Address, 3 Richardson, op. cit. supra note 16, at 305.

57. Compare Frankfurter, op. cit. supra note 9, at 69.

58. 8 Adams, op. cit. supra note 11, at 315–316.

59. 11 Pet. at 139, 141.

60. Id. at 142.

61. The cases are cited in *Edwards v. California,* 314 U.S. 160, 176–177 (1941).

62. *Matter of Chirillo,* 283 N.Y. 417, 436 (1940) (dissenting opinion).

63. *Edwards v. California,* 314 U.S. 160, 177 (1941). For a more recent case, see *Shapiro v. Thompson,* 394 U.S. 618 (1969).

64. Swisher, op. cit. supra note 24, at 309.

65. 11 Pet. at 552.

66. 5 How. 504, 583 (U.S. 1847).

67. See *Passenger Cases,* 7 How. 283, 424 (U.S. 1849).

68. *West River Bridge v. Dix,* 6 How. 507, 532 (U.S. 1848).

69. 7 Cush. 53 (Mass. 1851).

70. *State v. Searcy,* 20 Mo. 489, 490 (1855).

71. Corwin, The Doctrine of Due Process of Law before the Civil War, 24 *Harvard Law Review* 460, 461 (1911).

72. *Charles River Bridge v. Warren Bridge,* 11 Pet. at 547.

73. *License Cases,* 5 How. at 579.

74. Supra note 53.

75. 5 How. 504 (U.S. 1847).

76. 7 How. 283 (U.S. 1849).

77. Rutledge, *A Declaration of Legal Faith* 33 (1947).

78. Id. at 45.

79. Compare *Gibbons v. Ogden,* 9 Wheat. 1, 226 (U.S. 1824).

80. 11 Pet. at 158.

81. 2 Pet. 245 (U.S. 1829).

82. Id. at 251.

83. *License Cases,* 5 How. at 579.

84. Ibid.

85. 9 Wheat. 1 (U.S. 1824); supra p. 47.

86. Id. at 181.

87. Id. at 178.

88. Frankfurter, op. cit. supra note 9, at 24.

89. 13 How. 299 (U.S. 1852).

90. Letter from Benjamin R. Curtis to Mr. Ticknor, Feb. 29, 1852, 1 *Memoir of Benjamin Robbins Curtis, LL.D.* 168 (1879).

91. *Dred Scott v. Sandford,* 19 How. 393 (U.S. 1857).

92. Blaustein and Mersky, Rating Supreme Court Justices, 58 *American Bar Association Journal* 1183, 1185 (1972).

93. Quoted in 2 Friedman and Israel, *The Justices of the United States Supreme Court* 905 (1969).

94. He did not graduate, having left halfway through his course to work in a law office.

95. For the Curtis argument, see The Case of the Slave Med, 2 op. cit. supra note 90, at 69.

96. Quoted in Swisher, *History of the Supreme Court of the United States: The Taney Period 1836–64,* 239 (1974).

97. Frankfurter, op. cit. supra note 9, at 57.

98. Warren, op. cit. supra note 2, at 429.

99. Swisher, *American Constitutional Development* 205 (1943).

100. Op. cit. supra note 90, at 168.

101. Compare Powell, *Vagaries and Varieties in Constitutional Interpretation* 152–153 (1956).

102. 9 Wheat. at 14.

103. 12 How. at 318.

104. Id. at 319.

105. Ibid.

106. Ibid.

107. *Crandall v. Nevada,* 6 Wall. 35, 42 (U.S. 1868).

108. Op. cit. supra note 90, at 168.

109. The phrase of Holmes, J., in *Le Roy Fibre Co. v. Chicago, Mil. & St. P. Ry.*, 232 U.S. 340, 354 (1914).

110. *California v. Zook,* 336 U.S. 725, 728 (1949).

111. *Southern Pacific Co. v. Arizona,* 325 U.S. 761, 767 (1945).

112. *United States V. South-Eastern Underwriters Assn'n.,* 322 U.S. 533, 548 (1944).

113. *Parker v. Brown,* 317 U.S. 341, 362 (1943).

114. Gillette, in op. cit. supra note 93, at 901.

115. Frankfurter, op. cit. supra note 9, at 164.

116. Jackson Bank Veto Message, Richardson, op. cit. supra note 16, at 590.

117. William Leggett, quoted in Commager, *The Era of Reform,* 1830–1860, 94 (1960).

118. 3 Richardson, op. cit. supra note 16, at 305–306.

119. Speech by Taney, Aug. 6, quoted in Swisher, op. cit. supra note 24, at 297.

120. Quoted in Smith, op. cit. supra note 25, at 67.

121. Corporations, 4 *American Jurist* 298 (1830), in *The Golden Age of American Law* (Haar ed. 1965).

122. Letter from Peter V. Daniel to Martin Van Buren, Dec. 16, 1841, quoted in Frank, *Justice Daniel Dissenting: A Biography of Peter V. Daniel, 1784–1860,* 164 (1964).

123. 13 Pet. 519 (U.S. 1839).

124. Warren, op. cit. supra note 2, at 324.

125. Ibid.

126. Ibid.

127. 13 Pet. at 567.

128. Id. at 592.

129. Compare Lewis, op. cit. supra note 8, at 292.

130. Compare Frankfurter, op. cit. supra note 9, at 64–65.

131. Quoted in Tyler, op. cit. supra note 29, at 288.

132. Quoted in Warren, op. cit. supra note 2, at 332.

133. *Barrow Steamship Co. v. Kane,* 170 U.S. 100, 106 (1898).

134. Letter from John J. Crittenden to J. Meredith, 1842, Charles Hamilton, Auction No. 19, Item 340 (1967).

135. Concurring, in *Brown v. Allen,* 344 U.S. 443, 540 (1953).

136. Taney had been a leader of the Federalist party in Maryland before the War of 1812.

137. 4 *The Diary of James K. Polk during His Presidency* 137 (Quaife ed. 1910).

138. Id. at 138.

139. Letter from Roger B. Taney to Martin Van Buren, May 8, 1860, quoted in Lewis, op. cit. supra note 8, at 164.

140. Ibid.

141. Charge to the grand jury, Circuit Court of the U.S., April Term, 1836, Taney's Circuit Court Reports 615, 616.

142. Letter from Roger B. Taney to the Secretary of the Treasury, Feb. 16, 1863, quoted in Tyler, op. cit. supra note 29, at 433.

143. 21 How. 506 (U.S. 1859).

144. Id. at 514, 525.

145. Id. at 515, 517.

146. Id. at 518, 522–523.

147. Letter from J. H. Eaton to Andrew Jackson, Apr. 13, 1829, Charles Hamilton, Auction No. 25, Item 141 (1968).

148. See Richardson, op. cit. supra note 16, at 458.

149. *Worcester v. Georgia,* 6 Pet. 515 (U.S. 1832).

150. 8 op. cit. supra note 11, at 262–263.

151. Compare Warren, op. cit. supra note 2, at 219, with James, *The Life of Andrew Jackson* 603–604 (1938).

152. See Freehling, *Prelude to Civil War: The Nullification Controversy in South Carolina, 1816–1836,* 233 (1966).

153. Letter from Andrew Jackson to John Coffee, Apr. 7, 1832, 4 Bassett, op. cit. supra note 27, at 430.

154. Compare Frankfurter, op. cit. supra note 9, at 71.

155. Acheson, Roger Brooke Taney: Notes upon Judicial Self Restraint, 31 *Illinois Law Review* 705 (1937).

156. The famous term of Frankfurter, J., in *Colegrove v. Green,* 328 U.S. 549, 556 (1946).

157. Dissenting, in *Pennsylvania v. Wheeling & B. Bridge Co.,* 13 How. 518 (U.S. 1852).

158. 13 How. 518 (U.S. 1852).

159. Quoted in Warren, op. cit. supra note 2, at 509.

160. Quoted in Frank, op. cit. supra note 122, at 198.

161. The Court had original jurisdiction over such an action brought by a state.

162. Compare Frank, loc. cit. supra note 160.

163. 10 Stat. 112 (1852).

164. *Pennsylvania v. Wheeling & B. Bridge Co.,* 18 How. 421 (U.S. 1856).

165. *Decatur v. Paulding,* 14 Pet. 497, 516 (U.S. 1840).

166. *Kentucky v. Dennison,* 24 How. 66, 109–110 (U.S. 1861).

167. 7 How. 1 (U.S. 1849).

168. Id. at 42.

169. Id. at 43.

170. Now 10 U.S.C. § 331.

171. 7 How. at 43.

172. See Acheson, op. cit. supra note 155, at 714.

173. Swisher, op. cit. supra note 96, at 12.

174. 1 Hoar, *Autobiography of Seventy Years* 141 (1905).

175. Though Justices McLean and Wayne had served briefly under Marshall, they played no significant role in his Court.

176. Op. cit. supra note 10, at 277.

177. Swisher, op. cit. supra note 96, at 45.

178. 8 op. cit. supra note 11, at 304.

179. 3 Warren, op. cit. supra note 2, at 122.

180. 2 id. at 543.

181. Ibid.

182. Ibid.

183. Swisher, op. cit. supra note 96, at 47.

184. Warren, op. cit. supra note 2, at 644.

185. Weisenberger, *The Life of John McLean* 140 (1937).

186. Id. at 141.

187. White, op. cit. supra note 1, at 297.

188. Op. cit. supra note 90, at 168.

189. 1 Friedman and Israel, op. cit. supra note 93, at 609.

190. White, op. cit. supra note 1, at 294.

191. Ibid.

192. Swisher, op. cit. supra note 96, at 55.

193. *Autobiography of Martin Van Buren* 578 (1973 reprint).

194. White, op. cit. supra note 1, at 298.

195. Swisher, op. cit. supra note 96, at 55.

196. 2 Warren, op. cit. supra note 2, at 293.

197. 8 op. cit. supra note 11, at 315–316.

198. Op. cit. supra note 10, at 277.

199. 1 Bryce, *The American Commonwealth* 73 (1889).

200. 20 Wall. ix.

201. Swisher, op. cit. supra note 24, at 427.

202. Swisher, op. cit. supra note 96, at 717–718.

203. 3 Warren, op. cit. supra note 2, at 84.

204. Frankfurter, op. cit. supra note 9, at 48.

205. Compare McLaughlin, *A Constitutional History of the United States* 456 (1935).

206. Frankfurter, *Of Law and Men: Papers and Addresses, 1939–1956,* 133 (Elman ed. 1956).

207. Jackson, Farewell Address, 3 Richardson, op. cit. supra note 16, at 306.

208. Wright, *Economic History of the United States* 388 (1941).

209. Evans, *Business Incorporations in the United States* 13 (1948).

210. Faulkner, *American Economic History* 243 (Spriggs ed. 8th ed. 1960).

211. Hughes, Roger Brooke Taney, 17 *American Bar Association Journal* 787 (1931).

212. 12 How. 443 (U.S. 1852).

213. *The Thomas Jefferson,* 10 Wheat. 428 (U.S. 1825).

214. 12 How. at 457.

215. The term used in 2 Warren, op. cit. supra note 2, at 513.

216. 12 How. at 465.

217. Quoted in Steiner, *Life of Roger Brooke Taney* 292 (1922).

218. Op. cit. supra note 49, at 462.

219. Frankfurter, op. cit. supra note 9, at 71.

220. Quoted in 2 Warren, op. cit. supra note 2, at 290.

221. Lewis, op. cit. supra note 8, at 477.

222. Frankfurter, op. cit. supra note 9, at 72–73.

Chapter 4

1. Dissenting, in *Northern Securities Co. v. United States,* 193 U.S. 197, 401 (1904).

2. *Dred Scott v. Sandford,* 19 How. 393 (U.S. 1857).

3. *Cong. Globe,* 38th Cong., 2d Sess. 1013.

4. Lewis, *Without Fear or Favor: A Biography of Chief Justice Roger Brooke Taney* 470, 471 (1965).

5. Swisher, *Roger B. Taney* 578 (1961 ed.).

6. Jackson, *The Struggle for Judicial Supremacy* 327 (1941).

7. *Felix Frankfurter on the Supreme Court* 554 (Kurland ed. 1970).

8. But see Ehrlich, *They Have No Rights: Dred Scott's Struggle for Freedom* 173 (1979): "Bernard Schwartz was too kind in calling it merely a 'mistake' on the Court's part 'to imagine that a flaming political issue could be quenched by calling it a "legal" question.' It was not a mistake; it was a tragedy."

9. 1 Stat. 50 (1789).

10. 1 Stat. 106 (1790).

11. 3 Stat. 545 (1820).

12. 4 *Memoirs of John Quincy Adams* 502 (C. F. Adams ed. 1876).

13. Quoted in Coit, *John C. Calhoun* 146 (1950).

14. 2 *The Diary of James K. Polk during His Presidency* 75 (Quaife ed. 1910).

15. 3 id. at 366.

16. Quoted in Van Deusen, *The Jacksonian Era: 1828 to 1848,* 245 (1959).

17. Compare Dumond, *Antislavery Origins of the Civil War in the United States* 76–77 (1939).

18. Op. cit. supra note 12, at 530.

19. 5 id. at 5.

20. 4 *The Works of John C. Calhoun* 343 (Cralle ed. 1854).

21. Id. at 347.

22. Id. at 344–345.

23. Spain, *The Political Theory of John C. Calhoun* 24 (1951).

24. Op. cit. supra note 20, at 348.

25. Jefferson Davis, Notes for W.T.W. (n.d.), Charles Hamilton, Auction No. 31, Item 83 (1968).

26. Op. cit. supra note 20, at 348.

27. Mendelson, in S. I. Kutler, *The Dred Scott Decision: Law or Politics* 153 (1967).

28. 4 op. cit. supra note 14, at 297–298.

29. Compare Morison, *The Oxford History of the American People* 567 (1965).

30. 4 op. cit. supra note 14, at 20.

31. *Cong. Globe,* 30th Cong., 1st Sess. 950.

32. Id. at 1002; 4 op. cit. supra note 14, at 21.

33. *Cong. Globe,* 30th Cong., 1st Sess. 950.

34. 4 op. cit. supra note 14, at 207.

35. 4 Richardson, *A Compilation of the Messages and Papers of the Presidents, 1789–1897,* 642 (1896).

36. 5 id. at 431.

37. Jefferson Davis, Notes for W.T.W. (n.d.), Charles Hamilton, Auction No. 31, Item 83 (1968).

38. *Cong. Globe Appendix,* 31st Cong., 1st Sess. 95. See also id. at 154.

39. 9 Stat. 446, 449, 453, 454 (1850).

40. 9 Stat. 446, 450, 453, 456 (1850).

41. McLaughlin, *Constitutional History of the United States* 534 (1935).

42. *Cong. Globe,* 31st Cong. 1st Sess. 1155.

43. See Kutler, op. cit. supra note 27, at 156.

44. *Cong. Globe Appendix,* 33rd Cong., 1st Sess. 232. See also *Cong. Globe,* 35th Cong., 2d Sess. 1258.

45. *Cong. Globe Appendix,* 34th Cong., 1st Sess. 797.

46. To be sure, *Dred Scott* itself did not reach the Supreme Court by the procedural route provided in the 1850 Compromise or the Kansas-Nebraska Act;

yet it did dispose of the substantive issue contemplated by those laws. Kutler, op. cit. supra note 27, at 160.

47. 2 *The Collected Works of Abraham Lincoln* 355 (Basler ed. 1953). But see 4 id. at 67.

48. *Washington Union,* quoted in Lewis, op. cit. supra note 3, at 420.

49. Defendant's name was misspelled in the official report, so it is as *Dred Scott v. Sandford* that the case is still known.

50. The quote is from Emerson's "The Snow-Storm."

51. Letter from Roswell Field to Montgomery Blair, Dec. 24, 1855, quoted in Marke, *Vignettes of Legal History* 85 (1965).

52. Quoted in Hopkins, *Dred Scott's Case* 38 (1967).

53. Aristotle, *Politics* bk. 3, 5.

54. 1 *Memoir of Benjamin Robbins Curtis, LL.D.* 179 (1879).

55. Swisher, op. cit. supra note 5, at 493.

56. Klein, *President James Buchanan* 269 (1962).

57. The Catron letters are summarized in Swisher, op. cit. supra note 5, at 496.

58. Lawrence, *James Moore Wayne: Southern Unionist* 143 (1943).

59. Op. cit. supra note 54, at 235.

60. Lawrence, op. cit. supra note 58, at 155.

61. 2 Curtis, *Constitutional History of the United States* 275 (1896). Other commentators have asserted that dissents on the merits planned by Justices Curtis and McLean led to Justice Wayne's motion and its adoption—a view I formerly held. See Schwartz, *From Confederation to Nation: The American Constitution 1835–1877,* 118–119 (1973).

62. Curtis, op. cit. supra note 61, at 274–275.

63. Op. cit. supra note 54, at 206.

64. Quoted in Swisher, *History of the Supreme Court of the United States: The Taney Period, 1836–64,* 591 (1974).

65. Hopkins, op. cit. supra note 52, at 56.

66. Ibid.

67. 3 Warren, *The Supreme Court in United States History* 17 (1924).

68. Op. cit. supra note 47, at 466.

69. The actual order of reading was somewhat different, since the dissenters read their opinions first on March 7, followed by Justices Daniel, Grier, Campbell, and Wayne.

70. Warren, op. cit. supra note 67, at 27.

71. Justice Nelson alone stuck to that ground; he filed as a separate concurrence the opinion written by him as the original opinion of the Court.

72. According to the monumental study on the law of slavery, 5 Catterall, *Judicial Cases Concerning American Slavery and the Negro* 121 (1968), the decision on the third point was "unquestionably correct."

73. Notably *Strader v. Graham,* 10 How. 82 (U.S. 1850).

74. 19 How. at 455.

75. Lewis, op. cit. supra note 3, at 420–421.

76. Op. cit. supra note 7, at 212.

77. Justices Wayne, Grier, Daniel, Campbell, and Catron.

78. *Cong. Globe,* 35th Cong., 1st Sess. 617.

79. 19 How. at 450.

80. Benton, *Historical and Legal Examination of That Part of the Decision of the*

Supreme Court of the United States in the Dred Scott Case Which Declares the Unconstitutionality of the Missouri Compromise Act 11–12 (1857).

81. Taney, C.J., 19 How. at 449.

82. *De Lima v. Bidwell,* 182 U.S. 1 (1901); *Dooley v. United States,* 182 U.S. 222 (1901); *Downes v. Bidwell,* 182 U.S. 244 (1901), infra p. 186.

83. *Reid v. Covert,* 354 U.S. 1, 6 (1957).

84. 13 N.Y. 378 (1856).

85. See 3 Schwartz, *A Commentary on the Constitution of the United States: The Rights of Property* 31 (1965).

86. See, e.g., *Annals of Cong.,* 16th Cong., 1st Sess. 1262, 1521.

87. Baldwin, J., in *Groves v. Slaughter,* 15 Pet. 449, 515 (U.S. 1841).

88. *Greene v. Briggs,* 1 Curtis 311 (C.C.R.I. 1852). See also *Greene v. James,* 2 Curtis 187 (C.C.R.I. 1854). The Curtis approach here was not exactly that of substantive due process, but it went far in that direction.

89. Op. cit. supra note 54, at 173.

90. See Hopkins, op. cit. supra note 52, at 137.

91. *Cong. Globe,* 42nd Cong., 1st Sess. 576.

92. Kutler, op. cit. supra note 27, at 49.

93. 19 How. at 403.

94. Id. at 405, 406.

95. Id. at 407.

96. Ibid.

97. Id. at 416, 427.

98. Id. at 572, 575.

99. Id. at 614.

100. Id. at 614, 616.

101. 1 Stat. 50 (1789).

102. 19 How. at 623, 621.

103. Id. at 572.

104. North Carolina, Massachusetts, New Hampshire, New York, and New Jersey. Id. at 572–574.

105. Id. at 575.

106. Id. at 420.

107. Opinions of the Justices, 44 Maine 505, 573 (1857).

108. Ibid.

109. 1 Op. Att'y Gen. 506 (1821); 7 Op. Att'y Gen. 746, 753 (1856). See also an unpublished 1832 Taney opinion to such effect quoted in Swisher, op. cit. supra note 5, at 154 (1961).

110. E.g., *Amy v. Smith,* 1 Littell 326 (Ky. 1822); *Crandall v. State,* 10 Conn. 339 (Conn. 1834); *Hobbs v. Fogg,* 6 Watts 553 (Pa. 1837).

111. 4 Deveraux and Battle 144 (N.C. 1839).

112. 5 Iredell 203 (N.C. 1840).

113. Id. at 206–207.

114. See Hopkins, op. cit. supra note 52, at 99.

115. Op. cit. supra note 47, at 500.

116. Id. at 407.

117. Loc. cit. supra note 26.

118. 19 How. at 420.

119. Taney's term, id. at 451.

120. *Downes v. Bidwell,* 182 U.S. 244, 274 (1901).

121. Id. at 275.

122. Fehrenbacher, *Slavery, Law, and Politics: The Dred Scott Case in Historical Perspective* 304 (1981).

123. *Remarks of the Hon. Stephen A. Douglas on Kansas, Utah, and the Dred Scot Decision* 6 (1857).

124. Op. cit. supra note 47, at 453.

125. Id. at 467.

126. *Barron v. Mayor of Baltimore*, 7 Pet. 243 (U.S. 1833). See also 3 op. cit. supra note 27, at 100–101, where Lincoln assumed that the Fifth Amendment was applicable to the states.

127. Jefferson Davis, Notes for W.T.W., Charles Hamilton, Auction No. 31, Item 83 (1968). This apparently unpublished manuscript is not dated, but appears, from its condition and context, to have been written shortly after the Civil War.

128. 12 Stat. 432 (1862).

129. Loc. cit. supra note 127.

Chapter 5

1. Political Causes of the American Revolution, in Acton, *Essays on Freedom and Power* 196 (Himmelfarb ed. 1948).

2. *Texas v. White,* 7 Wall. 700, 725 (U.S. 1869).

3. *The Spirit of Liberty: Papers and Addresses of Learned Hand* 189–190 (3d ed. 1960).

4. *The Great Rights* 90 (Cahn ed. 1963).

5. Harper, *Lincoln and the Press* 109 (1951).

6. *Ex parte Merryman,* 17 Fed. Cas. 144, 153 (D. Md. 1861).

7. 17 Fed. Cas. 144 (D. Md. 1861).

8. Id. at 153.

9. Ibid.

10. 5 *The Collected Works of Abraham Lincoln* 436–437 (Basler ed. 1953).

11. See Randall, *Constitutional Problems under Lincoln* 161 (rev. ed. 1951); Sprague, *Freedom under Union* 43–44 (1965).

12. Jackson, *The Supreme Court in the American System of Government* 76 (1955).

13. Mikell, in 4 *Great American Lawyers* 188–189 (W. D. Lewis ed. 1908).

14. Dunning, *Essays on the Civil War and Reconstruction* 20–21 (1910).

15. Randall, op. cit. supra note 11, at 1.

16. Id. at 2.

17. 4 Lincoln op. cit. supra note 10, at 281.

18. 7 id. at 100.

19. Id. at 281.

20. 5 id. at 394.

21. Id. at 372.

22. 7 id. at 488.

23. 5 id. at 343.

24. Ibid.

25. Id. at 261, 265.

26. Id. at 264.

27. *Ex Parte Milligan,* 4 Wall. 2 (U.S. 1866).

28. 1 Wall. 243 (U.S. 1864).

29. 2 Black 635 (U.S. 1862).

30. Sandburg, *Abraham Lincoln* 275 (1966).

31. 7 Moore, *A Digest of International Law* 190 (1906).

32. *The Protector,* 12 Wall. 700, 702 (U.S. 1872).

33. *Prize Cases,* 17 L. Ed. 459, 465 (U.S. 1862). The Evarts argument is not given in the official report of the case.

34. 2 Black at 669.

35. Rossiter, *The Supreme Court and the Commander-in-Chief* 75 (1951).

36. *Williams v. Bruffy,* 96 U.S. 176, 189 (1878).

37. *Prize Cases,* 2 Black at 669–670.

38. Id. at 666.

39. This was the view of the dissent, id. at 690.

40. Id. at 668.

41. Compare Jackson, J. dissenting, in *Terminiello v. Chicago,* 337 U.S. 1, 37 (1949).

42. A. Lincoln to W. H. Herndon, Feb. 15, 1848, 1 op. cit. supra note 10, at 451.

43. Letter from John Quincy Adams to Gerrit Smith, July 31, 1839, Charles Hamilton, Auction No. 10, Item 1a (1965).

44. Ibid.

45. 4 op. cit. supra note 10, at 432–433.

46. Id. at 435.

47. Oliver Ellsworth, in 3 Farrand, *The Records of the Federal Convention of 1787,* at 241 (1911).

48. 4 Churchill, *A History of the English Speaking Peoples* 176 (1958).

49. Dabbs, *The Southern Heritage* 116 (1958).

50. 7 Wall. 700 (U.S. 1869).

51. Id. at 726.

52. Cooley, *Constitutional History of the United States* 49 (1889).

53. 7 Wall. at 725.

54. Bradley, J., concurring, in *Legal Tender Cases,* 12 Wall. 457, 554–555 (U.S. 1871).

55. 6 *The Works of John C. Calhoun* 309–311 (Cralle ed. 1857).

56. Id. at 311.

57. Maine, *Popular Government* 245 (1886).

58. Woodward, *Reunion and Reaction: The Compromise of 1877 and the End of Reconstruction* 14 (1956).

59. Warren, C.J., in op. cit. supra note 4, at 106.

60. *Ex parte Milligan,* 4 Wall. 2 (U.S. 1866).

61. *Cross v. Harrison,* 16 How. 164 (U.S. 1853).

62. *Texas v. White,* 7 Wall. 700, 725 (U.S. 1869).

63. Wright, The Programme of Peace, by a Democrat of the Old School 18 (1862), quoted in Hyman, *New Frontiers of the American Reconstruction* 25 (1966).

64. McKittrick, *Andrew Johnson and Reconstruction* 102 (1960).

65. House of Representatives, June 13, 1866, quoted in 1 Schwartz, *Statutory History of the United States: Civil Rights* 282 (1970).

66. Stampp, *The Era of Reconstruction: 1865 to 1877,* 87 (1966).

67. *Cong. Globe,* 39th Cong., 1st Sess. 142.

68. John Jay to Charles Sumner, Feb. 12, 1862, in McPherson, *The Struggle for Equality: Abolitionists and the Negro in the Civil War and Reconstruction* 238 (1964).

69. 7 Wall. 700 (U.S. 1869).

70. Id. at 726.

71. Id. at 727.

72. Id. at 730.

73. See *Dooley v. United States,* 182 U.S. 222 (1901); *Madsen v. Kinsella,* 343 U.S. 341 (1952).

74. See *Dooley v. United States,* 182 U.S. at 234.

75. 7 Wall. at 727–728.

76. 7 How. 1 (U.S. 1849).

77. 7 Wall. at 730.

78. *Georgia v. Stanton,* 6 Wall. 50 (U.S. 1868).

79. *Baker v. Carr,* 369 U.S. 186, 225 (1962).

80. Belz, *Reconstructing the Union* 207 (1969).

81. Woodward, in Hyman, op. cit. supra note 63, at 131.

82. 14 Stat. 428 (1867).

83. Though no death sentence could be executed without presidential approval.

84. Burgess, *Reconstruction and the Constitution* 113, 111 (1902).

85. 4 Wall. 2 (U.S. 1866).

86. Op. cit. supra note 4, at 100.

87. *Cong. Globe,* 39th Cong., 2d Sess. 251.

88. 4 Wall. at 121.

89. Fairman, *History of the Supreme Court of the United States: Reconstruction and Reunion, 1864–88, Part One* 232 (1971).

90. 7 Wall. 506 (U.S. 1869).

91. Fairman, op. cit. supra note 89, at 437.

92. 14 Stat. 385, 386 (1867).

93. *Ex parte McCardle,* 6 Wall. 318 (U.S. 1868).

94. 3 *The Diary of Gideon Welles* 314 (Beale ed. 1960).

95. *Cong. Globe,* 40th Cong. 2d Sess. 489.

96. Op. cit, supra note 94, at 258.

97. *Cong. Globe,* 40th Cong. 2d Sess. 1204, 1428.

98. 15 Stat. 44 (1868).

99. 7 Wall. at 514, 515.

100. See Fairman, op. cit. supra note 89, at 494; Hughes, Salmon P. Chase: Chief Justice, 18 *Vanderbilt Law Review* 586, 591 (1965).

101. Op. cit. supra note 94, at 320.

102. 3 Warren, *The Supreme Court in the United States History* 199 (1924).

103. Id. at 205.

104. Corwin, *The Constitution of the United States of America: Analysis and Interpretations* 615 (1953).

105. Roberts, Now Is the Time: Fortifying the Court's Independence, 35 *American Bar Association Journal* 1, 4 (1949).

106. *Ex parte Yerger,* 8 Wall. 85, 104 (U.S. 1869).

107. *United States v. Bitty,* 208 U.S. 393, 400 (1908).

108. Ratner, Congressional Power over the Appellate Jurisdiction of the Supreme Court, 109 *University of Pennsylvania Law Review* 157, 181 (1960).

109. 7 Wall. at 515.

110. Under the 1867 statute previously referred to.

111. Under § 14 of the first Judiciary Act, 1 Stat. 73, 81 (1789). Under it, a person confined under color of federal authority and denied release by a circuit court could petition the Supreme Court for habeas corpus, as well as for the common-law writ of certiorari to bring up the record below. The Supreme Court, in issuing habeas corpus in such a case, after its denial by a circuit court, has been held to be acting in the exercise of its appellate jurisdiction. *Ex parte Yerger,* 8 Wall. at 102.

112. 8 Wall. 85 (U.S. 1869).

113. Id. at 96.

114. 8 Wall. at 102–103.

115. Id. at 103.

116. Compare Hart and Wechsler, *The Federal Courts and the Federal Judicial System* 312 (1953).

117. *The Diary of Edward Bates* 187 (1933).

118. 1 Stat. 23 (1789).

119. 12 Stat. 326 (1861).

120. See Hyman, *Era of the Oath* 2 (1954).

121. 12 Stat. 502 (1862).

122. Letter from Judah P. Benjamin to Mr. Mason, Oct. 25, 1866, Charles Hamilton, Auction No. 31, Item 78 (1968).

123. 15 Stat. 2 (1867).

124. § 9, 15 Stat. at 16.

125. 15 Stat. 344 (1869).

126. See 13 Op. Att'y Gen. 390 (1871).

127. 12 Stat. 610 (1862).

128. Ibid.

129. See Hyman, op. cit, supra note 120, at 20–21.

130. 13 Stat. 424 (1865).

131. 12 Stat. 424 (1865).

132. Clemenceau, *American Reconstruction, 1865–1870,* 84–85 (1928).

133. Lincoln, op. cit. supra note 10, at 284.

134. 4 Wall. 333 (U.S. 1867).

135. 4 Wall. 277 (U.S. 1867).

136. *United States v. Brown,* 381 U.S. 437, 447 (1965). In addition, the law at issue in *Garland* was held an invalid infringement upon the presidential power of pardon.

137. *Cong. Globe,* 41st Cong., 3d Sess. 886.

138. 23 Stat. 21 (1884).

Chapter 6

1. 2 *The Collected Works of Abraham Lincoln* 405–407 (Basler ed. 1953).

2. T. Paine, *Rights of Man* 155 (Heritage Press ed. 1961) (italics omitted).

3. Frederick Douglass, quoted in Lynd, *Class Conflict, Slavery, and the United States Constitution* 155 (1967).

4. Jefferson Davis, Notes for W.T.W., Charles Hamilton, Auction No. 31, Item 83 (1968).

5. Quoted in McPherson, *The Struggle for Equality: Abolitionists and the Negro in the Civil War and Reconstruction* 100 (1964).

6. Lincoln, op. cit. supra note 1, at 323.

7. 2 Boutwell, *Reminiscences of Sixty Years in Public Affairs* 29 (1902).

8. 3 Warren, *The Supreme Court in United States History* 135 (1924).

9. Belden and Belden, *So Fell the Angels* 138 (1956).

10. Wambaugh, in 5 *Great American Lawyers* 344 (Lewis ed. 1908).

11. Hughes, Salmon P. Chase, Chief Justice, 18 *Vanderbilt Law Review* 568, 572 (1965).

12. Circular, "S. P. Chase, Attorney, Solicitor and Counsellor of Cincinnati, Ohio," attached to letter to John H. James, Dec. 14, 1839 (in author's possession).

13. 2 *The Diary of Gideon Welles* 187 (Beale ed. 1960).

14. Warren, op. cit. supra note 8, at 122.

15. Adams, *The Education of Henry Adams* 250 (1931 ed).

16. Magrath, *Morrison R. Waite: The Triumph of Character* 281 (1963).

17. Fairman, *History of the Supreme Court of the United States: Reconstruction and Reunion 1864–88, Part One* 26–27 (1971).

18. 16 Wall. 36 (U.S. 1873), infra p. 158.

19. *In re Neagle,* 135 U.S. 1 (1890).

20. Frankfurter, Mr. Justice Holmes and the Constitution, 41 *Harvard Law Review* 121, 141 (1927).

21. Fairman, op. cit. supra note 17, at 63, 66.

22. Haskins and Johnson, *History of the Supreme Court of the United States: Foundations of Power: John Marshall 1801–15,* 384–386 (1981).

23. Fairman, op. cit. supra note 17, at 66.

24. Ibid.

25. Schwartz, *The American Heritage History of the Law in America* 87 (1974).

26. Swisher, *History of the Supreme Court of the United States: The Taney Period 1836–64,* 250 (1974).

27. Id. at 258.

28. Fairman, op. cit. supra note 17, at 4.

29. Id. at 541–545.

30. Bowers, *The Tragic Era: The Revolution after Lincoln* v (1929).

31. Kutler, *Judicial Power and Reconstruction Politics* 6 (1968).

32. See id. at 114. Kutler cites as the two previous decisions invalidating congressional acts *Marbury v. Madison,* 1 Cranch 137 (U.S. 1803) and the *Dred Scott* case. Like most commentators he overlooks *Hodgson v. Bowerbank,* 5 Cranch 303 (U.S. 1809), where a section of the Judiciary Act was declared unconstitutional.

33. *Gordon v. United States,* 2 Wall. 561 (U.S. 1865); *Reichart v. Felps,* 6 Wall. 160 (U.S. 1868); *The Alicia,* 7 Wall. 571 (U.S. 1869); *United States v. Dewitt,* 9 Wall. 41 (U.S. 1870); *The Justices v. Murray,* 9 Wall. 274 (U.S. 1870); *Collector v. Day,* 11 Wall. 113 (U.S. 1871); *United States v. Railroad Company,* 17 Wall. 322 (U.S. 1873). Of these, only *Collector v. Day* was of great potential importance, but it had no immediate effect because the federal income tax at issue expired a few months after the decision. It may also be doubted that *United States v. Railroad Company* belongs among such decisions, since it turned on statutory interpretation, though the constitutional issue was dealt with by way of obiter.

34. 8 Wall. 603 (U.S. 1870).

35. *Legal Tender Cases,* 12 Wall. 457 (U.S. 1871).

36. Bradley, J. concurring, id. at 570.

37. 13 Wall. 128 (U.S. 1872).

38. See Schwartz, *Constitutional Law: A Textbook* 20 (2d ed. 1979).

39. *Hart v. United States* 118 U.S. 62 (1886) (Congress need not appropriate funds to satisfy claims of pardoned persons).

40. 4 Wall. 333 (U.S. 1867).

41. 4 Wall. 277 (U.S. 1867).

42. Galbraith, *Money: Whence It Came, Where It Went* 91 (1975).

43. 8 Wall. 603 (U.S. 1870).

44. Adams, op. cit. supra note 15, at 250.

45. 7 *American Law Review* 146 (1872).

46. *Legal Tender Cases,* 12 Wall. at 652–653, per Field, J., dissenting.

47. Id. at 653.

48. Id. at 583–584, per Chase, C.J., dissenting.

49. Johnson, *A Dictionary of the English Language* (1755).

50. 2 Farrand, *The Records of the Federal Convention of 1787,* 168 (1911).

51. The debate extracts and Madison notes are in id. at 309–310.

52. 3 id. at 172.

53. *Legal Tender Cases,* 12 Wall. at 529.

54. Warren, op. cit. supra note 8, at 236.

55. 14 Stat. 209 (1866).

56. 16 Stat. 44 (1869).

57. 12 Wall. 457 (U.S. 1871).

58. See Fairman, op. cit. supra note 17, at 1395.

59. Warren, op. cit. supra note 8, at 247.

60. Hughes, *The Supreme Court of the United States* 52 (1936).

61. 16 Wall. 36 (U.S. 1873).

62. Warren, op. cit. supra note 8, at 261.

63. Fairman, op. cit. supra note 17, at 1349.

64. 16 Wall. at 79.

65. Corwin, *The Constitution of the United States of America: Analysis and Interpretation* 965 (1953).

66. 16 Wall. at 81.

67. Id. at 105.

68. Id. at 116.

69. Id. at 122.

70. Supra p. 117.

71. Compare Frankfurter, Mr. Justice Holmes and the Constitution, 41 *Harvard Law Review* 141 (1927).

72. Referring to *Walker v. Sauvinet,* 92 U.S. 90, 93 (1876).

73. Hough, Due Process of Law—Today, 32 *Harvard Law Review* 226 (1919).

74. Samuel Shellabarger, in *In Memoriam—Morrison Remick Waite,* 126 U.S. 585, 599–600 (1888).

75. Warren, op. cit. supra note 8, at 283.

76. Frankfurter, *The Commerce Clause under Marshall, Taney and Waite* 76–77 (1964).

77. Quoted in Fairman, *Mr. Justice Miller and the Supreme Court* 373 (1939).

78. *Felix Frankfurter on the Supreme Court* 476 (Kurland ed. 1970).

79. Id. at 250.

80. Id. at 505.

81. Magrath, op. cit. supra note 16, at 299.

82. Ibid.

83. Id. at 182.

84. Id. at 271.

85. Fairman, op. cit. supra note 77, at 384.

86. Fairman, *History of the Supreme Court of the United States: Reconstruction and Reunion 1864–88, Part Two* 529 (1987).

87. Op. cit. supra note 78, at 476.

88. Schwartz, *Super Chief: Earl Warren and His Supreme Court* 259 (1983).

89. Magrath, op. cit. supra note 16, at 151.

90. Op. cit. supra note 78, at 477.

91. See Magrath, op. cit. supra note 16, at 300.

92. Ibid.

93. Id. at 301.

94. *Munn v. Illinois,* 94 U.S. 113 (1877) and its companion cases.

95. Frankfurter, op. cit. supra note 76, at 83.

96. *Munn v. Illinois,* 94 U.S. at 126.

97. See Fairman, The So-Called Granger Cases, 5 *Stanford Law Review* 592 (1953).

98. Of private right.

99. Sir Matthew Hale, De Portibus Maris, in Hargrave, *Collection of Tracts Relative to the Law of England* 77–78 (1787).

100. Note, 25 *American Law Register* 545 (1877).

101. Compare Hamilton, Affectation with a Public Interest, 39 *Yale Law Journal* 1092, 1097 (1930).

102. Frankfurter, supra note 76, at 86.

103. See *Wolff Packing Co. v. Industrial Court,* 262 U.S. 522, 536 (1923).

104. Brewer, J., dissenting, in *Budd v. New York,* 143 U.S. 517, 549 (1892).

105. Supra note 103.

106. *Nebbia v. New York,* 291 U.S. 502 (1934).

107. 18 Stat. 433 (1871).

108. 1 Schwartz, *Statutory History of the United States: Civil Rights* 727 (1970).

109. Pierce, *Memoir and Letters of Charles Sumner* 598 (1893).

110. 109 U.S. 3 (1883).

111. Id. at 24, 11.

112. Id. at 48.

113. Magrath, op. cit. supra note 16, at 145.

114. *Shelley v. Kramer,* 334 U.S. 1, 13 (1948).

115. Notably Senators Allen G. Thurman and James K. Kelly. See Schwartz, op. cit. supra note 108, at 671–676, 703–707.

116. Id. at 764.

117. 78 Stat. 241 (1964).

118. Schwartz, op. cit. supra note 108, at 764.

119. *Heart of Atlanta Motel v. United States,* 379 U.S. 241 (1964).

120. 347 U.S. 483 (1954).

121. See Black, J., dissenting, in *Connecticut General Life Ins. Co. v. Johnson,*

303 U.S. 77, 87 (1938). The argument in question occurred in *San Mateo County v. Southern Pac. R.R. Co.,* 116 U.S. 138 (1885).

122. Quoted in Graham, "The Conspiracy Theory" of the Fourteenth Amendment, 47 *Yale Law Journal* 371 (1938). The Conkling argument to such effect is not contained in the law reports.

123. Quoted in id. at 378.

124. The best-reasoned rejection of the Conkling thesis is to be found in the Graham article, referred to in the two prior notes. See also Corwin, *Liberty against Government: The Rise, Flowering, and Decline of a Famous Juridical Concept* 191–193 (1948). It should, however, be noted that earlier writers, following the lead of Beard and Beard, *Rise of American Civilization* 111–113 (1927), tended to follow the Conkling view.

125. Black, J., dissenting, in *Connecticut General Life Ins. Co. v. Johnson,* 303 U.S. 77, 87 (1938).

126. Compare Harris, *The Quest for Equality: The Constitution, Congress and the Supreme Court* 40 (1960).

127. Black, J., dissenting, in *Adamson v. California,* 332 U.S. 46, 74 (1947).

128. Schwartz, op. cit. supra note 108, at 305–306.

129. Which, in the Fifth Amendment, has always been construed to include corporations.

130. See Faulkner, *Economic History of the United States* ch. 9 (1938).

131. Especially *Bank of Augusta v. Earle,* 13 Pet. 519 (U.S. 1839), supra p. 89.

132. Supra note 94.

133. 118 U.S. 394 (1886).

134. Id. at 396.

135. Douglas, J., dissenting, in *Wheeling Steel Corp. v. Gander,* 337 U.S. 562, 576–577 (1949).

136. Id. at 576.

137. Id. at 574, per Jackson, J.

138. Freund, in Fairman, *History of the Supreme Court of the United States: Five Justices and the Electoral Commission of 1877,* xiii (1988).

139. Haworth, *The Hayes–Tilden Disputed Presidential Election of 1876,* 168 (1966 ed.).

140. Ibid.

141. Quoted in Woodward, *Reunion and Reaction: The Compromise of 1877 and the End of Reconstruction* 120 (1956).

142. Quoted in Magrath, op. cit. supra note 16, at 289.

143. Jackson, *The Struggle for Judicial Supremacy* xi (1941).

144. Woodward, op. cit. supra note 141, at 33.

145. Magrath, op. cit. supra note 16, at 291.

146. 19 Stat. 227 (1877).

147. McLaughlin. *A Constitutional History of the United States* 707 (1935).

148. 24 Stat. 373 (1887).

149. There was also an Oregon statute permitting the electors to fill any vacancy in their ranks.

150. Magrath, op. cit. supra note 16, at 293.

151. Id. at 294.

152. Adams, op. cit. supra note 15, at 277.

153. Id. at 280–281.

154. Rep. Charles Foster, 5 *Cong. Rec.* 1708.

Chapter 7

1. Holmes, *Collected Legal Papers* 26 (1920).
2. Holmes, *The Common Law* 1 (1881).
3. Dissenting, in *Lochner v. New York,* 198 U.S. 45, 75 (1905).
4. *Planned Parenthood v. Casey,* 112 S.Ct. 2791, 2812 (1992).
5. King, *Melville Weston Fuller* 109–110 (1950) [hereinafter cited as King].
6. King 114.
7. Schiffman, in 2 Friedman and Israel, *The Justices of the United States Supreme Court* 1479 (1969).
8. *Felix Frankfurter on the Supreme Court* 476 (Kurland ed. 1970).
9. King 125, 127.
10. Op. cit. supra note 8, at 476, 477.
11. King 138; op. cit. supra note 8, at 477–478.
12. Friedman and Israel, op. cit. supra note 7, at 1480.
13. Op. cit. supra note 8, at 477.
14. Ibid.
15. King 134.
16. King 123.
17. 1 *Holmes–Laski Letters* 579 (Howe ed. 1963).
18. King 158, 149.
19. Strong, Relief for the Supreme Court, *North American Review* 567, 570 (1881).
20. Fairman, *Mr. Justice Miller and the Supreme Court* 404 (1939).
21. King 150.
22. Supra p. 164.
23. *Budd v. New York,* 143 U.S. 517, 548, 551 (1892).
24. Friedman and Israel, op. cit. supra note 7, at 1521.
25. Id. at 1577.
26. Id. at 1603.
27. 1 *Holmes–Laski Letters* 356.
28. 198 U.S. 45 (1905).
29. Bickel, *The Unpublished Opinions of Justice Brandeis* 164 (1967).
30. Acheson, *Morning and Noon* 65 (1965).
31. Bickel, loc. cit. supra note 29.
32. Holmes, op. cit. supra note 1, at 184.
33. *Allgeyer v. Louisiana,* 165 U.S. 578 (1897), infra note 45.
34. *Lochner v. New York,* 198 U.S. 45 (1905).
35. *Mr. Justice Holmes* 78 (Frankfurter ed. 1931).
36. *Adkins v. Children's Hospital,* 261 U.S. 525, 568 (1923).
37. *American Federation of Labor v. American Sash Co.,* 335 U.S. 538, 543 (1949).
38. Compare *Hume v. Moore-McCormack Lines,* 121 F.2d 336, 339 (2d Cir. 1941).
39. Loc. cit. supra note 37.
40. Ibid.
41. Except for recognized physical and mental disabilities. See *State v. F. C. Coal & Coke Co.,* 33 W.Va. 188, 190 (1889).
42. *People v. Gillson,* 109 N.Y. 389, 398 (1888).
43. *People v. Budd,* 117 N.Y. 1, 48 (1889).

44. Venable, Growth or Evolution of Law, 23 *American Bar Association Reports* 278, 298 (1900).

45. 165 U.S. 578 (1897).

46. Id. at 590–591.

47. Id. at 589.

48. *People v. Gillson,* 109 N.Y. at 405.

49. *People v. Budd,* 117 N.Y. at 69.

50. 16 Wall. 36 (U.S. 1873), supra p. 158.

51. *Munn v. Illinois,* 94 U.S. 113 (1877) and its companion cases, supra p. 164.

52. 94 U.S. at 134.

53. *Railroad Commission Cases,* 116 U.S. 307, 331 (1886).

54. *Chicago & C. Railway Co. v. Minnesota,* 134 U.S. 418, 458 (1890).

55. See *Smyth v. Ames,* 169 U.S. 466, 526 (1898).

56. *Matter of Application of Jacobs,* 98 N.Y. 98, 105 (1885).

57. Ibid.

58. Hough, Due Process of Law—Today, 32 *Harvard Law Review* 218, 228 (1919).

59. Op. cit. supra note 8, at 31.

60. Frankfurter, Mr. Justice Holmes and the Constitution, 41 *Harvard Law Review* 121, 142 (1927).

61. Hough, supra note 58, at 228.

62. Loc. cit. supra note 37.

63. Jackson, *The Struggle for Judicial Supremacy* 48 (1941).

64. Dissenting, in *Poe. v. Ullman,* 367 U.S. 497, 517 (1961).

65. Supra p. 47.

66. 128 U.S. 1 (1888).

67. 156 U.S. 1 (1895).

68. Id. at 16.

69. Dissenting, in *Lochner v. New York,* 198 U.S. 45, 75 (1905).

70. Ibid.

71. King 193.

72. 157 U.S. 429, 158 U.S. 601 (1895).

73. 39 L. Ed. at 786.

74. 157 U.S. at 532.

75. Id. at 533.

76. 39 L. Ed. at 807.

77. 158 U.S. at 622.

78. 157 U.S. at 569.

79. See Corwin, *Court over Constitution* 196 (1937); King 220.

80. Corwin, op. cit. supra note 79, at 194.

81. 158 U.S. at 674, 684, 685.

82. Latham, *The Great Dissenter: John Marshall Harlan* 114 (1970).

83. King 216.

84. 157 U.S. at 607.

85. *DeLima v. Bidwell,* 182 U.S. 1 (1901); *Dooley v. United States,* 182 U.S. 222 (1901): *Downes v. Bidwell,* 182 U.S. 244 (1902).

86. Bander, *Mr. Dooley on the Choice of Law* 52 (1963).

87. Id. at 47.

88. 182 U.S. at 249.

89. Id. at 341–342.

90. Op. cit. supra note 8, at 484.

91. King 265.

92. 182 U.S. at 380.

93. 195 U.S. 138 (1904).

94. Latham, op. cit. supra note 82, at 141.

95. 163 U.S. 537 (1896). Nor is it mentioned in 3 Warren, *The Supreme Court in United States History* (1924).

96. *Planned Parenthood v. Casey,* 112 S.Ct. 2791, 2813 (1992).

97. 163 U.S. at 551, 544.

98. *To Secure These Rights, Report of the President's Committee on Civil Rights* 81 (1947).

99. 163 U.S. at 562.

100. Id. at 559.

Chapter 8

1. 198 U.S. 45 (1905).

2. Supra p. 35.

3. Bowen, *Yankee from Olympus: Justice Holmes and His Family* (1944).

4. Bartlett, *Familiar Quotations* 519 (15th ed. 1980).

5. Bowen, op. cit. supra note 3, at 201.

6. Kaplan, Encounters with O. W. Holmes, Jr., 96 *Harvard Law Review* 1828, 1829 (1983).

7. See Bowen, op. cit. supra note 3, at 285.

8. Ibid.

9. Holmes, The Path of the Law, in *Collected Legal Papers* 167, 180 (1920).

10. Holmes, *The Common Law* 1 (1881).

11. Ibid.

12. Biddle, *Mr. Justice Holmes* 61 (1986 ed.).

13. Supra p. 178.

14. Ibid.

15. 117 N.Y. 1 (1889).

16. *Munn v. Illinois,* 94 U.S. 113 (1877) and its companion cases, supra p. 164.

17. 117 N.Y. at 46, 45.

18. Id. at 46, 47.

19. Id. at 69.

20. Id. at 68, 71.

21. 3 Friedman and Israel, *The Justices of the United States Supreme Court* 1693 (1969).

22. Brief for plaintiff in error 18.

23. Butler, *A Century at the Bar of the Supreme Court of the United States* 172 (1942).

24. Notably, in *Holden v. Hardy,* 169 U.S. 366 (1898).

25. King, *Melville Weston Fuller* 298 (1950).

26. Novick, *Honorable Justice: The Life of Oliver Wendell Holmes* 463 (1989).

27. Supra p. 180.

28. *Holden v. Hardy,* 169 U.S. 366 (1898).

29. 198 U.S. at 53.

30. Id. at 54, 57, 56.

31. Id. at 57.

32. Ibid.

33. Id. at 58, 59.

34. Id. at 61, 62.

35. Id. at 61.

36. Id. at 63, 64.

37. *Selected Writings of Benjamin Nathan Cardozo* 81 (Hall ed. 1947).

38. Id. at 134.

39. 198 U.S. at 76, 75.

40. Compare Posner, *Law and Literature* 283 (1988).

41. 198 U.S. at 75.

42. "Every man has freedom to do all that he will, provided he infringes not the equal freedom of any other man." Spencer, *Social Statics* 55 (abridged and revised ed. 1892).

43. 198 U.S. at 75.

44. Ibid.

45. *Holden v. Hardy,* 169 U.S. 366 (1898); *Otis v. Parker,* 187 U.S. 606 (1903); *Jacobson v. Massachusetts,* 197 U.S. 11 (1905).

46. 198 U.S. at 75–76.

47. Id. at 76.

48. Ibid.

49. Posner, op. cit. supra note 40, at 285.

50. Compare Posner, *The Federal Courts* 106–107 (1985).

51. Posner, op. cit. supra note 40, at 285 (emphasis added).

52. Supra p. 179.

53. *Home Life Ins. Co. v. Fisher,* 188 U.S. 726 (1903).

54. King, op. cit. supra note 25, at 291.

55. 198 U.S. at 56.

56. Posner, op. cit. supra note 40, at 285.

57. 198 U.S. at 76.

58. Loc. cit. supra note 56.

59. 1 *Holmes–Laski Letters* 51 (Howe ed. 1953).

60. *Adkins v. Children's Hospital,* 261 U.S. 525, 570 (1923).

61. *Hebe Co. v. Shaw,* 248 U.S. 297, 303 (1919).

62. See Holmes, J., dissenting, in *Meyer v. Nebraska,* 262 U.S. 390, 412 (1923).

63. Frankfurter, J., dissenting, in *West Virginia Board of Education v. Barnette,* 319 U.S. 624, 647 (1943).

64. Pollock, Note, 21 *Law Quarterly Review* 211, 212 (1905).

65. *Ferguson v. Skrupa,* 372 U.S. 726, 731–732 (1963).

66. Id. at 732.

67. King, op. cit. supra note 25, at 109.

68. *Matter of Jacobs,* 98 N.Y. 98, 104–105, 115 (1885).

69. Supra note 42.

70. Supra p. 178.

71. *Budd v. New York,* 143 U.S. 517, 551 (1892).

72. *Poe v. Ullman,* 367 U.S. 497, 517 (1961).

73. *People v. Budd,* 117 N.Y. at 47.

74. Acheson, *Morning and Noon* 211 (1965).

75. Stevens, Judicial Restraint, 22 *San Diego Law Review* 437, 448 (1985).

76. Siegan, Rehabilitating *Lochner,* 22 *San Diego Law Review* 453 (1985).

77. Posner, *Economic Analysis of the Law* 409 (3d ed. 1986).

78. Id. at 593.

79. Fox and Sullivan, Retrospective and Perspective: Where Are We Coming From? Where Are We Going? 62 *New York University Law Review* 936, 957 (1987).

80. Posner, The Constitution as an Economic Document, 56 *George Washington Law Review* 4, 20, and note 25 (1987).

81. Id. at 20.

82. See *Hume v. Moore-McCormack Lines,* 121 F.2d 336, 339–340 (2d Cir. 1941).

83. *American Federation of Labor v. American Sash Co.,* 335 U.S. 538, 543 (1949).

84. Jackson, *The Struggle for Judicial Supremacy* 48 (1941).

85. *Hume v. Moore-McCormack Lines,* 121 F.2d at 340.

86. Holmes, op. cit. supra note 9, at 184.

87. *Baldwin v. Missouri,* 281 U.S. 586, 595 (1930).

88. *Otis v. Parker,* 187 U.S. 606, 609 (1903).

89. 1 *Holmes–Pollock Letters* 167 (Howe ed. 1961).

90. Holmes, op. cit. supra note 9, at 295.

91. *Commonwealth v. Perry,* 155 Mass. 117, 123 (1891).

Chapter 9

1. *Felix Frankfurter Reminisces* 86 (1960).

2. Quoted in Jackson, *The Supreme Court in the American System of Government* 54 (1955).

3. Ibid.

4. Rodell, *Nine Men* 179 (1955).

5. 1 Pringle, *The Life and Times of William Howard Taft* 529 (1964).

6. Id. at 530.

7. Id. at 531.

8. Id. at 532, 533.

9. 1 Pusey, *Charles Evans Hughes* 281 (1963).

10. *Felix Frankfurter on the Supreme Court* 481 (Kurland ed. 1970).

11. Id. at 480.

12. 241 U.S. xvii.

13. Umbreit, *Our Eleven Chief Justices* 372 (1938).

14. *Guinn v. United States,* 238 U.S. 347 (1915); *Buchanan v. Warley,* 245 U.S. 60 (1917).

15. Pringle, op. cit. supra note 5, at 536.

16. 2 id. at 971.

17. Op. cit. supra note 10, at 487.

18. Bickel and Schmidt, *History of the Supreme Court of the United States: The Judiciary and Responsible Government 1910–21,* 54–55 (1984).

19. Id. at 42.

20. Frank, *Marble Palace* 44 (1958).

21. Bickel and Schmidt, op. cit. supra note 18, at 334.

22. 2 *Holmes–Pollock Letters* 113 (Howe ed. 1961).

23. Pringle, op. cit. supra note 5, at 536.

24. Bickel and Schmidt, op. cit. supra note 18, at 9.

25. 2 Pringle, op. cit. supra note 5, at 854.

26. 1 *Holmes–Pollock Letters* 190.

27. Bickel and Schmidt, op. cit. supra note 18, at 80.

28. 1 *Holmes–Laski Letters* 579 (Howe ed. 1953).

29. Loc. cit. supra note 27.

30. Op. cit. supra note 1, at 101.

31. Bickel and Schmidt, op. cit. supra note 18, at 81.

32. Pusey, op. cit. supra note 9, at 275.

33. Frankfurter, *Of Law and Men* 112 (Elman ed. 1956).

34. Bickel and Schmidt, op. cit. supra note 18, at 82.

35. Id. at 83.

36. Id. at 84.

37. Id. at 85.

38. Id. at 97.

39. *Standard Oil Co. v. United States,* 221 U.S. 1 (1911); *United States v. American Tobacco Co.,* 221 U.S. 106 (1911).

40. 3 Friedman and Israel, *The Justices of the United States Supreme Court* 1650 (1969).

41. 221 U.S. at 66.

42. Acheson, *Morning and Noon* 62 (1965).

43. Bickel and Schmidt, op. cit. supra note 18, at 109.

44. Ibid. The quotes are from the oral dissent delivered by Harlan. They do not appear in the printed version.

45. 221 U.S. at 63.

46. Loc. cit. supra note 42.

47. Frankfurter, *Law and Politics* 4 (1962 ed.).

48. Bickel and Schmidt, op. cit. supra note 18, at 201.

49. 13 *Columbia Law Review* 294 (1913).

50. To show this, Warren cited, among others, *Minnesota Iron Co. v. Kline,* 199 U.S. 593 (1905); *Chicago, B. & Q. R.R. v. McGuire,* 219 U.S. 549 (1911); *Atkin v. Kansas,* 191 U.S. 207 (1903): *Muller v. Oregon,* 208 U.S. 412 (1908).

51. *Second Employers' Liability Cases,* 223 U.S. 1 (1912).

52. Bickel and Schmidt, op. cit. supra note 18, at 207.

53. *New York Central R.R. v. Winfield,* 244 U.S. 147, 165 (1917).

54. Smith, Sequel to Workmen's Compensation Acts, 27 *Harvard Law Review* 235, 251 (1914).

55. *Arizona Employer's Liability Cases,* 250 U.S. 400, 433 (1919).

56. 250 U.S. 400 (1919).

57. Id. at 452.

58. Acheson, op. cit. supra note 42, at 67.

59. Bickel and Schmidt, op. cit. supra note 18, at 588.

60. 2 *Holmes–Pollock Letters* 15.

61. *Lochner v. New York,* 198 U.S. at 76.

62. 250 U.S. at 431–432.

63. Id. at 419.

64. McKenna, J., dissenting, id. at 436.

65. *Wilson v. New,* 243 U.S. 332 (1917).

66. Bickel and Schmidt, op. cit. supra note 18, at 473.

67. 1 *Holmes–Laski Letters* 69.

68. 243 U.S. at 426.

69. Op. cit. supra note 1, at 102.

70. 208 U.S. 412 (1908).

71. Friedman and Israel, op. cit. supra note 40, at 1732.

72. Supra p. 194.

73. 243 U.S. at 435, 438.

74. Id. at 438.

75. *Coppage v. Kansas,* 236 U.S. 1 (1915); *Hitchman Coal & Coke Co. v. Mitchell,* 245 U.S. 229 (1917); *Duplex Printing Press Co. v. Deering,* 254 U.S. 443 (1921).

76. 247 U.S. 251 (1918).

77. Supra p. 183.

78. 1 *Holmes–Pollock Letters* 267.

79. Ibid.

80. 247 U.S. at 280.

81. Pringle, op. cit. supra note 5, at 535.

82. 2 id. at 957.

83. Id. at 967.

84. Op. cit. supra note 1, at 85.

85. 2 Pringle, op. cit. supra note 5, at 961.

86. Op. cit. supra note 10, at 488.

87. Mason, *William Howard Taft: Chief Justice* 233 (1965).

88. 1 *Holmes–Pollock Letters* 555; 2 id. at 113–114; 1 *Holmes–Laski Letters* 290.

89. 1 *Holmes–Laski Letters* 79.

90. Mason, op. cit. supra note 87, at 199.

91. Bindler, *The Conservative Court 1910–1930,* 205 (1986).

92. Mason, op. cit. supra note 87, at 165.

93. Schwartz, *Super Chief: Earl Warren and His Supreme Court* 279 (1983).

94. Friedman and Israel, op. cit. supra note 40, at 2024.

95. Mason, op. cit. supra note 87, at 216–217.

96. Id. at 215.

97. 1 *Holmes–Laski Letters* 493.

98. Strum, *Louis D. Brandeis: Justice for the People* 293 (1984).

99. Mason, op. cit. supra note 87, at 74.

100. Loc. cit. supra note 70.

101. Brandeis, Brief for Defendant in Error, *Muller v. Oregon* 10.

102. Frankfurter, Hours of Labor and Realism in Constitution Law, 29 *Harvard Law Review* 353, 365 (1916).

103. Compare Holmes, *Collected Legal Papers* 187 (1920).

104. Acheson, op. cit. supra note 42, at 82.

105. 1 *Holmes–Laski Letters* 209.

106. *American Federation of Labor v. American Sash Co.,* 335 U.S. 538, 543 (1949).

107. Mason, *Brandeis: A Free Man's Life* 581 (1946).

108. *The Words of Justice Brandeis* 154 (Goldman ed. 1953).

109. Mason, op. cit. supra note 87, at 228.

110. 2 Pringle, op. cit. supra note 5, at 960.

111. Bindler, op. cit. supra note 91, at 197.

112. Op. cit. supra note 10, at 488.

113. 2 Pringle, op. cit. supra note 5, at 1000.

114. Id. at 998.

115. Op. cit. supra note 10, at 488.

116. Frankfurter and Landis, *The Business of the Supreme Court: A Study in the Federal Judicial System* 280 (1927).

117. 2 Pringle, op. cit. supra note 5, at 967.

118. 257 U.S. 312 (1921).

119. 2 Pringle, op. cit. supra note 5, at 967.

120. 257 U.S. at 342.

121. *Bailey v. Drexel Furniture Co.*, 259 U.S. 20 (1922).

122. *Hammer v. Dagenhart,* supra note 76.

123. 259 U.S. at 37.

124. 2 Pringle, op. cit. supra note 5, at 1013–1014.

125. Mason, op. cit. supra note 87, at 247–248.

126. Quoted id. at 292–293. The decisions referred to were *Adkins v. Children's Hospital,* infra note 127; *Burns Baking Co. v. Bryan,* 264 U.S. 504 (1924); *Tyson Brothers v. Banton,* 273 U.S. 418 (1927); *Ribnik v. McBride,* 277 U.S. 350 (1928); *Baldwin v. Missouri,* 281 U.S. 586 (1930).

127. 261 U.S. 525 (1923).

128. *Planned Parenthood v. Casey,* 112 S.Ct. 2791, 2812 (1992).

129. 261 U.S. at 554–555, 557–558.

130. Id. at 546.

131. Op. cit. supra note 1, at 103.

132. Ibid.; id. at 104.

133. 1 *Holmes–Laski Letters* 495.

134. 2 *Holmes–Pollock Letters* 117.

135. Schwartz, op. cit. supra note 93, at 46.

136. Frankfurter, The Early Writings of O. W. Holmes, Jr., 44 *Harvard Law Review* 717, 724 (1931).

137. *Truax v. Corrigan,* 257 U.S. at 343–344.

138. 1 *Holmes–Pollock Letters* 167.

139. *Baldwin v. Missouri,* 281 U.S. at 595.

140. *Missouri, Kansas and Texas Ry. Co. v. May,* 194 U.S. 267, 270 (1904).

141. See Jackson, *The Struggle for Judicial Supremacy* 323 (1941).

142. 2 *Holmes–Laski Letters* 1209.

143. Compare *Burns Baking Co. v. Bryan,* 264 U.S. at 534.

144. See *North Dakota Board of Pharmacy v. Snyder's Drug Stores,* 414 U.S. 156, 167 (1973).

145. See *Duke Power Co. v. Carolina Environmental Study Group,* 438 U.S. 59, 84 (1978).

146. *New Orleans v. Dukes,* 427 U.S. 297, 303 (1976).

147. Compare Cardozo, *The Nature of the Judicial Process* 79 (1921).

148. Loc. cit. supra note 106.

149. Frankfurter, *Mr. Justice Holmes and the Supreme Court* 50 (1938).

150. *United States v. Schwimmer,* 279 U.S. 644, 654–655 (1928).

151. Frankfurter, op. cit. supra note 149, at 51.

152. 250 U.S. 616 (1919).

153. Lerner, *The Mind and Faith of Justice Holmes* 306 (1989 ed.)

154. Compare id. at 290.

155. 250 U.S. at 630.

156. 1 *Holmes–Laski Letters* 153.

157. Frankfurter, op. cit. supra note 149, at 51.

158. 250 U.S. at 630.

159. Id. at 628, 629.

160. Id. at 630–631.

161. *Schenck v. United States,* 249 U.S. 47, 52 (1919).

162. *Schaefer v. United States,* 251 U.S. 466, 482 (1920).

163. Supra note 161.

164. Compare Chafee, *Thirty Five Years with Freedom of Speech* 7 (1952).

165. Hughes, *The Supreme Court of the United States* 68 (1936).

166. 2 *Holmes–Laski Letters* 1219.

167. Holmes, *The Common Law* 1, 35 (1881).

Chapter 10

1. Mason, *Harlan Fiske Stone: Pillar of the Law* 406 (1956).

2. 2 Pringle, *The Life and Times of William Howard Taft* 1076 (1964).

3. Mason, *William Howard Taft: Chief Justice* 137 (1965).

4. Id. at 136.

5. 2 Pusey, *Charles Evans Hughes* 651 (1963).

6. 3 Friedman and Israel, *The Justices of the United States Supreme Court* 1903 (1969).

7. *Felix Frankfurter on the Supreme Court* 491 (Kurland ed. 1970).

8. Frankfurter, *Of Law and Men* 149 (Elman ed. 1956).

9. Id. at 141.

10. Op. cit. supra note 7, at 492.

11. Freund, Book Review, 65 *Harvard Law Review* 370 (1951).

12. Mason, op. cit. supra note 1, at 789.

13. Holmes, *Collected Legal Papers* 292 (1920).

14. The quote is from Emerson, The Snow-Storm.

15. Supra p. 218.

16. Dissenting, in *Baldwin v. Missouri,* 281 U.S. 586, 595 (1930).

17. Op. cit. supra note 7, at 517.

18. Id. at 528.

19. Schwartz, *The American Heritage History of the Law in America* 200 (1974).

20. Frankfurter, op. cit. supra note 8, at 202.

21. Posner, *Cardozo: A Study in Reputation* 32 (1990).

22. Cardozo, *The Nature of the Judicial Process* 28, 102 (1921).

23. Posner, op. cit. supra note 21, at 126.

24. Frankfurter, op. cit. supra note 8, at 148.

25. Pringle, op. cit. supra note 2, at 1044.

26. Ibid.

27. 290 U.S. 398 (1934).

28. Article I, section 10.

29. Mason, op. cit. supra note 1, at 362.

30. 291 U.S. 502 (1934).

31. Op. cit. supra note 7, at 523.

32. *Railroad Retirement Board v. Alton,* 295 U.S. 330 (1935).

33. *The Public Papers and Addresses of Franklin D. Roosevelt* 133 (1941).

34. Id. at 14, 1933 vol. (1938).

35. *Schechter Poultry Corp. v. United States,* 295 U.S. 495 (1935); *United States v. Butler,* 297 U.S. 1 (1936).

36. *Carter v. Carter Coal Co.,* 298 U.S. 238 (1936); *Ashton v. Cameron County Dist.,* 298 U.S. 513 (1936); *Louisville Joint Stock Land Bank v. Radford,* 295 U.S. 555 (1935).

37. Hughes, *The Supreme Court of the United States* 95 (1928).

38. See, e.g., Jackson, *The Struggle for Judicial Supremacy* 174 (1941).

39. Id. at 175.

40. *Morehead v. New York ex rel. Tipaldo,* 298 U.S. 587 (1936).

41. Jackson, op. cit. supra note 38, at 175.

42. Op. cit. supra note 33, at 126.

43. Dissenting, in *Lochner v. New York,* 198 U.S. 45, 75 (1905).

44. *Mandeville Island Farms v. American C.S. Co.,* 334 U.S. 219, 230 (1948).

45. Jackson, op. cit. supra note 38, at v.

46. Corwin, *Constitutional Revolution, Ltd.* (1941).

47. Op. cit. supra note 33, at lxix.

48. Mason, op. cit. supra note 1, at 363.

49. Roberts, *The Court and the Constitution* 61 (1951).

50. *Planned Parenthood v. Casey,* 112 S.Ct. 2791, 2812 (1992).

51. Roberts, op. cit. supra note 49, at 62.

52. *West Coast Hotel Co. v. Parrish,* 300 U.S. 379 (1937).

53. Pusey, op. cit. supra note 5, at 757.

54. Powell, quoted in Mason, *The Supreme Court: Vehicle of Revealed Truth or Power Group* 39 (1953).

55. *West Coast Hotel Co. v. Parrish,* 300 U.S. 379 (1937).

56. Supra supra note 40.

57. Jackson, op. cit. supra note 38, at 207–208.

58. *Wright v. Vinton Branch,* 300 U.S. 440 (1937); *Virginian Ry. v. Federation,* 300 U.S. 515 (1937); *Sonzinsky v. United States,* 300 U.S. 506 (1937).

59. Jackson, op. cit. supra note 38, at 213.

60. Corwin, op. cit. supra note 46, at 65.

61. 301 U.S. 1 (1937).

62. Jackson, op. cit. supra note 38, at 214.

63. 301 U.S. at 41.

64. *Helvering v. Davis,* 301 U.S. 619 (1937).

65. *Steward Machine Co. v. Davis,* 301 U.S. 548 (1937); *Carmichael v. Southern Coal Co.,* 301 U.S. 495 (1937).

66. *The Supreme Court under Earl Warren* 135 (Levy ed. 1972).

67. Douglas, *Go East Young Man: The Early Years* 450 (1974).

68. Gerhart, *America's Advocate: Robert H. Jackson* 274 (1958).

69. *The Fourteenth Amendment Centennial Volume* 34 (Schwartz ed. 1970).

70. Holmes, The Path of the Law, 10 *Harvard Law Review* 457, 469 (1897).

71. Dunne, *Hugo Black and the Judicial Revolution* 414 (1977).

72. 5 Burke, *Works* 67 (rev. ed. 1865).

73. Hugo Black, Jr., *My Father: A Remembrance* 239 (1975).

74. Hugo Black to Alan Washburn, Dec. 17, 1958, Black Papers, Library of Congress.

75. Frankfurter, op. cit. supra note 8, at 133.

76. Simon, *The Antagonists: Hugo Black, Felix Frankfurter and Civil Liberties in Modern America* 61 (1989).

77. Id. at 64.

78. Stanley Reed to Felix Frankfurter, n.d., Frankfurter Papers, Library of Congress.

79. Schwartz, *Super Chief: Earl Warren and His Supreme Court* 268 (1983).

80. 310 U.S. 381 (1940).

81. 307 U.S. 38 (1939).

82. *Waialua Agricultural Co. v. Maneja,* 216 F.2d 466, 476 (9th Cir. 1954).

83. *Maneja v. Waialua Agricultural Co.,* 349 U.S. 254, 259 (1955).

84. 301 U.S. at 99.

85. 312 U.S. 100 (1941).

86. Supra p. 212.

87. 312 U.S. at 117.

88. Id. at 113.

89. Compare Holmes, J., dissenting, in *Lochner v. New York,* 198 U.S. 45, 76 (1905).

90. *American Federation of Labor v. American Sash Co.,* 335 U.S. 538, 543 (1949).

91. 198 U.S. at 75.

92. *West Coast Hotel Co. v. Parrish,* 300 U.S. at 391.

93. *Olsen v. Nebraska,* 313 U.S. 236 (1941), overruling *Ribnik v. McBride,* 277 U.S. 350 (1928).

94. *Williamson v. Lee Optical Co.,* 348 U.S. 483, 488 (1955).

95. *Ferguson v. Skrupa,* 372 U.S. 726, 730 (1963).

96. Dissenting, in *Adkins v. Children's Hospital,* 261 U.S. at 570.

97. Jackson, op. cit. supra note 38, at xv–xvi.

Chapter 11

1. Quoted in Schwartz, *A Basic History of the U.S. Supreme Court* 172 (1968).

2. *Felix Frankfurter on the Supreme Court* 491 (Kurland ed. 1970).

3. 2 Pusey, *Charles Evans Hughes* 788 (1951).

4. Mason, *Harlan Fiske Stone: Pillar of the Law* 569 (1956).

5. Id. at 790.

6. Op. cit. supra note 2, at 492–493.

7. Mason, op. cit. supra note 4, at 791.

8. Frank, *Marble Palace* 81 (1958).

9. Mason, op. cit. supra note 4, at 792.

10. Ibid.

11. Lash, *From the Diaries of Felix Frankfurter* 152 (1974).

12. Frank, loc. cit. supra note 8.

13. Simon, *The Antagonists: Hugo Black, Felix Frankfurter and Civil Liberties in Modern America* (1989).

14. Harold H. Burton Diary, Library of Congess.

15. With Phil Kurland, n.d., Frankfurter Papers, Library of Congress.

16. *Brown v. Allen,* 344 U.S. 443, 540 (1953).

17. *Ex parte Quirin,* 317 U.S. 1, 35 (1942).

18. *Hirabayashi v. United States,* 320 U.S. 81, 100 (1943).

19. 323 U.S. 214 (1944).

20. 323 U.S. 283 (1944).

21. Id. at 304.

22. Id. at 310.

23. Jackson, *The Supreme Court in the American System of Government* 60 (1955).

24. *Selective Draft Law Cases,* 245 U.S. 366 (1918).

25. *Lichter v. United States,* 334 U.S. 742, 756 (1948).

26. Id. at 755.

27. *United States v. Bethlehem Steel Corp.,* 315 U.S. 289, 305 (1942).

28. 321 U.S. 414 (1944).

29. *Steuart & Bro. v. Bowles,* 322 U.S. 398 (1944).

30. *Felix Frankfurter Reminisces* 62 (1960).

31. Lash, op. cit. supra note 11, at 270.

32. Id. at 274.

33. Philip Elman to Frankfurter, Sept. 3, Frankfurter Papers, Library of Congress.

34. Lash, op. cit. supra note 11, at 274, 283.

35. Rodell, *Nine Men* 311 (1955).

36. Kluger, *Simple Justice: The History of Brown v. Board of Education and Black America's Struggle for Equality* 585 (1975).

37. Gerhart, *America's Advocate: Robert H. Jackson* 260 (1958).

38. Frankfurter to C. C. Burlingham, Oct. 27, 1954, Frankfurter Papers, Library of Congress.

39. Jackson to Frankfurter, June 19, 1946, Frankfurter Papers, Harvard Law School.

40. Jackson to Frankfurter, Sept. 20, 195[?], Frankfurter Papers, Library of Congress.

41. Black to Jerome Cooper, 1946, *"Sincerely your friend": Letters of Mr. Justice Hugo L. Black to Jerome A. Cooper* (n.d.).

42. Rodell, op. cit. supra note 35, at 310.

43. Berry, *Stability, Security, and Continuity: Mr. Justice Burton and Decision-Making in the Supreme Court 1945–1948,* vii (1978).

44. Id. at 89.

45. Burton to Frankfurter, Apr. 29, 1964, Frankfurter Papers, Harvard Law School.

46. Clark to Warren, Oct. 24, 1955, Clark Papers, University of Texas.

47. Harlan to Clark, Postcard, July 29, 1959, Clark Papers, University of Texas.

48. Miller, *Plain Speaking* 225–226 (1974).

49. Frankfurter to C. C. Burlingham, Sept. 8, 1956, Frankfurter Papers, Library of Congress.

50. 341 U.S. 494 (1951).

51. Id. at 510.

52. Id. at 589.

53. *Harisiades v. Slaughnessy,* 342 U.S. 580 (1952).

54. *Garner v. Los Angeles Board,* 314 U.S. 716, 724 (1951).

55. *Bailey v. Richardson,* 341 U.S. 918 (1951).

56. Dissenting, in *West Virginia Board of Education v. Barnette,* 319 U.S. 624, 665 (1943).

57. *Youngstown Sheet and Tube Co. v. Sawyer,* 343 U.S. 579 (1952).

58. Id. at 587, 589, 587.

59. Id. at 597.

60. 310 U.S. 586 (1940).

61. Frankfurter to Stone, May 27, 1940, Frankfurter Papers, Harvard Law School.

62. 319 U.S. 624 (1943).

63. Id. at 641.

64. Loc. cit. supra note 61.

65. Freedman, *Roosevelt and Frankfurter: Their Correspondence 1928–1945*, 701 (1967).

66. 319 U.S. at 639.

67. *Kovacs v. Cooper*, 336 U.S. 77, 95 (1949).

68. Ibid.

69. Mason, op. cit. supra note 4, at 626.

70. *United States v. Carolene Products Co.*, 304 U.S. 144, 152, n.4 (1938).

71. The most famous was that in *Brown v. Board of Education*, 347 U.S. 483, 494, n.11 (1954).

72. Loc. cit. supra note 70.

73. 323 U.S. at 216.

74. *Smith v. Allwright*, 321 U.S. 649 (1944).

75. *Shelley v. Kraemer*, 334 U.S. 1 (1948).

76. 163 U.S. 537 (1896), supra p. 188.

77. *Sipuel v. Board of Regents*, 332 U.S. 631 (1948).

78. *Sweatt v. Painter*, 339 U.S. 629, 633 (1950).

79. The term used by Harlan, J., dissenting, in *Plessy v. Ferguson*, 163 U.S. 537, 562 (1896).

Chapter 12

1. Frankfurter to Fred Vinson, n.d., Frankfurter Papers, Library of Congress.

2. 1 Bryce, *The American Commonwealth* 274 (1917).

3. Frankfurter to Reed, Apr. 13, 1939, Frankfurter Papers, Library of Congress.

4. Yeats, Easter 1916.

5. *Brown v. Board of Education*, 347 U.S. 483 (1954), infra Chapter 13.

6. *Reynolds v. Sims*, 377 U.S. 533 (1964).

7. Weaver, *Warren: The Man, The Court, The Era* 44 (1967).

8. Pollack, *Earl Warren: The Judge Who Changed America* 193 (1979).

9. Dunne, *Justice Joseph Story and the Rise of the Supreme Court* 91 (1970).

10. Id. at 307–308.

11. *N.Y. Times,* July 10, 1974, p. 24.

12. Lash, *From the Diaries of Felix Frankfurter* 152 (1975).

13. June 15, 1983, at A16.

14. Supra note 5.

15. 163 U.S. 537 (1896).

16. Schwartz, *Super Chief: Earl Warren and His Supreme Court* 4 (1983).

17. Woodward and Armstrong, *The Brethren: Inside the Supreme Court* (1979).

18. Douglas, *The Court Years 1939–1975,* 173 (1980).

19. 347 U.S. 483, 494, n.11 (1954).

20. Dunne, *Hugo Black and the Judicial Revolution* (1977).

21. Hutchinson, Hail to the Chief: Earl Warren and the Supreme Court, 81 *Michigan Law Review* 922, 923 (1983).

22. Dear Chief, June 23, 1969, Black Papers, Library of Congress.

23. Douglas, op. cit. supra note 18, at 240.

24. June 15, 1983, at A16.

25. Rodell, *Nine Men* 284 (1955).

26. Frankfurter, *Of Law and Men* 133 (1956).

27. Supra note 15.

28. Frankfurter to C. C. Burlingham, Apr. 24, 1955, Frankfurter Papers, Library of Congress.

29. Clark to Harlan, Sept. 12, Clark Papers, University of Texas.

30. Clayton, *The Making of Justice: The Supreme Court in Action* 217 (1964).

31. Douglas, op. cit. supra note 18, at 250.

32. *Jacobellis v. Ohio*, 378 U.S. 184, 197 (1964).

33. *N.Y. Times,* March 18, 1986, at 7.

34. Clayton, op. cit. supra note 30, at 43.

35. Schlesinger, *Robert Kennedy and His Times* 379 (1978).

36. Clayton, op. cit. supra note 30, at 159.

37. Minton to Frankfurter, Oct. 22, 1964, Frankfurter Papers, Library of Congress.

38. Clayton, op. cit. supra note 30, at 293.

39. Pound, *Interpretations of Legal History* 1 (1923).

40. Holmes, *The Common Law* (1881).

41. Id. at 1, 35–36.

42. Compare Cardozo, J., in *Jacob and Youngs v. Kent,* 230 N.Y. 239, 242–243 (1921).

43. Compare Cardozo, *Paradoxes of Legal Science* 57 (1927).

44. Lewis, *Portrait of a Decade: The Second American Revolution* 139 (1964).

45. 384 U.S. 436 (1966).

46. 1 *Holmes–Pollock Letters* 167 (Howe ed. 1961).

47. *U.S. News & World Report,* July 15, 1968, at 64.

48. *Reynolds v. Sims,* 377 U.S. 533 (1964).

49. *Johnson v. Virginia,* 373 U.S. 61, 62 (1963).

50. *Brown v. Board of Education,* 349 U.S. 294 (1955).

51. 377 U.S. 218 (1964).

52. 391 U.S. 430 (1968).

53. E.g., *Bell v. Maryland,* 378 U.S. 226 (1964); *Brown v. Louisiana,* 383 U.S. 131 (1966).

54. E.g., *Cox v. Louisiana,* 379 U.S. 536, 559 (1965); *Amalgamated Food Employees Union v. Logan Valley Plaza,* 391 U.S. 308 (1968).

55. 109 U.S. 3 (1883); supra p. 166.

56. 379 U.S. 241 (1964).

57. *South Carolina v. Katzenbach,* 383 U.S. 301 (1966).

58. 369 U.S. 186 (1962).

59. *Colegrove v. Green,* 328 U.S. 549, 556 (1946).

60. 377 U.S. 533 (1964).

61. Id. at 562, 568.

62. Pollock, op. cit. supra note 8, at 209.

63. *Fourteenth Amendment Centennial Volume* 34 (Schwartz ed. 1970).

64. 351 U.S. 12 (1956).

65. Id. at 19.

66. 372 U.S. 335 (1963).

67. Id. at 344.

68. 384 U.S. 436 (1966).

69. 367 U.S. 643 (1961).

70. Warren, The Law and the Future, *Fortune* 106, 126 (Nov. 1955).

71. 304 U.S. 144 (1938); supra p. 261.

72. Letter of Stone, J., Apr. 12, 1941, quoted in Mason, The Core of Free Government, 1938–40: Mr. Justice Stone and "Preferred Freedoms," 65 *Yale Law Journal* 597, 626 (1956).

73. Compare *Kovacs v. Cooper*, 336 U.S. 77, 95 (1949).

74. *Barron v. Mayor of Baltimore*, 2 Pet. 243 (U.S. 1833).

75. Black, J., dissenting, in *Adamson v. California*, 332 U.S. 46, 71–72 (1947).

76. *Benton v. Maryland*, 395 U.S. 784 (1969).

77. *Malloy v. Hogan*, 378 U.S. 1 (1964).

78. *Duncan v. Louisiana*, 391 U.S. 145 (1968).

79. *Klopfer v. North Carolina*, 386 U.S. 213 (1967).

80. *Pointer v. Texas*, 380 U.S. 400 (1965).

81. These are listed in Schwartz, *The Law in America: A History* 174 (1974).

82. See *New York Times Co. v. United States*, 403 U.S. 713, 761 (1971).

83. *Edwards v. South Carolina*, 372 U.S. 229 (1963); *Cox v. Louisiana*, 379 U.S. 536 (1965).

84. *New York Times Co. v. Sullivan*, 376 U.S. 254 (1964).

85. See 4 Schwartz, *A Commentary on the Constitution of the United States*, pt. 3, *Rights of the Person* 374 et seq. (1968).

86. Id. at 313 et seq.

87. *Poe v. Ullman*, 367 U.S. 497, 521 (1961).

88. 381 U.S. 479 (1965).

89. *N.Y. Times*, July 7, 1966, at 22.

90. Compare Hand, Mr. Justice Cardozo, 52 *Harvard Law Review* 361 (1939).

91. 4 Friedman and Israel, *The Justices of the United States Supreme Court* 2727 (1969).

Chapter 13

1. *Brown v. Board of Education*, 347 U.S. 483 (1954).

2. May 20, 1954, Frankfurter Papers, Harvard Law School.

3. Kluger, *Simple Justice: The History of Brown v. Board of Education and Black America's Struggle for Equality* 709 (1975).

4. Id. at 614.

5. 163 U.S. 537 (1896).

6. The conference quotes are from notes taken by Justice Burton, in his papers in the Library of Congress, and Justice Douglas, contained in Tushnet, What Really Happened in *Brown v. Board of Education*, 91 *Columbia Law Review* 1867, 1902–1907 (1992).

7. Id. at 1908.

8. Kluger, op. cit. supra note 3, at 601.

9. Burton Diary, Dec. 12, 1952, Burton Papers, Library of Congress.

10. Kluger, op. cit. supra note 3, at 614.

11. Ibid.

12. *Brown v. Board of Education,* 345 U.S. 972 (1953).

13. The memo is reprinted in Nomination of Justice William Hubbs Rehnquist, Hearings before the Committee on the Judiciary, United States Senate, 99th Cong., 2d Sess. 324 (1986). The original is in the *Brown* file, Robert H. Jackson Papers, Library of Congress.

14. Supra Chapter 8.

15. This, of course, is from the dissent by Justice Holmes in *Lochner v. New York,* 198 U.S. 45, 75 (1905).

16. Myrdal, *An American Dilemma* (1944).

17. *Washington Post* July 28, 1986 (national weekly edition), at 8.

18. See, e.g., supra note 13, at 322, 328–333.

19. Kluger, op. cit. supra note 3, at 609.

20. Id. at 606–609.

21. Memorandum by Mr. Justice Jackson, Mar. 15, 1954, Brown file, Jackson Papers, Library of Congress.

22. Frankfurter Memorandum, Sept. 29, 1959, Frankfurter Papers, Harvard Law School.

23. Frankfurter, Memorandum for the Conference, n.d., Frankfurter Papers, Harvard Law School.

24. 347 U.S. at 489.

25. Burton Diary, Dec. 17, 1953.

26. Ulmcr, Earl Warren and the Brown Decision, 33 *Journal of Politics* 689, 698 (1971).

27. Frankfurter, Memorandum, Jan. 15, 1954, Frankfurter Papers, Library of Congress.

28. Frankfurter Papers, Harvard Law School. These notes have not been used by other writers on the *Brown* case.

29. Warren, *Memoirs* 285 (1977).

30. Kluger, op. cit. supra note 3, at 692.

31. Id. at 698.

32. Ibid. The clerk in question confirms this statement.

33. Reed to Frankfurter, May 21, 1954, Frankfurter Papers, Harvard Law School.

34. Frankfurter, "Dear Brethren," Jan. 15, 1954, Burton Papers, Library of Congress.

35. Loc. cit. supra note 29.

36. Warren, To the Members of the Court, May 7, 1954, Tom Clark Papers, University of Texas. For the text of Warren's draft, see Schwartz, *The Unpublished Opinions of the Warren Court* 451 (1985).

37. 5/5 54-II. The first draft of this memo is also in Warren's writing.

38. A comparison with Earl Pollock's bench memo in *Brown* also shows that the Warren draft was not in any way based on that memo.

39. 347 U.S. 497 (1954).

40. Burton Diary.

41. These are discussed in Schwartz, *Super Chief: Earl Warren and His Supreme Court* 97–98 (1983).

42. May 18, 1954, quoted in Kluger, op. cit. supra note 3, at 713.

43. 347 U.S. at 494, note 11.

44. *Argument: The Oral Argument before the Supreme Court in Brown v. Board of Education of Topeka, 1952–55,* xxxvii (Friedman ed. 1969).

45. Kluger, op. cit. supra note 3, at 706.

46. Ibid.

47. Douglas to Warren, May 11, 1954.

48. Burton Diary.

49. Warren, op. cit. supra note 29, at 3.

50. Id. at 2.

51. See Kluger, op. cit. supra note 3, at 701.

52. The quotes from the Brown opinion are in 347 U.S. at 492–495.

53. Warren, op. cit. supra note 29, at 3.

54. *N.Y. Times,* May 18, 1954, quoted in Kluger, op. cit. supra note 3, at 113.

55. Scudder interview, Earl Warren Oral History Project, Bancroft Library, University of California, Berkeley.

56. Kluger, op. cit. supra note 3, at 709.

57. Frankfurter to Warren, May 17, 1954, Warren Papers, Library of Congress.

58. Frankfurter to Warren, May 13, 1954, Warren Papers, Library of Congress.

59. 347 U.S. at 500.

60. *Dawson v. Mayor,* 220 F.2d 386 (4th Cir. 1955).

61. *Mayor v. Dawson,* 350 U.S. 877 (1955).

62. *Holmes v. Atlanta,* 350 U.S. 879 (1955).

63. *Gayle v. Browder,* 352 U.S. 903 (1956).

64. *Johnson v. Virginia,* 373 U.S. 61 (1963).

65. *New Orleans Park Improvement Assn. v. Detiege,* 358 U.S. 54 (1959).

66. Loc. cit. supra note 64.

67. *Watson v. Memphis,* 373 U.S. 526 (1963).

68. *Burton v. Wilmington Parking Authority,* 365 U.S. 715 (1961).

69. *Johnson v. Virginia,* 373 U.S. 61, 62 (1963).

70. Burton Papers, Library of Congress.

71. *McCulloch v. Maryland,* 4 Wheat. 315, 407 (U.S. 1819).

72. Goldberg, Equality and Governmental Action, 39 *New York University Law Review* 205 (1964).

Chapter 14

1. Justice Scalia, *N.Y. Times,* Feb. 2, 1988, at A16.

2. Rehnquist, *The Supreme Court: How It Was, How It Is* 290 (1987).

3. *N.Y. Times,* Mar. 3, 1985, Magazine, at 35.

4. *Gonzalez v. Freeman,* 534 F.2d 570 (D.C. Cir. 1964).

5. Harlan to Burger, May 21, 1970, Harlan Papers, Princeton.

6. Savage, *Turning Right: The Making of the Rehnquist Supreme Court* 4 (1992).

7. *N.Y. Times,* Feb. 20, 1983, Magazine, at 20.

8. Drury, *Decision* 61 (1983).

9. *Washington Post,* July 7, 1986 (national weekly edition), at 8.

10. *N.Y. Times,* Feb. 22, 1988, at A16. This statement was made in 1986, while Burger was still Chief Justice.

11. WHR, Re: *Goldwater v. Carter,* Memorandum to the Conference, Dec. 10, 1979.

12. *Mapp v. Ohio,* 367 U.S. 643 (1961); *Miranda v. Arizona,* 384 U.S. 436 (1966).

13. Infra p. 322.

14. Harlan to Burger, June 9, 1990, Harlan Papers, Princeton.

15. Harlan to Frankfurter, Aug. 21, [1963], Frankfurter Papers, Library of Congress.

16. *N.Y. Times,* Mar. 8, 1986, at 7.

17. Infra p. 322.

18. Schwartz, *Swann's Way: The School Busing Case and the Supreme Court* 178 (1986).

19. Loc. cit. supra note 16.

20. On *Communist Party v. Whitcomb,* 414 U.S. 441 (1974).

21. Schwartz, *The Unpublished Opinions of the Burger Court* 412 (1988).

22. Schwartz, *Behind Bakke: Affirmative Action and the Supreme Court* 53 (1988).

23. Infra Chapter 15.

24. *N.Y. Times,* Feb. 20, 1983, Magazine, at 20.

25. Infra p. 324.

26. Supra note 11.

27. *Guardians Association v. Civil Service Commission,* 463 U.S. 582 (1983).

28. *Lau v. Nichols,* 414 U.S. 563 (1974).

29. July 23, 1979, p. 68.

30. *N.Y. Times,* July 23, 1984, at 8.

31. *The Burger Court: The Counter-Revolution That Wasn't* 252 (Blasi ed. 1983).

32. *N.Y. Times,* Jan. 17, 1986, at A14.

33. Rehnquist, op. cit. supra note 2, at 301.

34. Oct. 5, 1981, p. 22.

35. Apr. 19, 1982, p. 49.

36. *N.Y. Times,* Mar. 8, 1986, at 7.

37. *Moran v. Burbine,* 475 U.S. 412 (1986); *Oregon v. Elstad,* 470 U.S. 298 (1985).

38. *Garcia v. San Antonio Metropolitan Transit Authority,* 469 U.S. 528, 580 (1985) (dissent).

39. *Metropolitan Life Insurance Co. v. Ward,* 470 U.S. 869, 884 (1985) (dissent); *Akron v. Akron Center for Reproductive Health,* 462 U.S. 416, 453 (1983) (dissent).

40. *Mississippi University for Women v. Hogan,* 458 U.S. 718 (1982).

41. *Wygant v. Jackson Board of Education,* 476 U.S. 267, 284 (1986).

42. *Minnesota Star Co. v. Commissioner of Revenue,* 460 U.S. 575 (1983).

43. *McKaskle v. Wiggins,* 465 U.S. 168, 187–188 (1984).

44. Supra p. 203.

45. *Washington Post,* Oct. 1, 1984 (national weekly edition), at 33.

46. Ibid.

47. 1 Tocqueville, *Democracy in America* 290 (Bradley ed. 1954).

48. *Economist,* July 12, 1983, p. 16.

49. *United States v. Nixon,* 418 U.S. 683 (1974).
50. Infra Chapter 15.
51. *Dred Scott v. Sandford,* 19 How. 393 (U.S. 1857).
52. *Pollock v. Farmers' Loan & Trust Co.,* 157 U.S. 429 (1895).
53. Supra Chapter 13.
54. *Powell v. McCormack,* 395 U.S. 486 (1969).
55. *Frontiero v. Richardson,* 411 U.S. 677 (1973).
56. *Roe v. Wade,* infra Chapter 15.
57. *O'Connor v. Donaldson,* 422 U.S. 563 (1975).
58. *Houchins v. KQED,* 438 U.S. 1 (1978).
59. *Goldberg v. Kelly,* 397 U.S. 254 (1970).
60. *Richmond Newspapers v. Virginia,* 448 U.S. 555 (1980).
61. Supra Chapter 13.
62. *Brown v. Board of Education,* 349 U.S. 294, 301 (1955).
63. 396 U.S. 19 (1969).
64. Schwartz, op. cit. supra note 18, at 85–86.
65. 396 U.S. at 20.
66. 402 U.S. 1 (1971).
67. Reprinted in Schwartz, op. cit. supra note 18, at 208.
68. 402 U.S. at 15, 30.
69. *United States v. Montgomery County Board of Education,* 395 U.S. 225, 231 (1969).
70. *Keyes v. School District No. 1,* 413 U.S. 189 (1973).
71. 418 U.S. 717 (1974).
72. Schwartz, *The Ascent of Pragmatism: The Burger Court in Action* 266 (1990).
73. 426 U.S. 229 (1976).
74. *Regents of the University of California v. Bakke,* 438 U.S. 265 (1978).
75. Schwartz, op. cit. supra note 22, at 54.
76. Reprinted id. at 198.
77. *Massachusetts Board of Retirement v. Murgia,* 427 U.S. 307, 321 (1976).
78. *Frontiero v. Richardson,* 411 U.S. 677 (1973).
79. *Craig v. Boren,* 429 U.S. 190, 197 (1976).
80. *Mississippi University for Women v. Hogan,* 458 U.S. 718 (1982).
81. *Weinberger v. Weisenfeld,* 420 U.S. 636 (1975).
82. *Roberts v. United States Jaycees,* 468 U.S. 609 (1984).
83. *Orr v. Orr,* 440 U.S. 268 (1979).
84. *Reed v. Reed,* 404 U.S. 71 (1971).
85. *Taylor v. Louisiana,* 419 U.S. 522 (1975).
86. *Sugarman v. Dougall,* 413 U.S. 634 (1973); *Graham v. Richardson,* 403 U.S. 365 (1971).
87. *Trimble v. Gordon,* 430 U.S. 762 (1977).
88. 411 U.S. 1 (1973).
89. *Massachusetts Board of Retirement v. Murgia,* 427 U.S. 307 (1976).
90. *Cleburne v. Cleburne Living Center,* 473 U.S. 432 (1985).
91. *Memorial Hospital v. Maricopa County,* 415 U.S. 250 (1974).
92. *Dunn v. Blumstein,* 405 U.S. 330 (1972).
93. *Boddie v. Connecticut,* 401 U.S. 371 (1971).
94. *Zablocki v. Redhail,* 434 U.S. 374 (1978).
95. 411 U.S. at 35.

96. *Lynch v. Household Finance Corp.*, 405 U.S. 538, 552 (1972).

97. *Greer v. Spock*, 424 U.S. 828, 852 (1976).

98. Dissenting, in *Abrams v. United States*, 250 U.S. 616, 630 (1919).

99. *Valentine v. Chrestenson*, 316 U.S. 52 (1942).

100. 425 U.S. 748 (1976).

101. Id. at 762.

102. *Bates v. State Bar*, 433 U.S. 350 (1977).

103. *Buckley v. Valeo*, 424 U.S. 1 (1976).

104. *Stromberg v. California*, 283 U.S. 359 (1931).

105. 418 U.S. 405 (1974).

106. *Wooley v. Maynard*, 430 U.S. 705 (1977).

107. Supra p. 283.

108. 408 U.S. 753 (1972).

109. Id. at 762–763.

110. *Southeastern Productions v. Conrad*, 420 U.S. 546 (1975).

111. *Amalgamated Food Employees Union v. Logan Valley Plaza*, 391 U.S. 308 (1968).

112. *Hudgens v. National Labor Relations Board*, 424 U.S. 507 (1976).

113. 403 U.S. 713 (1971).

114. Id. at 730.

115. *Nebraska Press Association v. Stuart*, 427 U.S. 539 (1976).

116. *Richmond Newspapers v. Virginia*, 448 U.S. 555 (1980).

117. *Houchins v. KQED*, 438 U.S. 1 (1978).

118. *Branzburg v. Hayes*, 408 U.S. 665 (1972).

119. *Estes v. Texas*, 381 U.S. 532 (1965).

120. *Chandler v. Florida*, 449 U.S. 560 (1981).

121. Schwartz, *Super Chief: Earl Warren and His Supreme Court* 763 (1983).

122. Ibid.

123. *Gideon v. Wainwright*, 372 U.S. 335 (1963); *Mapp v. Ohio*, 367 U.S. 643 (1961); *Miranda v. Arizona*, 384 U.S. 436 (1966).

124. 407 U.S. 25 (1972).

125. Id. at 37.

126. Stewart to Douglas, Apr. 12, 1972.

127. *Mayer v. Chicago*, 404 U.S. 189 (1971).

128. *Ake v. Oklahoma*, 470 U.S. 68 (1985).

129. *Batson v. Kentucky*, 476 U.S. 79 (1986).

130. *Coolidge v. New Hampshire*, 403 U.S. 443, 492 (1971).

131. *Massachusetts v. Sheppard*, 468 U.S. 981, 987–988 (1984).

132. Ibid.; *United States v. Leon*, 468 U.S. 897 (1984).

133. *Rhode Island v. Innis*, 446 U.S. 291, 304 (1980).

134. *Harris v. New York*, 401 U.S. 222 (1970).

135. *New York v. Quarles*, 467 U.S. 649, 656 (1984).

136. 470 U.S. 298 (1985).

137. Id. at 306.

138. *Moran v. Burbine*, 475 U.S. 412, 424 (1986).

139. *The Burger Court: The Counter-Revolution That Wasn't* (Blasi ed. 1983).

140. *N.Y. Times*, Feb. 28, 1988, section 4, at 1.

141. *N.Y. Times*, Mar. 3, 1985, Magazine, at 35.

142. Id. at 34, 35.

143. Supra note 123.

144. *Argersinger v. Hamlin,* supra note 124.

145. *Coleman v. Alabama,* 399 U.S. 1 (1970).

146. *Faretta v. California,* 422 U.S. 806 (1975).

147. 351 U.S. 12 (1956).

148. *Ake v. Oklahoma,* 470 U.S. 68 (1985).

149. *Boddie v. Connecticut,* 401 U.S. 371 (1971).

150. Supra Chapter 13.

151. Supra note 66.

152. Supra p. 324.

153. Supra p. 289.

154. *Wygant v. Jackson Board of Education,* 476 U.S. 267 (1986).

155. *The Burger Years: Rights and Wrongs in the Supreme Court 1969–1986,* xx (H. Schwartz ed. 1987).

156. Op. cit. supra note 139, at ix.

157. Ibid.

158. *United States v. Will,* 449 U.S. 200 (1980); *Buckley v. Valeo,* 424 U.S. 1 (1976).

159. *Oregon v. Mitchell,* 400 U.S. 112 (1970).

160. *Northern Pipeline Construction Co. v. Marathon Pipe Line Co.,* 458 U.S. 50 (1982).

161. *Frontiero v. Richardson,* 411 U.S. 677 (1973).

162. The cases are listed in op. cit. supra note 139 at 306 n. 14.

163. *Immigration & Naturalization Service v. Chadha,* 462 U.S. 919 (1983).

164. *Bowsher v. Synar,* 478 U.S. 714 (1986).

165. Op. cit. supra note 139 at 200.

166. 418 U.S. 683 (1974).

167. Op. cit. supra note 139, at 212–213.

168. Supra p. 333.

169. Fortas, in *The Fourteenth Amendment Centennial Volume* 34 (Schwartz ed. 1970).

170. Op. cit. supra note 139, at 198.

171. Id. at 211.

172. *N.Y. Times,* Sept. 25, 1986, at B10.

173. Supra p. 272.

174. Compare op. cit. supra note 139, at 216.

175. Id. at 211.

176. Compare Pound, *Administrative Law* 56 (1942).

177. Op. cit. supra note 139, at 216.

Chapter 15

1. 410 U.S. 113 (1973).

2. Woodward and Armstrong, *The Brethren: Inside the Supreme Court* 238 (1979).

3. *McGovern v. Van Riper,* 43 A.2d 514, 518 (N.J. 1945).

4. Douglas, J., dissenting, in *Public Utilities Commission v. Pollak,* 343 U.S. 451, 467 (1952).

5. 381 U.S. 479 (1965).

6. *Mapp. v. Ohio,* 367 U.S. 643, 656 (1961).

7. In their seminal article, Warren and Brandeis, The Right to Privacy, 4 *Harvard Law Review* 193 (1890).

8. Dissenting, 381 U.S. at 510, n.1.

9. Citing *Pierce v. Society of Sisters,* 281 U.S. 370 (1925).

10. 381 U.S. at 484.

11. *Carey v. Population Services International,* 431 U.S. 678, 687 (1977).

12. *Eisenstadt v. Baird,* 405 U.S. 438, 453 (1972).

13. Re: *Abortion Cases,* Memorandum to the Conference, May 31, 1972.

14. 410 U.S. at 116.

15. The conference notes I used read "getting" but this seems an error.

16. See Woodward and Armstrong, op. cit. supra note 2, at 170.

17. *Washington Post,* July 4, 1972, at 1.

18. For its text, see Schwartz, *The Unpublished Opinions of the Burger Court* 93 (1988).

19. The draft is reprinted in id. at 103.

20. 402 U.S. 62 (1971).

21. For its text, see Schwartz, op. cit. supra note 18, at 120.

22. Reprinted id. at 141.

23. Supra note 20.

24. 408 U.S. 919 (1972).

25. *Poe v. Ullman,* 367 U.S. 497 (1961).

26. *Griswold v. Connecticut,* supra note 5.

27. 410 U.S. at 155.

28. Ibid.

29. Woodward and Armstrong, op. cit. supra note 2, at 233.

30. 410 U.S. at 155.

31. Id. at 162.

32. Id. at 173.

33. Ibid.

34. Ibid.

35. Ibid.

36. Stewart to Lewis F. Powell, Feb. 8, 1973.

37. 198 U.S. 45 (1905), supra Chapter 8.

38. *Ferguson v. Skrupa,* 372 U.S. 726, 731 (1963).

39. Re: No. 76-811 *Regents of the University of California v. Allen Bakke,* Memorandum to the Conference, Nov. 11, 1977.

40. Compare Rehnquist, J., dissenting, in *Weber v. Aetna Casualty & Surety Co.,* 406 U.S. 164, 179 (1972).

41. Particularly in *San Antonio School District v. Rodriguez,* 411 U.S. 1 (1973).

42. *Gitlow v. New York,* 268 U.S. 652 (1925).

43. *Buckley v. Valeo,* 424 U.S. 1, 64 (1976).

44. Kozinski, It Is a Constitution We Are Expounding: A Debate, 1987 *Utah Law Review* 977, 980.

45. Bork, in *The Great Debate: Interpreting Our Written Constitution* 48, 49 (1986).

46. Id. at 11.

47. Dissenting, in *Morrison v. Olson,* 487 U.S. 654, 711 (1988).

48. Bork, *The Tempting of America* 242 (1989).

49. *Lamont v. Postmaster General,* 381 U.S. 301, 308 (1965).

50. 381 U.S. at 491.

51. Id. at 492.
52. Id. at 499.
53. 410 U.S. at 210–211.
54. Ibid.
55. Dissenting, in *Olmstead v. United States,* 277 U.S. 438, 478 (1928).
56. Strunsky, The Invasion of Privacy: The Modern Case of Mistaken Identity, 28 *The American Scholar* 219 (1959).
57. The phrase is from Browning's "Paracelsus."
58. *Pavesich v. New England Life Ins. Co.,* 50 S.E. 68, 70 (Ga. 1905).
59. 410 U.S. at 213 (italics omitted).
60. *McGowan v. Maryland,* 366 U.S. 420 (1961).
61. *Miller v. School District No. 167,* 495 F.2d 658, 664, n.25 (7th Cir. 1974).
62. 381 U.S. at 496.
63. Id. at 496.
64. Ibid.
65. The conference was on *Poe v. Ullman,* 367 U.S. 497 (1961).
66. Id. at 540, 541, 542–543.
67. Ibid.
68. *In re Winship,* 397 U.S. 358 (1970).
69. Id. at 372.
70. *Poe v. Ullman,* 367 U.S. at 542.
71. Id. at 541.
72. *Richmond Newspapers v. Virginia,* 448 U.S. 555, 580 (1980) (opinion per Burger, C.J.).

Chapter 16

1. Compare Judge Learned Hand, in 317 U.S. xi (1942).
2. *N.Y. Times,* Mar. 3, 1985, Magazine, at 100.
3. L. Hand, supra note 1.
4. *N.Y. Times,* supra note 2.
5. 1 Bryce, *The American Commonwealth* 274 (1917).
6. *Newsweek,* July 23, 1979, at 68.
7. *N.Y. Times,* July 12, 1981, § 4, at 22.
8. *N.Y. Times,* Feb. 28, 1988, § 4, at 1.
9. *N.Y. Times,* Mar. 3, 1985, Magazine, at 33.
10. Id. at 31.
11. *Brown v. Board of Education,* 347 U.S. 483 (1954).
12. *Plessy v. Ferguson,* 163 U.S. 537 (1896).
13. The Rehnquist memo is reprinted in Nomination of Justice William Hubbs Rehnquist, Hearings before the Senate Judiciary Committee, 99th Cong., 2d Sess. 324 (1986).
14. *N.Y. Times,* supra note 9, at 32.
15. WHR to WJB, Re: No. 75-1064 *Kremens v. Bartley,* Mar. 8, 1977.
16. *Time,* Oct. 8, 1984, at 28.
17. *Rummell v. Estelle,* 445 U.S. 263 (1980).
18. WHR, Memorandum to the Conference, Feb. 21, 1980.
19. *Time,* loc. cit. supra note 16.
20. *N.Y. Times,* Oct. 8, 1986, at A32.

21. This was, of course, a takeoff on A. E. Housman, "To An Athlete Dying Young."

22. WHR, Memorandum to the Chambers of All Active and Retired Justices, June 12, 1973, Earl Warren Papers, Library of Congress.

23. Savage, *Turning Right: The Making of the Rehnquist Supreme Court* 16 (1992).

24. O'Brien, *Storm Center: The Supreme Court in American Politics* 189 (1986).

25. *N.Y. Times,* Dec. 13, 1987, at 37.

26. *N.Y. Times,* Mar. 3, 1985, Magazine, at 35.

27. Ibid.

28. *N.Y. Times,* supra note 26.

29. *N.Y. Times,* Mar. 8, 1986, at 7.

30. *N.Y. Times,* Sept. 25, 1986, at B10.

31. 2 *Almanac of the Federal Judiciary* 7 (1992).

32. *Planned Parenthood v. Casey,* 112 S.Ct. 2791 (1992).

33. *The Douglas Letters* 146 (Urofsky ed. 1987).

34. Wyzanski, *Whereas—A Judge's Premises: Essays in Judgment, Ethics, and the Law* 61 (1985).

35. Rehnquist, *The Supreme Court: How It Was, How It Is* 261 (1987).

36. *N.Y. Times,* Apr. 21, 1962, at 17.

37. Supra p. 208.

38. Rehnquist, Who Writes Decisions of the Supreme Court? *U.S. News & World Report,* Dec. 13, 1957, at 74.

39. *The Times (London),* July 11, 1986.

40. *N.Y. Times,* Sept. 20, 1987, Book Review, at 40.

41. Stevens, Madison Lecture at New York University Law School, Oct. 27, 1982.

42. Miky, Mike, & Ricki to WJB, Monday, Nov. 23, [19   ].

43. Rehnquist, op. cit. supra note 35, at 263.

44. Op. cit. supra note 33, at 141.

45. Douglas, *The Court Years 1939–1975,* 173 (1980).

46. *Harvard Law School Bulletin,* Winter 1986, p. 28.

47. Rehnquist, op. cit. supra note 35, at 299–300.

48. Id. at 300.

49. *Brown v. Board of Education,* 347 U.S. 483, 494 n.11 (1954).

50. Supra note 46.

51. William O. Douglas, Memorandum to the Conference, Oct. 23, 1961, Hugo Black Papers, Library of Congress.

52. Compare Posner, *The Federal Courts: Crisis and Reform* 106–107 (1985).

53. Compare id. at 111.

54. *A Dialogue about Legal Education as It Approaches the 21st Century* 29 (J. Kelso ed. 1987).

55. *Richmond v. J. A. Croson Co.,* 488 U.S. 469 (1989).

56. *Wards Cove Packing Co. v. Antonio,* 490 U.S. 642 (1989).

57. *McCloskey v. Kemp,* 481 U.S. 279 (1987).

58. *Nollan v. California Coastal Commission,* 483 U.S. 825 (1987).

59. *Planned Parenthood v. Casey,* 112 S.Ct. 2791 (1992).

60. *Gideon v. Wainwright,* 372 U.S. 335 (1963); *Mapp v. Ohio,* 367 U.S. 643 (1961); *Miranda v. Arizona,* 384 U.S. 436 (1967); supra pp. 280–281.

61. *Board of Estimate v. Morris,* 489 U.S. 688 (1989).

62. *N.Y. Times,* May 26, 1991, § 4, at 1.

63. *McCleskey v. Zant,* 111 S.Ct. 1454 (1991).

64. *California v. Acevedo,* 111 S.Ct. 1982 (1991).

65. *Yates v. Evatt,* 111 S.Ct. 1884 (1991).

66. *Rust v. Sullivan,* 111 S.Ct. 1759 (1991).

67. *Employment Division v. Smith,* 494 U.S. 872 (1990).

68. Cardozo, A Ministry of Justice, 35 *Harvard Law Review* 113, 126 (1921).

69. *Olmstead v. United States,* 277 U.S. 438, 478 (1928).

70. *National Treasury Employees Union v. Von Raab,* 489 U.S. 656 (1989).

71. *Texas v. Johnson,* 491 U.S. 397 (1989); *United States v. Eichmann,* 110 S.Ct. 2404 (1990); *R.A.V. v. St. Paul,* 112 S.Ct. 2538 (1992).

72. Faulkner, Privacy—The American Dream: What Happened to It? *Harper's,* July 1955, at 33, 36.

73. Harlan to Felix Frankfurter, Aug. 21, [1963], Frankfurter Papers, Library of Congress.

74. 399 U.S. 1 (1970).

75. *Miranda v. Arizona,* 384 U.S. 436 (1966).

76. *Planned Parenthood v. Casey,* 112 S.Ct. 2791 (1992).

77. Id. at 2809. In addition, the overruling must not lead to "serious inequity to those who have relied upon it or significant damage to the stability of the society governed by the rule." Ibid.

78. 198 U.S. 45 (1905), supra Chapter 8.

79. 163 U.S. 537 (1896), supra p. 188.

80. 112 S.Ct. at 2813–2814.

81. Id. at 2814.

82. Id. at 2866.

83. E.g., *N.Y. Times,* July 5, 1992, § 4, at 1.

84. *Planned Parenthood v. Casey,* 112 S.Ct. at 2854–2855.

Epilogue

1. Quoted in Dicey, *Law of the Constitution* 1 (9th ed. 1939).

2. Yeats, *Explorations* 351 (1962).

3. Hughes, *Addresses of Charles Evans Hughes* 185 (2d ed. 1916).

4. Pound, *Interpretations of Legal History* 1 (1967).

5. Holmes, *The Common Law* 1 (1881).

6. *McCulloch v. Maryland,* 4 Wheat. 316, 407 (U.S. 1819).

Bibliography

Abraham, Henry J. *Freedom and the Court: Civil Rights and Liberties in the U.S.* 5th ed. New York: Oxford University Press, 1988.

Abraham, Henry J. *Justices and Presidents: A Political History of Appointments to the Supreme Court.* 3rd ed. New York: Oxford University Press, 1991.

Baker, Leonard. *Brandeis and Frankfurter: A Dual Biography.* New York: Harper & Row, 1984.

Baker, Leonard. *John Marshall: A Life in Law.* New York: Macmillan, 1974.

Baker, Liva. *Felix Frankfurter.* New York: Coward-McCann, 1969.

Baker, Liva. *The Justice from Beacon Hill: The Life and Times of Oliver Wendell Holmes.* New York: Harper Collins, 1991.

Ball, Howard, and Phillip J. Cooper. *Of Power and Right: Hugo Black, William O. Douglas, and America's Constitutional Revolution.* New York: Oxford University Press, 1992.

Bates, Ernest S. *The Story of the Supreme Court.* South Hackensack: Fred B. Rothman & Co., 1982.

Baum, Lawrence. *The Supreme Court.* 3rd ed. Washington: Congressional Quarterly, 1988.

Belden, Thomas Graham, and Marva Robins Belden. *So Fell the Angels.* Boston: Little, Brown, 1956.

Berry, Mary. *Stability, Security and Continuity: Mr. Justice Burton and Decision-Making in the Supreme Court 1945–1958.* Westport: Greenwood Press, 1978.

Beth, Loren P. *John Marshall Harlan: The Last Whig Justice.* Lexington: University Press of Kentucky, 1992.

Beveridge, Albert Jeremiah. *The Life of John Marshall.* 4 vols. Boston: Houghton Mifflin, 1916–1919.

Bickel, Alexander M. *Politics and the Warren Court*. New York: Harper & Row, 1965.

Bickel, Alexander M. *The Least Dangerous Branch: The Supreme Court at the Bar of Politics*. Indianapolis: Bobbs-Merrill, 1962, 1986.

Bickel, Alexander M. *The Supreme Court and the Idea of Progress*. New York: Harper & Row, 1970.

Bickel, Alexander M. (ed.). *The Unpublished Opinions of Mr. Justice Brandeis: The Supreme Court at Work*. Chicago: University of Chicago Press, 1967.

Biddle, Francis. *Mr. Justice Holmes*. New York: Scribner, 1942.

Black, Hugo, Jr. *My Father: A Remembrance*. New York: Random House, 1975.

Blasi, Vincent (ed.). *The Burger Court: The Counter-Revolution That Wasn't*. New Haven: Yale University Press, 1986.

Blue, Frederick J. *Salmon P. Chase: A Life in Politics*. Kent: Kent State University Press, 1987.

Boles, Donald E. *Mr. Justice Rehnquist, Judicial Activist: The Early Years*. Ames: Iowa State University Press, 1987.

Boudin, Louis Boudianoff. *Government by Judiciary*. New York: W. Godwin, 1932.

Bowen, Catherine Drinker. *Yankee from Olympus: Justice Holmes and His Family*. Boston: Little, Brown, 1944.

Brown, William Garrott. *The Life of Oliver Ellsworth*. New York: Da Capo Press, 1970.

Bryce, James. *The American Commonwealth*. 2 vols. London and New York: Macmillan, 1889, 1917.

Cahn, Edmond (ed.). *Supreme Court and Supreme Law*. Bloomington: Indiana University Press, 1954.

Cardozo, Benjamin N. *The Nature of the Judicial Process*. New Haven: Yale University Press, 1921.

Cate, Wirt Armistead. *Lucius Q. C. Lamar, Secession and Reunion*. Chapel Hill: University of North Carolina Press, 1935.

Choper, Jesse H. *Judicial Review and the National Political Process: A Functional Reconsideration of the Role of the Supreme Court*. Chicago: University of Chicago Press, 1980.

Christman, Henry (ed.). *The Public Papers of Chief Justice Earl Warren*. New York: Simon & Schuster, 1959.

Clayton, James M. *The Making of Justice: The Supreme Court in Action*. New York: Dutton, 1964.

Clinton, Robert L. *Marbury v. Madison and Judicial Review*. Lawrence: University Press of Kansas, 1989.

Corwin, Edward Samuel. *Court over Constitution: A Study of Judicial Review as an Instrument of Popular Government*. Princeton: Princeton University Press, 1938.

Corwin, Edward Samuel. *John Marshall and the Constitution: A Chronicle of the Supreme Court*. New Haven: Yale University Press, 1919.

Corwin, Edward Samuel. *The Twilight of the Supreme Court: A History of Our Constitutional Theory*. New Haven: Yale University Press, 1934.

Cox, Archibald. *The Court and the Constitution*. Boston: Houghton Mifflin, 1988.

Cox, Archibald. *The Role of the Supreme Court in American Government*. New York: Oxford University Press, 1976.

Currie, David P. *The Constitution in the Supreme Court: The First Hundred Years, 1789–1888*. Chicago: University of Chicago Press, 1986.

Currie, David P. *The Constitution in the Supreme Court: The Second Century, 1888–1986*. Chicago: University of Chicago Press, 1990.

Curtis, Benjamin R., Jr. (ed.). *A Memoir of Benjamin Robbins Curtis*. New York: Da Capo Press, 1970.

Davis, Sue. *Justice Rehnquist and the Constitution*. Princeton: Princeton University Press, 1989.

Documentary History of the Supreme Court of the United States, 1789–1800. 4 vols. New York: Columbia University Press, 1985–1992.

Douglas, William O. *Go East Young Man: The Early Years*. New York: Random House, 1974.

Douglas, William O. *The Court Years 1939–1975*. New York: Random House, 1980.

Dunham, Allison, and Philip B. Kurland (eds.). *Mr. Justice*. Chicago: University of Chicago Press, 1956.

Dunne, Gerald T. *Hugo Black and the Judicial Revolution*. New York: Simon & Schuster, 1977.

Dunne, Gerald T. *Justice Joseph Story and the Rise of the Supreme Court*. New York: Simon & Schuster, 1970.

Elsmere, Jane Shaffer. *Justice Samuel Chase*. Muncie: Janevar Publ. Co., 1980.

Estreicher, Samuel, and John Sexton. *Redefining the Supreme Court's Role: A Theory of Managing the Federal Judicial Process*. New Haven: Yale University Press, 1987.

Fairman, Charles. *Mr. Justice Miller and the Supreme Court, 1862–1890*. Cambridge: Harvard University Press, 1939.

Fine, Sidney. *Frank Murphy*. 3 vols. Ann Arbor: University of Michigan Press; Chicago: University of Chicago Press, 1975–1984.

Flanders, Henry. *The Lives and Times of the Chief Justices of the Supreme Court of the United States*. Buffalo: William S. Hein, [Reprint of the 1881 edition] n.d.

Frank, John Paul. *Justice Daniel Dissenting: A Biography of Peter V. Daniel, 1784–1860*. Cambridge: Harvard University Press, 1964.

Frank, John Paul. *Marble Palace: The Supreme Court in American Life*. New York: Knopf, 1958.

Frank, John Paul. *Mr. Justice Black: The Man and His Opinions*. New York: Knopf, 1949.

Frank, John Paul. *The Warren Court*. New York: Macmillan, 1964.

Frankfurter, Felix. *Felix Frankfurter Reminisces*. New York: Doubleday, 1962.

Frankfurter, Felix. *Mr. Justice Holmes and the Constitution*. Cambridge: Dunster House Bookshop, 1927.

Frankfurter, Felix. *Mr. Justice Holmes and the Supreme Court*. 2d ed. Cambridge: Harvard University Press, 1961.

Frankfurter, Felix. *Of Law and Men: Papers and Addresses of Felix Frankfurter*. New York: Harcourt Brace, 1956.

Frankfurter, Felix. *The Commerce Clause under Marshall, Taney and Waite*. Chapel Hill: University of North Carolina Press, 1937, 1960.

Frankfurter, Felix, and James M. Landis. *The Business of the Supreme Court: A Study in the Federal Judicial System*. New York: Macmillan, 1927.

Freund, Paul A. *On Understanding the Supreme Court*. Boston: Little, Brown, 1949; New York: Greenwood, 1977.

Friedman, Leon (ed.). *The Justices of the United States Supreme Court: Their Lives and Major Opinions.* Vol. 5, *The Burger Court, 1969–1978.* New York: Chelsea House, 1979.

Friedman, Leon, and Fred Israel (eds.). *The Justices of the United States Supreme Court 1789–1969: Their Lives and Major Opinions.* 4 vols. New York: Chelsea House, 1969.

Gerhart, Eugene C. *America's Advocate: Robert H. Jackson.* Indianapolis: Bobbs-Merrill, 1958.

Goldman, Roger. *Thurgood Marshall: Justice for All.* New York: Carroll & Graf, 1992.

Goldstein, Joseph. *The Intelligible Constitution: The Supreme Court's Obligation to Maintain the Constitution as Something We the People Can Understand.* New York: Oxford University Press, 1992.

Haines, Charles Grove. *The Role of the Supreme Court in American Government and Politics, 1789–1835.* New York: Russell & Russell, 1960.

Harper, Fowler Vincent. *Justice Rutledge and the Bright Constellation.* Indianapolis: Bobbs-Merrill, 1965.

Hart, Albert Busnell. *Salmon Portland Chase.* Boston; New York: Houghton Mifflin, 1899.

Hellman, George Sidney. *Benjamin N. Cardozo, American Judge.* New York: McGraw-Hill, 1940.

Hendel, Samuel. *Charles Evans Hughes and the Supreme Court.* New York: King's Crown Press, 1951.

Hirsch, H. N. *The Enigma of Felix Frankfurter.* New York: Basic Books, 1981.

Howard, J. Woodford. *Mr. Justice Murphy: A Political Biography.* Princeton: Princeton University Press, 1968.

Howe, Mark De Wolfe. *Justice Oliver Wendell Holmes.* 2 vols. Cambridge: Harvard University Press, 1957.

Hughes, Charles E. *The Supreme Court of the United States.* New York: Columbia University Press, 1936, 1966.

Huston, Luther. *Pathway to Judgment: A Study of Earl Warren.* Philadelphia: Chilton Books, 1966.

Jackson, Robert Houghwout. *The Struggle for Judicial Supremacy: A Study of a Crisis in American Power Politics.* New York: Knopf, 1941.

Jackson, Robert Houghwout. *The Supreme Court in the American System of Government.* Cambridge: Harvard University Press, 1955.

Kalman, Laura. *Abe Fortas: A Biography.* New Haven: Yale University Press, 1990.

Katcher, Leo. *Earl Warren: A Political Biography.* New York: McGraw-Hill, 1967.

King, Willard Leroy. *Lincoln's Manager, David Davis.* Cambridge: Harvard University Press, 1960.

King, Willard Leroy. *Melville Weston Fuller, Chief Justice of the United States, 1888–1910.* New York: Macmillan, 1950.

Kluger, Richard. *Simple Justice: The History of Brown v. Board of Education and Black America's Struggle for Equality.* New York: Knopf, 1975.

Konefsky, Samuel Joseph. *Chief Justice Stone and the Supreme Court.* New York: Macmillan, 1945.

Konefsky, Samuel Joseph. *The Legacy of Holmes and Brandeis: A Study in the Influence of Ideas.* New York: Macmillan, 1956.

Kurland, Philip B. *Mr. Justice Frankfurter and the Constitution.* Chicago: University of Chicago Press, 1971.

Kurland, Philip B. (ed.). *Felix Frankfurter on the Supreme Court: Extrajudicial*

Essays on the Court and the Constitution. Cambridge: Harvard University Press, 1970.

Kurland, Phillip B., and Gerhard Casper (eds.). *Landmark Briefs and Arguments of the Supreme Court of the United States: Constitutional Law.* Arlington: University Publishers of America, 1977–19[   ].

Lamb, Charles M., and Stephen C. Halpern (eds.). *Burger Court: Political and Judicial Profiles.* Champaign: University of Illinois Press, 1990.

Latham, Frank Brown. *The Great Dissenter: John Marshall Harlan, 1833–1911.* New York: Cowles Book Co., 1970.

Lawrence, Alexander A. *James Moore Wayne: Southern Unionist.* Chapel Hill: University of North Carolina Press, 1943; Westport: Greenwood Press, 1970.

Levy, Leonard W. (ed.). *The Supreme Court under Earl Warren.* New York: Quadrangle Books, 1972.

Lewis, Anthony. *Gideon's Trumpet.* New York: Random House, 1964.

Lewis, Anthony. *Portrait of a Decade: The Second American Revolution.* New York: Random House, 1964.

Lewis, Walker. *Without Fear or Favor: A Biography of Chief Justice Roger Brooke Taney.* Boston: Houghton Mifflin, 1965.

MacKenzie, John P. *The Appearance of Justice.* New York: Scribner's, 1974.

Magrath, C. Peter. *Morrison R. Waite: The Triumph of Character.* New York: Macmillan, 1963.

Mason, Alpheus Thomas. *Harlan Fiske Stone: Pillar of the Law.* New York: Viking Press, 1956.

Mason, Alpheus Thomas. *The Supreme Court from Taft to Burger.* Baton Rouge: Louisiana State University Press, 1979.

Mason, Alpheus Thomas. *William Howard Taft: Chief Justice.* New York: Simon & Schuster, 1965.

Mason, Alpheus Thomas, and William M. Beaney. *The Supreme Court in a Free Society.* Englewood Cliffs: Prentice-Hall, 1959.

McClellan, James. *Joseph Story and the American Constitution.* Norman: University of Oklahoma Press, 1971.

McCloskey, Robert Green. *The Modern Supreme Court.* Cambridge: Harvard University Press, 1972.

McDevitt, Matthew. *Joseph McKenna.* New York: Da Capo Press, 1974.

McLean, Joseph Erigina. *William Rufus Day, Supreme Court Justice from Ohio.* Baltimore: Johns Hopkins Press, 1946.

Mendelson, Wallace. *Justices Black and Frankfurter: Conflict in the Court.* Chicago: University of Chicago Press, 1961.

Mendelson, Wallace. *The Supreme Court: Law and Discretion.* Indianapolis: Bobbs-Merrill, 1967.

Morgan, Donald Grant. *Justice William Johnson: The First Dissenter.* Columbia: University of South Carolina Press, 1954.

Morris, Richard Brandon. *John Jay, the Nation and the Court.* Boston: Boston University Press, 1967.

Murphy, Bruce Allen. *Fortas: The Rise and Ruin of a Supreme Court Justice.* New York: Morrow, 1988.

Murphy, Bruce Allen. *The Brandeis/Frankfurter Connection.* New York: Oxford University Press, 1982.

Murphy, James B. *L.Q.C. Lamar: Pragmatic Patriot.* Baton Rouge: Louisiana State University Press, 1973.

Newmyer, R. Kent. *Supreme Court Justice Joseph Story: Statesman of the Old Republic.* Chapel Hill: University of North Carolina Press, 1985.

Novick, Sheldon M. *Honorable Justice: The Life of Oliver Wendell Holmes.* Boston: Little, Brown, 1989.

O'Brien, David M. *Storm Center: The Supreme Court in American Politics.* 2d ed. New York: W. W. Norton, 1990.

Palmer, Jan. *The Vinson Court Era: The Supreme Court's Conference Votes, Data and Analysis.* New York: AMS Press, 1990.

Paper, Lewis J. *Brandeis.* Englewood Cliffs: Prentice-Hall, 1983.

Parrish, Michael E. *Felix Frankfurter and His Times: The Reform Years.* New York: Free Press, 1982.

Paschal, Joel Francis. *Mr. Justice Sutherland: A Man Against the State.* Princeton: Princeton University Press, 1951.

Pellew, George. *John Jay.* Boston; New York: Houghton Mifflin, 1890.

Pohlman, H. L. *Justice Oliver Wendell Holmes, Free Speech and the Living Constitution.* New York: New York University Press, 1991.

Pollack, Jack Harrison. *Earl Warren: The Judge Who Changed America.* Englewood Cliffs: Prentice-Hall, 1979.

Pollard, Joseph Percival. *Mr. Justice Cardozo: A Liberal Mind in Action.* New York: Yorktown Press, 1935.

Posner, Richard A. *Cardozo: A Study in Reputation.* Chicago: University of Chicago Press, 1990.

Posner, Richard A. (ed.). *The Essential Holmes: Selections from the Letters, Speeches, Judicial Opinions and Other Writings of Oliver Wendell Holmes, Jr.* Chicago: University of Chicago Press, 1992.

Pringle, Henry F. *The Life and Times of William Howard Taft: A Biography.* 2 vols. New York; Toronto: Farrar & Rinehart, 1939, 1964.

Pritchett, Charles Herman. *The Roosevelt Court: A Study in Judicial Politics and Values, 1937–1947.* New York: Macmillan, 1948.

Pusey, Merlo J. *Charles Evans Hughes.* 2 vols. New York: Macmillan, 1951, 1963.

Rehnquist, William H. *The Supreme Court: How It Was, How It Is.* New York: Morrow, 1987.

Rodell, Fred. *Nine Men: A Political History of the Supreme Court from 1790 to 1955.* New York: Random House, 1955.

Rostow, Eugene V. *The Sovereign Prerogative: The Supreme Court and the Quest for Law.* New Haven: Yale University Press, 1962; New York: Greenwood, 1974.

Savage, David G. *Turning Right: The Making of the Rehnquist Supreme Court.* New York: Wiley, 1992.

Schubert, Blendon A. *Constitutional Politics: The Behavior of the Supreme Court Justices and the Constitutional Policies That They Make.* New York: Holt, Rinehart and Winston, 1960.

Schubert, Glendon A. *The Judicial Mind: The Attitudes and Ideologies of the Supreme Court Justices, 1946–1963.* Evanston: Northwestern University Press, 1965.

Schwartz, Bernard. *Behind Bakke: Affirmative Action and the Supreme Court.* New York: New York University Press, 1988.

Schwartz, Bernard. *Super Chief: Earl Warren and His Supreme Court—A Judicial Biography.* New York: New York University Press, 1983.

Schwartz, Bernard. *The Ascent of Pragmatism: The Burger Court in Action.* Reading: Addison-Wesley, 1990.

Schwartz, Bernard. *The Law in America: A History*. New York: McGraw-Hill, 1974.

Schwartz, Bernard. *The Reins of Power: A Constitutional History of the United States*. New York: Hill and Wang, 1963.

Schwartz, Bernard. *The Supreme Court: Constitutional Revolution in Retrospect*. New York: Ronald Press, 1957.

Schwartz, Bernard. *The Unpublished Opinions of the Burger Court*. New York: Oxford University Press, 1988.

Schwartz, Bernard. *The Unpublished Opinions of the Warren Court*. New York: Oxford University Press, 1985.

Shogan, Robert. *A Question of Judgment: The Fortas Case and the Struggle for the Supreme Court*. Indianapolis: Bobbs-Merrill, 1972.

Sickels, Robert J. *John Paul Stevens and the Constitution: The Search and the Balance*. University Park: Pennsylvania State University Press, 1988.

Siegan, Bernard H. *The Supreme Court's Constitution*. New Brunswick: Transaction, 1987.

Simon, James F. *Independent Journey: The Life of William O. Douglas*. New York: Harper & Row, 1980.

Simon, James F. *The Antagonists: Hugo Black, Felix Frankfurter and Civil Liberties in Modern America*. New York: Simon & Schuster, 1989.

Smith, Charles William. *Roger B. Taney: Jacksonian Jurist*. Chapel Hill: University of North Carolina Press, 1936.

Smith, Page. *James Wilson, Founding Father, 1742–1798*. Chapel Hill: University of North Carolina Press, 1956.

Story, William Wetmore. *Life and Letters of Joseph Story, Associate Justice of the Supreme Court of the United States, and Dane Professor of Law at Harvard University*. 2 vols. Boston: Little and J. Brown, 1851.

Streamer, Robert J. *Chief Justice: Leadership and the Supreme Court*. Columbia: University of South Carolina Press, 1986.

Strum, Phillippa. *Louis D. Brandeis: Justice for the People*. Cambridge: Harvard University Press, 1984.

Swindler, William Finley. *Court and Constitution in the Twentieth Century*. 2 vols. Indianapolis: Bobbs-Merrill, 1969, 1974.

Swisher, Carl Brent. *Roger B. Taney*. New York: Macmillan, 1935.

Swisher, Carl Brent. *Stephen J. Field: Craftsman of the Law*. Hamden: Archon Books, 1963.

Swisher, Carl Brent. *The Supreme Court in Modern Role*. Rev. ed. New York: New York University Press, 1965.

Thomas, Helen Shirley. *Felix Frankfurter: Scholar on the Bench*. Baltimore: Johns Hopkins Press, 1960.

Tocqueville, Alexis de. *Democracy in America*. 2 vols. New York: Vintage Books, 1954.

Tribe, Laurence H. *God Save This Honorable Court: How the Choice of the Supreme Court Justices Shapes Our History*. New York: Random House, 1985.

Twiss, Benjamin. *Lawyers and the Constitution: How Laissez Faire Came to the Supreme Court*. Princeton: Princeton University Press, 1942; New York: Greenwood, 1974.

Umbreit, Kenneth Bernard. *Our Eleven Chief Justices*. New York: Harper & Brothers, 1938.

Urofsky, Melvin I., and Philip E. Urofsky (eds.). *The Douglas Letters: Selections from the Private Papers of Justice William O. Douglas.* Bethesda: Adler & Adler, 1987.

Warner, Hoyt Landon. *The Life of Mr. Justice Clarke: A Testament to the Power of Liberal Dissent in America.* Cleveland: Case Western Reserve University Press, 1959.

Warren, Charles. *The Supreme Court in United States History.* 3 vols. Boston: Little, Brown, 1922, 1924.

Warren, Earl. *The Memoirs of Earl Warren.* New York: Doubleday, 1977.

Wasby, Stephen L. (ed.). *He Shall Not Pass This Way Again: The Legacy of Justice William O. Douglas.* Pittsburgh: University of Pittsburgh Press, 1990.

Weaver, John D. *Warren: The Man, The Court, The Era.* Boston: Little, Brown, 1967.

White, G. Edmund. *Earl Warren: A Public Life.* New York: Oxford University Press, 1982.

Wiecek, William M. *Liberty under Law: The Supreme Court in American Life.* Baltimore: Johns Hopkins University Press, 1988.

Witt, Elder. *Congressional Quarterly's Guide to the U.S. Supreme Court.* 2d ed. Washington: Congressional Quarterly, 1990.

Woodward, Bob, and Scott Armstrong. *The Brethren: Inside the Supreme Court.* New York: Simon & Schuster, 1979.

Wright, Benjamin Fletcher. *The Growth of American Constitutional Law.* New York: H. Holt, 1942.

Oliver Wendell Holmes Devise

History of the Supreme Court of the United States. New York: Macmillan, 1971–1988.

Volume I: *Antecedents and Beginnings to 1801,* by Julius Goebel, Jr. (1971).

Volume II: *Foundations of Power: John Marshall, 1801–15,* by George L. Haskins and Herbert A. Johnson (1981).

Volumes III–IV: *The Marshall Court and Cultural Change, 1815–35,* by G. Edward White (1988).

Volume V: *The Taney Period, 1836–64,* by Carl B. Swisher (1974).

Volume VI: *Reconstruction and Reunion, 1864–88, Part One,* by Charles Fairman (1971).

Volume VII: *Reconstruction and Reunion, 1864–88, Part Two,* by Charles Fairman (1987).

Supplement to Volume VII: *Five Justices and the Electoral Commission of 1877,* by Charles Fairman (1988).

Volume IX: *The Judiciary and Responsible Government, 1910–21,* by Alexander M. Bickel and Benno C. Schmidt, Jr. (1984).

List of Cases

447

Index

Shielding the Poor

Social Protection
in the Developing World

Nora Lustig
Editor

Brookings Institution Press

Inter-American Development Bank

Washington, D.C.
2001

Copyright © 2001
INTER-AMERICAN DEVELOPMENT BANK
All rights reserved. No part of this publication may be reproduced or transmitted in any form or by any means without permission in writing from the Brookings Institution Press.
e-mail: permissions@brook.edu; fax: (202) 797-6195

To order this book, contact:
IDB Bookstore
1300 New York Avenue, N.W.
Washington, D.C. 20577
Tel: 1-877-PUBS IDB/(202) 623-1753
Fax: (202) 623-1709
E-mail: idb-books@iadb.org
www.iadb.org/pub

Brookings Institution Press
1775 Massachusetts Avenue, N.W.
Washington, D.C. 20036
Tel: 1-800-275-1447 / (202) 797-6258
Fax (202) 797-2960
www.brookings.edu
e-mail: bibooks@brookings.edu

Library of Congress Cataloging-in-Publication data

Shielding the poor: social protection in the developing world / Nora Lustig, editor.
      p. cm.
Includes bibliographical references and index.
  ISBN 0-8157-5321-7 (pbk. : alk. paper)
  1. Poor—Developing countries. 2. Public welfare—Developing countries. 3. Poverty—Developing countries. 4. Human services—Developing countries. 5. Structural adjustment (Economic policy)—Social aspects—Developing countries. I. Lustig, Nora.
  HV525 .S54 2000   00-010531
  362.5'8'091724Cdc21   CIP

The paper used in this publication meets minimum requirements of the American National Standard for Information Sciences—Permanence of Paper for Printed Library Materials—ANSI.48-1992

Printed by R. R. Donnelley and Sons
Harrisonburg, Virginia

Contents

Preface

Most countries in the developing world do not have effective mechanisms in place for softening the impact of adverse shocks on the poor. The contributions presented in *Shielding the Poor: Social Protection in the Developing World* explain why the poor are particularly vulnerable to adverse shocks and discuss appropriate policy responses for minimizing the impact of shocks on poverty and how to exploit the growth-enhancing elements of safety nets and social protection more generally. The volume covers a broad range of issues in the social protection agenda, including an analysis of the empirical evidence of the impact of shocks on poverty and inequality in Latin America, unemployment insurance and employment programs, the safety net role of microfinance, the role of social investment funds in helping the poor manage risk, old age security for the poor, the impact of health shocks on the poor, and lessons learned from social protection programs in the developed world.

The articles included in this book were presented at the conference, "Social Protection and Poverty," held at the Inter-American Development Bank (IDB) in February 1999 in Washington, D.C. The authors benefited greatly from comments by the discussants who participated in the conference, including Marguerite Berger, Gary Burtless, Gaurav Datt, Ruthanne Deutsch, Christiaan Grootaert, Carmen Pagés, Inder Ruprah, William Savedoff, Miguel Székely, and Andras Uthoff, as well as from anonymous reviewers.

Many people collaborated in the preparation of this volume. In particular, Alexander Kazan coordinated the logistics of the editorial process with the support of Gustavo Yamada and Daniel Myers. Celine Charveriat—with the collaboration of Ellen Connors and Heather McPhail—was the logistics coordinator of the conference and was supported by Miguel Almeyda, Soledad Bustos, César Cantú, Laura Sotomayor, and Luis Tejerina. We would like to thank Sandra Gain from the Publications Section of the IDB for her editorial input. We extend our warm appreciation to the Brookings Institution Press, especially Christopher Kelaher, acquisitions editor, and Janet Walker, managing editor. Theresa Walker edited the manuscript, Tanjam Jacobson proofread it, and Shirley Kessel prepared the index.

CHAPTER ONE

Introduction

Nora Lustig

Social protection consists of the set of public initiatives that can lessen the impact of adverse shocks on the income of the population. In more technical terms, social protection is the set of public interventions designed to assist individuals and households in better managing economic risks. These interventions typically include labor market interventions, social safety nets, and pensions. They also include public actions aimed at reducing risk such as prudent fiscal policy to prevent macroeconomic crises, large-scale reforestation to prevent natural disasters, or public health campaigns to reduce the incidence of illness. Measures designed to better equip the population to protect itself such as building a more solid asset base (through land distribution and titling, for example) and access to credit and insurance markets belong to the social protection agenda as well.

The primary focus of this book is not social protection in general but social protection for the poor in the context of a developing country. That is, we are concerned with providing social protection to the segment of the population that has little or no access to state-sponsored social insurance schemes (because it does not participate in a contributory system because of legal or de facto restrictions) or private market insurance or credit mechanisms (because of "cream skimming" practices and moral hazard issues); cannot save in adequate amounts precisely because it is poor; and has little or no voice to demand the protection of pro-poor programs and the implementation of safety nets in times of fiscal retrenchment. The mechanisms considered are those that serve to smooth downward risks, that is, adverse shocks.

The key objectives of social protection for the poor can be summarized as follows:

• To lessen the vulnerability of the poor through ex ante measures that reduce the occurrence of adverse shocks or mitigate their impact, and through ex post measures that help the poor to maintain adequate consumption and access to basic services once the shock occurs.

• To allow for better consumption smoothing over the life cycle of poor families through market and nonmarket mechanisms.

• To enhance equity by ensuring that the poor are not disproportionately exposed or hurt by adverse shocks.[1]

Why may social protection for the poor be an important concern for policymakers? One obvious reason is because policy interventions can improve the well-being of the poor simply by preventing sharp downfalls in income or consumption. Poor people in the developing world give high priority to economic security.[2] Empirical studies show that large fluctuations in income are common for the poor and that a large proportion of people fall into poverty at one point or another in their lives.[3] Large aggregate shocks such as economywide crises result in sharp increases in poverty (table 1–1). As seen in table 1–2, panel data indicate that the share of households that are "sometimes poor" is considerable and almost always exceeds the proportion of households that are "always poor." Because the poor are less equipped to smooth consumption, income downfalls will translate into large consumption downfalls.[4]

However, an equally compelling reason is that social protection can be growth enhancing as well. If the poor have access to mechanisms that protect them from sharp downfalls in income, they will be more likely to undertake riskier initiatives in the production and labor market spheres, and these initiatives could result in a higher return for the poor and for the economy overall. Similarly, if social protection helps prevent or at least mitigates irreversible damage to the accumulation of human capital (such as a rise in abusive child labor, malnutrition, or school dropouts), it will also be beneficial for overall growth and contribute to poverty reduction on a more permanent basis and not just during the period of the shock. In table 1–3 we present examples of the impact of economic crises on education and health and nutrition indicators.[5] Christiaan Grootaert finds that in Côte d'Ivoire, in re-

---

[1] See World Bank (1999a, p. 14).

[2] World Bank (1999b, 2000a).

[3] World Bank (2000b, chap. 8). At the more microeconomic level, Townsend (1994) finds that the coefficients of variation of income from the main crops in two Indian villages are between .37 and 1.01.

[4] Jalan and Ravallion (1997), for example, show that 40 percent of an income shock is passed on as lower consumption for the poorest 10 percent of households in China, while for the richest third only 10 percent is passed on.

[5] See also Lustig (1995, 1999).

Table 1–1. Poverty Headcount Ratio Before, During, and After Crisis

Country	Year of crisis	Before crisis		During crisis		After crisis			Change in GDP per capita relative to year	
		Ratio	Year	Ratio	Change	Ratio	Year	Change	Of crisis	Before crisis
Argentina (Greater Buenos Aires)	1985	10.1	1980	20.6	+	25.2	1987	+	+	–
Argentina (Greater Buenos Aires)	1989	25.2	1987	47.3	+	33.7	1990	+	+	–
Argentina (Greater Buenos Aires)	1995	16.8	1993	24.8	+	26.0	1997	+	+	+
Brazil (all metropolitan areas)	1990	27.9	1989	28.9	+					
Chile (metropolitan areas) §	1982	40.3	1980			48.6	1987	+	+	–
Costa Rica *	1982	29.6	1981	32.3	+	29.7	1983	+	+	–
Dominican Republic *	1985	37.3	1984			38.2	1986	+	+	+
Dominican Republic *	1990	35.7	1989			39.5	1992	+	+	–
Guatemala §	1982	65.0	1980	18.9		68.0	1986	+	–	–
Indonesia *	1998	11.3	1996	16.7	+	11.7	1999			
Jordan *	1989	3.0	1987			14.9	1992	+	+	+
Korea (urban) *	1998	8.6	1997	19.2	+					
Mexico	1986	28.5	1984			32.6	1989	+	+	+
Mexico §	1995	36.0	1994			43.0	1996	+	+	–
Panama *	1983	40.6	1980			44.0	1986	+	–	–
Panama *	1988	44.0	1986			50.0	1989	+	–	–
Peru §	1983	46.0	1979			52.0	1986	+	+	–
Peru (urban) *	1988	32.2	1985			50.0	1991	+	–	–
Russia **	1998	21.9	1996	32.7	+					
Thailand	1998	11.4	1996	12.9	+			+		
Uruguay §	1982	11.0	1981			15.0	1986	+	–	–
Venezuela §	1983	25.7	1982	32.7	+	34.8	1985	+	–	–
Venezuela §	1989	40.0	1988	44.4	+	41.5	1990	+	+	–
Venezuela §	1994	41.4	1993	53.6	+	48.2	1996	+	–	–

+ Increase.
– Decrease.
§ Based on household income.
* Based on per capita expenditure.
** Based on household expenditure.

Note: Headcount based on individual per capita household income and national poverty lines unless otherwise noted. For Argentina, Brazil, Chile, Korea, and Peru there was no information at the national level.

Source: World Bank (2000a); real GDP per capita data from World Bank (2000b); for Argentina, Ministerio de Economía de Argentina (1998) and Morley and Alvarez (1992); for Brazil, Barros, Mendonça, and Rocha (1995); for Chile, Lustig (1995, table 1–1); for Costa Rica, the Dominican Republic, and Panama, Londoño and Székely (1997); for Guatemala, Peru (1983), and Uruguay, ECLAC (1996); for Indonesia, Korea, and Thailand, World Bank (1999a); for Jordan, World Bank (1994); for Mexico (1986), Lustig and Székely (1998); for Mexico (1995), ECLAC (1999); for Peru (1988), Escobal, Saavedra, and Torero (1998); for Russia, Lokshin and Ravallion (2000); and for Venezuela, Ruprah and Marcano (1998).

Table 1–2. Households by Poverty Status in Selected Developing Countries, Various Years

Percent

Country	Period	Always poor	Sometimes poor	Never poor
China	1985–90	6.2	47.8	46.0
Côte d'Ivoire	1987–88	25.0	22.0	53.0
Ethiopia	1994–97	24.8	30.1	45.1
Pakistan	1986–91	3.0	55.3	41.7
Russian Federation	1992–93	12.6	30.2	57.2
South Africa	1993–98	22.7	31.5	45.8
Zimbabwe	1992/93–1995/96	10.6	59.6	29.8

Source: Baulch and Hoddinott (forthcoming).

sponse to a severe economic recession, the poorest households increased the labor force participation of children the most. Hanan Jacoby and Emmanuel Skoufias find that in rural India households used child labor as a way to respond to seasonal income fluctuations. In Zimbabwe, John Hoddinott and Bill Kinsey find that the 1994–95 droughts reduced annual growth rates of the height of small children.[6] These responses show how transient shocks can affect the ability of the children of poor families to grow out of poverty when they reach adulthood.

Finally, if the poor are protected from the income variability associated with openness and flexible labor markets, they are more likely to support stabilization programs and growth-enhancing reforms. Recent work has shown that the combination of weak institutions—including among them the lack of adequate social safety nets—and divided societies lies at the bottom of the growth collapses experienced in the past twenty-five years.[7]

A TYPOLOGY OF ADVERSE SHOCKS

Although adverse shocks are accompanied by a downturn in income or consumption, they are not all economic in origin. Economic shocks are those resulting from macroeconomic mismanagement, terms-of-trade shocks, volatility in capital flows,

---

[6] Grootaert (1998); Jacoby and Skoufias (1997); Hoddinott and Kinsey (1998).

[7] Rodrik (1997).

Table 1–3. Health and Educational Impact of Economic Crisis

	Argentina, 1995	Mexico, 1995	Indonesia, 1998
Main crisis indicators	Per capita GDP fell 4.1 percent. Per capita private consumption fell 5.6 percent.	Per capita GDP fell 7.8 percent. Per capita private consumption fell 11.1 percent.	Per capita GDP fell 14.6 percent. Per capita private consumption fell 5.1 percent.
Health	Per capita daily protein intake fell 3.8 percent in 1995 but increased 1.9 percent in 1996.	Among children under age 1, mortality from anemia increased from 6.3 deaths per 100,000 live births in 1993 to 7.9 in 1995. Among children age 1–4, the rate rose from 1.7 to 2.2.	The share of women whose body mass index is below the level at which morbidity and mortality risks increase was 25 percent. Most indicators of child nutritional status remained constant. The exception may be the weight (conditional on height) of children under age 3, suggesting that families may be investing in some members at the expense of others.
Education	Growth in gross primary enrollment declined from 2.2 percent in 1993 to 0.8 percent in 1996.	Gross primary school enrollment increased 0.44 percent in 1994 but fell 0.09 percent in 1995.	The dropout rates for children age 7–12 in the poorest quartile rose from 1.3 percent in 1997 to 7.5 percent in 1998. For children age 13–19, the rate rose from 14.2 percent to 25.5 percent. In both cohorts, the poorest quartile experienced the largest increase in dropout rates. The share of children age 7–12 in the poorest quartile not enrolled in school rose from 4.9 percent in 1997 to 10.7 percent in 1998. For children age 13–19, the rate rose from 42.5 to 58.4 percent. In both cohorts, the poorest quartile experienced the largest increase.

Source: World Bank (2000b).

and so on. Physical shocks include ill health, disability, and death in the family as well as large-scale epidemics. Natural shocks include droughts, pests, hurricanes, floods, and earthquakes. Social or political shocks include wars, conflicts, massive strikes, upheavals, and violence in various forms (domestic or otherwise). Environmental shocks include pollution, deforestation, and nuclear disasters. Table 1–4 summarizes the types of shocks that people may face.

Depending on the number of individuals or households that are simultaneously affected, shocks are either idiosyncratic or covariate (aggregate) (table 1–4). Idiosyncratic shocks are those that occur when only one or a few individuals or households in a community suffer losses. Typical idiosyncratic shocks are noncommunicative illness or frictional unemployment. Covariate shocks occur when large numbers of households are hit at the same time. Covariate shocks can affect entire villages, communities, or regions within a country as occurs, for example, with climatic events, downsizing of the public sector, and sharp capital outflows or terms-of-trade shocks. Entire countries are affected by economywide crises such as financial meltdowns and large-scale natural disasters such as El Niño; and groups of countries experienced the debt crisis of the 1980s. The global economy felt the impact of the Great Depression and the two world wars.

Some types of shocks are few and far between, such as the death of the breadwinner of a household, and others occur with frequency, such as a bad crop because of weather conditions. Some shocks are serially correlated. For example, natural disasters can be followed by sickness and death, compounding the initial impact of the environmental event.

Some shocks, even if they are infrequent, have a long-lasting effect, such as death or disability of the breadwinner or technological redundancy of skills. Such *catastrophic* adverse shocks may require permanent transfers to the affected households. There are other shocks that might be of high frequency but whose effects are not very severe, such as transient illness or temporary unemployment. In such cases the required relief is temporary.

STRATEGIES FOR MANAGING ADVERSE SHOCKS

The strategies for managing adverse shocks can be classified into three categories: nonmarket, market-based, and publicly mandated or provided (table 1–5). *Nonmarket* arrangements include the safety nets provided by social networks such as marriage, the extended family, and mutual community support, as well as the self-insurance mechanisms used by individuals and households, such as saving in

Table 1–4. Main Sources of Risk

Type of risk	At the household or individual level (idiosyncratic)	At the community level (covariate)	At the nationwide level (covariate)
Natural	Rainfall	Earthquakes Landslides Volcanic eruption	Floods Drought High winds
Health	Illness Injury Disability Old age Death	Epidemic	
Social	Crime Domestic violence	Terrorism Gangs	Civil strife War Social upheaval
Economic	Frictional unemployment	Resettlement Harvest failure	Growth collapse Balance-of-payments, financial, or currency crisis Technology- or trade-induced terms-of-trade shocks
Political		Riots	Political default on social programs Coup d'état
Environmental	Pollution	Pollution Deforestation Nuclear disaster	

Source: Adapted from World Bank (2000); Holzmann and Jørgensen (2000); Sinha and Lipton (1999).

the form of goods and real assets (food, farm animals, land), crop and field diversification, the use of safer technology, labor market decisions (migration, occupational choice, labor force participation), schooling decisions, and so on. *Market-based* arrangements include financial intermediaries and insurance companies. *Publicly mandated* or provided arrangements include the rules and regulations that mandate or provide insurance for unemployment, old age, disability, survivorship, accident and sickness. They also include the array of safety nets and social assistance programs designed to ameliorate the impact of adverse shocks on the poor regardless of their origin.

By their very nature the poor in developing countries are more likely to rely on nonmarket and self-insurance arrangements. Because of market failures arising from asymmetric information, moral hazard, and "cream skimming" practices, the poor are less likely to have access to formal credit and insurance markets. But while some informal and self-insurance arrangements might be effective for coping with idiosyncratic shocks, their effectiveness against covariate shocks is limited. Informal or self-insurance arrangements may be suboptimal even in the case of idiosyncratic shocks because they could result in lower potential incomes such as would be the case with safer but less productive technologies, inefficient crop and field diversification, or the decision to discontinue school attendance. In all such cases public intervention is warranted to improve the access of the poor to market-based arrangements and to reduce the use of self-destructive informal and self-insurance schemes to cope with adverse shocks.[8]

Government action is also fundamental in the prevention of adverse shocks. Reducing the likelihood of adverse shocks includes, for example, measures in the international financial architecture and economic policy realm for preventing economywide crises; environmental and population measures to reduce the likelihood that an environmental-climatic event results in a calamity; and public health policy to reduce the occurrence of preventable health shocks.

The purpose of this book is to discuss alternative interventions that can reduce and mitigate the impact of adverse shocks on the poor as well as allow for better consumption smoothing over the life cycle of poor families in the most efficient way. The latter implies paying particular attention in designing the interventions so as to exploit the growth-enhancing elements of safety nets, minimize leakage of the benefits to the nonpoor (targeting issues), and avoid perverse incentives. Essentially, the book will concentrate on the italicized concepts in table 1–5, that is, publicly provided risk-coping measures, such as employment programs and social assistance for health shocks and old age; and risk reduction and mitigation instruments, such as microfinance and social investment funds. It will also include a discussion of social protection programs in the developed world and the

---

[8] Extreme cases of self-destructive behavior in coping with shocks exist throughout the world. In India, for instance, it was discovered that poor women were forfeiting a kidney to pay back money they had borrowed to feed their families (University of California, 1999).

Table 1–5. Mechanisms for Managing Risk

	Informal mechanisms		Formal mechanisms	
	Individual and household	Group based	Market-based	Publicly provided
Risk reduction	Preventive health practices Migration Less risky income sources	Collective action for infrastructure, dikes, terraces Common property resource management		Sound macro-economic policy Environmental policy Education and training policy Public health policy Infrastructure (dams, roads) Labor market policies
Risk mitigation Portfolio diversification	Crop and plot diversification Income source diversification Investment in physical and human capital	Occupational associations Rotating savings and credit associations	Savings accounts in financial institutions *Microfinance*	Agricultural extension Open up trade opportunities Protection of property rights
Insurance	Marriage and extended family Sharecrop tenancy Buffer stocks	Investment in social capital (networks, associations, rituals, reciprocal gift giving)	Old age annuities Accident and disability insurance	*Pension systems* *Unemployment insurance* Health and disability insurance
Risk coping	Sale of assets Loans from moneylenders Child labor Reduced food consumption	Transfers from networks of mutual support	Sale of financial assets Loans from financial institutions	*Social assistance* *Workfare* Subsidies *Social funds* Cash transfers

Source: World Bank (2000a, chap. 8); adapted from Holzmann and Jørgensen (2000).

role of informal safety nets. Although the topics covered are by no means exhaustive, the chapters provide lessons from experience and a good overview of the issues that policymakers will have to face in designing appropriate ways of shielding the poor from adverse shocks.[9] While a few of the chapters are very technical in nature, others are primarily descriptive and accessible to a wide audience. The more technical chapters show the elements that have to be considered when attempting to strike a balance between social protection and efficiency.

Because of its focus on the uninsured poor, this book has great relevance for developing countries and a very limited one, if any, for the industrial world. As development proceeds in the less developed world, one would expect to see a transition away from self-insurance and social assistance to market-based risk management strategies and publicly provided social risk management instruments such as sick pay, health care, disability and old-age insurance, and unemployment insurance. One key question is what set of policies can accelerate the process of formalizing the informal labor market. A common view is that many of the labor market regulations designed to protect the labor force from abuse are major impediments to the latter because their costs and design make it rational to evade and avoid those regulations. Although of utmost importance, this discussion has been dealt with elsewhere and will not be a topic of this book.[10] Two other areas are not addressed: weak institutions and weak public finances. Although the latter are usually cited as a reason for not implementing more aggressive publicly funded consumption smoothing mechanisms, evidence shows that this factor has been exaggerated.

A ROAD MAP

The chapters in this book address various topics: the impact of economic crises on poverty and inequality and the importance of a safety net to shield poor people from their impact; mechanisms to address unemployment; health shocks and old age among the poor; the role of social funds as safety nets; microfinance to smooth consumption; and lessons from the developed world.

---

[9] For a broader discussion of risks and social protection, see Inter-American Development Bank (2000) and World Bank (2000a, chaps. 8, 9).
[10] See, for example, Edwards and Lustig (1997).

The Costs of Economic Crises

Chapter two, by Alain de Janvry and Elisabeth Sadoulet, shows how economywide crises in Latin America can result not only in sharp increases in poverty but also in inequality, making it harder to reduce poverty in the future even if growth at previous levels is resumed.[11] Using data for 48 growth and recession spells for 12 countries in Latin America between 1970 and 1994, the authors find that "there are strong asymmetries in the relation between income and poverty/inequality according to growth episode: recession is systematically devastating on poverty and inequality." They find that a 1-percent decline in per capita gross domestic product during the 1980s eliminated the gains in urban (rural) poverty reduction achieved by 3.7 (2) percent growth in the 1970s. Recession episodes in the 1980s were found to have a strong ratchet effect on inequality, since the higher level of inequality is not reversed with subsequent growth.

These results, together with those shown in table 1–1, should suffice to demonstrate how important it is for countries to reduce the likelihood of economic crises. They also indicate the importance of *countering* with the appropriate countercyclical safety nets to help the poor cope with the impact of economic crises. Pro-poor programs must be protected from budget cuts when a nation is introducing fiscal austerity measures to restore macroeconomic balance.[12]

Unemployment Insurance and Employment Programs

In chapter three Gustavo Márquez succinctly describes existing programs and their limitations in the region. During the 1990s Latin America experienced very high unemployment rates in general. According to data from the Economic Commission for Latin America and the Caribbean, the open unemployment rate in Latin America (excluding the Caribbean) reached 8.4 percent in 1998, up from 5.8 percent in 1992.[13] Furthermore, 12 out of 22 countries in the region with regular data

---

[11] That crises result in increases in inequality is not always the case. Economic downturns in the recent East Asian crises, for example, have not been accompanied by a rise in inequality. Sometimes inequality falls during a crisis.

[12] For more on this subject, see Lustig (1995, 2000); Inter-American Development Bank (2000, chaps. 1, 5); World Bank (2000a, chap. 9).

[13] ECLAC (1999).

had an unemployment rate close to or above 10 percent in 1997.[14] What is striking from this overview is how limited is the protection awarded for unemployment hazards in a region that has been facing major structural changes resulting from the introduction of market-oriented reforms and recurrent economic downturns. Although part of the unemployment problem would be solved if hiring and firing become less restrictive and costly, some of the available evidence does not indicate that the gains from reforming the labor market regulations would be large.[15]

In chapter four Hugo A. Hopenhayn and Juan Pablo Nicolini use modern optimal contract theory to discuss what the effects of heterogeneity are on the design of an optimal unemployment insurance scheme. Heterogeneity is understood in two senses: systematic differences in workers' reemployment rates and cyclical variations in reemployment probabilities. The authors find that for workers whose reemployment rates differ because of age and skill differences—but not in search effort—unemployment benefits should have a steeper profile: that is, they should be reduced more quickly. Overall, higher-risk workers—that is, those with lower reemployment probabilities—should have more lifetime coverage than low-risk workers. The authors also find that it is optimal to fully insure all aggregate risk and that the reemployment tax should be lowered during recessions. When recessions mostly affect baseline reemployment probabilities, the benefits should be decreased more slowly.

Hopenhayn and Nicolini's analysis allows us to interpret the advantages of workfare and training programs in a new light. It is very hard to monitor the employment status of workers in the informal sector. A very strong incentive problem occurs because an unemployed worker receiving benefits would not have incentives to report having found a job. One way to cope with this problem is to require that beneficiaries of the program follow a schedule, for instance, do public works. Examples are workfare programs such as the Maharashtra employment program in India, *Trabajar* in Argentina, and the minimum employment program in Chile in the past.[16] Furthermore, if the nonlabor costs are decentralized to the operating unit of the program, the monitoring of the employment status of the beneficiary is done in an incentive-compatible way. The operating unit finds it in its best interest to enforce the participation of the worker. In other words, workfare

---

[14] The countries are Argentina, Barbados, Colombia, Dominican Republic, Ecuador, Jamaica, Nicaragua, Panama, Peru, Trinidad and Tobago, Uruguay, and Venezuela.

[15] See Kugler (1999).

[16] See Lipton (1996); Ravallion (1998); Subbarao and others (1997).

programs can be interpreted as an unemployment insurance contract with a technology to monitor the employment status of the beneficiary. An alternative way of monitoring would be to require workers to attend training programs. The main objective of such programs may not be the productivity-enhancing effects but the monitoring services they supply.

Social Investment Funds

Chapter five by Steen Lau Jørgensen and Julie Van Domelen shows how to help the poor better manage risks by building up their social capital and physical infrastructure. Social funds are agencies that finance demand-driven projects in several sectors targeted to benefit a country's poor and vulnerable; these projects must meet a set of eligibility criteria. The first fund was established in Bolivia in 1987. At present there are social funds in almost all countries in Latin America and the Caribbean, Africa, the Middle East, Eastern Europe, Central Asia, and a few in Asia. Most of the funds have focused on building or refurbishing social infrastructure, particularly health posts, schools, and water supply and sanitation. Originally, the social funds were set up to provide temporary employment and relief from a crisis situation through labor-based income transfers and subsidization of social services and infrastructure. Although social funds continue to respond to emergency situations, such as Hurricane Mitch in Central America, fall-out from the wars in Cambodia and Angola, an earthquake in Armenia, or a drought in Zambia, they are evolving into permanent structures with multiple objectives. Nevertheless, for social funds to fulfill their emergency and nonemergency roles a number of institutional changes will have to be introduced. Systematic impact evaluation studies are also needed to identify what works best in the implementation of social funds.

The authors argue in favor of rethinking the use of social funds in the broader context of a social risk management framework. Community development funds, decentralization funds, and infrastructure funds can be used to reduce and mitigate risks by, for example, building earthquake proof buildings and dams, introducing reforestation programs, helping households relocate to safer areas, and so on to reduce the risk of natural disasters. Social funds can strengthen the informal networks and support risk-mitigating strategies of informal insurance. Employment generation and social assistance funds can provide sources of livelihood to communities hit by an adverse situation and protect the human capital (nutrition, health, and education) of the children of communities hit by a shock.

Coping with Health Shocks

In chapter six Paul Gertler compares the welfare gains from providing social insurance for major illness versus small health shocks.

Major or catastrophic illness has two important economic costs for households: the cost of medical care used to diagnose and treat the illness and the loss in income associated with reduced labor supply and productivity. Given the high cost and unpredictability of major illness, poor families in developing countries may not be able to smooth their consumption. Drawing on panel data for China and Indonesia, Gertler shows that while households are able to insure (through the mechanisms mentioned above) the economic costs of small health shocks, they are not able to insure against the costs of major or catastrophic illness. The results of the empirical exercise show that reducing the variation in income associated with major illness can have large welfare gains. Since poor families in developing countries do not have access to formal insurance owing to market failures (or, even if they could have access, they may not be able to afford it), there is a role for social insurance for income loss because of disability and medical care expenses. However, the fact that households are able to insure against the costs of small health shocks suggests that relying on user fees to expand publicly delivered health care services will have little impact on welfare.

Averting an Old-Age Crisis for the Poor

Estelle James points out in chapter seven that the majority of workers and old people in developing countries are not covered by formal social security programs. Coverage rates range from less that 10 percent in Sub-Saharan Africa and South Asia and less than 30 percent in most of East Asia, to 50 to 60 percent in middle-income countries in South America, and 70 to 80 percent in Eastern European transition economies. The uninsured fall into two categories: workers who have jobs that are not covered by contributory programs (self-employed rural workers and workers in small firms, for example); and women who have worked in the household rather than in the labor market for most of their lives.

As development proceeds, coverage will rise, but to achieve near full coverage will take quite some time. Until that happens, a large portion of the population will remain uninsured or partially so. While recent pension reforms tying benefits more closely to contributions are desirable from the point of view of incentives and fiscal soundness of the contributory systems, they may reduce coverage among the poor. In particular, benefits are reduced substantially for those who contribute for only part of their working lives, hence they may not be eligible for the redistributive pillar of the new pension systems. Because the minimum amount of years that workers must have contributed is rather large, workers who do not anticipate such a long participation in a contributory system or in the labor market will have an incentive to stay out of the system.

James proposes the implementation of the requirement to purchase survivors' benefits and joint annuities to cover the spouses who worked in the home as part of the household division of labor. For workers who participated in noncovered jobs and were too poor to save for old age, social assistance is essential. To reduce moral hazard problems, social assistance should be financed out of general revenues and should offer less than the redistribution given to the low-income groups who participate in contributory systems.

In chapter eight Carmelo Mesa-Lago provides an overview of the characteristics of social protection programs for health and old age. While some countries have very developed national health systems, a recurrent problem is that coverage in the rural areas is lower and poorer in quality than in urban areas (the incidence of poverty is higher in rural areas and most of the poor live in rural areas in the poorest countries of the region). The author advocates establishing national health care systems that cover all the population and argues in favor of using government resources in the prevention of health hazards by such means as vaccination campaigns, health education, potable water, and sewerage systems. The latter would bring expenses required in curative care down and free up resources for the inevitable cases. Mesa-Lago suggests establishing mandatory programs for the incorporation of low-income groups such as the self-employed, domestic servants, and employees of microenterprises, and creating schemes with lower financing burdens and benefits.

Improving the Poor's Ability to Mitigate Risks: The Role of Microfinance Programs

In chapter nine Manfred Zeller explores the role of microfinance in reducing the downward risk of falling below some minimum threshold levels of consumption for poor households. The author argues that the role of microfinance to smooth income is limited. However, "access to financial services can have a far greater role for smoothing consumption, and thereby increasing the risk-bearing capacity of households for increasing future income." In particular, the largest potential for microfinance is seen for helping the poor address idiosyncratic risks such as ill health, disability, old age, and divorce. Viewed this way microfinance goes beyond the traditional role of assisting the poor in earning income from microenterprises to a safety net role.

The author discusses several of the innovative microfinance institutions that offer financial products to respond to the above-mentioned idiosyncratic risks. The most common ones are precautionary savings services. Some microfinance institutions offer explicit lines of consumption credit. This is true of many village banks in Latin America and Sub-Saharan Africa. In addition, some microfinance institutions have developed insurance products such as life insurance. Broadening the outreach of financial services will carry higher risks. That is why microfinance institutions should circumscribe themselves—at least at first—to offer the new services to areas with low covariate risks such as illness, death, divorce, or disability.

Microfinance used for consumption smoothing purposes is likely to crowd out informal schemes. Given that microfinance services are likely to be indirectly subsidized by the government, for example, by grants for product innovation, staff training, and institutional expansion, formal financial services can have social costs that exceed their benefits. But Zeller argues, "evidence from recent research suggests that the informal responses are far from adequate, and that publicly supported institutional innovations in microfinance can offer in many circumstances a viable policy instrument that generates net social benefits."

How to Avoid Crowding Out Informal Insurance

Orazio Attanasio and José-Víctor Ríos-Rull develop an analytical model in chapter ten to explore the impact of the provision of a safety net on informal insurance arrangements. They find that the provision of a safety net from some external agency such as an international organization or the central government could, under certain assumptions, reduce the amount of idiosyncratic insurance achieved by a private contract such as that provided by what the authors call the "extended family." In other words, "the simple provision of aggregate insurance that just shrinks the variance of aggregate shocks without considering the possible crowding out of private insurance is not necessarily optimum." Moreover, such crowding out could, in certain circumstances, lead to an overall welfare decrease.

Regardless of whether the introduction of aggregate insurance leads to a welfare decrease, the authors stress that their results imply that it is worth thinking of insurance schemes that avoid these problems, though designing aggregate insurance schemes that do not crowd out private insurance arrangements is difficult. Attanasio and Ríos-Rull propose some possible mechanisms to avoid the crowding-out effect. For example, when the government can identify the "extended families" in the village, they can make the payment of aggregate insurance to each of the two members conditional on the agreement of the other partner. Therefore, a reversion to autarky would imply not only losing the benefit of the informal insurance agreement but also the access to the aggregate safety net. This would give members of the extended family a powerful mechanism to punish the individuals who renege on the informal insurance agreement. As the crowding out is generated by increasing the value of autarky, this kind of scheme would avoid it.

Whether an aggregate insurance scheme crowds out private informal arrangements depends on the specific functioning of these arrangements as well as the characteristics of the shocks that households face. As a result, the authors end their chapter by making a series of recommendations on how the relevant information could be collected by longitudinal household surveys.

Lessons from the Developed World

The first lesson one can learn from reading chapter eleven by Timothy M. Smeeding and Katherin Ross Phillips is that spending on social protection in the developed world makes a difference in terms of poverty reduction. A second lesson is that the developed world makes an effort to measure the impact of its social insurance and social assistance programs on household income. In contrast, most surveys in developing countries do not collect reliable information on these components of income.

In terms of specific programs, the authors argue that social insurance has the greatest impact on poverty reduction for working age adults (including the unemployed and those who do not participate in the labor market) and for the elderly. Social assistance plays a significant role in some countries (for example, Australia and the United Kingdom) and for some specific groups such as single parents and the elderly. All in all, while most of the countries have responded well to the more traditional risks such as extended unemployment, old age, and disability, not all have done so. Furthermore, only Sweden and to a lesser extent France, Spain, and the Netherlands appear to have dealt well with the new risk of single parenthood.

While social insurance schemes have a strong impact on reducing poverty without stigma, they have two problems: their large cost and their disincentive effects on the labor market. In addition, social insurance schemes for the aged in the current pay-as-you-go pension systems are not financially sustainable under current demographic trends. The authors conclude that tax-transfer systems in the style of a developed country are not likely to be fiscally affordable for developing countries, and they are liable to generate large economic costs because of their impact on work effort. The developing world will have to rely more heavily on targeted and self-targeted social assistance programs for the poor and on less expensive social insurance schemes.

References

Barros, Ricardo, Rosane Mendonça, and Sonia Rocha. 1995. "Brazil: Welfare, Inequality, Poverty, Social Indicators, and Social Programs in the 1980s." In Nora Lustig, ed., *Coping with Austerity*. Washington, D.C.: Brookings Institution.

Baulch, Bob, and John Hoddinott. Forthcoming. "Economic Mobility and Poverty Dynamics in Developing Countries." *Journal of Development Studies*.

Economic Commission for Latin America and the Caribbean (ECLAC). 1999. *Social Panorama of Latin America*. United Nations: Santiago de Chile.

Edwards, Sebastian, and Nora Lustig, eds. 1997. *Labor Markets in Latin America: Combining Market Flexibility with Social Protection*. Washington, D.C.: Brookings Institution.

Escobal, Javier, Jaime Saavedra, and Máximo Torero. 1998. *Los activos de los pobres en el Perú*. Documento de trabajo no. 26. Grupo de Análisis para el Desarrollo, Lima, Peru.

Grootaert, Christiaan. 1998. *Child Labor in Côte d'Ivoire—Incidence and Determinants*. Policy Research Working Paper no. 1905. World Bank, Washington, D.C.

Hoddinott, John, and Bill Kinsey. 1998. "Child Growth in the Time of Drought." International Food Policy Research Institute, Washington, D.C. Unpublished.

Holzmann, Robert, and Steen Jørgensen. 2000. *Social Risk Management: A New Conceptual Framework for Social Protection and Beyond*. Discussion Paper no. 0006. World Bank, Washington, D.C.

Inter-American Development Bank. 2000. *Social Protection for Equity and Growth*. Washington, D.C.: IDB.

Jacoby, Hanan, and Emmanuel Skoufias. 1997. "Risk, Financial Markets and Human Capital in a Developing Country." *Review of Economic Studies* 64 (3): 311–35.

Jalan, Jyotsna, and Martin Ravallion. 1997. *Are the Poor Less Well-Insured? Evidence on Vulnerability to Income Risk in Rural China*. Policy Research Working Paper no. 1863. World Bank, Washington, D.C.

Kugler, Adriana. 1999. *The Impact of Firing Costs on Turnover and Unemployment: Evidence from the Colombian Labour Market Reform*. Economics Working Papers. Department of Economics and Business, Universitat Pompeu Fabra, Barcelona, Spain.

Lipton, Michael. 1996. *Successes in Anti-poverty*. Discussion Paper no. 8. International Labor Office, Geneva.

Lokshin, Michael, and Martin Ravallion. 2000. "Welfare Impact of Russia's 1998 Financial Crisis and the Response of the Public Safety Net." World Bank, Washington, D.C. Unpublished.

Londoño, Juan Luis, and Miguel Székely. 1997. *Persistent Poverty and Excess Inequality: Latin America, 1970–1995*. Washington, D.C.: Inter-American Development Bank.

Lustig, Nora, ed. 1995. *Coping with Austerity: Poverty and Inequality in Latin America*. Washington, D.C.: Brookings Institution.

Lustig, Nora. 2000. "Crises and the Poor: Socially Responsible Macroeconomics." *Economía, Journal of the Latin American and Caribbean Economic Association*. Washington, D.C.: Brookings Institution.

Lustig, Nora, and Miguel Székely. 1998. *Economic Trends, Poverty and Inequality in Mexico*. Washington, D.C.: Inter-American Development Bank.

Ministerio de Economía de Argentina. 1998. "Informe Económico 28." Buenos Aires, Argentina.

Morley, Samuel, and Carola Alvarez. 1992. *Recession and the Growth of Poverty in Argentina.* Working Paper no. 92. Vanderbilt University, Nashville, TN.

Ravallion, Martin. 1998. *Appraising Workfare Programs.* Technical Study. SDS/POV, Inter-American Development Bank, Washington, D.C.

Rodrik, Dani. 1997. "Where Did All the Growth Go? External Shocks, Social Conflict, and Growth Collapses." Harvard University, Cambridge, MA. Unpublished.

Ruprah, Inder, and Luis Marcano. 1998. "Work in Progress." Inter-American Development Bank, Washington, D.C. Unpublished.

Sinha, Saurabh, and Michael Lipton. 1999. "Damaging Fluctuations, Risk and Poverty: A Review." In *World Development Report* 2000/2001. Commissioned Paper. Brighton and Washington, D.C.: Sussex University and World Bank.

Subbarao, Kalanidhi, and others. 1997. *Safety Net Programs and Poverty Reduction: Lessons from Cross-Country Experience.* Washington, D.C.: World Bank.

Townsend, Robert M. 1994. "Risk and Insurance in Village India." *Econometrica* 62 (May): 539–91.

University of California. 1999. *Berkeley Magazine.* Summer, p. 19.

World Bank. 1994. *Hashemite Kingdom of Jordan Poverty Assessment.* Report 12675-JO. Washington, D.C.

———. 1999a. "Social Protection Sector Strategy Paper." First Draft (February 15).

———. 1999b. *Poverty Trends and the Voices of the Poor.* Poverty Reduction and Economic Management. Washington, D.C.

———. 2000a. *World Development Report 2000/1: Attacking Poverty.* Washington, D.C.

———. 2000b. *World Development Indicators.* Washington, D.C.

CHAPTER TWO

Has Aggregate Income Growth Been Effective in Reducing Poverty and Inequality in Latin America?

Alain de Janvry and Elisabeth Sadoulet

Compared with other regions of the world, Latin America is characterized by high levels of poverty and inequality given the prevailing levels of per capita income. This has been referred to as "excess" poverty and inequality.[1] Latin American populations have also been subjected to unusually high income variations, most particularly during the past 30 years with rapid debt-led growth, the debt crisis, implementation of stabilization and adjustment policies, economic recoveries, and more recently the peso crisis and repercussions of shocks in Asia and Russia. Again, compared with other regions of the world, there has been "excess" instability. Poverty, inequality, and instability are thus issues of concern as they have high social costs. They reduce long-term economic growth (as demonstrated by sustained growth and lower levels of poverty, inequality, and instability in Asia for more than three decades), and they can create political backlashes on economic reforms.[2] They are sources of social breakdown with symptoms like crime, violence, and deterioration of social norms.

It is common knowledge that aggregate income growth, as measured by GDP per capita (GDPpc), is the main source of poverty reduction and potentially of inequality reduction.[3] Yet Latin America has not been short of successful growth over the long run. This suggests some features of Latin American growth and its context

---

We are indebted to Miguel Székely for useful suggestions.

[1] Londoño and Székely (1997).

[2] See Aghion and Howitt (1998) and *The Economist* (1996).

[3] World Bank (1990).

may be limiting the capacity of growth to make a dent in poverty and inequality. These features are clearly unequally present across countries. Indeed, while there are general features of Latin America as a region, poverty and inequality vary widely across countries, implying that, over the long run, growth has been differentially successful in affecting poverty and inequality.[4] If there is a concern with poverty and inequality, it is important to identify these features, so they can be modified through policy interventions that may render aggregate income growth more effective for reduction of poverty and inequality.

Based on these considerations, we address three questions in this chapter:

- How effective has aggregate income growth been in reducing poverty and inequality, and under what conditions has it been more or less effective?
- Given the continuing history of economic instability, what are the relative gains and costs in poverty and inequality of growth versus recession? Are they symmetrical in the sense that the elasticity of poverty and inequality with respect to income is the same whether income rises or falls?
- Latin America has gone through different "styles" of growth, shifting from import substitution industrialization before the debt crisis ("early" growth) to more open economy growth after structural adjustment ("late" growth). Is aggregate income growth under these two models differentially effective in reducing poverty and inequality?

We address these issues using econometric analysis to isolate the relationships among income and poverty and inequality from other determining factors. Surprisingly, virtually no econometric analysis of this relationship has been made. The growth-welfare relation has typically instead been analyzed by simple correlation or by constructing two-way tables with income growth/income recession crossed with increases/decreases in poverty and inequality.[5] This leaves uncontrolled a host of spurious correlations, which we attempt to control for in this chapter. It also does not allow us to identify how the context in which growth occurred affected poverty and inequality outcomes, a conditional analysis needed for the design of policy reforms.

---

[4] IDB (1998).

[5] Morley (1995); Psacharopoulos and others (1995).

DATA AND METHODOLOGY

It is clearly difficult to develop a consistent database on poverty and inequality across a sufficient number of countries and for a sufficient number of years to allow econometric identification of the determinants of poverty/inequality. Yet, a sustained effort at developing such data has been done, principally by Oscar Altimir at CEPAL, offering information from 1970 to 1994 for 12 countries for the years when household income and expenditure surveys were conducted.[6]

The timing of episodes of early growth, recession, and late growth varies sharply across countries. For this reason, distinguishing episodes of early growth, recession, and late growth by fixed dates—for instance, by decades, associating the 1970s with early growth, the 1980s with recession, and the 1990s with late growth, as is commonly done—is inadequate to capture "styles" of growth.[7] In addition, the way these episodes are captured by the available data varies across countries owing to the timing of the household surveys in relation to these episodes. Some countries do not have observed episodes of recession (Chile, Colombia, Costa Rica), others do not have data for early growth (Venezuela), some do not escape from recession (Brazil), and yet others fall back into recession after experiencing recoveries from recession (Honduras and Venezuela). As shown in table 2–1, we have organized the data in 53 spells of early growth (spells with positive GDPpc growth starting in 1970 and extending up to the debt crisis), recession (negative GDPpc), and late growth (spells with positive GDPpc growth originating after the 1970s), with dates that are idiosyncratic to each country. There is of course some arbitrariness in classifying spells by episodes of early growth, recession, and late growth, since the spells observed between data points may hide subperiods of growth or recession.[8] The data characterize urban poverty, rural poverty, and national-level inequality.

The variables to be explained are the rate of growth in the number of urban poor over a spell, the rate of growth in the number of rural poor, and the rate of growth in the Gini coefficient as a measure of inequality. We use a specification of a

---

[6] Altimir (1995). Most of these data are reported by CEPAL in *Social Panorama for Latin America* (1994, 1995, 1996). Details on data construction are given in de Janvry and Sadoulet (1998).

[7] See, for example, Londoño and Székely (1997).

[8] This correct observation was made by Miguel Székely. There is, however, no way out of this dilemma since we do not have annual survey data. By chance, there is a relatively good correspondence between the years of the surveys and the economic turning points in most countries.

Table 2–1. Growth Spells and GDP Per Capita Annual Growth Rates, Latin America, 1970–94

Average annual growth rates in percent

Country	Early growth		Recession		Late growth	
	Period	Rate	Period	Rate	Period	Rate
Argentina	1970–80	0.84	1980–86	−1.99	1990–92	7.31
			1986–90	−3.29	1992–94	5.44
Brazil	1970–79	5.85	1987–90	−1.92		
	1979–87	0.61	1990–93	−0.53		
Chile	1970–80	0.19			1980–87	0.43
					1987–90	5.34
					1990–92	7.37
					1992–94	3.73
Colombia	1970–80	2.89			1980–86	0.80
					1986–90	2.29
					1990–92	1.18
					1992–94	3.59
Costa Rica	1970–81	2.38			1981–88	0.33
					1988–90	1.87
					1990–92	2.87
					1992–94	3.14
Guatemala			1980–86	−3.86	1986–90	0.73
Honduras	1970–86	0.76	1992–94	−0.72	1986–90	0.72
					1990–92	1.30
Mexico	1970–84	2.96	1984–89	−1.47	1989–92	1.65
					1992–94	0.21
Panama	1970–79	1.25	1986–89	−7.93	1989–91	4.96
	1979–86	1.52			1991–94	4.56
Peru	1970–79	0.85	1979–86	−1.85	1991–94	3.33
			1986–91	−5.88		
Uruguay	1970–81	2.80	1981–86	−3.28	1986–90	1.53
					1990–92	4.80
					1992–94	3.92
Venezuela			1970–81	−0.33	1990–92	5.40
			1981–86	−2.55		
			1986–90	−1.48		
			1992–94	−3.44		
Number of spells	12		15		26	

Source: World Bank (1997).

poverty equation where the rate of change in poverty is explained by aggregate income growth, characteristics of the macroeconomic performance during the growth spell, and characteristics of the structural context in which growth occurred, measured at the beginning of the corresponding spell. This specification is similar to those used by Martin Ravallion and Gaurav Datt.[9] The equation explaining inequality is similarly specified. Hence, we are assuming that aggregate income growth is a determinant of household income poverty and inequality as opposed to jointness. In making this assumption, we note that GDPpc contains many elements beyond household income, and that there is consequently no simple relation that relates income growth to poverty and inequality indicators. However, the qualitative nature of growth (early, recession, and late) and the macroeconomic and structural contexts in which growth occurs are determinants of poverty and inequality outcomes. We also give importance to analyzing how a given growth rate affects poverty and inequality differentially according to the macroeconomic and the structural conditions where growth occurs. This is done by specifying selected interactions between GDPpc growth and macro and structural characteristics. Most important among these are the initial levels of poverty and inequality, the initial level of education, and the length of the episodes of growth or recession.

By specifying the regression equations in rates of change, we control for country-idiosyncratic characteristics that would explain levels of poverty. To control for residual country fixed effects, we ran regressions with country dummies, but these were globally not significant and are consequently not reported here.

The explanatory variables used in the poverty and inequality equations are:

- the rate of growth in GDPpc over the corresponding spell classified in three episodes
- GDPpc growth during early growth episodes
- GDPpc growth during recession episodes
- GDPpc growth during late growth episodes.

The following are characteristics of macroeconomic performance:

- the rate of growth in the real exchange rate over the spell
- the incidence of hyperinflation, defined as a rate of growth in the CPI that exceeds 100 percent a year

---

[9] Ravallion and Datt (1996, 1999).

- instability of growth during the spell measured by the coefficient of variation of GDPpc around its trend
- length of the regime of growth or recession, defined as the total number of successive years of growth or recession during and before the spell
- sectoral composition of growth measured by the growth differential between agriculture and nonagriculture, and growth of the services sector.

The following are characteristics of the structural context in which growth occurred:

- the level of GDPpc at the beginning of the spell
- the share of agriculture in GDP at the beginning of the spell
- the natural growth rate of population during the spell
- the share of urban population at the beginning of the spell
- the predicted level of rural-urban migration during the spell
- the level of secondary education at the beginning of the spell
- the level of inequality at the beginning of the spell
- the incidence of poverty at the beginning of the spell.

URBAN POVERTY

Analysis of the determinants of growth on urban poverty in table 2–2 shows that no significant decline in poverty took place owing to aggregate income growth under early growth. The elasticity of urban poverty with respect to GDPpc is –0.32, and it is not significantly different from zero. Recession, however, severely increased urban poverty, with an elasticity of –1.11, meaning that for every 1 percent decline in GDPpc there was an increase in the number of urban poor of 1.11 percent. There consequently was a strong asymmetry between the role of growth under import substitution industrialization and the role of recession: the 1 percent decline in GDPpc under recession eliminated the gain in urban poverty reduction achieved by as much as a 3.7 percent increase in GDPpc under early growth.

Contrast in the roles of early growth and recession in urban poverty illustrates the fallacy of analyzing the relationship between income and poverty without separating periods: pooling together years of early growth and recession would have yielded a negative relation between aggregate income growth and poverty, an encouraging result. However, this relation comes from recession, not from growth. Hence, while existence of a negative relation is correct, the policy implication that

Table 2–2. Determinants of Change in Urban Poverty

Variable	Coefficient	Student t
Aggregate GDP per capita growth		
Early growth episode	–0.32	–0.5
Recession episode	–1.11	–2.2
Late growth episode	–1.25	–2.1
Macroeconomic performance		
Real exchange rate growth	0.31	2.5
Hyperinflation dummy	3.94	2.4
Structural context		
GDP per capita (thousands of 1987 dollars)	–1.96	–1.0
Share of agriculture in GDP	0.09	0.6
Population growth	1.75	0.4
Urban population share	0.0004	0.0
Rural-urban migration (predicted rate)	1.10	0.3
Secondary education	0.001	0.0
Initial inequality	–4.45	–0.5
Initial incidence of urban poverty	–0.10	–0.9
Intercept	4.18	0.2
Number of observations	48	
R^2	0.73	

Note: The endogenous variable is the annual growth rate in the number of urban poor by spell.
Source: Authors' calculations.

growth reduces poverty is totally misleading, a mistake that permeates much of the quantitative analysis on poverty.

While early growth was not effective for urban poverty reduction, this is not the case for late growth. Results show that the income elasticity of poverty for late growth is –1.25. This is not unexpected if we believe that removal of distortions on the price of capital allowed for a more labor-intensive growth path, resulting in greater ability for growth to reduce poverty than under import substitution. This is indeed an encouraging result that deserves further attention. Among other determinants of change in urban poverty, structural variables have no role, while what matters is the macroeconomic performance. Both real exchange rate depreciation (associated with stabilization policies) and the occurrence of bouts of hyperinflation have strong nefarious contemporaneous effects on urban poverty.

FIGURE 2–1.

Determinants of Urban Poverty in Argentina

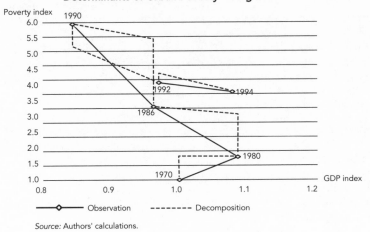

Source: Authors' calculations.

The ratchet effect of instability in GDPpc on urban poverty is illustrated for Argentina in figure 2–1 using the estimated equation in table 2–2. The solid line represents the observed relation between GDPpc growth and urban poverty growth. The data for Argentina cover one period of early growth, two periods of recession, and two periods of late growth. The dotted line is the predicted role of income using the equation estimated in table 2–2. The vertical line from each point is the change in poverty explained by exogenous variables other than GDPpc and by the error term in the equation. These vertical shifts show that factors other than GDPpc, both explained and unexplained, are important in predicting changes in poverty. The graph also clearly shows that recession was devastating for the rural poor, with declining aggregate income leading to a sharp increase in poverty.

The context in which growth occurs is a determinant of the effect that income growth can have on poverty reduction. We analyze the role of these contextual variables on growth by introducing interaction terms between context and GDPpc growth. In table 2–3, we report only the coefficients of the direct and interaction terms and only of the episodes when significant, not the full corresponding regression. There are four important results.

Role of initial level of inequality. When GDPpc is interacted with the initial level of inequality in the corresponding spell, the poverty reduction effect of aggregate income growth is diminished by high inequality. Ravallion observes that "the higher

Table 2–3. Effect of Initial Level in Determinants of Change in Urban Poverty

Variable	Coefficient	Overall effect of growth	
		Lowest	Highest
Effect of initial level of inequality on			
GDPpc growth: early growth episode		(Costa Rica)	(Colombia)
GDPpc growth	–4.44*	–2.29*	0.48
GDPpc growth*initial inequality	7.39*		
Effect of initial level of inequality on			
GDPpc growth: late growth episode		(Uruguay)	(Guatemala)
GDPpc growth	–9.26**	–3.84**	0.29
GDPpc growth*initial inequality	18.02**		
Effect of initial level of poverty on			
GDPpc growth: late growth episode		(Uruguay)	(Honduras)
GDPpc growth	–2.66**	–2.23**	0.82
GDPpc growth*initial level of poverty	0.053°		
Effect of initial level of education (percent			
secondary enrollment) on GDPpc			
growth: late growth episode		(Honduras)	(Uruguay)
GDPpc growth	2.60°	–0.63	–2.50**
GDPpc growth*initial level of education	-0.06**		
Effect of sectoral composition of growth and			
initial inequality on GDPpc growth:			
late growth episode		(Uruguay)	(Guatemala)
Services growth	–5.64**	–2.28**	0.27
Services growth*initial inequality	11.15*		

° Significant at the 85 percent level.
* Significant at the 90 percent level.
** Significant at the 95 percent level.
Note: The endogenous variable is the annual growth rate in the number of urban poor by spell.
Source: Authors' calculations.

the initial level of inequality, the less effective aggregate income growth is in reducing poverty."[10] With high inequality, the tails of the distribution of income are thick, and a change in the mean income level has little effect on frequency in the tails. Recall that, across all countries, the elasticity of urban poverty with respect to GDPpc is –0.3 in early growth. We can illustrate how this overall effect changes by using

[10] Ravallion (1997).

the level of inequality prevailing in countries at the extremes of the distribution of inequality. If we use the level of inequality prevailing in Costa Rica (0.29, the lowest in the region for early growth observations), growth was effective in reducing poverty, with a significant elasticity of –2.3. By contrast, in Colombia with the higher Gini among early growth observations (0.67 in 1970), the elasticity is an insignificant 0.48. For late growth, the elasticity across all countries is –1.3. For Uruguay, with the lowest observed level of inequality among late growth observations (0.30), this elasticity is a large –3.84, while in Guatemala, which has the highest level of inequality (0.53), the poverty reduction effect is completely erased, resulting in an elasticity of 0.29. The results hence support Ravallion's contention that inequality can erase the beneficial poverty-reducing effects of growth, even under late growth. High-inequality countries cannot consequently rely on growth to reduce inequality.

Role of initial level of poverty. Growth is similarly found to be effective for poverty reduction if the initial level of poverty is not too high. Under late growth, the income elasticity of poverty is a significant –2.2 at the poverty incidence level prevailing in Uruguay (0.08, lowest in the sample), while it is an insignificant 0.8 at the poverty incidence level prevailing in Honduras (0.66, highest in the sample). This suggests that scale is significant in poverty reduction, at least within the range observed in Latin America: it is easier to reduce urban poverty if there is less urban poverty to start with.

Role of secondary education. Results show that late growth is only effective in reducing poverty if the initial levels of secondary school enrollment are sufficiently high. Thus, in Uruguay, with the highest level of secondary school enrollment, the income elasticity of poverty is –2.5 with a secondary school enrollment of 81 percent, while it falls to –0.6 with the enrollment levels prevailing in Honduras (32 percent). Education is thus key if growth is to serve as an effective instrument for poverty reduction.

Sectoral composition of growth. Interacting growth in services and initial level of inequality shows that, in late growth episodes, service sector growth combined with low initial levels of inequality is effective for urban poverty reduction. Indeed, PREALC observes that the informal sector (with a large service component) has been the most effective at employment creation since the debt crisis.[11]

We thus conclude that growth is only effective as an instrument for poverty reduction if the initial levels of inequality and poverty are not too high, if secondary education is sufficiently prevalent, and if it is accompanied by high service

---

[11] PREALC (1992).

Table 2–4. Determinants of Change in Rural Poverty

Variable	Twelve countries		Nine countries[a]	
	Coefficient	Student t	Coefficient	Student t
Aggregate GDP per capita growth				
Early growth episode	–0.27	–0.8	–0.23	–0.6
Recession episode	–0.60	–2.0	–0.60	–1.9
Late growth episode	–0.99	–2.9	–0.97	–2.4
Macroeconomic performance				
Real exchange rate growth	0.07	1.1	0.08	1.0
Hyperinflation dummy	0.30	0.3	0.51	0.3
Structural context				
GDP per capita (thousands of 1987 dollars)	–2.11	–2.3	–1.67	–0.9
Share of agriculture in GDP	–0.15	–1.4	–0.09	–0.6
Rural population natural growth	1.13	1.0	0.57	0.3
Rural-urban migration (predicted rate)	–0.75	–1.4	–0.57	–0.9
Secondary education	–0.003	–0.1	–0.02	–0.3
Initial inequality	–1.67	–0.3	–4.00	–0.5
Initial incidence of rural poverty	–0.06	–1.8	–0.05	–1.1
Intercept	8.39	1.6	9.00	1.4
Number of observations	40		35	
R^2	0.61		0.61	

a. Data for Argentina, Colombia, and Uruguay are omitted.
Note: The endogenous variable is the annual growth rate in the number of rural poor by spell.
Source: Authors' calculations.

sector growth in a context of low inequality. These are all contextual characteristics that can be molded by policy interventions to make growth more effective for poverty reduction.

RURAL POVERTY

Data for rural poverty are not as solid as for urban poverty, and the explanatory power of a poverty equation is consequently lower. Some observations are dubious (Argentina, Colombia, and Uruguay) and the analysis is consequently repeated deleting them, reducing the number of countries to nine.[12] Results in table

---

[12] Personal communication from Nora Lustig.

FIGURE 2–2.

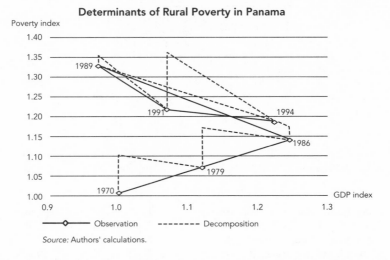

Determinants of Rural Poverty in Panama

Source: Authors' calculations.

2–4 show similar patterns to those for urban poverty, although muted, as agricultural incomes do not respond to the economic cycle as strongly as urban incomes, in part because the migration buffer exists unilaterally from rural to urban sectors, and in part because production for home consumption reduces the impact of price shocks. Early growth is not effective at reducing poverty. Recession has a strongly significant negative elasticity of –0.6 (meaning an increase in poverty as income is falling). There is consequently again a strong asymmetry between early growth and recession. A 1-percent decline in income erases the poverty reduction effect of 2 percent of early growth. Late growth is, however, quite effective at poverty reduction, with an elasticity of –0.99, although lower than the effect of growth in the urban sector.

The other determinants of change in rural poverty are structural, as opposed to derived from macroeconomic performance in the case of urban poverty. The initial level of GDPpc lowers the growth rate in poverty reduction, indicating that there is convergence as GDPpc rises. The initial incidence of rural poverty also lowers the growth rate of rural poverty, showing again that scale is relevant in poverty reduction.

When suspicious data for Argentina, Colombia, and Uruguay are removed, the sample is reduced to nine countries and 35 observations. The results are reported in table 2–4. We see that eliminating these data makes no difference in the results, stressing the robustness of the findings.

The asymmetrical effects of growth and recession are illustrated with data for Panama in figure 2–2. The data for Panama cover two spells of early growth, one

Table 2–5. Effect of Length of Regime in Determinants of Change in Rural Poverty

Variable	Elasticity	Overall effect of growth	
		Lowest	Highest
Estimation with 12 countries		(1 year)	(4 years)
GDP per capita growth	–1.35**	–1.13**	–0.50*
Length of regime*GDP per capita growth	0.21*		
Estimation with 9 countries		(1 year)	(4 years)
GDP per capita growth	–1.43**	–1.18**	–0.45
Length of regime*GDP per capita growth	0.24*		

* Significant at the 90 percent level.
** Significant at the 95 percent level.
Note: Values show the effect of length of regime on GDPpc growth. The endogenous variable is the annual growth rate in the number of rural poor by spell.
Source: Authors' calculations.

spell of recession, and two spells of late growth. The large vertical segments show that GDPpc is not a strong predictor of observed changes in rural poverty, except during recession and the first period of economic recovery, where GDPpc growth explains most of the observed changes in poverty. Recession has a strong ratchet effect on poverty. Yet, the encouraging observation is the strong poverty reduction effect of late growth that outperforms (in a positive direction) the impact of recession per percentage point of change in income.

The length of the recession period affects the income elasticity of rural poverty. As shown in table 2–5, a 1-percent decline in GDPpc in the context of a one-year recession is more devastating than a 1-percent decline in a longer recession. Thus, the elasticity is –1.18 with a one-year recession, while it is –0.45 with a four-year recession. These results stay the same when countries with suspicious rural poverty data are removed. Longer recessions allow the poor to engage in risk management. This shows that the poor lack access to risk-coping instruments and can reduce the costs of declining income through risk management over the longer run. Giving access to risk-coping instruments such as social funds should thus be important in helping the poor reduce the cost of short-term income fluctuations.

INEQUALITY

Inequality, as measured by the Gini coefficient, is even harder to explain than rural poverty. The results in table 2–6 are quite disturbing for the potential of growth to

Table 2–6. Determinants of Change in Inequality

Variable	Coefficient	Student t
Aggregate GDP per capita growth		
Early growth episode	0.32	0.9
Recession episode	–0.44	–2.2
Late growth episode	–0.05	–0.2
Qualitative features of growth		
Differential growth agriculture-nonagriculture		
Early growth episode	–0.26	–0.6
Recession episode	0.04	0.1
Late growth episode	–0.24	–1.0
Coefficient of variation of GDP per capita	–0.43	–1.8
Macroeconomic performance		
Real exchange rate growth	0.06	1.0
Hyperinflation dummy	1.16	1.4
Structural context		
GDP per capita (thousands of 1987 dollars)	–0.69	–1.1
Share of agriculture in GDP	–0.12	–1.6
Population growth	–0.72	–0.5
Urban population share	–0.08	–0.7
Rural-urban migration (predicted rate)	0.45	0.4
Secondary education	0.002	0.1
Initial inequality	–10.12	–2.0
Intercept	13.71	1.2
Number of observations	49	
R²	0.50	

Note: The endogenous variable is the annual growth rate of the Gini coefficient by spell.
Source: Authors' calculations.

reduce inequality: neither early nor late growth has significant effects on inequality. Recession, by contrast, has a powerful effect, but evidently in the unfortunate direction: every 1-percentage point of decline in GDPpc increases inequality by 0.44 percent. Structural factors affect inequality, particularly the share of agriculture in GDP and the initial level of inequality, which both help reduce the growth in inequality.

Using Panama again as an illustration, figure 2–3 shows the devastating effect of recession on inequality, with a 1-percent decline in income eliminating the gains from 9 percent in late income growth. The figure again illustrates how wrong

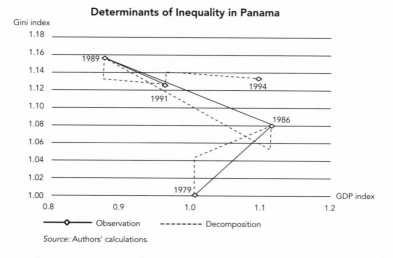

FIGURE 2–3.

Determinants of Inequality in Panama

Source: Authors' calculations.

an analysis of the relationship between income growth and inequality could be if it did not decompose the relation by periods. In this case, with nonsignificant effects of early and late growth, the negative relation between income and inequality would wholly come from recession. The policy implication that growth reduces inequality would thus be totally unfounded.

The length of the regime of growth under early growth shows that growth was neutral on inequality only if the number of years of sustained growth was large enough. Thus, with the shortest period of early growth observed in Panama

Table 2–7. Effect of Length of Regime on Determinants of Change in Inequality

		Overall effect of growth	
Variable	Coefficient	Lowest	Highest
		(Panama, 4 years)	(Panama, 21 years)
GDP per capita growth	2.11**	1.59**	−0.60
Length of regime*GDP per capita growth	−0.13*		

* Significant at the 90 percent level.
** Significant at the 95 percent level.
Note: Values show the effect of length of regime on GDPpc growth for early growth episodes. The endogenous variable is the annual growth rate of the Gini coefficient by spell.
Source: Authors' calculations.

(four years), growth increased inequality with an elasticity of 1.59 (table 2–7). By contrast, sustained growth over 21 years, the longest sequence of years of sustained growth, also observed in Panama, eliminates the recessive effect of growth, with a nonsignificant elasticity of –0.6 (table 2–7). Short bouts of growth are thus particularly destabilizing on the distribution of income, concentrating opportunities in the hands of a few. The sustainability of growth is important to mitigate negative inequality effects.

CONCLUSION

This study used a data set on poverty and inequality across 12 Latin American countries over 25 years that is far from perfect. While the authors of the data made remarkable efforts in seeking to achieve consistency across space and time, the data are not as solid as desired, particularly for the rural sector. It should be remembered that the results presented[13] are consequently conditional on the quality of this data set. As better data become available, the estimations we have presented will need to be run again, possibly with different results. Yet, it is remarkable that the data yield strong regularities, confirming many of the theoretical expectations on the relation between growth and poverty and inequality, and qualifying these results by models of Latin American economic development and by contexts in which growth and recession occurred. If the data had simply been white noise, these regularities would not have emerged as systematically and significantly as they did. Removing suspicious data for rural poverty leaves these results unaltered, vouching for the robustness of the findings.

The following table summarizes the income elasticities of poverty and inequality that were obtained in this study.

Income elasticity	Urban poverty	Rural poverty	Inequality
Early growth	–0.32	–0.27	0.32
Recession	–1.11**	–0.60**	–0.44**
Late growth	–1.25**	–0.99**	–0.05

** Significant at the 95 percent level.

---

[13] See Lustig (1994).

There are strong asymmetries in the relations among income and poverty and inequality according to growth episode: recession is systematically devastating on poverty and inequality. A 1-percent decline in GDPpc in a recession episode eliminates the gains in urban poverty reduction achieved by 3.7 percent growth in GDPpc under early growth, the gains in rural poverty reduction achieved by 2 percent growth under early growth, and the gains in inequality reduction achieved by 9 percent growth under late growth. Recession has a particularly strong ratchet effect on inequality since subsequent growth is unable to compensate for the higher level of inequality thus achieved. Reducing aggregate income shocks, in particular by lessening external vulnerability, should thus be an important policy goal, even if the opportunity cost is somewhat lower growth.[14] Economies can indeed be made more resilient to external shocks, and this is all the more important when poverty is high. The dilemma of this trade-off can be lessened by providing the poor with access to risk-coping instruments in order to protect them from the poverty and inequality effects of downturns. This includes building permanent programs of social protection for food security, guaranteeing employment in public works programs, keeping children in school, and maintaining health services whatever the phase of the economic cycle, and minimizing budget cuts in social services during recessions.[15]

The style of growth matters for welfare. Early growth (import substitution industrialization) was not effective for poverty and inequality reduction. Late growth (open economy) is encouragingly very effective for poverty reduction. The precise mechanisms by which this happens need to be analyzed. But late growth is disappointingly ineffective for inequality reduction.

Econometric estimates of income elasticities of poverty and inequality obtained without distinguishing growth episodes are misleading: a negative elasticity may come from recession instead of growth, especially for inequality in general and for poverty under early growth and recession, leading to fallacious policy implications regarding the potential of growth to reduce poverty and inequality under these circumstances.

Aggregate income growth is only effective for poverty and inequality reduction if a set of contextual conditions holds. For urban poverty, aggregate income growth is only effective if the levels of inequality and poverty are not too high, if

[14] Altimir (1998).
[15] Nelson (1999).

the levels of secondary education are sufficiently high, and if growth is reinforced by growth in the service sector in a context of sufficiently high equality. For rural poverty, the cost of a recession per percentage point of decline in GDPpc is higher if the income shock is short. And for inequality, short episodes of growth are more destabilizing of the distribution of income.

The overarching conclusion is that inequality needs to be attacked directly by asset redistribution measures in order for growth to be effective for poverty reduction. Latin America remains the region of the world where income is most unequally distributed, and inequality robs growth from creating the expected welfare gains.[16] Education, in particular, has a powerful role to play in reconciling aggregate income growth and poverty reduction.

---

[16] IDB (1998).

References

Aghion, Philippe, and Peter Howitt. 1998. *Endogenous Growth Theory.* Cambridge, MA: MIT Press.

Altimir, Oscar. 1995. *Changes in Inequality and Poverty in Latin America.* Santiago, Chile: CEPAL.

———. 1998. "Inequality, Employment, and Poverty in Latin America: An Overview." In V. Tokman and G. O'Donnell, eds., *Poverty and Inequality in Latin America: Issues and New Challenges.* Chicago, IL: University of Notre Dame Press.

CEPAL. 1994, 1995, 1996. *Social Panorama in Latin America.* Santiago, Chile.

de Janvry, Alain, and Elisabeth Sadoulet. 1998. *Poverty and Inequality in Latin America: A Causal Analysis, 1970–1994.* Working Paper. Department of Agricultural and Resource Economics. University of California at Berkeley, Berkeley, CA.

The Economist. 1996. "The Backlash in Latin America: Gestures against Reform." November 30: 19-21.

Inter-American Development Bank (IDB). 1998. *Facing Up to Inequality in Latin America: Economic and Social Progress in Latin America, 1998–1999 Report.* Baltimore, MD: Johns Hopkins University Press.

Londoño, Juan Luis, and Miguel Székely. 1997. *Persistent Poverty and Excess Inequality: Latin America, 1970–1995.* Working Paper Series no. 357. Inter-American Development Bank, Washington, D.C.

Lustig, Nora. 1994. *Measuring Poverty in Latin America: The Emperor Has No Clothes.* Washington, D.C.: Brookings Institution.

Morley, Samuel. 1995. *Poverty and Inequality in Latin America: The Impact of Adjustment and Recovery in the 1980s.* Baltimore, MD: Johns Hopkins University Press.

Nelson, Joan. 1999. "Shock-Resistant Growth?" ODC Viewpoint. Washington, D.C.: Overseas Development Council.

PREALC/International Labour Office. 1992. *Empleo y transformación productiva en América Latina y el Caribe.* Documento de trabajo no. 369. Santiago, Chile.

Psacharopoulos, George, and others. 1995. "Poverty and Income Inequality in Latin America during the 1980s." *Review of Income and Wealth* 41 (September): 245–64.

Ravallion, Martin. 1997. "Can High-Inequality Developing Countries Escape Absolute Poverty?" *Economic Letters* 56: 51–57.

Ravallion, Martin, and Gaurav Datt. 1996. "How Important to India's Poor Is the Sectoral Composition of Economic Growth?" *World Bank Economic Review* 10 (January): 1–25.

———. 1999. *When Is Growth Pro-Poor? Evidence from the Diverse Experiences of India's States.* Washington, D.C.: World Bank.

World Bank. 1990. *World Development Report 1990: Poverty.* Washington, D.C.: World Bank.

———. 1997. *World Development Indicators*, CD-ROM. Washington, D.C.

CHAPTER THREE

Social Protection for the Unemployed: Programs in Latin America

Gustavo Márquez

Macroeconomic volatility seems to be a recurrent feature of the Latin American economies. There is some evidence that unemployment is more sensitive to downswings than it was in the past. Furthermore, openness exposes workers to more unemployment risks. Traditional legally mandated severance payment mechanisms have failed to provide the income support needed by unemployed and displaced workers primarily because of the narrow scope of its coverage. This has led governments in Latin America, faced with sharp economic instability since 1995, to develop a series of attempts at setting up mechanisms to support the incomes of groups of the population hurt by unemployment and declining incomes. This chapter presents an overview of these programs, pointing out their limitations and potentials.

UNEMPLOYMENT INSURANCE

Table 3–1 presents a summary description of unemployment insurance systems in the region. As can be seen, very few countries in the region have legally or administratively enacted unemployment insurance systems, and even fewer have working unemployment insurance schemes. This is a consequence of the very weak incentives that exist for the development of unemployment insurance and other more socialized forms of income protection, given that severance payments work as privately provided income insurance for workers in full-benefit employment contracts who are laid off.

The author thanks Carola Alvarez (IDB), Gaurav Datt (IFPRI), and three anonymous reviewers for insightful comments and suggestions.

Table 3–1. Unemployment Insurance in the Region

Country	Law	Funding	Replacement rate[a]	Benefit duration	Benefits min/max	Coverage requirements[c]
Argentina	1991 reform 1995	Worker: 1 percent wages Employer: 1.5 percent payroll	60 percent	4–12 months Max: 4 m.w.	Min: 1 m.w.	Employees 1 (12), 2, 3
Barbados	1982	Worker: 1.5 percent wages Employer: 1.5 percent payroll	60 percent 10 weeks 40 percent 16 weeks	26 weeks in a 52-week period		Employees 1 (6) 16–64 years old
Brazil	1986 1990	FAT (.65 percent tax on total sales)	1–3 m.w.	4 months	Min: 1 m.w.	Employees 4 (36, 4), 5, 6
Chile	1981	Government	$37 monthly for the first 6 months, $18 last 6 months	Max. 1 year[b]		Employees 2, 4 (12, 2), 5
Ecuador	1958 1988	Worker: 2 percent salary Employer: 1 percent payroll	One-time subsidy, amounts decided each year			Employees 1 (24), 7 (30)
Mexico		Social security pension	95 percent	5 years max		Employees between 60–65 years old
Uruguay	1981	Contributions to social security	Up to 50 percent	6 months	Min: 0.5 m.w. Max: 4 m.w.	Employees 1 (6), 5, 3, 8 in commerce and industry
Venezuela	1989 reform 1998	Worker: .7 percent wages Employer: 1.5 percent payroll	Up to 60 percent	13–26 weeks	Max: $44	Employees 1 (12), 2

m.w. Minimum wage.

a. Percentage of last wage.

b. Beneficiaries receive also family support, medical, and maternity benefits.

c. Requirements: 1 (s) be employed s months before receiving subsidy, 2 availability to work, 3 does not receive other social security benefits, 4 (s, j) not having received more than s months of benefits in the last j years, 5 unemployed for reasons outside the conduct and willingness of worker, 6 subject to economic need, 7 (x) waiting period of x days, 8 at least 12 months between periods of receiving subsidy.

Source: Lora and Pagés (1999); U.S. Dept. of Health and Human Services (1995).

In those countries that do have unemployment insurance systems, coverage is limited to workers that have contributed, while they were employed, to the financing of the system. In other words, only workers in full-benefit employment contracts and working in payroll tax–paying firms enjoy the benefits of the unemployment insurance system. This excludes from the protection a sizable fraction of the workforce that works in the unregulated segment of the labor market, presumably those who because of their human and social capital deficits are the neediest in terms of income protection. The level and duration of benefits provided are low relative to unemployment insurance systems in more developed countries. Replacement rates are normally on the order of 50 to 60 percent of last wage, with caps linked to the minimum wage for higher salaries. Benefits are granted for periods typically not longer than four months.

The unemployment insurance system in Argentina is quite limited in the number of beneficiaries and has remained so in spite of strong increases in the number of unemployed workers. Jacqueline Mazza reports that the number of beneficiaries has remained stable, around 100 thousand to 125 thousand workers, of whom more than 70 percent are prime age males, and more than 50 percent are not household heads.[1] She also reports that an analysis of beneficiaries in their personal and previous job characteristics shows that there is a definite trend toward serving younger and middle-class displaced workers. This suggests that unemployment insurance is not fulfilling a safety net role for the poor in the case of Argentina.

Brazil has the biggest unemployment insurance system in the region, with around 300,000 to 400,000 beneficiaries. Mazza reports that unemployment insurance in Brazil is also serving younger (more than 50 percent of beneficiaries are younger than 30) and more educated (45 percent of beneficiaries have completed eighth grade or higher) workers. As Mazza assesses, the unemployment insurance system reflects wage inequality, in the sense that benefits accrue to the middle deciles in the distribution of income.[2]

In Venezuela, the unemployment insurance system was enacted in 1989, but it was never implemented. The system was reformed in 1998. The new system will protect beneficiaries through a mix of individual and collective insurance operated by competitive insurance providers, but implementation has not yet begun as of this date. Given that only workers with regulated, tax-paying contracts are entitled

---

[1] Mazza (1999).
[2] Mazza (1999).

to benefits, it is likely that the pattern of distribution of beneficiaries will be very similar to that of Argentina and Brazil.

Mexico and Uruguay have unemployment insurance programs operated by the social security system. In both cases coverage is quite limited, and in the former it is just an advance payment of old age pensions for a maximum of five years. In the case of Barbados, the unemployment insurance system is very small in coverage, though quite well adapted to the needs of an island economy with frequent but short episodes of unemployment concentrated in workers in the tourism industry.[3]

In general, unemployment insurance systems lack connection with other labor market intermediation and placement services. Even when the unemployment insurance system is operated through the Labor Ministry (as in Brazil), workers are not required to register in the intermediation service, and payment of the benefit is not contingent on verification of search effort. On the one hand, this lack of connection generates opportunity for fraud. Even if it is illegal to have a job and receive unemployment insurance payments simultaneously, most operators complain of their lack of capacity to control what is perceived to be widespread fraud and collusion between firms and workers.[4] On the other hand, this lack of connection with labor market intermediation services makes the system a pure income transfer that does not ease the transition of the unemployed into a new job.

Most unemployment insurance systems are financed through payroll taxes, which are already quite high in the region. This partly explains why coverage is limited, replacement rates are low, and periods of coverage short. Any expansion of the system to cover hitherto unprotected segments of the population is likely to face substantial opposition by its own present beneficiaries and by firms operating in the regulated sector of the economy. Only in Brazil has some expansion to new groups been made (to traditional fishermen and to workers affected by the drought in the Northeast), but the expansion has been temporary and financed through the use of excess funds. If unemployment insurance is to work as part of the safety net in a crisis, the expansion of coverage would have to be produced just when the flow of benefits to already protected workers was highest, creating financial strains

---

[3] Mazza (1999).

[4] Mazza (1999) reports that some efforts have been made in Argentina to detect if workers receiving unemployment insurance were working, by using a common taxpayer identification number. It was found that a sizable number of workers were not only working but also contributing to the social security plan in a new job while they continued to receive the unemployment insurance payment.

on the system and the need for additional funding. The question is whether to attempt this through the unemployment insurance system or by creating an alternative mechanism for income transfer better suited to the needs of workers with different labor market participation.

It has also been argued that the implementation of unemployment insurance requires considerable institutional resources in terms of accounting and recordkeeping. However, mandatory savings-based schemes in place in Brazil, Colombia, Ecuador, and Peru also require considerable institutional resources of the same type. Furthermore, pension system reforms in several countries in the region have created a network of institutions that hold individual workers' accounts and that can be used for recordkeeping in the unemployment insurance system with few additional costs.[5]

In conclusion, the design and target population of unemployment insurance make it suited to protect workers who have full-benefit employment contracts and who acquire rights to it through their contributions while employed. In terms of labor market distortions, the low level of benefits and their short duration apparently do not create incentives against the search for employment. In fact, the reports on fraud in Argentina and Brazil rather suggest that workers use unemployment insurance as a means to obtain additional income while in a new job. As Hugo Hopenhayn and Juan Pablo Nicolini (in this volume) show, it is possible to design optimal unemployment insurance schedules that do not induce reduction in search efforts. Furthermore, unemployment insurance schemes based on nominative contributions to individual accounts that can be rolled over into retirement funds can minimize negative impacts on search effort.[6]

In terms of ability to expand and contract countercyclically, unemployment insurance expenditure is an ideal mechanism. By definition, outlays increase when unemployment is rising and contract with the recuperation of employment.

The most problematic aspect of unemployment insurance, however, is related to its coverage. Workers must bear at least part of the cost of insurance to prevent moral hazard problems. For high-productivity workers, wages are high enough to make the benefit of paying for unemployment insurance (the expected value of benefits when unemployed) higher than the cost of the current income forgone by pay-

---

[5] Most notably Chile but also Argentina, Uruguay, Peru, and Venezuela.
[6] For a proposal of an unemployment insurance system along these lines, see Cortázar and others (1995) and the Venezuelan social security law of 1997.

ing the contribution. However, for low-productivity workers, the utility gain from an increase in current income will be big enough to generate incentives to negotiate with employers a contract without benefits in exchange for a higher current income.

EMPLOYMENT GENERATION PROGRAMS

Employment generation programs are a natural reaction of governments to increasing unemployment. Politically they show the concern of the government with the workers' plight and, by providing jobs, they directly attack unemployment. For analytical purposes it is convenient to separate labor-intensive public works from wage subsidies to the private sector.

Labor-Intensive Public Works

Labor-intensive public works have been the tools of choice to deal with economywide shocks. The number and variety of programs in place in the region show that governments choose to spend greater additional resources on employment generation than on other mechanisms to provide income support to unemployed workers. One of the main advantages of these programs is that they are self-targeted and, therefore, can be implemented without the delays necessary to implement a targeting mechanism.[7]

Three characteristics of labor-intensive public works are crucial in their success as income support mechanisms. In the first place, these programs are financed by the central government and executed by local organizations—be it local governments or nongovernmental organizations (NGOs)—who normally are in charge of selecting the works to be performed and the selection of beneficiaries. Thus, labor-intensive public works require an extensive and solid network of institutions at the local level, with the technical and operational capacity to choose the works to be done, organize the production process, and channel resources to the needy poor. A large part of the success of these programs hinges on how well structured the relationship is between the central government and the executing agencies. There is not a unique way of designing this relationship. To mention just two examples, Argentina chooses to finance works that are approved by a central government agency and executed mostly by local governments, while Brazil chooses to allocate resources

---

[7] Grosh (1994); Ravallion (1998).

semiautomatically on a regional needs base and have works selected by the subnational governments. In any case, what is important is that the design of the relationship between financing and work execution be adequate to the institutional and political structure of the country. Federalist countries should respect local autonomy in work selection and allocate budgets on objective criteria, while more centralized countries will be more able to select works and distribute resources at the central level while keeping responsibility for execution at the local level.

In the second place, the wage level and the criteria for selection of beneficiaries are set at the central level, while local organizations are in charge of the selection of beneficiaries. Thus, a certain tension prevails between the criteria set at the central level and the local political and social reality within which the selection of beneficiaries takes place. There are multiple ways to solve or at least mitigate the consequences of this tension. Community oversight is useful to ensure that resources are not diverted through political favoritism or other forms of corruption, but there is no guarantee that the needed level of community participation will exist. A useful complement to community oversight is a system of random sampling of projects and beneficiaries by the central government agency in charge of overseeing the program to check whether resources are being diverted. This step implies a nontrivial investment of resources in sampling and supervision, but these resources will pay for themselves in greater transparency and better targeting of beneficiaries.

In the third place, to target resources on needy groups and to avoid inducing distortions in local labor markets, wages in labor-intensive public works are frequently set below the market wage of the relevant labor market. The literature on workfare in the developed world suggests that this targeting mechanism is not without costs in terms of stigmatizing workers who participate in the program, and in terms of political and social discrimination among workers by program administrators.[8] There is no solution to this problem short of raising wages to market levels, which in most cases will be impossible given resource constraints.

In summary, labor-intensive public works do not generate important labor market distortions to the extent that they offer wages below the relevant market and can provide a source of income to workers temporarily unemployed. Their coverage depends on the resources allocated to the program, but there is no intrinsic reason why coverage of low-skill workers could not be as ample as needed to reduce unemployment to the target level. This same property, however, brings us

---

[8] Lightman (1995); Rose (1994).

to the problem of their countercyclical nature. Because the amount of resources dedicated to the program is a political decision, there is no way of guaranteeing that the program will move in sync with the economic cycle, expanding in downturns and shrinking in upturns. In fact, the experience in the region shows that once the programs are in place, it is very difficult to reduce their size. In the well-known cases of programs that were phased out during the 1980s (PEM and POJ in Chile and PAIT in Peru), the closing seems to have been mostly a reaction to widespread problems of design and political manipulation.[9]

Wage Subsidies

Subsidized private sector jobs are much less prevalent than labor-intensive public works programs. Argentina is the only case where wage subsidies were widely used, and their scope has shrunk recently, owing to criticisms from the union movement.

Wage subsidies work through reducing the payroll tax or severance payments in employment contracts for particular groups of workers (youth, women, ex-combatants, and so on). This characteristic makes them suitable for the introduction of more flexible (or precarious) employment contracts in a process of labor market regulation reform. In fact, this was the role these programs fulfilled in Argentina in 1995. But at the same time, this feature makes them the center of a political debate on labor market "flexibility," which in large measure explains why these programs were phased out in the face of union opposition in 1998.

However, because wage subsidies are targeted on particular groups, they change the relative prices of different types of workers in favor of the target group and induce large labor market distortions, not the least of which is the substitution of nonsubsidized for subsidized workers.[10] To mitigate this problem, there is normally an "additionality" requirement, by which subsidies are granted only for net new hires that expand the payroll. In turn, this rule requires the determination of a baseline number of employees and a control on new hires. Theoretically, the Ministries of Labor fulfill this task in the normal course of their business. In practice, the ministries are extremely weak and have a very low enforcement capability. This

---

[9] Graham (1994).

[10] More formally, deadweight effects appear when the subsidized jobs would have been created anyway, without the subsidy, while substitution effects appear when subsidized workers replace nonsubsidized ones. See Calmfors (1994). The additionality requirement addresses the deadweight effect, while substitution effects are only prevented at the margin.

weakness makes it impossible to determine base lines and control hires of subsidized workers, therefore making worker substitution a widespread problem. As a consequence, it is not clear whether these programs really create more jobs than would have been created without the subsidy.

In summary, these programs generate large and important labor market distortions by attempting to change the relative salaries of different types of workers. Because they have to be explicitly targeted by design, they require a comprehensive and often nonexistent enforcement apparatus, making the problem of targeting the program an intractable one. In terms of their countercyclical nature, expanding and shrinking the program requires an administrative decision. To the extent that these programs are often perceived as a mechanism to introduce more flexible (or more precarious) employment contracts, they can become the center of an often ardent political debate and make decisions about program implementation politically very costly. This has been the experience of Argentina, where these programs were phased out jointly with the rejection of more far-reaching labor regulation reforms during 1998.

Table 3–2 summarizes the employment generation programs in seven countries in the region at the end of 1995. The list was extracted from a joint ILO-IDB volume on active labor market policies in Argentina, Brazil, Chile, Costa Rica, Jamaica, Mexico, and Peru. These countries represent a wide spectrum of variation in policy development, operational capabilities, and exposure to volatility in international capital markets. Program descriptions and characteristics are summarized by Francisco Verdera in that volume, and a more thorough discussion of programs is presented in the accompanying national reports.[11] An itemized description of the programs is presented in table 3A–1 in the appendix to this chapter.

Argentina is the country with the most varied set of employment generation programs, comprising a combination of public works and subsidies to private employment. Public subsidies to private sector employment, in the form of subsidies to firms that increase the number of employees, were widely used under various mechanisms. Workers displaced from the public sector and unemployed workers receiving unemployment insurance were given vouchers that employers could use to pay tax liabilities. Firms could opt for tax rebates if they were hiring particular groups of workers (youth, women, ex-combatants, and so on) under promotional contractual forms. Firms in particular activities (like reforestation) were subsidized if they hired

---

[11] Verdera (1998).

Table 3–2. Employment Generation Programs in Seven Countries in the Region

Country	Beneficiaries		Expenditure	
	Thousands	Percent of total labor force	Millions of U.S. dollars	Percent of GDP
Argentina	892.2	9.31	249.2	0.09
Brazil	221.8	0.49	1,188.8	0.21
Chile	4.3	0.10	1.4	0.00
Costa Rica	8.1	0.71	3.3	0.04
Jamaica	6.0	0.61	21.2	0.50
Mexico	1,024.0	4.42	1,802.0	0.51
Peru	27.8	0.93	100.0	0.19

Source: Data from Verdera (1998), modified by author. For a complete listing, see appendix tables in this chapter.

new workers. But the most visible mechanism of subsidization was the use of "promotional employment contracts" established in a series of decrees in 1995. These promoted contracts were more precarious than regular full-benefit contracts, did not originate rights to severance payments, and had lower payroll tax liabilities.

Argentina's federal government also financed labor-intensive public works as an employment generation device. The *Trabajar* and similar programs were financed and supervised by the federal government using the *Fondo Nacional de Empleo* (a fund financed through payroll taxes). The resources were used to build small-scale and labor-intensive public works (in many cases social infrastructure, but also roads and small sanitation works), with the works being executed by a wide variety of agencies, from local and state governments to NGOs.

The *PROGER* program in Brazil is a contrasting mechanism for employment generation. The program operates through the establishment of credit lines offered through the national development banking system to small enterprises, cooperatives, NGOs, and other civil society associations. This mechanism circumvents the subnational governments for execution of works in order to avoid the creation of budgetary entitlements. Partial and incomplete evaluations of *PROGER*, however, are not too optimistic about the results for employment generation.[12]

Chile does not have any employment generation program as such, though it has a number of very small and narrowly targeted programs to address living conditions that may hinder the labor market participation of particular groups.

Costa Rica uses public works, wage subsidies, and credit to small enterprises as mechanisms to promote employment generation. Credit to promote employment generation in small firms is also widely used in Jamaica in a battery of programs, some of which also include a form of short-term training. Jamaica has a training and temporary employment program for unemployed youth, aimed at easing their labor market insertion.

Mexico uses public works (rural roads and other social infrastructure) as employment generation devices. The programs are financed by allocations from general revenues (not from payroll taxes) in the federal government budget, and states and local governments execute the works.

Finally, Peru uses legal incentives, a social investment fund, and a micro- and small-enterprise credit program as tools for employment promotion. The labor law reform of 1991 introduced several more precarious forms of employment contracts, allowing firms to hire workers without generating rights to severance payments under fixed-term contracts. FONCODES, a social investment fund, is also used as an employment generation device that can be quickly adjusted to the situation of local labor markets. However, it is not clear how much capacity or interest FONCODES management has in employment generation as opposed to the physical execution of civil works.[13]

SHORT-TERM TRAINING PROGRAMS

Short-term training programs work as an income support device through the provision of scholarships to trainees during the classroom training and apprenticeship periods, which are normally between four and six months. The scholarships are below the relevant market wage, and the apprenticeships are developed in private firms with which the training providers sign an agreement. The short duration of the classroom training makes these programs more suited to young new entrants

---

[12] Government of Brazil (1998).
[13] Verdera (1998).

in the labor market with job search skills than to workers who need skill updating or upgrading and are being displaced from declining sectors.

The main challenge in the design of these training programs arises from the existence of a national training institution, normally a monopolistic public provider of training financed through a payroll tax, with no incentive whatsoever to adapt the nature of its activities and clientele to the challenges of high unemployment. To circumvent this obstacle the programs are organized through the setting up of a separate pool of resources managed by a specialized agent at the central government level. This agent in turn bids out resources to private providers that execute the training programs in a decentralized fashion. As already mentioned, these decentralized providers must enter into agreements with private sector firms to ensure that trainees will have an apprenticeship stage, making private firms the effective gatekeepers of the quality and relevance of the training programs. Another interesting by-product of this process is the development of stronger connections between firms and training providers, which make the latter effectively providers of job search assistance services.

Training programs tend to be more expensive on a per beneficiary basis than labor-intensive public works, given that a larger part of the resources goes to pay the training provider. However, calculations of benefits should include the long-term change in the structure of the training system and the development of job search assistance services, which are very large positive externalities of these programs.[14]

The organization of the programs makes it easy for the program organizer to administratively target groups of the population, and the programs have been quite successful in attracting unemployed youth. However, the programs can be "too effective" in attracting the target group: in Mexico in 1996 youth participation rates increased so much that even if the employment rate of the group rose, so did its unemployment rate. Although there is no formal proof that this was the result of the expansion of training programs (particularly PROBECAT) in that year, a suggestive association exists among expansion of these programs, decline in school

---

[14] These emergency training programs have created the opportunity to introduce institutional innovation into a training system characterized by the monopolistic power of payroll-tax-financed institutions. Disseminating these innovations to the mainstream vocational training system will make it much more successful in addressing the needs of workers caught in the normal process of job churning, who need to upgrade skills.

Table 3–3. Training Programs in Seven Countries in the Region

| Country | Beneficiaries | | Expenditure | |
	Thousands	Percent of total labor force	Millions of U.S. dollars	Percent of GDP
Argentina	133.0	1.4	95.6	0.04
Brazil	740.5	1.6	310.2	0.06
Chile	36.6	0.8	18.3	0.03
Costa Rica	13.1	1.2	60.6	0.73
Jamaica	43.5	4.4	18.6	0.44
Mexico	410.3	1.8	135	0.04
Peru	1.5	0.1	5.0	0.01

Source: Data from Verdera (1998), modified by author. For a complete listing, see appendix tables in this chapter.

enrollment rates, and increase in labor force participation and employment of the target groups.

In summary, these programs tend to generate positive labor market externalities beyond the training process itself, by easing the entry of young workers and creating experience in the operation of labor market intermediation mechanisms (job search assistance). The nature of the training makes the programs suitable for unemployed youth and, as with any training program, one should not expect them to create new jobs but rather to provide new entrants with some labor market experience. Because youth unemployment is a permanent problem in the labor market, one should not think about these programs as countercyclical devices, but rather as permanent features of a well-functioning labor market intermediation system, which could be expanded and contracted following demand in a countercyclical way.

Table 3–3 presents a summary description of the training programs that were being used as income transfer devices in seven countries in the region by the end of 1995.[15] An itemized description of these programs is presented in table 3A–2 in the appendix to this chapter. Training programs were widely used as a mechanism to

---

[15] Verdera (1998).

transfer income, particularly to unemployed youth, through scholarships during the classroom training period (normally three to six months) and sometimes through job search assistance or apprenticeship in private firms. Most of the time these training programs were financed by the government and delivered by private and NGO training providers, with little or no intervention by the traditional national training institutions.

The basic operational technology of these training programs was based on *Chile Joven*, a pioneering youth training program that combined a scholarship for classroom training with a three-month paid apprenticeship in a private firm. Instead of direct purchasing of training services, resources were used to create a fund that was managed by a central government agency. The managing agency requested proposals for training projects, and funds were granted through open bidding. The proposals had to describe the content of the courses to be taught and include a commitment from private sector firms to accept the trainees as apprentices for a period of time (normally three months). The provision of scholarships served as an income transfer to beneficiaries, took them out of the unemployment queue, and gave them some labor market experience during the apprenticeship. These three beneficial effects of the *Joven* program were quite adequately suited to situations characterized by high youth unemployment rates.[16] However, other countries in the region emulated the contracting methodology of the *Joven* program to cater to the needs of other population groups.

Among the countries in the study reported here, Argentina, Chile, and Peru have programs inspired by the *Chile Joven* design, targeting low-income unemployed youth. Argentina has also used the contracting mechanisms of the *Joven* program to develop training programs for other groups of the population and has granted subsidies to private employers who hire apprentices under promotional employment contracts.

Brazil also uses competitive bidding for training provision, but the program operates in a highly decentralized way. The *PLANFOR* program is financed through the FAT, a payroll-tax-financed fund, and funds are allocated to states and local

---

[16] The contracting mechanism of *Chile Joven* was a way to create incentives for training providers to deliver courses of good quality and with content relevant to the labor market. This created pressures for an institutional and content revamping of the training system, as firms accepting apprentices acted as controllers and gatekeepers of the relevance and adequacy of the training provided. The program was therefore rightly perceived as a tool to modernizing and connecting the training system with productive activities.

governments, who in turn hire different providers (private and public) through competitive bidding. States must present annual training plans to the *PLANFOR* administration, and funds are allocated in proportion to each state's share of the total workforce. This method of allocation is presently being changed to reflect the state level of poverty and education and past experience with the execution of annual training programs. Interestingly, the national training institutions (in Brazil the SENAI-SENAC system) participate in the bidding process as another provider of training services, thus creating a financial and institutional dynamic in the overall training system.

Costa Rica used instead the national training institution (INA) as a channel for delivery of training services to semiskilled and skilled unemployed workers. Thus, INA schedules and provides training programs for low-income workers in marginal urban areas, for displaced public sector workers, and for handicapped workers using its own facilities and instructors. A special line of action was established to enable INA to contract out other training institutions, but no special targeting mechanism has been used.

Jamaica uses several programs to provide training for unskilled and young unemployed workers, but the mechanism for income transfer is temporary jobs rather than scholarships during training.

Mexico has the biggest training with income transfer program in the region, and it has been effectively used as a protective device for unemployed and displaced workers and expanded and contracted according to the economic cycle. The PROBECAT program provides a scholarship for the beneficiaries, and the state offices of the Labor Ministry organize various training programs that are delivered locally. Different program evaluations have found that the program has been somewhat successful as a training program, increasing incomes and likelihood of employment for beneficiaries, even though positive effects tend to increase with higher levels of education of the beneficiaries.[17]

---

[17] Government of Mexico (1995).

Table 3A–1. Description of Employment Generation Programs in Seven Countries in the Region

Country, program	Beneficiaries		Expenditure	
	Thousands	Percent of total labor force	Millions of U.S. dollars	Percent of GDP
Argentina		9.31		0.09
Public works financed with public resources				
Solidarity Assistance Program (PROAS)				
Unemployed household heads in public works; joint program by Ministry of Social Development and state governments	260.0	2.7	54.5	0.020
Occupational Training Program (PRENO)	94.0	1.0	20.0	0.007
Community Service Program (ASISTIR)				
Female household heads in community development activities	25.0	0.3	2.6	0.001
Trabajar Program				
Unemployed household heads in public works; program by local governments and NGOs	233.0	2.4	44.9	0.017
Private sector employment promotion				
Private Employment Program for Small- and Medium-Sized Enterprises				
Subsidy for new jobs for unemployed workers in firms with less than 100 employees	254.0	2.7	42.4	0.016
National Forestation Program (FORESTAR)				
Subsidy for new jobs for unemployed workers in new agricultural/forestry firms	21.0	0.2	4.4	0.002
Labor Reintegration Program				
Subsidy to workers who find a job while receiving unemployment insurance	–		–	
Geographic Mobility Program				
Subsidy to workers who have to move from place of residence to keep job	–		–	
Private Employment Creation Voucher Program (BOCEP)				
Fiscal credit for workers displaced from state's payroll; new employer can use as collateral for credit from public banks	5.2	0.1	73.4	0.027
Brazil[a]	221.8	0.49	1,188.8	0.21
Income and Employment Generation Program (PROGER)				
Special credit lines to MSMEs, cooperatives and informal sector	221.8	0.5	1,188.8	0.21

Table 3A–1. (continued)

Country, program	Beneficiaries		Expenditure	
	Thousands	Percent of total labor force	Million of U.S. dollars	Percent of GDP
Chile	4.3	0.10	1.4	0.00
Temporary Work Program				
Child-care and educational services for children of agricultural temporary workers	4.3	0.1	1.2	0.002
Indigenous Microentrepreneur Development Program				
Strengthening of economic networks of indigenous groups through ME creation and support	–		0.2	
Costa Rica	8.1	0.71	3.3	0.04
National Employment Generation Program				
Transfer of a minimum wage to unemployed workers who participate in construction of social services infrastructure and service delivery	2.1	0.2	0.1	0.001
Pro Trabajo Work Training Program				
Incentives for labor reintegration and temporary work–subsidy of 50 percent of minimum wage for on-the-job training for unemployed/vulnerable workers	3.4	0.3	2.1	0.026
Productive ideas–support to ME creation	2.6	0.2	1.1	0.013
Jamaica	6.0	0.61	21.2	0.50
Micro Investment Development Agency (MIDA)				
Credit for ME development	6.0	0.6	7.6	0.181
The Government of Jamaica/Government of the Netherlands Micro Enterprise Project (GoJ/GoN MEP)				
Credit for ME development	–			0.000
The Government of Jamaica/European Union Programme				
Credit for ME development	–		1.4	0.034
Mel Nathan Institute for Development and Social Research (MMI)				
Community development services	–		1.6	0.038
Enterprise Development Trust (EDT)				
Credit for ME development	0.0	0.0	0.2	0.004
The Women's Construction Collective (WCC)				
Training and credit for female construction workers	–		–	

(continued)

Table 3A–1. Employment Generation Programs (continued)

Country, program	Beneficiaries		Expenditure	
	Thousands	Percent of total labor force	Millions of U.S. dollars	Percent of GDP
Jamaica (*continued*)				
ASSIST Ltd.				
Credit for ME development	–		0.1	0.002
Bee Keeping and Honey Bee Project				
Training and employment for youth in bee-keeping activities	–		0.3	0.007
SESP				
Training and temporary employment for unemployed workers	–		10.0	0.237
Mexico	1,024.0	4.42	1,802.0	0.51
Rural Roads Conservation Program				
Rural public works for unemployed youth, federal government-financed works organized by state and local governments	712.0	3.1	350.0	0.099
Physical Infrastructure and Productive Employment Works Program				
Social infrastructure public works for unemployed youth, federal government-financed works organized by state and local governments	312.0	1.3	1,452.0	0.410
Lions Club and Rotary International Private Social Programs	–	–	–	–
Peru[b]	27.8	0.93	0.1	0.19
Microenterprise and Self-employment Program (PRODAME)				
Training and credit for ME creation and support	4.2	0.1	0.1	0.000
FONCODES				
Social investment fund builds small public works using local workforce	23.6	0.8	100.0	0.002

– Not available

a. PROEMPREGO is excluded from the Brazilian list of employment generation programs as it is an investment program. It obviously has employment consequences, but its primary objective is improvements in sanitation, environmental infrastructure, urban transport, and so on through BNDES lines of credit.

b. Peru has also implemented a number of its employment generation programs as labor-intensive investment subprojects complementary to the normal investment activities of institutions such as the National Development Institute (INADE), National Program of Nutrition Assistance (PRONAA), National Construction Company (ENACE), National Housing Fund (FONAVI), National Institute of Health and Educational Infrastructure (INFES), SEDAPAL, CORDECALLAO, CORDELIMA, INABIF, Municipal Compensation Fund, PROMANACHCS (Agriculture Ministry), and the Transportation Ministry.

Table 3A–2. Description of Training Programs in Seven Countries in the Region

| Country, program | Beneficiaries | | Expenditure | |
	Thousands	Percent of total labor force	Millions of U.S. dollars	Percent of GDP
Argentina	133.0	1.4	95.6	**0.04**
Project Youth				
Scholarships and stage in temporary job for low-income, nonskilled, unemployed youth	53.0	0.6	71.7	0.027
Microentrepreneurship Project				
Entrepreneurship training for experienced, unskilled workers	5.4	0.1	6.5	0.002
Imagen Program (Employment Guidance)				
Job-search assistance	27.0	0.3	1.2	0.000
Occupational Workshops Program (PTO)				
Support to NGOs on setting up training institutions	18.0	0.2	4.2	0.002
Occupational Training Program				
Training of unemployed and SME personnel	24.0	0.3	7.3	0.003
Employment Training Program				
Scholarships and stage in temporary job for low-income, nonskilled, unemployed, and displaced workers	1.7	0.0	2.3	0.001
Learning Program				
Financing of health and accident insurance for young workers hired under *Contratos de Aprendizaje*	1.9	0.0	–	
Starting Program				
Financing of training cost for workers in new firms	2.0	0.0	2.4	0.001
Fiscal Credit Program				
Tax exception for training firms	–		–	
Brazil	740.5	1.6	310.2	0.06
PLANFOR				
FAT-financed training program executed at the federal and state levels by independent training institutions				
State and Federal Programs				
Federal and state programs for vulnerable groups	340.8	0.7	149.8	0.03
Emergency Programs				
Emergencies from drought and declining/restructuring sectors	399.7	0.9	159.4	0.03

(continued)

Table 3A–2. Training Programs (continued)

Country, program	Beneficiaries		Expenditure	
	Thousands	Percent of total labor force	Millions of U.S. dollars	Percent of GDP
Chile	36.6	0.8	18.3	0.03
Chile Joven Youth Employment Program				
Stipend and stage in temporary job for low-income, nonskilled, unemployed youth	17.9	0.4	10.4	0.019
Support Program for Women Heads of Low-Income Households				
Training, daycare, health, and other services to improve labor market insertion of poor women	15.0	0.3	4.9	0.009
Women and Microenterprise Program				
Entrepreneurship training for female household heads with some education	0.1	0.0	0.3	0.001
Labor Reintegration Program				
Job search and relocation assistance to displaced carbon and textile workers	0.2	0.0	0.8	0.002
Regular Scholarships Programs				
Scholarships for training at official institutions for vulnerable groups (temporary workers in agriculture, ports, and fishing)	1.3	0.0	0.3	0.001
Support Project for Labor Reintegration for Handicapped People				
Policy formulation and pilot program for labor market insertion of handicapped workers	0.1	0.0	0.1	0.000
Labor Training and Insertion for Handicapped People	0.6	0.0	0.9	0.002
Rehabilitation, Training, and Labor Insertion Program for Handicapped People	0.2	0.0	0.1	0.000
Labor Training and Formation Program				
Adult training program privately operated	1.2	0.0	0.4	0.001
Costa Rica	13.1	1.2	60.6	0.73
Llave en Mano Training Program				
Contracting out training activities by the public training institution (INA)	–		–	
Training and Restructuring for the Mobilized				
Training for displaced public sector workers	1.5	0.1	–	
Public Workshops				
Training low-income workers in marginal urban areas	6.2	0.6	–	
Professional Training for the Handicapped				
Training handicapped workers	1.0	0.1	–	

(continued)

Table 3A–2. (continued)

Country, program	Beneficiaries		Expenditure	
	Thousands	Percent of total labor force	Millions of U.S. dollars	Percent of GDP
Costa Rica (*continued*)				
Labor and Social Security Ministry's Program for				
Employment Training Scholarships				
Scholarships for training workers with				
secondary education	4.4	0.4	0.1	
Jamaica	43.5	4.4	18.6	0.44
Skills 2000				
Training for out-of-school and unskilled				
unemployed workers	40.0	4.1	11.4	0.3
Special Training Empowerment Programme (STEP)				
Youth training	0.6	0.1	4.6	0.1
Strategies to Rehabilitate Inner Cities through				
Viable Enterprises (VIABLE)				
Urban youth training	–		–	
National Youth Service (NYS)				
Training for temporary employment for				
unemployed youth	2.9	0.3	2.6	0.06
Mexico	410.3	1.8	135	0.04
Unemployed Training Scholarship Program				
(PROBECAT)				
Training and scholarships for unemployed				
workers	410.3	1.8	135	0.038
Peru	1.5	0.1	5.0	0.01
Youth Labor Training Program (PROJOVEN)				
Scholarships and training for unemployed youth	1.5	0.1	5.0	0.01

– Not available.

References

Calmfors, Lars. 1994. "Active Labour Market Policy and Unemployment—a Framework for the Analysis of Crucial Design Features." *OECD Economic Studies 22*. Paris.

Cortázar, Rene, and others. 1995. "Hacia un nuevo diseño del sistema de protección a cesantes." *Colección Estudios CIEPLAN 40.*

Government of Brazil. 1998. Ministério do Trabalho, Brasília. *Relatório da Força-tarefa sobre Políticas de Emprego – Diagnóstico e Recomendações.* August.

Government of Mexico. 1995. *Capacitación y empleo: evaluación del programa de becas de capacitación para desempleados*, Sec. de Trabajo y Previsión Social, México DF. August.

Government of the United States. 1995. *Social Security Programs throughout the World.* Department of Health and Human Services.

Graham, Carol. 1994. *Safety Nets, Politics, and the Poor: Transitions to Market Economies.* Washington, D.C.: Brookings Institution.

Grosh, Margaret. 1994. *Administering Targeted Social Programs in Latin America.* World Bank Regional and Sectoral Studies. World Bank, Washington, D.C.

Lightman, E.S. 1995. "You Can Lead a Horse to Water, but . . . : The Case against Workfare in Canada." In J. Richards and others, eds., *Helping the Poor: A Qualified Case for Workfare.* Toronto: Howe Institute.

Lora, E., and C. Pagés. 1997. "La legislación laboral y el proceso de reformas estructurales de América Latina y el Caribe." In M. Cárdenas, ed., *Empleo y distribución del ingreso en América Latina, Hemos avanzado?* Bogotá: Fedesarrollo.

Mazza, Jacqueline. 1999. *Unemployment Insurance: Case Studies and Lessons for the Latin American and Caribbean Region.* Technical Study RE2/SO2. Inter-American Development Bank, Washington, D.C.

Ravallion, Martin. 1998. *Appraising Workfare Programs.* Technical Study. SDS/POV, Inter-American Development Bank, Washington, D.C.

Rose, Nancy E. 1994. *Put to Work: Relief Programs in the Great Depression.* Monthly Review Press.

Verdera, Francisco. 1998. "Análisis comparativo de los programas de empleo e ingresos en América Latina y el Caribe." In G. Márquez and D. Martínez, eds., *Programas de empleo e ingreso en América Latina y el Caribe.* Lima, Peru, and Washington, D.C.: Inter-American Development Bank and International Labour Organisation.

CHAPTER FOUR

Heterogeneity and Optimal Unemployment Insurance

Hugo A. Hopenhayn and Juan Pablo Nicolini

The purpose of this chapter is to explore the effects of heterogeneity on the design of optimal unemployment insurance (UI). The problem is by all means important to policymakers. Most existing UI programs offer the same contract to all workers, while optimal contract theory suggests that optimal contracts depend on the risk exposure of agents. The evidence on private insurance markets suggests heterogeneity is important, too: the older one becomes, the more expensive life insurance is; the faster one drives—and therefore the more accidents one has in a given year—the more expensive auto insurance is next year; the closer to California your house is, the more expensive earthquake insurance is. If private firms find it optimal to offer different contracts to customers that have different observable characteristics, why would it be optimal to offer the same unemployment insurance to different workers?

Maybe existing contracts are offering too much insurance to some workers and too little to others. If this is the case, welfare could be increased and distortions on incentives reduced with the same budget, by optimally designing contracts for groups of workers. The purpose of this chapter is to contribute to this discussion.

The provision of insurance has a negative impact on incentives in environments with private information. Thus, UI has effects on average unemployment duration and therefore on equilibrium unemployment rates. In fact, most features of the UI programs have been allegedly designed with the aim of reducing these distortions. For instance, the benefit received is only a fraction of the previous wage and lasts for a limited time. Also, a certain number of previous working periods are required to qualify for benefits.

This paper was prepared for the LACEA/IDB/World Bank Network on Inequality and Poverty. We thank Carmen Pagés for useful suggestions.

In previous work, we used optimal dynamic contract theory under asymmetric information to assess the optimality of the existing restrictions to deal with incentive problems and characterized optimal unemployment insurance contracts when asymmetric information creates a trade-off between insurance and incentives.[1] We showed that along the optimal contract, the benefit the unemployed worker receives is a decreasing function of the length of the unemployment spell. We also showed that a reemployment tax that increases with the length of the unemployment spell could substantially improve the efficiency of the contract.

A major drawback of existing models is that all unemployed workers are assumed to face the same risk in all periods. In this chapter we relax this assumption in two dimensions. First, we use the model to understand how important systematic differences are in workers' reemployment hazard rates for the design of unemployment insurance. Second, we want to understand the effect of cyclical variations in reemployment probabilities.

As we mentioned above, understanding these issues seems critical from a policy perspective. Current unemployment insurance programs give similar profiles to all unemployed workers. However, the unemployment risk is very uneven across the population. For instance, in Argentina the average unemployment rate from May 1992 to May 1995 was 3.6 percent, 9.7 percent, and 14.5 percent for professionals, white-collar, and blue-collar workers, respectively.[2] In addition, there is not much contingency of the program on aggregate conditions, though in some cases the governments make discretionary adjustments.[3] And aggregate conditions vary a lot, particularly in Latin American countries. The experience of Chile in the early 1980s and that of Argentina in 1995, when unemployment rates skyrocketed to 27 percent and 18 percent, respectively, are eloquent examples.

All we know about optimal contract theory suggests that the particular details of the contract are sensitive to variations in the risk exposure of agents, so it is natural to investigate the optimality of unemployment insurance contracts that vary with observable characteristics of unemployed workers. This issue is particularly important when there is policy concern regarding the well-being of the less fortunate in society, since unemployment risk is higher in the low-skill and low-education portion of the working population.

---

[1] See Hopenhayn and Nicolini (1997 and 1999).
[2] See Pessino (1997) for details.
[3] Some U.S. states increase the coverage during recessions discretionally; see Meyer (1990).

The model and approach of this chapter draw heavily on our previous work.[4] We extend the analysis to allow for risk heterogeneity across workers and over time. This chapter proceeds as follows. First, we derive some theoretical results in a simple two-period model, for the purpose of highlighting the main forces at work in the problem of designing optimal unemployment insurance contracts in the presence of risk heterogeneity. A full dynamic treatment of the problem is substantially more complicated and beyond the scope of this chapter. Next we generalize the model to an infinite time horizon and solve it numerically to compute the effects on the optimal contract of variations in the risk exposure of unemployed workers. There is clear evidence that the reemployment probability depends critically on observed characteristics of agents, like education or age. Thus, we first fit a logit equation to unemployment termination rates in Argentina, using data from a household survey (*Encuesta Permanente de Hogares*) to quantify the degree of unemployment risk heterogeneity. We use this evidence to calibrate the model. We particularly draw attention to the dependence of the optimal effort level on the risk characteristics of the agents. After that, we provide a nontechnical summary of the results and discussion of the main policy implications derived from the analysis, together with a discussion of a policy experiment ongoing in Argentina since 1996. Finally, we close the chapter. The reader not interested in the technical discussion should go directly to our closing remarks.

SOME THEORETICAL RESULTS

In this section we characterize the optimal unemployment insurance in a two-period model with two alternative sources of heterogeneity. First, we consider a setup where workers are heterogenous in their unemployment risk exposure. Second, we consider variations of risk exposure over time, depending on aggregate conditions.

As we mentioned in the introduction, the theoretical analysis will be done in a two-period model. This model is straightforward to solve, and the intuition behind the results is very clear. The infinite period version is technically very demanding and beyond the scope of this chapter.[5]

We consider the problem of providing insurance to a worker who is unemployed in the first period. In this same period, the worker chooses the effort de-

---

[4] Hopenhayn and Nicolini (1997, 1998).
[5] For infinite versions of the model without heterogeneity, see Hopenhayn and Nicolini (1997, 1999).

voted to finding a job for the second period. The key feature of the environment is that the probability of finding a new job depends on the effort devoted by the unemployed worker, and the government cannot monitor this effort. A contract specifies an unemployment benefit in the first period, a benefit in the second period if the worker is still unemployed, and a tax in the second period if the worker does find a job. The optimal contract maximizes the utility of the worker subject to a budget constraint for the government. This budget constraint is given by the political will of the government; in particular, it could be zero. This is the case of a self-financed unemployment insurance.[6]

Heterogeneity

We will first study how the optimal contract depends on the risk characteristics of the agents. The preferences of the worker are given by

$$(4\text{-}1) \qquad U(c) - a + \beta[(1 - p - \Delta) U(c^u) + (p + \Delta) U(c^e)],$$

where $a \in \{0,1\}$ is the search effort chosen by the worker in the first period, p is the probability of finding a job if the search effort is zero, while $p + \Delta$ is the probability if the effort level is 1, c^j is consumption in period 2 in state $j = e$ (employment), u (unemployment), and c is first period consumption. The function U is increasing and concave and β is the discount factor, assumed to be the same one as that used by the government.

In the context of our model, different risk exposures amount to heterogeneity on the probability to get a job when the effort level is high. Thus, let us assume that there are $j = 1, 2, 3, \ldots J$ different classes of workers, such that

$$p^j = p_0^j + \Delta_j.$$

The question we address in this section is how the features of the optimal contract vary when p varies. Heterogeneity may arise from differences in the baseline probability, p_0^j, or in the marginal effect of effort, Δ_j. In this section we will consider variations in both. Note that we allow for the worker to find a job even without

---

[6] Most existing UI programs spend more than what they collect and must be financed with other taxes.

searching. The key is that the probability of finding a job is higher if the worker chooses the high effort level.

We follow the literature and assume that the principal can control the consumption of the agent, so we preclude borrowing and lending contracts. We also assume that jobs are homogeneous and pay a wage w.[7] Even though our emphasis is in heterogeneity, we will suppress individual superscripts j in the notation that follows, since they will not be important in the algebra.

As the effort level is not observable, if the government wants to induce the worker to choose the high effort level, the contract must satisfy the following incentive compatibility constraint:

(4-2) $$\beta\Delta(U(c^e) - U(c^u)) \geq 1.$$

This condition guarantees that the worker will weakly prefer to choose the high effort level. The value for the government, measured in goods, of the contract is given by

(4-3) $$\beta[(p + \Delta)(c^e - w) + (1 - p - \Delta)c^u] + c = B.$$

As is well known, there is a family of optimal contracts that are the solution of a Pareto problem. To solve for a point in the Pareto frontier, we can maximize the utility of the worker given a budget B for the government. Alternatively, we can solve the dual, that is, we can minimize the budget given a value for the worker's utility.

Note that the two problems have different interpretations regarding how different workers are treated. If we fix the budget, we are assuming that the government is allocating the same budget to each worker. Thus, along the optimal contract, workers who have lower probabilities of finding a job will have lower utility. However, if the contract fixes the utility of each worker at the same level, then it has to be the case that a higher budget is allocated to workers with lower

---

[7] In the context of this model, this is a harmless assumption if wage offers are observable, since the principal will fully insure the agent against wage risk. If wage offers are not observable, there is an additional moral hazard problem owing to the effect of the insurance on the reservation wage of the worker. However, in Hopenhayn and Nicolini (1998) we show that this moral hazard problem is equivalent to the one we model, and it can be embodied in the analysis without any change in the theory.

reemployment probabilities. Thus, in the first problem there is no redistribution across workers, while in the second one there is. We do not directly address this redistribution issue here, since it may be the object of a broader social security scheme that considers other income risk beyond unemployment risk. We will solve the problem assuming that the government allocates the same budget to each worker. However, it is worth mentioning that all the theoretical results proved in this chapter also hold if we solve the problem assuming that the contract gives all workers the same utility level.

The optimal contract problem is therefore to maximize the utility function 4-1 subject to the incentive compatibility constraint 4-2 and to the budget constraint 4-3, where, as we mentioned before, B is the per worker budget that the government allocates to the UI program. Note that the objective function is concave and the restrictions define a convex set, so the first-order conditions fully characterize the solution.

It is straightforward to verify that the first-order conditions can be combined to yield

(4-4)
$$\frac{1}{U'(c)} = \frac{p+\Delta}{U'(c^e)} + \frac{1-p-\Delta}{U'(c^u)}.$$

This equation and the two constraints can be used to find solutions for c, c^u, and c^e as functions of p and Δ. Note that the incentive compatibility constraint implies that consumption tomorrow if employed must be higher than consumption tomorrow if unemployed. But then, equation 4-4 implies that

$$c^e > c > c^u,$$

which means that the unemployment benefit tomorrow must be lower than today's, while consumption tomorrow if employed must be higher than today's. The intuition for these results is standard in the moral hazard literature. To provide incentives, the contract must punish unlucky workers by lowering the benefit and compensate lucky workers by increasing consumption.[8]

---

[8] These results generalize to infinite periods with repeated unemployment spells; see Hopenhayn and Nicolini (1997, 1999).

We are interested in understanding how the values of the benefit (c, c^u) and of the tax $(w - c^e)$ depend on the risk characteristics of the agents (p, Δ). In particular, we want to know how high-risk workers should be treated, compared with low-risk workers. A comparative statics exercise provides the answer to the question.

Differentiating totally the three equations that implicitly solve the system, we obtain

$$
\begin{bmatrix}
\dfrac{U''(c)}{U'(c)^2} & \dfrac{-(1-p-\Delta)U''(c^u)}{U'(c^u)^2} & \dfrac{-(p+\Delta)U''(c^e)}{U'(c^e)^2} \\[2em]
0 & -\beta\Delta U'(c^u) & \beta\Delta U'(c^e) \\[2em]
-1 & -(1-p-\Delta)\beta & -(p+\Delta)\beta
\end{bmatrix}
\begin{bmatrix}
dc \\[2em] dc^u \\[2em] dc^e
\end{bmatrix}
$$

$$
=
\begin{bmatrix}
\left(\dfrac{1}{U'(c^e)} - \dfrac{1}{U(c^u)}\right) & \left(\dfrac{1}{U'(c^e)} - \dfrac{1}{U(c^u)}\right) \\[2em]
0 & -[U(c^e) - U(c^u)] \\[2em]
\beta(c^e - w - c^u) & \beta(c^e - w - c^u)
\end{bmatrix}
\begin{bmatrix}
dp \\[2em] d\Delta
\end{bmatrix}.
$$

The determinant of the first matrix must be negative, since this is a well-defined maximum problem. Let D be the value of the determinant. Applying Cramer's rule, it can be shown that

$$
\frac{\partial c}{\partial p} = \frac{\beta^2 \Delta}{D}\left\{\left[\frac{1}{U'(c^u)} - \frac{1}{U'(c^e)}\right][(p+\Delta)\,U'(c^u) + (1-p-\Delta)\,U'(c^e)]\right.
$$
$$
\left. + [c^e - w - c^u]\left[(1-p-\Delta)\frac{-U''(c^u)\,U'(c^e)}{U'(c^u)^2} + (p+\Delta)\frac{-U''(c^u)\,U'(c^u)}{U'(c^e)^2}\right]\right\}.
$$

Since U is increasing and concave, the second term in square brackets of each of the two terms on the right-hand side are positive. But as c^u is lower than c^e, the first bracket in the first term is negative. Finally, note that w represents a contribution to the budget for the government when the agent finds a job, while $c^e - c^u$ is the incremental cost. Since the incentive compatibility constraint holds with equality at an optimum, workers get the same utility whether they exert search effort or not. A positive effort will thus be optimal if it contributes positively to the budget, thus allowing for higher levels of consumption in all states. Hence, if supporting positive effort is optimal, it must be the case that

$$(w - c^e + c^u) > 0,$$

so the first term in the second bracket is also negative. As D is negative, we have established that when the baseline probability of finding a job goes up, the first period benefit does too. To get the intuition of this result, it is revealing to look at the first-order condition 4-4 from a different point of view. Recall that

$$\frac{1}{U'(c)} = [U'(c)]^{-1}.$$

But the inverse of the marginal utility in the first period is the marginal cost of providing utility in that first period. Thus, the first-order condition can be written as

$$MgC(u(c)) = (1 - p - \Delta)\, MgC(u(c^u)) + (p + \Delta)\, MgC(u(c^e))$$

or

$$MgC(u(c)) = MgC(u(c^u)) + (p + \Delta)\, (MgC(u(c^e)) - MgC(u(c^u))).$$

As p goes up, the probability that the worker will be employed next period is higher, and therefore it is more likely that the government will collect the tax, $(w - c^e)$ instead of paying the benefit c^u. Therefore, the present expected value of the budget is higher, so total expected consumption should be higher. As the marginal cost is equalized in the two periods, this "income" effect raises the utility of consumption in the two periods.[9] However, the increase in p also increases the mar-

---

[9] This effect is similar to increases in the total budget, B.

ginal cost tomorrow, since it increases the weight in the most expensive state.[10] Thus, consumption tomorrow becomes more expensive for the principal; this "substitution" effect reinforces the increase in first-period consumption.

We can also find the effect of changes in the baseline probability on second-period consumption:

$$\frac{\partial c^u}{\partial p} = \frac{-\beta \Delta U'(c^e)}{D} \left\{ \left[\frac{1}{U'(c^u)} - \frac{1}{U'(c^e)} \right] + \beta [c^e - w - c^u] \frac{U''(c)}{U'(c)^2} \right\}.$$

Note that the first term is negative, while the second is positive, so the sign is undetermined. The intuition should be clear, given the discussion above. The "income" effect, given by the second term, increases consumption in the second period if unemployed, but the "substitution" effect reduces it. The final result depends on which effect dominates. Note that the incentive compatibility constraint implies that when p changes, both c^e and c^u move in the same direction. The intuition is the same.

To summarize, workers with a higher baseline probability should obtain higher replacement ratios—the ratio of benefit received to the wage—in the first period. However, owing to the substitution effect, it is not clear whether benefits in the second period should also be higher. This suggests that workers with higher baseline probabilities will have a steeper pattern of benefits over time. It is possible, however, that if the income effect is stronger for c^u than for c, the path could be steeper for workers with lower baseline probabilities.

Similarly, we can find the effect on the values of consumption of changes in the parameter Δ. Note that changes in Δ not only affect the incentive compatibility constraint, but also total employment probability. The effect of changes in the probability have already been discussed, so to isolate the effects of changes in the marginal impact of effort, we assume that $d\Delta = -\varepsilon$, $dp = \varepsilon$, so that $d(p + \Delta) = 0$. The total effect of changes in Δ results from the combination of the effects discussed above and the one that follows. Applying Cramer's rule, we obtain

$$\frac{\partial c^u}{\partial \Delta = -\partial p} = -\frac{U(c^u) - U(c^e)}{D}(p + \Delta) \left\{ -\beta \frac{U''(c)}{U'(c)^2} - \frac{U''(c^e)}{U'(c^e)^2} \right\},$$

---

[10] This effect would be absent if there were no incentive constraints, since in that case the marginal utilities in the second period would be the same.

which is negative. Thus, a worker with a lower Δ but compensating higher baseline probability—such that $p + \Delta$ remains constant—has a lower benefit in the following period if unemployed. On the other hand,

$$\frac{\partial c^e}{\partial \Delta = -\partial p} = \frac{U(c^u) - U(c^e)}{D} (1 - p - \Delta) \left\{ -\beta \frac{U''(c)}{U'(c)^2} - \frac{U''(c^u)}{U'(c^u)^2} \right\},$$

which is positive, so the tax is lower when Δ falls, keeping $p + \Delta$. The intuition is also simple. As Δ falls, it is harder to provide incentives, because the probability of receiving the reward (higher consumption) is lower. Thus, the reward must be increased, and the way to do so is by punishing more in the unemployment state (reducing c^u) and increasing the reward in the employment state (increasing c^e).

Finally, we can also compute

$$\frac{\partial c}{\partial \Delta = -\partial p} = -\frac{U(c^u) - U(c^e)}{D} \beta(1 - p - \Delta) \, (p + \Delta) \left\{ \frac{U''(c^u)}{U'(c^u)^2} - \frac{U''(c^e)}{U'(c^e)^2} \right\},$$

which, since the second derivatives of the utility function are negative, is indeterminate. The intuition is also clear. As it is harder to give incentives, consumption tomorrow if the worker is unemployed goes down, reducing the marginal cost tomorrow, but consumption if the worker finds a job is higher, increasing tomorrow's marginal cost. This may change the marginal cost to provide utility tomorrow, in which case, to preserve optimality, the marginal cost today must change too. Thus consumption today could go up or down, depending on whether marginal cost tomorrow goes up or down.

So far, the analysis assumed that changes in the parameters do not change the optimal effort level. However, note that both the reduction in the baseline probability, p, and the reduction in the marginal effect of effort, Δ, reduce the value of search. However, a decrease in p also lowers the worker's utility if it is not optimal to recommend high effort level, but changes in Δ do not. Thus, as Δ falls, the value of implementing high effort goes down, while the value of implementing low effort does not. For sufficiently low value of the search effectiveness parameter Δ, it is optimal to recommend the low effort, and full insurance is provided.

The results discussed in this subsection can be summarized as follows (these comparisons assume the same budget is allocated to different worker types):

• Workers that have a lower than average baseline reemployment probability have lower initial benefits, but these benefits decrease at a lower rate.

• Workers that are less effective at searching—holding the total probability constant—should receive benefits that fall faster over time, provided the optimal recommended search effort level does not change.

• On the other hand, for those same workers, if a lower search effort is to be recommended, a flatter scheme of benefits should be provided.

Cyclical Variation

In this section we explore how the optimal contract varies when there are cyclical variations in the risk exposure of agents. This issue is of particular relevance given that job creation and destruction do exhibit cyclical movements, so the risk exposures do too. In particular, we are concerned with changes in the optimal coverage when particularly large shocks hit the economy, like the recession in Chile in 1982 or the recessions in Mexico and Argentina in 1995.

To keep things simple, we will assume that labor market conditions are given by a state variable $s \in \{n, r\}$, where n indicates normal times and r indicates a recession. Let π be the probability of entering a recession. A recession is defined as period where the reemployment probability is lower. We will consider cases where only the baseline probability is lower and cases where search effectiveness is also lower. We also allow the wage to be lower during recessions.

A superscript n indicates the value of the variable if there is no recession, while r indicates the value if there is a recession. The optimal insurance scheme is the solution to the maximum of

$$
\begin{aligned}
V = {}& \pi\{U(c^r) - a^r + \beta[(1 - p^r - \Delta^r)U(c^{u,r}) + (p^r + \Delta^r)U(c^{e,r})]\} \\
& + (1 - \pi)\{U(c^n) - a^n + \beta[(1 - p^n - \Delta^n)U(c^{u,n}) + (p^n + \Delta^n)U(c^{e,n})]\},
\end{aligned}
$$

(4-5)

subject to

$$
\beta\Delta^r(U(c^{e,r}) - U(c^{u,r})) \geq a^r
$$

$$
\beta\Delta^n(U(c^{e,n}) - U(c^{u,n})) \geq a^n
$$

and

$$B = \pi(c^r + \beta[(p^r + \Delta^r)c^{e,r} + (1 - p^r - \Delta^r)c^{u,r}] - w^r(p^r + \Delta^r)\beta$$
$$+ (1 - \pi)(c^n + \beta[(p^n + \Delta^n)c^{e,n} + (1 - p^n - \Delta^n)c^{u,n}] - w^n(p^n + \Delta^n).$$

The solution is characterized by the following first-order conditions:

$$U'(c^r) = U'(c^n)$$

$$\frac{1}{U'(c^r)} = \frac{p^r + \Delta^r}{U'(c^{e,r})} + \frac{1 - p^r - \Delta^r}{U'(c^{u,r})}$$

$$\frac{1}{U'(c^n)} = \frac{p^n + \Delta^n}{U'(c^{e,n})} + \frac{1 - p^n - \Delta^n}{U'(c^{u,n})}.$$

The first condition just shows that the consumption of the worker the first period should not depend on the aggregate shock. This is natural, since there is no moral hazard associated with that shock, so full insurance is optimal. The other two conditions are similar to the one before. The marginal cost condition has to hold in both states of nature.

Note that the first condition ties down the marginal cost in the first period, so the marginal cost in the second period has to be the same, independent of the aggregate shock. Using this fact, it is straightforward to characterize the optimal unemployment insurance. Note that the following two equations solve for consumption in the second period:

(4-6)
$$k = \frac{p^j + \Delta^j}{U'(c^{e,j})} + \frac{1 - p^j - \Delta^j}{U'(c^{u,j})}$$

(4-7)
$$\beta\Delta^j(U(c^{e,j}) - U(c^{u,j})) \geq 1$$

for $j = u, e$, where k does depend on exogenous variables but is the same for u and e. The two equations form a system that is depicted in figure 4–1. Equation 4-6 is the downward sloping curve G, while equation 4-7 is the upward sloping curve F.

The natural way to interpret a recession is to assume that either the baseline probability, or the marginal effect of effort, or both are lower during a recession.

FIGURE 4–1.

Consumption in the Second Period

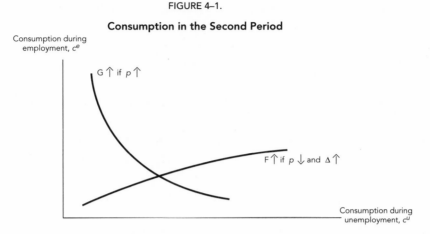

Consider first a recession where the marginal effect of search is the same as in normal times, but the baseline probability is lower. Thus, the G function for the recession state is above the one for normal times, while the F function is the same in both states. This means that consumption during the recessions must be higher than during normal times in both states, u and e. The intuition of the result is related to the "income" effects discussed above. As the reemployment probability is lower during a recession, the weight in the marginal cost of providing utility in the case of employment is lower. As the marginal cost of providing utility in the employment state is higher, this reduces the expected marginal cost of providing utility tomorrow if there were a recession, and that is why consumption is increased in that state. This implies that during a recession, benefits should not be lowered that much, while reemployment taxes should be reduced.

Finally, consider a recession where search effectiveness falls and the baseline probability increases, so that the total probability of employment remains unchanged.[11] This does not change the G curve, but moves the F curve upward. This implies that consumption when workers find a job during a recession is higher than if they find a job in normal times, so the reemployment tax must go down during recessions. On the other hand, consumption during recessions if unemployed is lower than during normal times. Thus, the benefit should go down faster during recessions. Again the intuition is simple. As it is harder to give incentives, the tax must be lowered and the benefit reduced during recessions.

---

[11] As before, the effect of a fall in Δ is the same as the joint effects discussed in this chapter.

To summarize, during recessions the reemployment tax should be lowered, while the effect on replacement ratios is not clear. To the extent that the effect of the fall in the baseline probability is stronger than the one in the marginal effect of effort, the benefit should be increased, while the opposite is true if the marginal effect dominates.

Finally, a word of caution should be raised regarding the effect on the optimal effort level.[12] Recall that when the marginal effect falls enough, it becomes optimal to recommend the low effort level. In this case, as we argued above, the optimal policy is to provide full insurance. This means that

$$c^n = c^r = c^{r,u} = c^{r,e}.$$

So the benefit must be kept constant during recession, while the tax should be increased to capture all the gains of working. This last result is due to the assumption that workers do not dislike working, otherwise the wage differential must compensate for that disutility. To summarize, recessions are likely to change the optimal effort level. This should decrease the rate at which benefits fall with length of unemployment.

A final point worth emphasizing is the management of funds of the insurance program. The budget constraint imposed above implicitly assumes that the government has access to complete markets, meaning that there is not only a credit market but also a contingent market through which the government can trade goods in different states. In particular, consider the case of a recession where only the baseline probability falls. As we discussed above, this is likely to increase consumption and the expected discounted cost of the program. For the sake of argument, assume that the wage in both states is the same. As the probability of finding a job (and therefore of collecting taxes) is lower in a recession, the expected value of revenues is lower during a recession:

$$(p^r + \Delta)(w - c^{e,r}) < (p^n + \Delta)(w - c^{e,n}).$$

---

[12] The conventional wisdom is that in fact during deep recessions like the one in Argentina in 1995, the probabilities of finding a job are very low regardless of the search intensity, but, to the best of our knowledge, there is no clear evidence to support that claim.

On the other hand, expected expenditures in a recession are higher than in normal times:

$$(1-(p^r+\Delta))\,c^{r,u}+(p^r+\Delta)\,c^{r,e} > (1-(p^n+\Delta))\,c^{n,u}+(p^n+\Delta)\,c^{n,e}.$$

Thus, the government must transfer resources from periods of high demand to periods of recession. The policy recommendation is obvious. The government must have a contingency fund that provides the required resources to finance the deficit of the unemployment insurance in times of recession. The results of this subsection can be summarized as follows:

- During recessions, the wage tax must be lowered.
- During recessions, the behavior of the benefit is not clear. If the recession is characterized by a fall in the baseline probability, the benefit should be higher than in normal times. However, if the fall is in the incremental effect of effort, the benefit should be lower than during normal times, if the optimal effort level does not change much.
- If the recession is characterized by a reduction in search effectiveness, then the optimal search effort level may fall. This could have a positive impact on the level of unemployment benefits.

COMPUTATIONS

In this section we provide some preliminary computations to illustrate the magnitude of the effects discussed above. We first describe the method used for assigning parameters to the model. Then we provide the results of the numerical experiments performed.

Calibration

We consider an infinite periods version of the model discussed above. Two types of computations are considered. In the first, we suppress all exogenous shocks and focus on heterogeneity in reemployment risk. In the second, we consider aggregate shocks to reemployment risk, while suppressing heterogeneity. We calibrate reemployment rates using estimated hazard rates from a linked panel obtained from the household surveys for the greater Buenos Aires area, from 1993 to 1997. The unit time period is six months, which corresponds to the periodicity of the

Table 4–1. Analysis of Maximum Likelihood Estimates

Variable	DF	Parameter estimate	Standard error	Wald chi-square	Pr > chi-square	Standardized estimate	Odds ratio
Intercept	1	1.4591	0.4076	12.8123	0.0003		
Age	1	–0.0296	0.00569	26.9904	0.0001	–0.18656	0.971
Schooling							
Level 1	1	–0.1657	0.2107	0.6182	0.4317	–0.042718	0.847
Level 2	1	–0.2983	0.2289	1.6982	0.1925	–0.068106	0.742
Level 3	1	–0.2945	0.238	1.531	0.216	–0.06086	0.745
Level 4	1	0.0747	0.2715	0.0756	0.7833	0.012133	1.078
Level 5	1	–0.0389	0.2903	0.018	0.8933	–0.005613	0.962
Gender	1	0.2746	0.129	4.5324	0.0333	0.074175	1.316
May 1994	1	–0.4217	0.3604	1.3694	0.2419	–0.057417	0.656
May 1995	1	–0.9429	0.3094	9.2866	0.0023	–0.203122	0.39
May 1996	1	–0.0935	0.3161	0.0874	0.7675	–0.018323	0.911
October 1993	1	–0.7132	0.3709	3.6986	0.0545	–0.09219	0.49
October 1994	1	–0.9513	0.3194	8.87	0.0029	–0.184257	0.386
October 1995	1	–0.9296	0.3063	9.2098	0.0024	–0.20825	0.395
October 1996	1	–0.7429	0.3189	5.4251	0.0198	–0.141352	0.476

Association of predicted probabilities and observed responses
Concordant, 63.7 percent   Somers' D, 0.279
Discordant, 35.8 percent   Gamma, 0.281
Tied, 0.5 percent   Tau-a, 0.136
(331,240 pairs)   c, 0.640

Source: Authors' calculations.

survey. The discount factor chosen is 2.5 percent per unit time period, reflecting a 5 percent annual real interest rate.

Reemployment hazard rates were estimated for all those workers that declared being unemployed in a survey and were either unemployed or employed in the following one. This suppresses those unemployed workers that withdrew from the labor force, approximately one-third of the pool. This criterion identifies workers committed to searching for a new job. Owing to reporting errors, we discarded those unemployed workers who reported having been employed for more than one year in the following survey. This procedure could result in a downward bias in reemployment rates. The pooled sample obtained consists of a total of 1,166 unemployed workers, of whom 490 were recorded as holding a job six months later with less than one year of seniority. This implies a reemployment rate of 42 percent. If we had not excluded the workers with duration over one year, the average reemployment rate would have been 54 percent. As a consequence, we set the benchmark rate at 50 percent. During this period, owing to the existence of temporary contracts, it is quite likely that multiple transitions occured within the six-month interval between surveys. At this stage, we have no good procedure to correct for this time aggregation problem. Our choice would tend to oversample those workers who obtained a job and were able to keep it.

To estimate the hazard rate we used a logit model, taking as explanatory variables age, sex, schooling dummies, and temporal dummies for each of the surveys included in our sample. The results are presented in table 4-1. Interestingly, the schooling variables do not appear to be highly significant.[13] Age has a very high negative effect on reemployment: an additional year reduces the probability of reemployment by 2.9 percent. Reemployment rates of male workers are 32 percent higher than for females. On the other hand, the survey time dummies show a large and significant variation. The benchmark value is for the survey in May 1993. Three periods can be distinguished: higher reemployment rates from May 1993 to May 1994, followed by low (approximately half as large) from October 1994 to October 1995, and a return to higher reemployment rates starting in May 1996.

These estimates suggest that during booms hazard rates are approximately twice as high as in recessions and that the average duration of high and low reemployment periods is three semesters. Based on these numbers, we calibrate the probability of staying in the same state to be two-thirds. We take the baseline hazard rate in high reemployment periods to be 50 percent, and in low reemployment periods 25 percent. For the computations based on heterogeneity only, we take these two hazard rates for groups with high and low reemployment rates, respectively.

In our model, reemployment probabilities are given by $p = p_0 + \Delta$, where p_0 corresponds to an exogenous arrival of job offers, and Δ to the incremental probability due to search. We interpret the data as if all the agents in our sample are effectively searching. Our data do not allow us to identify the role of these two components in explaining the observed differences in hazard rates. For illustration purposes, we take the following—arbitrary—combination of parameters:

---

[13] It is worth noting, however, that according to some previous estimates of one of the authors, schooling significantly increases the chances of getting a permanent vis-à-vis temporary contract.

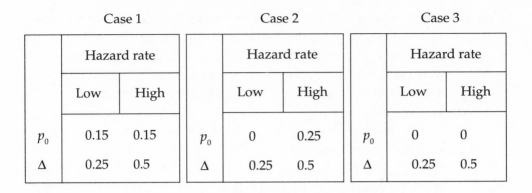

Case 1				Case 2				Case 3		
	Hazard rate				Hazard rate				Hazard rate	
	Low	High			Low	High			Low	High
p_0	0.15	0.15		p_0	0	0.25		p_0	0	0
Δ	0.25	0.5		Δ	0.25	0.5		Δ	0.25	0.5

Results

We first consider the results for the case of heterogeneity. Table 4–2 gives consumption levels while unemployed and employed. In all cases, we normalize the salary of an employed worker to 100. Hence the consumption values given in the table reflect percentage values of a period salary. The first two columns correspond to a worker with a high reemployment rate. The second two columns correspond to a worker with a low reemployment rate, when the UI gives the worker the same initial replacement ratio (100 percent). The third column gives the consumption pair for the same group of workers, when the initial replacement ratio is chosen so that the total expected budget matches that of a high reemployment worker. This total budget turns out to be approximately the equivalent of one year of salary. The budget corresponding to the middle pair is almost twice as large in all cases, in correspondence to the difference in hazard rates. The following observations can be made:

  • As p_0 increases, the profile of subsidies becomes steeper and the difference in consumption in the two states (employed/unemployed) becomes larger.
  • When the two groups do not differ in search effectiveness but in the baseline probability (case 2) and they start with the same replacement ratio, the low reemployment group gets a higher consumption profile. Notice that this does not imply that this group is necessarily better off, since it also exhibits higher unemployment duration.
  • When search is necessary for reemployment for both groups (case 3), and the low hazard group is less effective at searching, the unemployment benefits follow a similar pattern, but the reemployment tax (subsidy) is higher (lower) for the high hazard group.

Table 4–2. Consumption Levels for High and Low Hazard Groups

Case, month	High reemployment rate group		Low reemployment rate group		Low reemployment rate group with same budget as high rate group	
	Unemployed	Employed	Unemployed	Employed	Unemployed	Employed
Case 1						
0	100.3	⋯	100.3	⋯	95.7	⋯
6	98.6	101.8	97.2	109.8	92.5	104.9
12	96.7	100.0	94.0	106.5	89.4	101.7
18	94.9	98.1	90.8	103.2	86.3	98.5
24	93.1	96.3	87.7	100.0	83.3	95.3
30	91.2	94.5	84.7	96.8	80.3	92.2
36	89.5	92.8	81.7	93.7	77.4	89.1
Case 2						
0	100.3	⋯	100.3	⋯	95.9	⋯
6	97.8	102.6	99.1	103.9	94.6	99.4
12	95.3	100.0	97.8	102.6	93.4	98.1
18	92.7	97.4	96.5	101.3	92.1	96.8
24	90.2	94.9	95.2	100.0	90.8	95.5
30	87.7	92.4	93.9	98.7	89.6	94.3
36	85.3	90.0	92.6	97.4	88.3	93.0
Case 3						
0	100.3	⋯	100.3	⋯	95.9	⋯
6	99.1	101.3	99.1	103.9	94.6	99.4
12	97.8	100.0	97.8	102.6	93.3	98.1
18	96.5	98.7	96.5	101.3	92.0	96.8
24	95.2	97.4	95.2	100.0	90.8	95.5
30	93.9	96.1	93.9	98.7	89.6	94.3
36	92.7	94.9	92.6	97.4	88.3	93.0

Note: In all cases, the salary of an employed worker is normalized to 100.
Source: Authors' calculations.

- In the intermediate case, where both groups have a positive and equal baseline probability, the profile is much steeper for the low hazard group and the spread is also higher. This reflects the fact that providing search incentives becomes much harder for this low hazard group.
- The patterns obtained by looking at the profile for the low group at the same budget level are similar, except that the starting point is much lower. This starting point implies a permanent income approximately 4 percent lower for this group.

Table 4–3. Consumption Levels during Expansion and Recession

Case, month	Expansion		Recession	
	Unemployed	Employed	Unemployed	Employed
Case 1				
0	100.3	...	100.3	...
6	98.6	101.8	97.2	109.8
12	96.7	100.0	94.0	106.5
18	94.9	98.1	90.8	103.2
24	93.1	96.3	87.7	100.0
30	91.2	94.5	84.7	96.8
36	89.5	92.8	81.7	93.7
Case 2				
0	100.3	...	100.3	...
6	97.8	102.6	99.1	104.0
12	95.3	100.0	97.7	102.7
18	92.7	97.4	96.4	101.3
24	90.2	94.9	95.0	100.0
30	87.7	92.4	93.7	98.6
36	85.3	90.0	92.4	97.3
Case 3				
0	100.3	...	100.3	...
6	99.1	101.3	99.1	104.0
12	97.8	100.0	97.7	102.7
18	96.5	98.7	96.4	101.3
24	95.1	97.4	95.0	100.0
30	93.8	96.1	93.7	98.6
36	92.5	94.8	92.4	97.3

Note: In all cases, the salary of an employed worker is normalized to 100.
Source: Authors' calculations.

• Though there are differences between the UI program for low and high hazard groups, these differences do not appear to be very large. This suggests that, except for some special groups, the payoffs to designing "tailor made" UI programs for different groups may not be that large.

Table 4–3 provides the results for the optimal unemployment insurance program with exogenous fluctuations in reemployment hazard rates. Each pair of columns has the following interpretation. The first pair traces the path for the unemployment benefits and reemployment consumption throughout an expansion. The second pair traces the corresponding path for a recession. Both benefit paths start with equal replacement ratios, as corresponds to the optimal insurance across the two initial states. Thereafter, the paths look identical to the ones obtained in the first four columns of table 4–2. Hence, the above remarks apply.

DISCUSSION

Our focus in this chapter was to study the effect of heterogeneity on the features an optimal insurance contract ought to have in the presence of incentive problems. In particular, we focused on the cases in which the existence of unemployment insurance reduces the incentives unemployed workers have to look for a job, therefore increasing equilibrium unemployment rates. In this section we provide a nontechnical discussion of the results. We also briefly review other incentive problems that are related to the ones discussed in this chapter.

We first addressed the issue of unemployment insurance design when workers differed in their risk exposure. The logit estimation we performed shows that variations in experience or age can generate wide ranges of reemployment probabilities. Aggregate conditions are important too. In all cases, the degree of heterogeneity is large and we can account for workers with half the risk of remaining unemployed than others, while this risk can double for every worker during recessions. The insurance contract consists of a benefit the worker receives while unemployed and a reemployment wage tax, both of which are potentially contingent on the length of the unemployment spell. We analyze how this contract should vary for different worker types.

Our theoretical analysis indicates that the source of heterogeneity is important. If the cause of the heterogeneity is that some workers are more likely to find jobs because of differences in human capital, experience, and the like, but there is no significant difference in the additional chances they obtain by searching, then workers with higher probability of reemployment should have steeper profiles of unemployment benefits. The effect this has on reemployment wage taxes is unclear, depending, among other things, on the level of risk aversion and on how it changes with wealth. However, if the main difference is that high reemployment probability workers are more effective at searching, the effect on starting benefits is not obvious, but the profile would be steeper for low probability workers. On the other hand, it may be optimal for those with lower search effectiveness to search less, which would tend to flatten the level of benefits given to this group. Finally, there is an additional effect that arises when the heterogeneity is in the additional probability unemployed workers obtain by search effort. In this case, it is possible that for some workers it is efficient for them to choose lower effort levels. In this case, much more insurance can be provided, reinforcing the concept that the benefit profile for high-risk workers should be less steep than for low-risk workers. All these results suggest that high-risk workers should have more lifetime coverage than low-risk workers.

The second problem we analyzed is the effect of aggregate fluctuations on the optimal contract. We showed first that initial benefits should not depend on the aggregate reemployment state, a natural result since there is no moral hazard associated with this shock. This means that it is optimal to fully insure all aggregate risk. On the other hand, the reemployment tax should be lowered during recessions, while the effect on benefits is not clear. When recessions mostly affect baseline probabilities, our results suggest that benefits should decrease more slowly. In contrast, when recessions affect mostly search effectiveness, the optimal profile could be steeper.

Finally, we have also indicated that proper management of the insurance should provide for these contingencies, recognizing that the expected cost of the program will increase in recessions. Active participation in world insurance markets is required to provide for the financing of the program in times of recessions. Interestingly, a similar scheme is currently being managed by the Argentinian government to provide liquidity to the banking sector in case of a crunch. Our analysis suggests a similar scheme should be managed to provide funds for unemployment insurance in case of a deep recession.[14]

It is worth emphasizing that the results obtained are very general, in the sense that they hold both when the budget allocated to every individual is the same and when the total utility of each agent is the same. The two cases amount to different preferences over individuals. Take the case in which the total budget is the same for both individuals. As some workers have higher unemployment risk, those workers will have lower utility in the optimal contract. Thus, in the case that the contract offers the same utility, it is clear that the expected budget for the high unemployment probability workers will be higher. Thus, our results hold even if one is willing to allocate higher budgets to high-risk groups.

---

[14] The current scheme in Argentina is not fully comparable with the one this analysis suggests, since it only provides liquidity. It is not an insurance contract in the principal, only in the interest payments.

State Verifiability

Our focus in discussing optimal unemployment insurance has been the group of workers whose unemployment risk is higher, namely, the less educated and less experienced workers. Often, the members of this group find job opportunities mostly in the informal sector of the economy. Therefore, it may be very hard to monitor the employment status of the worker. Our investigation assumed that while search effort is not observable, employment status is. A strong incentive problem arises when the latter does not hold, since an unemployed worker receiving benefits would not have incentives to disclose having found a job.

One way to cope with this problem is to design programs that require those receiving benefits to appear at the insurance office, perhaps at random times. An extreme version of this is to force the beneficiary to hold a schedule. This can be done through government-sponsored working programs, like the *Plan de Empleo Mínimo* in Chile in the early 1980s or the *Programa Trabajar* currently functioning in Argentina. This last program has been in operation for three years, and its budget is used to fully subsidize labor in social projects managed by nonprofit organizations. These organizations are responsible for other costs of the project, that is, materials and capital. Wages paid are below the minimum wage, which reflects the fact that this program is geared to low-income groups. Furthermore, the regional allocation of the program's budget is affected by regional unemployment rates. The duration of the projects ranges from three to six months. Each worker must dedicate a minimum of six hours a day to working in the project.

Given the discussion above, a program like this one is attractive in that it decentralizes the monitoring of the employment status of the beneficiary in an incentive compatible way. The nonprofit organizations finance the other inputs of the program, so it is in their best interest to enforce the presence of the worker.

In terms of the analysis of this chapter, this program can be understood as an unemployment insurance contract plus a technology to monitor the working status of the worker. To the extent that the problem of monitoring employment status is more problematic for low-income groups, it is reasonable that these programs should be focused on these groups.

An alternative way in which this monitoring takes place is by requiring unemployed workers who collect benefits to attend educational and retraining programs. Note that the main objective may not be the instruction per se (although the more it increases the marginal productivity of the worker, the better), but the monitoring services it supplies. It is not clear, though, how the monitoring in these programs is performed, since it is not obvious that it is in the best interest of the school to monitor participants' attendance.

It should be emphasized that these monitoring schemes may come at a cost. In the analysis performed in this chapter, the key variable that increases the probability of reemployment is the effort of the worker. Although it is not obvious that effort is just measured as total daily time allocated to search activities, this is indeed a natural interpretation. Under this interpretation, then, by forcing the worker to allocate a significant fraction of the time endowment to the monitoring technology, the time left to allocate to search activities is very low. Thus, while the programs do ensure that the worker is not taking advantage of the insurance while working, they also reduce the available time for search activities and eventually reduce the reemployment probability. This is only a problem if the recommended action is the high effort level. On the contrary, if the optimal effort level is zero, which, as we suggested in this chapter, may be the case, these mechanisms can be a reasonable way to solve the monitoring problem.

In the case that the time interpretation of effort is appropriate, a possible way out of the trade-off between monitoring the employment state and letting the unemployed worker allocate a sizable amount of time to search activities is a part-time job. The idea is to force the worker to allocate the minimum possible amount of time to the monitoring technology and minimize the probability that the worker is in fact employed. Examples of strategies that could be used with that purpose are part-time jobs whose time requirements each week are stochastic. Thus, the worker has half a day to allocate to search activities but does not know, ex ante, when. Under the assumption that working requires a stronger commitment to a time schedule than searching, this may improve upon the efficiency of the program.

It should also be mentioned, however, that the time interpretation of effort that we considered in the previous paragraph is not the only way to interpret the moral hazard problem. And this is important to assess the potential cost in terms of a reduction of the reemployment probability of the program. An alternative interpretation, which is formally equivalent, is that job offers exogenously come to the unemployed worker with a certain probability.[15] The wage of each offer is drawn from a given probability distribution, so with certain probability the worker receives low wage offers, and with other probability high wage offers. As is standard in job search models, the worker will accept the high wage offers and reject the low

---

[15] See Hopenhayn and Nicolini (1999) for details.

wage ones. In fact, the optimal behavior of the worker is characterized by a reservation wage, such that all offers above that wage will be accepted and all offers below that wage will be rejected.

In such an environment, an unemployed worker receiving benefits will be more demanding than a worker without coverage, so the probability of accepting a job will be lower. This incentive problem can be cast along the lines of the model analyzed in this chapter and exactly the same theoretical results follow. In fact, if we observe time series of the working status of the agents and of which of the unemployed workers is receiving benefits, it is impossible to tell from the data if the moral hazard problem is due to a reduction in the time devoted to search or an increase in the reservation wage.

From a theoretical standpoint, this equivalence does not present any complications, since, as we have mentioned already, the results do not depend on the source of the moral hazard problem. However, it is key to assess the effect that forcing the unemployed workers to allocate time to monitoring activities has on their reemployment probability. In the case that the moral hazard problem is due to reduced time devoted to search, taking the worker's time reduces the chances of reemployment, while if it is due to increases in the reservation wage, it does not.[16]

A final word regarding the monitoring problem. Note that the insurance scheme discussed above contemplates levying a tax on the workers once they get a job. Thus, if it is too costly to monitor the worker's employment status, incentives for self-reporting must be given. As in any problem with private information, the fact that one of the parties can reveal information can be used in the optimal design problem. Contributed funds have been suggested as a way of curtailing this problem. The idea of the contributed funds is that each worker has a personal account, very similar to a pension plan, to which the worker contributes in the working state and withdraws from in the unemployment state. Thus, the incentives to contribute arise from the effect present contributions have on future benefits. This program shows how the future benefits can be used to provide incentives to the workers to reveal their state. However, if these funds simply replicate outside saving opportunities, workers would have very little incentives to report. Hence, additional benefits should be provided to induce self-selection. This could be done by

---

[16] Note that in the shorter search scenario, it is perfectly reasonable for unemployed workers to refuse to enter into this program, particularly those who have a marginal effect of effort that is high. This creates an adverse selection problem because the ones that more willingly participate in this program are the ones who get a small increase in their employment probability by choosing the high effort level.

subsidizing the return or providing an option value by conditioning future unemployment benefits to specific employment durations.

In most cases these funds, as is the case in pension plans, are fully funded by each individual. That is, total contributions and total withdrawals satisfy a present value condition for each individual account. As such, there is no insurance provided. Full insurance only imposes ex ante present value conditions, using fair prices to value alternative states of nature. Thus, while the contributions can definitely have informational content that is valuable in the design of the optimal mechanism, imposing ex post present value conditions amounts to providing no insurance. When informational constraints are relevant, full insurance is not optimal, but in the trade-off between incentives and insurance, there is no presumption that the solution is the corner with no insurance.

References

Hopenhayn, Hugo, A., and Juan Pablo Nicolini. 1997. "Optimal Unemployment Insurance." *Journal of Political Economy* 105 (April): 412–38.

————. 1998. *Optimal Unemployment Insurance: The Adverse Selection Case.* Working Paper. Universidad Torcuato Di Tella, Buenos Aires, Argentina.

————. 1999. *Optimal Unemployment Insurance and Employment History.* Working Paper. Universidad Torcuato Di Tella, Buenos Aires, Argentina.

Meyer, B. 1990. "Unemployment Insurance and Unemployment Spells." *Econometrica* 58 (July): 757–82.

Pessino, Carola. 1997. "Argentina: The Labor Market during the Economic Transition." In Sebastian Edwards and Nora Lustig, eds., *Labor Markets in Latin America: Combining Social Protection with Market Flexibility.* Washington, D.C.: Brookings Institution.

CHAPTER FIVE

Helping the Poor Manage Risk Better: The Role of Social Funds

Steen Lau Jørgensen and Julie Van Domelen

In a world of increasing opportunities and risks because of globalization and technological and political change, there is a need to reassess what role social funds should play. Social funds have established themselves as important instruments for social protection in many parts of the developing world. This chapter will show the important role that social funds can fulfill in an approach to social protection, which moves us away from simply looking at social protection as a response to adverse shocks toward a more holistic, institution-oriented definition that puts social protection squarely at the center of the fight against poverty and social exclusion.

Initial steps have been made, with fairly comprehensive qualitative information available on most social funds through beneficiary assessments. Improvements in quantitative information, particularly about benefits to poor households and sustainability of social fund investments, are under way in several countries with support from the World Bank–financed Social Funds 2000 Impact Evaluation Study.

WHAT IS A SOCIAL FUND?

There is no universally agreed definition of a social fund. We propose to define social funds as follows: agencies that finance projects in several sectors targeted to benefit a country's poor and vulnerable groups based on a participatory manner of demand generated by local groups and screened against a set of eligibility criteria. There are agencies that would meet these criteria but are not called social funds, and there are agencies called social funds that do not meet these criteria.

In general, social funds present the following characteristics. Social funds establish menus, procedures, and targeting criteria to support investments benefiting the poor. They appraise, finance, and supervise the implementation of small social projects but do not (in general) identify, implement, and maintain or operate the projects. Almost all social funds insist on cofinancing from the beneficiaries to ensure that projects are not just responding to need but to demand. However, while they respond to demand from local groups (community groups, nongovernmental organizations [NGOs], local governments, or local representatives of regional or national governments), most have a set menu of eligible projects or a negative list of ineligible projects. Even though most are part of the public sector, the funds often have operational autonomy and enjoy exceptions from public sector rules such as civil service rules or procurement and disbursement rules. Most tend to be like private firms in their operational practices, with a small staff employed on the basis of performance contracts, higher salaries, and higher performance standards. Management is usually private sector style, that is, driven more by results than by rules. Because of their operational autonomy, most funds operate under strict accountability and transparency criteria through independent audits and intense public scrutiny. Although most social funds are heavily dependent on external financing, they are run by nationals of the country and do not rely on long-term expatriate technical assistance.

Since the first internationally known social fund, the *Fondo Social de Emergencia* in Bolivia, was established in 1987, the world has seen an explosion in the number of these institutions and a proliferation of objectives and modes of operation. Today almost all countries in Latin America and the Caribbean have social funds or development projects (such as the one in North-East Brazil) that share the same operational characteristics as social funds. In Sub-Saharan Africa, at last count social funds or their sister Public Works and Employment Projects (AGETIPs, by their French acronym) existed in 24 countries, with at least half a dozen more countries at various stages of preparing or piloting social funds.[1] In the Middle East and North Africa there are four social funds operating, one of which, the Egypt Social Fund, is the world's largest, with at least two more under preparation. In Eastern Europe and Central Asia, about five are currently in operation, with another half dozen at various stages of preparation. The region that has the fewest social funds is Asia, with only three agencies in operation that are called social funds and with five more under preparation. However, several agencies do exist in countries such as India and Indonesia that share many operational characteristics with social funds.

---

[1] Frigenti and Harth (1998).

Table 5–1. Portfolio Distribution of Social Fund Investments in the Middle East and North Africa

Percent

Program	Micro-enterprise	Roads	Other infras-tructure	Education	Health	Water and sanitation	Other
West Bank and Gaza–Community Development Project		40	24	20	6	10	
West Bank and Gaza–NGO Project				54	28		17
Yemen SFD	8		4	56	11	20	1
Egypt–SFD Phase I	58	4	20	6	5	2	5
Algeria Safety Net Program		40	31			21	7

Source: Van Domelen (1998).

In terms of the level and focus of activity of social funds, they are most widely known for their investments in social infrastructure, particularly health, education, water supply, and sanitation, although this allocation varies greatly by country. For the regions where summary statistics are available, Latin America and the Middle East and North Africa, tables 5–1 and 5–2 summarize the distribution of investments. Investment in health, education, and water supply (infrastructure and noninfrastructure) is the leading area in all funds except those in Egypt, Chile, the West Bank, the Gaza Community Development Project, Algeria, and the original Emergency Social Fund of Bolivia.

Growth in the number and volume of activity of social funds makes them one of the most successful examples of institutional replicability and adaptability in the short history of development efforts.[2] While international agencies were largely responsible for the extension of the basic model between regions, the homegrown demand from countries for this type of program has fueled their adoption and adaptation to local circumstances. The fact that social funds allow governments to build on local groups' ability and resources, and thereby leverage scarce fiscal or aid money, has meant that these funds are now occupying important niches in many countries.

---

[2] The Inter-American Development Bank and the World Bank alone have invested more than $3.5 billion in social funds.

Table 5–2. Portfolio Distribution of Selected Social Fund Investments in Latin America and the Caribbean

Percent

Program	Economic infrastructure	Social infrastructure	Productive projects	Other
Bolivia				
ESF (1986–91)	44	43	3	9
SIF (1991–95)		85		15
Chile				
FOSIS (1991–95)			46	54
Ecuador				
FISE (1993–95)	11	85	4	
El Salvador				
FIS (1990–96)		84	13	3
Guatemala				
FIS (1993–95)	3	62	2	33
Haiti				
FAES (1995–96)	26	67		7
Honduras				
FHIS (1990–95)	10	65	7	18
Nicaragua				
FISE (1991–94)	19	63	1	17
Peru				
FONCODES (1991–96)	22	53	13	12

Source: Goodman and others (1997).

However, as part of a country's social protection strategy, it is worth pointing out that social funds remain a very small part of the social protection activities in the vast majority of countries. In a recent review of social funds financed by the Inter-American Development Bank, only one fund in Latin America spent more than 1 percent of GDP (Nicaragua).[3] On average in the Latin American region, less than U.S.$10 is spent per year per poor person through social funds. In the Middle East and North Africa, in spite of the presence of one of the world's largest social funds in Egypt, which has committed roughly U.S.$1 billion since its inception in 1991, social fund spending is a relatively small share of total effort on safety net pro-

---

[3] Morley in Bigio (1998, p. 46); Goodman and others (1997).

grams. In general, social funds remain highly dependent on external resources. Exceptions to the rule are Chile, with under 10 percent from foreign sources, Colombia with 20 percent external financing, FONEPAZ in Guatemala at 12 percent, and Peru's FONCODES, with 58 percent donor support. Only Egypt has moved to shift more of the share of financing to local sources, from only 6 percent at the outset to 22 percent at present. Data for Africa, Eastern Europe, and Asia are not available.

Originally, social funds were set up to provide temporary employment and provide "a bridge over the crisis," through labor-based income transfers and the subsidization of social services and infrastructure.[4] As the institutions have evolved, most are now seen as more permanent components of a country's social development strategy. The social funds still respond to emergencies, such as Hurricane Mitch in Central America, the fall-out from the wars in Cambodia and Angola, an earthquake in Armenia, or a drought in Zambia.

Although many social funds were initiated with fairly simple objectives, today most social funds must balance multiple objectives, all of which fall broadly under the umbrella of efforts to improve the living conditions of the poor. Most social funds incorporate to a lesser or greater extent objectives in the five categories listed below. Please note that these objectives are not mutually exclusive, and several social funds have changed emphasis over time:

1. The improvement in a country's *infrastructure*, such as the current Bolivian Social Investment Fund and the funds in Central America, Peru, Ethiopia, Malawi, Armenia, Angola, and Cambodia. These funds have tended to focus on addressing unmet needs of poor communities through basic social and economic infrastructure.

2. The *employment* funds, typical of the initial stage of funds created in response to emergencies, such as in Bolivia and Egypt. In the absence of an emergency, job creation also appears as a prime objective in other funds, such as the AGETIPS in Africa or the planned Bulgaria fund, whose main objective is the provision of short-term employment primarily through the repair of infrastructure.

3. Broader-based *community development*, exemplified in Argentina, Romania, Malawi, and Zambia, where a major objective of the social funds is to build community capacity to demand and manage development resources. This is most frequently done through a "learning-by-doing" process where the social funds finance mainly infrastructure projects that the communities manage and implement.

---

[4] Avila and others (1992).

4. Improvement in the delivery of *social services*, as typified by the funds in Chile, Argentina, and Romania, where a major emphasis is put on financing private-public partnerships in social service provision, including a large emphasis on training.

5. *Support for decentralization*, promoted by the funds in Chile, Honduras, Bolivia, and Ethiopia, where a major objective of the fund is to work closely with local governments to support the decentralization effort of the country. Some funds pass on their expertise to governments (Zambia, Honduras), while others (like Chile) transfer successful pilot interventions to local governments.

There is hardly a uniform trend in where social funds are going, and any knowledgeable social funds person will be able to come up with a dozen funds that are not following any of the trends given here. In any case, in a general sense some of the trends that can be observed are as follows:

• Social funds are generally becoming more permanent, more integrated into a country's overall social and economic development efforts—this implies more and better coordination with line agencies, local governments, and civil society.

• There is a relative increase (but from a very small base) in the share of resources from social funds that go to social services.

• Increasingly social funds pay more attention to popular participation, both to enhance sustainability and to build social capital.

• Social funds are increasingly seen as, and are moving to operate more as, supporters of decentralization.

• Social funds are faced with increasing demand for income-generating subprojects, but the experience so far has been mixed. The funds with better performance in the microfinance area have usually done a combination of two things. First, they have selected appropriate intermediaries, and second, they have adopted policies that take into consideration best practice in the microfinance area. The Chile social fund presents an interesting case in terms of its successful support for income generation.

From ten-plus years of experience with social funds, several stylized facts can be developed about what works and what does not.[5] On the positive side, social

---

[5] While these stylized facts are the authors' own, many are supported by the findings of assessments such as Bigio (1998); Frigenti and Harth (1998); Goodman and others (1997); Pradhan, Rawlings, and Ridder (1998); and Subbarao and others (1997).

funds have proved very good at adjusting to changed circumstances, as decentralization moves forward or as a natural disaster happens.[6] Funds tend to be more participatory than other development projects, but they have the potential to do even better, and there is wide variety across social funds. Social funds are well targeted to the poor and have reached the poor in many cases. They have low overheads and administrative costs and generally manage to provide infrastructure at much lower costs than traditional public sector agencies. In terms of both financial and public accountability the funds tend to outperform other development interventions, and where they work well, they help generate trust in the public sector among communities and build social capital. Funds can work in very different situations: for example, in Armenia, Argentina, Cambodia, Rwanda, and Haiti.

Social funds have a mixed record on sustainability. Social funds that started as emergency operations rarely focused on sustainability as a prime issue. As funds have evolved and become more focused on medium-term impacts, sustainability has become a systemic concern, particularly given the poor track record of the line ministries and local governments often responsible for operating and maintaining the investments after the social fund intervention. On health and education investments they tend to do better than traditional ministries owing to the emphasis on community participation; on economic infrastructure they do as well or as poorly as other agencies depending on the institutional framework in the country.[7]

Originally, autonomy from line ministries was seen as fundamental for a social fund to operate. However, there are several successful counterexamples, including social funds in Chile and Zambia under the Ministries of Planning and the Argentina social fund, which is a program of the Ministry of Social Development. In terms of operating procedures, some funds work more directly with community groups (Peru, Argentina, Zambia, Malawi, Romania, and Armenia), while others work more closely with intermediaries like local government (Honduras, Nicaragua, and Bolivia). In terms of the types of investments included in social fund menus, some funds focus more narrowly on social infrastructure, while others have more

---

[6] Some examples include Honduras, where in response to Hurricane Mitch the FHIS shifted to emergency assistance and reconstruction by changing procedures and quadrupling its capacity; Chile, where after a strategic planning exercise FOSIS revised its menu of eligible interventions and shifted to a geographic rather than programmatic focus; and Bolivia, where the FIS now works solely with local governments in response to the new decentralization policies.

[7] Bigio (1998).

expanded menus to include significant investments in productive activities, training, and social services. In general, it appears that optimal institutional design is better determined by country need and circumstance than standard prescription.

Social funds generally have not done well in microcredit activities, and they are not well integrated with the rest of the public sector. Because of their operational autonomy, in some cases funds have ended up running as almost parallel governments, confusing beneficiaries and not contributing to capacity building. While most social funds were designed as temporary instruments, there has been little success in training and transferring the positive aspects of social fund experience to line ministries. Some critics claim that the operational success of the social funds has distracted attention from the longer-term institutional reforms necessary in the permanent public agencies.

While social funds have been very successful at reaching underserved areas and marginal populations, there has also been leakage of benefits to the nonpoor and gaps in coverage of the poorest of the poor (while social funds do in fact reach the lowest income deciles, not all people in those deciles benefit from social fund interventions). These observations are largely due to the demand-driven model, which relies upon community initiative and capacity; the focus on providing access to broad public services (health, education), where exclusion of less-poor community members is not feasible; and inclusion of certain types of programs that may be less well targeted by their nature (for example, small and microenterprise support, urban sewerage).

Social funds have also been less adept at providing massive assistance, especially in terms of employment generated. Moreover, targeting of employment benefits has tended to exclude women and be less pro-poor than programs that use wages lower than market-based wages.

Two of the main difficulties in coming to hard and fast conclusions about social funds are the diversity of experience and the dearth of effective evaluations of social fund performance and impact. The last point may seem contradictory when one looks at the lengthy bibliographies and research pieces devoted to social funds. However, most evaluations have been limited by the lack of data on what is happening to program participants at the household level and a lack of information that would allow comparison of social funds to other delivery mechanisms. To address the second point, the World Bank launched the Social Funds 2000 Impact Evaluation Study in 1998 to evaluate social fund performance in terms of poverty targeting, impacts of benefits at the household level, sustainability of these benefits, and cost effectiveness of interventions compared with other delivery mechanisms in each of six case study countries (Bolivia, Honduras, Zambia, Armenia, Nicaragua, and Peru). Results are expected for the first quarter of 2000.

For social funds to remain effective contributors to social protection, the institutional issues raised above will need to be addressed in a sustained fashion. Where social funds have a narrower sectoral focus, sharing tools and information and joint evaluations with line ministries and local governments may lead to either better rationalization of efforts, mutual strengthening of institutional capacity, and/or eventual phasing out of social fund support in certain areas.[8] In other instances, closer social fund integration with local governments, combined with greater decentralization, may lead to an absorption of social fund financing within fiscal transfer schemes. In other circumstances, social funds may take on a more pre-eminent role in assisting poor communities to organize and express their demands. By addressing these institutional coherency and effectiveness issues, social funds may evolve into more permanent actors in a country's social protection and poverty reduction framework.

SOCIAL FUNDS IN A SOCIAL RISK MANAGEMENT FRAMEWORK

One of the reasons for the relative success of social funds has been their ability to work with a wide variety of agencies, private contractors, line ministries, local authorities, decentralized agencies, international and local NGOs, community-based organizations, and the communities themselves. Social risk management is focused on helping individuals manage risk better, but individuals' risk management strategies employ a variety of institutions or economic agents. The most basic unit is the family—where a lot of the information asymmetries are minimized. NGOs and community-based organizations also help through information intermediation between the families in a community and the outside world. Similarly, market-based institutions are employed through the labor or financial markets. Finally, social funds work with various public sector agencies. It is not surprising that the beneficiaries (and sometimes the public at large) often regard social funds as fully responsive to community and household priorities and, therefore, as an important agent of public support for their own risk management.[9]

---

[8] An example of transfer of models back to line ministries is Chile's FOSIS support for forestry initiatives.
[9] Van Domelen and Owen (1998). As funds evolve toward becoming more permanent instruments, they run the risk of losing some of the characteristics that have made them so popular in the first place, namely, agility and flexibility.

FIGURE 5–1.

Social Funds in the Social Risk Management Framework

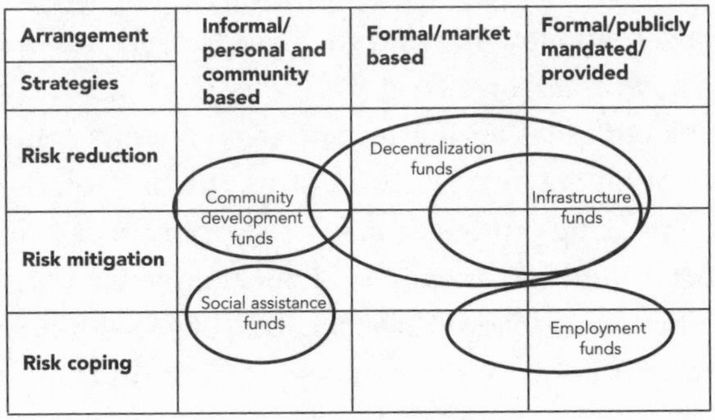

Arrangement Strategies	Informal/ personal and community based	Formal/market based	Formal/publicly mandated/ provided
Risk reduction		Decentralization funds	
Risk mitigation	Community development funds		Infrastructure funds
Risk coping	Social assistance funds		Employment funds

Figure 5–1 shows a mapping of the different types of social funds into a matrix of social risk management. The employment funds are set up to help people cope with the effect of crises. What differentiates social funds from traditional public works programs is that active participation from the private sector and civil society is encouraged through the use of private sector contractors and civic organizations as sponsors, and thus the social funds are able to move out of the bottom right corner of the matrix toward the middle of the last row. Some recent social funds with a public works component, such as the Malawi Social Action Fund, have managed to include some elements of community participation, spreading the coverage of these funds into the first column as well.

The community development funds fit within the cells of support to informal mitigation and reduction mechanisms. They help in mitigation by building social capital (one more asset for the portfolio of the vulnerable) and in reducing certain risks such as local conflict through the support for locally generated joint efforts.

The social assistance funds have so far mainly focused on supporting households' informal coping mechanisms (such as support for AIDS victims, helping the poor get access to existing transfers) or within mitigation (through support for building human capital through nutrition, training, and other human development services). The support for decentralization funds is working across the market-based and public sector aspects of risk mitigation and coping. By building the capacity of local governments to interact better with the private sector and with communities, the funds are helping lower the information gap, which has in the past caused government failure in the provision of some social risk management services at this level.

The trends in social funds' characteristics toward more permanent impacts beyond temporary employment, more social services, more participation, more decentralization, and more income generation would seem to indicate that social funds are shifting upward in the matrix toward risk reduction as opposed to risk coping.

Several social fund–type mechanisms have been created with temporary employment as a prime objective, for instance, in Bolivia after the closure of the tin mines, in Egypt to deal with the effects of the Gulf War, in the West Bank and Gaza in response to closures of the border with Israel, and in Ecuador as a response to the economic contraction during adjustment. To think of a social fund within a social risk management framework means to assess, first, whether temporary employment is needed (for example, is open unemployment the issue for the vulnerable?), and then, whether a social fund instrument is better at delivering such services than other perhaps more centralized and top-down interventions.

Even though social funds have done well on many scores, employment creation has not been their strong suit.[10] For instance, social funds have not been very effective in targeting a specific type of worker to benefit from these temporary jobs, be they ex-miners or redundant public sector workers. Although considered "vulnerable," such groups often have coping mechanisms (severance pay, higher skill and education levels, and so on) which make direct employment generation through public works less attractive. In general, even the larger social funds with explicit employment creation objectives have generated temporary jobs equivalent to well below 1 percent of the labor force. While funds may serve as an important political tool during difficult periods of transition and shocks, as a social risk minimization strategy its effects reach a relatively small number of households at risk.

The same holds true for social fund operations as a poverty alleviation or compensation measure. Although the number of people benefiting from improved access to and quality of social infrastructure and services is far greater than the potential employment impacts, the amounts disbursed are minor. One study discussed above found that the value of goods and services being transferred by a social fund to the poor typically averages well below 5 percent of the per capita income of the poor.[11] The finding is similar to a recent review of social funds in the Middle East and North Africa region, which finds that in all cases the annual amount transferred was less than 4 percent of the poverty line income.[12] Therefore, the so-

---

[10] For the results on Bolivia, see Newman, Jørgensen, and Pradhan (1991).
[11] Goodman and others (1997).
[12] Van Domelen (1999).

cial protection effects of social funds, either in terms of employment creation or in the provision of basic services to the poor, have been important for the beneficiaries but limited in their coverage.[13]

WHITHER SOCIAL FUNDS?

Social funds can be an effective tool to support risk mitigation at the community level since there are more assets available for a community to manage in a portfolio sense after the social fund has financed new or improved infrastructure. To move the social funds squarely into the risk-reducing area, their investments need to help prevent shocks. This would mean making sure that the water supply system indeed does provide clean water over a period of time to prevent water-borne diseases, and making sure that learning is taking place in the school, so the risk of future low earnings is reduced. In other words, social funds need to pay more attention to the flow of benefits from the infrastructure they have created, including more attention to operation and maintenance.

Education investments account for a significant share of current social fund portfolios. In most cases, grants are given for school rehabilitation or construction of new classrooms at the primary level. The potential impacts of these investments vary between projects. These benefits range from extending the useful life of a building to creating space for increased enrollment, increasing the number of years offered at the school, and improving teacher and community morale and hence the quality of education. Under a social risk management strategy, the benefits of building repair are far outstripped by the benefits of increasing enrollment and number of years completed, as these will have the largest effects on the capacity of poor households to reduce risks over time.

Taking social risk management as a primary consideration, social funds would become more discerning in their education investments, placing relatively more resources in projects that had greater potential to affect either enrollment (directly, through creating more spaces, or indirectly, through reduced drop-out rates) or years of schooling completed. By focusing their attention on impacts in educational attainment, social funds will be better able to steer themselves away from becoming simply a substitute for national school construction and maintenance programs.

---

[13] Bigio (1998).

To date, social funds have been more focused on outputs than outcomes, understandable in the context of social crises and the need to prove their operational capacity. Moving to a greater focus on outcomes will require that social funds become better "learning organizations" capable not only of action but in-depth monitoring and evaluation. Mainstreaming impact evaluation methodologies and ensuring that learning takes place across social funds, local governments, and sectors is a significant challenge for the future.

Given the limited resources available to social funds compared with the poverty problems of the countries, difficult decisions about whom to reach are unavoidable. In general, the targeting strategies of social funds use a broad focus on poor communities, not distinguishing by vulnerability. To improve their effectiveness at risk management, social funds should seek to identify communities, households, and individuals within the broad pool of the poor, which are by their nature more vulnerable and marginalized. If one of the goals of social risk management is to improve equity, assisting the most vulnerable will increase the impact of social fund investments. This will be difficult given the demand-driven nature of the funds and fierce competition for resources coming from eligible communities. Nonetheless, social funds should consider several strategies, many of which are already used by selected social funds. Such strategies might include a sliding scale of community contributions, with less counterpart required of the most marginalized participants; expansion of the menu to include projects explicitly oriented to such vulnerable groups as the elderly or indigenous groups; and a greater emphasis on resources to enable communities to tap into other government programs.[14]

Using a social risk management approach calls for a reconsideration of the menu of eligible social fund micro projects. Priority investments would include those interventions that have the most profound effect on reducing the risks faced by the most vulnerable populations. This means an expansion from the traditional area of social infrastructure investment. Financing projects that address such issues as legal assistance to help vulnerable groups obtain property rights, financing transportation to facilitate remote communities' access to health and education ser-

---

[14] Romania's Social Development Fund is financing programs that allow marginalized groups to get access to existing government benefits such as child or elderly allowances. The Argentina Participatory Social Fund finances empowerment and leadership workshops for women's groups that have, among other elements, training for how to access municipal services. Another Argentine example is a subproject that provides legal services to an indigenous group to enable its members to have national identity cards and hence access to entitlement programs.

vices, and supporting empowerment training for women are examples that might be envisioned under a social risk management strategy.

To date, there has been relatively less emphasis placed on community economic development (which would help reduce and mitigate risk) than on short-term employment creation and delivery of basic social infrastructure. There are some notable exceptions, such as the cases of Egypt, Chile, and Albania, where significant resources have gone to microfinance and technical support to entrepreneurs. These programs help to accumulate assets at the household level, a key element in a social risk management strategy. If social funds accept their place in a broad social risk management strategy for a country, this will mean more emphasis on support for community economic development, an area where social funds have done less well in general.[15]

PARTICIPATION AND CAPACITY BUILDING

Social funds contribute to social risk management through the creation of local capacity. Besides the impacts of the investments themselves, social funds further this local capacity building in two important ways. First, social funds have been an important source of resources and learning by doing for decentralized, locally based entities, including local governments, NGOs, local offices of line ministries, and community groups. This is consistent with the notion that vulnerable communities are better served by public interventions that are executed in a decentralized fashion. The impact of local agencies more able to address local problems is difficult to quantify but has been observed in many impact assessments of social funds.

To maximize this impact, the design of social funds should go beyond a more narrow focus on local agencies and groups as executing agencies, or channels for investments, and seek to obtain further institutional impacts. Many social funds have made important strides. For example, in Zambia, district officers are fully integrated in the project cycle and receive an important complement of training. In Argentina, participatory provincial and local councils have been established to further coordination, information sharing, and resource optimization around social investments, including those made by the social fund. In Honduras, the FHIS has

---

[15] Where microfinance or other income-generating activities have been successful, the majority of beneficiaries are women, especially women heads of household, so a move in this direction would also help develop more gender-balanced social risk management. That men do not apply is not only because of targeting but also because market failure is less prevalent for men than for women.

sponsored one of the first forays into town hall type meetings, or *cabildos abiertos*, to identify community needs and priorities in a participatory fashion.

The second area of process impact is on the "social capital" of poor communities. Due to their demand-driven, participatory approach, social fund interventions may increase both household and community social capital by increasing community cohesion, furthering community propensity to act jointly for the benefit of members of the community, and building trust and empowerment. In most cases, this effect is attributable to processes that increase social capital through the skills, networks, and confidence gained by the community at large in the identification of its needs and by project committee members who manage the implementation of the micro projects. This increased community capacity to address problems is often observed in increased participation rates in community-initiated activities and improved perception of the community by its residents, as borne out in beneficiary assessments carried out on social funds.[16] For instance, in Malawi, a beneficiary assessment of community participants found that their trust in government in general had increased because of their experience in working with the Malawi social fund, MASAF.

Social funds that have been more successful at building social capital appear to be those that have processes that give maximum responsibility to communities for the design and implementation of micro projects. For instance, many funds use a formal community assembly mechanism to identify and prioritize needs. Several funds channel financing directly to community project committees, who are then responsible for project implementation, including selection of contractors or service providers, administration, and supervision. These mechanisms have helped raise awareness of the broad range of community perceptions of needs, forge links of shared concerns between community members, mobilize general participation, and give valuable organizational experience to selected community members.

In some instances, there may be an apparent trade-off between building capacity of local agencies and increasing social capital of poor communities. For instance, social funds that channel money directly to community groups are often criticized as short-circuiting local government's prerogatives. However, social funds, which rely to a large degree on intermediaries (be they governmental or nongovernmental agencies), usually have less intense community participation and responsibility built into their project cycles. In fact, optimal social fund design should

---

[16] Van Domelen and Owen (1998).

seek to combine the two elements. Strengthening both local institutional capacity and social capital of communities would best further the goal of social risk management.

CONCLUSION

Social funds have played a role in social risk management in the past, but mainly in the area of risk coping, with some impact on risk mitigation. Their relative operational efficiency and ability to work with a variety of actors involved in social risk management makes them potentially important vehicles for risk reduction and mitigation as well.

References

Avila, Seifert, and others. 1992. *Un puente sobre la crisis*. La Paz, Bolivia: Fondo Social de Emergencia.

Bigio, A., ed. 1998. *Social Funds and Reaching the Poor–Experiences and Future Directions*. Washington, D.C.: World Bank.

Frigenti, L., and A. Harth. 1998. *Local Solutions to Regional Problems: The Growth of Social Funds and Public Works and Employment Projects in Sub-Saharan Africa*. Washington, D.C.: World Bank.

Goodman, M., and others. 1997. *Social Investment Funds in Latin America: Past Performance and Future Role*. Washington, D.C.: Inter-American Development Bank.

Newman, J., S. Jørgensen, and M. Pradhan. 1991. "How Did Workers Benefit from Bolivia's Emergency Social Fund?" *World Bank Economic Review* 5 (May).

Pradhan, M., L. Rawlings, and G. Ridder. 1998. "The Bolivian Social Investment Fund: An Analysis of Baseline Data for Impact Evaluation." *World Bank Economic Review* 12 (September): 457–82.

Subbarao, K., and others. 1997. *Safety Net Programs and Poverty Reduction: Lessons from Cross-Country Experience*. Washington, D.C.: World Bank.

Van Domelen, J. 1998. *Review of Social Investment Funds in the MENA Region*. Working Paper. World Bank, Washington, D.C.

———. 1999. "Social Funds in the Middle East and North Africa." Draft internal report. Washington: World Bank (January).

Van Domelen, J., and D. Owen. 1998. *Getting an Earful: A Review of Beneficiary Assessments of Social Funds*. Social Protection Discussion Paper Series 9816. Social Protection Unit, World Bank, Washington, D.C.

CHAPTER SIX

Insuring the Economic Costs of Illness

Paul Gertler

One of the most sizable and least predictable shocks to the economic opportunities of families is major illness. There are two important economic costs associated with illness: the cost of the medical care used to diagnose and treat the illness and the loss in income associated with reduced labor supply and productivity. The size and unpredictability of both of these costs suggest that families may not be able to smooth their consumption over periods of major illness, especially in developing countries where few individuals are covered by formal health and disability insurance.[1] The possibility that there is less than full consumption smoothing through these mechanisms suggests a potentially large loss in welfare from this shock to the household's resources. Many developing countries, recognizing this potential loss in welfare and the failure of private health insurance markets, have or are considering social insurance to help smooth the economic costs of illness.

This chapter investigates the potential welfare gain from social insurance. In particular, it pays attention to the possibility that social insurance may crowd out or replace private informal insurance. While families with sick members in developing countries are not able to gain access to formal insurance markets, they do rely on private informal coping mechanisms such as drawing on savings, selling assets, transfers from their family and social support networks, and borrowing from local credit markets.[2] Estimates of the welfare gain from social insurance must net out the crowd-out effect.

I am grateful to John Giles for useful comments and advice. The views expressed are mine alone.
[1] World Bank (1993, 1995a).
[2] Morduch (1999) provides a useful summary of this literature.

The extent to which families are able to smooth consumption over periods of illness is also important for the design of social insurance programs. In particular, as is discussed later, the extent to which families are able to smooth small health shocks has implications for user fees and the ability of social insurance to finance the rarer expensive health shocks.

To determine the extent to which households are able to employ private informal insurance mechanisms to smooth health shocks, the ability of families in Indonesia and China to smooth consumption over periods of major illness is investigated. To do so, the chapter uses unique panel data that contain excellent measures of health status combined with data on consumption.

While there is a growing literature on consumption smoothing in developing countries, little explicit attention has been paid to smoothing of health shocks.[3] Robert Townsend includes in his regression analysis the "percentage of the year sick" and finds no effect on consumption changes. Anjini Kochar models wage income and informal borrowing as a function illness, as measured by a member of the family experiencing a loss of work due to illness.[4] She finds that illness to the male lowers wage income and increases informal borrowing during peak periods in the agricultural cycle, but that there are no effects during slack periods and no effects of female illnesses. These studies appear to indicate that families living in low-income countries are able to smooth illness shocks fairly well.[5]

A key limitation of past work, however, is that the measures of health employed may reflect only small, and even potentially anticipated, changes in health status, not the kind of unexpected major illnesses that may be difficult to smooth. Paul Gertler and Jonathan Gruber overcome these problems by using measures of individuals' physical abilities to perform activities of daily living (ADLs).[6] ADLs have been proved reliable and valid measures of physical functioning ability in both developed and developing countries and distinguish the type of serious exogenous health problems that are likely to be correlated with changes in labor market and consumption opportunities. Gertler and Gruber find that while households are able to smooth 70 percent of the costs of moderate health shocks, they can only smooth about 40 percent of the costs of serious illness.

---

[3] See Morduch (1995) and Townsend (1995) for reviews of the consumption smoothing literature.
[4] Townsend (1994); Kochar (1995).
[5] In contrast, Cochrane (1991) finds that consumption in the United States is sensitive to major illness, defined as being ill for more than 100 days.
[6] Gertler and Gruber (1997).

POLICY FRAMEWORK

The classic reason for most governments to intervene in health care markets is the inherent uncertainty in health status. No one knows what tomorrow will bring. Seemingly healthy individuals can be struck by cancer, injured in accidents, or experience severe diarrhea. The uncertainty is compounded the longer one looks into the future and the less one knows about one's current health. While the costs associated with most illnesses are small, the costs associated with rare serious illness can be quite large. When a serious illness hits unpredictably, the economic consequences for the family can be significant. Given aversion to risk, families prefer to insure these risks and thereby have predictable, smooth nonmedical consumption. Despite the demand, families have difficulty purchasing insurance from private sources because of two problems created by information asymmetries: adverse selection and cream skimming.[7] Private insurance market failure suggests the potential for welfare gains from government intervention. The main problem in insurance market failure is that participation is voluntary, so that good risks can choose not to buy insurance and bad risks can be denied coverage. Many countries solve this problem through mandatory social insurance (SI). In developing countries, SI takes two main forms.

The first is universal publicly financed and delivered health care modeled after the British National Health System. In these systems, governments provide medical care through public facilities that are accessed by paying at most a nominal user fee. These systems are financed through some combination of general tax revenues and payroll taxes. There is a heated policy debate about raising user fees at public health care facilities. Governments have or are actively considering raising user charges at public facilities as a means of financing improvements in the

---

[7] Rothschild and Stiglitz (1976). Adverse selection arises because insurers are not able to observe differences in health status among different people, so they are forced to offer insurance based on the population's average medical care expenditures. The terms of the contract are good for bad-risk individuals, but bad for good risks. The incentive is for the good risks to drop out of the market, leaving the bad to insure among themselves. This substantially drives up the price of insurance, making it potentially unaffordable to large segments of the population. Cream skimming occurs when insurers can observe poor health. Insurers try to select good risk and avoid individuals with pre-existing conditions such as cancer or AIDS, who are bad risks with predictably high medical care expenditures. In addition, since insurance contracts are usually written for discrete periods of time, individuals who develop serious illness are prohibited from renewing their insurance.

health sector.[8] Vocal opponents are concerned that increased fees will adversely affect the poor's access to medical care and, consequently, their health outcomes.[9] This debate, however, has ignored the possible role of public subsidies as insurance. Subsidies reduce risk by spreading the medical costs of uncertain illness across healthy and sick times; taxes are incurred when individuals are healthy and are used to finance medical care purchased when individuals are sick. As a result, raising user fees in a world of imperfect consumption insurance has an important welfare cost: higher user fees "tax families while they are down," imposing higher costs at exactly the point where the marginal utility of consumption is highest.

The second approach is to finance medical care through mandatory payroll taxes and allow beneficiaries to purchase medical care from both private and public providers. The movement toward this model has been motivated by the desire to reduce financial pressure on government budgets.[10] SI is seen as a way to shift a portion of the public burden of delivering and financing health care to the private sector. SI reduces the out-of-pocket prices at the time of purchase of higher quality private care relative to lower quality public care. As a result, SI provides an incentive to choose the private sector over the public sector, thereby lowering the demand for publicly delivered services. Since SI is financed through additional off-budget earmarked taxes, it also relieves pressure from the general budget.

Low-income countries, however, have limited abilities to tax. Therefore, the resources available for SI are severely constrained, which greatly diminishes their ability to provide insurance. In such poor environments, there is a strict budget constraint on SI benefits. SI plans thus face the trade-off between providing a large number of individuals with a small benefit or a small number of people with a large benefit. This means that a very large deductible (and possibly a large copayment) would be required to provide uncapped benefits for the rare large financial risks (for example, those associated with rare catastrophic illnesses such as cancer). The high deductible would ensure that benefits were available for expensive catastrophic illnesses and were not used up on less expensive higher-probability events (for example, influenza). Because of the budget constraint, lowering the deductible would require capping benefits. In the limit, a zero deductible implies the lowest possible benefit cap and least effective insurance against catastrophic illness.

---

[8] For example, World Bank (1987); Jiménez (1996).

[9] For example, Cornia, Jolly, and Stewart (1987); Ready (1996).

[10] Gertler (1998).

All the same, this is exactly what many countries have done. Paul Gertler and Orville Solon show that many low-income countries have adopted first-dollar coverage and therefore have placed the lowest cap possible on benefits.[11] In essence, they have chosen to provide the minimum benefits for all illnesses rather than full insurance for rare high-cost illnesses.

A number of powerful political interest groups see a first-dollar capped benefit design as in their self-interest. The most obvious interest group is the collection of international donors and other political groups who are worried about the poor and who want to use the health care system as a means of redistribution.[12] First-dollar coverage ensures universal access to medical care regardless of income. It alleviates the widespread concern that even small out-of-pocket costs may deter utilization, especially among the very poor.[13] Politicians also support first-dollar coverage. Since the median voter is poor in most of these countries, first-dollar coverage puts money into more voters' pockets. Employers also have strong financial incentives to support capped-benefit first-dollar coverage. Typically, social insurance premiums are cofinanced by employers. In many countries, large employers historically have provided workers with limited health benefits as a means of reducing absenteeism.[14] However, quick treatment of minor illnesses reduces absenteeism more than the treatment of catastrophic illnesses. Employers capped benefits since it was cheaper to fire severely ill individuals who had little chance of returning to work. For similar reasons, employers benefit more from the capped first-dollar coverage that is more likely to reduce absenteeism than from catastrophic coverage with high deductibles that is less likely to affect workforce productivity.

The solution to both the user fee debate and the debate over first-dollar coverage depends in part on the extent to which families are able to smooth the costs of small health shocks. If yes, then there is little welfare loss to charging small user fees or using co-pays and deductibles.

---

[11] Gertler and Solon (1998).

[12] Besley and Gouveia (1994).

[13] Cornia, Jolly, and Stewart (1987). Indeed, a good portion of public intervention in health care markets is justified by the tenet of universal access to basic minimum medical care, regardless of income, as embodied in the populist slogan "health for all by the year 2000." Most countries recognize that poor individuals may not be able to afford health care and therefore subsidize the participation of poor individuals in universal insurance schemes. This explains, in part, why most countries set up large universal public health care delivery systems that charge at most nominal user fees (Jiménez 1987; World Bank 1987).

[14] Gertler and Sturm (1997).

WELFARE MEASUREMENT

One measure of the welfare cost of not being able to fully insure the costs of illness is the amount that households are willing to pay to eliminate consumption variability owing to illness. This measures households' ex ante valuation of insurance that would fill the gap in existing insurance markets for the income loss due to illness, arising either through reduced earnings or increased medical expenditures.

The willingness to pay is calculated in a certainty equivalence framework. Let C^* be consumption when healthy and $L(H_i)$ be the economic cost of illness with severity H_i, which occurs with probability π_i. Then the welfare loss from uncertain illness is the amount W, such that the welfare from getting $C^* - W$ with certainty is equal to the expected welfare when the loss is uncertain:

$$(6\text{-}1) \qquad u\left(\frac{C^* - W}{C^*}\right) = E\left[u\left(\frac{C^* - L(H_i)}{C^*}\right)\right].$$

However, the willingness to pay formula overstates the welfare gain from social insurance because it ignores the fact that households will smooth some of the shocks through private informal mechanisms. So, if we let γ represent the share of the loss that cannot be smoothed, then (6-1) can be written as

$$(6\text{-}2) \qquad u\left(\frac{C^* - W}{C^*}\right) = E\left[u\left(\frac{C^* - \gamma L(H_i)}{C^*}\right)\right].$$

Assuming a constant relative risk aversion form for the utility function, where ρ is the coefficient of relative risk aversion, (6-1) can be rewritten as

$$(6\text{-}3) \qquad \frac{\left(\dfrac{C^* - W}{C^*}\right)^{1-\rho}}{1-\rho} = \sum_j \pi_j^* \frac{\left(\dfrac{C^* - \gamma L_j}{C^*}\right)^{1-\rho}}{1-\rho},$$

where there are j discrete health states. Rearranging terms, the certainty equivalent can be expressed as a percentage of consumption when healthy:

$$(6\text{-}4) \qquad \frac{W}{C^*} = 1 - \left(\Sigma_j \, \pi_j^* \left(\frac{C^* - \gamma L_j}{C^*} \right)^{1-\rho} \right)^{\frac{1}{1-\rho}} .$$

W/C^* measures the value of insurance that fully smoothes consumption across illness states as a percentage of baseline consumption. This measure is a lower bound of the willingness to pay for insurance, however, since it is calculated based on the variation in consumption due to illness after families have already used informal mechanisms to smooth some of the costs of illness. These smoothing activities themselves have costs that are not reflected in the calculation. For example, there is some cost to family and friends from private transfers of resources to the ill household head; similarly, if consumption smoothing is occurring through increased labor supply by family members, the value of the reduced leisure to those family members is not reflected here.

The key to estimating (6-4) is γ, the share of the costs of illness that cannot be insured. Here it is estimated in the context of the theory of full insurance, as discussed by John Cochrane, Angus Deaton, and Robert Townsend.[15] This theory posits that households will fully share the risk of idiosyncratic shocks so that the growth in household consumption will not depend on changes in household resources once the change in aggregate community resources has been taken into account. This is formalized in the next section.

INDONESIA

Indonesia is the fourth most populous country in the world, with tremendous cultural and economic diversity. Until recently, economic growth has been impressive with an average real annual per capita growth rate of 3.9 percent over the past 15 years. Despite this growth, per capita incomes were still low, even before the onset of the crisis, at U.S.$880 per year in 1996.[16] Indonesia had also seen remarkable improvements in health status.[17] Between 1960 and 1990 life expectancy at birth increased by 24 percent to 59 years, and child mortality decreased 68 percent to 111 per thousand.

---

[15] Cochrane (1991); Deaton (1992a); Townsend (1994).
[16] Asian Development Bank (1997).
[17] World Bank (1993).

Indonesia has invested heavily to develop a comprehensive government-operated health care delivery system that individuals are able to access by paying a modest user fee. In 1991, there was at least one primary health center and several subcenters in each of Indonesia's 3,400 subdistricts. A large network of government-operated hospitals at the district, provincial, and central levels backs up this large primary care system. Despite this system, Indonesia's health care expenditures remain low relative to those of its neighbors.[18] In 1990 annual expenditures on health care from both public and private sources were only about $12 per person, which amounts to roughly 2 percent of GDP.

Few individuals in Indonesia are covered by health insurance other than the implicit insurance provided through the almost free public health care system; on average, user fees at public facilities amount to 5 percent of average costs.[19] While the public health care system provides extensive primary care services, its hospital care is more limited. Moreover, many individuals opt to pay out of pocket for higher quality private sector services, as over half of all utilization is provided by the private sector.[20] About 10 percent of the population is covered by health insurance provided to civil servants. However, this insurance only covers utilization at public facilities and, therefore, the benefit to the individual is only to cover the small user fees. An additional 4 percent of the population is covered by health insurance offered through employers, but this insurance typically has capped benefits, minimizing absenteeism for minor illnesses but not paying the costs of major illness.[21] Similarly, there is limited disability insurance as there is no government program, more than two-thirds of workers are self-employed, and few firms provide extensive sick leave.

Data and Sample

The data used in this analysis, collected as part of the Indonesian Resource Mobilization Study (IRMS), come from a panel survey of households designed to evaluate an experimental increase in user fees charged at public medical care facilities in two of Indonesia's 27 provinces. The two study provinces are West Nusa Tengarah (NTB), which is composed of the two islands just east of Bali, and East Kalimantan

[18] World Bank (1993).
[19] World Bank (1995b).
[20] Gertler and Molyneaux (1996).
[21] Dow and Gertler (1997).

(KalTim), which is located on the east coast of the island of Borneo. Together they account for about 6 million residents. KalTim has the third highest per capita income among all 27 provinces, while NTB ranks twenty-second. The data were collected in 1991 and 1993, allowing us to examine health, income, and consumption changes over a two-year period. The data were collected for each household at the same point in the year in both waves, so that seasonality effects are conditioned out of the differences models.

The sample consists of all households that were in the survey in both rounds, whose heads were at least 18 years old in the second round, and who have nonmissing data on the health measures described below. Paul Gertler and Jack Molyneaux, and William Dow and others discuss attrition from this sample and conclude that it does not cause significant sample selection problems.[22]

The Risk of Illness

The key to the analysis is that there are unusually good measures of the change in the health status of household members. The analysis explores the effects of two types of health measures: self-reported illness symptoms (symptoms) and limitations in the physical ability to perform activities of daily living (ADLs). Self-reported illness symptoms are similar to the measures used by the previous literature. Illness symptoms are measured by a dummy for whether the individual reports any symptom (ill), and a dummy for whether they report a symptom that has lasted more than one month (chronically ill). This measure aggregates the 10 categories of self-reported specific symptoms (for example, fever, respiratory congestion, and so on) for adults.

As an alternative the analysis therefore relies on a second measure that assesses an individual's physical ability to perform activities of daily living. These physical functioning measures are based on individuals' self-ratings of ability to engage in specific activities, not based on general assessments of illness symptoms that are more likely to be endogenous to labor supply decisions. Initially developed for studying levels of disability among the elderly, these measures are used increasingly to study the health status of all adults. Physical functioning measures have been tested extensively for reliability (consistency between tests and interviewers) and validity (consistency between individual assessments of differ-

---

[22] Gertler and Molyneaux (1996); Dow and others (1996).

ent skills). In addition, in contrast to self-reported symptoms, these measures tend to be negatively correlated with income and education in both the United States and low-income samples.[23]

Activities of daily living are divided into two categories. Intermediate ADLs consist of the ability to carry a heavy load for 20 meters; sweep the floor or yard; walk for five kilometers; take water from a well; and bend, kneel, or stoop. Basic ADLs consist of the ability to bathe yourself; feed yourself; clothe yourself; stand from sitting in a chair; go to the toilet; and rise from sitting on the floor. A limitation in any of these activities, particularly basic ADLs, clearly represents a major change in health status.

The responses to these questions on the survey are coded as "can do it easily" (a value of 1), "can do it with difficulty" (2), and "unable to do it" (3). The responses to these questions were then combined in accordance with the following algorithm developed for the RAND Medical Outcome Study:[24]

$$Health = \left(\frac{Score - \text{Min } Score}{\text{Max } Score - \text{Min } Score} \right),$$

so that the ADL index takes on a value of 1 if the individual can perform all ADLs without difficulty, and zero if the individual cannot perform any ADLs. This chapter's central model uses an overall index of ADL limitations. Results for a disaggregation of this ADL index into both its intermediate and basic components are presented below.

The means and standard deviations of the health outcome measures are presented in table 6–1, part A. The table shows the means for period 1 levels, and for changes from period 1 to period 2. In period 1, a large proportion of adults, 29 percent, reported some ADL limitation. In addition, substantial change in health status occurs over time. Between 1991 and 1993, more than 33 percent of the sample reported changes (either upward or downward) in ADL limitations.

---

[23] See Strauss and others (1993); Kington and Smith (1996); Gertler and Zeitlin (1996). In the United States and South East Asia, ADLs have been found to be reliable and valid self-assessments with a high degree of internal consistency. See Andrews and others (1986); Guralnik and others (1989); Ju and Jones (1989); Strauss and others (1993); Ware, Davies-Avery, and Brook (1980). They are routinely used in studies of labor supply in the United States (for example, Bound 1991; Bound, Schoenbaum, and Waidman 1995; Stern 1989), and are the key measures of health status in the new Health and Retirement Survey. See Wallace and Herzog (1995).

[24] Stewert and others (1990).

Table 6–1. Means and Standard Deviations of Health Outcome Measures, Earnings, and Medical Care Expenditures in Indonesia

Variable	Mean
Part A. Means of health measures	
Period 1 levels	
ADL index	0.966
	(0.082)
Some ADL limitations	0.29
Illness symptoms	0.60
Chronic illness symptoms	0.14
Changes	
Change in ADL index	0.005
	(0.088)
Any ADL change	0.337
Change in illness	–0.015
Change in chronic illness symptoms	0.161
Part B. Means of other variables in period 1	
Nonmedical consumption per capita	36,350
	(31,868)
Head's hours of work	36.6
	(24.6)
Head's earnings per capita	17,573
	(19,256)
Head not working	0.19
Family medical spending per capita	335
	(1,020)
Male	0.86
Married	0.79
Spouse's age	35.8
	(11.6)
Family size	4.80
	(2.13)
Education	
None	0.33
1–5 years	0.32
6 years	0.19
7 years or more	0.16

Note: Tabulated by the author from IRMS data. Standard deviations are in parentheses. N = 3,933.
Source: Author's calculations.

If one looks at the self-reported symptom measures, one finds that more than one-half of the sample reported an illness symptom last month in the first survey round. This raises questions about the usefulness of this indicator for investigating consumption smoothing as its huge frequency indicates that it is picking up many minor health problems that do not need expensive medical care or affect labor supply. However, a much smaller share reports chronic symptoms lasting more than one month. While there is some reduction in symptoms across these two years, there is a very large increase in chronic symptoms, which may be expected to some extent as this cohort ages.

The Cost of Illness

A prerequisite for there to be an effect of illness on consumption through imperfect consumption insurance is that there must be a sizable cost of illness. In this section, the cost of illness is quantified in terms of reduced labor supply, lost earnings, and increased medical spending.

Earnings and medical care spending equations can be estimated using the following fixed effects specification:

$$(6\text{-}5) \qquad\qquad \Delta L_{ij} = \beta \Delta h_{ij} + \upsilon_j + \varepsilon_{ij},$$

where ΔL_{ij} is the change in labor supply (or earnings, or medical care spending) for individual i living in community j, Δh_{ij} is the change in health for that individual, and υ_j is a community-level error component.

Equation 6-5 regresses first differenced labor outcomes and medical care spending against the change in health and aggregate determinants of labor supply (or medical spending). A full set of community dummies is included to control for these aggregate determinants.[25] Also included are demographic controls to capture other secular trends in the labor supply of household heads: the head's sex, age, education, and marital status; the wife's age and education; and the change in log family size. To measure a change in the indicator variables for symptoms, a variable is defined which is 0 if there is no change, 1 if the person moves from ill to healthy, and –1 if the person moves from healthy to ill. The change for ADLs is simply the change in the ADL index value.

---

[25] Communities for our purposes are defined as IRMS "enumeration areas," which are village sampling clusters.

The model is a fixed effects specification, and as such controls for unobserved heterogeneity. In particular, the first differencing sweeps out correlation from omitted unobserved individual characteristics (such as preferences and health endowments) that confound identification of the effect of illness on labor market outcomes. However, there may be unobserved correlates of income changes and changes in health outcomes that confound identification. One major source of spurious correlation, shocks to the local community economy, such as weather, which affect both permanent income and health, is controlled by including a set of community fixed effects.[26]

Labor supply is meaningful in two ways: as the changes in hours worked and as a dummy for participation in the labor force. Earnings and wages are only reported in the IRMS data for the one-third of heads who work in the market. We impute wages to all workers based on these market rates by first taking an average of hourly market wages by province (NTB or KalTim), age (<25, 25–49, 50+), education (the four categories denoted at the bottom of table 6–1, part B), and gender. This cell-specific average wage is then matched to all persons in the cell, regardless of whether they worked in the market.[27] This imputed hourly wage is then multiplied by hours per week to get weekly earnings, and by 4.3 to get monthly earnings, in order to match our monthly consumption figures.

The means and standard deviations of the earnings and medical care expenditures variables are reported in table 6–1, part B. Earnings are measured in real per capita terms in order to match the consumption specification below.[28] Among heads, average hours of work are almost 37; more than 80 percent of heads work in period 1.

Spending on medical care is measured as the product of reported medical utilization and prices from the sites at which medical care was delivered, following Gertler and Molyneaux.[29] Descriptive statistics for both are reported in table 6–1, part B. Spending on medical care is quite low, averaging less than 1 percent of

---

[26] A related source of concern is idiosyncratic changes in household income that feed back into health; for example, job loss that results in a deterioration of health (perhaps through mental depression). But our pattern of results suggests that this alternative explanation does not account for our findings. In particular, we find that larger health shocks are associated with bigger income losses and larger consumption losses. Therefore, if our results reflect effects of labor supply on health, this feedback mechanism would have to operate more strongly the larger the negative income shock. This means, for example, that the effect on health from a job loss would be bigger for high-wage individuals than low-wage individuals. This type of feedback seems to us to be unlikely.

[27] The valuation of nonmarket work at the market wage is only appropriate if labor markets clear; this assumption is supported for Indonesia by Pitt and Rosenzweig (1986) and Benjamin (1992).

[28] All figures are reported in 1991 urban NTB rupiah.

[29] Gertler and Molyneaux (1996).

Table 6–2. Coefficients for Illness and Change in Hours Worked, Indonesia

Variable	Model		
	1	2	3
Change in symptoms	−0.52		
	(0.80)		
Change in chronic symptoms		−1.04	
		(1.02)	
Change in ADLs			30.85
			(5.08)
Male head	3.14	3.23	3.21
	(2.28)	(2.32)	(2.30)
Age of head	−0.26	−0.26	−0.31
	(0.21)	(0.21)	(0.21)
Age squared/100	0.22	0.22	0.26
	(0.20)	(0.20)	(0.19)
Education			
None	2.78	2.66	2.82
	(1.62)	(1.62)	(1.62)
1–5 years	2.69	2.64	2.76
	(1.47)	(1.46)	(1.46)
6 years	4.71	4.59	4.67
	(1.59)	(1.59)	(1.59)
Single	0.39	0.47	0.05
	(3.27)	(3.27)	(3.26)
Wife's age	−0.08	−0.08	−0.08
	(0.07)	(0.07)	(0.06)
Change in log family size	−1.49	−1.39	−1.51
	(2.28)	(2.28)	(2.27)

Note: Standard errors are in parentheses. Estimates are from models such as (6-2) in the text. N = 3,933.
Source: Author's calculations.

nonmedical consumption. This reflects both low levels of utilization and the extensive subsidization of medical care costs by the public sector. Even conditional on having some positive spending, mean spending on medical care is only about 2 percent of nonmedical consumption, although roughly 5 percent of sample households spend more than 10 percent on nonmedical consumption.

Table 6–2 reports the full regression specification for our first measure of labor supply, change in hours worked. For symptoms, there is a negative effect of becoming ill on hours of work, but neither coefficient is significant. The result suggests that having chronic symptoms is associated with a reduction in labor supply of 1 hour per week.

Table 6–3. Coefficients for Illness, Labor Supply, and Medical Spending, Indonesia

Variable	Symptoms	Chronic symptoms	ADLs
Change in hours	−0.52	−1.04	30.85
	(0.80)	(1.02)	(5.08)
Change in labor force participation	0.031	0.029	−0.738
	(0.012)	(0.014)	(0.080)
Change in earnings (in Rp. 10,000)	−0.128	−0.060	2.02
	(0.060)	(0.076)	(0.35)
Change in medical spending (in Rp. 10,000)	0.022	0.015	−0.118
	(0.004)	(0.006)	(0.026)

Note: Standard errors are in parentheses. Coefficients are for change in health in the regression that includes all covariates shown in table 6–2. N = 3,933.
Source: Author's calculations.

The third column shows the results for the ADL measures; here, illness is represented by a reduction in the index, so that a positive coefficient indicates that illness reduces labor supply. There is a sizable and significant effect of ADL changes. The coefficient implies that moving from completely healthy (index = 1) to completely sick (index = 0) would lower hours of work by almost 31 hours per week, which is a fall of 84.3 percent of baseline hours worked. In other words, if the head moved from being able to perform all of the ADLs to being unable to perform even one ADL, his hours of work per week would fall by 2.8 hours (7.6 percent of baseline hours).[30] The control variables are generally insignificant, except that the most educated heads are found to work more hours.

Table 6–3 presents the coefficients of interest for other measures of labor supply. The first row replicates the findings from table 6–2. The next row shows the results for change in labor force participation. The finding parallels that of table 6–2: positive effects of symptoms (becoming ill raises nonparticipation), and negative effects of ADL changes (improved physical functioning lowers nonparticipation). In this case, the effects are significant for all of our health status measures, although much stronger for ADLs. Indeed, moving from being able to perform all of the ADLs to being able to perform none implies a 74 percent likelihood of becoming a

---

[30] Note that this evaluation can be done for all of the ADL coefficients by simply multiplying the coefficient by 0.0909, which is the change in the ADL index arising from a movement from being able to do all ADLs to being completely unable to do one ADL.

nonparticipant, while experiencing an illness symptom or chronic illness increases the likelihood of not participating by about 3 percent.

The third row of table 6-3 shows the effect on imputed earnings, expressed in 10,000 rupiah units. Surprisingly, the effect of chronic symptoms on earnings is actually lower than for nonchronic symptoms, despite a larger effect on hours worked. This implies that the population for which chronic symptoms are associated with reduced work is a relatively low (predicted) wage population. Although the imputation of wages by demographic characteristics limits the generality of this result, it is consistent with the notion that individuals who are marginally attached to the labor force are justifying their exit from the labor force by reporting a chronic symptom.

For ADL change, the coefficient is once again much stronger. It implies that moving from being completely able to perform ADLs to being completely unable to perform ADLs would lower earnings by Rp. 20,170. This is roughly as large as baseline mean earnings, suggesting that such a shift would (unsurprisingly) leave the head with small earnings. Moving from being completely able to perform all ADLs to being unable to perform one ADL lowers earnings by Rp. 1,834, or about 10 percent of baseline earnings.

Finally, the last row of table 6-3 shows the effects of illness on medical spending. There are significant effects in the expected direction for all three measures (having symptoms = more spending; lower ADLs = more spending). But these effects are trivially small relative to the effects on earnings. This is not surprising since publicly provided care is heavily subsidized (that is, user fees are well below the cost of care).

Do Households Fully Insure Consumption?

The previous sections demonstrated that major illnesses as measured by changes in basic ADLs are associated with large financial costs to households. This section tests whether households are insuring consumption against these unexpected costs of illness.

The empirical specification is derived from the theory of full insurance, which casts consumption insurance in terms of interhousehold risk sharing.[31] In practice, however, the empirical specification used here follows the previous developing

---

[31] See, for example, Cochrane (1991); Deaton (1994); and Townsend (1994).

country literature in examining consumption *smoothing*, either through insurance from others or through self-insurance (that is, savings). Indeed, the empirical tests do not distinguish between these two channels of consumption smoothing. The reason for briefly laying out the full insurance model is to highlight a key assumption of the empirical testing: state independence in consumption.

The key empirical insight of the theory of full insurance is that mechanisms for pooling risks will equalize the growth in the marginal utility of consumption across households within communities. The easiest way to derive this condition is from the first-order conditions to the central planner's problem of allocating resources under uncertainty given a set of household social weights. The first-order conditions in logarithmic form are $\ln(MU(C_{ijt})) = \ln(\lambda_{jt}) - \ln(\omega_{ij})$, where $MU(C_{ijt})$ is marginal utility of consumption of household i living in community j, λ_{jt} is the Lagrange multiplier associated with the aggregate resource constraint for community j in period t, and ω_{ij} is the social weight associated with the household. The social weight does not vary over time and therefore is just a household fixed effect. Taking differences of both sides of the first-order conditions to eliminate the fixed effect finds that with full insurance $\Delta \ln(MU(C_{ijt})) = \Delta \ln(\lambda_{jt})$. In words, the growth rate of each household's marginal utility within a community is equalized.

The empirical analogue depends on the shape of the marginal utility function and other factors that affect intertemporal and interhousehold differences in tastes. Here a form of the constant relative risk aversion utility function suggested by Deaton, where the utility of per capita consumption is multiplied by the size of the family, is used.[32] Letting n_{ijt} be the number of household members, the utility function is

$$U_{ijt}(C_{ijt}) = \theta_{ijt} n_{ijt} \left(C_{ijt} / n_{ijt}\right)^{1-\rho} / (1-\rho),$$

where θ_{ijt} is an unobservable taste parameter that accounts for other variations in preferences.

In this case, the differenced logarithmic first-order condition becomes

$$\Delta \ln\left(\frac{C_{ij}}{n_{ij}}\right) = \frac{1}{\rho}[\Delta \ln(\lambda_j) - \Delta \ln(\theta_{ij})],$$

---

[32] Deaton (1994).

which can be expressed as

$$\Delta \ln\left(\frac{C_{ij}}{n_{ij}}\right) = \frac{1}{\rho}\Delta \ln(\lambda_j) + \varepsilon_{ij}.$$

This implies that while the growth in the marginal utilities of consumption is constant within a community, the growth in household consumption will differ due to intertemporal and interhousehold differences in preferences (due, for example, to aging or change in family size). Therefore, the theory of full insurance implies that the growth in each household's consumption will not depend on changes in household resources that are uncorrelated with shifts in preferences once the growth in community resources has been taken into account.

With the use of the above results one can test whether families are able to insure consumption against illness by estimating the following equation:

(6-6) $$\Delta \ln\left(\frac{C_{ij}}{n_{ij}}\right) = \alpha\Delta \ln(C_j) + \beta\Delta h_{ij} + \varepsilon_{ij},$$

which is a regression of the growth in per capita (nonmedical care) consumption against the change in health (h_{ij}), controlling for the growth in community resources by including the change in community-level consumption. In addition, preference shifts associated with changes in family size or structure are controlled for by including the change in log family size and a series of measures of the change in the shares of the family that are male or female family members ages 0–5, 6–17, 18–49, and 50 plus. And, as above, other potential taste shifters that might be correlated with illness are controlled for: the head's sex, age, education, and marital status; and the wife's age and education. Conditional on these taste shifters, then, if there is full smoothing of illness, there will be no effect of the change in health on the change in consumption.

The dependent variable for the analysis is the change in the log of monthly nonmedical consumption per capita. The means for consumption expenditures are shown in table 6–1, part B. Like earnings, consumption is reported in real terms by deflating for price differences across locales and over time.

The estimates of equation 6-6 are presented in table 6–4. For illness symptoms, the hypothesis of full insurance cannot be rejected. The coefficients on both measures are insignificant; indeed, they are wrong-signed, indicating that illness is associated with higher levels of consumption, not lower.

Table 6–4. Regression of the Growth in Nonmedical Care Consumption, Indonesia

Variable	Model 1	Model 2	Model 3
Change in symptoms	0.004		
	(0.012)		
Change in chronic symptoms		0.013	
		(0.014)	
Change in basic ADLs			0.194
			(0.080)
Male head	0.020	0.019	0.021
	(0.037)	(0.037)	(0.037)
Age of head	0.002	0.002	0.002
	(0.003)	(0.003)	(0.003)
Age squared/100	−0.003	−0.003	−0.002
	(0.003)	(0.003)	(0.003)
Education			
None	−0.028	−0.028	−0.028
	(0.023)	(0.023)	(0.023)
1–5 years	−0.019	−0.019	−0.018
	(0.022)	(0.022)	(0.022)
6 years	0.033	0.033	0.033
	(0.024)	(0.024)	(0.024)
Single	0.080	0.079	0.079
	(0.052)	(0.052)	(0.052)
Wife's age	0.0003	0.0003	0.0003
	(0.001)	(0.001)	(0.001)
Change in log family size	−0.464	−0.465	−0.464
	(0.036)	(0.036)	(0.036)
Change in community consumption	0.366	0.365	0.370
	(0.033)	(0.033)	(0.033)

Note: Standard errors are in parentheses. Coefficients on change in share of family in age/sex groups are not reported. N = 3,933.
Source: Author's calculations.

In contrast, when the ADL index is used, the full insurance hypothesis is strongly rejected. Changes in the ADL index have a significant and sizable effect in the expected direction; negative increments to health are associated with reductions in consumption. Moving from being able to perform all ADLs to being able to perform none of them would lower consumption by almost 20 percent. A move from being completely able to being unable to perform one ADL would lower consumption by 1.8 percent.

The control variables show the expected pattern of effects. Consumption growth rates are higher for male heads, for older heads (although the effect increases with age at a diminishing rate), and for more educated heads. Per capita log consumption changes fall with the change in log family size, indicating some economies of scale in consumption; there is no clear pattern to the (unreported) coefficients on the changes in demographic shares, which are mostly insignificant. And there is a strong positive association with community consumption, but the estimated coefficient is much less than one. This is consistent with the rejection of full consumption smoothing at the community level in Townsend and Deaton.[33]

Moreover, the more severe illnesses measured by ADL changes are very strongly associated with consumption changes. This provides a striking refutation of the full insurance hypothesis at the household level. These latter types of illness changes appear to represent shocks to a family's opportunity set that cannot be smoothed.

How Incomplete Is Insurance?

The results in tables 6–1 through 6–4 provide a convincing demonstration that there is incomplete consumption smoothing of illness in Indonesia. The natural question to ask is "how incomplete is this insurance?" This magnitude is critical for assessing the importance of these findings for welfare and for considering their policy implications. Therefore, the magnitude of lack of consumption smoothing against illness as the share of the costs of illness that are financed out of consumption is measured. To do so, the previous consumption smoothing literature is followed by estimating a model of the effect of changes in (net of medical spending) income on the growth of nonmedical care consumption:

$$(6\text{-}7) \qquad \Delta \ln\left(\frac{C_{ij}}{n_{ij}}\right) = \alpha \Delta \ln(C_j) + \mu \Delta \ln(n_{ij}) + \gamma \Delta y_{ij} + \varepsilon_{ij},$$

where y_{ij} is earnings minus medical care expenditures. Then the share of the costs of illness that are financed out of reduced consumption is simply γ/C_{ij}.[34]

---

[33] Townsend (1994); Deaton (1992a).

[34] The level of income is used instead of the log, since roughly one-quarter of cases where there is a change in the ADL index have zero earnings in one period and these cases should not be excluded.

Table 6–5. Estimating Magnitude of Consumption Insurance, Indonesia

Type of estimation	Coefficient	Implied effect of income changes on consumption changes, γ/C_{t-1}
OLS	0.008	0.03
	(0.004)	
IV: ADL	0.096	0.35
	(0.042)	
IV: Symptoms	−0.025	
	(0.070)	
IV: Chronic symptoms	−0.099	
	(0.113)	

Note: Standard errors are in parentheses. Regressions include all controls shown in table 6–4 and the note to that table. Coefficients are for change in earnings of head minus change in medical spending from regressions of the form of equation 6-7. The first row estimates this model by OLS, while remaining rows estimate 2SLS models, with the instrument mentioned.
Source: Author's calculations.

Estimating equation 6-7 by OLS forms the basis for Townsend's and Deaton's test of full insurance.[35] The results from this estimation are shown in the first row of table 6–5. They show only the coefficient of interest—that on change in income—from regressions that include all of the regressors shown in table 6–4; income is expressed in units of Rp. 10,000. In fact, a significant, but very small, relationship is found between income changes and consumption changes and is consistent with Townsend's results. A Rp. 10,000 increase in income is estimated to increase consumption by only 0.8 percent, or Rp. 300. That is, as shown in the second column, this implies that for each rupiah that income falls, consumption falls by only Rp. 0.03. This is a trivial change, which would indicate very close to full consumption smoothing.

However, there are two potential problems with estimating equation 6-7 by OLS, both of which would bias toward a finding of consumption smoothing. The first, as noted by Jonathan Morduch, is that the growth in income is correlated with the error term through the production process; risk adverse families may choose the variation in income so that consumption can be smoothed using available mechanisms.[36] The second is measurement error in the growth of income, particularly since earnings have been imputed in the data.

---

[35] Townsend (1994); Deaton (1992a).
[36] Morduch (1990).

To solve these problems, an instrumental variables approach is used, which uses the change in the illness variables to instrument for the change in income. This instrument is valid given that the utility function is not state dependent, that there is no feedback from changes in consumption to changes in health, and that measurement error in health changes is uncorrelated with measurement error in income changes. The first two of these conditions are demonstrated by the tests above for the change in the ADL index, while the last seems reasonable. In this case, this regression allows an assessment of whether the major changes in income due to illness are smoothed differently than average income changes.

Once income is instrumented by the change in ADLs in the second row of table 6–5, the coefficient rises dramatically and becomes significant. The estimate indicates that for every Rp. 10,000 of income lost due to illness, there is a fall in consumption of 9.6 percent, or Rp. 3,490. That is, for each rupiah that income falls, consumption falls by Rp. 0.35 (as shown in the second column). This suggests that families are able to smooth only 65 percent of the loss in income from ADL changes on average.

The other illness measures are used in the remaining rows of table 6–5. As one could infer, the estimates here are actually wrong-signed and are insignificant. As noted earlier, there are two alternative explanations for this finding of no impact of illness-induced income changes on consumption. Either these types of high frequency/low severity illness events are easily smoothed, or these are not exogenous shifts in the family's opportunity set (and thus they are not valid instruments for this exercise). In order to consider the first alternative in more detail, the chapter next considers the impact of variations in our ADL measure.

The results thus far have aggregated all of the available ADL information into one index. While this provides a convenient summary measure, it masks underlying heterogeneity in the response of consumption to different types of health changes. In particular, households may be better able to smooth the modest income loss associated with minor health changes than they are the larger income loss associated with major health changes. This would arise if individuals had available limited self-insurance (for example, savings) that can only cover small income losses, or if consumption insurance (for example, transfers and loans from extended family) were available in small but not large amounts.

This issue is explored in table 6–6 by disaggregating the ADL index into changes in intermediate and changes in basic ADLs. As noted earlier, the latter set of limitations are much more serious; while 24 percent of the sample has some intermediate ADL limitation, only 2 percent has some basic ADL limitation. There-

Table 6–6. Heterogeneity, Indonesia

Index	γ	γ/C_{t-1}
Overall ADL index	0.096	0.35
	(0.042)	
Intermediate ADL index	0.079	0.29
	(0.039)	
Basic ADL index	0.165	0.60
	(0.095)	

Note: Standard errors are in parentheses. Each regression includes the controls shown in table 6–4 and the note to that table. The coefficient in the first column is that on change in earnings of head minus change in medical spending from regressions of the form of equation 6-7, for the instruments mentioned. Figures in the second column are implied effects of income changes on consumption changes.
Source: Author's calculations.

fore, the instrument set used to estimate equation 6-3 is varied by IV. The coefficients in the table are estimates of the effect of income variation on consumption, where the instruments are not just the overall ADL index, but also the separate indexes for basic and intermediate ADLs. The IV coefficients in each case therefore represent the impact of income variation induced by less and more severe changes in illness. In other words, they provide an assessment of whether there is better ability to smooth less severe health changes (the intermediate ADL changes in row 2) than more severe health changes (the basic ADL changes in row 3).

The results suggest that the impacts of basic ADL limitations on consumption are much more sizable. They find that each Rp. 10,000 of income loss due to intermediate ADL changes causes consumption to drop by 7.9 percent, but that each Rp. 10,000 of income loss due to basic ADL changes causes consumption to drop by 16.5 percent. That is, the findings estimate that families can smooth 71 percent of the income loss associated with intermediate ADL changes, but only 40 percent of the loss associated with basic ADL changes. This is a striking difference, and it suggests that there is definite heterogeneity in the ability of families to smooth illness shocks.

Insurance Market Policies

The results thus far demonstrate that families are not able to smooth the economic costs arising from serious illness to the household head, and as the extent of ability to smooth falls, the larger the shock. This incompleteness in private insurance markets suggests the potential for welfare gains from government provision of insurance against income loss and medical illness. In this section, the magnitudes of these welfare gains from social insurance are considered. It abstracts from the fundamental issue of the justification for public intervention, except to note that there is a substantial and well-known literature on insurance market failures in this context.[37] In addition, the section focuses solely on the welfare gains from more complete insurance and abstracts from other important potential welfare gains such as improvements in health status and gains in social welfare from redistribution.

This section implements the welfare measurement approach discussed earlier. It considers two alternative social insurance policies, disability and medical insurance. In each case, both the application of the policy to the overall change in ADLs and the application to just basic changes in ADLs are considered to reflect the fact that a policy more tightly targeted to the most severe changes will have the largest welfare gain relative to payouts. The benefits of providing disability insurance to everyone, and just to workers (as is done in most developed countries) are also considered.

Disability Insurance

This section contrasts the benefits and costs of formal disability insurance that fully smoothes consumption over the loss in earnings arising from illness. The gain to the household from such insurance is the expected value of the transfer from the insuring agency plus the welfare gain from consumption smoothing. The cost to the government is the expected value of the transfer plus a markup for administrative costs, the cost of moral hazard through increased reported illness in response to the existence of this program, and any deadweight loss from financing these benefit payments. That is, the expected benefit payout is just a transfer from the government to households; the ultimate efficiency of disability insurance policy rests on a comparison of the welfare gains from consumption smoothing and the inefficiencies inherent in operating a disability insurance program. Measuring these inefficiencies is beyond the scope of this chapter. But, by comparing the welfare gain from consumption smoothing to the expected benefits payout (the transfer), the chapter can offer a sense of how large these costs would have to be in percentage terms to offset the consumption smoothing benefits of disability insurance.

---

[37] See, for example, Rothschild and Stiglitz (1976).

Table 6–7. Welfare Gains from Disability and Medical Insurance, Indonesia

Type of insurance	Expected insurance payouts (percent of consumption)	Welfare gain (percent of consumption)	Gain/cost
Disability insurance for all			
Overall ADLs	0.89	0.36	0.40
Basic ADLs only	0.25	0.18	0.72
Disability insurance for workers only			
Overall ADLs	0.99	0.51	0.52
Basic ADLs only	0.32	0.40	1.25
Medical insurance for all			
Overall ADLs	0.30	0.14	0.47
Basic ADLs only	0.13	0.11	0.85

Note: The first two columns show, as a percentage of consumption, the expected insurance payout and welfare gain (respectively) of providing full insurance against either disability or medical expenditures. The last column shows the ratio of welfare gains to expected insurance payouts.
Source: Author's calculations.

The section begins by estimating the expected payout from a disability insurance policy that fully replaces the earnings loss to those who become ill by the ADL metric. The loss in earnings from an illness, L_j, is measured by using the estimates of equation 6-2 reported in the third row of table 6–3 to predict the loss in earnings from downward movements in the ADL indexes.[38] The probability of experiencing the loss, π_j, is measured using the observed frequency distribution of downward movements in the ADL indexes. The expected loss in earnings, then, is the sum of the π_j times L_j. The estimate for the expected insurance payout for earnings losses is 0.89 percent of baseline consumption.

The estimated insurance payouts, which are equivalent to overall expected earnings losses from illness, are reported in the first column of table 6–7. The expected payout for overall changes in ADLs is about 0.9 percent of consumption. The expected payout for more serious illnesses, as measured by movements in ba-

---

[38] It is inappropriate to incorporate the consumption increases from upward movements in health, which simply reflect recovery from earlier downward shifts. The results for the consumption smoothing effects of changes in the ADL index are very similar if we just use downward shifts to identify our estimates.

sic ADLs, is 0.25 percent of consumption. These results are quite small as a share of consumption. Despite the fact that the expected earnings loss conditional on occurrence of an ADL change is very high, the frequency of occurrence of serious illness is very low, so that overall expected insurance payouts are low as well. Similarly, the expected payouts for more serious illnesses are much lower than for less serious illnesses; this reflects the fact that more serious illnesses occur with much less frequency.

Next, equation 6-4 is used to estimate the private willingness to pay to eliminate the variation in consumption due to the income loss from serious illness. This chapter has already discussed how π_j and L_j are measured. The coefficients reported in the second column of table 6–5 are used as estimates of γ. There is no direct estimate of the coefficient of relative risk aversion, ρ. Instead, we evaluate equation 6-4 for a range of values from 2 to 4, which is the range estimated by most previous studies using individual microdata.[39] The results are fairly insensitive to values in this range.

The results of this exercise for $\rho = 3$ are presented in the second column of table 6–7. We first show the welfare loss from illness, which is (as noted above) a lower bound on the willingness to pay for insurance as a percentage of ex ante consumption. For overall changes in ADLs, this is 0.36 percent of consumption. This is once again quite small, despite the large economic cost of these rare illnesses, due to the infrequency of illness. This also reflects the fact that individuals can smooth 65 percent of the cost of illness through other mechanisms, so that to some extent disability insurance will crowd out those other sources of support. We calculate that if no smoothing from other sources were available, the welfare gain from complete disability insurance would be 1.2 percent of consumption.

But, while small as a share of baseline consumption, this welfare gain is fairly large relative to expected insurance payouts, as shown in the third column of table 6–7. The welfare gain amounts to roughly 40 percent of insurance payouts. Restricting the analysis to only the most serious basic ADL changes, there is once again a very small welfare loss from illness, 0.18 percent of consumption. However, the welfare gain from insuring these more severe illnesses is 72 percent of the insurance payout under disability insurance.

The second panel of table 6–7 restricts the analysis to workers only. In this case, not only do we find that there is a larger payout under disability insurance, but the welfare gains are larger as well. Indeed, for overall ADL changes, the wel-

---

[39] Zeldes (1989); Engen (1993).

fare gains from insurance amount to over one-half of insurance payouts. For basic ADL changes, the welfare gains are actually larger than the insurance payouts.

These findings of large welfare gains from insurance, relative to expected payouts, suggest the potential for welfare improvements from government insurance provision. Only if the deadweight loss of government provision, through administrative costs, moral hazard, and the marginal cost of public funds, amounts to half or more of expected payouts will there be no welfare improvement from formal disability insurance. And, if the government is able to target the disability program to workers and to the most severely disabled, there will be welfare improvements so long as these incremental costs (including, of course, the costs of targeting) do not exceed 125 percent of the transfer.

The Insurance Value of Public Medical Care Subsidies

There is a heated policy debate in developing countries about raising user fees for services obtained at public health care facilities. Governments have or are actively considering raising these charges as a means of financing improvements in the health sector and improving the efficiency with which medical care is delivered.[40] Vocal opponents are concerned that increased fees will adversely affect the access of the poor to medical care and, consequently, their health outcomes.[41] Policymakers are also promoting lowering subsidies for hospitalization and shifting them to primary and preventive care.[42] This proposal is justified based on the argument that primary and preventive care are more cost-effective methods of improving a population's overall health.

This debate, however, has ignored the possible role of public subsidies as consumption insurance. Subsidies reduce risk by spreading the medical costs of uncertain illness across healthy and sick times; taxes are incurred when healthy people finance medical care purchased when sick. As a result, raising user fees in a world of imperfect consumption insurance has an important welfare cost: higher user fees "tax families while they are down," imposing higher costs at exactly the point where the marginal utility of consumption is highest. Thus, given the imperfect consumption smoothing that we document, there may be an additional consumption smoothing motivation for low user fees.

---

[40] See, for example, World Bank (1987); Jiménez (1996).

[41] See, for example, Cornia, Jolly, and Stewart (1987); Ready (1996).

[42] World Bank (1993).

These consumption smoothing models indicate that families are able to fully smooth the costs of medical care associated with small health shocks that do not affect physical functioning. However, since families are not able to smooth rare large shocks, shifting subsidies away from the treatment of these illnesses will come at a cost of reduced welfare from lower insurance.

This section estimates the insurance value of these public medical care subsidies. First, it estimates what medical care expenditures would be in a world with no subsidies. User fees at public facilities are estimated to be about 10 percent of the cost of providing care.[43] Using these same data, Gertler and Molyneaux estimate the price elasticity of demand for medical care to be −0.4.[44] Therefore, if prices were increased to the full costs of care—a tenfold increase—this would raise medical spending by 600 percent. The unsubsidized medical care expenditures for each change in ADLs is measured by the subsidized expenditure predicted from table 6–3, increased by a factor of 6.

Using the estimates of π_{j}, the expected unsubsidized medical care expenditures arising from ADL changes are calculated. The results are reported in the first column of the third panel of table 6–7. Even unsubsidized, expected medical care expenditures are only about one-third of the expected loss in earnings from illness.

The willingness to pay to eliminate the variation in consumption due to medical care expenditures in a world with no formal disability insurance is reported in the second column of the third panel of table 6–7. The willingness to pay computation follows that above, but uses the unsubsidized value for medical care expenditures in addition to the earnings loss, raising the welfare cost of imperfect consumption smoothing. Then the difference between the willingness to pay to insure total income loss, including unsubsidized medical spending, and the willingness to pay to insure the earnings loss only is taken.

Not surprisingly, the welfare gain from full medical insurance as a percent of consumption is small; for overall ADLs, it is only 0.14 percent of consumption. However, the welfare gain as a percentage of expected medical care expenditures is quite large. Overall, this gain is almost 50 percent as large as expected expenditures. For basic ADL changes, the gain is 85 percent as large. The welfare gains are large relative to payouts because the unsubsidized medical care losses are incurred on top of income losses. This is the point where the marginal utility of consumption is highest and, therefore, the welfare loss per dollar is highest.

---

[43] World Bank (1995a).
[44] Gertler and Molyneaux (1996).

These results suggest that user fees for frequent small illnesses are affordable in the sense that families are able to smooth consumption over these shocks. This also suggests that user fees for primary and preventive care are affordable. However, since families are not able to afford rare large shocks, shifting subsidies by raising user fees for hospitalization will come at a cost of reduced welfare from lower insurance. Our results suggest that there is likely to be some welfare gain from subsidizing inpatient care for rare expensive illnesses, which families are least able to smooth and for which there is the lowest moral hazard cost.

CHINA

During the 1980s and 1990s, China astonished the world with annual GDP growth rates averaging over 8 percent in most years. These numbers mask the tremendous differences in economic growth across China's regions, as rural areas of the hinterland witnessed much slower growth over this period. Much of the same story can be told with respect to both access and quality of health care during the reform period. Variation in access can be quite striking—in 1993, for example, the number of hospital beds per thousand was 5.50 for Shanghai and 6.24 for Beijing, but only 1.1 in China's rural areas.[45]

Improved access to health care services actually predated the reform era. China's rural residents benefited from a 1965 State Council directive that called for health reform and more emphasis on rural services and led to the training of barefoot doctors and extension of basic health services down to the village.[46] Dramatic improvements in health outcomes followed. The under-five mortality rate, for example, fell from 144 per thousand live births in 1965 to 60 in 1980, and further to 44 by 1990.[47] Since 1980, the basic institutions of the rural health care system developed in the 1960s have remained preserved within the postreform township and village institutions.

The upper tier of the rural health care system run by the County Public Health Bureau is composed of one or more general hospitals, an epidemic prevention station, and a maternal and child health station. Township health centers (*weishengyuan*) form the middle tier of the rural health care system and generally include a small

---

[45] State Statistical Bureau (1994); Ministry of Public Health (1994).
[46] West (1997).
[47] World Bank (1996). The under-five mortality rate is defined as the number of children who die between birth and their fifth birthday.

hospital, an outpatient clinic, and an office for maternal and child health care. Finally, the lowest tier of the rural health system is the village health office *(weishengsuo)*. Part-time rural health aides typically treat only common medical problems and refer serious illnesses to the township health center. Besides family planning services, rural health aides are responsible for immunization treatment and provide general health education.[48]

On the eve of reform in the late 1970s, costs of health care for rural residents were quite low, and collective insurance coverage was quite broad. Dating to the 1950s, one of three forms of insurance was available to rural residents. Government health insurance *(gongfei yiliao)*, available to state cadres, teachers, and township government workers, was funded through cost reimbursement. Labor health insurance *(laodong baoxian)* was provided to any rural residents employed in state-owned enterprises. Finally, cooperative health insurance *(hezuo yiliao)* was set up by villages and managed in coordination with township health centers.[49] By the early 1980s, the majority of China's rural population had access to some form of risk-pooling arrangement that guaranteed access to care. Various estimates place the uninsured population at between 10 and 29 percent in 1981.[50] With introduction of the household responsibility system in agriculture and the dismantling of the communal welfare fund that supported cooperative health insurance, however, the uninsured population exploded to almost 80 percent of rural households by 1993.[51] The villages used in the analysis of this chapter reflect this trend. As of 1997, residents in only one-quarter of them participated in any type of health insurance plan.

At present, the Ministry of Public Health is experimenting with different types of community-financing programs for rural residents. Most small-scale experiments provide a form of coinsurance requiring residents to pay part of the cost of health services at the point of service.[52] Whether health insurance should be compulsory or not has been a matter of debate within policy circles. While a 1994 policy announcement emphasized that participation in community-organized coinsurance programs should be voluntary at the individual level, there have been reports of experiments with compulsory participation as well.[53]

---

[48] West (1997).

[49] Wei (1995); World Bank (1996).

[50] West (1997); World Bank (1984).

[51] Wei (1995).

[52] World Bank (1996).

[53] *Peoples Daily,* July 2, 1994.

Data

The analyses of health shocks in this chapter use household survey data provided by the Survey Department of the Research Center on the Rural Economy (RCRE) at the Ministry of Agriculture in Beijing. Annual household surveys from 104 villages of Shanxi, Jiangsu, Anhui, Shandong, Henan, and Shaanxi provinces and the Shanghai suburbs spanning the period from 1986 to 1997 are used to both analyze the impact of health shocks on household consumption and evaluate potential demand for health insurance in rural China.

RCRE has collected data from a panel of households since 1986, but the survey was not conducted in 1992 or 1994 because of funding difficulties. Households are asked a range of questions regarding income from on-farm activities and off-farm employment, household consumption, land use, asset ownership, savings, formal and informal access to and provision of credit, and transfers from both village members and friends and family outside the village. Values of nonmarketed grain that show up in income, consumption, and grain balance sections of the survey are adjusted to reflect market prices following a procedure outlined by Shaohua Chen and Martin Ravallion.[54] County agricultural research offices that collect expenditure, income, and labor allocation information from households on a monthly basis monitor the household survey. A staff person from the office works with households to clear up inconsistencies in the survey.

In the analysis below, changes in expenditures on health care are used to identify the occurrence and severity of a health shock. While small expenditures generally reflect routine preventative care administered at village or township health offices, large expenditures reflect catastrophic shocks that require visits to more expensive fee-for-service hospitals at the township or county level.

Health Care Costs

Until the mid-1980s the rural health care system was financed largely through transfers from the central government. Since the mid-1980s, however, there has been increasing pressure on local governments to contribute matching funds for the construction of health centers and offices. With respect to the provision of services, a switch from salaried compensation from local government budgets to fee-for-ser-

---

[54] Chen and Ravallion (1996).

vice financing exacerbated the effect of deteriorating mechanisms for risk pooling at the village level and contributed to the growth in household out-of-pocket expenses. Nationally, patient fees represented roughly 14 percent of total expenditures on health care in rural areas in 1980, but by 1992 patient fees accounted for 34 percent of total expenditures on health care.[55] Data from the RCRE household survey also reflect this trend. From table 6–8 we see that in constant 1986 yuan, the share of households spending more than 100 yuan on health expenditures doubled between 1987 and 1997. For the households in this sample, an expenditure of 100 yuan is roughly 8 percent of total household expenditures for the year, making this a sizable health shock.

As in other countries around the world, the data from this survey indicate that most expenditures on health care are devoted to treating the catastrophic illnesses faced by a small proportion of the population. The Lorenz curve plots the cumulative share of the population versus the cumulative share of health expenditures (figure 6–1). It is evident from figure 6–1 that roughly 20 percent of the population in this sample accounts for 75 percent of the expenditures on health care. Lorraine West has noted that in 1993 the household portion of payment for major surgery was roughly 150 yuan, implying that expenditures of over 100 yuan signify major shock.[56]

While households might be able to cover small health shocks relatively easily, catastrophic shocks have become a more serious problem with the introduction of fee-for-service payment schemes in China's rural hospitals. To cover fees for serious illnesses, households must deplete savings, if they exist, or rely on informal loans from family members. Financing medical care to cover the serious illness of a family member can have significant long-term consequences for households in rural China. As the health policy community in Beijing strives to develop a new rural insurance system, the clear task it faces is to find a way to insure against the economic impact of catastrophic shocks.

Consumption Smoothing and the Welfare Loss from Lack of Insurance

In the case of Indonesia the illness shocks were observed directly. In China only medical care expenditures are observed. Moreover, since income is not observed, the impact of illness on income cannot be estimated and equation 6-5 cannot be

---

[55] West (1997).
[56] West (1997).

Table 6–8. Increase in Household Expenditures on Health Care, 1987–97, China

Values in 1986 RMB yuan

Expenditure	1987	1989	1991	1993	1995	1997
Average household consumption of nondurable goods	1,360	1,280	1,221	1,221	1,433	1,342
Average household health care expenditure	31	32	37	45	54	60
Share of household health expenditures over 100 RMB yuan	0.09	0.11	0.11	0.14	0.17	0.18

Note: Nondurable goods include food, clothing, fuel, and services.
Source: RCRE Rural Household Survey.

directly estimated. Instead, (6–5) must be estimated by replacing the change in income with the change in medical care expenditures. The coefficient times baseline consumption, then, is interpreted as how much consumption falls for each yuan of medical care spending. However, the falls in consumption might be due either to medical care spending or to associated reductions in income from lost work due to illness. In the case of China the two cannot be separated.

The change in medical care expenditures is used in place of the change in income in (6–5) to avoid the measurement error problem. However, there could be feedback from the change in consumption to the change in medical care spending. Families with higher income spend more on medical care. The first-order effect is solved by using a difference model that controls for heterogeneity in permanent income. Then by including village-time fixed effects, community-level changes in permanent income are controlled for, as are changes in human capital at the household level. Therefore, the remaining sources of concern include changes in household-level idiosyncratic shocks to permanent income. While feedback from changes in consumption to medical care expenditures cannot be completely ruled out, the degree to which it is likely to affect the results is limited. Moreover, feedback from consumption to medical care expenditures should be positive, while the effect of medical expenditures on consumption should be negative. Therefore, to the extent there is feedback, it biases the coefficient toward zero. This suggests that results are biased toward finding insurance. Hence, the estimates of the welfare loss from not being able to insure the economic costs of illness are lower bound estimates.

Table 6–9 reports the results for two specifications of equation 6-5. The first specifies the changes in medical care expenditures linearly, and the second specifies

FIGURE 6–1

Lorenz Curve of Health Care Expenditures

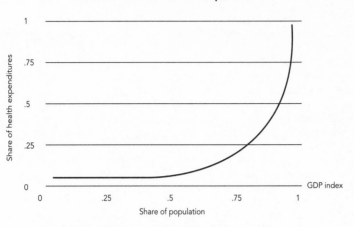

Source: RCRE Household Surveys, 1987-97. Ministry of Agriculture, Beijing

them as piecewise linear splines with knots at 50 and 250. The splines allow nonlinear responses to the health shock. This specification tests the hypothesis that households are able to smooth small shocks, but less able to smooth big shocks.[57] The results overwhelmingly indicate that households are not able to fully insure medical care expenditures. In the linear specification, the coefficient on medical care expenditures indicates that 94 percent of medical care expenditures come out of household consumption, or that households can smooth only about 6 percent of medical care costs. The spline specification, however, indicates that households are fully able to smooth small health shocks under 50 yuan, but not able to smooth larger shocks above 50 yuan. In fact, consumption falls by 1.06 yuan for each yuan of medical spending for spending levels between 50 and 249 yuan, and consumption falls by 1.11 yuan for each yuan of medical spending for levels above 250 yuan. The latter results could be interpreted as households not being able to insure all medical care costs above 50 yuan or that there are other costs associated with large expenditures such as lost income, transportation, and food costs associated with inpatient stays in hospitals.

---

[57] Note that about 27.9 percent of the households have no medical care expenditures in a given year, 53.3 percent have expenditures of less than 50 yuan, 16.3 percent have expenditures between 50 and 250 yuan, and 2.5 percent have shocks greater than 250 yuan.

Table 6–9. Smoothing the Consumption Effects of Shocks to Nondurable Consumption in Rural China

Item	Model		Mean [standard deviation]
	1	2	
Lag household prime laborers	−0.031	−0.031	2.522
	(0.001)	(0.001)	[1.138]
Lag household dependents	−0.005	−0.005	1.852
	(0.001)	(0.001)	[1.158]
Lag male share of prime laborers	0.026	0.026	0.516
	(0.008)	(0.008)	[0.216]
Lag land per capita	0.002	0.002	1.434
	(0.003)	(0.003)	[1.012]
Lag share of laborers with elementary education	0.006	0.007	0.352
	(0.006)	(0.006)	[0.329]
Lag share of laborers with lower middle school education	0.015	0.015	0.323
	(0.007)	(0.007)	[0.325]
Lag share of laborers with upper middle school education	0.010	0.010	0.071
	(0.010)	(0.009)	[0.188]
Lag share of laborers with special skill	0.007	0.007	0.102
	(0.008)	(0.008)	[0.205]
Change in health expenditures	−0.00071		36.530
	(0.00002)		[80.110]
Small changes in health expenditures (less than 50 yuan RMB)		0.00009	
		(0.00008)	
Medium changes in health expenditures (50 to 249 yuan RMB)		−0.00080	
		0.00005	
Large changes in health expenditures (greater than 250 yuan RMB)		−0.00092	
		(0.00003)	
Number of observations	45,263	45,263	45,263
R^2	0.051	0.053	
Village*year fixed effects, $F(780, 44,473)$	9.567	9.626	

Note: The dependent variable is Δln(nondurable consumption). Average nondurable consumption was 1,321 RMB yuan per household (in 1986 yuan), with a standard deviation of 705 RMB yuan. Standard errors are in parentheses.
Source: Author's calculations.

The willingness to pay is calculated to eliminate the variation in consumption due to medical care expenditure shocks using the methods presented earlier. The results of the spline model are used to estimate γ, and the frequency distribution of medical care expenditures to estimate π_j and L_j. Using the same estimates of risk aversion as in the Indonesian case, it is estimated that households are on average willing to pay 1.87 percent of household consumption. This is approximately six times average medical care spending.

CONCLUSIONS

Using data from Indonesia and China, this chapter finds that while households are able to insure the economic costs of small health shocks, they are not able to insure the costs of major illness. The results indicate that there are large welfare gains from reducing the variation in consumption from the economic costs of major illness. However, households are unable to purchase insurance from the private sector due to market failures. This suggests a role for government to improve welfare through social insurance for income loss due to disability and medical care expenditures. The fact that households are able to insure against the costs of small illnesses suggests that employing user fees to finance the expansion of publicly delivered health care services will have little impact on welfare. Moreover, this result implies that first-dollar capped social insurance benefit structures provide little welfare gain. Indeed, such benefit structures just crowd private informal insurance. Rather, the big welfare gains are from insuring the rare large illnesses.

References

Andrews, G., and others. 1986. *Aging in the Western Pacific*. Manila, Philippines: World Health Organization.

Asian Development Bank. 1997. *Asian Development Outlook 1996 and 1997*. Manila, Philippines: Asian Development Bank.

Attanasio, Orazio, and Steven Davis. 1996. "Relative Wage Movements and the Distribution of Consumption." *Journal of Political Economy* 104 (December): 1227–62.

Benjamin, Dwayne. 1992. "Household Composition, Labor Markets, and Labor Demand: Testing for Separation on Agricultural Household Models." *Econometrica* 60 (March): 287–322.

Besley, Timothy, and Miguel Gouveia. 1994. "Alternative Systems of Health Care Provision." *Economic Policy* (October): 201–58.

Bound, J. 1991. "Self-Reported versus Objective Measures of Health in Retirement Models." *Journal of Human Resources* 26: 106–38.

Bound, J., M. Schoenbaum, and T. Waidman. 1995. "Race and Education Differences in Disability Status and Labor Force Participation." *Journal of Human Resources* 30: S227–S267.

Chen, Shaohua, and Martin Ravallion. 1996. "Data in Transition: Assessing Rural Living Standards in Southern China." *China Economic Review* 7 (Spring).

Cochrane, John. 1991. "A Simple Test of Consumption Insurance." *Journal of Political Economy* 99 (October): 957–76.

Cornia, G., R. Jolly, and F. Stewart. 1987. *Adjustment with a Human Face*. Oxford: Clarendon Press.

Deaton, Angus. 1992a. "Saving and Income Smoothing in Côte d'Ivoire." *Journal of African Economics* 1: 1–24.

———. 1992b. *Understanding Consumption*. Oxford: Clarendon Press.

———. 1994. *The Analysis of Household Surveys: Microeconometric Analysis for Development Policy*. Monograph. World Bank, Washington, D.C.

Dow, William, and Paul Gertler. 1997. "Private Health Insurance and Public Expenditures in Indonesia." RAND, Santa Monica, CA. Unpublished.

Dow, William, and others. 1996. "Health Care Prices, Health and Labor Outcomes: Experimental Evidence." RAND, Santa Monica, CA. Unpublished.

Dynarski, Susan, and Jonathan Gruber. 1997. "Can Families Smooth Variable Earnings?" *Brookings Papers on Economic Activity* 1:1997, 229–304.

Engen, Eric. 1993. "A Stochastic Life-Cycle Model with Mortality Risk: Estimation with Panel Data." UCLA, Los Angeles, CA. Unpublished.

Gertler, Paul. 1998. "On the Road to Social Health Insurance." *World Development* 26 (4): 717–32.

Gertler, Paul, and Jonathan Gruber. 1997. *Insuring Consumption against Illness*. Working Paper. National Bureau of Economic Research, Cambridge, MA.

Gertler, Paul, and Jack Molyneaux. 1996. "The Effect of Medical Care Prices on Utilization and Health Outcomes: Experimental Results." RAND, Santa Monica, CA. Unpublished.

Gertler, Paul, and Orville Solon. 1998. "Who Benefits from Social Insurance in Developing Countries?" Haas School of Business, UC-Berkeley, Berkeley, CA. Unpublished.

Gertler, Paul, and Sturm. 1997. "Private Health Insurance and Public Expenditures." *Journal of Economics* 77 (2): 237–57.

Gertler, P., and J. Zeitlin. 1996. "The Returns to Childhood Investments in Terms of Health Later in Life." RAND, Santa Monica, CA. Unpublished.

Gruber, Jonathan. 1996. *Cash Welfare as a Consumption Smoothing Mechanism for Single Mothers*. Working Paper no. 5738. National Bureau of Economic Research, Cambridge, MA.

———. 1997. "The Consumption Smoothing Benefits of Unemployment Insurance." *American Economic Review* 82 (March): 182–205.

Guralnik, J., and others. 1989. "Physical Performance Measures in Aging Research." *Journal of Gerontology* 44 (September): 141–46.

Hayashi, Fumio, Joseph Altonji, and Laurence Kotlikoff. 1996. "Risk Sharing between and within Families." *Econometrica* 64 (March): 261–94.

Jiménez, E. 1987. *Pricing Policy in the Social Sectors: Cost Recovery for Education and Health in Developing Countries*. Baltimore, MD: Johns Hopkins University Press.

———. 1996. "Human and Physical Infrastructure." In J. Behrman and T. N. Srinavasan, eds., *Handbook of Development Economics*. Amsterdam, Netherlands: North Holland.

Ju, A., and G. Jones. 1989. *Aging in ASEAN and Its Socio-economic Consequences*. Singapore: Institute of Southeast Asian Studies.

Kington, R., and J. Smith. 1996. "Socio-Economic Correlates of Adult Health." *Demography* 33 (1): 25–36.

Kochar, Anjini. 1995. "Explaining Household Vulnerability to Idiosyncratic Income Shocks." *American Economic Review* 85 (May): 159–64.

Mace, Barbara. 1991. "Full Insurance in the Presence of Aggregate Uncertainty." *Journal of Political Economy* 99 (October): 928–56.

Ministry of Public Health (MPH). 1994. *Chinese Health Statistical Digest, 1993.*

Morduch, Jonathan. 1990. "Risk, Production, and Saving: Theory and Evidence from Indian Households." Harvard University, Cambridge, MA. Unpublished.

———. 1995. "Income Smoothing and Consumption Smoothing." *Journal of Economic Perspectives* 9 (Summer): 103–14.

———. 1999. "Between Market and State: Can Informal Insurance Patch the Safety Net?" *World Bank Research Observer* 16 (2): 122–34.

Nelson, Julie. 1994. "On Testing for Full Insurance Using Consumer Expenditure Survey Data." *Journal of Political Economy* 102 (April): 384–94.

Paxson, Christina. 1992. "Using Weather Variability to Estimate the Response of Savings to Transitory Income in Thailand." *American Economic Review* 82 (March): 15–33.

Pitt, M., and M. Rosenzweig. 1986. "Agricultural Prices, Food Consumption, and the Health and Productivity of Farmers." In I. Sing, L. Squire, and J. Strauss, eds., *Agricultural Household Models: Extensions and Applications*. Baltimore, MD: Johns Hopkins University Press.

Ready, Sanjy. 1996. "A Critical Review of User Charges for Basic Services." *Policy Review* 136.

Rothschild, Michael, and Joseph E. Stiglitz. 1976. "Equilibrium in Competitive Insurance Markets: An Essay on the Economics of Imperfect Information." *Quarterly Journal of Economics* 90 (November): 629–50.

Schultz, T. P., and A. Tansel. 1997. "Wage and Labor Supply Effects of Illness in Côte d'Ivoire and Ghana: Instrumental Variable Estimates for Days Disabled." *Journal of Development Economics* 53 (August): 251–86.

Sindelar, J., and D. Thomas. 1991. *Measurement of Child Health: Maternal Response Bias*. Discussion Paper no. 663. Economic Growth Center, Yale University, New Haven, CT.

State Statistical Bureau (SSB). 1994. *Zhongguo Tongji Nianjian 1994* (A statistical survey of China). Beijing, China: Zhongguo Tongji Chubanshe.

Stern, S. 1989. "Measuring the Effect of Disability on Labor Force Participation." *Journal of Human Resources* 24 (Summer): 361–95.

Stewert, A., and others. 1990. *Measurement of Adult Health Status: Physical Health in Terms of Functional Status.* Cambridge, MA: Harvard University Press.

Strauss, John, and Duncan Thomas. 1996. "Human Resources: Empirical Modeling of Household and Family Decisions." In J. Behrman and T. N. Srinavasan, eds., *Handbook of Development Economics.* Amsterdam, Netherlands: North Holland.

Strauss, J., and others. 1993. "Gender and Life-Cycle Differentials in the Patterns and Determinants of Adult Health." *Journal of Human Resources* 28 (Fall): 791–837.

Townsend, Robert. 1994. "Risk and Insurance in Village India." *Econometrica* 62 (May): 539–91.

———. 1995. "Consumption Insurance: An Evaluation of Risk-Bearing Systems in Low-Income Economies." *Journal of Economic Perspectives* 9 (Summer): 83–102.

Wallace, R., and A. Herzog. 1995. "An Overview of Health Status Measures in the Health and Retirement Survey." *Journal of Human Resources* 30 (Winter): S84–S107.

Ware, J., A. Davies-Avery, and R. Brook. 1980. *Conceptualization and Measurement of Health Status for Adults in the Health Insurance Study: Vol. IV, Analysis of Relationships among Health Status Measures.* R-1987/6-HEW. RAND, Santa Monica, CA.

Wei, Ying. 1995. "An Introduction to Health Financing Patterns in China." National Health Economics Institute (Beijing). Paper presented at a health care conference in Beijing, (May).

West, Lorraine. 1997. "Provision of Public Services in the PRC." In Christine P. W. Wong, ed., *Financing Local Government in the People's Republic of China.* Asian Development Bank and Oxford University Press.

World Bank. 1984. *China: The Health Sector.* A World Bank Country Study. World Bank, Washington, D.C.

———. 1987. *Financing Health Services in Developing Countries.* World Bank Policy Study. World Bank, Washington, D.C.

———. 1993. *World Development Report: Investing in Health.* Oxford: Oxford University Press.

———. 1995a. *Averting the Old Age Crisis.* Oxford: Oxford University Press.

———. 1995b. *Indonesia: Public Expenditure, Prices and the Poor.* Washington, D.C.: World Bank.

———. 1996. *China: Issues and Options in Health Financing.* Washington, D.C.: World Bank.

Zeldes, Stephen P. 1989. "Consumption and Liquidity Constraints: An Empirical Investigation." *Journal of Political Economy* 97 (April): 305–46.

CHAPTER SEVEN

Coverage under Old Age Security Programs and Protection for the Uninsured: What Are the Issues?

Estelle James

The majority of workers and old people in developing countries are uninsured by formal social security programs. Coverage ranges from less than 10 percent in Sub-Saharan Africa and South Asia and less than 30 percent in most of East Asia to 50–60 percent in the middle-income countries of South America, 70–80 percent in the Eastern European transition economies, and 90–100 percent in the small group of countries in the Organization for Economic Cooperation and Development (OECD).[1]

Economic development is the major determinant of coverage rates, but policies chosen by governments also matter. The structure of industry, the limited taxing capacity of governments, and the high discount rate and liquidity constraints faced by low earners limit the feasible scope of contributory schemes in developing countries. We argue that they also limit the desirability of contributory schemes for low-income workers in these countries. If the contribution rate is borne by workers, it may reduce their take-home pay at a point in the life cycle when they need more income rather than less; and if borne by employers, it may reduce the number of jobs in the economy. A low contribution rate and a high rate of return can reduce these disincentives and distortions that inhibit optimal coverage.

The uninsured fall into two main groups: workers who have labor market jobs that are not covered by contributory programs (for example, the self-employed, the informal sector), either because they cannot find covered jobs or because they (or their employers) prefer to operate in the informal sector where

---

[1] World Bank (1994).

taxes and regulations are smaller; and women who have worked in the household rather than the labor market for most of their lives, expecting to be supported by the family system, which may fail them in old age. The second group can be protected by requiring the purchase of survivors' insurance and joint annuities by workers in the contributory scheme—thereby institutionalizing the informal family system into the formal social security system. In a multipillar scheme, this cost would be borne by the married workers directly involved, rather than being passed on to others. For the first group of uninsured, social assistance programs targeted toward the lowest earners outside of the formal system seem to be essential—creating the need to design such programs efficiently and take their costs into account in planning the reform. The challenge is how to maximize the proportion of money that reaches the targeted groups while minimizing leakage and moral hazard problems.

This chapter discusses how contributory social security systems imply a class of uninsured; argues that a high coverage level under mandatory contributory schemes is neither necessary nor desirable for low-income countries; examines voluntary programs and universal benefits as alternatives to mandatory contributory schemes; suggests institutionalizing the implicit family contract into formal pension systems to protect women who have worked in the home rather than the formal labor market—requiring spouses to purchase survivors' insurance and joint annuities; and analyzes the use of social assistance for the lowest-income groups who are left out of the formal system. Salient issues include the trade-off between social assistance and human capital creation, how to provide social assistance without diminishing the incentive to be in the contributory scheme (the moral hazard problem), how to target benefits while keeping transactions costs and other leakages low, and how much priority to give to social assistance to the old versus young families with children.

HOW SOCIAL SECURITY CREATES A CLASS OF UNINSURED

Most countries, including almost all developing countries, finance old age security through earmarked taxes, called "contributions," rather than through general revenues. This emphasis on contributory systems with benefits contingent on contributions is used to increase the public's willingness to pay and to decrease distortionary, evasionary techniques. But it has the side effect of creating a class of uninsured or partially insured individuals who have contributed little or nothing in their working years and may be left in poverty in old age.

Why Are Most Social Security Schemes Financed by Earmarked Payroll Taxes, or "Contributions"?

Most mandatory pension schemes, including almost all those in developing countries, are financed by payments that people make specifically for this purpose, rather than through general revenues. The payments are mandatory and in this sense they are taxes, but they are earmarked for a specific service and for this reason are usually called "contributions." The programs are for those who make contributions rather than universal, and the benefits they pay depend on the level of contributions.

The basic idea is that when people perceive that they are getting a specific service in return for their payments, they are more willing to pay and less anxious to evade. Both political opposition and economic distortions are likely to be smaller for earmarked taxes than for general taxes. In this sense, the government's spending frontier is extended when earmarked taxes linked to size of benefits are used. For this reason, such arrangements are common for the financing of quasi-public services such as education, medical care, and old age insurance, where exclusion and differentiation in type of service is feasible. People who do not contribute do not get access to these services.

The earmarked tax or contribution for social security is usually based on wages, subject to a ceiling and occasionally a floor. The returns to capital are not taxed to finance these programs, nor is property taxed. Benefits also depend on wages—sometimes lifetime wages and sometimes final year wages. The theory, again, is that this indirectly links benefits to contributions, thereby increasing peoples' willingness to pay the price.

But why use a payroll tax base? Why not base contributions on total income or on some flat amount? One rationale for using a payroll base is that pensions in old age are designed to replace the wages that people receive when they are able to work, hence the benefits should be tied to wages. A close benefit-contribution linkage then requires that contributions also be based on wages. If benefits depended on wages but were financed by general revenues, capital as well as labor would be taxed, thereby making the programs more redistributive. Holders of capital would oppose this financing method, giving us a second, political economy, reason for its infrequent use. A third, more pragmatic, reason for payroll tax finance is that such deductions are the easiest way administratively to reach large segments of the population, who do not file income tax returns in many countries. A sales or value-added tax would also be administratively feasible, but would make it more difficult to keep track of the taxes paid by each individual, and hence to connect benefits and contributions. Payroll taxes, in contrast, can be collected from employers while records are maintained on each worker—administratively an easier job.

To some extent this theory is violated by reality. On the one hand, some groups have been able to extract benefits that far exceed their contributions, due to easy eligibility, lax disability requirements, and early retirement. These behaviors ultimately made the system unsustainable in Latin America and led to a wave of multipillar reforms that tied benefits more closely to earmarked contributions.

On the other hand, the political economy of some countries (for example, Australia, Denmark, Switzerland) has allowed them to use general revenue finance or to forego a ceiling on taxable wages, thereby delinking benefits from contributions and making the system more redistributive from rich to poor. But in recent years, fiscal pressures have caused these arrangements to be downsized and supplemented by contributory pillars. Most mandatory systems now include components that require wage-based taxes and return benefits that depend in some way on wages or contributions.

The Consequence: Groups without Formal Labor Market Experience Are Not Covered

While possibly ameliorating the political and economic limits to taxation and government spending, contributory programs based on earmarked payroll taxes create a new problem—a distinction between covered and noncovered groups that depends on labor market experience. The uncovered group consists of two subsets:

- Those who engage in home work, instead of market work (primarily women).
- Those who engage in market work but whose jobs are not covered by contributory schemes (for example, the self-employed and agricultural workers), either because they cannot find covered jobs or because they (or their employers) choose to operate in the informal sector in order to avoid taxes and regulations.

Women presumably expect their monetary needs to be met through the family system, so they work in the household, without earning wages or pension rights. Their problem is that this expectation in their youth may not be realized when they grow old. Workers who engage in market work that is not covered earn wages to satisfy their monetary needs when young but fail to accumulate pension rights that

FIGURE 7-1

Relationship between Public Pension Coverage and Income per Capita

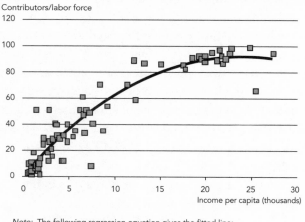

Note: The following regression equation gives the fitted line:
$y = -0.17X^2 + 7.79x - 0.34$
$R^2 = 0.89$
Source: Calculations by R. Palacios and M. Pallares, Washington, D.C., World Bank.

will provide an income when they grow old. Sometimes they contribute just enough to qualify for benefits, albeit modest, and evade thereafter, thereby making the system fiscally unsustainable even though their pension remains modest.

In all these cases, the family system has been the traditional means of old age support, but if this system breaks down, these groups are in trouble, and if they are living at the edge of poverty, their problem becomes a social problem. Indeed, a mandatory old age system developed in part to gather the resources to avoid this social problem. What can be done about these groups who are outside the formal old age systems?

IS INCREASED COVERAGE BY CONTRIBUTORY SCHEMES THE SOLUTION?

Should governments seek to increase coverage in the contributory scheme? While this is possible within limits, I argue that vastly increased coverage is neither feasible nor desirable in low-income countries.

Figure 7-1 demonstrates the close relationship between per capita income and coverage of workers under formal social security programs. Per capita income alone explains 89 percent of the variance in coverage. We observe that in low-income countries such as India and Sri Lanka, coverage of the adult population is as low as 10 percent, while in high-income countries it is close to 100 percent. We also observe some (small) variance in coverage for any given level of income. This suggests that, while coverage can be influenced to a minor degree by country policies, structural factors tied to stage of development play the major role in determining coverage by contributory programs. These structural factors come from two sources—the low tax-collecting capacities of governments at early stages of development combined with the prevalence of small enterprises and self-employment, which make it infeasible to extend coverage; and the fact that it may not be in the best interest of low-income workers to participate in contributory old age schemes, which makes coverage undesirable as well. It is very difficult to implement a mandatory program unless most workers perceive it as in their best interest.

The Difficulties in Collecting from Small Enterprises and the Self-Employed

The rationale for mandatory old age programs is that people may be myopic, may not make provisions themselves on a voluntary basis, and may hope to fall back on society's largesse should the need arise. The government mandate is designed to overcome these problems of myopia and moral hazard. But it leaves the government with a large enforcement problem, as workers try to evade the mandatory payments that they would not have made on a voluntary basis. Governments in developing countries often lack the necessary enforcement capabilities. The structure of the economy makes it difficult for them to compel compliance. Thus they face a trade-off between maximizing nominal coverage and minimizing evasion. After some point the increase in evasion may exceed the increase in nominal coverage, so effective coverage may decline if the government tries to expand the system beyond its capacities—evasion is a contagious social disease.

It is relatively easy to collect from large companies but more difficult to collect from small enterprises or the self-employed or subsistence agriculture or transient workers. Small enterprises have short life spans; they may come and go before they are registered and taxed. The self-employed, who must pay both the worker's and employer's share, have a double incentive to evade and find it easy to underreport their earnings. Keeping track of transient workers who work irregularly for different employers is a daunting task. Self-employment, small enterprises, subsistence production, and transient workers dominate in agriculture, the mainstay of most developing economies.

These problems exist in industrial countries as well, but they are multiplied in developing countries, where the "difficult" groups are disproportionately large and the government's capacity is weak. Many developing countries do not even try to cover these groups, and those that try often fail. For example, the self-employed, who constitute about a third of the labor force, are not covered in Chile.[2] They are covered in Argentina, which is considering excluding them because of high evasion. In many Asian countries employers with fewer than 10 or 20 workers are not covered. In most African countries only employees of the government and large state or multinational companies are covered. It may be wise for developing countries to concentrate their limited enforcement capacities in sectors where they are most likely to succeed—but this leaves the majority of workers uninsured.

Rational Reasons for Nonparticipation among the Poor

Even if increased effective coverage were feasible, it might not be desirable. The costs of coverage must be paid either by workers or employers, depending on the elasticity of labor supply and demand. Many workers may be better off outside the formal retirement old age security system, with higher take-home pay, which would be reduced by social security contributions. And the economy may be better off with more jobs, coming from lower labor costs, if employers operate outside the social security system. Policymakers thus face a trade-off between higher coverage and higher take-home pay for workers, hence greater current consumption; and between higher coverage and lower labor costs for employers, hence greater employment. While this trade-off may be decreased if a low target replacement rate and required contribution rate are chosen, some trade-off always remains.

Low-income workers may have perfectly rational utility-maximizing reasons for preferring to stay out of the old age system and for evading contributions if they are nominally covered. Often they are living close to the poverty level. They have relatively short expected lifetimes, so it may make more sense for them to use their meager incomes to survive at present rather than saving for the distant future, when they may not be alive. This effect is accentuated if, at the annuity stage, they are merged with high-income workers who have greater expected longevity, thereby depressing benefits and returns for the poor. This practice is common in mandatory social security systems, making it rational for low-income workers to evade such systems.

---

[2] World Bank (1994); Queisser (1998).

Moreover, even when they save, the best rate of return for them may come from investing in land, homes, tools, or the education of their children, who will return the loan by supporting them in the future. In most low- and middle-income countries, older people live in multigenerational households and their consumption level therefore depends on the earnings of their children more than on their own pensions. Investing in the human capital of their children may be the best old age security program for them. Investing in a family business may be the next best alternative. Lacking access to well-functioning credit markets and facing a high risk premium, farmers, the self-employed, and low-income groups generally are forced to pay exceedingly high borrowing rates or to use personal savings to finance these investments. They may, understandably, be reluctant to lock up their modest savings in a long-term retirement program that will not be available to meet shorter-term investment, educational, health, or other emergency needs.

Consistent with this hypothesis, a study of contribution patterns in Peru shows that the self-employed, farmers, and low-income workers are less likely to contribute regularly.[3] Empirical evidence from saving programs targeted to the poor in Mexico and Indonesia shows that these groups will indeed save, but they place a high value on liquidity and therefore choose short- rather than long-term financial instruments. Moreover, such savings are invariably small, much less than needed for old age security.[4] Experiments with informal systems show that workers are willing to save small amounts to meet short-term contingencies, in contrast to old age security arrangements that require large long-term illiquid payments.[5] Extending coverage by requiring low-income informal sector workers to contribute to old age security programs would not be in the best interests of these workers in such circumstances, even if the government had the capacity to enforce the mandate.

Usually employers are responsible for part of the contribution, giving them an incentive to operate out of the system if they see this as a way to reduce labor cost. While the market may eventually require a compensating wage increase for employers who are outside the formal old age system, employers may not perceive this in the short run, or even in the long run if they can attract workers who do not place a high value on social security benefits. If employers can keep their labor costs low by staying out of the system, this increases their international competitiveness and consequently the level of employment—especially important in coun-

[3] Queisser (1998).
[4] Aportela (1999).
[5] Van Ginneken (1999).

tries with high levels of unemployment or underemployment. Governments must weigh carefully the questions of who will bear the payroll tax if effective coverage is extended and how high the tax can be to avoid negative consequences on employment.

Will a Closer Link between Benefits and Contributions Encourage Participation?

Multipillar social security reforms in recent years have featured a strengthening of the benefit-contribution link. A second, funded defined-contribution pillar has been added, in which benefits ultimately depend exclusively on contributions plus investment income. In addition, these schemes usually include a public pillar that is redistributive and applies only to those who have contributed to the second pillar; it provides a safety net to the low earners among the contributors. In a sense, this can be regarded as an example of the risk category differentiation mentioned above. The hope is that this will increase the incentive of low-earning workers and their employers to participate in the formal sector and thereby reduce the number of uninsured.

These reforms should enable revenues to cover obligations and hence make the system more sustainable for those who do participate. Since fiscal sustainability is a precondition for responsible coverage expansion, these reforms may set the stage for actions by the government to extend coverage. Moreover, they may encourage compliance among long-term workers and their employers and enhance the welfare effects of participation, owing to the smaller tax element and the hope of a higher rate of return.

However, compliance may be discouraged among those who no longer receive windfall gains—some of whom were rich and some poor. And benefits are reduced substantially for those who contribute for only part of their working lives, and hence may not be eligible for the redistributive first pillar. Thus, pension coverage among the old poor may actually decrease.

For example, Chile provides a minimum pension guarantee of 25 percent of the average wage to workers who have contributed for at least 20 years to their individual accounts in the second pillar, and many other countries have followed this example. Accumulations in the second pillar are supplemented by the government to bring the annual benefit to this level. This guarantee will protect low-income covered workers, especially those who have contributed for only 20 years. For this reason, many low-income workers may stay in the system for 20 years. But workers who do not anticipate 20 years of participation will have a continued incentive to stay out of the system. A guarantee that increased with years of contributions might have been more equitable and effective at constraining evasion.

The Brazilian social security system has long included an "age" pension which, at a specified age (65 and 60 for urban men and women, 60 and 55 for rural men and women, respectively), pays 70 percent of the wage base to workers who have contributed for at least five years. The typical pension was one times the minimum salary, which is about 30 percent of the average wage. The Brazilian system also included a much more generous pension based on length of service, which required 30 years of covered employment and paid five to six times the minimum salary (150 percent of the average wage) to the average beneficiary. The "length of service" pension went mainly to urban men who worked in the formal labor force for most of their lives and earned relatively high salaries. The age pension went mainly to women, especially low-income rural women. For example, in 1997 out of 5.2 million recipients of the age pension, 75 percent were rural dwellers and 62 percent were women, while 83 percent of the 2.9 million recipients of the length of service pensions were urban men.[6]

Because of its low employment requirement, the age pension was a near-universal benefit, targeted toward rural areas and women. However (as a consequence of this and other features), Brazil faces severe fiscal and evasion problems as workers were increasingly tempted to escape to the informal sector, contribute for only five years, and collect the age pension. As part of the reform process that began in the mid-1990s and is ongoing today, the contribution requirement for the age pension will gradually increase to 15 years.[7] This change will likely improve urban compliance and sustainability, but rural women and others who do not have a chance to participate in the formal labor market for 15 years may become uninsured.

As another example, Uruguay previously had an age pension that required 10 years of covered employment, but the required contributory period was raised to 15 years in Uruguay's recent pension reform.[8] Undoubtedly, this will have the same beneficial effects on fiscal sustainability, but the fate of the uninsured is unclear.

---

[6] Instituto Nacional do Seguro Social (1998).
[7] World Bank (1998).
[8] Queisser (1998); Law 16.713, chapter II, article 68.

Policy Changes That Might Increase Coverage at the Margin

Figure 7–1 shows that per capita income strongly influences but does not completely determine coverage by formal programs. What kinds of policies might increase coverage, in an enforceable and welfare-enhancing way, at the margin?

Low contribution and target replacement rates. Many developing countries choose a relatively high replacement rate target of 60–70 percent, which requires a high contribution rate for sustainability. A lower target replacement rate and contribution rate would decrease the trade-off with take-home pay and unemployment, thereby encouraging workers and employers to participate. Thailand recently instituted a scheme for private sector workers with a target replacement rate of 20 percent.

Paying a high rate of return on funded plans. One would expect that workers would be more likely to use retirement savings accounts if the rate of return were high and administrative costs low. However, since these funds are committed for the long term, workers would have to trust that high returns would continue for many years; it is not clear that such assurances could be given.

Increasing the credibility of the contributory scheme. The incentive to participate in the system will increase if workers believe it is financially sustainable and will survive to pay the promised benefits in the future when they retire. That is one object of multipillar systems—but it may take many years for their credibility to be established.

Permitting borrowing against retirement funds or lump sum withdrawals upon retirement. This would make retirement funds more liquid and therefore diminish resistance to participation—but these depleted accounts might never be replenished and lump sums might be quickly spent, defeating the original purpose of the old age program.

Offering better terms to low earners in view of their lower life expectancy and higher opportunity cost. This may take the form of lower contributions or higher promised benefits. Such incentives are widely viewed as redistribution. They may alternatively be an implicit recognition of the fact that low earners belong in a different risk category from high earners, because they are likely to live shorter lives; hence if both groups face the same contribution-benefit ratio, perverse redistribution from poor to rich goes on, and it is quite rational for the poor to try to stay out of the system.

Differentiated risk categories have, in effect, been introduced in the multipillar systems of many countries: the Netherlands has a flat benefit formula in the first pillar; Mexico makes a flat contribution to each worker's individual account; Switzerland places a ceiling on first-pillar benefits while having no ceiling on taxable wages; and in Uruguay, low- and middle-income contributors to the new funded pillar receive an extra benefit.[9] In Colombia a "solidarity tax" of 1 percent is imposed on salaries above a specified level and used to finance subsidies to low-income contributors.[10]

These better annual payoffs or lower charges may marginally encourage participation by low earners—although the high discount rate and liquidity demand of this group limit this effect. At the same time, if such measures are viewed as redistribution rather than risk categorization, they may encourage evasion by high earners and may simply not be viable for political economy reasons. Moreover, if the differentiation is not justified on actuarial grounds, it may make the system financially unsustainable. Thus, there are real limits to the ways in which policies can be shaped to make inclusion in a contributory program desirable for large groups of workers in low-income countries.

In sum, until the government's capacity to enforce tax collections increases, the structure of the economy changes to facilitate this, and the earning capacity of the bottom half of the labor force grows—all of which occurs with the process of economic development—it is difficult and not necessarily desirable to extend contributory old age security coverage to the entire population.

VOLUNTARY AND UNIVERSAL SOLUTIONS OUTSIDE THE CONTRIBUTORY SCHEME

Some analysts have urged that voluntary contributions should be permitted to extend pension insurance to those who do not have covered jobs. In Japan, men are encouraged to make flat contributions for their wives in exchange for the promise of a flat benefit. In China, workers in township and village enterprises are subject to social pressure to contribute to their individual accounts on a "voluntary" basis. Making coverage voluntary avoids the evasion and unemployment problems discussed above. In several countries community organizations such as nongovernmental organizations (NGOs) have tried to set up small-scale self-help schemes for informal sector workers.[11]

---

[9] Queisser (1998).
[10] Valdes-Prieto (1998).
[11] Van Ginneken (1999).

Are Voluntary Contributions the Answer to the Coverage Problem?

While the availability of voluntary retirement savings instruments is probably utility improving, I believe we should not expect them to accomplish very much. After
all, a basic reason for the existence of mandatory programs is that many people,
especially low-income people, will not save voluntarily for their retirement, and
the basic reason for limited coverage is that, even when the program is mandatory,
many workers and employers will try to avoid contributing because they believe
that participation does not make them better off. In addition, the transactions costs
of collecting many small voluntary contributions might be relatively high.
Voluntarism and self-help schemes are more likely to succeed in programs when
the costs are small and the benefits immediate (as for microfinance or primary health
care). It is likely to be only a small part of the solution to a large long-term old age
security problem.

In addition, I would offer at least three caveats to this approach. First, if annuities are promised in the voluntary program, they should be actuarially fair, except
for deliberate redistribution that is planned and funded from the start; otherwise,
the voluntary program could explode into a large, unfunded, unexpected obligation. Second, in an individual account saving plan, workers should be given accurate information about the real rate of return they will receive and the replacement
rate it will provide. In China, where some new enterprises have begun to cover
workers on a "voluntary" basis (augmented by social pressure to pay), workers
have been led to expect a high nominal rate of return based on the assumption of a
high rate of inflation. Workers may not realize that this nominal rate will fall if
inflation falls, so its real value is minuscule. Third, voluntary contributions are likely
to be small, at best. In China, the negative real rate of return combined with the
small size of the voluntary contributions will not provide much security in old age.

Will Universal Benefits Solve the Problem of the Uninsured?

Some countries do not have a problem of "uninsured old" because they have universal flat (uniform) or very broad means-tested old age security benefits. These
include many OECD countries, such as the Netherlands, Denmark, Norway, Canada,
New Zealand, and Australia. In these countries, employment and contributions
are not required for inclusion. Instead, the old age benefit is typically financed out
of general revenues, and all residents are eligible to receive it once they reach the
specified age. When these countries adopt a multipillar system, this universal ben-

efit in effect becomes their first pillar. This approach solves the problem of coverage since there are no uninsured, and it eliminates poverty in old age so long as the benefit is above the poverty line.

However, it poses several other problems, chief among them being fiscal problems. Universal flat old age benefits are costly and will become more costly as populations age. A contributory program with earmarked taxes and with more narrowly targeted redistributions would cost less. To finance these large expenditures with aging populations requires either a large increase in tax rates, which may be distortionary, or a cut in other important social programs. This approach also poses political economy problems, stemming from the need to reach a collective agreement on the level of the uniform benefit and from the redistribution inherent in such programs.

Are universal uniform general-revenue-financed old age benefits a good option for developing countries? Recently Bolivia established such a first pillar in the form of the "bonosol," a universal benefit financed from the proceeds of a "collective capitalization fund" that contains the government's shares of state enterprises in the process of being privatized. The benefit initially was slated to be 11 percent of the average wage, 50–85 percent of the income of poor workers.[12] However, it was quickly cut, and it is even less clear what will happen when the capitalization fund is exhausted. Probably for most developing countries, a universal flat old age benefit is a luxury they cannot afford, nor is it the best use for their limited public resources.

The great income inequality in developing countries also makes a universal uniform benefit implausible, because it would be hard to reach a collective decision on its size and method of financing. When income is unequal, a uniform benefit that is reasonable from the point of a poor worker would be negligible for a rich worker, who would therefore be uninterested in supporting it. But a benefit that is high enough for the rich worker would exceed the wage level of a poor worker and would be very expensive for the economy as a whole. Relatedly, when incomes are very unequal, typically only a minority of people pay general taxes, and these people would oppose financing a universal benefit—making it infeasible from a political economy point of view. Bolivia, where incomes are very unequal, tried to avoid these problems by using proceeds associated with a privatization program, but it is not clear that the bonosol will last. Note that the OECD countries with universal benefits all have a high degree of income equality.

---

[12] Queisser (1998); von Gersdorff (1997).

HOW TO PREVENT POVERTY AMONG OLDER WOMEN: FORMALIZING THE INFORMAL FAMILY SYSTEM

What, then, will work? This chapter proposes two solutions—one aimed at women who are married to covered men and the other aimed at members of both genders who did not have covered jobs when young and are close to the poverty line when old.

The majority of old people are women, and this is even truer of the very old. Among the old that are poor and uninsured, women are disproportionately represented. They often lack the labor force participation that would entitle them to contributory benefits, and even if covered, they are usually only "partially insured" because their levels of education, wages, and years of service are low. They are less likely than men to have inherited property, and in some cultures, assets acquired by women are taken over and owned by men. Their greater longevity means that they are dominant among the very old, who are most likely to be poor, having used up whatever savings they previously accumulated.

The absence of labor force participation and asset ownership among women was part of a traditional family system in which husbands participated in the formal markets and wives worked in the home. Women provided nonmonetized services, especially when young, while their monetary needs were supposed to be covered by their spouses, and eventually their children. But in many cases this system fails, especially in old age, when women are at the receiving end of the lifetime contract. Marriages break up, and the husband is the one with the formal income. Husbands die earlier than wives, with their retirement benefits used up, and often do not leave adequate resources to support the surviving spouse.[13] Children move away or have income problems of their own. In these cases, the monetary support that the family was supposed to provide is not forthcoming, and the low personal income of women becomes a social problem.

Social security systems could be designed to enable women to enforce the implicit family contract that was agreed to earlier in life. Eventually women are likely to participate more broadly in the labor market and to be covered on their own, but in the meantime public policies can ensure that the family support system they counted on when young continues into old age.

---

[13] For evidence that families do not choose adequate survivors' insurance, even in countries where this is available, see Auerbach and Kotlikoff (1991).

Some traditional defined-benefit social security systems provide dependents' and survivors' benefits to wives of covered workers; the wives are covered by virtue of their husbands' coverage. But this means that society at large, rather than the individual husband, takes responsibility for dependent wives. The benefits to housewives are financed partially by taxes paid and benefits foregone by unmarried men and by wives who participate in the labor market—a high implicit tax that discourages female labor force participation and accentuates the problem. Men who marry much younger women late in life are heavily subsidized, and women who are not married to covered men do not receive any benefit. This system may work well when almost all men and women are married, at socially determined ages, and few females work in the formal labor market. But it raises serious efficiency and equity problems when marital and labor force participation patterns change and become more discretionary.

In the context of these changing individualized patterns and multipillar systems, which attempt to link the individual's benefits with his or her contributions, the following measures might be considered to incorporate the informal family contract into the formal old age security system:

- The required purchase of adequate survivors' benefits by those inside the contributory system and the availability of low cost survivors' benefits to those outside
- The requirement that insured workers contribute toward the personal accounts of their nonworking spouses or that mandatory retirement savings be considered the joint property of both spouses
- Mandatory joint annuitization, with price indexation, so that the money accumulated in workers' accounts is not quickly used up and the lifetimes of both spouses are covered
- The use of unisex mortality tables, so that women do not receive lower annual benefits than men because of their greater longevity (this implies a redistribution from men to women that will be controversial and may be difficult to implement in a competitive annuities market)
- Splitting the accrued benefits and retirement accumulations between the spouses, a provision that becomes especially important in case of divorce
- Increased emphasis on female education and labor market equality to augment the earning power and pensions of women
- Changing inheritance, property, and divorce laws to give women equal rights.

Measures such as these would take care of the needs of the largest group that is not covered—spouses who have not participated in the labor market for much of their lives—and as such would go far toward eliminating poverty among the uninsured old.

SOCIAL ASSISTANCE AND MEANS-TESTING

For individuals who remain outside the formal old age system and are poor, we are driven to the need for means-tested social assistance that is universal and noncontributory. Indeed, most countries have some such social assistance program, aimed at the poorest groups. And these programs have been increasing in some countries to supplement new multipillar systems with a close benefit-contribution link.

In recent years several OECD countries have replaced their single-pillar universal systems with multipillar systems because of the growing fiscal strain. That is, the universal flat benefit, in reduced form, has become the first pillar, while a second mandatory pillar that is contributory, funded, and privately managed has been added. (In these countries, the second pillar generally builds on preexisting plans established by collective bargaining and now extended by government.) The existence of the second, contributory, pillar permits cutbacks in the size of benefits from the first, universal, pillar, but it also creates a new problem of the "partially uninsured." Commonly, this has been addressed by offering larger means-tested benefits for those who are not in or who receive only small benefits from the contributory second pillar.

For example, Denmark recently decided to raise contributions to funded occupational defined-contribution plans (its second pillar) to 9–12 percent of wages, which should eventually provide a replacement rate of 40–45 percent, and to decrease the size of the universal flat benefit (its first pillar) to 25 percent of the average wage. Of course, this means that those with limited employment experience (women, self-employed, farmers) will receive smaller benefits than others in their cohort and less than they would have previously. In this sense, they are only partially insured. To offset this result, the government will offer a means-tested benefit to those without second-pillar pensions. So, it is supplementing the first (public universal) pillar with a second (private contributory) pillar on the one hand, and a means-tested "zero" pillar for the partially insured on the other hand.[14] The United

---

[14] Ploug (1993) and discussions with author, 1998.

Kingdom has decreased the value of its flat basic pension relative to the average wage and increased the roles of both private defined-contribution pensions and public means-tested supplements.[15]

Key issues that must be dealt with in designing a well-functioning social assistance program are: How large should the program be relative to other social programs? How does the availability of noncontributory assistance affect the fiscal sustainability of the contributory program and, conversely, how does the structure of a contributory program affect the demands upon social assistance? How can moral hazard problems be avoided? How is eligibility for assistance determined? Should these criteria be different for the old and the young? And primarily, how can the program be structured to maximize the probability that assistance will reach the targeted groups, with a minimum of leakage to others?

Tradeoff between Social Assistance and Human Capital Creation

In setting up their social assistance programs for the old, governments face a tradeoff with other public programs, such as education and health services for the young, that may help people build human capital and diminish reliance on social assistance in the long run. How much should be spent on social assistance for the old versus job creation for the young and other public goods? In the face of severe budget constraints in developing countries, there is no easy answer and no one right answer for all. But the question must be asked in all cases.

Interaction between Contributory Programs and Social Assistance: Moral Hazard

Social assistance is paid to mitigate hardships on the noninsured old, but it also creates incentives to become noninsured—the moral hazard problem. Low-income workers may fail to participate in the contributory scheme, which may eventually lead to its collapse, if they think that in this way they will qualify for social assistance. Despite this disincentive, society may feel it must offer social assistance to the truly needy. The end result may be both inadequate social assistance and unsustainable social insurance.

Partly in response to this problem, many contributory programs include a redistributive component—for example, the first pillar in multipillar systems pro-

---

[15] Johnson (1998); Whitehouse (1998).

vides a safety net for contributors. This arrangement recognizes that low earners really belong in a different risk category than high earners because of their lower life expectancy. It also encourages compliance by giving them better terms. Access to a safety net within the contributory scheme helps to overcome the moral hazard problem by making participation for low earners more attractive. The impact on evasion and fiscal sustainability depends on the generosity of the social assistance program relative to the redistribution in the contributory program. The latter should be greater than the former to encourage contributions. So society faces a dilemma because of the moral hazard problem: if social assistance benefits are generous, they make the contributory program less sustainable; if they are miserly, they leave the uninsured in poverty, even those who had no opportunity to get a covered job.

This negative impact of social assistance on the contributory program is heightened if it is financed out of the social security budget, as in Brazil and Uruguay prior to their recent reforms, where the social security system was charged for beneficiaries who had only five or 10 years of contributions. While reducing the benefits from contributing, this simultaneously increases the tax burden on contributors, hence their incentive to participate in the contributory program is cut from both directions, and the program ultimately becomes unsustainable. General revenue finance, which has a broader base, is preferable, both on efficiency and equity grounds, for universal means-tested programs.

How to Target Benefits: Keeping Official and Unofficial Transactions Costs Low

The essence of means-tested social assistance is that it is targeted to low-income groups. Depending on data availability and country standards, "means" may be defined in terms of income (commonly), assets (as in Australia), or the presence or absence of scarce consumer goods such as water, electricity, and motorcycles in the households (appropriate in developing countries). Chile offers a small social assistance benefit, about 12 percent of the average wage, to the poorest of the noninsured groups over age 65, using traditional means-testing techniques. The size of the total social assistance budget is predetermined, as is the benefit level. This automatically constrains the number of beneficiaries—below the current number of eligible households. Thus, many localities have waiting lists of qualified individuals without access to benefits. Not surprisingly, most recipients are women who did not have an opportunity to participate in the labor market for enough years to qualify for the contributory guaranteed benefit.

But targeting incurs transactions costs. In cases where beneficiaries are poor, this may lead to a large leakage of funds to the middle-class bureaucrats who administer the system. Besides the official salaries that they receive, there is ample opportunity for unofficial side payments to induce rapid and favorable treatment. For example, in several Indian states, old people complain about patronage and the side payments they must make to get their applications processed.[16]

Traditional means-testing may also lead to take-up problems as some people do not apply because of ignorance or stigma, and criteria may not be applied uniformly. In Thailand, village elders identify the rural poor, mostly widows without children. This system may work well in some villages, but one can imagine personal favoritism playing a role in others.[17] Finally, means- and asset-testing create a moral hazard problem: people may be discouraged from saving for their own old age.

Realizing these disadvantages of traditional means-tested programs, countries have begun experimenting with nontraditional approaches and with proxies for need, which reduce these transactions costs. Such methods may not target precisely, but the savings from reduced leakage may more than compensate. For example, in the *Progresa* program in Mexico, a computerized model that aggregates several socioeconomic variables is used to identify poor communities, especially those in rural villages, and their residents. The econometric model is structured to give heavy weight to families with children and to provide an incentive for these children to attend school. But old people also benefit—and the relative weights given to school-attending children versus the old become a political issue.

A categorical approach is also used to reduce transactions costs: very old age may be a proxy for need. The very old who are women are often among the poorest groups, so this is an even narrower proxy for need. Argentina targets the "very old" in its social assistance program. All people whose age exceeds 70 and who have contributed for 10 years qualify. Presumably the transactions costs of this program are lower than in Chile. But given the correlation between income level and longevity, many poor people die before they ever collect, while many of those who collect are well above the poverty line. Benefits in Argentina are 19 percent of the average wage.[18] This contrasts with Brazil and Uruguay, where 15 years of contributions are required for the age-based social assistance pension but benefits are

---

[16] Van Ginneken (1999) and fieldwork by the author.
[17] Van Ginneken (1999).
[18] Ley de Seguridad 24.241; Vittas (1997).

higher, and Chile, where benefits are lower but can be received at an earlier age and contributions are not required. In general, we observe a tradeoff between tightness of eligibility criteria and size of benefits.[19]

Still another approach to means-testing involves self-selection: to offer assistance in a form for which mainly low-income people will apply. Self-selection can be achieved by requiring queues for receipt of small cash benefits, a cost that high-income people are less likely to be willing to incur, or by offering in-kind benefits such as free lunches that only low-income people would accept. NGOs may provide the service at lower cost and in a less bureaucratic way than the government, particularly when small-scale ventures are involved. In some countries the poorest old are accommodated by soup kitchens or dormitories run by NGOs but financed by governments. The advantage of self-selection is that it avoids the transactions costs and possible misidentification of an application process. The disadvantage is that the benefit and quality levels may not be optimal, and many needy old people may end up not participating.

At this stage, we do not really know which of these methods entails higher transactions costs and other leakages and which is more effective at targeting needy old people. This should be a high priority topic for further research.

Old versus Young Candidates for Social Assistance

Should different criteria apply to old versus young candidates for social assistance, and how much priority should be given to poor families with children versus the poor old? These two questions are interrelated.

On the one hand, some analysts argue that eligibility criteria should be more stringent for the young, since they can work and should be encouraged to seek work, while the presumption is that the old cannot work or have low productivity when they work. The old, therefore, can be offered social assistance without the labor disincentive effects that would be incurred by the young.

Of course, the expectation of receiving assistance when old may discourage saving when young, a different type of disincentive problem. In effect, means- and asset-tested social assistance impose a high marginal tax rate on savings. In Australia, the young who are unemployed and the old without adequate income and assets are guaranteed the same level of benefits, but with different eligibility crite-

---

[19] For a discussion of these tradeoffs in the contributory program as well, see James (1998).

ria regarding efforts to find employment, since the presumption is that the young can work (hence work incentives should be retained) while the old cannot. But the government in Australia feared that saving when young might be discouraged by its means- and asset-tested age pension, so it recently established a contributory mandatory saving plan for workers. This will eventually reduce the moral hazard problem regarding saving, leaving different work requirements for the old and the young.

On the other hand, one can argue that priority for social assistance should be given to young families with children, who have their entire lives ahead of them. According to this line of thought, children should not be penalized for the failure of their parents to obtain a well-paying job. Helping the children may be a better long-term investment for society. Of course, money given to families may not better the condition of the children—this depends on how the marginal income is spent. The Mexican *Progresa* program is interesting in this regard because it makes school attendance one of the criteria for aid, and the money is given directly to the mothers, who have been shown to be more likely to spend it to enhance the welfare of the children.

The Role of the Extended Family in Social Assistance Programs

The family is the oldest form of social insurance system.[20] If the old and the young live together in multigenerational households, the tradeoff between them in the allocation of social assistance is less critical. To illustrate: in South Africa a means-tested pension is paid to most older blacks who are living in rural areas. This pension originated in apartheid days and was intended for the small number of urban whites who had failed to accumulate their own private occupational pensions. A much smaller stipend was paid to blacks. But with the elimination of apartheid, the entire black population became eligible for the larger stipend, which has cut-off points and benefit amounts that are very high relative to rural black incomes. Often, family income goes up substantially when a member reaches the eligible age. Since old and young live together in multigenerational households, both groups benefit from the age stipend. But the tradeoff is not completely eliminated. The program is very costly and other uses for the money may be more targeted toward the young and may have a greater social payoff, such as increased spending on education. This is a controversial issue in South Africa today.

---

[20] See Kotlikoff and Spivak (1981) on risk sharing through the family.

When the family support system is strong, it is necessary to determine whether the income and assets of the entire family should count in applying the means test, or only those of the old person. In Western industrial societies, the move toward individual responsibility has meant that the government replaces the family as the social safety net and only the individual's means are counted. In contrast, in several Asian societies, such as Hong Kong and Singapore, children have a legal responsibility to take care of their parents, and old people can enforce this legally, albeit at great personal price. In Hong Kong, before the means-tested benefit is paid, children must testify that they are unable to support their parents. China is thinking of adopting a similar system. Indeed, in multigenerational households it is difficult to separate out the means of the parent and the child, since both share common living arrangements. But the share of total household consumption that accrues to different age groups is unknown to outsiders. Giving the older member a small stipend may increase his or her bargaining power to receive a pro rata share and in this sense may improve the welfare of the old beyond the stipend cost.

This leads to a broader question: how can governments offer social assistance while encouraging the continuation of family responsibility? How can penalties and incentives be structured to complement and crowd in, rather than crowd out, family care? Earlier work has shown that every dollar of social security benefits partially displaces private family transfers.[21] Incentives that governments have put in place to counteract this effect are tax rebates for children who care for their parents in Malaysia and for children who expand their homes to accommodate parents in Japan, Sweden, and Norway; and day care centers or respite care to give caregivers temporary relief in Hong Kong, Singapore, France, Germany, and the United Kingdom.[22] But in developing countries, where family support is strong and intergenerational households are the norm, it seems likely that such public subsidies might have only a small marginal impact, mainly constituting a financial relief for families who would have provided the services anyway. I am not aware of any careful research evaluating the efficacy of these measures. Such research would be worth doing, to inform other countries that might be considering these policies.

---

[21] Cox and Jiménez (1990).
[22] World Bank (1994).

CONCLUSIONS

The growth of formal coverage will accompany the process of economic development. Until that happens, a large proportion of the population will be uninsured or partially insured. The recent pension reforms tying benefits more closely to contributions are a step in the right direction for the contributory systems and are a necessary precondition for fiscally sound coverage expansion, but they cannot be expected to increase coverage in the short run and may even have the opposite effect. This chapter has surveyed the issues that policymakers need to address as they consider how to provide old age protection for the uninsured. While economic growth is the key to higher coverage, good policies also help.

Coverage expansion in contributory programs may be marginally encouraged by policies such as putting the social security system on a financially sustainable basis to enhance its credibility, choosing a modest target replacement rate that requires a relatively low contribution rate, allowing workers to receive a high (competitive) rate of return on their long-term retirement savings, and offering low-income workers access to safe saving instruments and partial benefits such as survivors' insurance (term life insurance), on a voluntary basis. These policies may reduce the number of "uninsured," but I would expect the impact to be small. Nonparticipation in formal old age security programs is a rational response among low-income workers, given their short expected lifetimes, high discount rates, and strong liquidity needs. For these reasons, forcing low earners to contribute to a formal program may not be optimal or feasible. But it leaves society with the problem of how to deal with the uninsured who survive to old age, are poor, and are unable to work.

This chapter has suggested two subgroups and courses of action that respond to their needs in an affordable way. First, for spouses of covered employees, who worked in the home rather than the market as part of the household division of labor, specific measures (such as the requirement to purchase survivors' benefits and joint annuities) might ensure that the implicit family contract is institutionalized and continued into old age. Second, for workers who participated in the labor market in noncovered jobs, earning enough to support themselves when young but with no surplus to save for old age, social assistance is essential. Social assistance should be financed out of general revenues and should offer less than the redistribution given to the low-income groups who have contributed, to reduce moral hazard problems.

Means-testing should be used to target social assistance, but this practice often entails high transactions costs and potential abuses. Computerized econometric models, use of proxies and categorical eligibility, self-selection mechanisms, and provision of in-kind benefits by NGOs (financed by government) are worth serious consideration in lieu of traditional targeting mechanisms. How to minimize moral hazard and leakages while maximizing the proportion of expenditures that reaches the targeted group is the key challenge—for practitioners and for researchers. As Latin American countries consider their second generation of pension reforms, they should be, and in some cases are, moving in these directions.

References

Aportela, F. 1999. "Effects of Financial Access on Savings by Low-Income People." Massachusetts Institute of Technology, Cambridge, MA.

Auerbach, Alan, and Laurence Kotlikoff. 1991. *Life Insurance Inadequacy—Evidence from a Sample of Older Widows*. Working Paper no. 3765. National Bureau of Economic Research, Cambridge, MA.

Cox, Donald, and Emmanuel Jiménez. 1990. "Achieving Social Objectives through Private Transfers: A Review." *World Bank Research Observer* 5: 205–18.

Instituto Nacional do Seguro Social. 1998. *Anuário Estatístico da Previdência Social—AEPS 1997*. Ministério da Previdência e Assistência Social, Brasília, Brazil.

James, Estelle. 1998. "Pension Reform in Latin America: Is There an Efficiency-Equity Tradeoff?" In N. Birdsall, C. Graham, and R. Sabot, eds., *Beyond Tradeoffs: Market Reforms and Equitable Growth in Latin America*. Washington, D.C.: IDB and Brookings Institution.

Johnson, Paul. 1998. "Pension Reform in the United Kingdom." *Annals of Public and Cooperative Economics* 69 (December): 517–32.

Kotlikoff, Laurence, and Avia Spivak. 1981. "The Family as an Incomplete Insurance Market." *Journal of Political Economy* 89: 372–91.

Ploug, Niels. 1993. *Compulsory Complementary Pension Schemes*. The Danish National Institute of Social Research, Denmark.

Queisser, Monica. 1998. *The Second-Generation Pension Reforms in Latin America*. Paris: OECD.

Valdes-Prieto, Salvador. 1998. "Pension Reform in Latin America: Transition and Implementation Problems." *Annals of Public and Cooperative Economics* 69 (December): 483–516.

Vittas, Dimitri. 1997. *The Argentine Pension Reform and Its Relevance for Eastern Europe*. Policy Research Working Paper no. 1819. World Bank, Washington, D.C.

Van Ginneken, Wouton. 1999. "Social Security for the Informal Sector: A New Challenge for the Developing Countries." *ISSA Review*.

von Gersdorff, Hermann. 1997. *Pension Reform in Bolivia: Innovative Solutions to Common Problems*. Policy Research Working Paper no. 1832. Financial Sector Development Department, World Bank, Washington, D.C.

Whitehouse, Edward. 1998. *Pension Reform in Britain*. Discussion Paper no. 98-10. Social Protection Group, World Bank, Washington, D.C.

World Bank. 1994. *Averting the Old Age Crisis: Policies to Protect the Old and Promote Growth*. New York: Oxford University Press.

———. 1998. *Informal Report on Social Security in Brazil*. Washington, D.C.: World Bank.

CHAPTER EIGHT

Social Assistance on Pensions and Health Care for the Poor in Latin America and the Caribbean

Carmelo Mesa-Lago

This chapter analyzes social (public) assistance protection for the poor and certain low-income groups in Latin America and the Caribbean (LAC) in old age, disability, death, and sickness. Social assistance can be informal or formal. The informal variety is based on solidarity, tradition, and custom, and is voluntarily provided by family, friends, community, or work groups. For instance, among rural families in LAC, old or disabled family members unable to work and sustain themselves are helped by younger active members. And yet the processes of modernization, creation of job opportunities, urbanization and rural-to-urban migration, shift from extended to nuclear families, and change in cultural patterns have significantly eroded such informal help, particularly in the more developed countries. In the 1980s, only 8 to 9 percent of the population above 65 years old in Argentina and Chile (among the most urbanized countries in the region) received income from their family, but 73 to 74 percent received income from pensions, while in Costa Rica (much more rural) the proportions were 23 percent and 46 percent, respectively.[1] In another type of informal group solidarity, coworkers or members of a trade or occupation contribute to a common pot in order to help those afflicted by sickness, temporary disability, or death (funeral expenses). This second type of as-

The author gratefully acknowledges the materials and comments supplied on Argentina by Fabio Bertranou, professor of economics at Universidad de Cuyo; on Brazil by Helmut Schwarzer, Técnico de Planejamento e Pesquisa at IPEA; on Chile by Mónica Valencia Corvalán, secretary general of Superintendencia de Seguridad Social, and Alberto Arenas de Mesa, chief of the Research Center of Ministerio de Hacienda; and comments on the whole study by two anonymous reviewers.
[1] World Bank (1994).

sistance, nevertheless, is little extended and lacks permanency and sufficient resources to support old members of the group when they become unable to work, as
well as inactive dependents of a deceased member. For reasons of space limitations
and treatment elsewhere, I do not discuss informal social assistance in this chapter.[2]

Formal social assistance is legally established and institutionalized, as part of
a general social security system that also includes social *insurance*. The latter is
mandatory and constitutes a right generated through payroll contributions paid
by the insured and usually the employer (often by the state also, in the form of
subsidies or payroll contributions). Social *assistance* is neither insurance nor a right
(is not based on such contributions), but a government concession often based on
need and conditioned to the availability of fiscal resources. The above-mentioned
processes of modernization and development, which eroded informal means of
protection, have conversely led to an expansion of social security, but the insurance
scheme has grown considerably more than the assistance program. Within the latter, this chapter focuses on health care and pensions for old age, disability, and
death (survivors). Excluded are other social security schemes such as unemployment insurance and emergency employment programs, as well as social safety nets
(discussed in other chapters of this book). In any event, the poor are never covered
by unemployment insurance, while social safety funds do not grant pension assistance, although they may offer certain basic health services. Because of space limitations and lack of data, I also exclude formal types of assistance to the poor outside of social security, such as those provided by charity institutions (religious,
nongovernmental organizations [NGOs]).

The main target population group of this chapter is the poor, that is, those who
are under the overall poverty line, measured by the cost of a basket of food and
nonfood basic needs. In addition, other low-income, vulnerable groups are considered: nonsalary workers in the urban informal sector (for example, self-employed),
rural workers and peasants, and some salary earners who receive a low wage and
work in certain occupations (for example, domestic servants, employees of informal
microenterprises). Although this second group does not always overlap with the poor,
it is not commonly covered by social insurance and, hence, lacks social protection.

A major obstacle I confronted is the lack of data on this subject, especially
statistics. This vacuum is explained by several reasons: social assistance is of considerably lesser importance and extension than social insurance; it is not based on

---

[2] World Bank (1994); Zeller in this book.

a right and lacks an organized constituency capable of exercising pressure to get information; and few countries in LAC have social assistance programs that go beyond charity and a token help for a minimal fraction of those in need. For instance, the U.S. Social Security Administration in its biannual report *Social Security Programs throughout the World* only includes six out of 34 countries in LAC as having social assistance programs. The International Labour Office in its latest triennial report *The Cost of Social Security* published social assistance expenditures for only 10 of those countries. The World Bank report *Averting the Old Age Crisis* includes only a couple of statistical tables and very scarce information on social assistance programs in LAC, while the 1999 World Bank annual report does not contain any data at all. The latter is also the case with the United Nations Development Programme's *Human Development Report*.[3] Partly because of those reasons and despite the growing interest and number of publications on poverty in the 1980s and 1990s, technical and academic literature on this topic and region is scarce, and a good part of it is my own work.[4]

COVERAGE OF THE TARGET POPULATION BY SOCIAL ASSISTANCE

In analyzing protection of the poor and other vulnerable groups it is necessary to distinguish between legal entitlement and statistical coverage. The former is stipulated by law but not necessarily enforced in practice, and the latter is the estimate by social security institutions of the number of affiliates to the system. Although the statistical coverage is much more accurate than the legal one, it does not necessarily reflect reality, due to estimation flaws; figures on coverage of the poor are usually nonexistent. Census and survey data are more reliable but seldom provide data on coverage by social assistance.

Health Care

At the start of the 1990s, the Pan American Health Organization (PAHO) roughly estimated that 130 million poor (about 70 percent of the total) had no access to health care in LAC. A similar estimate is not available for the end of the century, but this section reviews the most recent legal and statistical data.[5]

---

[3] U.S. SSA (1997); ILO (1996); World Bank (1994); UNDP (1998).
[4] Mesa-Lago (1983, 1990, 1992a, 1992b, 1994a, 1994b, 1997, 2000a).
[5] The general source is Mesa-Lago (1992a).

Legal coverage of health care for the total population in 33 LAC countries is summarized in table 8–1 (no data are available on Suriname). In 15 countries there is a unified and standardized national health system, usually managed by the Ministry of Health, which covers all residents: in all the non-Latin Caribbean (NLC), Brazil, and Cuba. In the remaining 18 countries of Latin America (LA), there is a dual health care system: one provided by the social insurance scheme, which mainly covers the salaried labor force, and another by the Ministry of Health, which offers public health care to the noninsured poor and low-income population (Nicaragua had the first system in the 1980s but shifted to the second in the 1990s). Besides health care, table 8–1 exhibits coverage of cash benefits (for example, sickness and maternity paid leave): in the countries with a national health system such benefits are granted by social insurance (and are separately shown in the table for salaried, self-employed, domestic servants, and rural workers); while in the countries with a dual health system, coverage in the table refers to both health care and cash benefits.

The national health system entitles all *residents* to health care and, hence, legally the poor and low-income groups have access to the same basic care as the rest of the population. Under the dual system in LA, 10 countries entitle *all* the salaried labor force to health care by social insurance, eight extend that protection only to *part* of the labor force, and Haiti lacks health insurance (table 8–1). The poor and low-income groups in LA are legally under the care of the ministry, which traditionally is underfunded and offers worse quality care than does social insurance. Within the social insurance scheme, only two countries legally extend mandatory coverage to self-employed workers (but of dubious enforcement), 10 permit voluntary affiliation, and seven exclude them all together. Nine countries grant mandatory coverage to domestic servants, two by voluntary affiliation, and eight exclude them. Finally, half of the countries provide mandatory coverage to salaried rural workers and a few to members of cooperatives, and the other half excludes them. In all these countries, peasants and unpaid family workers are always excluded, as well as the long-term unemployed. Under the national health system all these groups are entitled to health care.

Costa Rica has the most extensive and equal coverage in LA under the social insurance scheme, with compulsory coverage for domestic servants, rural workers, employees of microenterprises, and the unemployed (for a period after dismissal), while self-employed workers have voluntary coverage but are subsidized, and virtually all of them are covered; furthermore, all the dispossessed (*indigentes*) are freely covered by the social assistance (noncontributory) program administered by social insurance, and their treatment is the same as that of the insured. In Brazil, a law of 1990 mandated universal coverage through the United Health System, guaranteeing health care as a basic social right. In Chile, *indigentes* and low-income groups are covered by the public health program, while part of the middle-income and virtually all the high-income strata are affiliated to private insurance, which offers better quality of care at a cost unaffordable to the poor and low-income strata. In Argentina and Uruguay, the poor and low-income groups are also covered but under a stratified system of care, virtually all of them by public health, while the insured are protected by union-managed schemes currently undergoing reform (in Argentina), and mutual aid societies and cooperatives (Uruguay).

Statistical coverage for the total population of health care is exhibited in table 8–2 for all LA countries (except Haiti) and three NLC countries: the third column shows coverage by social insurance alone, and the fourth column combines all health care programs, normally smaller in the former group than in the latter. The most socially developed group of countries in LA have close to universal coverage under all programs combined: 92 to 96 percent in Argentina, Brazil, Chile, Costa Rica, Cuba, and Uruguay. Poverty incidence in these countries ranges from 13 to 24 percent of households (except in Brazil, where it is about 41 percent), the lowest in the region, which means that a large majority of the poor and low-income groups are effectively covered.[6] Conversely, the group of least developed countries in LA has very low coverage under social insurance (6 to 22 percent) and higher but still quite low under all programs combined (34 to 59 percent) in Bolivia, Dominican Republic, El Salvador, Guatemala, Honduras, Paraguay, and Peru. Poverty incidence in these countries is the highest of the region (52 to 73 percent), hence, the poor and the low-income groups are not protected. Finally, LA countries in the middle group have a combined coverage of about three-fourths of the population: 75 to 79 percent in Colombia, Mexico, Panama, and Venezuela. Poverty incidence in these countries ranges from 30 to 49 percent; therefore, the majority of the poor lack effective protection. Data from three NLC countries indicate that they have reached a level of coverage under their national health systems similar to that of the most socially developed countries of LA: from 89 to 98 percent in the Bahamas, Barbados, and Jamaica, hence effectively protecting a large majority of the poor, particularly in the first two countries.

---

[6] Poverty data from CEPAL (1996, 1997).

Table 8–1. Legal Coverage of Health Care Benefits by National Health Systems and/or Social Insurance in Latin America and the Caribbean, 1997

Country	All residents	Salaried employees		Potentially poor groups		
		All[a]	Part[b]	Self-employed	Domestic servants	Rural workers[c]
Social insurance						
Argentina		x		x[d]	x	x
Bolivia		x		x		
Chile		x		x[d]	x	x
Colombia		x		x[d]	x[d]	x
Costa Rica		x		x[d]	x	x
Dominican Republic			x			
Ecuador			x		x	
El Salvador			x	x		
Guatemala			x[e]			
Haiti						
Honduras			x[e]	x[d]		
Mexico			x	x[d]	x[d]	x
Nicaragua			x	x[d]		x
Panama		x		x[d]	x	x
Paraguay		x		x[d]	x[f]	
Peru		x				
Uruguay		x			x	x
Venezuela		x[e]			x	
National health system						
Antigua and Barbuda	x	x		x		x
Bahamas	x	x		x	x	x
Barbados	x	x		x[g]	x	x

Belize	X			X
Bermuda	X			
Brazil	X	X^d	X^h	X
Cuba	X			X
Dominica	X			X
Grenada	X	X		X
Guyana	X		X	X
Jamaica	X		X^i	
St. Kitts and Nevis	X	X		X
St. Lucia	X	X		X
St. Vincent	X			X
Trinidad and Tobago	X		X	X

a. Practically all countries exclude unpaid family workers and eight countries also exclude temporary workers.

b. Normally covers permanent employees in industry, commerce, mining, transportation, communications, civil service, and public utilities. Usually excludes agriculture and domestic service, as well as temporary, home, and unpaid family workers.

c. Refers to salaried work and, in some countries, to cooperatives; in Uruguay, includes small producers too. For self-employed in agriculture, see self-employed column. In Brazil, rural workers are covered under a special program; in Colombia, only some regions are covered; in Mexico, coverage is gradually being expanded to salaried work, co-ops, and small communal farms; in Panama, temporary and seasonal workers will be covered by regulations; in Cuba, excludes private farmers.

d. Voluntary coverage; in Panama, members of trade unions are compulsorily covered; in Brazil, Chile, and Nicaragua, the agricultural self-employed are not covered.

e. Coverage is limited geographically to capital city and large urban areas.

f. Only those who work in businesses, not in homes.

g. Voluntary continuation of coverage is available for those who shift from salaried work to self-employment.

h. In-kind benefits only.

i. Only in case of maternity.

Note: In the non-Latin Caribbean, Brazil, and Cuba there is a national health system (except Bermuda, which has compulsory hospitalization private insurance) with coverage of all residents, which provides health care. In addition, these countries usually have social insurance that grants cash benefits (these are shown in the table for salaried employees, the self-employed, domestic servants, and rural workers). In the remaining countries, coverage refers to social insurance for both benefits in cash and in kind.

Source: Author's calculations, based on U.S. SSA (1997) and additional information.

Table 8–2. Statistical Coverage for the Economically Active and Total Populations of Pensions and Health Care in Latin America and Selected Caribbean Countries, 1990–95

Percent

Country	Year[a]	Economically active population[b]	Total population By social insurance[c]	Total population Global coverage[d]
Latin America				
Argentina		81.4	–	92
Bolivia		13.6	21.3	34
Brazil		61.8	–	92
Chile		80.0[e]	100.0[e]	93
Colombia	1985–88	30.2	16.0	75
Costa Rica		55.0	86.2[f]	96
Cuba	1980	93.0[g]	100.0[g]	–
Dominican Republic		12.7	5.6	71
Ecuador		28.0	17.2	61
El Salvador		22.6	14.2	59
Guatemala		27.6	16.3	50
Honduras	1985–88	12.8	10.3	46
Mexico		43.7	58.4	77
Nicaragua		14.3	13.0	69
Panama		61.0	54.0	79
Paraguay		8.7	22.3	54
Peru		32.0	23.8	44
Uruguay	1985–88	73.0	87.7[h]	96
Venezuela	1985–88	54.3	49.9	76
Non-Latin Caribbean				
Bahamas		–	98.0	–
Barbados	1985–88	96.9	–	97
Jamaica	1985–88	93.2	–	89

– Not available.

a. Most recent data for more than half of the countries are from 1990–95; for the rest, the most recent year available is noted.

b. Coverage for pensions.

c. Coverage for health care by sickness-maternity program of social insurance. Excludes coverage by Ministry of Public Health, except in countries with national health systems such as Cuba.

d. Gross estimate of total population coverage combining all health care programs.

e. Official figures on coverage of the economically active population are inflated and the figure is a rough estimate; the figure for population coverage is probably inflated too.

f. Includes coverage of the poor *(indigentes)*; if coverage by the Ministry of Health is added, total coverage is almost universal.

g. Based on legal coverage; no statistics are available.

h. Includes the Social Insurance Bank, the Ministry of Health, the armed forces, and Mutual Aid Societies.

Source: Mesa-Lago and Bertranou (1998) and additional information.

Pensions

Legal coverage for the economically active population of pensions is smaller than that of health care, because employment is a condition for entitlement: out of the 33 countries, in 25 all salaried workers are mandatorily covered (virtually all in NLC and 12 in LA), and in another eight only part of the salaried labor force is covered.[7] Legal entitlement to social assistance programs of the poor and other vulnerable groups in LAC is summarized in table 8–3. According to the U.S. Social Security Administration only three LA countries (Cuba, Nicaragua, and Uruguay) provide social assistance or noncontributory pensions for the poor, and three more in the NLC (Antigua and Barbuda, the Bahamas, and Bermuda).[8] Checks on the legislation actually show that four other LA countries (Argentina, Brazil, Chile, and Costa Rica), as well as at least two in the NLC (Barbados and Trinidad and Tobago), provide social assistance pensions for the poor (on the other hand, the Nicaraguan program no longer appears to be in operation). A total of 11 countries, therefore, legally have this program.

In addition, 13 countries grant mandatory coverage to self-employed workers and 10 grant voluntary coverage, while 10 exclude them altogether. Seventeen countries entitle domestic servants to mandatory coverage, one provides voluntary coverage, and 16 exclude them. No special pension programs are available for rural workers except those who are salaried in large plantations. Unemployed and unpaid family workers, as well as peasants, are always excluded.

Statistical coverage for the economically active population of contributory social insurance pensions is presented in table 8–2. Similar to health care, the most advanced LA countries, as well as those in the NLC for which data are available, show the highest coverage (but lower than in health care): 73 to 97 percent in Argentina, Barbados, Chile, Cuba, Jamaica, and Uruguay. Coverage of the middle LA group ranges from 30 to 64 percent, and in the least developed countries coverage ranges from 13 to 28 percent. As the proportion of coverage of pensions is lower than that of health care, it is obvious that the poor are uninsured, although they might be eligible for assistance pensions in a few countries. In the 1980s the following proportions of the population above 65 years appeared to receive assistance pensions in six countries: Costa Rica and Brazil, 20 to 22 percent; Jamaica and Uruguay,

---

[7] Mesa-Lago and Bertranou (1998).
[8] U.S. SSA (1997).

Table 8–3. Legal Coverage of Social Assistance Pensions for the Poor and Other Vulnerable Groups in Latin America and the Caribbean, 1997

Country[a]	Noncontributory (social assistance) pensions for the poor[b]	Contributory (social insurance) pensions for vulnerable groups	
		Self-employed	Domestic servants[c]
Latin America			
Argentina	x	x	x
Bolivia		x[d]	
Brazil	x	x	x
Chile	x	x[d]	x
Colombia		x[d]	x
Costa Rica	x	x[d]	x
Cuba	x	x	
Dominican Republic			x
Ecuador		x[d]	x
El Salvador		x[d]	
Honduras		x	
Mexico		x[d]	x[d]
Nicaragua	x	x[d]	
Panama		x[d]	x
Peru		x[d]	x
Uruguay	x	x	x
Venezuela			x
Non-Latin Caribbean			
Antigua and Barbuda	x		
Bahamas	x	x	x
Barbados	x	x	x
Belize		x	x
Bermuda	x	x	
Guyana		x	x
Jamaica		x	x
St. Kitts and Nevis		x	
Trinidad and Tobago	x	x	x

a. Dominica, Guatemala, Haiti, Paraguay, St. Lucia, and St. Vincent do not have any programs for the poor and other vulnerable groups.

b. Means-tested. No country provides flat rate universal pensions. Argentina, Barbados, Brazil, Chile, Costa Rica, and Trinidad and Tobago do have social assistance pensions but are not included in the U.S. SSA tables; conversely, Nicaragua is included but currently does not provide such pensions.

c. In some countries, these pensions are subject to special conditions and/or receive some type of subsidy.

d. Voluntary affiliation.

Source: Author's calculations, based on U.S. SSA (1997) and additional information.

16 percent; Venezuela, 12 percent; and Argentina, 3 percent—the last figure is surprisingly low and should be higher.[9]

Note that Costa Rica, which has virtually universal coverage in health care,
only covers 55 percent of the economically active population for pensions (table
8–2); however, this figure does not take into account social assistance pensions,
hence, total coverage should be higher but not close to universal. Affiliation in Costa
Rica's contributory pension program among the self-employed is only 9 percent
(contrasted with almost universal coverage in health care) because their affiliation
is voluntary and they do not receive a fiscal subsidy as in health care. The highest
percentages of affiliation of self-employed workers, albeit still a minority, are found
in countries where coverage is mandatory: 25 to 48 percent in the Bahamas, Uruguay, and Barbados (coverage appears to be high in Argentina also). Data available
for other countries, where coverage happens to be voluntary, show much lower
percentages: 1 to 11 percent in Chile, Peru, and Mexico. But one should not infer
from these scarce data that making coverage mandatory would solve the problem,
because there are other factors involved such as the proportion of the labor force in
self-employment (for example, low in Uruguay and very high in Peru), the higher
financial burden of affiliation imposed on these workers, and the significant difficulties in affiliating them and collecting their contributions.[10]

ENTITLEMENT CONDITIONS AND BENEFITS

This section describes several programs of social assistance available in LAC (for
health care and pensions) and analyzes entitlement conditions and benefits in such
programs.

Entitlement Conditions

Social assistance can be granted for health care and pensions. For health care the
condition of poverty is not required under the national health system, as all residents regardless of income are entitled to free care. In the social insurance system
typical of LA, those not insured are normally entitled to free health care in the
public system managed by the Ministry of Health. In both systems only the poor

---

[9] World Bank (1994).
[10] Mesa-Lago (1990); Mesa-Lago and Bertranou (1998); more on this later.

might be exempted from paying user fees in countries that impose them. In a few countries of LA access of the noninsured to the assistance health program calls for a means test.

Social assistance pensions are of two main types. The most extensive type in the world and in LAC is the benefit based on need and, hence, limited to the poor; this is the most adequate type for developing countries that endure high poverty incidence and income inequality, because it is targeted, demands fewer resources, and has a progressive impact on distribution (particularly when financed by the income tax); but it has administrative costs (identification of the poor, means test) and conveys a stigma. Nonexistent in LAC is a universal benefit that is flat and granted regardless of income and wealth; this type is administratively simpler and cheaper than the first type and does not convey a stigma because it is universal. However, it might stimulate both evasion in the contributory scheme and free riders. This type of pension is more appropriate to developed countries as they have abundant resources and a more equal income distribution. Its regressive effect (because it is paid to middle- and high-income groups) could be eliminated by including the pension in the income tax, but this would be difficult to enforce in LAC countries because they have a low capacity to collect such a tax, and their main source of fiscal revenue is the usually regressive sales tax.[11] The first type of pension is the one found in at least 11 LAC countries, six in LA and five in the NLC (table 8–3). We have information on nine of those countries, and all but one requires the means test (table 8–4). In Barbados such a test was suspended in 1982, although the rapid increase in costs thereafter might have forced its restitution. The means test is commonly based on a minimum wage or pension level for the insured or his or her family. In addition, in some countries the recipient of the pension may not be supported by his or her family (Brazil, Uruguay), or a ceiling is set on the number of assistance pensions granted (Chile), or the overall sum depends on the resources available (Costa Rica). In the old Brazilian system, in operation in 1975–95, it was required that the beneficiary had contributed for at least one year to the social insurance program; that condition was eliminated in the new system, which replaced the old one in 1996 and led to a significant increase in pensioners.[12]

Social assistance pensions are invariably awarded for the risks of old age and disability, but less so for survivors. Table 8–4 shows that only four of the nine coun-

---

[11] World Bank (1994).
[12] IPEA (1998a, 1998b).

tries in LAC for which data are available grant survivors' pensions, an important difference from social insurance, which always provides this type of pension. Poor widows and young orphans, therefore, are more devoid of aid than the elderly and disabled.

Entitlement conditions for social assistance pensions are stricter than for social insurance pensions and depend on the risk covered. For instance, a minimum age is required for an old age pension between 65 and 70 years (table 8–4), higher than the ages required for retirement in the insurance scheme, and yet the poor have a life expectancy lower than the insured (who normally enjoy better living conditions). The higher minimum age is imposed to cut assistance expenses and discourage the nonpoor from obtaining that pension. Disability assistance pensions usually demand a medical test of the incapacity similar to that required from the insured, but there are no data on whether that test is equally administered in both cases. The new assistance pension system of Brazil expanded the definition of disability to include the congenital cases. The few countries that grant survivors' assistance pensions often require that the dependent relative is poor also. In Costa Rica, the widow should have children below 18 years of age or disabled, otherwise she must be older than 55 years or disabled. In Cuba, single mothers who have children qualify for a pension.[13]

Benefits

It has been mentioned already that the quality of health care usually available to the poor under the Ministry of Health is lower than that provided by social insurance and the private sector; hence, the poor receive (if effectively covered) the worst care available. The economic crisis of the 1980s led to a cut in social expenditures, and fiscal budgets for the Ministry of Health were substantially reduced in most countries of the region, investment was halted, and the availability and quality of care declined. A few countries tried to cope with the crisis, reassigning resources to the poor and the infant-maternal group, and a modest recovery took place in the late 1980s and 1990s. In Chile, the return of democracy in the 1990s led to an increase in the health budget and some improvement in the infrastructure and personnel. In Cuba the crisis was postponed until the 1990s, when the socialist camp collapsed and Soviet aid was terminated; in spite of an impressive physical plant,

---

[13] CCSS (1995); Mesa-Lago and Roca (1992).

Table 8–4. Entitlement Conditions for Social Assistance Pensions in Latin America and the Caribbean, 1997–98

Country	Year of inception	Risks covered			Age required for old age pension	Family per capita income	Means-tested	Other limitations
		Old age	Disability	Survivor				
Argentina	1948, 1991	x	x	[a]	70	—	x	Resources available
Bahamas[b]	1957–58, 1967	x	x	x	65	—	x	—
Barbados[b]	1957–58	x			65	—	[c]	—
Brazil	1974, 1996	x	x		70/67[d]	Less than 25 percent of minimum wage	x	Beneficiary can't be supported by family
Chile	1975	x	x		65	Less than 50 percent of minimum pension in social insurance	x	Amount set in fiscal budget
Costa Rica	1974	x	x	x	65	Less than 50 percent of minimum pension in social insurance	x	Resources available

Cuba[e]	1970s	x		–	–	x[f]	–
Uruguay	1919	x	x	70	Less than old age minimum pension	x	Beneficiary can't be supported by family
Trinidad and Tobago	1970s	x	x	65	Less than U.S.$100 monthly	x	–

– Not available.

a. Mothers with seven children or more, and the surviving widower and minor children who were dependent.

b. Data are for 1987.

c. Eliminated in 1982, might have been reestablished.

d. Old and new systems.

e. Data are for 1990.

f. Provided to noninsured without means whose essential needs are not satisfied.

Source: Argentina from Schulthess (1995) and Bertranou (1999); Bahamas and Barbados from Mesa-Lago (1994); Brazil from IPEA (1998a, 1998b); Chile from SSS (1999); Costa Rica from CCSS (1997); Cuba from Mesa-Lago and Roca (1992); Trinidad and Tobago from IDB (1999); and Uruguay from BPS (1998).

equipment, and personnel, the health sector is suffering an acute crisis owing to the lack of medicine, spare parts, and other crucial inputs.[14]

Both the number and expenditures of social assistance pensions are usually lower than those of social insurance pensions, because of the former's tougher entitlement conditions and the considerably fewer resources assigned. Table 8–5 supports that general rule in five of seven countries for which data are available; the table exhibits the proportions of assistance pensioners over total pensioners and of assistance pension expenditures over total pension expenditures: 9.1 and 5.6 percent in Uruguay, 8.2 and 4 percent in Argentina, 10.2 and 5.7 percent in Brazil, 34.7 and 7.4 percent in Chile, and 49.7 and 15.9 percent in Costa Rica. The opposite is true in the two NLC countries: 58.5 and 39.9 percent in Barbados, and 76.5 and 45.5 percent in the Bahamas. There, the proportion of assistance pensioners is higher than that of insured pensioners (in LA the proportion of insured pensioners is higher). Such abnormally high proportions are explainable by the financial and administrative systems, the relative low number of insurance pensions in young schemes, and the liberalization of entitlement conditions for assistance pensions in both countries in the 1980s—in Barbados, in the midst of political campaigns for national elections, the means test was suspended, the age was reduced, and the pension amount was increased.[15]

The average social assistance pension is and should be smaller than the insurance pension in order to avoid both disincentives for the insured's compliance and incentives for free riding (if the amount paid in the two types of pensions is close, why affiliate and pay contributions to social insurance if one can get a similar pension free?). Table 8–5 confirms this assertion for all eight countries, but note that while the ratio of insurance over assistance pensions is 5.2 in Costa Rica, it declines to 2.9–2.4 in Chile, Argentina, and Cuba; 1.9–1.8 in Brazil and Uruguay; and 1.5–1.4 in Barbados and the Bahamas. In the last two countries the gap between the two types of pensions is very narrow, hence generating adverse effects. In 1987 insured workers in these two countries complained that their pensions were very close to the assistance pensions and that part of their contributions to the insurance scheme was used to finance the assistance pensions; this criticism was stronger in Barbados after the elimination of the means test.[16]

The social assistance pension should be sufficient to cover the essential needs

---

[14] Mesa-Lago (2000a, 2000b).

[15] Mesa-Lago (1988, 1994a).

[16] Mesa-Lago (1988); the author was unable to gather more recent information on this issue.

Table 8–5. Benefits of Social Assistance Pensions in Some Latin American and Caribbean Countries, 1997–98

Country	Percentage of social assistance over total social security		Ratio of social insurance over social assistance average pension	Monthly average social assistance pension (U.S. dollars)
	Number of pensioners[a]	Pension expenditures		
Argentina	8.2	4.0	2.5	150.00[b]
Bahamas[c]	76.5	45.5	1.5	–
Barbados[c]	58.5	39.9	1.4	–
Brazil	10.2	5.7	1.9	108.72
Chile	34.7	7.4	2.9	52.37
Costa Rica	49.7	15.9	5.2	31.18
Cuba[d]	–	–	2.4	1.90
Uruguay	9.1	5.6	1.8	134.13

– Not available.
a. In some countries refers to number of pensions (one person may receive more than one pension).
b. This figure might be inflated because it is the average of several programs not all of which are assistance.
c. Data are for 1986.
d. Data in the third column are for 1995.
Source: Argentina from Schulthess (1995) and Bertranou (1999); Bahamas and Barbados from Mesa-Lago (1994a); Brazil from IPEA (1998a, 1998b); Chile from SSS (1997, 1999); Costa Rica from CCSS (1997) and Mesa-Lago (1998b); Cuba from UNDP (1997) and Rivero (1999); and Uruguay from BPS (1998).

of the poor. Although we lack exact comparative data on the cost of living in these countries, table 8–5 indicates that the average monthly assistance pension ranges from U.S.$108 to U.S.$150 in Argentina, Brazil, and Uruguay but is considerably lower (U.S.$31 to U.S.$52) in Chile and Costa Rica, and extremely low in Cuba (U.S.$1.90). The cost of living in Chile is close to that in Argentina, Brazil, and Uruguay, and Chile's social assistance pension is less than half that of the other countries; the cost of the basket to cover basic needs in Chile in mid-1998 was 50 percent higher than the social assistance pension.[17] Costa Rica has a lower cost of living than the other four countries (Argentina, Brazil, Chile, and Uruguay), but its assistance pension is 40 percent less than that of Chile and 71 to 79 percent less than the assistance pensions in Brazil, Uruguay, and Argentina.

In Cuba, in the 1980s, the average value of a pension was low, but pensioners received a basic package of rationed goods at subsidized prices, their house rent was fixed and reduced if their income level was very low, transportation was very

---

[17] Based on SSS (1999).

cheap, and health care was free and of adequate quality. The crisis of the 1990s reversed those compensatory benefits: in 1998 the minimum social insurance pension was 60 pesos, or U.S.$2.86 (at the rate of exchange in state houses), and the flat assistance pension was 40 pesos, or U.S.$1.90; furthermore, the package of rationed goods has been dramatically reduced, prices in free markets have skyrocketed, transportation has been cut to one-tenth, and health care has deteriorated.[18]

In Brazil, the old-system assistance pension was raised to equal the minimum salary in 1991 (with retroactive effects to pensions paid since 1988), and that level was maintained by the new system that began in 1996. The old system also eliminated in 1991 the difference in the amounts of pensions paid in urban and rural areas, hence raising the latter where the poverty incidence was higher: at the end of 1997, the proportions of pensioners and pension amounts in urban areas were 11 and 5 percent of the totals, respectively, while those in rural areas were 8.9 and 8.8 percent, respectively.[19]

FINANCING

This section analyzes the aggregate cost of social assistance, its revenue sources, financial aid needed to incorporate special labor groups, and impact on income distribution.

The Cost of Social Assistance

The amount usually assigned to social assistance programs in LAC is small in relation to both total social security benefit expenditures and GDP, although available data are probably underestimated. The International Labour Office only reports data on social assistance expenditures for 12 countries in LAC (see table 8–6; Brazil was added by the author), the majority of them in NLC.[20] Argentina, Chile, and Uruguay do not appear in the table, although they have social assistance pensions. The ILO figures are underestimated because expenditures of noncontributory pension and health care programs seem to be included as social insurance instead of social assistance, and expenditures of some public health programs under the ministry are often excluded. Unfortunately these are the only data available and, in

---

[18] Mesa-Lago (1997); UNDP (1997); Rivero (1999).
[19] IPEA (1998a, 1998b).
[20] ILO (1996, 1999).

Table 8–6. Social Assistance Expenditures as Percentages of Total Social Security Benefit Expenditures and GDP in Latin America and the Caribbean, 1986–94

Country[a]	Year	Percentage of total social security benefit expenditures	Percentage of GDP
Latin America			
Brazil[b]	1994	5.0	0.27
Costa Rica	1993	3.9	0.29
Cuba	1990	3.4	0.52
Ecuador	1986	17.2	0.51
Nicaragua	1992	12.9	0.07
Panama	1989	0.4	0.04
Non-Latin Caribbean			
Barbados	1986	5.5	0.25
Belize	1989	9.4	0.09
Grenada	1989	6.2	0.17
Guyana	1989	1.6	0.03
Jamaica	1992	30.8	0.32
Suriname	1989	31.7	0.82
Trinidad and Tobago	1989	17.1	0.41

a. Only countries that show social assistance expenditures are included.
b. Data are estimated by the author.
Source: Based on ILO (1996, 1999).

eight countries, the most recent year reported by the ILO is either 1986 or 1989. The World Bank gives data on social assistance pensions as a percentage of total old-age pensions in six countries in the 1980s, including Venezuela, which is not reported on either by the ILO or by the U.S. Social Security Administration.[21]

The proportion assigned to social assistance out of total social security benefit expenditures is lower than 10 percent in eight countries (5 percent or smaller in five of them), it increases to 13–19 percent in three, and reaches 31–32 percent in the other two. In no country does social assistance expenditures as a percentage of GDP reach 1 percent , and in 10 countries it is below 0.5 percent (it has been estimated that 0.5 to 1 percent of GDP in transfers would suffice to eradicate extreme poverty).[22] In spite of the flaws mentioned, these data suggest that very little is spent on social assistance in the region. The overwhelming majority of social secu-

---

[21] World Bank (1994).
[22] Lustig and Deutsch (1998).

rity expenditures, therefore, go to social insurance, although in half of the countries of LA less than one-third of both the economically active population and the total population are covered by that program (table 8–2).

The scarcity of resources assigned to social assistance is often aggravated by the failure of the state or other institutions to properly allocate those resources. The overall amount for assistance is normally fixed without clear priorities, resulting in a struggle among various dispossessed groups for the meager funds available and encouraging political patronage.

Sources of Revenue

Social assistance in LAC has three main sources of revenue: a percentage contribution on the payroll earmarked for social assistance (separated from that for social insurance); fiscal resources; and transfers from social insurance funds (this often happens when the other two sources are insufficient to finance assistance costs). Table 8–7 shows the sources of social assistance pensions in eight countries; financing of health care for the poor is generally done out of the state budget; some peculiarities of these sources are explained below.

In Argentina and Cuba the only source of revenue for the two noncontributory programs is the state budget. In Chile, social assistance health care is totally financed by the state, while noncontributory pensions are mainly financed by the state but with the minor aid of a payroll contribution imposed on those insured in the old social insurance system (those in the new private pension system do not pay that contribution). In Costa Rica the two programs have different legal financing: health care for the poor is a state obligation, and fiscal transfers must be made to the social insurance institute to cover the cost of care of *indigentes*; noncontributory pensions are financed by an autonomous fund (FODESAF) whose sources come from an ad hoc payroll tax and sales taxes, and 20 percent of that fund is earmarked for such pensions. In practice, neither the state nor FODESAF transfers all the resources owed to the social insurance institute. In addition, the state has cut the FODESAF budget by 50 percent, does not transfer to FODESAF all the tax revenue collected, and has charged it with part of the cost of health care for the poor. As a result, the social insurance institute is forced to cover the deficit of both programs, and the public debt has been significant for many years.[23] In Brazil, the old assis-

---

[23] FCN (1998b).

Table 8–7. Financing and Administration of Social Assistance Pensions in Latin America and the Caribbean, 1997–98

Country	Percentage of payroll	Source of revenue					
		Transfers from		Social insurance and assistance pension funds		Administered by	
		State	Social insurance	Common	Separated	Social insurance	State
Argentina		x			x		x
Bahamas[a]		x	x	x		x	
Barbados[a]	x		x	x		x	
Brazil	x[b]	x[b]	x[b]	x[b]	x[b]	x[c]	x[c]
Chile	x	x			x		x
Costa Rica	x		x		x	x	
Cuba		x		[d]	[d]		[e]
Uruguay[f]		x	x	x		x	

a. Data are for 1987.

b. Contributions to social insurance (transfers) were used to finance the old system, hence, there is a common fund; the new system is entirely financed by the state and the social insurance fund should not be touched, but in practice it might be.

c. Social insurance manages the old system. The new system is administered by the Ministry of Social Insurance and Social Assistance, decentralized, with participation of local organizations.

d. There are no pension funds.

e. State designs policy, and administration is by organizations of people's power.

f. Data are for 1990.

Source: See table 8–4.

tance pension system was funded (and still is for those currently under that system) by payroll contributions to social insurance (transfers, in reality), but the new assistance system is financed by the state mainly by a tax on the gross turnover of private enterprises.[24] Barbados has a separate payroll contribution for social assistance pensions, but it is insufficient, and transfers are made from social insurance. In the Bahamas and Uruguay social assistance pensions are to be financed by the state, but the amount assigned is insufficient, thus leading to transfers from social insurance; the proportion of assistance pensions financed by the state in the Bahamas declined in the 1980s, while transfers from social insurance increased.[25]

In general, it is better to finance social assistance pensions from fiscal resources, particularly if the major state revenue is the income tax, because the impact on

[24] IPEA (1998a).

[25] Mesa-Lago (1988, 1994a).

distribution would be progressive. The risk is that the state controls the budget for those pensions and can cut them. A payroll contribution earmarked for social assistance could avoid that problem but create others noted above. A valuable lesson learned from past experience is that social insurance and social assistance pensions should not be mixed but must have clear and separate sources of revenue, accounts, and funds.

Financial Aid to Incorporate Special Labor Groups

Financial aid is needed to make possible the extension of health care and pensions to other groups of the population with low income and special labor conditions. When discussing the low percentage of self-employed workers who are covered by social insurance, it was argued that the financial burden imposed on them is one important cause. In the overwhelming majority of countries, the law imposes on the self-employed a percentage of contribution equal to the sum of the percentages that the salaried worker and his or her employer pay, the reason being that the self-employed lacks an employer. As a result, the percentage paid by the self-employed is two or three times that paid by a salaried worker; because most of the self-employed have an income below the minimum wage, establishing the latter as the tax base does not solve the problem. It was shown that in Costa Rica, the self-employed have a very high coverage by the social insurance health care program but a very low coverage by the pension program. Apart from the issue of priorities of the insured (health care being more urgent than long-run income security), a crucial explanation for the difference is that the percentage contribution of the self-employed to health care is slightly lower than that paid by the salaried worker but the contibution is three times higher for pensions.[26] One of the reviewers of this chapter rejected my point that the self-employed have a heavier tax burden than the salaried worker arguing that "there is no meaningful distinction between the portion of an employment tax [social security contribution] paid by the employer and the employee. The employer is not going to pay a gross wage that exceeds the worker's marginal productivity." And yet there is a long debate on whether the employer actually pays that contribution or transfers it to the worker or to prices; in the first and third possibilities the employee does not have the burden of such a contribution.

---

[26] FCN (1998a, 1998b).

To cope with the problem discussed above and avoid paying an assistance pension to the low-income elderly self-employed, three alternatives could be considered: establishing a lower level of income as the tax base, reducing that contribution and adjusting the pension accordingly (making it actuarially fair), or subsidizing the self-employed contribution for pensions. Probably, a combination of the first and second options would be the best, because they do not require a fiscal subsidy that could encourage a reclassification of work from wage to self-employed. And yet, if the amount of the pension were excessively low, some type of subsidy would be needed to effectively incorporate this group. Concerning health care, national health systems or integrated social insurance systems, as in Costa Rica, are adequate solutions for incorporating the low-income self-employed and similar groups mentioned below.

Coverage of domestic servants tends to be somewhat higher than that of the self-employed because they do have an employer (mandatory affiliation appears to be an important explanatory factor here also), but the special nature of this contractual relationship and the obstacles that impede the state's enforcement of the law are factors that contribute to low coverage.[27] Peasants are also difficult to incorporate into a pension program for several reasons: income that is below the minimum wage and that may be unstable; lack or frequent changes of employer; isolation and dispersion that make it very arduous to register, collect contributions from, and pay benefits to them (more so than the urban self-employed); extremely hard work and poor living conditions that reduce their life expectancy (the worker may be dismissed when his or her ability to work declines with age); complex and long bureaucratic procedures to prove their years of work and process a pension; and the prevailing culture that their children will take care of them in old age, although such informal protection is rapidly disappearing.[28] In Brazil, workers in the rural sector receive a pension financed by a tax on agricultural production.[29] Special social insurance schemes and methods should be designed, tailored to the peculiarities of these occupations, in order to facilitate affiliation, collection of contributions, and incentives to join.

---

[27] Mesa-Lago (1990).
[28] Mesa-Lago (1994b; 1998).
[29] Schwarzer (1999).

Impact on Income Distribution

It has been amply documented that state subsidies to social security in LA normally are not targeted to social assistance for the poor and extension of coverage to low-income strata but are mainly assigned to social insurance and middle-income strata that are already covered and often receive relatively good benefits. Such regressive effects are illustrated by the following examples.

Studies conducted in the 1980s on the distributive impact of health care in several countries of LAC indicate that public programs administered by the Ministry of Health (especially prevention and primary care), social assistance programs for the poor, and special programs for rural areas were those with the most progressive effects, while social insurance health programs and those for privileged groups (for example, the armed forces) had the most regressive effects. A reallocation of state subsidies toward public health, prevention, and primary care, social assistance, and rural areas, as well as extension of effective coverage to the poor and low-income groups would considerably improve the progressive impact on redistribution and help those in need.[30]

For pensions, in Brazil most social security expenditures and fiscal subsidies are concentrated on private employees and civil servants living in cities and developed areas, who are earning relatively high salaries and are entitled to costly seniority pensions that result in a significant regressive effect. At the end of 1997, the average seniority pension of private employees was about five times the average social assistance pension; the average seniority pension for federal civil servants was 2.5 times that of private employees, and that of federal judicial and parliamentary servants was 7.5 times higher. Pensions in the new social assistance system appear to have a progressive effect on regional distribution as they are concentrated in poor regions such as the Northeast, but their share of fiscal subsidies is so small that it cannot compensate for the regressive effect of seniority pensions.[31]

Costa Rica has one of the fairest income distributions and one of the most developed social security systems in LAC, and yet until very recently, fiscal subsidies were focused on 19 independent pension programs for civil servants, congressmen, judges, teachers, and so forth, who are among the best paid in the country; they accounted for 20 percent of the total number of pensioners but received 42 percent of the total amount of benefits; part of those pensions was fully financed by

---

[30] Mesa-Lago (1992a); World Bank (1993).
[31] IPEA (1998a, 1998b).

the state, and the rest received substantial fiscal subsidies. Reforms implemented in the 1990s are reducing such inequalities by gradually incorporating all those privileged groups (except the judiciary) into the general social insurance system, and eventually their entitlement conditions should become standardized.[32] In Chile, although a good many of the inequalities of the old social insurance pension system were eradicated, in 1997 at least 3.7 percent of GDP was spent by the state to finance the pension deficit from the old system and subsidize the new fully funded pension system, but less than 0.1 percent of GDP went to social assistance pensions, which, as already noted, are insufficient to meet essential needs.[33] All over LA (except in Costa Rica), members of the armed forces enjoy the most generous pensions and liberal entitlement conditions, and in most countries, also the best hospitals; the state heavily subsidizes those programs. Reassigning state subsidies away from middle-income and some high-income groups and directing them toward the poor and low-income strata would help to extend coverage of pensions, reduce poverty, and reverse the current regressive impact on distribution.[34]

ADMINISTRATION

There is an important need throughout LAC for the coordination of social assistance with social insurance, as well as other antipoverty programs, such as social safety nets, the health policy, and so forth. Different agencies are in charge of the administration of social assistance in the region.

Health Care

The Ministry of Health manages integrated national health systems. In only one country (Costa Rica), does the social insurance institute administer the noncontributory health program through an integrated system (which unifies all preventive and curative care), while the ministry sets policy, oversees the system, and provides some minor services. The advantage of these two approaches is that their services are integrated, and the poor tend to receive similar care as the rest of the population (I have confirmed such equality of treatment in Costa Rica). When the health system is dual or multiple, stratification results: the middle-income group is

---

[32] Mesa-Lago (1994a, 1998).
[33] Bustamante (1998); SSS (1998).
[34] Mesa-Lago (1983, 1990, 1992a); World Bank (1994).

covered by social insurance, the poor and low-income groups are legally left to the care of the ministry, and the high-income and some of the upper-middle-income groups are covered by the private sector (in Chile health maintenance organizations covered 27 percent of the total population in 1997). The best services are those of the private sector and, normally, the armed forces, followed by those of social insurance, and the worst services are those of the ministry. In about half of the countries in LA, a minority of the population is affiliated to social insurance but receives the large majority of the health care revenue; conversely the majority of the population is legally assigned to the public program of the Ministry of Health, which receives a small share of the budget.

With few exceptions, efforts to unify the services of the ministry and social insurance and decentralize the provision of services have failed, in spite of numerous reform attempts and recommendations of diverse international agencies (ILO, PAHO, World Bank). In the early 1980s Chile implemented a thorough health care reform, and a few other countries are doing the same in the second half of the 1990s (Argentina, Colombia, Peru); it is too soon to evaluate the results of this second round of reforms.[35]

Pensions

The administration of social assistance pensions is normally centralized. It is in the charge of the social insurance institute in five countries: the Bahamas, Barbados, Brazil (old system), Costa Rica, and Uruguay; and directly by the state in the other four countries: Argentina, Brazil (new system), Chile, and Cuba (table 8–7). In the Bahamas and Barbados, the management of social assistance was shifted from the state to the social insurance institute in 1974 and 1982, respectively, while the opposite has been occurring in Brazil since 1995–96. At least in two countries, there is some degree of decentralization and input from below.

Brazil's old social assistance system was fully administered (and still is for those already covered by it in 1996) by the social insurance institute. The new system began with a complete reorganization of social assistance and is based on principles of decentralization, but the social insurance institute on behalf of the state still pays pensions, although this function is expected to be eventually transferred to municipalities; popular participation is secured through local representative coun-

---

[35] Mesa-Lago (1992a); Cruz-Saco and Mesa-Lago (1999).

cils of social assistance, municipal services, and private institutions.[36] In Cuba the Ministry of Labor and Social Security designs the social assistance policy and supervises the system, while local organizations of people's power (OPP) grant the pensions; more information is needed on the OPP functions and whether they actually identify who are the poor, administer means tests, make suggestions on how to improve the system, and so forth.

It is not rare to find abuse and free riders in social assistance programs: pensions paid to those who are not poor, through political patronage or bureaucratic connections. Recent reports on pensions in Brazil and Costa Rica assert that there are irregularities such as the simulation of poverty (indigence), underdeclaration of age, false witnesses' statements, clientelism, and political interference in the selection of the beneficiaries.[37]

Some countries (for example, Costa Rica, Mexico) have tried to facilitate the incorporation of and collection of contributions from peasants and self-employed workers (an obstacle mentioned already) by using their cooperatives and associations to register and collect from them, but, although positive, the results have been small, owing to the scarce managerial ability of such intermediaries and lack of incentives offered by the social insurance institute for their effort.[38] Social insurance institutes should help to train their associations or cooperatives as efficient intermediaries and pay a commission based on the number of affiliations and amount of contributions collected. A question of administrative arrangement that has significant financial implications is whether the social assistance and social insurance pensions have separate funds or they are together in a common fund (table 8–7). In the Bahamas, Barbados, and Uruguay there is a common fund for both programs, thus facilitating the transfers from insurance to assistance. In Cuba, there are no pension funds at all, and the state pays both types of pensions out of general revenue. In Costa Rica, the two funds are separated, but due to FODESAF's incomplete or complete but insufficient transfers to social insurance, the latter ends up absorbing the difference (in the past, state debts have usually been negotiated in and paid with government bonds, but resulted in losses for social insurance). In Brazil, the old system had and still has a common fund (a minimum of 12 monthly contributions to social insurance is required to qualify for the old assistance pensions), while the new system is financed by the newly created state Fund for Na-

---

[36] IPEA (1998a).

[37] IPEA (1998b); FCN (1998b).

[38] Mesa-Lago (1998).

tional Social Assistance (FNAS). Technically, the social insurance fund is separate now and cannot be used to finance social assistance pensions but, in practice, the FNAS delays the transfer to the social insurance institute to pay such pensions, resulting in a bitter fight between the two institutions. Finally, Argentina and Chile have a separate social insurance fund that cannot be touched for social assistance pensions, which are directly paid by the state.

In view of the negative experience of several countries in LAC, it would be better if the social insurance institute is not put in charge of the administration of social assistance pensions. Even if the social insurance institute directly receives the revenue of a special tax or payroll contribution, it would be responsible for paying assistance pensions if that tax/contribution is insufficient to cover costs. The same would happen if the owed state subsidy or transfer fails to materialize or is insufficient to cover all costs. It could be argued that transfers from social insurance to social assistance have a progressive redistribution effect, but it is more transparent and less complex to achieve that end by reassigning fiscal subsidies in order to target the poor.

TWO RECENT TYPES OF REFORM: BRAZIL AND COSTA RICA

This chapter has argued that a national health system or a universal, integrated health care system is the best way to protect the poor and low-income groups, and several countries of the NLC and Costa Rica should be models for LA. The same is not true of adequate models for social assistance pensions, and this section provides two examples of them: the recent reform of Brazil (1991–96), and the proposal for such reform in Costa Rica (1998). These two countries are also important for the peculiarities of their systems: the two have the highest coverage of social assistance pensions of the population above 65 years in the region, and they have different types of administration. Costa Rica's system is managed by social insurance, while Brazil's is managed by the state. Brazil's new system is decentralized, with participation from below; and Costa Rica's proposed reform was the outcome of a process of national consensus and advocates the universalization of the old age assistance pension and the extension of coverage among self-employed with low income.

Brazil

The Organic Law of Social Assistance, widely discussed in Brazil since 1989, enacted in 1993, and regulated in 1995, established in 1996 a new national social assistance scheme.[39] It has integrated several previous institutions and programs, is decentralized, institutionalizes the participation of representative organizations, and claims to have abolished the old vices of the past: fragmentation and lack of coordination, clientelism, and corruption.[40] Three agencies that dealt with social assistance were integrated into the Secretary of Social Assistance, which is one of the two main branches of the Ministry of Social Insurance and Social Assistance (MPAS); the ministry elaborates the budget proposal and coordinates and supervises the social assistance policy at the national level. A newly created National Council of Social Assistance approves the national policy and assistance budget, registers the various institutions devoted to social assistance policy, and designs the criteria for transfer of resources to such institutions. The federal district, states, and municipalities have funds that receive the resources from the Union, contribute their own share, and manage the funds according to previous agreements signed with the MPAS. The implementation of the programs is done at the local level by Councils of Social Assistance; trade unions, municipalities, and NGOs cooperate with the councils. Norms for the social assistance policy, approved at the end of 1997, proclaim the principles of universalization, equality in access to services, efficiency, and transparency.

In 1998 an internal evaluation of the reform process reported that 67 percent of the municipalities have organized their councils, 57 percent have established the funds, and 32 percent have developed their plans. Some difficulties are noted in the report such as the need to develop managerial capacity at the local level to manage the projects in order to secure an effective decentralization process. The importance of coordinating social assistance activities at the three levels—national, state, and local—is also noted. In addition, the evaluation focused on quantities of services provided instead of their quality and targeting efficiency. Several municipalities are under severe financial stress and cannot provide their needed share for social assistance.

The system includes five programs: social assistance pensions for the poor who are old or disabled; lump sums for birth and death for poor families; assistance services; other social assistance programs; and projects to fight poverty. The key features and results of the first three programs are summarized as follows. Social assistance pensions are totally financed by the Union budget and paid through the social

---

[39] Lei Orgânica de Assistência Social (1993).
[40] This section is based on IPEA (1998a, 1998b).

insurance institute. Entitlement conditions and benefits have been described already; the number of these pensions increased twofold in 1996–97 and reached 38 percent of the total number of assistance pensions being paid in the nation (it should be recalled that the old system is closed but still is paying pensions, although the number is declining as the beneficiaries die). There are no social assistance survivor pensions in Brazil, but the new system grants lump sums for birth and death to families with a monthly per capita income below one-fourth of the minimum wage. Finally, assistance services (preventive, curative, and promotion of health) are currently provided to 15 percent of the elderly poor, as well as services of rehabilitation and promotion to 4 percent of the poor who are disabled. With the exception of pensions, other benefits are still modest, but the system has been in operation for only three years and the evaluation covered only the first two.

Attractive features of the Brazilian reform that should be followed are the integration of the social assistance system, its decentralization, and participation from below. An outside evaluation would be useful to assess the impact of the new system on poverty, whether pensions are sufficient to cover basic needs, the financial shares contributed at the three levels, effective implementation at the local level, managerial efficiency, and so forth.

Costa Rica

A Forum for National Consensus was held in Costa Rica in 1998 with wide representation from most pertinent sectors of the population (workers, employers, cooperatives, peasants, women, minorities, political parties, the Executive, NGOs) to discuss several crucial issues, one of them being pension reform. At the end of September, a document with recommendations had been elaborated by the forum and sent to the government; reportedly, a legal draft had been finished at the end of 1998 and submitted to congress for its consideration in 1999 (it was approved in 2000). The document includes two important reforms: the universalization of a social assistance pension and the extension of social insurance pension coverage among low-income groups.[41]

Principles of the document are the right of all people to a pension sufficient to cover basic needs, the extension of coverage of the social security system to the uninsured, especially among the poorest, the universalization of a noncontributory pension for the poor based on solidarity, and the state obligation to guarantee

---

[41] This section is based on FCN (1998a, 1998b); Mesa-Lago (1998).

such a pension. A noncontributory basic pension would be granted to all the population more than 70 years old and not covered by current pension schemes, starting with the least developed counties and gradually extending to the entire nation in five years. A new permanent Solidarity Fund for that purpose would be established, separate from the insurance pension fund, with the current resources provided by FODASEF (guaranteed by the government) and others from government agencies, municipalities, and communities. The new pension, it is estimated, will cost from 0.16 percent to 0.26 percent of GDP in the next twenty years. Costa Rica already has a noncontributory pension for the poor older than 65, but it has a ceiling, and a significant part of the target population does not receive such a pension. Apparently, the new program would not eliminate the current one but would be added to it. It is not clear, however, whether the new pension would be universal regardless of income or based on need and submitted to a means test. The amount of the new pension would be 50 percent of the minimum insurance pension, which suggests it might be higher than the current average assistance pension (equal to one-fifth of the average insurance pension) and close somewhat the existing gap between insurance and assistance pensions.

The power to extend coverage to low-income self-employed workers, who are not voluntarily affiliated to the insurance program, is left to the social insurance institute, which will decide to establish mandatory coverage for various sectors according to their characteristics, based on a public timetable. To facilitate the incorporation of these workers, the state will subsidize the portion of the percentage contribution assigned to employers, totally or partially depending on the worker's income. The pension will be at least equal to the minimum pension in the insurance pension program, a controversial aspect because, combined with the explained subsidy, it could encourage salaried workers (in combination with their employers) to report that they are self-employed. No estimates have been released on the cost of this program. The proposal does not mention other groups in the labor force that are difficult to incorporate into the contributory pension program (for example, peasants), but says that the social insurance institute should evaluate its agreements with associations or cooperatives of such groups and promote and help their affiliation. A special program is proposed to encourage voluntary affiliation by housewives to the contributory pension program.

The Forum document is generally positive, and most of its recommendations appear to be feasible. The proposed universalization of the social assistance pension follows most of the recommendations of this chapter, but two of its features are not clear: the type of the assistance pension and its relationship with the average insurance pension. The estimated cost of this program, as a percentage of GDP, is small, but details on the calculation are lacking. If accurate, the program should be financially viable in Costa Rica. The proposal to extend coverage to the self-employed also follows this chapter's recommendations, except, perhaps, for the determination of the level of the pension for the self-employed. The process of building a national consensus to design the crucial elements of a pension reform in Costa Rica is so far unique in the region and should be a model to follow.

CURRENT AND FUTURE PROBLEMS AND RECOMMENDATIONS

This section summarizes the major problems currently faced by social assistance and the recommendations of this chapter (organized by the four sections of the study) and explores potential future difficulties in this field.

Coverage

Problems

LAC countries with national health systems provide their services to all residents, and hence appear to cover virtually all of the population, including the poor and low-income groups; this is also true of at least the four most developed countries with social insurance systems in LA, through a combination of social insurance and assistance. In the rest of the countries with social insurance systems, total population coverage combining all programs ranges from 75 percent to 34 percent and, therefore, leaves out most or all the poor and low-income strata. Those legally entitled to protection by the public health system managed by the Ministry of Health do not have effective access to care, or the quality of the services they receive is very poor. Only one country with a social insurance system (Costa Rica) has integrated all health services and provides coverage to the poor (under social assistance) as well as low-income groups (who receive subsidies), and their treatment is equal to that of the insured. Health care coverage in rural areas (where poverty incidence is higher) is lower and poorer in quality than in urban areas; indigenous populations are usually poor, concentrated in rural areas, and largely unprotected by health care. Informal workers in urban areas, most of whom are poor, also lack effective health coverage.

Coverage of the economically active population by social insurance pensions tends to be lower than that by health care and excludes the poor with very few exceptions: in the four most developed LA countries and two NLC countries, such coverage ranges from 73 to 97 percent and, in some of them, a proportion of the poor might be covered by social assistance. Legal and statistical coverage of the self-employed, domestic servants, rural workers, and other low-income groups is considerably smaller than that by health care too. In about eleven countries, social assistance pensions are legally established for the poor, but the scarce data available suggest that they do not cover the majority of them.

Recommendations

National health care systems or integrated social insurance health systems that cover all the population with primary health care should be established in order to protect the poor; ex ante coverage by social assistance of health (prevention, health education, potable water, and waste disposal) is better and cheaper than ex post curative care; where resources are very scarce to expand coverage, priorities should be given to health care over assistance pensions; the least developed countries should also target rural areas (and indigenous populations where they exist) over urban areas; facilities should be given to middle- and high-income strata to buy additional coverage or better protection through different providers, including social insurance and the private sector but without any fiscal subsidy; social assistance pensions should be expanded to the poorest population after universal coverage in primary health care has been achieved; and the incorporation into social insurance of low-income groups, such as the self-employed, domestic servants, and employees of microenterprises could be facilitated by establishing mandatory programs for some of them or creating ad hoc schemes with lower financing burden and benefits (subsidized contributory programs ex ante are cheaper than and avoid the stigma of social assistance ex post).

Entitlement Conditions and Benefits

Problems

Although comprehensive and accurate data are not available, it appears that about one-third of the countries of LAC have social assistance pension programs in operation. All of them are based on need, and all, with the possible exception of one, are means tested. No country offers a universal, flat pension regardless of income, which is more appropriate to developed countries. Assistance pensions are granted to the poor in old age and disability; only three countries legally provide pensions to survivors (the Bahamas, Costa Rica, and Cuba), hence, poor widows and minor orphans are left without protection. Minimum ages for old age assistance pensions are higher than those required for contributory programs and range from 65 to 70 years; certain workers whose labor conditions are very harsh cannot in practice gain access to the contributory pensions and must wait a longer period to qualify for the assistance pension. We lack comparative data on how the medical test for disability is administered. In at least two countries (the Bahamas and Barbados), the levels of the social insurance and social assistance pensions are very close, hence creating disincentives for affiliation to the contributory program and encouraging free riders. Three countries (Argentina, Brazil, and Uruguay) provide minimum assistance pensions that appear sufficient to cover basic needs (in Brazil, to avoid indigence), but in other countries (Chile, Costa Rica, and Cuba) those minimums seem to be insufficient. Cuba used to provide low minimum pensions, combined with a social safety net that protected the poor, but the crisis of the 1990s has drastically reduced that minimum in real terms and virtually destroyed the additional social safety net.

Recommendations

The social assistance pension based on needs and means tested is recommended for most of LAC because of the region's scarcity of resources, high poverty incidence, and income inequality; poor widows with minor children and single mothers with a large number of children should be protected by social assistance (workfare, nutrition, health care, childcare, and training programs should be preferable to cash transfers when feasible); there must be a sufficient difference between the pension paid by social insurance and social assistance, but the reduction of the latter may result in a sum grossly insufficient to cover basic needs (changes in social assistance, therefore, should be coordinated with a reform of social insurance pensions); and ad hoc pension programs should be designed for groups of the labor force working under very harsh conditions.

Financing

Problems

The available data on social assistance expenditures are scarce and plagued by improper definitions. Such data indicate, nevertheless, that only a small proportion of social security is devoted to social assistance, and most of that goes to social insurance, despite the fact that, in half of LA, two-thirds of the population and labor force are not covered. As a percentage of GDP, assistance expenditures are usually lower than 0.5 percent, suggesting that a more significant effort is needed and could be financially feasible in many countries, particularly the most developed, if there is the political will. Ceilings are normally set to the overall sum assigned to assistance pensions, without clear priorities, which leads to a struggle for the scarce resources available. Very high percentage contributions imposed on the self-employed worker (due to the lack of an employer) are triple the percentage contribution assigned to the salaried worker, making very difficult the incorporation of the self-employed and increasing the chances that they will eventually become assistance cases. Evidence from several countries (Brazil, Chile, Costa Rica) shows that the bulk of fiscal subsidies is allocated to social insurance pensions for privileged groups (for example, congressmen, the judiciary, other civil servants, members of the armed forces), and very little is assigned to social assistance for pensions and health care, with a regressive impact on income distribution.

Recommendations

A higher proportion of social security expenditures and GDP could be devoted to social assistance programs (an increase in the proportion of GDP must be preceded by a careful feasibility evaluation); when ceilings on the amount of assistance pensions are set, clear priorities should be established to select the beneficiaries. One of the following three alternatives or a combination of them should be considered to facilitate the incorporation of the low-income self-employed into social insurance: establish a lower level of income as the tax base, reduce the contribution and adjust the pensions accordingly, or subsidize the contribution. Assistance programs for health care and pensions for the poor and low-income groups should receive fiscal subsidies currently assigned to the social insurance that covers middle-income groups and generous pensions for privileged groups.

Administration

Problems

A major obstacle for the study, evaluation, and policy design of social assistance programs in LAC is the very scarce data available on them; only the ILO provides some financial statistics (incomplete and mostly outdated), and the remaining international and regional organizations do not publish any data. There is a lack of coordination among antipoverty programs, including social assistance, and between this scheme and social insurance. The administration of health care in LA is normally under numerous institutions that provide unequal treatment to various segments of the population, generating stratification and inequalities. The administration of social assistance pensions is highly centralized, without input from local levels and beneficiaries (the poor). In a good number of countries, the pension funds for social insurance and social assistance are not separated or the state does not fulfill its financial social assistance obligations, thus resulting in transfers from social insurance to assistance, which erode the financial and actuarial stability of the former. Enforcement of the means test is not always efficient, and there are cases of fraud, political interference, and corruption.

Recommendations

An effort should be made to coordinate all antipoverty programs (social assistance, social safety nets, emergency employment), as well as other related programs such as primary health care, and those targeting vulnerable groups (children, women, ethnic groups); the current stratification in the administration of health care should be eliminated through an integrated but decentralized system capable of securing at least primary care for the poor and low-income groups, as well as facilitating their participation; the administration of social assistance pensions should also be integrated and decentralized, stimulating active participation from local levels and beneficiaries; social insurance and assistance pension schemes should be coordinated, but their funds must be separated and the state should fulfill its financial obligations to avoid transfers from and destabilization of the insurance scheme; associations or cooperatives of low-income groups should be stimulated and helped (training personnel, paying commissions) to become intermediaries that affiliate and collect contributions from them; the means test must be applied periodically (to check changing poverty conditions) in a simple and efficient manner (relying

more heavily on the information provided by local communities than on centralized bureaucratic procedures, and without political interference and fraud); and
statistical data and information on social assistance programs should be gathered
and published by countries and international organizations to better understand
and evaluate those schemes and design adequate policies.

The Inter-American Development Bank has considerable resources and a well-
designed poverty reduction policy but little experience in direct transfers to the
poor and social protection of informal sector workers.[42] The Bank could help in this
important policy area by providing financial and technical aid on the following
aspects, among others: developing information and statistics on social assistance
programs; assessing the financial feasibility of establishing these programs in LAC
countries or reforming those in existence; targeting the poor and designing simple
but efficient means tests; studying effective mechanisms for incorporation of the
informal sector in both health care and pension noncontributory programs; and
promoting administrative decentralization and participation.

Lessons from the Experience of Brazil and Costa Rica

Brazil and Costa Rica have recently introduced systems of universal social assistance pensions and, because these countries already have the highest regional coverage of social insurance pensions for those above 65 years, they should reach all
the elderly population including the poor. The Brazilian system has the following
features: it is managed by the state and totally financed by the Union, it integrates
all previous social assistance programs, it is decentralized at the local level and
procures participation from representative organizations. An outside evaluation of
the system is needed to assess its impact on poverty, whether pensions are sufficient to cover basic needs, its effective implementation at the local level, and its
managerial efficiency. The result of a process of national consensus, the Costa Rican
system will universalize social assistance pensions for all of the population 70 years
and older and extend social insurance pensions for low-income self-employed with
a state subsidy that will totally or partially substitute for the employer's contribution. It is important to clarify whether the assistance pension will be universal regardless of income or submitted to an income test, the calculation of the cost of this
program requires more precision, and the administration appears to be centralized

---

[42] Lustig and Deutsch (1998).

without representation. Features of both systems that should be emulated are the provision of a universal social assistance pension for the elderly poor (in Costa Rica, also a subsidized social insurance pension for low-income self-employed), the full financing of such pensions out of fiscal revenue, and the separation of finances for social insurance and assistance pensions. Administrative decentralization and representation from below in Brazil and the process of building national consensus in Costa Rica are additional commendable features.

CONCLUSION

Several potential future problems can be envisioned. The number of poor has been growing in LA since the beginning of the 1980s and reached between 150 million and 196 million in the 1990s. The poverty incidence of the total population rose from 41 percent to 46 percent in 1980–90, while such incidence among households increased from 31 percent to 41 percent in that period but declined to 39 percent in 1994. Although the incidence of poverty has decreased in the majority of countries, it has risen at least in Argentina, Mexico, and Venezuela.[43] The crisis of 1998–99 (particularly in Brazil) may result in an increase in the number of poor and incidence of poverty in the region, thus making it more difficult and costly to protect them. The least developed countries have the highest poverty incidence and the lowest resources to help the poor. Hence, their problem is the gravest. Poverty incidence in rural areas is much higher than in urban areas: among the total population it was 61 and 39 percent in rural and urban areas, respectively, in 1990, while among households it was 55 and 34 percent, respectively, in 1994. As the poor are concentrated in rural areas, dispersed, and often isolated, it is more expensive to provide health care to them. Yet the rural population is declining in LAC, hence, this problem should be reduced in the long run, but that does not exonerate the leadership from its current responsibility to help the rural poor.

The urban informal sector is also affected by poverty, but access to health care is relatively easier there than it is in rural areas, and yet this is not the case with pensions. Low-income groups in the urban sector, such as self-employed and unpaid family workers, employees of microenterprises, and domestic servants, constitute the bulk of the informal sector that has been expanding since the 1980s. These people either lack an employer or have one who often evades registration

---

[43] CEPAL (1992, 1996); Lustig and Deutsch (1998).

and payment of contributions. The immense majority of them are not covered by social insurance and in many cases do not meet the requirements to qualify for social assistance, particularly in pensions. As their numbers expand, this problem worsens, and the focus of public social policy should change.

The poor are uneducated, receive the lowest income, and are not organized. Hence, they lack political power to press for government help. Conversely, the most powerful groups of insured are well educated, have relatively high income, and are strongly organized (for example, civil servants, teachers). Hence, they exercise effective pressure to improve their coverage and benefits, as well as obtain fiscal support. In some countries, like Argentina and Uruguay, pensioners are organized into very powerful groups, which successfully lobby for the protection of their pensions. The risk of political-economic destabilization will increase in the future unless the poor are organized and exercise pressure on the state to provide essential services (or elect political leaders willing to do that job) or the state takes the initiative to socially protect the poor.[44]

A few LA countries have gone through the demographic transition and have aging populations and the oldest pension programs in the Americas (Argentina, Cuba, Uruguay), which means that expenditures on pensions and health care for the old will continue to expand. The majority of countries of LA are entering the demographic transition and still have relatively young populations, but that situation will change soon and fast. In 1990 the proportion of the population 60 years and older was 16.4 percent in Uruguay, 13.1 percent in Argentina, and 11.8 percent in Cuba. Those proportions will jump in 2030 to 22.5, 19.3, and 27.2 percent, respectively. However, the proportions of the youngest countries (the least developed: Bolivia, Guatemala, Honduras, Nicaragua) in 1990 were 4.2 to 5.4 percent, but in 2030 will increase to 9 to 10 percent, still lower than the 1990 figures of the oldest countries.[45] The combination of aging with increasing poverty (the "aging of poverty") could become a grave problem, hence the need to tackle now the protection of the poor and low-income groups.[46]

---

[44] Lustig and Deutsch (1998).

[45] World Bank (1994).

[46] Lustig and Deutsch (1998).

References

Banco de Previsión Social (BPS). 1998a. *La seguridad social en Uruguay.* Montevideo: Asesoría Económica y Actuarial.

————. 1998b. *Boletín estadístico 1998.* No. 53. Montevideo.

Bertranou. 1999. Personal communication.

Bustamante, Julio. 1998. "17 años del sistema chileno de pensiones." In Alejandro Bonilla and Alfredo Conte-Rand, eds., *Pensiones en América Latina: dos décadas de reforma.* Lima, Peru: OIT.

Caja Costarricense del Seguro Social (CCSS). 1995. *Reglamento del régimen no contributivo de pensiones por monto básico.* San José, Costa Rica.

————. 1997. *Anuario estadístico 1997.* San José, Costa Rica.

Comisión Económica de América Latina y el Caribe (CEPAL). 1992. *El perfil de la pobreza en América Latina.* Santiago, Chile.

————. 1996. *Statistical Yearbook for Latin America and the Caribbean 1996.* Santiago, Chile.

————. 1997. *Panorama social de América Latina 1997.* Santiago, Chile.

Cruz-Saco, María Amparo, and Carmelo Mesa-Lago, eds. 1999. *Do Options Exist? The Reform of Pension and Health Care Systems in Latin America.* Pittsburgh: University of Pittsburgh Press.

Foro de Concertación Nacional (FCN). 1998a. *La reforma del sistema nacional de pensiones: una propuesta.* San José, Costa Rica.

————. 1998b. *Informe final.* San José, Costa Rica.

Instituto de Pesquisa Econômica Aplicada (IPEA), Diretoria de Política Social. 1998a. *Assistência Social 1995-1998: Quatro Anos de Transformações.* (Background paper for the report.) Brasília, Brazil.

————. 1998b. *Previdência Social.* Brasília, Brazil.

Lei Orgânica de Assistência Social. 1993. Brasília, Brazil.

Inter-American Development Bank (IDB). 1999. Presentation at IDB conference by an official of Trinidad and Tobago (February).

International Labour Office (ILO). 1996. *The Cost of Social Security 1987-1989.* Geneva, Switzerland.

————. 1999. http://www.ilo.org/public/english/110secso/cssinder.htm.

Lustig, Nora, and Ruthanne Deutsch. 1998. *The Inter-American Development Bank and Poverty Reduction: An Overview.* Working Paper Series POV-101-R. Inter-American Development Bank, Washington, D.C.

Mesa-Lago, Carmelo. 1983. "Social Security and Extreme Poverty in Latin America." *Journal of Development Economics* 12: 83–110.

————. 1988. "Social Insurance: The Experience of Three Countries in the English-Speaking Caribbean." *International Labour Review* 127: 479–96.

————. 1990. *La seguridad social y el sector informal.* No. 32. Organización Internacional del Trabajo, PREALC, e Investigaciones sobre Empleo, Santiago, Chile.

————. 1992a. *Health Care for the Poor in Latin America and the Caribbean.* PAHO Scientific Publication no. 539. Pan American Health Organization and Inter-American Foundation, Washington, D.C.

————. 1992b. "Protection of the Informal Sector in Latin America and the Caribbean by Social Security or Alternative Means." In Víctor Tokman, ed., *Beyond Regulation: The Informal Economy in Latin America*. Boulder, CO: Lynne Rienner Publishers.

————. 1994a. *Changing Social Security in Latin America: Towards the Alleviation of Social Costs of Economic Reform*. Boulder, CO: Lynne Rienner.

————. 1994b. "Expansion of Social Protection to the Rural Population in Latin America." *Social Security in Developing Countries*. New Delhi, India: Har-Anand Publications.

————. 1997. "La seguridad social y la pobreza en Cuba." *La seguridad social en América Latina: seis casos diferentes*. Buenos Aires, Argentina: CEDLA-Konrad Adenauer Stiftung.

————. 1998. "Análisis y recomendaciones sobre la propuesta del gobierno en el foro de concertación nacional sobre el sistema de pensiones de Costa Rica" y "Evaluación del Acuerdo de la Comisión de Pensiones del FCN en Costa Rica." San José, Costa Rica: Friedrich Ebert Stiftung (August and September).

————. 2000a. "Achieving and Sustaining Social Development with Limited Resources: The Experience of Costa Rica." In Dharam Ghai, ed., *Social Development and Public Policy: Some Lessons from Successful Experiences*. London, UK: Macmillan.

————. 2000b. *Market, Socialist and Mixed Economies: Comparative Policy and Performance–Chile, Cuba and Costa Rica*. Baltimore, MD: Johns Hopkins University Press.

Mesa-Lago, Carmelo, and Sergio Roca. 1992. "Cuba." In John Dixon and David Macarov, eds., *Social Welfare in Socialist Countries*. London, UK: Routledge.

Mesa-Lago, Carmelo, and Fabio Bertranou. 1998. *Manual de economía de la seguridad social en América Latina*. Montevideo, Uruguay: CLAEH.

Ministério da Previdência e Assistência Social (MPAS). 1998. *Anuário Estatístico da Previdência Social 1997*. Brasília, Brazil.

————. 1998. *Boletín Estatístico da Previdência Social* 3 (December).

Oficina Nacional de Estadística. 1998 *Annuario Estadístico de Cuba 1996*. Havana, Cuba.

Rivero, Raúl. 1999. "La penuria acusa a cientos de jubilados cubanos [Report from Havana]." *El Nuevo Herald*. Miami, FL, January 17.

Schulthess, Walter E. 1995. "Efectos sobre la distribución del ingreso de las prestaciones no contributivas." *Previsión Social* 19: 3–30.

Schwarzer, Helmut. 1999. *Impactos Socio-Econômicos do Sistema de Aposentadorias Rurais no Brasil*. Brasília, Brazil: IPEA.

Superintendencia de Seguridad Social (SSS). 1997, 1998. *Estadísticas mensuales de seguridad social*. Santiago, Chile. (January-June).

————. 1999. *Information on Social Assistance and Social Insurance*. Santiago, Chile (January).

United Nations Development Programme (UNDP). 1997. *Investigación sobre el desarrollo humano en Cuba 1996*. Havana, Cuba: Caguayo S.A.

————. 1998. *Human Development Report 1998*. Oxford: Oxford University Press.

U.S. Social Security Administration (SSA). 1997. *Social Security Programs throughout the World 1997*. Washington, D.C.: Government Printing Office.

World Bank. 1993. *World Development Report: Investing in Health*. Oxford: Oxford University Press.

————. 1994. *Averting the Old-Age Crisis: Policies to Protect the Old and Promote Growth*. Oxford: Oxford University Press.

————. 1999. *World Development Report 1998/99*. Oxford: Oxford University Press.

CHAPTER NINE

The Safety Net Role
of Microfinance for Income
and Consumption Smoothing

Manfred Zeller

This chapter explores the role of microfinance for income and consumption smoothing. In a nutshell, improved access to financial services can have two principal effects on household outcomes. First, it can raise the expected value of income and, therefore, of consumption and future investment and asset accumulation. This is the traditional and often sole argument for provision of services by microfinance institutions (MFIs). Second, it can decrease the downward semivariances of income or consumption. It is the second effect that is relevant for the subject of this chapter.[1]

For the food-insecure, it is particularly important to reduce the downward risk of falling below some minimum threshold levels for consumption of food and other basic needs. Therefore, the poor tend to value financial services that address the risk-coping motive more whereas the wealthy can afford to demand more of financial services that generate income and accumulate assets. For example, while the rich and well-cushioned in developed countries buy stocks, middle- and lower-income families prefer to hold more certificates of deposit, and the poor keep their money in a checking account or under the pillow. Similar behavior, albeit using different financial products, including myriad informal financial substitutes, can be observed among the wealthy and poor in developing countries.

This chapter seeks to assess the role of microfinance for income and consumption smoothing by the poor.[2] The principal policy implication is that the role of

---

[1] I note that it can sometimes be more efficient to reduce the downward risk in consumption by increasing the mean income, for example, through adoption of technology.

[2] For the definition of these terms, see Morduch (1995).

microfinance for risk-coping mechanisms is not well recognized and therefore underutilized in policy and microfinance practice. Although it is admittedly more difficult to offer savings and insurance services than credit, recent product innovations by a few microfinance institutions suggest that there is room to exploit this potential more efficiently.

Generating extra income (or growth) is the traditional argument for the provision of credit and savings services.[3] Financial services that potentially raise the income of households are microenterprise credit, seasonal agricultural credit, medium- and long-term investment credit, and term deposits and savings accounts that earn interest income. For this type of service I use the term *financial services for income generation*. These services are fairly common among MFIs and constitute most often the only type of financial services they offer.

Credit, savings, and insurance services that address the demand for reducing ex ante the variance of income, or ex post the variance of consumption, are rarely offered by MFIs. Such services include insurance, the provision of savings services that are liquid and can be withdrawn at short notice, and the provision of consumption credit, or less controversially expressed, the provision of general household credit for maintaining family labor and the household's human and social capital. These services provide a shield against future risks and can thereby enable households to bear more risks. Since technology adoption and the level of production and investment increases with risk-bearing capacity, the provision of financial services for consumption smoothing (FCs) can have an indirect and positive effect on ex ante income generation.[4] FCs can potentially reduce the cost of income and consumption smoothing by, for example, substituting for some higher-cost informal savings or higher-cost informal sources of consumption credit. FCs are particularly demanded in environments of considerable interannual and seasonal income fluctuations and are, therefore, particularly relevant for rural households depending mainly on agriculture for their livelihood. Moreover, FCs gain in relative importance over MFIs for disadvantaged clientele groups such as women and wage laborers. Labor, their major production factor, is exposed to a number of health risks that can jeopardize earnings income at any time.

Policy may be well advised to recognize not only the microfinance nexus for poverty alleviation through growth but also its potential for providing social protection that can complement other measures for public and informal safety nets.

---

[3] See Zeller and others (1997).

[4] See Eswaran and Kotwal (1990).

COPING WITH COVARIANT AND IDIOSYNCRATIC RISKS THROUGH MICROFINANCE SERVICES

In this section I attempt to systematize the risks that poor households in developing countries face and that motivate the households' demand for financial services for income and consumption smoothing. I contrast this demand with the type of services commonly supplied by microfinance institutions. The gap between current supply and demand by the poor defines areas for potential policy action as well as further research.

Tables 9–1, 9–2, and 9–3 list various categories of risk that affect the process of income generation or consumption by households. These risks cause income to fluctuate and may create additional unexpected expenses that need to be met by ex post consumption smoothing measures. The second column in the three tables lists examples of typical informal responses to these risks, whereas the last column indicates the relevance of microfinance policy for addressing these risks.

When considering the risks listed in the tables, it is important to distinguish between idiosyncratic and covariant risks, that is, risks that affect only individuals or larger groups of people in the same locality, respectively. This is because the informal responses to risk that are differentiated in the second column of the tables are less effective in covering covariant risks than in protecting households against idiosyncratic risks. In general, informal responses are of a localized nature, mostly based on actions by individual household members or by informal institutions at the local community level. Mark Rosenzweig and Kenneth I. Wolpin find that sales of bullocks in India are motivated by the need to smooth consumption. Yet the effectiveness of traditional forms of savings can be severely hampered by covariant risk such as drought. Czukas and others explore the role of livestock as a form of precautionary savings in Burkina Faso.[5] Their results show that livestock transactions play less of a role in consumption smoothing than is often assumed. This phenomenon suggests that drought as a covariant risk can equally threaten the effectiveness of specific forms of precautionary savings. This is particularly true if poorly integrated markets for the assets lead to drastic declines in prices exactly at a time when a large part of households seeks to sell.

Table 9–1 systematizes the risks related to the generation of income and distinguishes between income from self-employment in farm and nonfarm microenterprises as well as wage labor income. While the latter covers the risk of

---

[5] Rosenzweig and Wolpin (1993); Czukas, Fafchamps, and Udry (1995).

Table 9–1. Risks Affecting Income Generation of Households and Their Members

Risks related to	Examples of informal responses to risk	Relevance for microfinance policy
Input markets (availability and quality of production inputs, including shortages of family labor due to ill health)	Diversifying income sources (nonfarm, on-farm, wage labor, temporary or permanent migration of household members) Establishing reliable input sources through formal contracts or through investment in social relations with input dealers Entering into bonded patron-client relationships by poor entrepreneurs with wealthy input suppliers (for example, tenant-landlord) Holding costly reserves of inputs (for example, seeds or raw material for microenterprises) Investing in social capital (informal groups that provide labor)	If input markets do not function well, credit for inputs (in cash) to microentrepreneurs may not create much benefit Organization of MFI clients to reap economies of scale, scope, and risk in purchasing inputs
Production function (for example, covariant weather risks or idiosyncratic risks affecting business, crop, or livestock enterprise)	Diversifying income (that is, foregoing profits from specialization) Risk-reducing inputs (for example, irrigation, pesticides, vaccination of animals) Postponing decisions (for example, sowing later) Diversifying operations spatially (for example, plot diversification) Choosing low-return enterprises that have lower risks	Credit and savings services for diversification in new enterprises Provision of production insurance (crop, livestock insurance)
Output markets (risks in finding a buyer and price risks)	Diversifying income Establishing contracts/informal relationships with output buyers (including bonded patron-client relationships) Producing more for home consumption than for the market (emphasizing autarky and foregoing gains from trade)	Addressing bottlenecks in marketing (again, lack of access to financial services may not be the primary cause of income fluctuation)

Table 9–2. Risks Affecting Consumption with Chronic, Permanent Effects on the Ability to Earn Income

Risk related to	Examples of informal responses to risk	Relevance for microfinance policy
Sliding into chronic poverty in its worst form (loss of all productive assets, including ability to work), for example, often caused by covariant risks, such as natural disasters, war, political upheaval and major economic crises, HIV/AIDS	Informal social welfare (for example neighborhood help, giving to beggars, raising children in foster homes, remittances by extended family) Informal precautionary savings and investment in human capital (having more children) and social capital (having access to networks that provide help)	No role for credit as there is no viable project to be financed and no repayment capacity Provision of precautionary savings services Other safety net measures are more relevant (public transfers to replenish assets, such as disaster relief or social security) Very limited role for insurance, except if coupled with international reinsurance
Permanent inability to work	Same as above	Disability insurance and precautionary savings services
Old age or death of family member	Informal precautionary savings (long-term investments in physical, human, and social capital that can provide income in old age)	Precautionary savings services Life insurance

Table 9–3. Risks Affecting Consumption with Usually Transitory Effects on the Ability to Earn Income

Risk related to	Examples of informal responses to risk	Relevance for microfinance policy
Health (temporarily affecting ability to work)		
1. Covariant health risks (for example, malaria, flu)	Reducing exposure to health risk if causes are known Holding precautionary savings Investing in social capital that provides labor, food, and care (but capacity of network for service provision may be weakened, too, because of covariance)	Public health policy (including health insurance) is most relevant MF policy can complement by providing - precautionary savings services with emphasis on low transaction costs for withdrawal and liquidity rather than return - consumption credit
2. Idiosyncratic health risks (for example, many human diseases, accident, pregnancy)	Like with covariant risks, but investment in social capital is much more likely to be effective	In addition to the above, member-based MFIs can self-finance the demand for consumption credit out of internal savings or can retail specific insurance services
Claims of social network (for example, financing social events, helping out friends and relatives in need) and communal conflicts that undermine access to essential resources for production and human welfare	Holding precautionary savings, as above	Provision of liquid savings services for unexpected claims and term deposits for anticipated claims
Divorce, domestic violence, and other causes of household disintegration	Maintaining ownership/control over assets brought into/accumulated during marriage Investing in social networks accessible by the individual household member	Promoting savings accounts and credit lines for individuals, in particular for women

unemployment, the former are specific risks related to the availability of inputs (with respect to quantity, quality, and price risks), the stochastic production function of the enterprise, and the availability of markets where products of the household and its enterprises can be sold. For brevity, I chose not to differentiate the risks affecting income generation in idiosyncratic and covariant risks. It should be noted, however, that many of these risks are covariant. For example, risks related to the conduct and performance of input, output, and labor markets have similar effects on households that engage in the same enterprises. The less diversified the local economy, the larger the share of the population that is potentially affected by the same source of risk. In other words, the resilience and ability of informal networks to deal with these types of covariant risk factors diminish with greater specialization of the local economy. Negative effects on income are of course exacerbated by poorly integrated labor, financial, and commodity markets. The proper functioning of these markets often critically depends on infrastructure.

Table 9–1 highlights the potential of microfinance policy to partially address these risks. The principal remedy to address these risks may not necessarily lie in improving financial markets but in investing in road infrastructure, technology development and transfer, or improving the performance of commodity markets. The extent to which microfinance matters ultimately depends on the specific circumstances. With respect to risks occurring in the availability and quality of inputs, credit disbursed in cash may be of little use, and addressing the underlying bottlenecks and imperfections in input markets is likely to be more relevant in many circumstances. Yet, member-based financial institutions can exploit economies of scale, scope, and risk by collective acquisition of inputs.

The role of microfinance tends to increase when one considers risks related to the production function itself. Access to credit can help households to adopt risk-reducing inputs, such as investment in irrigation or use of disease-resistant crop varieties and pesticides. It can further assist to diversify risks by entering into new enterprises for which profits are weakly correlated with the traditional income portfolio of the household. For certain types of production risks that can be easily monitored and therefore insured, sustainable provision of insurance is possible.[6] However, as far as farm enterprises are concerned, the provision of crop and livestock

---

[6] Hazell (1992) distinguishes three characteristics that make a risk insurable. First, the likelihood of the event must be readily quantifiable. Second, the damage it causes must be easy to attribute and evaluate. Third, neither the occurrence of the event nor the damage it causes should be affected by the insured's behavior (that is, absence of moral hazard).

insurance is riddled with many difficulties, although a number of crop insurance schemes exist that are linked with credit.[7] Yet, research points out that these schemes are heavily subsidized and tend to benefit larger farmers over smaller ones.[8]

The principal difficulties in crop insurance increase further when one considers the conditions of small-scale farming in developing countries. New information technology and satellite imaging that can decrease the cost of monitoring may change the future prospects for sustainable insurance of risks in smallholder agriculture. However, at present, the role of financial sector policy in addressing these risks appears fairly limited. Sensible loan repayment schedules, especially the flexibility to reschedule loans in case of crop failure, can mitigate the borrowers' risk but may also introduce the problem of moral hazard. Last, for risks related to output markets, reasoning similar to that for input markets holds. Insofar as access to finance can enable households to diversify their portfolio of enterprises to smooth income risks, microfinance could possibly make a contribution. However, for most circumstances, lack of road infrastructure and communications and policy distortions in output markets are likely to play a greater role in volatility of household incomes.

The discussion of risks related to income volatility points to a somewhat limited role of savings, credit, and insurance services related to income smoothing. The principal direct role that can be identified is that savings and credit services can enable households to acquire the necessary start-up capital for establishing new enterprises for which profits are weakly correlated with their existing portfolio. Moreover, access to credit and savings services can facilitate household investment in risk-reducing inputs such as irrigation or pesticides.

As is discussed next, access to financial services can have a far greater role for smoothing consumption and thereby increasing the risk-bearing capacity of households for increasing future income. Table 9–2 refers to rather infrequent but very large risks that can wipe out the productive capacity of a household, whereas table 9–3 lists risks that frequently occur and cause transitory shocks to consumption.[9]

---

[7] See Hazell, Pomareda, and Valdes (1983).

[8] Hazell, Pomareda, and Valdes (1983).

[9] Insofar as these risks concern the productive capacity of the household by affecting the ability of household members to work and generate income, these risks could also be viewed as affecting income generation and be listed under labor inputs in table 9–1. However, I chose to list these risks as ex post shocks as they create additional potential demand for unanticipated consumption expenditures (such as the treatment of human diseases).

The household's ability to deal with large, infrequent risks—such as war, political upheaval, successive major droughts, and other natural disasters—through informal responses is quite weak (see first row in table 9–2). This vulnerability is caused by the covariant nature of these risks (and the related weakness of informal responses to deal with such risks) or by the large impact of the risk on the household. Regarding these covariant and large risks, the role of insurance and credit is fairly limited. Insofar as these sources of risk are covariant, the provision of sustainable insurance schemes appears quite impossible under the conditions of most low-income countries unless the insurance company is well diversified at the national level and can possibly benefit from reinsurance services so that it can spread the risks over a large client base. In most cases, it is the state that is called upon to be the implicit insurer by providing social assistance. This assistance can take the form of permanent income transfers to secure a minimum standard of living, for example, in the case of permanent disability that impedes earning an income, or temporary transfers to replenish productive assets of households and to treat conditions of workers' disability. Once the ability to earn an income is restored through private or public assistance so that the capacity to repay a loan and to save is regained, savings and credit services can assist households to expand the productive capital in successive periods. However, moral hazard problems may emerge once the government is relied upon as the insurer of last resort.[10]

One may argue that temporary transfers by the state to replenish assets could be given on a loan instead of a grant basis. If the administrative network to properly administer such loans is in place and can be used with low transaction costs to the government and the target groups, it could be justified to choose a loan over a grant system. Yet, if governments use—as often is the case—local-level employees of certain line ministries who are inexperienced in the handling of credit, the repayment rates for disaster loans—such as after droughts or floods—are often extremely low. Repayment rates that hover in the teens and twenties, combined with additional administrative costs of loan provision and recovery, may well lead to total costs of service provision that are far higher for loans than for grants. Moreover, loosely monitored and ill-targeted disaster credit schemes by the state run the risk of destroying repayment motivation.

For all three types of risks listed in table 9–3, precautionary savings services could be important. A particularly large potential appears to exist for cushioning

---

[10] See Besley (1995).

the risk of permanent disability and for the case of old age and the death of family members. However, in the case of old age or permanent disability that is caused by idiosyncratic risk such as an accident, insurance services can play an important role, too. For these risks, however, there appears to be no role for credit simply because the risk under consideration wipes out the capacity to earn an income and, therefore, to repay the loan. However, if the disabled person possesses assets that provide a source of income (such as a rental house) or are good collateral to the bank, consumption credit can in principle be offered.

Table 9–3 lists risks that usually have transitory effects on the ability to earn an income. They therefore cause transitory shortfalls in consumption if informal responses are inadequate. A major source of risk for the poor is ill health caused by covariant diseases, such as malaria and flu, or by many idiosyncratic diseases. The impact of health risks increases with the level of poverty because labor is the major production factor the poor have. The rich may substitute for their own family labor by acquiring hired labor in case of temporary illness. Just as in the case of imperfect commodity markets, if the public health system does not function well, so that proper medical care and medicines are not available, access to financial services may not do much good. It appears, therefore, generally more appropriate to invest in health infrastructure and in access to safe water and sanitation that can directly tackle these health risks. Only if a health infrastructure is in place and is accessible by the poor can financial services make a difference. In studies by the International Food Policy Research Institute, the short-term impact of access to financial services on nutrition was found insignificant in all cases.[11] In the long term, however, access to financial services may increase the income of households and thereby enable communal action to use part of that income to invest in health infrastructure by, for example, funding a communal water borehole. If health services can be purchased locally, access to precautionary savings services and to credit are expected to have a considerable potential for assisting the poor in dealing with transitory health risks. The role of financial services is equally important for financing consumption goods during illness.

Other sources of transitory risks causing volatility in the poor's consumption include the manifold claims that the social network can voice. These claims include the need to advance or reciprocate help to the extended family, friends, and neighbors, and requirements for financing social events to satisfy cultural norms, such as

---

[11] See Zeller and Sharma (1998); Sharma and Schrieder (2000).

marriage and burial. For these types of transitory events, the provision of precautionary savings appears very appropriate. Since these shocks can frequently occur, and some are hard to anticipate, a range of precautionary savings services that differ with respect to liquidity and return could be offered. For example, long-term savings products are more appropriate for predictable events such as marriage, whereas frequent and unanticipated claims by the social network could be dealt with by means of current accounts and highly liquid savings services. Another source of social risk that arises from the networks at the community level is that of communal conflict regarding access to and use of resources by different socioeconomic groups, such as drinking water, land, and other natural resources that are essential for income generation or for human welfare.

The above discussion pointed to several specific risks, mostly related to consumption smoothing, that potentially can be addressed by MFIs. These risks are mainly of an idiosyncratic nature, and the dominant financial service that appears most feasible to be implemented by microfinance institutions as a response to these risks is precautionary savings and credit. The willingness of the poor to pay for financial services for income and consumption smoothing depends of course on the effectiveness and costs of informal responses, including informal forms of precautionary savings, consumption credit, and insurance.[12] Importantly, formal financial services responding to these safety net aspects of finance can crowd out informal responses, implying a smaller net benefit of formal services. If formal services are subsidized by the state, they can create social costs that exceed social benefits. Having said that, the evidence shows that informal responses are far from adequate.

To find the right mix between publicly and privately provided safety nets is, then, the true challenge. In a nutshell, some form of public assistance is necessary to alleviate poverty and protect the poor from major shocks. The main question is which policy, or even better, which bundle of policies addresses this problem in the most efficient manner. Moreover, informal responses are greatly weakened in their effectiveness if risks are correlated over time. They are also less effective for the vulnerable and socially excluded in society, that is, those who lack sufficient access to informal self-help networks. Thus, informal responses are likely to provide adequate cushioning for some, but not for others, particularly the poor. Secular trends, such as the break-up of the extended family through migration and

---

[12] On informal responses see also Alderman and Paxson (1992); Cox and Jiménez (1992); Townsend (1995); Walker and Jodha (1983); Udry (1990).

urbanization, and demographic shifts, such as fertility decline and extended life expectancy, tend to reduce over time the efficiency of informal responses, particularly regarding old age and disability insurance. Because of this weakening of informal networks over time, the demand for publicly provided safety nets as well as the demand for financial services for consumption smoothing that is provided by microfinance institutions is likely to increase in low-income countries.

RECENT INNOVATIONS OF MICROFINANCE INSTITUTIONS

In the following, I mainly focus on idiosyncratic risks, for which the implementation potential of microfinance appears to be largest and for which product innovations have already been introduced by microfinance institutions.

Since most MFIs in developing countries at present are too small in terms of size of clientele and geographical coverage, they are often unable to effectively cover covariant risks, either by direct insurance services or by pooling emergency funds financed by clients. However, as MFIs grow over time and reach operational scales like those achieved by the Bank Rakyat Indonesia (BRI), BRAC, or the Grameen Bank, there is also considerable potential for sustainable coverage of covariant risks. For example, the Grameen Bank and BRI both have rescheduled loans to clients in areas of natural disasters. BRI can do this without assistance from the state because of its high profits and business conviction that losing a good borrower is also a loss to BRI. The Grameen Bank has also rescheduled loans in the past for clients affected by flood. The Grameen Bank obligates members to deposit small amounts of savings in a so-called emergency fund. The pooling of such funds over larger areas can in principle address covariant types of risks.

The major sources of idiosyncratic risk that cause consumption to fluctuate are listed in table 9–4 and summarized in the first column: health risks, including pregnancy and temporary or permanent disability caused by accident or disease; old age and death of family members (again, as far as death is not caused by covariant risks such as war and AIDS); claims by the social network or expenses for social events that need to be met by the household; and social risks such as the break-up of families because of divorce and other reasons that leave vulnerable household members at risk, especially children, women, and the elderly. The second column in table 9–4 describes innovations in financial products that specifically address these risks. The third column gives examples of MFIs that provide such services to their clients.

The provision of health insurance for low-income people in developing countries faces a number of great challenges that are not discussed in this chapter. In developed countries, and in the case of formal sector employees in developing countries, health insurance is usually provided by specialized nonbanking institutions. Therefore, I view the role of microfinance institutions in providing health insurance as quite limited. Yet microfinance institutions can provide precautionary savings services and consumption credit that can indirectly address health risks. For example, village banks that follow the FINCA model or the model developed by the French NGO Centre International de Développement et de Recherche (CIDR) raise funds for internal lending to their members.[13]

The village bank model allows the members to decide on interest rates for savings deposits and for internal loans. For example, the village banks supported by CIDR in Madagascar set savings rates between 24 and 36 percent a year, and on-lending rates at 36 to 48 percent a year, although the formal lending rate of the agricultural bank was only 14 percent. The lending rate decided by the village banks was found to be much higher than the one for loans from friends and relatives, but less than the lending rate of about 60 percent that socially distant moneylenders charge on seasonal consumption loans.[14] In many village banks, the members explicitly allowed for consumption loans financed by internal funds. Some of the village banks even provided interest "subsidies" to members in need of such loans. Other examples of MFIs that explicitly provide consumption credit include Caja Social in Mexico and BRAC in Bangladesh. BRAC members can borrow up to 75 percent of their savings deposit for emergency purposes. SEWA in India targets microloans to very poor women and allows its borrowers to stop loan repayment during pregnancy.

Health risks can also be addressed by the provision of precautionary savings services. This type of service is useful for all types of risk listed in table 9–4, provided that the maturity of the deposit, the interest rate, and the transaction costs for depositing and withdrawing funds at short notice are adjusted accordingly. For health risks that occur relatively frequently and demand immediate response, the costs and time for withdrawal must be minimal. A current account at a village bank or a nearby bank branch offers such features, as does a term deposit that can be withdrawn at short notice with a penalty. To protect savings deposits, banking laws

---

[13] Chao-Béroff (1996); Nelson and others (1996).
[14] Zeller (1998).

Table 9–4. Innovations in Savings, Credit, and Insurance Services by Microfinance Institutions

Risk related to	Product innovations by MFIs	Examples of MFIs that have implemented innovations
Health (temporarily affecting the ability to work, such as an accident, many diseases, and pregnancy, and that usually lead to higher consumption expenditures and to shortfalls in income)	Consumption credit lines that provide cash loans at short notice to clients Frequent condition for loan eligibility: borrower must already be client of MFI (but exceptions in case of lending funds accumulated by members themselves) Loan rescheduling in case of pregnancy Precautionary savings services, such as current accounts earning no interest, or term deposits with varying maturities, interest rates and penalties for early withdrawal	Caja Social, Mexico BRAC, Bangladesh (up to a certain amount of savings deposit) Village banks following the FINCA model (in many countries in Latin America and Africa consumption loans are funded with internal savings of members, and often given with interest rebates that are decided by members) Cooperative credit and savings institutions (such as in Cameroon and Madagascar) SEWA, India BancoSol (Bolivia), a commercial bank catering to the poor
Permanent disability	Disability insurance	Village banks following the FINCA model in Kenya. FINCA assists the village banks with buying group disability insurance for their members from an insurance company
Old age or death of family member	Life insurance Precautionary savings (as above, but long-term deposits with higher interest rates)	Bank Rakyat Indonesia: the life insurance only covers debt of borrower; in case of death of borrower, the insurance pays for any outstanding debt of borrower Bangladesh Rural Advancement Committee (BRAC): the life insurance is paid out to the

		person designated by BRAC member in case of death; the lump-sum payment to the heir provides an implicit incentive to take care of the BRAC member during old age
		Mostly microfinance institutions that are registered as banks
Claims by social network	Consumption credit lines	Author does not know of any MFI that explicitly provides loans for financing social events such as marriage or burial
	Holding precautionary savings, as above	
Divorce and other causes of household disintegration	Targeting of financial services to women	Most but not all MFIs: savings accounts and credit lines are registered under individual names (husband does not co-sign)
	Promotion of social change, gender equality, women's empowerment	

Sources: Rashid and Townsend (1993); Zeller and others (1997); Wisniwski and Hannig (2000); Nelson and others (1996); Goetz and Sen Gupta (1996).

often hinder semiformal MFIs (such as village banks and group-based savings and credit schemes) from offering and diversifying their savings products in response to customer demands.[15] Yet those MFIs that are registered under the banking or cooperative law often have a variety of savings products that respond to the demand for precautionary savings to cover risks of health, disability, social claims, or old age. Examples of banks that successfully offer savings services to a diverse clientele, including the urban and rural poor, are BancoSol in Bolivia and BRI in Indonesia.

Poor households may accept nominal interest rates for savings deposits that are below the inflation rate if the costs and time of withdrawal of savings are minimal compared with alternative informal sources of savings. Nonetheless, diverse savings products that provide different forms of tradeoffs between liquidity and return are required to address the full range of savings needs of the poor. The optimal choice of savings products can be conditioned by the clients' access to labor, food, and commodity markets. For example, if food markets during the hungry season are segmented and food prices are highly volatile, households may continue to save in the form of food, even if formal savings options with high liquidity and low transaction costs are accessible. Often such conditions are found in remote areas with poor infrastructure. For example, in the rice market of Madagascar, regional and seasonal price differences reach up to 300 and 100 percent, respectively.[16]

The imperfections in the food marketing system explain why the growth and performance of member-managed rice "banks" in Madagascar, linked with a cash credit program, were quite successful during the 1990s. The rice bank scheme offers groups of smallholders the option to store their rice after harvest when output prices are low and to take out cash loans to finance consumption and to invest in off-farm enterprises during the dry season. The rice serves as collateral. Four to six months after the harvest when rice prices are high, the farmers sell their rice and repay their consumption loans. This credit with an in-kind savings scheme is attractive to farmers who face volatile food markets as it allows households to more effectively smooth their consumption during the hungry season.

Another important type of risk for the poor is a disability that hinders or prevents working. Village banks in Kenya that are promoted by FINCA provide an innovative example. The members of the village banks can purchase group disability insurance from a specialized insurance company. FINCA assists in retailing these services to the members of the village banks.

---

[15] Wisniwski and Hannig (2000).
[16] Minten (1998).

A number of MFIs offer life insurance services to cover risks of death or lack of care during old age (table 9–3). Most often, however, the insurance contract only covers the outstanding debt of the borrower in case of his or her death. This is the case, for example, for BRI in Indonesia or ASA in Bangladesh. BRAC, however, offers a life insurance contract to its members that pays a predetermined sum in case of death of the member.[17] The insurance contract can respond to two principal motives. First, in the case of women in particular, in rural Bangladesh the death of a husband usually results in the woman's loss of access to all the major assets of the household. The widow is then completely dependent on her children, brothers, parents, and father- or brothers-in-law. By buying life insurance and designating a beneficiary in her family, the woman can gain increased bargaining power to obtain care during old age. Second, women in single-parent households can provide some security to their children by buying life insurance.

Because of sociocultural constraints, women often cannot get a loan unless they are married and their husband is a cosigner on the loan application. Microfinance institutions ought to insist that such discrimination is not practiced for their loan and savings products. By providing women with individual credit lines and savings accounts, their bargaining power during marriage could increase (although this effect may not materialize).[18] Moreover, individual accounts for women would enable them to have a much stronger economic position in case of separation from the family, for example, because of divorce or the death of the husband.

CONCLUSIONS

Access to microfinance has the potential not only to assist the poor in earning income from microenterprises but also to smooth their income and consumption. The first potential effect is the traditional argument for microfinance, which one may call the growth argument for microfinance. It is presently the primary motivation for the microfinance movement. Yet the second effect gains relative importance with the increasing poverty level of MFI clients. This is the safety net argument for public support of microfinance institutions.

---

[17] When I visited Bangladesh in 1995, a BRAC member showed me her insurance certificate. In case of her death, the contract would pay 5,000 taka (about U.S.$110) to her son. When asked for her motive for buying this insurance, she replied that the insurance gives her children more security in case she dies early and gives her more security during old age, when she has to depend on her children.

[18] See Goetz and Sen Gupta (1996).

This chapter sought to distinguish these two principal effects of, and arguments for, public support of microfinance institutions. Microfinance can address aspects of growth as well as safety net policy. I entirely focused in this chapter on the safety net role and discussed the types of risks that cause fluctuations in income as well as in consumption. The largest potential for microfinance is seen in addressing idiosyncratic risks such as risks related to ill health, disability, old age, and divorce. When microfinance institutions grow in scale and reach out to diverse client groups, they also increase their potential to address covariant risks of their clientele.

Several innovative microfinance institutions offer financial products that respond to these risks. Most commonly found are precautionary savings services that provide clients with various products that offer choices concerning the transaction costs of withdrawal and the return earned on the deposit. Some MFIs offer explicit lines of consumption credit, especially the member-based financial institutions that give their members the flexibility to raise savings deposits for lending to members at terms freely decided by the members. Many village banks in Latin America and Sub-Saharan Africa offer consumption credit that is financed by internal savings collected from the banks' members. Some MFIs have ventured into insurance and developed their own insurance products, mainly life insurance. Other experiences suggest that MFIs have a potential for retailing insurance products from the formal insurance sector to their clients.

The poorer the declared target group of an MFI, the more important it is that the MFI offer financial services for income and consumption smoothing. By improving its product mix as recommended in this chapter, an MFI's costs of targeting to the poor may decrease, as the poor will have a greater incentive to become clients. However, when MFIs choose to broaden their outreach of financial services with safety net characteristics, they must be aware of the potentially greater portfolio and liquidity risks that such a strategy entails. I argued in the chapter that the MFIs will not need to worry much about idiosyncratic risks, but they need to do so for covariant risks. Prudent behavior would therefore suggest that MFIs first target areas with low covariant risks and only gradually expand client outreach in higher risk areas. Higher liquidity reserves and larger equity capital also appear to be adequate responses to covariant risks. Client-funded emergency funds that are pooled over large areas have the potential to spread these risks at sustainable levels.

The poor's willingness to pay for financial services for income and consumption smoothing will of course depend on the effectiveness and costs of informal responses, including informal forms of precautionary savings, consumption, and insurance. Thus the provision of financial services may crowd out informal responses. To the extent that services by MFIs are indirectly subsidized by the state— for example, by grants for product innovation, staff training, and institutional expansion—formal financial services can create social costs that exceed social benefits. Yet the evidence from recent research suggests that the informal responses are far from adequate and that publicly supported institutional innovations in microfinance can offer in many circumstances a viable policy instrument that generates net social benefits.

To find the right mix between publicly and privately provided safety nets remains, therefore, the true challenge. Under many conditions, it appears that MFIs could offer safety net-type services that are largely or exclusively financed by the clients. Alternative forms of safety net provision supported or directly implemented by the state, such as ex post income transfers or public works, can carry high administrative costs for delivery and targeting and may require considerable response times after the shock has already occurred. In comparison, precautionary savings, insurance, and consumption credit are demand driven. And by using local information, MFIs can adapt their services to the specific demand patterns of various clientele groups. Depending on the subsidy level of the MFI, the costs of service provision can be financed to a large extent or to a full extent by the clients themselves. MFIs that are already established can offer financial products for income and consumption smoothing at relatively low variable costs as the core business is already supported by growth-oriented financial services.

For these reasons, MFIs that want to increase their relevance for the poor are well advised to innovate financial services for income and consumption smoothing. Public action could further promote this strategy by supporting pilot projects and related action research. The latter is especially needed to evaluate the potential crowding-out effects on other formal and informal services and the net financial and economic benefit of the introduction of new financial products. Nonetheless, evaluations of MFIs that receive support from the government or donors so as to make a contribution to the alleviation of poverty ought to include checks on whether the MFI provides financial products for income and consumption smoothing such as precautionary savings services, emergency credit, insurance services, or implicit insurance substitutes. Such checks can be undertaken rapidly and at low cost by simply looking at the terms of the financial products currently offered, and they can identify further poverty-oriented product innovation that could easily be implemented and could increase the business volume and profitability of the MFI.

References

Alderman, H., and C. H. Paxson. 1992. *Do the Poor Insure? A Synthesis of the Literature on Risk and Consumption in Developing Countries.* Discussion Paper no. 169. Woodrow Wilson School of Public and International Affairs, Princeton University, Princeton, N.J.

Besley, T. 1995. "Credit, Savings, and Insurance." In J. Behrman and T. N. Srinivasan, eds., *Handbook of Development Economics,* vol. IIIA. Amsterdam, Netherlands: Elsevier.

Chao-Béroff, R. 1996. *Village Banks in Pays Dogon: A Successful Home-Grown Approach.* CGAP Newsletter no. 2. CGAP Secretariat, Washington, D.C.

Cox, D., and E. Jiménez. 1992. "Social Security and Private Transfers in Developing Countries: The Case of Peru." *World Bank Economic Review* 6 (January): 155–69.

Czukas, K., M. Fafchamps, and C. Udry. 1995. "Drought and Saving in West Africa: Are Livestock Really a Buffer Stock?" Northwestern University and Stanford University. Unpublished.

Eswaran, M., and A. Kotwal. 1990. "Implications of Credit Constraints for Risk Behavior in Less-Developed Countries." *Oxford Economic Papers* 42.

Goetz, A. M., and R. Sen Gupta. 1996. "Who Takes the Credit? Gender, Power and Control over Loan Use in Rural Credit Programs in Bangladesh." *World Development* 24 (January): 45–63.

Hazell, P. B. R. 1992. "The Appropriate Role of Agricultural Insurance in Developing Countries." *Journal of International Development* 4 (April): 567–81.

Hazell, P. B. R., C. Pomareda, and A. Valdes, eds. 1983. *Crop Insurance for Agricultural Development: Issues and Experience.* Baltimore, MD: Johns Hopkins University Press.

Minten, B. 1998. *Accessibilité au marché des produits agricoles et prix aux producteurs dans les villages ruraux à Madagascar.* IFPRI/FOFIFA Working Paper no. 17. Ministry of Scientific Research and FOFIFA, Antananarivo, Madagascar, and IFPRI, Washington, D.C.

Morduch, J. 1995. "Income Smoothing and Consumption Smoothing." *Journal of Economic Perspectives* 9 (3): 103–14.

Nelson, C., and others. 1996. *Village Banking—The State of Practice.* New York: SEEP Network and UNIFEM.

Rashid, M., and R. M. Townsend. 1993. "Targeting Credit and Insurance: Efficiency, Mechanism Design, and Program Evaluation." World Bank and University of Chicago. Unpublished.

Rosenzweig, M., and K. I. Wolpin. 1993. "Credit Market Constraints, Consumption Smoothing, and the Accumulation of Durable Production Assets in Low-Income Countries: Investments in Bullocks in India." *Journal of Political Economy* 101 (February): 213–24.

Sharma, M., and G. Schrieder. 2000. "Impact of Access to Credit on Household Income, Food Security and Nutrition: A Review of Empirical Evidence." In M. Zeller and others, eds., *Innovations in Microfinance for the Rural Poor: Exchange of Knowledge and Implications for Policy.* Proceedings of a workshop organized by the German Foundation for Development (DSE), the International Food Policy Research Institute (IFPRI), the International Fund for Agricultural Development (IFAD), and the Bank of Ghana, held in Accra, Ghana, 1998. DSE, Feldafing, Germany.

Townsend, R. M. 1995. "Financial Systems in Northern Thai Villages." *Quarterly Journal of Economics* 110 (November): 1011–46.

Udry, C. 1990. "Credit Markets in Northern Nigeria: Credit as Insurance in a Rural Economy." *World Bank Economic Review* (November): 251–59.

Walker, T. S., and N. S. Jodha. 1983. "How Small Farm Households Adapt to Risk." In P. B. R. Hazell, C. Pomareda, and A. Valdes, eds., *Crop Insurance for Agricultural Development: Issues and Experience.* Baltimore, MD: Johns Hopkins University Press.

Wisniwski, S., and A. Hannig. 2000. "Successful Mobilization of Small and Micro-savings: Experiences from Seven Deposit-Taking Institutions." In M. Zeller and others, eds., *Innovations in Microfinance for the Rural Poor: Exchange of Knowledge and Implications for Policy.* Proceedings of a workshop organized by the German Foundation for Development (DSE), the International Food Policy Research Institute (IFPRI), the International Fund for Agricultural Development (IFAD), and the Bank of Ghana, Ghana, November. DSE, Feldafing, Germany.

Zeller, M. 1998. "Determinants of Repayment Performance in Credit Groups: The Role of Program Design, Intragroup Risk Pooling, and Social Cohesion." *Economic Development and Cultural Change* 46 (April): 599–620.

Zeller, M., and M. Sharma. 1998. "Rural Finance and Poverty Alleviation." *Food Policy Report.* Washington: International Food Policy Research Institute (IFPRI).

Zeller, M., and others. 1997. "Rural Finance for Food Security of the Poor: Implications for Research and Policy." *Food Policy Review* 4. International Food Policy Research Institute (IFPRI), Washington, D.C.

CHAPTER TEN

Consumption Smoothing and Extended Families: The Role of Government-Sponsored Insurance

Orazio Attanasio and José-Víctor Ríos-Rull

The main aim of this chapter is to provide a conceptual framework to evaluate the provision of aggregate insurance schemes within environments characterized by both aggregate and idiosyncratic risk. Obviously the results we provide cannot be fully general, as they will depend on the particular institutional features that we discuss in our model. Our framework, however, stresses that to evaluate the desirability and the design of various insurance schemes, one has to pay attention to the way in which such schemes interact with existing private (and often informal) insurance mechanisms.

We focus on a situation in which individuals facing idiosyncratic risk can partly diversify it by entering a contractual agreement with another agent. The contract we study, however, cannot fully achieve the best possible allocation within the pair because of the presence of enforceability problems. In equilibrium, some agents will enter into pairwise relationships from which they have no incentives to deviate. We characterize the equilibrium and show that the amount of idiosyncratic risk that can be insured away depends, among other things, on the difference between the individual's intertemporal welfare and the amount she would achieve under "autarky."[1]

José-Víctor Ríos-Rull thanks the National Science Foundation for Grant SBR-9309514 and the University of Pennsylvania Research Foundation for their support. The authors are also grateful to Fabrizio Perri for his comments and for his help with the code and to Ethan Ligon and Robert Holzmann.

[1] This result has been proved in a number of studies, such as those by Thomas and Worrall (1988); Ligon, Thomas, and Worrall (1997); and Kocherlakota (1996).

In our model, we show what the effect is of reducing aggregate uncertainty for the functioning of the private insurance mechanism.[2] As we interpret the reduction in aggregate uncertainty as the provision of a "safety net" on the part of some external agent, such as an international organization or the central government, we can view our exercise as an attempt to quantify the extent to which such mechanisms might possibly crowd out private insurance mechanisms at the risk of worsening individual welfare.

The intuition behind our results is quite simple. If the provision of a "safety net" is equivalent to the elimination of the left tail of the distribution of aggregate shocks, it is possible that it reduces the amount of idiosyncratic risk insurance achieved by an enforceability compatible private contract. In other words, the provision of aggregate insurance, as it makes "autarky" outcomes less unattractive, might make the enforceability constraint more severe. The overall effect on welfare will depend on the ratio of aggregate to idiosyncratic variance and a variety of other model parameters.

The welfare computations to evaluate a proposed safety net involve a variety of components. First of all, one has to evaluate the direct effect of the transfers involved with the scheme. Obviously, by transferring resources to individuals we are increasing their welfare. To control for this effect we consider only actuarially fair schemes: that is, in "good times" we subtract a fair insurance premium from the flow of income of the individual involved in the scheme. Second, one has to evaluate the effect on aggregate welfare of the reduction in aggregate variance and compare it to the effect of the possible increase in idiosyncratic variance caused by the worsening of the enforceability constraint. The overall effect depends on the curvature of the utility function and, once again, on the relative variance of aggregate and idiosyncratic risks.

In a related but independent paper the properties of progressive taxation are explored.[3] These taxes are not distortionary. However, they change the relevant individual endowment and therefore the value of autarky. They show that the per-

---

[2] There is a slight abuse of language here. As will become clear below, for all pairs of individuals the uncertainty is aggregate. This is because the shocks to each member of the pair are not perfectly negatively correlated as in Kocherlakota (1996). Some of the uncertainty that they face is aggregate for the pair but not for the economy as a whole. The purely aggregate uncertainty is the one that the government might attempt to insure away. Therefore, when we refer to aggregate insurance, we will be referring to the villagewide aggregates, while when we refer to idiosyncratic, we mean idiosyncratic to the pair but not to the village as a whole.

[3] Krueger and Perri (1999).

verse effect that we study in this chapter may be very pervasive. Their model is different, and they study partial insurance mechanisms that involve all agents.

The considerations above suggest that the simple provision of aggregate insurance, which just shrinks the variance of aggregate shocks without considering the possible crowding out of private insurance, is not necessarily optimum. And even when such a scheme is welfare improving, it might be worth thinking about the possibility of alternative designs for safety nets that minimize the crowding out of private arrangements to insure idiosyncratic shocks. In particular, we consider the possibility that the provider of aggregate insurance requires the joint participation of the partners in the private insurance mechanism for the aggregate insurance. The ideas proposed here are somewhat similar to those behind the "peer monitoring" proposed to overcome adverse selection problems in credit markets with asymmetric information.[4]

The design of aggregate insurance mechanisms that satisfy the condition that they not interfere with existing private insurance arrangements are by no means easy. The main problem is likely to be the identification of the particular kind of mechanisms at play in a specific situation and the number of partners involved in it.

From what we have said so far, it is clear that the empirical relevance of our results depends on a variety of characteristics that can potentially be measured. For this reason, in the last part of the chapter, we discuss the implications of our result for the design of microeconomic surveys that could eventually be used for evaluating alternative safety nets. In particular, we discuss the necessity of measuring the relative importance of aggregate and idiosyncratic variance and of identifying the existence and the operation of private insurance mechanisms.

THE MODEL

We consider a stochastic endowment economy with only one good per period, which cannot be stored. There are a large number of identical separate islands that do not communicate with each other. Except when we talk about the government budget constraint, we look only at what happens on a generic island. Each island is populated by a large number of agents, normalized to be of measure one. Some of these agents are *paired* with another agent; by this we mean that they are enabled to enter a long-term relationship that will provide partial insurance. We think of these pairs

---

[4] See Armendariz and Grollier (1997); Armendariz (1998); Banerjee, Besley, and Guinnane (1994).

of agents as "extended families." We assume that these pairings are given exogenously and are immutable in the sense that they cannot be created or destroyed, and that not all agents are paired. A fraction $2\mu < 1$ of the agents is paired with one and only one other agent. The measure of such pairings is then $\mu < 1/2$. This measure may vary across islands. We think of islands where μ is large as being socially very cohesive in the sense that private institutions, the extended family, provide a mechanism to partially insure their members. On the other hand, we could think of islands with low μ as being ones where private social arrangements are weaker. We think of μ as a quantity that could potentially be measured and that is prone to vary substantially across environments.

There are different kinds of shocks in this economy. Let z denote an aggregate shock with finite support in Z. Furthermore, the shock z is Markov, with transition matrix $\Gamma_{z,z'} = \text{Prob}(z_{t+1} = z' \mid z_t = z)$. Let $s \in S$ denote an idiosyncratic Markov shock to each household that may be multivalued, so that it can incorporate both temporary and permanent elements. This shock also has finite support. The aggregate shock z is common to all agents on the same island. Given the large number of islands, there is no aggregate uncertainty in the economy as a whole. Conditional on two consecutive realizations of the aggregate shock, we write the stochastic process for s as having transition $\Gamma_{s,z,z',s'} = \text{Prob}(s_{t+1} = s' \mid z_{t+1} = z', z_t = z, s_t = s)$. In each state $\{s, z\}$ agents get endowment $e(z, s)$. We write compactly $\varepsilon \equiv \{z, s\}$ and its transition $\Gamma_{\varepsilon,\varepsilon'}$.

In general, agents can observe the aggregate shock and their own idiosyncratic shock, but not other individual agents' shocks. An important exception arises in members of a pair. These agents observe each other's endowment. Perhaps the best way of thinking of membership in a pair is that members have the ability to contact each other (and remember their past actions).[5] For paired agents, we use $y_{i,j} = (z, s_i, s_j)$, with the convention that the agent with the lowest name ($i < j$) is referred to as agent 1, and the highest name as agent 2. When this is understood, we use the compact notation y and we refer to its components as $\{z(y), s_1(y), s_2(y)\}$. We also write compactly the transition matrix of the pair as $\Gamma_{y,y'}$. We denote by $\gamma^*(y)$ the stationary distribution of the shocks.[6] Moreover, the history of shocks relevant to the pair up to t is denoted by $y^t = \{y_0, y_1, \ldots, y_t\}$. We use $\pi(y^t \mid y_{-1})$ to denote the probability of history y^t conditional on the initial state of the economy y_{-1}.

---

[5] This assumption about the observability and record-keeping properties of the shocks prevents the endogenous formation of pairs in the economy.

[6] We make sufficient assumptions on the Γ terms to ensure that there is a unique stationary distribution and there are no cyclically moving subsets.

There is a government in this model economy. The government does not observe the idiosyncratic components of household shocks, but it does observe the island specific shock z. For now, we assume that the government does not observe whether individual agents belong to a pair or not. However, the government knows the number of individuals that are paired, that is, it knows μ. The government can raise taxes across islands and uses the receipts to make transfers. In the process, it keeps a balanced budget. Given the lack of storage, these taxes and transfers, which are in effect a form of compulsive insurance, can be no better than actuarially fair. We denote these taxes (net of transfer) by $-\tau(z)$, or $-\tau(\varepsilon)$, or $-\tau(y)$, depending on the context. However, it is understood that the tax only depends on the aggregate state. This is the only role of the large number of islands that exist in the model, to simplify the characterization of government policies.

We assume that the agents of our model maximize the expectations of a standard intertemporally separable, strictly concave and differentiable utility function, in which future expected utility is discounted at a rate $\beta < 1$:

(10-1)
$$E_0\left\{\sum_t \beta^t u(c_t)\right\}.$$

For any given unpaired individual agent, we assume that there are no trading opportunities except for those involved by the government transfer. Therefore the consumption of an unpaired agent is $c(\varepsilon) = e(\varepsilon) + \tau(\varepsilon)$. We write the value of the autarkic agent recursively as

(10-2)
$$\Omega(\varepsilon) = u[e(\varepsilon) + \tau(\varepsilon)] + \sum_{\varepsilon'} \Gamma_{\varepsilon,\varepsilon'} \, \Omega(\varepsilon').$$

Paired agents are affected by each other's idiosyncratic shocks and their joint consumption is restricted by the pairwise feasibility constraint that now takes the form

(10-3)
$$c_1(y) + c_2(y) = e_1(y) + e_2(y) + 2\tau(y).$$

In the absence of enforceability problems, agents would equate their marginal utilities in all states of the world, taking into account the transfers from the government:

(10-4)
$$\frac{u'[c_1(y)]}{u'[c_2(y)]} = \text{a constant independent of } y.$$

While it is trivial to show that any optimal allocation has to satisfy equation 10-4,[7] theory is silent on how the surplus is split. Replication arguments and equality between the agents imply that a competitive equilibrium allocation within the pair would be symmetric. In any case, we denote with $W(y, 1)$ the value of the first best that treats both types symmetrically, starting from each of the possible states y.

Notice that in such a situation an actuarially fair aggregate insurance scheme would be welfare improving, as it would diversify island risk across all the islands. From the point of view of individual agents such a scheme would be equivalent to a reduction of the variance of aggregate shocks. Both paired and unpaired agents would gain from such a scheme, given the concavity of the utility function.

We characterize the degree of enforceability of contracts between the two members of a pair by a function $P(y)$. This function denotes the cost for an individual of breaking the agreed arrangement. When $P(y) = \infty$ we are in the standard perfect enforcement case. When $P(y) = 0$ (no commitment) there are no external means to enforce those contracts and it is the typical case studied in the literature. This function can be used to study special institutions, such as the family, where certain social activities can be used to increase the costs of breaking the agreement. We further assume that if an individual breaks a contract, she will not be able to enter any similar contract in the future and will be in a state of autarky that is equivalent to the disappearance of the pair to which the agent belongs. We could think of this as the most severe subgame-perfect punishment.[8]

Besides incurring cost $P(y)$, upon breaking the contract agents get utility $\Omega[\varepsilon(y)]$. This means, among other things, that we assume that the government cannot observe who broke a contract and who did not in order to select the transfer. If this were possible, the government could use the transfer to enhance the set of privately achievable allocations by reducing the value of autarky.

The paired agents can engage in a mutually advantageous relationship that may allow them to smooth consumption even without commitment.[9] Any allocation for the pair should satisfy enforcement constraints. That means that at each

---

[7] It just follows from strict concavity and the possibility of transferring resources across dates and states.

[8] See Abreu (1988).

[9] To describe how this is done we draw from Kehoe and Perri (1997), who in turn follow the recursive approach of Marcet and Marimon (1992, 1995). The characterization of the optimal contracts in a model with imperfect enforceability is stated in different terms in Ligon, Thomas, and Worrall (1997, 2000) and Alvarez and Jermann (1997). We find the approach that keeps track of the current ratio of utility weights both more transparent and computationally easier.

point in time and in every state of the world, y^t, the members of the pair prefer the allocation they receive to autarky (after incurring in the cost $P(y_t)$ of breaking away). These enforcement constraints, therefore, take the form

$$(10\text{-}5) \qquad \sum_{r=t}^{\infty} \sum_{y^r} \beta^{r-t} \, \pi(y^r | y^t) \, u[c_i(y^r)] \geq \Omega[\varepsilon(y_r)] + P(y_t) = \hat{\Omega}[\varepsilon(y_t)].$$

Let us consider the problem of maximizing a weighted sum of utilities subject to the resource constraints and the enforcement constraints, that is, the problem of choosing allocations $\{c_1(y^t), c_2(y^t)\}$ for all y^t to solve

$$(10\text{-}6) \qquad \max_{\{c_i(y^t)\}} \lambda_1 \sum_{t=0}^{\infty} \sum_{y^t} \beta^t \, \pi(y^t) \, u[c_1(y^t)] + \lambda_2 \sum_{t=0}^{\infty} \sum_{y^t} \beta^t \, \pi(y^t) \, u[c_2(y^t)],$$

subject to equations 10-3 and 10-5, where λ_1 and λ_2 are nonnegative initial weights. We can write the Lagrangian as

$$(10\text{-}7) \qquad \sum_{t=0}^{\infty} \sum_{y^t} \beta^t \, \pi(y^t) \left\{ \sum_{i=1}^{2} \lambda_i \, u[c_i(y^t)] \right.$$
$$\left. + \sum_{i} \mu_i(y^t) \left[\sum_{r=t}^{\infty} \sum_{y^r} \beta^{r-t} \, \pi(y^r | y^t) u[c_i(y^r)] - \hat{\Omega}_i[\varepsilon(y_r)] \right] \right\}$$

plus the standard terms that relate to the resource constraints.

Noting that $\pi(y^r | y^t)$ can be rewritten as $\pi(y^r) = \pi(y^r | y^t)\pi(y^t)$, we can rewrite the Lagrangian as

$$(10\text{-}8) \qquad \sum_{t=0}^{\infty} \sum_{y^t} \sum_{i} \beta^t \, \pi(y^t) \{ M_i(y^{t-1}) \, u[c_i(y^t)] + \mu_i(y^t) \, [u[c_i(y^t)] - \Omega_i[\varepsilon(y_r)]] \}$$

plus the terms that refer to the feasibility constraint. The newly introduced variable, $M_i(y^{t-1})$, is defined recursively as $M_i(y_{-1}) = \lambda_i$ and

$$(10\text{-}9) \qquad M_i(y^t) = M_i(y^{t-1}) + \mu_i(y^t).$$

Note that at time t, the $M_i(y^t)$ terms are equal to the original weights plus the cumulative sum of the Lagrange multipliers on the enforcement constraint at all periods from 1 to t. The first-order conditions that can be derived from this modified Lagrangian include

(10-10)
$$\frac{u'[c_1(y^t)]}{u'[c_2(y^t)]} = \frac{M_2(y^{t-1}) + \mu_2(y^t)}{M_1(y^{t-1}) + \mu_1(y^t)}$$

in addition to the complementary slackness conditions. The next step consists of renormalizing the enforceability multipliers by defining

(10-11)
$$\varphi_i(y^t) = \frac{\mu_i(y^t)}{M_i(y^t)} \quad \text{and} \quad x(y^t) = \frac{M_2(y^t)}{M_1(y^t)}.$$

The virtue of this normalization is that it allows us to keep track only of the relative weight x. Its transition law can be written as

(10-12)
$$x(y^t) = \frac{[1 - \varphi_1(y^t)]}{[1 - \varphi_2(y^t)]} x(y^{t-1})$$

by noting that $[1 - \varphi_1(y^t)] M(y^t) = M(y^{t-1})$.

We are now in a position to write this problem recursively. To do so we define a mapping from values into values, to a fixed point at which the value functions characterize the solution to our problem. To solve our model numerically, as we do in the next section, we actually follow this procedure, that is, we iterate from a certain initial set of value functions. Successive approximations have yielded in every case the desired fixed point. The state variables are the current value of the shocks y (recall that, due to the fact that the shocks are Markov, their current value is sufficient to evaluate conditional expectations) and the current value of the relative weights x. We use three value functions, one for the planner, denote it $V(y, x)$; and one each for the agents, denote them $V_i(y, x)$. These functions satisfy the following property:

(10-13)
$$V(y, x) = V_1(y, x) + x V_2(y, x).$$

To update the value functions, that is, to obtain $T(V)$, $T(V_1)$, and $T(V_2)$, we first solve the following auxiliary problem, where no incentive constraints are taken into account:

$$(10\text{-}14) \qquad \Phi(y,x) = \max_{c_1,c_2} \; u(c_1) + x\, u(c_2) + \beta \sum_{y'} \Gamma_{y,y'} \, V(y',x),$$

subject to the feasibility constraint (10-3), with solution c_i^Φ. Note that in this problem the relative weight x is constant. Next, we verify the enforceability of the solution to equation 10-14. This means verifying whether

$$(10\text{-}15) \qquad u[c_i^\Phi(y,x)] + \beta \sum_{y'} \Gamma_{y,y'} \, V_i(y',x) \geq \hat{\Omega}[\varepsilon(y)] \;\; \text{for} \;\; i = 1,2.$$

If equation 10-15 is satisfied, then $T(V) = \Phi(y,x)$, and $T(V_1)$ and $T(V_2)$ are given by its left-hand side. It is easy to see that equation 10-15 cannot be violated for both agents at the same time (just note that autarky is a feasible allocation). The only remaining problem is to update the value functions when the constraint is binding for one of the agents, say agent 1. In this case, we solve the following system of equations in $\{c_1, c_2, x'\}$:

$$(10\text{-}16) \qquad \hat{\Omega}[\varepsilon(y)] = u(c_1) + \beta \sum_{y'} \Gamma_{y,y'} \, V_1(y',x')$$

$$(10\text{-}17) \qquad x' = \frac{u'(c_1)}{u'(c_2)}$$

$$(10\text{-}18) \qquad c_1 + c_2 = e_1(y) + e_2(y) + 2\tau(y)$$

with solution $\{c_1^*, c_2^*, x^*\}$.[10] To update the value functions we let

$$(10\text{-}19) \qquad T(V_1)(y,x) = u(c_1^*) + \beta \sum_{y'} \Gamma_{y,y'} \, V_1(y', x^{*\prime})$$

$$(10\text{-}20) \qquad T(V_2)(y,x) = u(c_2^*) + \beta \sum_{y'} \Gamma_{y,y'} \, V_2(y', x^{*\prime})$$

---

[10] There will typically be only one solution, given the monotonicity of all the functions involved.

(10-21) $T(V)(y,x) = V_1(y,x) + x\, V_2(y,x).$

A fixed point of operator T gives us the value for the problem of maximizing a weighted sum of utilities.[11] Moreover, it also gives us a way to completely characterize the properties of such a solution by numerical methods. This means that for any parameterization we can tell whether the enforceable allocation is autarky, the first best, or anything in between. We can also study how the enforceable allocations are affected by changes in the environment.

One question that remains is how this allocation is actually implemented. Like in the first best, the theory is silent about how to split the surplus initially. Let's assume a symmetric split. This means that the starting value for x is 1. From there a contract can be implemented by a state-contingent transfer, say $\theta(y, x)$, that specifies what agent 1 gives to agent 2 (it can be negative) when the state is given by the pair $\{y, x\}$. This transfer is just the difference between the endowment and the solution to the problem above. The law of motion for the state variable x is also given by the procedure described above.

This completes our description of the model and its solution. The steps between equation 10-13 and equation 10-19 reflect the steps of the simulation program we use below to characterize the quantitative properties of some examples.

GOVERNMENT-PROVIDED INSURANCE

In the model above, we considered a particular form of government insurance. In particular, we assumed an actuarially fair insurance that depends only on aggregate shocks and that is distributed uniformly across individuals. In this section we evaluate this type of scheme and show that it can crowd out private insurance and, potentially, lead to a decrease in aggregate welfare. Obviously, the one we consider is not the only possible insurance scheme. On the one hand, it can be argued that it might be important to consider transfers that simply provide relief in exceptional circumstances, such as natural disasters. If these transfers were financed by international organizations, it would not be necessary to consider the premium that an actuarially fair insurance would imply in good times. Furthermore, a naive and careless insurance scheme in some circumstances might bring about a reduction in

---

[11] See Marcet and Marimon (1992, 1995) for details.

welfare by simply overinsuring the agents in the economy. On the other hand, one might argue that the government could devise more complicated insurance schemes to avoid or minimize possible interference by an aggregate scheme with the functioning of private insurance mechanisms.

As far as the first objection is concerned, it should be stressed that a simple transfer is very likely, especially if large in size, to increase the welfare of the agents who receive it. By focusing on an actuarially fair scheme, we want to consider not just the possible benefits of a proposed scheme but also its costs. Moreover, stressing the possible crowding out effects that an aggregate insurance scheme might have allows us to focus on its inefficiencies and possible ways to improve it. That is, regardless of whether a proposed insurance scheme increases or decreases welfare, the presence of crowding-out effects stresses that such a scheme might be suboptimal and, subject to some caveats, could be improved.

These considerations lead us to the second objection, the subject of the next two subsections. Under "A More Sophisticated Scheme," we consider more complex schemes that attempt to avoid the problems considered under "Simple Aggregate Insurance." It should be stressed, however, that in this respect the assumptions made about the information held by the government are crucial. Obviously, if the government were able to observe idiosyncratic shocks, or even observe who deviated from private insurance arrangements, it would be trivial to construct schemes that would avoid crowding out. Under "A More Sophisticated Scheme" we only consider situations in which the government does not observe idiosyncratic shocks or is unable to identify the individual responsible for the breaking up of an extended family. Indeed, we consider a situation in which the government does not even observe membership of an extended family. We assume only that the government has information on the nature of the various shocks and on the extent to which private arrangements are able to diversify idiosyncratic risk.

Simple Aggregate Insurance

In this subsection we describe the effects of a simple aggregate insurance scheme of the kind discussed above. The effect that simple aggregate insurance schemes might have on welfare and on the performance of the economy described by our model is complex and depends on a variety of factors. In particular, in addition to preferences, the effects depend crucially on the properties of the aggregate shocks and how they interact with individual shocks, on the amount of individual risk that can be diversified in equilibrium, and on the relative importance of aggregate and idiosyncratic shocks. The full characterization of the effects of the introduction of a government-sponsored insurance policy can only be done, within our model, with numerical simulations.

We are mainly interested in the long-term properties of the policies and not necessarily in those of the transition, that is, we define the properties of a policy in terms of the long-term averages that it implies. As the stationary distribution of the equilibrium values is hard to compute analytically, to compute these long-run averages we simulate the model economy for long periods of time. Different policies are valued by starting the economy at the same initial condition and letting it run for a long time. We plan to investigate the issues involved with the introduction of the policy in future work.[12]

Before presenting the numerical results, it is possible and useful to discuss the intuition behind them and describe the effects of aggregate insurance in some special cases. As we discussed above, the presence of enforceability constraints has the effect of limiting the amount of idiosyncratic risk that individuals can diversify by entering the private arrangements available to them in our model. The main reason for this is that the contracts individuals enter have to satisfy the constraint that each individual will never have the incentive to default and walk away from the arrangement.

The amount of risk sharing that can be achieved by these types of contracts depends on a variety of parameters, such as the discount factor, the variance and persistence of idiosyncratic and aggregate risk, and the cost of default (over and above the loss from being excluded from future contracts). In particular, we can construct scenarios in which either the full insurance outcome is reached or no private contract is possible. This is done in a very simple way by varying the dis-

---

[12] This means asking what the effects of a switch of policies are (for the introduction of a policy, we think of the previous one as being $\tau(y) = 0$ for all y). Doing this means taking into account that the economy is in some state at the time of the introduction of the new policy. In terms of our model, this implies that at a point of time, the island economy is characterized by an aggregate shock z, a distribution of unpaired individuals over their idiosyncratic shocks s with total measure $1 - \mu$, and a distribution of paired individuals over the pairs of idiosyncratic shocks and the current state of their relative weights x. This state is stochastic and depends on the history of shocks. To analyze policy switches, we will then generate a large number of possible initial states by simulation.

This is an important question, since there is no unique solution to the problem of which allocation gets picked by each paired household. We will follow the principle of maintaining the relative weight that households have. The problem shows up because the new policy will have changed the relevant range where x lies. We will assume that the share of the newly defined surplus is the one that obtains from keeping the relative weights x between the agents.

count rate: for low enough valuation of future consumption assessment only autarky can be implemented, while if agents care enough about the future (and, perhaps, are sufficiently risk averse) the first best can be implemented, since agents have a lot of distaste for autarky.

Introducing insurance against aggregate shocks has two effects. On the one hand, it reduces the variance of aggregate shocks and therefore increases welfare because utilities are concave. On the other hand, it reduces the amount of idiosyncratic risk that can be diversified by enforceable contracts. The reason for this is that increasing all individual endowments in bad states of the world makes autarky less unappealing, and therefore the enforceability constraints are more likely to be binding.

The net effect depends on which of these two effects prevails. Obviously, if we start from a situation in which no risk-sharing contract is enforceable (autarky equilibrium), the introduction of the aggregate insurance scheme cannot make things worse as it cannot crowd out any private insurance. However, if in the initial situation private arrangements are able to diversify a substantial part of idiosyncratic risk, there is potential for a substantial amount of crowding out, which might lead to a welfare reduction.

This result is not entirely surprising. Ethan Ligon, Jonathan P. Thomas, and Tim Worrall, for instance, show that in a model similar to that considered here, the introduction of storage possibilities can lead to a reduction in welfare.[13] The reason for their result is the same as that considered here. Giving the individual households the possibility of self-insuring via storage makes autarky less unappealing and therefore, via the enforceability constraints, crowds out some of the private insurance. Also, Dirk Krueger and Fabrizio Perri find that the private sector's ability to partially insure against shocks diminishes with a certain class of government-sponsored redistributive policies (in their case, progressive taxation).[14]

If one is interested in overall or average welfare, an important parameter is μ, the fraction of paired individuals. This parameter could be interpreted as reflecting how widespread is extended family or other forms of private and informal insurance arrangements. It is a parameter that, as we argue later, could be measured by appropriately designed surveys. Low values of μ make it more likely that a government program increases welfare, as there is less scope for crowding out private insurance mechanisms.

To evaluate the overall effects one has to use numerical simulations. In the

[13] Ligon, Thomas, and Worrall (2000).
[14] Krueger and Perri (1999).

rest of this section we present some simple results to illustrate that, indeed, simple aggregate insurance can be welfare reducing for parameter values that are not extreme. Furthermore, in addition to the effects on welfare, we try to quantify the amount of crowding out induced by the introduction of a simple aggregate insurance scheme. This is important to assess the amount of inefficiency implied by a certain scheme, regardless of its overall welfare effect. For such a purpose we consider two statistics: the average absolute amount of private transfers before and after the introduction of the scheme and the ratio of the variance of idiosyncratic endowments net of private transfers and aggregate shocks to the variance of idiosyncratic endowments net of aggregate shocks but gross of private transfers. Under full insurance the ratio is zero, as idiosyncratic shocks are completely diversified. Under autarky, however, the ratio is one. Therefore, the closer is the ratio of the variance to zero, the more that enforceable private arrangements can insure idiosyncratic risk.

As mentioned above, the effects of the aggregate insurance scheme depend on the nature and importance of aggregate and idiosyncratic shocks. We started by considering two types of aggregate shocks: multiplicative and additive. In the additive scheme, individual endowments are given by $z + s_i$. In the multiplicative scheme, individual endowments are given by zs_i. In both cases, the Markov process that describes the joint process $\{z, s_i\}$ is the one described above. Probably the multiplicative scheme is more realistic if one thinks of aggregate shocks as shocks linked to weather and the like. In this case an aggregate shock increases the variance of individual shocks. However, if we want to think of an aggregate insurance scheme as a scheme that reduces the variance of aggregate shocks, it is probably better to consider an additive shock. It is difficult to imagine, in the context of multiplicative shocks, that the provision of an insurance scheme reduces the variance of these shocks, as a government transfer would have to interact with the idiosyncratic shocks. Therefore, in the case of multiplicative shocks, we do not interpret the insurance scheme as reducing the variance of aggregate shocks but simply as providing an actuarially fair additive transfer. That is, we do not assume that the government is able to undo part of the effect of a multiplicative aggregate shock on individual endowments. In any case, the model that we have chosen encompasses additive and multiplicative shocks as special cases, since we think of the endowment as a generic function of the shocks $e(z, s)$.

We consider four simulations. In the first two we consider an additive aggregate shock and in the second two, a multiplicative shock. The preference parameters, transition probabilities matrixes, and values of the aggregate and idiosyncratic shocks (albeit not those of individual endowments) are the same in the two scenarios. In both the aggregate and idiosyncratic cases, we consider an actuarially fair scheme that consists of providing consumers with 0.001 units of consumption in bad aggregate times. In computing aggregate welfare, we only consider situations in which $\mu = 0.5$, that is when all agents are paired. This is not important, as we can make the set of unpaired consumers arbitrarily small. Furthermore, we have set the function $P(y)$ at zero, that is, we consider the case of no penalties (besides the breaking down of the relationship) imposed on the agent responsible for breaking down the extended family.

The functioning of the model is well illustrated by some simple pictures that correspond to a model economy with additive shocks; no government insurance; constant coefficient of relative risk aversion (CRRA) utility, with risk aversion parameter $\sigma = 0.8$ and discount factor $\beta = 0.85$; aggregate states $z \in \{1, 0.05\}$, with persistence of good and bad aggregate states $\{0.95, 0.8\}$ (diagonal elements of $\Gamma_{z,z}$); and idiosyncratic individual $s \in \{1, 0.015\}$, with persistence of good and bad individual states $\Gamma_{s,s'} = \{0.95, 0.75\}$ (independent of the aggregate states). In this economy there are eight possible states, corresponding to the different combinations of the realizations of the aggregate shock and the two individual idiosyncratic shocks.

In figure 10–1 we plot the consumption function against the negative of the log of the state variable,[15] the ratio of the weights in the surrogate social planner's problem, $\hat{x}$, in each of the eight states of the world. We plot the consumption function for the first best allocation, where we get a function that reflects the fact that the share of total output that goes to agent 1 is monotonically increasing in $\hat{x}$. The autarkic allocation is also plotted. It is independent of $\hat{x}$, which implies that it is a horizontal line. Finally, the enforceable allocation has the property that it coincides with the first best only in certain regions of the relative weights. Outside those regions, the first best is no longer enforceable. Agents can, however, still do better than autarky in some of the states and get a small transfer bounding away their allocations from the autarkic ones.

Figure 10–2 shows the value functions associated with $\hat{x}$ for each of the eight states for the enforceable allocation, the first best, and autarky. As we can see, the value of the first best is monotonically increasing and concave (note that given that we are plotting the functions relative to the logs, they are more concave than they seem). Note also that the autarky value function is independent of $\hat{x}$, as it should

---

[15] Negative so that it is increasing, log so that it is symmetric around zero. There is no loss of generality.

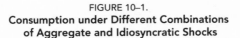

FIGURE 10–1.
**Consumption under Different Combinations
of Aggregate and Idiosyncratic Shocks**

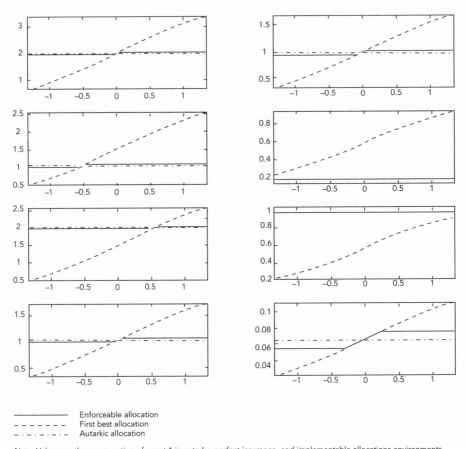

	Enforceable allocation
	First best allocation
	Autarkic allocation

Note: Values are the consumption of agent 1 in autarky, perfect insurance, and implementable allocations environments as a function of minus the log of the relative weights for each state of nature.
Source: Authors' calculations.

be. Moreover, note that the enforceable allocation is never below the autarkic one, and in some instances is equal to it. Finally, notice that for $x \hat{=} 0$, where the two agents are treated equally, the first best is strictly better than the enforceable equilibrium. The exceptions are states 5 and 6 (the third row, where agent 1 is in much better shape than agent 2 in both aggregate states), where in order to induce agent 1 not to go to autarky, he has to be offered more than the symmetric first best.

FIGURE 10–2.
**Value Functions under Different Combinations
of Aggregate and Idiosyncratic Shocks**

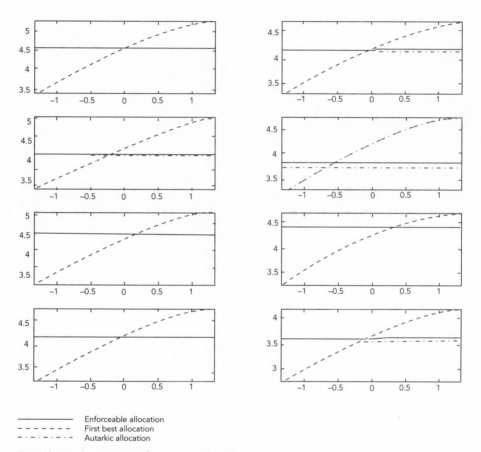

———————— Enforceable allocation
– – – – – – – First best allocation
– · – · – · – Autarkic allocation

Note: Values are the consumption of agent 1 in autarky, perfect insurance, and implementable allocations environments as a function of minus the log of the relative weights for each state of nature.
Source: Authors' calculations.

Figure 10–3 shows the evolution of the negative of the log of the ratio of marginal utilities $\hat{x}$ for each of the eight states of the economy. We see that for the first best, that ratio does not change over time and, hence, the graph shows a diagonal. On the same chord, the autarkic allocation varies the most and reflects the ratio of marginal utilities for the different endowment points. We represent this by a horizontal line since it does not depend at all on the previous period's ratio of marginal

FIGURE 10–3.
**Ratio of Marginal Utilities under Different
Combinations of Aggregate and Idiosyncratic Shocks**

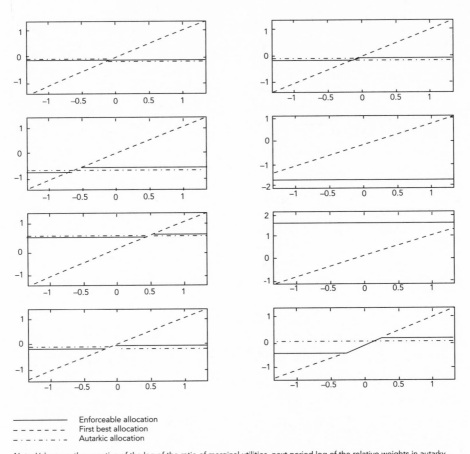

——————— Enforceable allocation
— — — — — First best allocation
— · — · — · — Autarkic allocation

Note: Values are the negative of the log of the ratio of marginal utilities, next period log of the relative weights in autarky, perfect insurance, and implementable allocations environments as a function of minus the log of the relative weights for each state of nature.
Source: Authors' calculations.

utilities. For the enforceable contract, we see that there are ranges over which the variable remains constant and ranges where it no longer varies, sometimes at the autarkic ratio of marginal utilities, sometimes at a different one that permits more consumption smoothing.

In figure 10–4 we show a typical consumption path for agent 1 for the three cases that we study. Note that for all arrangements—first best, enforceable, and autarky allocations—consumption is volatile due to the existence of aggregate un-

Table 10-1. Summary Statistics for Four Simulations

Statistic	Additive aggregate shocks		Multiplicative aggregate shocks	
	No insurance $\tau(1)=0$	Insurance $\tau(1)=.001$	No insurance $\tau(1)=0$	Insurance $\tau(1)=.001$
Average output per capita $\sum_y \gamma^*(y)[e_1(y)+e_2(y)]$	1.64583	1.64583	0.67702	0.67702
Average enforceable value function $\sum_y \gamma^*(y) V_i(y,1)$	4.44575	4.44558	3.30871	3.31925
Average symmetric value function (first best) $\sum_y \gamma^*(y) W(y,1)$	4.47292	4.47350	3.31717	3.32839
Average value function under autarky $\sum_y \gamma^*(y) \{\Omega[\in_1(y)] + \Omega[\in_2(y)]\}$	4.43563	4.43692	3.11841	3.13855
Sample average private transfers $\sum_y \gamma^*(y)[e_1(y)+\tau(y)-c_1(y,1)]$	0.01626	0.013780	0.18327	0.17971
Ratio of variances of private consumption and endowment (net of aggregate) $\sum_y \gamma^*(y) [c_1(y,1)-\sum_y \gamma^*(y) c_1(y,1)]^2$	0.88376	0.89550	0.40484	0.40537

$\sum_y \gamma^*(y) \{e_1(y,1)+\tau(y)-\sum_y \gamma^*(y)[e_1(y,1)+\tau(y)]\}^2$

Note: Values are computed statistics from the model economies, with the following parameters: $\sigma = .8$, $\beta = .85$, $z \in \{1, .05\}$, $\Gamma_{z_1,z_1} = .9$, $\Gamma_{z_2,z_2} = .8$, $s \in \{1, .015\}$, $\Gamma_{s_1,s_1} = .95$, $\Gamma_{s_1,s_1} = .75$, $P(y) = 0$.
Source: Authors' calculations.

certainty. Note also that the first best (or symmetric social planner) is least volatile, next is the enforceable, and finally autarky. Moreover, for this particular example, the enforceable allocation seems to be closer to autarky than to the first best. The same can be seen in figure 10-5, which shows the log of relative weights, or log-ratio of marginal utilities. The first best is set at zero, given our symmetric initial condition, and it remains there. The enforceable moves around, although less than the autarkic one. Note that since the good state of the idiosyncratic shock is more likely than the bad state, more than half the time the two agents have the same endowment.

In table 10-1 we report the summary statistics for our four simulations. The statistics that we report are the expected values with respect to the stationary distribution of the shocks of output per capita, welfare in the three equilibria (enforceable, first best, and autarky), and private enforceable transfers. In addition, we report

FIGURE 10–4.

Typical Consumption Path for Agent 1 under Three Cases

Consumption

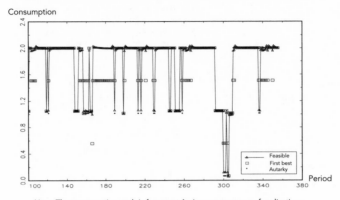

Note: The consumption path is for agent 1 given a sequence of realizations
for autarky, perfect insurance, and implementable allocations.
Source: Authors' calculations.

the ratio of the variance of idiosyncratic (net of aggregate) consumption and endowments. As we discussed above, this ratio is inversely related to the amount of
idiosyncratic risk that is diversified in equilibrium. The variances are computed as
the sample variances over a very long simulation.

As can be seen from the first two columns of the table, for the case of an
additive shock and the parameters considered, the introduction of an insurance
scheme reduces the average welfare that can be obtained in an enforceable equilibrium. As should be clear from the discussion above, this result is not the only possible one. With different parameters, one would get an overall improvement. However, the mechanism through which this result comes about is quite clear from the
table. Notice that the introduction of aggregate insurance increases the value of
autarky (and of the first best allocation, for that matter). The increase in the value of
autarky crowds out some private transfers, as is evident from the 20 percent reduction in average private transfers. This reduction more than compensates for the
increase in welfare induced by the reduction in the variance of aggregate shocks.
The amount of crowding out induced by the public transfer scheme is also evident
in the increase in the ratio of variances (the ratio equals 1 under autarky and zero
under perfect insurance).

The story in the last two columns, however, is very different. The introduction of aggregate insurance in the additive case improves welfare. The average size

FIGURE 10–5.
Marginal Utilities between Agents under Three Cases

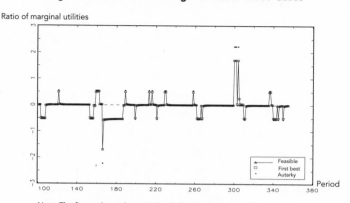

Note: The figure shows the typical path for the relative weights (ratios of marginal utilities) between agents given a sequence of realizations for autarky, perfect insurance, and implementable allocations.
Source: Authors' calculations.

of private transfers decreases, but not enough to reduce welfare. The ratio of variances increases somewhat. But again, in this case the insurance scheme does more good than harm, especially if we recall that in this case we are assuming that all households are paired and therefore have some access to private insurance arrangements.

A More Sophisticated Scheme

In the previous section, we have shown that the simple insurance scheme described earlier is not efficient and can even lead to a decrease in average welfare. It is therefore profitable to think of alternative schemes that might not interfere with the functioning of private insurance mechanisms. Obviously, the design of these schemes will depend on the knowledge, on the part of the government or the organization providing them, of the types of private insurance schemes available in the economy. In particular, it will be necessary to know the prevalence, importance, and nature of various arrangements.

Suppose that the government knows the structure outlined above and can identify the possible pairs in the village. Below we also analyze the possibility that the government, even if it knows the nature of the private arrangements described in the previous sections, cannot know which individuals are related by the private arrangements we have described. However, we will also assume that the government has no knowledge of idiosyncratic shocks and cannot even identify the guilty party if a private arrangement breaks down.

When the government can identify the extended families in the village, a simple way to minimize the effect that the aggregate insurance scheme has on private insurance would be to make the payment of the aggregate insurance conditional on the agreement of both partners. If one of the partners were not willing to sign the receipt of the aggregate scheme, both of them would lose the aggregate payment. This scheme might solve the issue of the crowding out of private insurance. Basically, this mechanism would give the individuals within the extended family a possibly very powerful punishment for the individuals who deviate from the agreement. A reversion to autarky would mean not only the loss of the individual insurance arrangement but also of the aggregate one. The same arguments that are used to guarantee that some idiosyncratic risk is shared in the absence of aggregate insurance can now be used to say that at least the same amount of risk is insured after the introduction of aggregate insurance.

The situation is a bit more complicated if the government cannot identify the members of the extended families and a fraction of the population is not actually linked to anybody else. In such a situation, a possibility is to make an individual register for the aggregate insurance scheme ex ante. Furthermore, those registering in couples could be given a small premium, which would induce them to prefer registration in couples (with a clause that makes future payment subject to the couple's agreement). The assumption that one needs to make this scheme work is that individuals not belonging to extended families would be able to find a partner to participate in the aggregate scheme, even if they are unable to find one to share individual risk. This assumption might not be very strong as it does not require the observation on the part of unpaired individuals of the idiosyncratic shocks of perspective partners. Furthermore, it requires that the paired individuals participate with their extended family partner in the aggregate insurance scheme. Again, this assumption is not too strong, as it does not require a change in the information structure of our economy.

Extensions

The model we sketched earlier can be extended in several directions. The first, obvious, extension is to allow for the possibility of storage. As discussed in Ligon, Thomas, and Worrall and by Fernando Alvarez and Urban Jermann, the problem becomes numerically much more complex because of the presence of nonconvexities implied by storage.[16] However, the main result obtained in this chapter, that simple aggregate insurance schemes are inefficient and can potentially decrease welfare, goes through. The only caveat one has to bear in mind is that the presence of storage in a model with enforceability constraints might put severe limitations on the amount of idiosyncratic risk that is diversified. This is because the possibility of self-insurance makes autarky much less unappealing than without storage.[17] When considering the introduction of aggregate insurance, therefore, we start from a situation in which there is potentially very little private insurance to crowd out.

These considerations, however, do not affect the result that the simple insurance can be improved upon and, depending on the particular features of the economy, could be counterproductive. Indeed, in a situation in which intertemporal allocation differs little from what would prevail under autarky because of the presence of an extremely binding enforceability problem, one could try to design aggregate insurance schemes to overcome these types of problems and induce a greater degree of risk sharing. In other words, in some situations, the role of the government might be more useful in inducing more risk sharing than in providing aggregate insurance.

IMPLICATIONS OF THE MODEL FOR THE DESIGN OF SURVEYS

In this section, we discuss the implications that the models discussed above have for the design of household surveys. While we do not detail the questions that might be included in a future questionnaire, we discuss some of the conceptual issues that arise from the discussions above and that could and should be informative for the design of these questions.

Clearly, four elements are crucial for the design of any proposed insurance scheme targeted toward aggregate shocks:

1. The prevalence, importance, and nature of private insurance schemes. One can think of this as an attempt at measuring empirically the parameter μ.

---

[16] Ligon, Thomas, and Worrall (1997); Alvarez and Jermann (1997).

[17] As mentioned above, Ligon, Thomas, and Worrall (1997) show that the presence of storage might decrease welfare through the same mechanism. This possibility arises in our model with the introduction of aggregate insurance.

2. The importance of enforceability constraints and the degree of risk sharing.
3. The variance and persistence of aggregate and idiosyncratic shocks.
4. The relative importance of aggregate and idiosyncratic shocks.

The main problems to be faced when one attempts to gather information on these issues are that surveys are typically not targeted toward a small village but are instead nationally representative surveys. They also typically lack a longitudinal dimension. These limitations are particularly relevant for the third and fourth points. It is therefore crucial to design questions that allow one to identify shocks and disentangle, on the one hand, the idiosyncratic and aggregate component, and on the other, the other permanent and transitory components.

Designing a number of questions on various types of private transfers and arrangements that individuals might have access to is essential. It is possible and desirable to collect information on the access to some schemes (credit, insurance, informal transfers from and to relatives), about the extent of their usage, and on their prevalence throughout the economy. It is important to quantify the amounts involved in the transfers and collect as much information as possible on the functioning of the relevant mechanisms. This information should be complemented with information about assets and the extent to which these assets can provide self-insurance. Finally, to be able to use these data, it is also crucial to complement the information on transfers, income, and so on with information about consumption.

Designing questions that would allow one to identify particular problems with the functioning of these arrangements (enforceability, asymmetric information, and so on) is important. The very nature of the enforceability problems might make the eliciting of this kind of information extremely difficult. One possible strategy would be to get at the problem indirectly by attempting to measure the degree of risk sharing among members of extended households. In this respect, the information on consumption and how consumption reacts to various shocks is particularly valuable. Obviously, deviations from perfect risk sharing could be explained by a variety of reasons other than enforceability problems, such as asymmetric information. Moreover, it is important to take into account the possibility that individual households might be engaged in different relationships providing different amounts of risk sharing.

Evaluating aggregate insurance and its optimal provision involves, by definition, having an idea about the mechanism of intertemporal allocation of resources and about the variances of the shocks received by individuals. As most surveys have a very short or no longitudinal dimension, it is crucial to design questions aimed at collecting information about the dynamics of the income processes faced by the individual households. These might include retrospective questions and questions about expectations. The former could gather information about past levels of income and perceived normal income and elicit comparisons of current and normal income. The latter could include direct questions on households' expectations about the future and, possibly, about perceived variances. Substantial progress has been made in survey design to obtain synthetic measures of perceived risk and variance.[18] Furthermore, questions about expectations can be used to obtain information about the perceived persistence of shocks.[19] The main advantage of this procedure and more generally of using direct information on expectations is that it cuts through the thorny issue of the difference between the information set of economic agents and that of the econometrician.

As discussed above, within the framework of our model it is crucial to distinguish aggregate versus idiosyncratic shocks. There is now substantial evidence about the fact that even in small and relatively homogeneous societies, such as rural villages, shocks that might be thought of as aggregate (such as the weather) have an important idiosyncratic component. To identify aggregate versus idiosyncratic shocks it is therefore important, when one does not have access to information about other households in the same village, to design questions targeted toward gathering information about the general environment in which the sampled households operate, about their perceptions of shocks compared with their neighbors and the village in general. It might be useful to elicit information not only from the sampled households but also from some village authorities (headmen) about village conditions.

CONCLUSIONS

In this chapter we have analyzed the optimal provision of aggregate insurance in a situation in which individuals in a small economy face both idiosyncratic and aggregate risk. While we allow risk sharing among members of what we call extended families, we are interested in situations in which idiosyncratic risk is less than fully

---

[18] A number of studies on income expectations and income variability have been performed at the Bank of Italy and at the University of Michigan.

[19] In a recent paper, Pistaferri (1998) has shown how to use information on actual and expected income in subsequent interviews to decompose exactly transitory and permanent shocks.

insured because of the presence of enforceability problems. We show that in such a situation, the provision of a simple insurance scheme is almost surely inefficient. Furthermore, we show that it is possible to construct scenarios in which the provision of aggregate insurance decreases aggregate welfare. The reason for this inefficiency is that aggregate insurance makes the enforceability constraints worse and therefore crowds out some private insurance.

We solve and simulate our model for the case in which individual households have access to no storage technologies. We conjecture, however, that the essence of our results carries through to the case of economies with storage.

We also discuss the possibility of designing an aggregate insurance scheme that avoids the problems just mentioned. Finally, in the last part of the chapter we present some thoughts on the implications of our model for the design of household surveys.

References

Abreu, D. 1988. "On the Theory of Infinite Repeated Games with Discounting." *Econometrica* 56 (March): 383–96.

Alvarez, F., and U. Jermann. 1997. "Asset Pricing When Risk Sharing Is Limited by Default." University of Pennsylvania. Unpublished.

Armendariz, B. 1998. "A Theory of Credit Unions." University College, London, UK. Unpublished.

Armendariz, B., and C. Grollier. 1997. "Peer Group Formation in an Adverse Selection Model." University College, London, UK. Unpublished.

Banerjee, A., T. Besley, and T. Guinnane. 1994. "Thy Neighbor's Keeper: The Design of a Credit Cooperative with a Theory and a Test." *Quarterly Journal of Economics* 109 (May): 491–516.

Kehoe, P., and F. Perri. 1997. *International Business Cycles with Endogenous Incomplete Markets.* Working Paper. Federal Reserve Bank of Minneapolis, Minneapolis, MN.

Kocherlakota, N. R. 1996. "Implications of Efficient Risk Sharing without Commitment." *Review of Economic Studies* 63 (October): 595–609.

Krueger, D., and F. Perri. 1999. *Risk Sharing: Private Insurance Markets or Redistributive Taxes?* Working Paper. Federal Reserve Bank of Minneapolis, Minneapolis, MN.

Ligon, E., J. P. Thomas, and T. Worrall. 1997. "Informal Insurance Arrangements in Village Economies." Unpublished.

———. 2000. "Mutual Insurance, Individual Savings, and Limited Commitment." *Review of Economic Dynamics* 3 (April): 216–47.

Marcet, A., and R. Marimon. 1992. "Communication, Commitment, and Growth." *Journal of Economic Theory* 58 (December): 219–49.

———. 1995. "Recursive Contracts." Universitat Pompeu Fabra, Barcelona, Spain. Unpublished.

Pistaferri, L. 1998. "Income Risk Dynamics and Heterogeneity." University College, London, UK. Unpublished.

Thomas, J. P., and T. Worral. 1988. "Self-Enfor

CHAPTER ELEVEN

Social Protection for the Poor in the Developed World

Timothy M. Smeeding and Katherin Ross Phillips

The purpose of this chapter is to review the recent evidence on the antipoverty effectiveness and other characteristics of social protection for the poor in the rich nations of the world. We will show that a wide range of poverty rates and antipoverty policies can be found among these countries. Within each country a unique set of antipoverty policies combines with other social protection policies to help reduce poverty. We examine the ways in which various private (though perhaps regulated or mandated by governments) and public policies affect poverty among the overall population and among several key groups: middle-aged workers, including those who are fully or partially employed and those with no earnings; childless families; families with children (including single parents); extended families (where living together produces economies of scale to reduce poverty); and the elderly. We examine the effect of education attainment on poverty as well.

    Our objectives are twofold: first, to describe the arithmetic effects of social protection policies on poverty, and second, to attempt to infer their lessons for the design of social protection systems and safety nets in the developing world. In doing so, we discuss the responsiveness of modern society to a number of social risks: traditional risks such as old age, unemployment, and disability, and new risks such as single parenthood, care for children when parents are employed, and the effects of demographic cycles on the costs of aging societies.

The authors would like to thank Kati Foley, Esther Gray, and Mary Santy for their help in preparing the manuscript, and Gary Burtless, Dennis Sullivan, and two anonymous referees for comments on an earlier version. Support for the chapter was provided by the IDB, Ford Foundation, and the MacArthur Network on Families and Children.

In the short space allotted to this chapter, we are limited in the extent to which we can examine different measures of poverty and specific programs. We present results for a set of rich nations at a point in time, with no direct analysis of poverty trends over time. We concentrate on money-based poverty, with only a summary discussion of the effects of noncash benefits on poverty. And we limit our poverty measures to relative income–based headcounts of the poor. We are less concerned about this final limitation than we would be if we were writing a paper on poverty measurement, where a number of poverty concepts and measures should be explored. Yet, because the antipoverty effects of social protection systems are similar whether one uses absolute or relative poverty concepts, the main points we make in this chapter can be argued regardless of the poverty concept employed.[1]

MEASURING THE EFFECTS OF POLICY ON POVERTY

Cross-national comparisons of poverty have focused primarily on the distribution of disposable money income after direct (income and employee payroll) taxes and after transfer payments.[2] While this definition of post-tax and transfer disposable income is broad, it falls considerably short of the Haig-Simons comprehensive income definition, typically by excluding much of capital gains, imputed rents, home production, and in-kind income (including employment-related benefits).[3] Most cross-national studies of poverty employ either a measure of income gross of all taxes or a measure that subtracts "direct taxes"—income and employee payroll taxes—alone. In general, studies do not count personal property or wealth taxes as direct taxes. Employer payroll taxes are implicitly assumed to fall on employees, and indirect taxes are ignored.[4]

---

[1] Kenworthy (1998); Smeeding (1997b).

[2] Direct taxes are most often estimated from tax imputation models rather than official tax records. For example, the after-tax data for Australia, Germany, and the United States are obtained using a tax imputation model at the level of the individual household to estimate direct taxes. Sweden uses official records of taxes paid.

[3] Still, this definition is broader than some. For instance, the U.S. Census Bureau's annually reported household income and poverty statistics use data from the Current Population Survey that include cash transfers but exclude taxes, thus making it difficult to ascertain the long-term effects of even income taxes on income inequality in the United States. U.S. Bureau of the Census (1998).

[4] Because of differential reliance on employer and employee social security contributions across nations, and because of the differential mix of personal, business, earnings, income, property, and goods (expenditure, V.A.T., sales) taxes across rich nations, the manner in which taxes are collected may have

Because we want to measure the effects of public policy on poverty alleviation, we also examine the impact of public taxes and transfers on well-being by
estimating the percentage of persons with incomes below half of the adjusted-
median disposable income, based on their adjusted market income (MI). MI includes all forms of earnings (wages, salaries, and self-employment income) plus
capital income. Next we factor in "private transfers," including occupational pension benefits, interhousehold transfers, and private transfers, such as child support. Private income transfers therefore include everything but government transfers
and taxes. We also separate out the effects of two types of transfers on poverty:
universal and social insurance transfers, including such items as child allowances
and unemployment, disability, and old age insurance. Next the effects of payroll
and income taxes are estimated as defined above. Finally, social assistance or means-
tested and emergency benefits are counted. The latter category includes cash and
near-cash transfers, which are assumed equivalent to cash income. These near-cash
benefits include such items as food stamps in the United States and housing allowances in Sweden. Each is easily measured in national currency terms. Once we
have added these together, we reach disposable personal income, or DI, which includes all types of income, including taxes and transfers.

These comparisons are designed to illustrate how universal benefits, social
insurance, and social assistance "welfare" programs—the social safety net—help
reduce poverty. They also tell us how the tax system, including negative taxes such
as refundable personal tax credits (for example, the U.S. earned income tax credit
[EITC] and the U.K. family tax credit), help raise the incomes of some families relative to others.

Because poverty is of greater concern when it is concentrated among vulnerable groups (children, aged, unemployed) compared with others (for example, able
childless adults), we present poverty rates for several groups as well as for all persons (figures 11–1 and 11–2 and table 11A–3 in the appendix to this chapter). We
first consider household poverty rates among households headed by a prime age
adult (25 to 64) in table 11–1. Here we break the aggregates into three groups: those
with a head or a spouse working full-year, full-time (to assess wage adequacy);

---

some effect on the results of cross-national comparative analyses of poverty. But in order to calculate the
burden of indirect taxes, a great deal of additional information is needed. Incidence assumptions (consumers, labor, and capital) need to be made, and relative types and amounts of consumption need to be
identified. Largely because of these additional requirements, we know of no studies of poverty that
include the effect of indirect as well as direct taxes.

those with only part-time workers (head or spouse) as a residual; and those with no earners (who are either full-year unemployed or not in the labor force, including the totally disabled). These analyses clearly focus on the questions of whether or not participation in the labor market can by itself reduce poverty and also how social protection affects poverty among working-age households.

We then turn to individual rates of poverty among adults (all persons aged 25 to 64) grouped into various demographic categories: couples (two adults present); adults in "extended families" (multigenerational families with children and adults other than the head and partner); childless prime age adults (adults 21–64 in households without children); and elderly (adults 65 and over) (table 11–2). We do not directly assess child poverty in this chapter. We do, however, investigate the poverty of children indirectly by assessing the economic status of their parents.

We return to the household concept in table 11–3, where we present poverty rates by education level. We have coded education groups into three categories— low, medium, and high—for the nations that have these data (all but France and the United Kingdom) in order to examine the relationship between one measure of human capital (education level of the head) and poverty. Because of low levels of human capital, policy implications for developing countries are perhaps most directly relevant. Income and poverty definitions are more completely summarized in the appendix to this chapter and table 11A–1.

The database used to carry out this analysis is the *Luxembourg Income Study* (LIS) database, which now contains information on child poverty for 27 nations in 100 databases covering the period 1967 to 1997.[5] The LIS consists of a set of existing household income microdata sets that have been "harmonized" (categories of income and demography are made consistent), producing output files that are more comparable than are the raw files. While the LIS process certainly raises the ratio of "signal" to "noise" in cross-national comparisons of income, poverty, and economic well-being, some of the noise remains. Hence, footnotes on noncomparabilities that have been reduced but not eliminated still are worthy of note.[6]

From the LIS (table 11A–2) list we have selected nine data sets to examine here: three young large Anglo-Saxon nations with "underdeveloped" welfare states (United States, Australia, Canada); five European nations (United Kingdom, Spain, France, Germany, and the Netherlands), which span the social policy spectrum;

---

[5] See LIS homepage at http://liss.ceps.lu and table 11A–2.

[6] Recent papers and publications on poverty, inequality and social protection using LIS include Gottschalk and Smeeding (1997, 2000); Danziger and Jäntti (2000); Smeeding (1997a); and Kenworthy (1998).

and one "advanced" Scandinavian welfare state (Sweden). While other choices of nations were available, this set fairly well represents the types of social protection systems available in rich nations.[7]

RESULTS

Our purpose is to assess the relative levels of poverty across the selected nations and the effect of social protection systems on these societies. We begin with two all-inclusive figures (based on table 11A–3) that paint the broad outline of poverty patterns and antipoverty effects across these nations. These pictures help set the stage for the detailed results that follow.

Overview

There is a wide range of relative income–based poverty rates based on disposable income (DI) for all persons across the nine countries, as seen in figure 11–1 (derived from table 11A–3). The United States is clearly the outlier at either the 40 or 50 percent poverty line, with an 18.4 percent rate at our preferred 50 percent of median standard. Australia comes next, at 15.7 percent, and then a grouping of the United Kingdom, Canada, Spain, and France, all in the 10 to 12 percent range. Finally, poverty is lowest in (West) Germany, Sweden, and the Netherlands, all in the 6 to 7 percent range. At the more stringent 40 percent poverty standard, only the United States has poverty in double digits, while Australia has an 8 percent rate. The next four nations (United Kingdom, Canada, Spain, and France) are all around the 6 percent poverty level, while the lowest three (Germany, Sweden, and the Netherlands) are all around 4 percent. Beyond the United States and Australia, which always rank highest, and the Netherlands which is always lowest (or tied for lowest), there is no unique ranking. Although country-by-country rankings vary by the level of median income at which poverty is measured, three or four distinct groupings of nations and large differences across these nations are apparent in figure 11–1. The range of poverty rates varies by two to three times across the extremes depending on which level of poverty line is selected.

---

[7] We deliberately exclude the newly reformed central and eastern European nations on the grounds that their welfare states are in some ways remnants of the former Warsaw bloc and are hence in a state of transition.

FIGURE 11–1.
Incidence of Poverty across Modern Nations

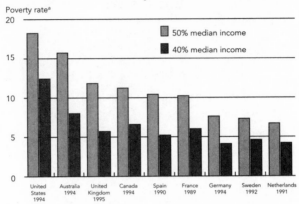

a. Percent of all persons with adjusted disposable incomes less than 40 or 50 percent of adjusted median disposable income. Forty percent of the median is chosen for comparison because it is almost exactly the ratio of the U.S. poverty line to the U.S. median.
Source: Authors' calculations from the Luxembourg Income Study, Smeeding and others (1998), and table 11A–3.

Market income (MI)–based poverty rates (figure 11–2) are more closely clustered than are DI-based rates, with all countries facing pre-tax and transfer poverty rates between 30 and 38 percent at the 50 percent of median poverty standard. The antipoverty effects of taxes and transfers, however, differ greatly. In fact, the United States and Australia begin with the two lowest MI-based poverty rates but end up with the highest DI-based rates (figure 11–2). Canada begins at a point close to the U.S. figure but then ends up with a better after-tax and transfer poverty rate. In the low-DI poverty countries (for example, Sweden and the Netherlands but also France and Germany), there is a much larger antipoverty effect but also a larger "target" MI-based pre-tax and transfer poverty group. The patterns at the 50 percent level are largely similar to those at the 40 percent poverty level (for the latter, see table 11A–4).

A closer look at table 11A–3 indicates that in every nation with the exception of Australia and the United Kingdom, universal and social insurance transfers have by far the largest impacts on poverty. In the United Kingdom, social assistance also has a large and roughly equal effect on poverty. While all other nations make use of social assistance payments, they play a far less significant role than does social insurance in most nations. In every nation, private transfers play a small positive role, while taxes play a small negative role, but neither is a prime mover for pov-

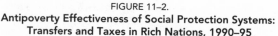

FIGURE 11–2.
**Antipoverty Effectiveness of Social Protection Systems:
Transfers and Taxes in Rich Nations, 1990–95**

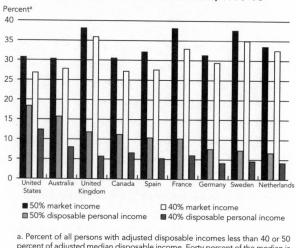

a. Percent of all persons with adjusted disposable incomes less than 40 or 50 percent of adjusted median disposable income. Forty percent of the median is chosen for comparison because it is almost exactly the ratio of the U.S. poverty line to the U.S. median.
Source: Authors' calculations from the Luxembourg Income Study and table 11A–3.

erty reduction. In the expansive welfare states of Sweden, Germany, France, and even Spain, social insurance benefits account for 80 percent or more of the poverty reduction derived from the social protection system. In Canada, the Netherlands, and the United States, about two-thirds of the antipoverty effect can be attributed to social insurance and universal transfers.[8]

Social insurance includes old age and survivors' benefits, temporary and permanent disability payments, unemployment compensation, and in some countries, maternity allowances. Universal benefits include child allowances, maternity allowances, and in some countries, guaranteed child support (child support assurance). Because the effects of social insurance may be dominated by one or more of these specific types of benefits, it behooves us to take a closer look at which types of benefits are most prevalent and which packages have the greatest impact on pov-

---

[8] While the terms "social insurance" and "universal benefits" are generally the same across all nations, Canada has recently begun to target its child allowance ("universal") program and unemployment insurance ("social insurance") program by phasing out the benefits at high income levels, for example, $65,000 and above. We return to this point in the discussion that follows.

erty. We accomplish this decomposition by examining impacts on more detailed demographic groups in the next section of this chapter. We are not able to complete a program-by-program analysis for each type of social assistance or social insurance benefit. Indeed, because there is no one particular type of social protection instrument that dominates across several nations, such a detailed analysis would be fruitless in any case. Rather we seek to demonstrate the general type of programs that affect the poor and to document the extent of the impacts for each type.

The preliminary figures suggest that there may be a relationship between social protection efforts (for example, as measured by the percentage of GDP spent on cash social protection) and reductions in poverty. Indeed, we examine the percentage change in poverty from MI to DI (as in tables 11A–3, 11–1, and 11–2), and compare it with social protection expenditures (for example, those from the OECD).[9] Figures 11A–2 and 11A–3 show that there is a strong relationship between social protection budgetary efforts and poverty reduction among the nonelderly (figure 11A–2) and among all persons including the elderly (figure 11A–3). In general, higher spending produces lower poverty rates. And this overall relationship is not solely driven by social retirement expenses because the result also holds true for the nonelderly.[10] In both charts the United States is an outlier, suggesting not only that it spends little on social protection (relative to GDP) but also that this spending is not well targeted to the otherwise poor (as denoted by its being far below the trend line in figures 11A–2 and 11A–3). For instance, among the nonelderly, Australia has a larger but still below average antipoverty impact for roughly the same level of expenditure, while among all persons, it drops closer to the U.S. level.[11] And among the midlevel countries in terms of expenditures on and poverty reduction for the nonelderly, France seems to achieve a larger impact than does the United Kingdom, Germany, or Canada. Sweden and the Netherlands achieve high levels of poverty reduction, but they also spend large fractions of GDP on social protection. To investigate these results more closely, we now turn to the more detailed results.

---

[9] OECD (1999). The OECD Social Expenditures database allows users to separate benefits paid to the elderly (households with a head or recipient 65 or older) and the nonelderly. It also permits us to separate health care spending from cash and near-cash benefits as in figures 11A–2 and 11A–3. Education benefits are, however, not included in these figures.

[10] The indirect effects of social expenditure on pre-tax and transfer poverty and infertility are discussed below.

[11] This is not to recommend the Australian income and means-tested social protection system, but just to note that targeted spending produces greater poverty reduction per dollar spent.

Working-Age Household Poverty and Social Protection

We begin by examining the effects of social protection on poverty among households headed by householders (household heads) of working age (25 to 64 years old). Because of the importance of labor market income supplements, we break this group into three subgroups in each country:

- households with either the head or spouse working full-year, full-time
- households with neither the head nor the spouse employed ("nonearner" households)
- households with a part-time employed head or spouse (or both) and with neither working full-year, full-time (the residual of the first two subgroups).

Overall poverty rates are also tabulated. In table 11–1 we examine the household (not the person). Because countries often try to construct "income packages" for different types of households, whereby all earnings, social insurance, and other factors are taken into account, one could argue that the household is the proper accounting unit and poverty reference group.[12] The breakdown into these types is to help tell us how various labor market groups are affected by the social protection systems in each country.[13] In both tables 11–1 and 11–2, column A presents MI poverty rates, column E presents DI poverty rates, and the last column presents the overall percent reduction in poverty from MI to DI.

There are both large and subtle differences across countries in these results (table 11–1). One of the most clear findings is that full-year, full-time workers begin with low poverty rates and improve from there. The highest poverty rates among this group (United States, 6.2 percent; Australia, 3.3 percent; Canada, 2.9 percent) are also low-wage countries, that is, those with a large fraction of workers earning less than two-thirds of the median wage.[14] But even in these countries and for full-year, full-time workers, the tax transfer system further reduces poverty. DI poverty is less than MI poverty in each nation.

At the other end of the spectrum, nonearners almost by definition have extremely high MI poverty rates and hence must rely on the transfer system to bring

---

[12] See Danziger, Rainwater, and Smeeding (1997). In table 11–2 we use individual poverty rates but maintain the same household accounting framework.

[13] In table 11–1 we exclude Spain and France because of the lack of comparable data on type of worker.

[14] Smeeding (1997b).

Table 11–1. Household Poverty Rates by Income Source and Household Working Status

Percentage of household heads 25 to 64 years old

Country, year, working status	Market income (A)	Column (A) + private income transfers (B)	Column (B) + universal and social transfers (C)	Column (C) – taxes (D)	Column (D) + social assistance transfers (E)	Percent change in columns A to E (F)
Australia, 1994						
Full-year, full-time worker[a]	5.1	4.9	4.9	5.2	3.3	–35.3
Part-time worker, other[b]	31.6	30.3	30.3	30.9	18.5	–41.5
Nonearners[c]	86.3	82.5	82.5	83.2	56.7	–34.3
Overall	23.2	22.2	22.2	22.8	14.8	–36.2
Canada, 1994						
Full-year, full-time worker	4.9	4.4	2.6	3.3	2.9	–40.8
Part-time worker, other	42.8	38.7	25.3	28.0	23.9	–44.2
Nonearners	90.7	77.9	65.0	66.9	58.8	–35.2
Overall	23.9	21.1	15.4	16.6	14.5	–39.3
Germany, 1994						
Full-year, full-time worker	1.4	1.4	1.0	1.7	1.4	0.0
Part-time worker, other	32.4	28.8	16.2	21.8	17.1	–47.2
Nonearners	89.8	85.5	49.8	50.3	38.3	–57.3
Overall	19.0	17.7	10.3	12.1	9.4	–50.5
The Netherlands, 1991						
Full-year, full-time worker	2.5	0.5	0.3	1.0	0.8	–68.0
Part-time worker, other	31.3	26.7	16.5	22.2	14.6	–53.4
Nonearners	91.2	69.8	32.6	36.8	17.9	–80.4
Overall	24.1	19.1	9.8	12.2	6.9	–71.4

Sweden, 1992

Full-year, full-time worker	4.4	4.3	1.2	2.3	1.8	−59.1
Part-time worker, other	29.2	28.0	6.4	10.2	3.5	−88.0
Nonearners	94.8	94.6	24.7	42.0	17.3	−81.8
Overall	20.7	20.1	5.0	8.5	3.8	−81.6

United Kingdom, 1995

Full-year, full-time worker	1.6	1.5	0.6	1.6	0.9	−43.8
Part-time worker, other	34.2	27.7	20.9	24.1	13.6	−60.2
Nonearners	77.2	66.6	56.8	57.6	34.0	−56.0
Overall	30.2	25.9	21.2	22.6	13.2	−56.3

United States, 1994

Full-year, full-time worker	6.5	6.0	5.4	7.2	6.2	−4.6
Part-time worker, other	43.7	39.7	34.3	38.1	35.4	−19.0
Nonearners	90.4	81.1	70.9	72.1	68.4	−24.3
Overall	23.2	21.0	18.4	20.5	18.9	−18.5

a. Either the head or the spouse (or both) works full-year, full-time. Full-year is defined as 50 or more weeks of employment. Full-time is defined as 35 or more hours of employment. For Australia, 1994, the number of weeks of employment is missing so full-year, full-time employment is identified by 35 or more hours and the labor force status of "employed full-time."

b. Either the head or the spouse (or both) works part-year or part-time and has earnings, but neither works full-year, full-time. This is the residual of the first and third categories.

c. Neither the head nor the spouse reports any earnings.

Note: Poverty is measured at 50 percent of median-adjusted household disposable income. See table 11A–1 in the appendix to this chapter for definitions of income categories and poverty rates.

Source: Authors' calculations.

these rates above the poverty level. Since the "nonearners" can run as high as 20 to 30 percent of all such households (for example, see the United Kingdom and the Netherlands in table 11A–6), this is a major problem in some nations. Social insurance and social assistance are combined to bring about large poverty reductions in some nations for this group (for example, the Netherlands, Sweden), while those that do not have such strong institutions are much less likely to reduce poverty rates to reasonable levels (for example, the United States).

In between these extremes, we find part-time (or part-year) worker households, where again outcomes vary according to the strength of the social protection system. Resulting DI poverty rates vary from 3.5 to 35.4 percent for this group, with social insurance playing the strongest role in poverty reduction efforts.

In every country, private income transfers and taxes play small, offsetting roles, with taxes raising poverty by 1 to 2 percentage points and private transfers having the opposite effect. The overall results at the bottom of each country's breakdowns reflect these patterns (and also the relative numbers of households in each of the three categories). In almost all of the countries, social insurance benefits, disability, unemployment, child allowances, workers' compensation, and maternity benefits play the largest role in reducing poverty. Only in Australia, which has a set of expansive income-tested social assistance schemes, and in the United Kingdom, where income-tested social assistance benefits are a relatively large part of the safety net, do we find that social insurance is not the largest source of poverty reduction. In all the rest of these nations, social insurance transfers provide two-thirds or more of the antipoverty effect of the social protection system.

Adults, Parents, and Elderly by Family Type

Another way to examine the effects of social protection is to look at individual adults, including parents with children in the household, according to their household living arrangement status, not their work status (table 11–2). Different nations treat adults in different ways, depending on their family situation: presence or absence of children; presence or absence of other adults (extended families or single parents). Because older retired households also receive large amounts of social transfers, we examine the population 65 and over as well.[15]

---

[15] The age line that separates the retired from workers is not always clear and may be below 65 in many countries. See Smeeding and Quinn (1998) on this topic.

The most striking findings here are the diversity of social transfer effectiveness across the population types and the continued importance of social insurance transfers in most nations. Adults 25 to 64 years old (tables 11–2 and 11A–4), not surprisingly, look by and large like adult households with heads in the same prime age range: social insurance drives the antipoverty system (with the exception of Australia and the United Kingdom). Overall, there is a wide range in adult MI and DI poverty rates, with the latter ranging from 3.1 percent in Sweden to 15.4 percent in the United States. Among childless adults and extended families, this same pattern persists: wide-ranging DI poverty rates and social insurance as the primary antipoverty tool.

Among families with children, social assistance plays a somewhat larger role. Couples with children still rely heavily on social insurance, but the presence of children adds to the role of social assistance in most nations, especially in the United Kingdom, but also in Canada, France, and Sweden. Couples with children have DI poverty rates that range from 2 percent in Sweden to double digits in Australia (10.6 percent), Spain (10.9 percent), the United States (11.8 percent), and the United Kingdom (12.3 percent).

Single parents are a quite varied group, with MI poverty rates from 40 percent in Sweden to 78 percent in the United Kingdom and the Netherlands and with DI poverty rates ranging from 4 percent in Sweden to more than 50 percent in Australia, Canada, Germany, and the United States. Even in France and the Netherlands, single parent poverty rates run in the 28 to 30 percent range. In France, Germany, and the Netherlands, we find that social assistance now tops social insurance in its antipoverty effect for single parents. Clearly most nations have not done well in providing social protection to this vulnerable group. In Sweden (and in Norway, Finland, and Denmark, not shown here), MI-based poverty rates run below the DI-based poverty rates in many other nations, indicating that Sweden (and to some extent France and Spain) has found a way to encourage single parents to become more self-supporting through part-time or full-time work, thus reducing MI poverty by a greater margin than other nations.

While the elderly are a much better protected group in all nations except Sweden, where everyone is well-protected, a wide range of DI poverty rates emerge, ranging from almost 33 percent in Australia (where an income-tested benefit system substitutes for social retirement) to below 5 percent in the Netherlands. Only Canada and Germany also have single-digit elderly poverty rates. In the United States 22.7 percent of the elderly are poor, as are 13 to 17 percent of the elderly in Spain, Germany, and France. For the first time, we see that private transfers, here in

Table 11–2. Adult Poverty Rates by Income Source

Poverty measured at 50 percent of median-adjusted household disposable income

Country, year adult category	Market income (A)	Column (A) + private income transfers (B)	Column (B) + universal and social transfers (C)	Column (C) – taxes (D)	Column (D) + social assistance transfers (E)	Percent change in columns (A) to (E) (F)
Australia, 1994						
All adults (25 to 64)	21.8	20.8	20.8	21.3	12.3	–43.6
Couples with children[a]	16.2	15.8	15.8	16.4	10.6	–34.6
Single parents[b]	69.8	67.7	67.7	69.3	48.5	–30.5
Adults in extended families[c]	19.8	19.8	19.8	20.5	8.2	–58.6
Childless adults[d]	23.1	21.7	21.7	22.1	12.2	–47.2
Elderly (65 and over)	79.5	73.0	73.0	73.2	32.8	–58.7
Canada, 1994						
All adults (25 to 64)	21.6	18.6	12.3	13.4	11.3	–47.7
Couples with children	16.3	15.6	10.1	11.4	9.9	–39.3
Single parents	61.8	59.4	52.3	53.3	47.6	–23.0
Adults in extended families	15.0	13.6	8.3	9.1	6.2	–58.7
Childless adults	23.5	18.8	11.9	12.9	10.9	–53.6
Elderly (65 and over)	78.9	61.6	8.4	8.9	6.1	–92.3
France, 1989						
All adults (25 to 64)	27.3	26.7	9.8	10.4	8.5	–68.9
Couples with children	20.1	19.7	8.1	8.5	6.1	–69.7
Single parents	47.9	46.3	40.5	41.3	28.5	–40.5
Adults in extended families	28.2	28.1	11.0	11.8	8.6	–69.5
Childless adults	31.6	30.8	9.5	10.2	9.3	–70.6
Elderly (65 and over)	86.6	86.2	17.9	18.7	16.7	–80.7

Germany, 1994						
All adults (25 to 64)	16.8	15.6	7.8	9.3	7.0	−58.3
Couples with children	9.0	9.0	6.3	7.9	5.9	−34.4
Single parents	62.5	56.5	51.2	55.8	50.4	−19.4
Adults in extended families	11.9	11.9	5.3	6.1	3.5	−70.6
Childless adults	19.9	18.0	7.1	8.6	6.2	−68.8
Elderly (65 and over)	88.0	77.6	9.3	9.5	8.3	−90.6
The Netherlands, 1991						
All adults (25 to 64)	22.0	16.8	7.4	9.7	5.9	−73.2
Couples with children	9.0	8.7	5.0	7.0	5.6	−37.8
Single parents	79.5	72.0	55.3	59.9	31.5	−60.4
Adults in extended families	11.1	10.1	4.4	6.1	5.1	−54.1
Childless adults	29.3	20.5	7.2	9.6	5.1	−82.6
Elderly (65 and over)	92.3	65.8	3.5	5.0	4.4	−95.2
Spain, 1990[e]						
All adults (25 to 64)	24.3	23.4	10.6	—	9.9	−59.3
Couples with children	15.3	14.7	11.2	—	10.9	−28.8
Single parents	53.0	43.6	32.4	—	32.4	−38.9
Adults in extended families	22.9	22.1	9.5	—	8.9	−61.1
Childless adults	31.4	30.4	10.5	—	9.5	−69.7
Elderly (65 and over)	72.0	68.6	15.6	—	13.0	−81.9
Sweden, 1992[f]						
All adults (25 to 64)	18.1	17.7	4.0	6.6	3.1	−82.9
Couples with children	10.7	10.6	3.1	4.5	2.2	−79.4
Single parents	40.5	34.5	9.3	13.5	3.7	−90.9
Adults in extended families	—	—	—	—	—	—
Childless adults	20.9	20.9	4.1	7.4	3.6	−82.8
Elderly (65 and over)	91.6	91.6	13.1	19.2	6.4	−93.0

Table continues on next page.

Table 11–2. Adult Poverty Rates by Income Source (continued)

Country, year adult category	Market income (A)	Column (A) + private income transfers (B)	Column (B) + universal and social transfers (C)	Column (C) – taxes (D)	Column (D) + social assistance transfers (E)	Percent change in columns A to E (F)
United Kingdom, 1995						
All adults (25 to 64)	27.2	22.5	17.1	18.5	11.0	−59.6
Couples with children	20.4	19.5	16.9	18.8	12.3	−39.7
Single parents	77.8	74.2	71.8	72.6	43.2	−44.5
Adults in extended families	23.1	22.2	15.8	20.2	9.6	−58.4
Childless adults	27.6	20.0	12.7	13.6	7.6	−72.5
Elderly (65 and over)	83.3	65.5	29.3	29.8	13.9	−83.3
United States, 1994						
All adults (25 to 64)	20.7	18.4	15.2	17.1	15.4	−25.6
Couples with children	13.1	12.6	11.3	13.3	11.8	−9.9
Single parents	59.0	55.2	52.0	55.0	48.7	−17.5
Adults in extended families	26.7	25.0	21.8	24.6	20.3	−24.0
Childless adults	20.7	17.2	12.9	14.4	13.7	−33.8
Elderly (65 and over)	73.8	60.2	23.5	23.8	22.7	−69.2

— Not available.
a. Adults, 25 to 64 years old, living in households with children headed by a married or cohabiting couple with no other adults present.
b. Unmarried household heads, 25 to 64 years old, living in households with children and with no other adults present.
c. Adults, 25 to 64 years old, living in households with children and adults other than the head and partner (if married or cohabiting).
d. Adults, 25 to 64 years old, living in households with no children present.
e. Tax information is not available for Spain, 1990.
f. Cannot identify extended families in Sweden, 1992.
Note: See table 11A–1 in the appendix to this chapter for definitions of income categories and poverty rates.
Source: Authors' calculations.

the form of occupational pensions, have a large role in reducing poverty, especially in the Netherlands, but also in the United Kingdom, Canada, Germany, and the United States. Social retirement still plays the largest role, but in Sweden, the United Kingdom, Canada, France, and Spain, social assistance also plays a not-insignificant role among the elderly.

Education and Income Sources

Our final breakdowns of poverty are by education status of the head of the household. Cross-national levels of education are not coded in a comparable way in any data set. In some, for example, the United Kingdom data set used by LIS, age of leaving school is the only variable that is present. However, two recent LIS papers have re-coded education into low, medium, and high levels and have assessed the robustness of these results.[16] We use these classifications in table 11–3.[17]

There is a clear and pronounced relationship between poverty status and head's educational attainment. The largest differences across education groups show up in the first column. Higher levels of education produce lower household poverty rates in every nation and this effect is most pronounced in the high-poverty nations like the United States, where there is a more than sixfold difference between the MI-based poverty status of the least educated compared with the highest educated. In every country smaller but similar differences occur, with single-digit MI-based poverty rates appearing in Germany and Spain as well. Tax and transfer policy reduces MI poverty in all nations and with similar "percentage change" has an impact across education categories in most nations. But the largest drops in the absolute numbers of the poor owing to tax and transfer policy take place among the least educated in most nations. Only in the United States do we find the lowest educated receiving the least antipoverty effect for social protection systems relative to other groups.

The net effect of education on MI plus taxes and transfers reduces poverty to 7 percent or less for the highly educated in all nations studied here. The least educated reach single-digit poverty rates only in Sweden. In every other nation, those with the least education have poverty rates of 10.8 percent or more, with rates of 25

---

[16] O'Connor (1994); Sullivan and Smeeding (1997).

[17] The actual re-codes of LIS education variables into these categories are available on the LIS website (http://www.lis.ceps.lu) or from Sullivan and Smeeding (1997), which is also available online from this same source.

Table 11–3. Household Poverty Rates by Income Source and Education Level of Household Head

Percentage of household heads 25 to 64 years old

Country, year, education level	Market income (A)	Column (A) + private income transfers (B)	Column (B) + universal and social transfers (C)	Column (C) – taxes (D)	Column (D) + social assistance transfers (E)	Percent change in columns A to E (F)
Australia, 1994						
Low	31.6	30.9	30.9	32.0	20.3	−35.8
Medium	15.9	14.9	14.9	16.7	10.4	−34.6
High	12.6	11.0	11.0	11.5	7.0	−44.4
Overall	23.2	22.2	22.2	22.8	14.8	−36.2
Canada, 1994						
Low	40.2	36.5	27.0	28.7	24.9	−38.1
Medium	20.7	18.1	12.9	14.2	12.3	−40.6
High	11.1	8.7	7.0	7.6	6.9	−37.8
Overall	23.9	21.1	15.4	16.6	14.5	−39.3
Germany, 1994						
Low	32.4	30.5	20.1	22.5	18.5	−42.9
Medium	18.2	17.3	9.5	11.1	8.3	−53.3
High	8.3	5.5	3.5	5.9	5.5	−33.7
Overall	19.0	17.7	10.3	12.1	9.4	−50.5
The Netherlands, 1991						
Low	39.4	32.4	15.9	19.6	10.8	−72.6
Medium	18.7	14.0	7.3	8.9	5.2	−72.2
High	12.8	10.6	6.5	8.7	4.5	−64.8
Overall	24.1	19.1	9.8	12.2	6.9	−71.4
Spain, 1990[a]						
Low	28.3	27.4	13.9	—	13.2	−53.4
Medium	10.0	8.8	4.6	—	4.5	−55.0
High	5.3	4.2	2.2	—	2.2	−58.5
Overall	23.1	22.1	11.3	—	10.8	−53.2

Sweden, 1992

Low	26.4	26.1	5.3	10.4	5.1	−80.7
Medium	19.5	18.7	4.0	6.7	3.2	−83.6
High	11.8	11.5	5.1	6.2	2.5	−78.8
Overall	20.7	20.1	5.0	8.5	3.8	−81.6

United States, 1994

Low	52.5	50.9	46.4	49.8	46.0	−12.4
Medium	23.0	20.5	17.6	19.9	18.2	−20.9
High	8.1	6.3	5.5	6.6	6.2	−23.5
Overall	23.2	21.0	18.4	20.5	18.9	−18.5

— Not available.

a. Tax information is not available for Spain, 1990.

Note: Poverty is measured at 50 percent of median-adjusted household disposable income. The three education levels are low, medium, and high attainment. For the United States, the break between low and medium is completion of high school, and between medium and high, the completion of a bachelor's degree in college. This conceptual definition transfers to Canada and Australia fairly well but less so to European countries. For example, a liberal definition of high, when applied to the Swedish and Dutch data, includes some persons with something similar to the American two-year associate's degree. At the same time, the German system relies more heavily on vocational education, and many German workers without a university degree possess job skills comparable to American college graduates of the same age. For details, see Sullivan and Smeeding (1997) and O'Connor (1994). See table 11A–1 in the appendix to this chapter for definitions of income categories and poverty rates. All households are headed by an adult, 25 to 64 years old.

Source: Authors' calculations.

percent in Canada and 46 percent in the United States. Clearly the better educated are the least poor, often by a wide margin, in every nation studied here.

Summary

The LIS data reveal a rich and varied pattern of social protection among the nations examined. Self-protection, in the form of low MI or pre-tax and transfer poverty rates, produces the best results for the highly educated and for childless couples, extended families, and households with at least one full-time earner. While they may not always be classified as a social protection, the labor market and the extended family are clearly strong antipoverty devices in all rich nations. Full employment policies and extended family have definite measurable economic benefits.

Private transfers and taxes largely offset one another for most nonelderly groups. Social assistance plays a large and often significant role in many nations (for example, Australia, the United Kingdom) and for some specific groups (for example, single parents, elderly). But two factors seem to hold the most promise for poverty reduction: the education system, which directly produces lower MI-based poverty in every country; and the overall expense, extent, and generosity of the social insurance system, which provides the bulk of antipoverty effect for working-age adults (including those who are not at all employed) and for the elderly in all nations (with the singular exception of Australia). While many nations have responded well to the "traditional" needs for social protection, for example, old age, extended unemployment, and disability, not all have done so. And only Sweden, and to a far lesser extent France, Spain, and the Netherlands, appear to have dealt at all well with social protection against the "new risk" of single parenthood.[18]

DISCUSSION AND CONCLUSION

The ultimate question posed for this chapter seems to be, what, if any, lessons can social protection policy for the poor in the developing world take from the social protection policies and results in the developed world? The short answer is, that

---

[18] Overbye (1997).

depends. Here we assess the findings above in light of the institutional, demographic, and economic situation of the developing world.

Expansive social insurance systems are a double-edged sword. On the one hand, large amounts of social protection have strong antipoverty effects as demonstrated above. While extensive social insurance systems prevent widespread poverty for most groups, without the problems of stigma or take-up found in social assistance schemes, three negative factors associated with these programs need also be taken into account: their aggregate expense; their effect on labor markets; and the current nonsustainability of social insurance for the aged in pay-as-you-go pension schemes. We will deal with each in turn.

As seen in figure 11–2, the more that a nation spends on social protection, the better the antipoverty effects for working-age adults and for the elderly and near elderly. But social protection is expensive: more than 12 percent of GDP for cash programs for the nonelderly alone in the Netherlands and Sweden; 18 to 21 percent of GDP or more in overall elderly and nonelderly cash outlays in the United Kingdom, France, and Germany; and 25 percent or more in Sweden and the Netherlands. And this does not count public expenditure for health care or public education. These large outlays have significant effects on labor markets in three ways.

First and foremost, large social retirement systems, complete with early retirement (at 55 or over) in the guise of disability transfers or unemployment insurance (or clearly stated as "early retirement" or "unemployment retirement" benefits), have reduced labor force participation for men at relatively young ages throughout Europe and Scandinavia. One striking statistic: only 16 percent of Dutch men 61 or over participate in the labor force. In the Netherlands, France, Germany, and many other European nations, the fraction of men who work is now less than 35 percent for 62-year-olds.[19] The extension of early retirement benefits leads to work stoppage in every nation studied, but especially in the high-unemployment nations of northern and central Europe. Here "joblessness" is passively fought by finance ministers and social ministers with social insurance programs, which effectively remove most older workers from the labor market. In the face of ever-expanding life expectancy in old age, these policies suggest the strong possibility of near future fiscal catastrophe as suggested below.

Second, extended unemployment benefits are notorious for their negative effects on work and labor supply behavior in such diverse nations as Poland and

---

[19] See Gruber and Wise (1998); Smeeding and Quinn (1998).

Canada.[20] Another rule of thumb is that the more recent the study, the greater the negative effects of social insurance on labor markets. Disability insurance at younger ages has similar impacts in every rich nation.[21]

Finally, income-tested (or means-tested) social assistance has negative effects on work in most nations, though these are probably of a lesser magnitude than is popularly believed. Some nations, for example, Sweden and France, have found good ways to mix work and income support for low-income single parents (or couples). Canada has found ways to phase out universal and social insurance policies such as child allowances and extended unemployment insurance at higher income levels.[22] Most nations, however, for example, the United Kingdom, have not done well on this front, creating social assistance systems with severe work disincentives or so-called poverty traps. Whether U.S.-style "welfare reform" will work in these nations is open to question.

Hence, the costs of reduced labor supply must be counted in when assessing such programs. Unfortunately, the negative effects of income transfers on work effort are not well studied in any of these nations. Robert Moffitt finds modest negative effects in the United States, where the tax and transfer system is the smallest of the nations studied.[23] An early comparative study of the United States and the Netherlands found large negative effects of the Dutch tax and transfer system on work effort compared to the United States.[24] But we know of no later similar studies for the overall transfer systems of other nations covered, much less for developing countries.

Most of the "classic" studies of the work-reducing effects of social transfers are largely out of date.[25] Many focus to a large extent on the third type of problem mentioned above—that is, social assistance—at the expense of studying extended unemployment or retirement income. The work-reducing effects of early retirement are also largely ignored in several studies.[26] The third major shortcoming of expansive pay-as-you-go social insurance systems for the elderly is their economic and demographic nonsustainability. The United States publicly worries about a

---

[20] Schmidt and Gora (1998); Lemieux and MacLeod (1998).

[21] Aarts, Burkhauser, and de Jong (1996).

[22] Banting (1997).

[23] Moffitt (1992).

[24] Haveman (1985).

[25] Danziger, Haveman, and Plotnick (1981).

[26] For example, Atkinson and Mogenson (1993); Burtless and Haveman (1987); and Moffitt (1992).

projected 2 percent of GDP shortfall between revenues and expenses for social retirement in the year 2030. The Germans, French, Canadians, and Dutch only wish
their situation were so favorable. Early retirement and generous benefits mix with
ever-growing life expectancy at older ages and declining birthrates to produce revenue shortfalls of 4 to 6 percent of GDP for social retirement schemes over this
same horizon in these nations.[27] Even at this time, attempts to raise retirement ages,
cut pensions, or build in added tiers for occupational retirement are meeting increased resistance.

Finally, we should mention measures to address the "new risks" of rich societies: social protection for single parents and work-enabling policies for mothers,
married and unmarried.[28] Few Western nations have met this challenge in a meaningful way. Child support by absent parents is either largely unpaid (United States,
Canada) or subsumed by "advance maintenance" social insurance benefits, which
provide for guarantees in the absence of payment by absent parents while more or
less ignoring the parental obligation.[29] The problem of adequate levels of support
for single parents is an issue that is unsolved by most rich societies.[30]

In summary, Western-style tax and transfer systems are not currently
budgetarily affordable by developing nations, and they are liable to have large economic costs in any case. While classic tax and transfer social protection systems are
liable to have large automatic stability effects on consumption levels, they are also
liable to retard economic growth in the developing world. Fortunately a more modest
set of policies also offers promises of universal social protection at lower costs.

---

[27] Smeeding and Sullivan (1998).

[28] Overbye (1997).

[29] Skévik (1997).

[30] For example, Smeeding and others (1998).

APPENDIX. DIFFERENCES IN CONCEPTS OF WELL-BEING AND POVERTY BETWEEN RICH AND POOR NATIONS

The measurement of economic poverty in all nations, rich or poor, involves the calculation of economic well-being or resources relative to needs. Economic well-being refers to the material resources available to households. (We use the terms *household* and *family* interchangeably. Our formal unit of aggregation is the household—all persons living together and sharing the same housing facilities—in almost all nations. Only in Sweden does "household" refer to a more narrow definition of the "family" unit.) The concern with these resources is not with material consumption itself but rather with the capabilities they give household members to participate in their societies.[31] These capabilities are inputs to social activities, and participation in these activities produces a particular level of well-being.[32] Measurement of these capabilities differs according to the context in which one chooses to measure them, particularly within rich nations compared with poor ones.

All advanced or rich societies are highly stratified socially. Some individuals have more resources than others. The opportunities for social participation are vitally affected by the resources at the disposal of the family, particularly in nations like the United States, where there is heavy reliance on the market to purchase such social goods as health care, education, and child care services.[33] Money income is the central resource in these societies. But there are still other important kinds of resources, such as social capital, noncash benefits, education, and access to basic health care, all of which add to human capabilities.[34] There are also many forces in rich societies that reduce well-being by limiting capabilities to participate fully in society, such as violent geographically and socially isolated neighborhoods and poor quality public education. Earnings and job instability also increase economic insecurity in many rich countries.

In poor nations, where poverty is more basic—often the difference between life and death—real consumption of food and shelter is the preferred measure of well-being. Economic poverty emerges and is measured by having too few resources for survival or living on life's edge. Here life expectancy, mortality rates at young ages, lack of access to public health, illiteracy, and other basic measures of poverty

---

[31] Sen (1992).
[32] Rainwater (1990); Coleman, Rainwater, and McClelland (1978).
[33] Rainwater (1974).
[34] Coleman (1988).

and social exclusion are much more common and much more easily measured than is income. And social capital in the form of family support may be the major form of social protection in developing countries, particularly in rural communities.

In rich societies, lower life expectancy and higher infant mortality are also correlated with poverty, though to a lesser extent than in developing countries.[35] But in rich countries, consumption—or the ability to consume—is the key measure of economic resources and the ability to avoid poverty, while income—consumption plus change in net worth—brings with it more complicated issues of period of measurement and life cycle considerations. However, income is a much more appropriate and, we would argue, more easily measured index of well-being for rich nations than is consumption.[36] Further, an emphasis on income, in addition to consumption, allows researchers to focus not only on today's consumption but also on ability to protect future consumption, that is, savings and access to credit markets.

In rich nations, one measures poverty based on annual disposable money income. Detailed comparable information exists on money income by source, taxes paid, and certain kinds of transfers that have a cashlike character, such as housing allowances, fuel assistance, and food stamps. We do not take into account the major in-kind benefits that are available in most countries, such as health care, education, day care and preschool, and general subsidies to housing. To the extent that the level and distribution of these resources are different in different countries, our analysis of money income must be treated with some caution. But since we are interested in the effects of safety nets on poverty, we prefer instead a measure of poverty that focuses on the short-term responsiveness of governments and other agencies in providing social protection to the poor.

Equivalence Scales and Economies of Scale

Households differ not only in terms of resources but also in terms of their needs. We take differing needs, owing to differences in household size and other factors (for example, urban-rural differences), into account by adjusting income for family size using an equivalence scale. The adjustment for household size is designed to account for the different requirements families of different sizes and different circumstances have for participating in society at a given level. Different equivalence scales will yield different distributions of well-being. Several studies in Europe, the

---

[35] Jung and Smeeding (1999).
[36] See Johnson and Smeeding (1998) on this topic.

United States, and Australia point to an equivalence scale that implies fairly large economies of scale in the conversion of money incomes to social participation among families with children and also among the aged.[37] Because choice of equivalence scale may favor small versus large families, depending on which scale is selected, we aim to find a middle ground value that is appropriate for measuring vulnerability for both large families (for example, those with two or more children) and smaller units (for example, single elderly women living alone).

Buhmann and others have proposed that disposable income be adjusted for family size in the following way:[38]

$$\text{Adjusted income} = \text{disposable income}/\text{size}^E.$$

The equivalence elasticity, or "equivalence factor," E, varies between 0 and 1; the larger is E, the smaller are the economies of scale assumed by the equivalence scale. The various studies reviewed in the survey make use of equivalence scales for analyses of per capita income ranging from $E = 0$ (or no adjustment for size) to $E = 1$ (which ignores all economies of scale).[39] Between these extremes, the range of possible values is evenly covered. The reader should keep in mind that all money income estimates in this chapter are based on adjusted or equivalent income calculated according to the above formula.

The obvious question is which measure of E to use for this study. Following Anthony Atkinson, Lee Rainwater, and Timothy Smeeding, we have selected an E value of 0.5, similar to that used by the OECD and Eurostat. For the most part, national rankings by *overall* poverty rates are not sensitive to the measure of E selected.[40]

However, subgroup poverty rates are very sensitive to the choice of equivalence scale. As demonstrated in appendix figure 11A–1 for Spain, poverty rates among the elderly (usually small families in rich nations) and children (larger families, particularly in developing nations and in richer Catholic nations) vary systematically according to the level of the equivalence factor. When $E = 0$, there are complete economies of scale and smaller households have higher poverty rates

---

[37] Buhmann and others (1988); Bradbury (1989); Rainwater (1990). For the aged see Burkhauser, Smeeding, and Merz (1996).

[38] Buhmann and others (1988).

[39] Buhmann and others (1988); Atkinson, Rainwater, and Smeeding (1995).

[40] Atkinson, Rainwater, and Smeeding (1995, especially chapters 2, 3, and 7). For OECD see Förster (1993), and for Eurostat see Hagenaars, De Vos, and Zaidi (1994). See also Burkhauser, Smeeding, and Merz (1996).

(owing to the correlation between income and household size) than do larger ones. The opposite result is obtained at higher levels of the equivalence factor, all the way to $E = 1$, where there are no economies of scale and each additional person needs as much as the first person to be nonpoor. Two important notes can be added. First of all, this same relationship obtains for every rich nation; the crossing of the lines in figure 11A–1 is not unique to Spain. Second, there is far too little research on the appropriate measure of E in developing nations. Simplistic measures of poverty such as "$1.50 per person per day" imply $E = 1$ equivalence scales and hence the likelihood of family size biases apparent in figure 11A–1.[41]

Having defined equivalent income in this way, we determine the equivalent income of all households and all individuals in each country. We then examine the distribution of equivalent incomes of households and of persons in households in relation to the selected poverty line. That is, we tabulate the percentage of persons who have given characteristics and the percentage of households with given characteristics. In technical terms, our person calculations are weighted by the number of persons of each type (all persons including children, adults, elderly) residing in each household type.

Relative versus Absolute Poverty

Needs can be measured in two ways, an absolute definition and a relative definition. Relative poverty involves deciding on the income concept for relativity (median or mean) and on the fraction of adjusted income that signifies poverty. Absolute poverty measurement means locating the "absolute" poverty line and then converting that poverty line into national currency.

We rely here on a relative concept of poverty, the percentage of persons with incomes below half of median income. This income is in line with a well-established theoretical perspective on poverty.[42] Such a measure is now commonly calculated by the European Commission, by the OECD, and by other international groups.[43] Only the British and one other major international study use a fraction of mean income as a standard, though Cantillion and others use both mean and median income–based poverty rates in their study.[44]

---

[41] World Bank (1990); Ravallion, Datt, and van de Walle (1991).
[42] Sen (1992); Townsend (1979).
[43] Hagenaars, De Vos, and Zaidi (1994); Ramprakash (1995); Förster (1993).
[44] Cantillion, Marx, and van den Bosch (1996).

In fact, most studies use the "average," or median, household as the point of reference, as do we. Using the average, or mean, income means measuring social distance from something other than the average household. Moreover, the decision to use one measure versus the other can lead to quite different results in poverty trends when inequality is changing. In the United States from 1973 to 1994, the mean income grew 15 percent more than the median income, thus ensuring that poverty measured relative to the mean grew much more than poverty relative to the median.[45]

The determination of "absolute" poverty lines requires both the selection of an absolute poverty line in one currency and its translation into other currencies. Such translations rely on "purchasing power parties" (PPPs), such as those constructed by Robert Summers and Alan Heston or by the OECD.[46] However, PPPs are based on aggregated data and income (consumption) concepts that are not well suited for use with microdata, which are highly sensitive to the price deflator used when rapid inflation takes place (as is often the case in Latin America), and which are sensitive to the overall quality of the income data reported on the survey in question. Hence, we rely on the relative poverty–based headcount measure alone.

While we stress the half of median measure, we use one additional measure of relative poverty to test the sensitivity of our headcount measures to alternative poverty lines. Forty percent of the median is chosen for comparison because it is almost exactly the ratio of the United States poverty line to the United States median. This poverty measure is used in figure 11–1 and table 11A–3.

---

[45] Burtless (1996).
[46] Summers and Heston (1991); OECD (1986).

FIGURE 11A–1.
Poverty Rates as a Function of the Equivalence Factor, Spain, 1990

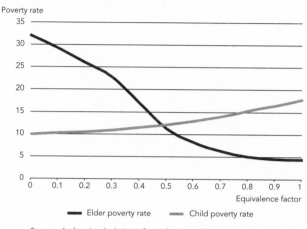

Source: Authors' calculations from the Luxembourg Income Study. See Smeeding and others (1998).

FIGURE 11A–2.
Relationship between Social Expenditure as a Percent of GDP and Poverty Reduction among Nonelderly Persons

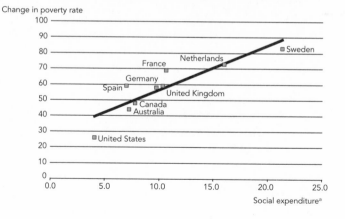

a. Social expenditure as a percent of GDP is taken from OECD (1999). The most recent year is used in cases where the exact year is not available. Social expenditure includes all public cash and near-cash expenditure for social protection. Health care is excluded. Poverty reduction is measured by the percentage reduction in poverty rates between market income and disposable income-based poverty rates (last column of table 11–2).
Source: Authors' calculations from the Luxembourg Income Study. See Smeeding and others (1998).

FIGURE 11A–3.
Relationship between Social Expenditure as a Percent of GDP and Poverty Reduction among All Persons

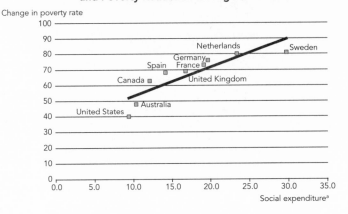

a. Social expenditure as a percent of GDP is taken from OECD (1999). The most recent year is used when the exact year is not available. Social expenditure includes all public cash and near-cash expenditure for social protection except for those received by the aged and survivors. Health care is also excluded. Poverty reduction is measured by the percentage reduction in poverty rates between market income and disposable income poverty (last column of table 11–2).
Source: Authors' calculations from the Luxembourg Income Study. See Smeeding and others (1998).

Table 11A–1. Poverty Measurement and Definitions of Categories That Affect Income

Poverty measurement

The poverty rate is the percentage of households (table 11–1), adults (tables 11–2 and 11A–4), or all persons (adults/elderly/children—figures 11–1 and 11–2 and table 11A–3) with income less than a given percent of median-adjusted disposable income for all persons. In tables 11–1 and 11–2, the poverty rate is 50 percent of the median income; in table 11A–4, it is 40 percent; in table 11A–3, rates for 50 and 40 percent of the median are shown. Incomes are adjusted by E = 0.5, where adjusted income equals actual income divided by household size to the power E. Adjusted income equals income/S^E.

Categories

All income amounts are adjusted by E = 0.5, as described above.

Market income	Earnings and cash property income.
Private transfers	Occupational pension income, alimony, child support, private interfamily transfers, and other cash income.
Universal and social transfers	Universal benefits and social insurance, including social retirement, survivors' benefits, unemployment compensation, short- and long-term disability, maternal and paternal benefits, sickness benefits, and child allowances.
Taxes	Payroll and income taxes.
Social assistance transfers	Income-tested benefits, means-tested (income- and wealth-tested) benefits, and emergency benefits, cash and near cash. The earned income tax credit in the United States and the family tax credit are counted as social assistance in these nations, not as "negative taxes."

Table 11A–2. Luxembourg Income Study Database List

Country	Historical databases	Wave I	Wave II	Wave III	Wave IV
Australia		1981	1985	1989	1994
Austria			1987		1995[a]
Belgium			1985	1988/1992	1997[a]
Canada	1971, 1975	1981	1987	1991	1994
Czech Republic				1992	1996[a]
Denmark			1987	1992	1995[b]
Finland			1987	1991	1995
France		1979/1981	1984A/1984B	1989	1994
Germany	1973, 1978	1981	1983/1984	1989	1994
Hungary				1991	1994
Ireland			1987		1995[b]
Israel		1979	1986	1992	1997[a]
Italy			1986	1991	1995
Luxembourg			1985	1991	1994
The Netherlands			1983/1986[a]/1987	1991	1994
Norway		1979	1986	1991	1995
Poland			1986	1992	1995
Portugal					1995[b]
R.O.C. Taiwan		1981	1986	1991	1995
Russia				1992	1995
Slovak Republic				1992	1996[b]
Spain		1980		1990	1995[b]
Sweden	1967, 1975	1981	1987	1992	1995
Switzerland		1982		1992	
United Kingdom	1969, 1974	1979	1986	1991	1995
United States	1969, 1974	1979	1986	1991	1994/1997[c]

a. Received; waiting to be harmonized.
b. Under negotiation.
c. State file 199567.

Table 11A–3. Poverty Rates for All Persons by Income Source

Country, year, poverty measure	Market income (A)	Column (A) + private income transfers (B)	Column (B) + universal and social transfers (C)	Column (C) – taxes (D)	Column (D) + social assistance transfers (E)	Percent change columns (A) to (E) (F)
Australia, 1994						
50 percent median income	30.3	28.6	25.6	26.1	15.7	−48.2
40 percent median income	27.8	25.8	22.8	23.0	8.0	−71.2
Canada, 1994						
50 percent median income	30.5	25.5	12.5	13.5	11.2	−63.3
40 percent median income	27.2	21.9	9.0	9.3	6.6	−75.7
France, 1989						
50 percent median income	38.1	37.1	11.9	12.5	10.2	−73.2
40 percent median income	32.9	31.7	6.8	7.3	6.0	−81.8
Germany, 1994						
50 percent median income	31.3	28.2	8.5	9.8	7.6	−75.7
40 percent median income	29.4	25.9	5.8	6.6	4.1	−86.1
The Netherlands, 1991						
50 percent median income	33.5	25.3	8.0	10.4	6.7	−80.0
40 percent median income	32.5	23.6	7.2	8.3	4.2	−87.1
Spain, 1990[a]						
50 percent median income	32.1	30.7	11.3	—	10.4	−67.6
40 percent median income	27.6	26.3	6.0	—	5.2	−81.2
Sweden, 1992						
50 percent median income	37.6	37.3	9.7	13.5	7.3	−80.6
40 percent median income	34.9	34.7	6.0	7.3	4.6	−86.8
United Kingdom, 1995						
50 percent median income	38.1	31.1	20.0	21.3	11.8	−69.0
40 percent median income	35.9	28.3	14.9	15.5	5.7	−84.1
United States, 1994						
50 percent median income	30.7	26.7	18.3	20.1	18.4	−40.1
40 percent median income	26.8	22.6	13.7	14.8	12.4	−53.7

— Not available.
a. Tax information is not available for Spain, 1990.
Note: See table 11A–1 for definitions of income categories and poverty rates.
Source: Authors' calculations.

Table 11A–4. Adult Poverty Rates by Income Source

Poverty measured at 40 percent of median-adjusted household disposable income

Country, individual category	Market income (A)	Column (A) + private income transfers (B)	Column (B) + universal and social transfers (C)	Column (C) – taxes (D)	Column (D) + social assistance transfers (E)	Percent change columns A to E (F)
Australia, 1994						
All adults (25 to 64)	19.1	17.9	17.9	18.1	6.3	-67.0
Couples with children[a]	13.0	12.6	12.6	12.9	5.7	-56.2
Single parents[b]	65.2	62.6	62.6	62.6	22.4	-65.6
Extended families[c]	16.0	15.7	15.7	15.8	3.2	-80.0
Childless adults[d]	21.0	19.3	19.3	19.5	6.3	-70.0
Elderly (65 and over)	78.0	70.1	70.1	70.1	14.4	-81.5
Canada, 1994						
All adults (25 to 64)	18.4	15.4	9.4	9.8	6.9	-62.5
Couples with children	12.8	12.2	7.0	7.3	5.3	-58.6
Single parents	56.9	54.2	46.4	46.7	29.8	-47.6
Extended families	12.0	10.8	5.9	6.3	3.5	-70.8
Childless adults	20.6	15.8	9.3	9.6	7.1	-65.5
Elderly (65 and over)	75.6	56.2	2.1	2.2	1.3	-98.3
France, 1989						
All adults (25 to 64)	21.9	21.2	5.9	6.4	5.2	-76.3
Couples with children	11.7	11.4	4.2	4.6	3.5	-70.1
Single parents	41.2	39.3	29.3	29.3	12.3	-70.1
Extended families	20.2	19.9	6.3	6.6	4.8	-76.2
Childless adults	28.9	27.9	6.1	6.8	6.2	-78.5
Elderly (65 and over)	84.2	83.8	8.9	9.5	9.1	-89.2
Germany, 1994						
All adults (25 to 64)	14.9	13.6	5.5	6.3	3.5	-76.5
Couples with children	7.2	7.0	4.3	5.3	2.7	-62.5
Single parents	57.5	53.1	45.3	49.5	32.7	-43.1

Extended families	6.3	6.1	3.4	4.8	2.2	−65.1
Childless adults	18.5	16.5	4.8	5.3	2.9	−84.3
Elderly (65 and over)	88.6	74.8	5.1	5.1	4.4	−95.0
The Netherlands, 1991						
All adults (25 to 64)	21.1	15.6	6.5	7.7	3.6	−82.9
Couples with children	8.3	8.0	4.3	5.3	3.6	−56.6
Single parents	78.6	70.6	51.9	54.4	14.3	−81.8
Extended families	9.9	8.1	4.4	4.4	2.8	−71.7
Childless adults	28.2	19.1	6.3	7.6	3.3	−88.3
Elderly (65 and over)	91.1	61.8	3.2	3.2	3.0	−96.7
Spain, 1990[e]						
All adults (25 to 64)	19.7	18.9	5.9	—	5.4	−72.6
Couples with children	10.7	10.2	6.3	—	6.2	−42.1
Single parents	46.3	31.4	17.2	—	17.2	−62.9
Extended families	16.8	16.1	5.6	—	5.1	−69.6
Childless adults	27.7	26.7	5.5	—	4.8	−82.7
Elderly (65 and over)	68.3	64.8	6.6	—	4.6	−93.3
Sweden, 1992[f]						
All adults (25 to 64)	15.8	15.6	3.1	4.1	1.8	−88.6
Couples with children	8.5	8.4	2.4	3.2	1.4	−83.5
Single parents	34.2	31.7	6.6	8.1	1.3	−96.2
Extended families	—	—	—	—	—	—
Childless adults	19.0	19.0	3.3	4.3	2.2	−88.4
Elderly (65 and over)	89.1	89.1	1.5	2.2	1.5	−98.3
United Kingdom, 1995						
All adults (25 to 64)	25.0	20.4	14.4	15.1	5.9	−76.4
Couples with children	17.9	17.2	14.4	15.4	7.2	−59.8
Single parents	75.4	71.0	65.8	67.3	16.2	−78.5
Extended families	20.7	19.2	13.5	15.0	3.7	−82.1
Childless adults	25.6	18.2	10.3	10.6	4.4	−82.8
Elderly (65 and over)	81.1	60.3	13.5	13.8	13.8	−83.0

Table continues on next page.

Table 11A–4. Adult Poverty Rates by Income Source (continued)

Country, individual category	Market income (A)	Column (A) + private income transfers (B)	Column (B) + universal and social transfers (C)	Column (C) – taxes (D)	Column (D) + social assistance transfers (E)	Percent change in columns A to E (F)
United States, 1994						
All adults (25 to 64)	17.2	14.9	11.7	12.9	10.6	-38.4
Couples with children	9.5	9.1	7.9	9.1	6.6	-30.5
Single parents	51.8	48.3	45.1	46.9	38.3	-26.1
Extended families	21.5	20.2	17.3	18.8	14.1	-34.4
Childless adults	17.9	14.4	9.9	10.8	9.8	-45.3
Elderly (65 and over)	70.0	54.8	14.8	15.0	13.3	-81.0

— Not available.

a. Adults, 25 to 64 years old, living in households with children headed by a married or cohabiting couple with no other adults present.

b. Unmarried household heads, 25 to 64 years old, living in households with children and no other adults present.

c. Adults, 25 to 64 years old, living in households with children and adults other than the head and partner (if married or cohabiting).

d. Adults, 25 to 64 years old, living in households with no children present.

e. Tax information is not available for Spain, 1990.

f. Cannot identify extended families in Sweden, 1992.

Note: Forty percent of the median is chosen because it is almost exactly the ratio of the U.S. poverty line to the U.S. median. See table 11A–1 for definitions of income categories and poverty rates.

Source: Authors' calculations.

Table 11A–5. Estimated Population of Individuals

Country, measure	Adults, 25 to 64 years old					Elderly, 65 and over	Total
	Couples with children	Single parents	Extended families	Childless	Overall		
Australia, 1994							
Thousands	2,905	233	776	4,864	8,779	1,924	10,703
Percent of total	27.1	2.2	7.2	45.4	82.0	18.0	100.0
Canada, 1994							
Thousands	4,860	500	1,542	8,391	15,293	3,243	18,536
Percent of total	26.2	2.7	8.3	45.3	82.5	17.5	100.0
France, 1989							
Thousands	9,782	549	2,684	13,480	26,496	7,271	33,767
Percent of total	29.0	1.6	7.9	39.9	78.5	21.5	100.0
Germany, 1994							
Thousands	13,045	979	3,112	23,735	40,871	12,278	53,149
Percent of total	24.5	1.8	5.9	44.7	76.9	23.1	100.0
The Netherlands, 1991							
Thousands	2,895	191	497	4,415	7,999	1,900	9,899
Percent of total	29.2	1.9	5.0	44.6	80.8	19.2	100.0
Spain, 1990							
Thousands	5,930	110	4,676	8,040	18,755	5,321	24,077
Percent of total	24.6	0.5	19.4	33.4	77.9	22.1	100.0
Sweden, 1992							
Thousands	1,629	215	—	2,528	4,372	1,518	5,889
Percent of total	27.7	3.6	—	42.9	74.2	25.8	100.0
United Kingdom, 1995							
Thousands	9,587	1,306	1,735	15,572	28,199	8,086	36,286
Percent of total	26.4	3.6	4.8	42.9	77.7	22.3	100.0
United States, 1994							
Thousands	40,383	5,466	17,223	68,516	131,589	31,241	162,830
Percent of total	24.8	3.4	10.6	42.1	80.8	19.2	100.0

— Not available.

Source: Luxembourg Income Study. See Smeeding and others (1998).

Table 11A–6. Estimated Population of Households by Working Status

Country	Full-year, full-time	Part-time	Non-earners	Overall
Australia, 1994				
Thousands	3,219	972	793	4,985
Percent of total	64.6	19.5	15.9	100.0
Canada, 1994				
Thousands	5,629	1,771	1,099	8,499
Percent of total	66.2	20.8	12.9	100.0
Germany, 1994				
Thousands	14,802	5,534	2,639	22,975
Percent of total	64.4	24.1	11.5	100.0
The Netherlands, 1991				
Thousands	2,769	930	879	4,578
Percent of total	60.5	20.3	19.2	100.0
Sweden, 1992				
Thousands	1,642	925	253	2,820
Percent of total	58.2	32.8	9.0	100.0
United Kingdom, 1995				
Thousands	8,433	2,335	4,931	15,698
Percent of total	53.7	14.9	31.4	100.0
United States, 1994				
Thousands	53,290	15,852	8,386	77,528
Percent of total	68.7	20.4	10.8	100.0

Note: Data are not available for France or Spain.
Source: Luxembourg Income Study. See Smeeding and others (1998).

References

Aarts, Leo J. M., Richard V. Burkhauser, and Philip de Jong, eds. 1996. *Curing the Dutch Disease: An International Perspective on Disability Reform.* Aldershot, UK: Avebury Press.

Atkinson, Anthony B., and Gunnar Mogenson. 1993. *Welfare and Work Incentives: A North European Perspective.* Oxford, UK: Oxford University Press.

Atkinson, Anthony B., Lee Rainwater, and Timothy M. Smeeding. 1995. *Income Distribution in OECD Countries: The Evidence from LIS.* Paris, France: OECD.

Banting, Keith. 1997. "The Social Policy Divide: The Welfare State in Canada and the United States." In Keith Banting, George Hoberg, and Richard Simon, eds., *Degrees of Freedom: Canada and the United States in a Changing World.* Montreal and Kingston, Ontario, Canada: McGill Queens University Press.

Bradbury, Bruce. 1989. "Family Size Equivalence and Survey Evaluations of Income and Well-Being." *Journal of Social Policy* 11: 383–408.

Buhmann, B., and others. 1988. "Equivalence Scales, Well-Being, Inequality and Poverty." *Review of Income and Wealth* 34 (June): 115–42.

Burkhauser, Richard V., Timothy M. Smeeding, and Joachim Merz. 1996. "Relative Inequality and Poverty in Germany and the United States Using Alternative Equivalence Scales." *Review of Income and Wealth* 42 (December): 242–63.

Burtless, Gary. 1996. "Trends in the Level and Distribution of U.S. Living Standards: 1973–1993." *Eastern Economic Journal* 22 (Summer): 271–90.

Burtless, Gary, and Robert Haveman. 1987. "Taxes and Transfers: How Much Economic Loss?" *Challenge* (March–April): 45-51.

Cantillion, Bea, Yves Marx, and Karel van den Bosch. 1996. "Poverty in Advanced Economies: Trends and Issues." Paper presented to the Twenty-Fourth General Conference of the International Association for Research on Income and Wealth (IARIW), Norway.

Coleman, James. 1988. "Social Capital in the Creation of Human Capital." *American Journal of Sociology* 94: S95–S120.

Coleman, Richard P., Lee Rainwater, and Kent A. McClelland. 1978. *Social Standing in America: New Dimensions of Class.* New York, N.Y.: Basic Books.

Danziger, Sheldon, Robert Haveman, and Robert Plotnick. 1981. "How Income Transfer Programs Affect Work, Savings, and Income Distribution: A Critical Review." *Journal of Economic Literature* 19 (September): 975–1028.

Danziger, Sheldon, and Markus Jäntti. 2000. "Income Poverty in Advanced Countries." In Anthony B. Atkinson and François Bourguignon, eds., *Handbook on Income Distribution.* Amsterdam, Netherlands: Elsevier Science Ltd.

Danziger, Sheldon, Lee Rainwater, and Timothy M. Smeeding. 1997. "Child Well-Being in the West: Toward a More Effective Antipoverty Policy." In Giovanni Andrea Cornia and Sheldon Danziger, eds., *Child Poverty and Deprivation in the Industrialized Countries 1945–1995.* London, UK: Oxford University Press..

Förster, Michael. 1993. *Comparing Poverty in 13 OECD Countries: Traditional and Synthetic Approaches.* Studies in Social Policy Paper no. 10. OECD, Paris, France.

Gottschalk, Peter, and Timothy M. Smeeding. 2000. "Empirical Evidence on Income Inequality in Industrialized Countries." In Anthony B. Atkinson and François Bourguignon, eds., *Handbook of Income Distribution,* vol. 1. Amsterdam, Netherlands: Elsevier Science Ltd.

———. 1997. "Cross-National Comparisons of Earnings and Income Inequality." *Journal of Economic Literature* 35 (June): 633–87.

Gruber, Jonathan, and David Wise. 1998. "Social Security and Retirement: An International Review." *American Economic Review* 88 (May): 158–63.

Hagenaars, Arie, Klas De Vos, and Azghar Zaidi. 1994. "Patterns of Poverty in Europe." Paper presented to the Twenty-Third General Conference of the International Association for Research on Income and Wealth (IARIW), Canada.

Haveman, Robert. 1985. "Does the Welfare State Increase Welfare?" Inaugural Lecture, Tinbergen Chair in Economics, Department of Economics, Erasmus University, The Netherlands.

Johnson, David, and Timothy M. Smeeding. 1998. "Measuring the Trend in Inequality among Individuals and Families: Consumption or Income?" Center for Policy Research, The Maxwell School, Syracuse University, Syracuse, N.Y. Unpublished.

Jung, Kwangho, and Timothy M. Smeeding. 1999. "Income Inequality and Population Health among 18 Developed Countries." Center for Policy Research, The Maxwell School, Syracuse University, Syracuse, N.Y. Unpublished.

Kenworthy, Lane. 1998. *Do Social Welfare Policies Reduce Poverty? A Cross-National Assessment*. LIS Working Paper no. 191. Luxembourg Income Study, Differdange, Luxembourg, and Syracuse University, Syracuse, N.Y.

Lemieux, Thomas, and William MacLeod. 1998. *Supply Side Hysteresis: The Case of Canadian Unemployment Insurance*. Working Paper no. 6732. National Bureau for Economic Research, Cambridge, MA.

Moffitt, Robert. 1992. "Incentive Effects of the U.S. Welfare System: A Review." *Journal of Economic Literature* 30 (March): 1–61.

O'Connor, Inge. 1994. *A Cross-National Comparison of Education and Earnings*. LIS Working Paper no. 116. Center for Policy Research, The Maxwell School, Syracuse University, Syracuse, N.Y.

Organization for Economic Cooperation and Development (OECD). 1998. *Purchasing Power Parities*. Paris: OECD.

———. 1999. *Social Expenditures Database*. Paris: OECD.

Overbye, Einar. 1997. "Policy Responses to Household Vulnerability: The Norwegian Case in an International Context." Paper presented to the Fourth International Research Seminar on Social Security, Sigtuna, Sweden.

Rainwater, Lee. 1974. *What Money Buys: Inequality and the Social Meanings of Income*. New York, N.Y.: Basic Books.

———. 1990. *Poverty and Equivalence as Social Constructions*. LIS Working Paper no. 91. Luxembourg Income Study, Syracuse University, Syracuse, N.Y.

Ramprakash, Deo. 1995. "Poverty in Europe." *European Journal of Social Policy* 15: 161–68.

Ravallion, Martin, G. Datt, and Dominique van de Walle. 1991. "Quantifying Absolute Poverty in the Developing World." *Review of Income and Wealth* 37: 345–61.

Schmidt, Christophe, and Marek Gora. 1998. "Long-Term Unemployment, Unemployment Benefits and Social Assistance: The Polish Experience." *Empirical Economics* 23(1-2): 55–85.

Sen, Amartya. 1992. *Inequality Reexamined*. Cambridge, MA: Harvard University Press.

Skévik, Anne. 1997. "The State-Parent Relationship after Family Break-Up: Child Maintenance in Norway and Britain." Paper presented to the Fourth International Research Seminar on Social Security, Sigtuna, Sweden.

Smeeding, Timothy M. 1997a. "Poverty in Developed Countries: The Evidence from LIS." *Poverty and Human Development, 1997*. New York: United Nations.

———. 1997b. "U.S. Income Inequality in a Cross-National Perspective: Why Are We So Different?" *Looking Ahead* 19(2-3): 41–50. Reprinted in David Auerbach and Richard Belous, eds., *The Inequality Paradox: Growth of Income Disparity*. Washington, D.C.: National Policy Association.

Smeeding, Timothy M., and Joseph F. Quinn. 1998. "Cross-National Patterns of Labor Force Withdrawal." In Peter Flora, ed., *The State of Social Welfare, 1997*. London, UK: Ashgate Publishers.

Smeeding, Timothy M., and Dennis Sullivan. 1998. "Generations and the Distribution of Economic Well-Being: A Cross-National View." *American Economic Review* 88 (May): 254–58.

Smeeding, Timothy M., and others. 1998. *Poverty and Parenthood across Modern Nations: Findings from the Luxembourg Income Study*. LIS Working Paper no. 194. Differdange, Luxembourg.

Sullivan, Dennis, and Timothy M. Smeeding. 1997. "Educational Attainment and Earnings Inequality in Eight Nations." *International Journal of Education Research* 27 (6): 513–25.

Summers, Robert, and Alan Heston. 1991. "The Penn World Tables (Mark 5): An Expanded Set of International Comparisons." *Quarterly Journal of Economics* 105 (2): 327–68.

Townsend, Peter. 1979. *Poverty in the United Kingdom: A Survey of Household Resources and Standards of Living*. Berkeley, CA: University of California Press.

U.S. Bureau of the Census. 1998. *Poverty in the United States: 1997*. Current Population Reports, Series P-60, no. 201. Government Printing Office, Washington, D.C.

World Bank. 1990. *World Development Report*. New York, N.Y.: Oxford University Press.

Authors

Orazio Attanasio is a Professor of Economics at University College, London.

Alain de Janvry is a Professor in the Department of Agricultural and Resource Economics at the University of California, Berkeley.

Paul Gertler is a Professor of Economic Analysis and Policy at the Haas School of Business at the University of California, Berkeley.

Hugo A. Hopenhayn is a Professor of Economics in the Economic College at the University of Rochester.

Estelle James is a Lead Economist in the Development Economics Research Group and the World Bank Institute at the World Bank.

Steen Lau Jørgensen is a Sector Manager in the Social Protection Unit of the Human Development Network at the World Bank.

Nora Lustig is Chief of the Poverty and Inequality Advisory Unit at the Inter-American Development Bank.

Gustavo Márquez is an Economist in the Research Department at the Inter-American Development Bank.

Carmelo Mesa-Lago is a Professor of Economics at the University of Pittsburgh.

Juan Pablo Nicolini is Chairman of the Department of Economics at Universidad Torcuato di Tella, Buenos Aires.

José-Víctor Ríos-Rull is a Professor of Economics at the University of Pennsylvania.

Katherin Ross Phillips is with the Urban Institute.

Elisabeth Sadoulet is a Professor in the Department of Agricultural and Resource Economics at the University of California, Berkeley.

Timothy M. Smeeding is a Professor and Director of the Center for Policy Research at Syracuse University.

Julia Van Domelen is a Senior Economist in the Social Protection Unit of the Human Development Network at the World Bank.

Manfred Zeller is a Professor at the Institute of Rural Development at the University of Göttingen.

Index